Programming Ruby 1.9

Programming Ruby 1.9

The Pragmatic Programmers' Guide

Dave Thomas

with Chad Fowler
and Andy Hunt

The Pragmatic Bookshelf
Raleigh, North Carolina   Dallas, Texas

This book is a heavily revised version of the book *Programming Ruby*, originally published by Addison Wesley. This book is printed with their permission.

Our Pragmatic courses, workshops, and other products can help you and your team create better software and have more fun. For more information, as well as the latest Pragmatic titles, please visit us at

http://www.pragmaticprogrammer.com

Printed in the United States of America.

ISBN: 1-934356-08-5
ISBN-13:   978-1-934356-08-1
Printing: P1.0, April 2009
Version: 2009-3-31

Text printed on acid-free paper.

Contents

PART III—RUBY CRYSTALLIZED

PART IV—RUBY LIBRARY REFERENCE

PART V—APPENDIXES

List of Tables

List of Figures

Foreword

I wrote forewords to the previous two edition of this book. For the first edition, I wrote about motivation. For the second edition, I wrote about miracles.

For this third edition, I'd like to write about courage. I always admire brave people. People around Ruby seem to be brave, like the authors of this book. They were brave to jump in to a relatively unknown language like Ruby. They were brave to try out new technology. They could have happily stayed with an old technology, but they didn't. They built their own world using new bricks and mortar. They were adventurers, explorers, and pioneers. By their effort, we have a fruitful result—Ruby.

Now I feel that I've created my own universe with help from those brave people. At first, I thought it was a miniature universe, like the one in "Fessenden's Worlds." But now it seems like a real universe. Uncountable brave people are now working with Ruby. They challenge new things every day, trying to make the world better and bigger. I am very glad I am part of the Ruby world.

I suppose that even the world itself could not contain the books that should be written. But now we have the first book, updated to the most recent. Enjoy.

Yukihiro Matsumoto, a.k.a. *"Matz"*
まつもと ゆきひろ
Japan, February 2009

Preface

This book is a new version of the PickAxe, as *Programming Ruby* is known to Ruby programmers. It is a tutorial and reference for the version 1.9 of Ruby programming language.

Ruby 1.9 is a significant departure from previous versions. There are major changes in string handling, the scoping of block variables, and the threading model. It has a new virtual machine. The built-in libraries have grown, adding many hundreds of new methods and almost a dozen new classes. The language now supports scores of character encodings, making Ruby one of the only programming languages to live fully in the whole world.

Given a choice between showing the 1.8 version of some Ruby construct and the 1.9 version, this book shows the new way. If you're planning to use Ruby 1.8 and not Ruby 1.9, then I'd recommend putting this book down and instead looking at the second edition of Programming Ruby.[1]

But, before you run off, I'd also like you to stop for a second and consider switching to Ruby 1.9. As a language, and as a programming environment, it really is a step up from previous versions of Ruby. It runs faster, it is more expressive, and it enables even more programming paradigms. Most frameworks (including Ruby on Rails) are now compatible with Ruby 1.9. And some Ruby implementations (such as MacRuby—a version of Ruby that is integrated into the Objective C runtime on the Mac) run only 1.9 code.

Why Ruby?

When Andy and I wrote the first edition, we had to explain the background and appeal of Ruby. Among other things, we wrote, "When we discovered Ruby, we realized that we'd found what we'd been looking for. More than any other language with which we have worked, Ruby *stays out of your way*. You can concentrate on solving the problem at hand, instead of struggling with compiler and language issues. That's how it can help you become a better programmer: by giving you the chance to spend your time creating solutions for your users, not for the compiler."

That belief is even stronger today. Almost eight years later, Ruby is still our language of choice: I use it for client applications and web applications. I use it to run our publishing business (our online store, http://pragprog.com, is more than 40,000 lines of Rails code), and I use it for all those little programming jobs I do just to get things running smoothly.

---

1. http://pragprog.com/titles/ruby

In those eight years, Ruby has progressed nicely. A large number of methods have been added to the built-in classes and modules, and the size of the standard library (those libraries included in the Ruby distribution) has grown tremendously. The community now has a standard documentation system (RDoc), and RubyGems has become the system of choice for packaging Ruby code for distribution. We have a best-of-breed web application framework, Ruby on Rails, with others waiting in the wings.

Ruby Versions

This version of the PickAxe documents Ruby 1.9.[2]

Exactly what version of Ruby did I use to write this book? Let's ask Ruby:

```
% ruby -v
ruby 1.9.1p0 (2009-01-30 revision 21907) [i386-darwin9.6.0]
```

This illustrates an important point. Most of the code samples you see in this book are actually executed each time I format the book. When you see some output from a program, that output was produced by running the code and inserting the results back into the book.

Changes in the Book

Throughout the book I've tried to mark changes between 1.8 and 1.9 using a small symbol in the margin, like the one here. One change I didn't make: I decided to continue to use the word *we* when talking about the authors in the body of the book. Many of the words come from the first edition, and I certainly don't want to claim any credit for Andy's work on that book.

Resources

Visit the Ruby website at http://www.ruby-lang.org to see what's new. Chat with other Ruby users on the newsgroup or mailing lists (see Appendix B).

And I'd certainly appreciate hearing from you. Comments, suggestions, errors in the text, and problems in the examples are all welcome. E-mail us at

    rubybook@pragprog.com

---

2.   Ruby version numbering used to follow the same scheme used for many other open source projects. Releases with even minor version numbers—1.6, 1.8, and so on—were stable, public releases. These are the releases that are prepackaged and made available on the various Ruby websites. Development versions of the software had odd minor version numbers, such as 1.5 and 1.7. However, in 2007 Matz broke with convention and made 1.9 a stable public release of Ruby.

If you tell us about errors in the book, I'll add them to the errata list at

    http://www.pragprog.com/titles/ruby3/errata.html

You'll find links to the source code for almost all the book's example code at

    http://www.pragprog.com/titles/ruby3

Acknowledgments

The first International Ruby Conference had something like 32 attendees. We could all fit into the tiny hotel bar and talk the night away. Things have changed since then. The annual conference now sells out many hundreds of seats within hours, and an increasing number of secondary conferences have sprung up to meet the needs of folks who can't get to RubyConf.

As the community has grown, so has Ruby. The language and its libraries are now many times bigger than they were back when the first edition of this book came out.

And as the language has grown, so has this book. The PickAxe is now massive, mostly because I still want to document every single built-in class, module, and method. But a book of this size can never be a solo undertaking. This edition builds on the work from the first two editions, which included major contributions from Chad Fowler and Andy Hunt. Just as significant, all three editions have been works created by the Ruby community. On the mailing lists, in the forums, and on this book's errata pages, hundreds of people have contributed ideas, code, and corrections to make it better. As always, I owe every one of you a big "thank you!" for all you have done and for all that you do. The Ruby community is still as vibrant, interesting, and (mostly) friendly as it ever was—that's quite an achievement given the explosive growth we've enjoyed.

Getting this book into production has also been a challenge. Many thanks to Kim Wimpsett for doing an amazing job on the copy edit, Steve Peter for finding ways to lay out all those awkward pages full of code, and Janet Furlow for keeping us all on track.

Finally, I'm still deeply indebted to Yukihiro "Matz" Matsumoto, the creator of Ruby. Throughout this period of growth and change, he has remained helpful, cheery, and dedicated to polishing this gem of a language. The friendly and open spirit of the Ruby community is a direct reflection of the person at its center.

Thank you all. Domo arigato gozaimasu.

Dave Thomas
THE PRAGMATIC PROGRAMMERS
http://www.pragprog.com

Notation Conventions

Throughout this book, we use the following typographic notations.

Literal code examples are shown using a typewriter-like font:

```
preface_2.rb
class SampleCode
  def run
    #...
  end
end
```

Within the text, Fred#do_something is a reference to an instance method (in this case do_something) of class Fred, Fred.new[3] is a class method, and Fred::EOF is a class constant. The decision to use a hash character to indicate instance methods was a tough one. It isn't valid Ruby syntax, but we thought that it was important to differentiate between the instance and class methods of a particular class. When you see us write File.read, you know we're talking about the class method read. When instead we write File#read, we're referring to the instance method read. This convention is now standard in most Ruby discussions and documentation.

The book contains many snippets of Ruby code. Where possible, we've tried to show what happens when they run. In simple cases, we show the value of expressions on the same line as the expression. For example:

```
preface_3.rb
a = 1
b = 2
a + b   # =>   3
```

Here, you can see that the result of evaluating a + b is the value 3, shown to the right of the arrow. Note that if you were to run this program, you wouldn't see the value 3 output—you'd need to use a method such as puts to write it out.

At times, we're also interested in the values of assignment statements, in which case we'll show them:

```
preface_4.rb
a = 1   # =>   1
b = 2   # =>   2
a + b   # =>   3
```

---

3. In some other Ruby documentation, you may see class methods written as Fred::new. This is perfectly valid Ruby syntax; we just happen to think that Fred.new is less distracting to read.

If the program produces more complex output, we show it below the program code:

`preface_5.rb`

```
3.times { puts "Hello!" }
```

produces:

```
Hello!
Hello!
Hello!
```

In some of the library documentation, we wanted to show where spaces appear in the output. You'll see these spaces as " ␣ " characters.

Command-line invocations are shown with literal text in a Roman font, and parameters you supply are shown in an *italic* font. Optional elements are shown in large square brackets.

ruby *[flags ...] [progname] [arguments ...]*

Road Map

The main text of this book has four separate parts, each with its own personality and each addressing different aspects of the Ruby language.

In **Part I,** *Facets of Ruby*, you'll find a Ruby tutorial. It starts with some notes on getting Ruby running on your system followed by a short chapter on some of the terminology and concepts that are unique to Ruby. This chapter also includes enough basic syntax so that the other chapters will make sense. The rest of the tutorial is a top-down look at the language. There we talk about classes and objects, types, expressions, and all the other things that make up the language. We end with chapters on unit testing and digging yourself out when trouble strikes.

One of the great things about Ruby is how well it integrates with its environment. **Part II,** *Ruby in Its Setting*, investigates this. Here you'll find practical information on using Ruby: using the interpreter options, using irb, documenting your Ruby code, and packaging your Ruby gems so that others can enjoy them. You'll also find tutorials on some common Ruby tasks: using Ruby with the Web and using Ruby in a Microsoft Windows environment (including wonderful things such as native API calls, COM integration, and Windows Automation). We'll also touch on using Ruby to access the 'net.

Part III, *Ruby Crystallized*, contains more advanced material. Here you'll find all the gory details about the language, the concept of *duck typing*, the object model, metaprogramming, tainting, reflection, and marshaling. You could probably speed-read this the first time through, but we think you'll come back to it as you start to use Ruby in earnest.

The ***Ruby Library Reference*** is **Part IV**. It's big. We document more than 1,250 methods in more than 54 built-in classes and modules (up from 800 methods in 40 classes and modules in the previous edition). On top of that, we now document the library modules that are included in the standard Ruby distribution (96 of them).

So, how should you read this book? Well, depending on your level of expertise with programming in general and OO in particular, you may initially want to read just a few portions of the book. Here are our recommendations.

If you're a beginner, you may want to start with the tutorial material in Part I. Keep the library reference close at hand as you start to write programs. Get familiar with the basic classes such as Array, Hash, and String. As you become more comfortable in the environment, you may want to investigate some of the more advanced topics in Part III.

If you're already comfortable with Perl, Python, Java, or Smalltalk, then we suggest reading Chapter 1 on page 3, which talks about installing and running Ruby, followed by the introduction in Chapter 2. From there, you may want to take the slower approach and keep going with the tutorial that follows, or you can skip ahead to the gritty details starting in Part III, followed by the library reference in Part IV.

Experts, gurus, and "I-don't-need-no-stinking-tutorial" types can dive straight into the language reference in Chapter 22, which begins on page 313, skim the library reference, and then use the book as a (rather attractive) coffee coaster.

Of course, nothing is wrong with just starting at the beginning and working your way through page by page.

And don't forget, if you run into a problem that you can't figure out, help is available. See Appendix B, beginning on page 887, for more information.

Part I

Facets of Ruby

## Chapter 1

Getting Started

Before we start talking about the Ruby language, it would be useful if we helped you get Ruby running on your computer. That way, you can try sample code and experiment on your own as you read along. In fact, that's probably essential if you want to learn Ruby—get into the habit of writing code as you're reading. We will also show you some different ways to run Ruby.

The Command Prompt

(Feel free to skip to the next section if you're already comfortable at your system's command prompt.)

Although there's growing support for Ruby in IDEs, you'll probably still end up spending some time at your system's command prompt, also known as a *shell prompt* or just plain *prompt*. If you're a Linux user, you're probably already familiar with the prompt. If you don't already have a desktop icon for it, hunt around for an application called Terminal or xterm. (On Ubuntu, you can navigate to it using Applications > Accessories > Terminal.) On Windows, you'll want to run cmd.exe, accessible by typing cmd into the dialog box that appears when you select Start > Run. On OS X, run Applications > Utilities > Terminal.app.

In all three cases, a fairly empty window will pop up. It will contain a banner and a prompt. Try typing echo hello at the prompt and hitting Enter (or Return, depending on your keyboard). You should see hello echoed back, and another prompt should appear.

Directories, Folders, and Navigation

It is beyond the scope of this book to teach the commands available at the prompt, but we do need to cover the basics of finding your way around.

If you're used to a GUI tool such as Explorer on Windows, or Finder on OS X, for navigating to your files, then you'll be familiar with the idea of *folders*—locations on your hard drive that can hold files and other folders.

When you're at the command prompt, you have access to these same folders. But, somewhat confusingly, at the prompt they're called *directories* (because they contain lists of other directories and files). These directories are organized into a strict hierarchy. On Unix-based systems (including OS X), there's one top-level directory, called / (a single forward slash). On Windows, there is a top-level directory for each drive on your system, so you'll find the top level for your C: drive at C:\ (that's the drive letter, C, a colon, and a single backslash).

The path to a file or directory is the set of directories that you have to traverse to get to it from the top-level directory, followed by the name of the file or directory itself. Each component in this name is separated by a forward slash (on Unix) or a backslash (on Windows). So, if you organized your projects in a directory called projects under the top-level directory and if the projects directory had a subdirectory for your time_planner project, the full path to the README file would be /projects/time_planner/readme.txt on Unix and C:\projects\time_planner\readme.txt on Windows.

To navigate to a directory, use the cd command. (Because the Unix prompt varies from system to system, we'll just use a single dollar sign to represent it here.)

```
$ cd /projects/time_planner        (on Unix)
C:\> cd \projects\time_planner      (on Windows)
```

Now, on Unix boxes, you probably don't want to be creating top-level directories. Instead, Unix gives each user their own *home directory*. So, if your username is dave, your home directory might be located in /usr/dave, /home/dave, or /Users/dave. At the shell prompt, the special character ~ (a single tilde) stands for the path to your home directory. You can always change directories to your home directory using cd ~, which can also be abbreviated to just cd.

To find out the directory you're currently in, you can type pwd (on Unix) or cd on Windows. So, for Unix users, you could type this:

```
$ cd /projects/time_planner
$ pwd
/projects/time_planner
$ cd
$ pwd
/Users/dave
$
```

On Windows, there's no real concept of a user's home directory:

```
C:\> cd \projects\time_planner
C:\projects\time_planner> cd \projects
C:\projects>
```

You can create a new directory under the current directory using the mkdir command:

```
$ cd /projects
$ mkdir expense_tracker
$ cd expense_tracker
$ pwd
/projects/expense_tracker
```

> **Spaces in Directory Names and Filenames**
>
> Most operating systems now allow you to create folders with spaces in their names. This is great when you're working at the GUI level. However, from the command prompt, spaces can be a headache, because the shell that interprets what you type will treat the spaces in file and folder names as being parameter separators and not as part of the name. You can get around this, but it generally isn't worth the hassle. If you are creating new folders and files, it's easiest to avoid spaces in their names.

Notice that to change to the new directory, we could just give its name relative to the current directory—we don't have to enter the full path.

I suggest you create a directory called pickaxe to hold the code you write while reading this book:

```
$ mkdir ~/pickaxe        (on Unix)
C:\> mkdir \pickaxe      (on Windows)
```

Get into the habit of changing into that directory before you start work:

```
$ cd ~/pickaxe           (on Unix)
C:\> cd \pickaxe         (on Windows)
```

Installing Ruby

Quite often, you won't even need to download Ruby. It now comes preinstalled on many Linux distributions, and Mac OS X includes Ruby (although the version of Ruby preinstalled on OS X is normally several minor releases behind the current Ruby version). Try typing **ruby -v** at a command prompt—you may be pleasantly surprised.

If you don't already have Ruby on your system or if you'd like to upgrade to a newer version (remembering that this book describes Ruby 1.9), you can install it pretty simply. But first, you have a choice to make: go for a prepackaged distribution or build Ruby from source?

Prepackaged Distributions

A packaged distribution of Ruby simply works out of the box. You install it, and it runs. Binary distributions are prebuilt for a particular operating environment and are convenient if you don't want to mess around with building Ruby from source. The downside of a packaged distribution is that you may have to take it as given: it may be a minor release or two behind the leading edge, and it may not have the optional libraries that you might want (although you may be able to install additional libraries using RubyGems, described in a moment). If you can live with that, you'll need to find a packaged distribution for your operating system and machine architecture.

Windows Distributions

In the old days (where *old* means Ruby 1.8), things were good for Windows users. There was a great "batteries included" package that would install not just Ruby but also a vast array of libraries and gems. This was called the *One-Click Installer*, or OCI.

However, with the advent of Ruby 1.9, the situation has changed somewhat. Ruby 1.9 hasn't been around long, so some of the libraries that were included in the 1.8 installer have not yet been made compatible with 1.9. As I write this, the OCI project is in a state of flux. The maintainer, Luis Lavena, is planning on releasing a Ruby 1.9 version of the OCI in early 2009, but it may well not contain as many libraries as the 1.8 version. The situation will improve over time. (And, if you feel strongly about this, I know Luis would welcome your help porting stuff over.)

So, you have a couple of choices for installing Ruby 1.9 on Windows. You can visit http://rubyforge.org/projects/rubyinstaller and see whether a one-click installer is available. If not, you can download a prebuilt binary from ruby-lang.org.[1]

Linux Distributions

Most modern Linux distributions use the apt-get system (or the Synaptic GUI) to find and install Ruby. As of November 2008, the following command installs Ruby, irb, and ri:

```
$ sudo apt-get install ruby1.9 libruby1.9 libreadline-ruby1.9 irb1.9
$ sudo apt-get install rdoc1.9 ri1.9
```

This installs all the Ruby commands with a 1.9 suffix, so you'll need to do this:

```
$ ruby1.9 -v
ruby 1.9.0 (2007-12-25 revision 14709) [i486-linux]
```

Be aware that the version of Ruby we just installed is many months behind the current version.

Note that you need to have superuser access to install global packages on a Unix or Linux box, which is why we use the sudo command.

OS X Distributions

Leopard (OS X 10.5) comes with Ruby 1.8 preinstalled.[2] If you want to make use of the new Ruby 1.9 features, you'll want to install Ruby yourself. You can do this from source,

---

1. Visit http://www.ruby-lang.org/en/downloads/, and look for *Ruby on Windows*.

2. At some point, it seems likely that Apple will include MacRuby. This is its own port of Ruby 1.9, tightly integrated into the Objective-C runtime. In the meantime, you can download MacRuby from http://www.macruby.org.

or you can use a package management system. I personally use MacPorts.[3] Once you have the basic ports system installed, as described on its website, installing Ruby is as simple as doing this:

```
$ sudo port install ruby19
```

As with apt-get for Linux, MacPorts currently installs the Ruby executables with a 1.9 suffix (ruby1.9, irb1.9, and so on). If you don't already have /opt/local/bin in your path, you'll need to add it. As an alternative, you could investigate `http://rubyosx.com/`, which claims to offer a packaged OS X installation.

Building Ruby from Source

Because Ruby is an open source project, you can download the interpreter's source code and build it on your own system. Compared to using a binary distribution, this gives you a lot more control over where things go, and you can keep your installation totally up-to-date. The downside is that you're taking on the responsibility of managing the build and installation process. This isn't onerous, but it can be scary if you've never installed an open source application from source.

The first thing to do is to download the source. This comes in three flavors, all from `http://www.ruby-lang.org/en/downloads`:

- The stable release in *tarball* format. A tarball is an archive file, much like a .zip file.
- The *stable snapshot*. This is a tarball, created nightly, of the latest source code in Ruby's stable development branch. The stable branch is intended for production code and in general will be reliable. However, because the snapshot is taken daily, new features may not have received thorough testing yet—the stable tarball in the previous bullet will be generally more reliable.
- The *nightly snapshot*. This is again a tarball, created nightly. Unlike the stable code in the previous two tarballs, this code is leading edge, because it is taken from the head of the development branch. Expect things to be broken in here.

If you plan on downloading either of the nightly snapshots regularly, it may be easier to subscribe to the source repository directly. The sidebar on page 9 gives more details.

Once you've loaded a tarball, you'll have to expand the archive into its constituent files. Use the tar command for this (if you don't have tar installed, you can try using another archiving utility, because many now support tar-format files).

```
$ tar xzf snapshot.tar.gz
ruby/
ruby/bcc32/
ruby/bcc32/Makefile.sub
ruby/bcc32/README.bcc32
     :    :    :
```

---

3.   `http://www.macports.org/`

This installs the Ruby source tree in the subdirectory ruby/. In that directory, you'll find a file named README, which explains the installation procedure in detail. To summarize, you build Ruby on Unix-based systems using the same four commands you use for most other open source applications: ./configure, make, make test, and make install. You can build Ruby under other environments (including Windows)—see README.win32 in the distribution's win32 subdirectory as a starting point.

Source Code from This Book

We have made the source code from this book available for download from our website at http://pragprog.com/titles/ruby3/code. Sometimes, the listings of code in the book correspond to a complete source file. Other times, the book shows just part of the source in a file—the program file may contain additional scaffolding to make the code run.

Running Ruby

Now that Ruby is installed, you'd probably like to run some programs. Unlike compiled languages, you have two ways to run Ruby—you can type in code interactively, or you can create program files and run them. Typing in code interactively is a great way to experiment with the language, but for code that's more complex or that you will want to run more than once, you'll need to create program files and run them. But, before we go any further, let's test to see whether Ruby is installed. Bring up a fresh command prompt, and type this:[4]

```
$ ruby -v
ruby 1.9.1p0 (2009-01-30 revision 21907) [i386-darwin9.6.0]
```

If you believe that you should have Ruby installed and yet you get an error saying something like "ruby: command not found," then it is likely that the Ruby program is not in your path—the list of places that the shell searches for programs to run. If you used the Windows One-Click Installer, make sure you rebooted before trying this command. If you're on OS X and installed Ruby from source, you'll probably have to add a line like this to the file .profile in your home directory:

```
PATH=/usr/local/bin:$PATH
```

Interactive Ruby

One way to run Ruby interactively is simply to type ruby at the shell prompt. Here we typed in the single puts expression and an end-of-file character (which is Ctrl+D on our system). This process works, but it's painful if you make a typo, and you can't really see what's going on as you type.

---

4. Remember you may need to use ruby1.9 as the command name if you installed using a package management system.

The Very Latest Ruby

For those who just have to be on the very latest, hot-off-the-press, and *untested* cutting edge (as we were while writing this book), you can get development versions straight from the developers' working repository.

The Ruby developers use Subversion (often abbreviated as SVN) as their revision control system. Subversion clients can be downloaded from http://subversion.tigris.org/. You can check files out as an anonymous user from their archive by executing the following SVN command:

```
$ svn co http://svn.ruby-lang.org/repos/ruby/trunk ruby
```

The complete source code tree, just as the developers last left it, will now be copied to a ruby subdirectory on your machine.

This command will check out the head of the development tree. If you want the Ruby 1.8 branch, change trunk to branches/ruby_1_8 in the checkout command.

```
% ruby
puts "Hello, world!"
^D
Hello, world!
```

For most folks, *irb*—Interactive Ruby—is the tool of choice for executing Ruby interactively. irb is a Ruby shell, complete with command-line history, line-editing capabilities, and job control. (In fact, it has its own chapter beginning on page 265.) You run irb from the command line. Once it starts, just type in Ruby code. It will show you the value of each expression as it evaluates it. Exit an irb session by typing exit or by using the end-of-file character on your operating system (normally Ctrl+D or Ctrl+Z).

```
% irb
irb(main):001:0> def sum(n1, n2)
irb(main):002:1>   n1 + n2
irb(main):003:1> end
=> nil
irb(main):004:0> sum(3, 4)
=> 7
irb(main):005:0> sum("cat", "dog")
=> "catdog"
irb(main):006:0> exit
```

We recommend that you get familiar with irb so you can try our examples interactively.

Ruby Programs

The normal way to write Ruby programs is to put them in one or more files. You'll use a text editor (Emacs, vim, TextMate, and so on) or an IDE (such as NetBeans) to create and maintain these files. You'll then run the files either from within the editor or IDE or from the command line. I personally use both techniques, typically running from within the editor for single-file programs and from the command line for more complex ones.

Let's start by creating a simple Ruby program and running it. Open a command window, and navigate to the pickaxe directory you created earlier:

```
$ cd ~/pickaxe          (unix)
C:\> cd \pickaxe        (windows)
```

Then, using your editor of choice, create the file myprog.rb, containing the following:

```
gettingstarted_2.rb
puts "Hello, Ruby Programmer"
puts "It is now #{Time.now}"
```

(Note that the second string contains the text Time.now between curly braces, not parentheses.)

You can run a Ruby program from a file as you would any other shell script, Perl program, or Python program. Simply run the Ruby interpreter, giving it the script name as an argument:

```
$ ruby myprog.rb
Hello, Ruby Programmer
It is now 2009-03-31 09:57:43 -0500
```

On Unix systems, you can use the "shebang" notation as the first line of the program file:[5]

```
gettingstarted_4.rb
#!/usr/local/bin/ruby -w

puts "Hello, Ruby Programmer"
puts "It is now #{Time.now}"
```

If you make this source file executable (using, for instance, chmod +x myprog.rb), Unix lets you run the file as a program:

```
$ ./myprog.rb
Hello, Ruby Programmer
It is now 2009-03-31 09:57:43 -0500
```

You can do something similar under Microsoft Windows using file associations, and you can run Ruby GUI applications by double-clicking their names in Explorer.

---

5. If your system supports it, you can avoid hard-coding the path to Ruby in the "shebang" line by using #!/usr/bin/env ruby, which will search your path for ruby and then execute it.

Ruby Documentation: RDoc and ri

As the volume of the Ruby libraries has grown, it has become impossible to document them all in one book; the standard library that comes with Ruby now contains more than 9,000 methods. Fortunately, an alternative to paper documentation exists for these methods (and classes and modules). Many are now documented internally using a system called *RDoc*.

If a source file is documented using RDoc, its documentation can be extracted and converted into HTML and ri formats.

Several websites contain a complete set of the RDoc documentation for Ruby, but `http://www.ruby-doc.org` is probably the best known. Browse on over, and you should be able to find at least some form of documentation for any Ruby library. The site is adding new documentation all the time.

The ri tool is a local, command-line viewer for this same documentation. Most Ruby distributions now also install the resources used by the ri program.

To find the documentation for a class, type ri *ClassName*. For example, the following lists the summary information for the GC class. (For a list of classes with ri documentation, type ri.)

```
$ ri GC
------------------------------------------------------------- Class: GC
     The GC module provides an interface to Ruby's mark and sweep
     garbage collection mechanism. Some of the underlying methods are
     also available via the ObjectSpace module.
------------------------------------------------------------------------

Class methods:
     count, disable, enable, malloc_allocated_size, malloc_allocations,
     start, stress, stress=

Instance methods:
     garbage_collect
```

For information on a particular method, give its name as a parameter:

```
% ri GC::enable
------------------------------------------------------- GC::enable
     GC.enable    => true or false
------------------------------------------------------------------
     Enables garbage collection, returning true if garbage
     collection was previously disabled.

        GC.disable   #=> false
        GC.enable    #=> true
        GC.enable    #=> false
```

If the method you pass to ri occurs in more than one class or module, ri will list all of the alternatives.

Reissue the command, prefixing the method name with the name of the class and a dot:

```
$ ri assoc
    More than one method matched your request.  You can refine your
    search by asking for information on one of:

Array#assoc [Ruby 1.9.1]
Array#rassoc [Ruby 1.9.1]
Hash#assoc [Ruby 1.9.1]
Hash#rassoc [Ruby 1.9.1]

$ ri Array.assoc
----------------------------------------------------------- Array#assoc
    array.assoc(obj)   ->  an_array  or  nil
-----------------------------------------------------------------------
    Searches through an array whose elements are also arrays
    comparing obj with the first element of each contained array
    using obj.==. Returns the first contained array that matches
    (that is, the first associated array), or nil if no match is
    found. See also Array#rassoc.
        :    :    :
```

For general help on using ri, type ri --help. In particular, you might want to experiment with the --format option, which tells ri how to render decorated text (such as section headings). If your terminal program supports ANSI escape sequences, using --format ansi will generate a nice, colorful display. Once you find a set of options you like, you can set them into the RI environment variable. Using my shell (zsh), this would be done using the following:

```
% export RI="--format ansi --width 70"
```

If a class or module isn't yet documented in RDoc format, ask the friendly folks over at suggestions@ruby-doc.org to consider adding it.

All this command-line hacking may seem a tad off-putting if you're not a regular visitor to the shell prompt. But, in reality, it isn't that difficult, and the power you get from being able to string together commands this way is often surprising. Stick with it, and you'll be well on your way to mastering both Ruby and your computer.

## Chapter 2

Ruby.new

Most books on programming languages look about the same. They start with chapters on basic types: integers, strings, and so on. Then they look at expressions, before moving on to if and while statements. Then, perhaps around Chapter 7 or 8, they'll start mentioning classes. We find that somewhat tedious.

Instead, when we designed this book, we had a grand plan (we were younger then). We wanted to document the language from the top down, starting with classes and objects and ending with the nitty-gritty syntax details. It seemed like a good idea at the time. After all, most everything in Ruby is an object, so it made sense to talk about objects first.

Or so we thought.

Unfortunately, it turns out to be difficult to describe a language that way. If you haven't covered strings, if statements, assignments, and other details, it's difficult to write examples of classes. Throughout our top-down description, we kept coming across low-level details we needed to cover so that the example code would make sense.

So, we came up with another grand plan (they don't call us pragmatic for nothing). We'd still describe Ruby starting at the top. But before we did that, we'd add a short chapter that described all the common language features used in the examples along with the special vocabulary used in Ruby, a kind of mini-tutorial to bootstrap us into the rest of the book. And that mini-tutorial is this chapter.

Ruby Is an Object-Oriented Language

Let's say it again. Ruby is a genuine object-oriented language. Everything you manipulate is an object, and the results of those manipulations are themselves objects. However, many languages make the same claim, and their users often have a different interpretation of what *object-oriented* means and a different terminology for the concepts they employ.

So, before we get too far into the details, let's briefly look at the terms and notation that *we'll* be using.

When you write object-oriented programs, you're normally looking to model concepts from the real world. Typically during this modeling process you'll discover categories of things that need to be represented in code. In a jukebox, the concept of a "song" could be such a category. In Ruby, you'd define a *class* to represent each of these entities. A class is a combination of state (for example, the name of the song) and methods that use that state (perhaps a method to play the song).

Once you have these classes, you'll typically want to create a number of *instances* of each. For the jukebox system containing a class called Song, you'd have separate instances for popular hits such as "Ruby Tuesday," "Enveloped in Python," "String of Pearls," "Small Talk," and so on. The word *object* is used interchangeably with *class instance* (and being lazy typists, we'll probably be using the word *object* more frequently).

In Ruby, these objects are created by calling a *constructor,* a special method associated with a class. The standard constructor is called new.

```
intro_1.rb
song1 = Song.new("Ruby Tuesday")
song2 = Song.new("Enveloped in Python")
# and so on
```

These instances are both derived from the same class, but they have unique characteristics. First, every object has a unique *object identifier* (abbreviated as *object ID*). Second, you can define *instance variables*, variables with values that are unique to each instance. These instance variables hold an object's state. Each of our songs, for example, will probably have an instance variable that holds the song title.

Within each class, you can define *instance methods*. Each method is a chunk of functionality that may be called in the context of the class and (depending on accessibility constraints) from outside the class. These instance methods in turn have access to the object's instance variables and hence to the object's state. A Song class, for example, might define an instance method called play. If the variable my_way referenced a particular Song instance, you'd be able to call that instance's play method and play a particular song.

Methods are invoked by sending a message to an object. The message contains the method's name, along with any parameters the method may need.[1] When an object receives a message, it looks into its own class for a corresponding method. If found, that method is executed. If the method *isn't* found... well, we'll get to that later.

This business of methods and messages may sound complicated, but in practice it is very natural. Let's look at some method calls. In this code, we're using puts, a standard Ruby method that writes its argument(s) to the console, adding a newline after each:

```
puts "gin joint".length
puts "Rick".index("c")
puts 42.even?
puts sam.play(song)
```

---

1.   This idea of expressing method calls in the form of messages comes from Smalltalk.

produces:

```
9
2
true
duh dum, da dum de dum ...
```

Each line shows a method being called as an argument to puts. The thing before the period is called the *receiver*, and the name after the period is the method to be invoked. The first example asks a string for its length, and the second asks a different string to find the index of the letter *c*. The third line asks the number 42 if it is even (the question mark is part of the method name even?). Finally, we ask Sam to play us a song (assuming there's an existing variable called sam that references an appropriate object).

It's worth noting here a major difference between Ruby and most other languages. In (say) Java, you'd find the absolute value of some number by calling a separate function and passing in that number. You could write this:

```
num = Math.abs(num)      // Java code
```

In Ruby, the ability to determine an absolute value is built into numbers—they take care of the details internally. You simply send the message abs to a number object and let it do the work:

```
num       = -1234    # =>   -1234
positive = num.abs   # =>   1234
```

The same applies to all Ruby objects. In C you'd write strlen(name), but in Ruby it's name.length, and so on. This is part of what we mean when we say that Ruby is a genuine object-oriented language.

Some Basic Ruby

Not many people like to read heaps of boring syntax rules when they're picking up a new language, so we're going to cheat. In this section, we'll hit some of the highlights—the stuff you'll just *need* to know if you're going to write Ruby programs. Later, in Chapter 22, which begins on page 313, we'll go into all the gory details.

Let's start with a simple Ruby program. We'll write a method that returns a cheery, personalized greeting. We'll then invoke that method a couple of times:

`intro_5.rb`

```
def say_goodnight(name)
  result = "Good night, " + name
  return result
end

# Time for bed...
puts say_goodnight("John-Boy")
puts say_goodnight("Mary-Ellen")
```

As the example shows, Ruby syntax is clean. You don't need semicolons at the ends of statements as long as you put each statement on a separate line. Ruby comments start with a # character and run to the end of the line. Code layout is pretty much up to you; indentation is not significant (but using two-character indentation will make you friends in the community if you plan on distributing your code).

Methods are defined with the keyword def, followed by the method name (in this case, say_goodnight) and the method's parameters between parentheses. (In fact, the parentheses are optional, but we like to use them.) Ruby doesn't use braces to delimit the bodies of compound statements and definitions. Instead, you simply finish the body with the keyword end. Our method's body is pretty simple. The first line concatenates the literal string "Good night,␣" and the parameter name and assigns the result to the local variable result. The next line returns that result to the caller. Note that we didn't have to declare the variable result; it sprang into existence when we assigned to it.

Having defined the method, we invoke it twice. In both cases, we pass the result to the method puts, which simply outputs its argument followed by a newline (moving on to the next line of output):

```
Good night, John-Boy
Good night, Mary-Ellen
```

The line

```
puts say_goodnight("John-Boy")
```

contains two method calls, one to the method say_goodnight and the other to the method puts. Why does one call have its arguments in parentheses while the other doesn't? In this case, it's purely a matter of taste. The following lines are both equivalent:

```
puts say_goodnight("John-Boy")
puts(say_goodnight("John-Boy"))
```

However, life isn't always that simple, and precedence rules can make it difficult to know which argument goes with which method invocation, so we recommend using parentheses in all but the simplest cases.

This example also shows some Ruby string objects. Ruby has many ways to create a string object, but probably the most common is to use *string literals*, which are sequences of characters between single or double quotation marks. The difference between the two forms is the amount of processing Ruby does on the string while constructing the literal. In the single-quoted case, Ruby does very little. With a few exceptions, what you type into the string literal becomes the string's value.

In the double-quoted case, Ruby does more work. First, it looks for substitutions (sequences that start with a backslash character) and replaces them with some binary value. The most common of these is \n, which is replaced with a newline character. When a string containing a newline is output, that newline becomes a line break:

```
puts "And good night,\nGrandma"
```

produces:

```
And good night,
Grandma
```

The second thing that Ruby does with double-quoted strings is expression interpolation. Within the string, the sequence #{*expression*} is replaced by the value of *expression*. We could use this to rewrite our previous method:

```
intro_10.rb
def say_goodnight(name)
  result = "Good night, #{name}"
  return result
end
puts say_goodnight('Pa')
```

produces:

```
Good night, Pa
```

When Ruby constructs this string object, it looks at the current value of name and substitutes it into the string. Arbitrarily complex expressions are allowed in the #{...} construct. In the following example, we invoke the capitalize method, defined for all strings, to output our parameter with a leading uppercase letter:

```
intro_11.rb
def say_goodnight(name)
  result = "Good night, #{name.capitalize}"
  return result
end
puts say_goodnight('uncle')
```

produces:

```
Good night, Uncle
```

For more information on strings, as well as on the other Ruby standard types, see Chapter 6, which begins on page 87.

Finally, we could simplify this method some more. The value returned by a Ruby method is the value of the last expression evaluated, so we can get rid of the temporary variable and the return statement altogether:

```
intro_12.rb
def say_goodnight(name)
  "Good night, #{name.capitalize}"
end
puts say_goodnight('ma')
```

produces:

```
Good night, Ma
```

We promised that this section would be brief. We have just one more topic to cover: Ruby names. For brevity, we'll be using some terms (such as *class variable*) that we aren't going to define here. However, by talking about the rules now, you'll be ahead of the game when we actually come to discuss class variables and the like later.

Ruby uses a convention that may seem strange at first: the first characters of a name indicate how the name is used. Local variables, method parameters, and method names should all start with a lowercase letter or with an underscore. Global variables are prefixed with a dollar sign ($), and instance variables begin with an "at" sign (@). Class variables start with two "at" signs (@@).[2] Finally, class names, module names, and constants must start with an uppercase letter. Samples of different names are given in Table 2.1 on the next page.

Following this initial character, a name can be any combination of letters, digits, and underscores (with the proviso that the character following an @ sign may not be a digit). However, by convention, multiword instance variables are written with underscores between the words, and multiword class names are written in MixedCase (with each word capitalized). Method names may end with the characters ?, !, and =.

Arrays and Hashes

Ruby's arrays and hashes are indexed collections. Both store collections of objects, accessible using a key. With arrays, the key is an integer, whereas hashes support any object as a key. Both arrays and hashes grow as needed to hold new elements. It's more efficient to access array elements, but hashes provide more flexibility. Any particular array or hash can hold objects of differing types; you can have an array containing an integer, a string, and a floating-point number, as we'll see in a minute.

You can create and initialize a new array object using an *array literal*—a set of elements between square brackets. Given an array object, you can access individual elements by supplying an index between square brackets, as the next example shows. Note that Ruby array indices start at zero.

```
intro_13.rb
a = [ 1, 'cat', 3.14 ]   # array with three elements
puts "The first element is #{a[0]}"
# set the third element
a[2] = nil
puts "The array is now #{a.inspect}"
```

produces:

```
The first element is 1
The array is now [1, "cat", nil]
```

You may have noticed that we used the special value nil in this example. In many languages, the concept of *nil* (or *null*) means "no object." In Ruby, that's not the case; nil is an object, just like any other, that happens to represent nothing. Anyway, let's get back to arrays and hashes.

---

2.   Although we talk about global and class variables here for completeness, you'll find they are rarely used in Ruby programs. There's a lot of evidence that global variables make programs harder to maintain. Class variables are not as dangerous—it's just that people tend not to use them much.

Table 2.1. Example Variable and Class Names

| Variables | | | | Constants and |
Local	Global	Instance	Class	Class Names
name	$debug	@name	@@total	PI
fish_and_chips	$CUSTOMER	@point_1	@@symtab	FeetPerMile
x_axis	$_	@X	@@N	String
thx1138	$plan9	@_	@@x_pos	MyClass
_26	$Global	@plan9	@@SINGLE	JazzSong

Sometimes creating arrays of words can be a pain, what with all the quotes and commas. Fortunately, Ruby has a shortcut: %w does just what we want:

intro_14.rb

```
a = [ 'ant', 'bee', 'cat', 'dog', 'elk' ]
a[0]   # =>   "ant"
a[3]   # =>   "dog"
# this is the same:
a = %w{ ant bee cat dog elk }
a[0]   # =>   "ant"
a[3]   # =>   "dog"
```

Ruby hashes are similar to arrays. A hash literal uses braces rather than square brackets. The literal must supply two objects for every entry: one for the key, the other for the value. The key and value are normally separated by =>.

For example, you may want to map musical instruments to their orchestral sections. You could do this with a hash:

```
inst_section = {
  'cello'    => 'string',
  'clarinet' => 'woodwind',
  'drum'     => 'percussion',
  'oboe'     => 'woodwind',
  'trumpet'  => 'brass',
  'violin'   => 'string'
}
```

The thing to the left of the => is the key, and the thing to the right is the corresponding value. Keys in a particular hash must be unique—you can't have two entries for "drum." The keys and values in a hash can be arbitrary objects—you can have hashes where the values are arrays, other hashes, and so on.

Hashes are indexed using the same square bracket notation as arrays. In this code, we'll use the p method to write the values to the console. This works like puts but displays values such as nil explicitly.

```
p inst_section['oboe']
p inst_section['cello']
p inst_section['bassoon']
```

produces:

```
"woodwind"
"string"
nil
```

As the previous example shows, a hash by default returns nil when indexed by a key it doesn't contain. Normally this is convenient, because nil means false when used in conditional expressions. Sometimes you'll want to change this default. For example, if you're using a hash to count the number of times each different word occurs in a file, it's convenient to have the default value be zero. Then you can use the word as the key and simply increment the corresponding hash value without worrying about whether you've seen that word before. This is easily done by specifying a default value when you create a new, empty hash. (The full source for the word frequency counter is on page 52.)

intro_17.rb

```
histogram = Hash.new(0)    # The default value is zero
histogram['ruby']  # =>   0
histogram['ruby'] = histogram['ruby'] + 1
histogram['ruby']  # =>   1
```

Array and hash objects have lots of useful methods; see the discussion starting on page 47, and the reference sections starting on pages 438 and 524, for details.

Symbols

Often, when programming, you need to create a name for something significant. For example, you might want to refer to the compass points by name, so you'd write this:

```
NORTH = 1
EAST  = 2
SOUTH = 3
WEST  = 4
```

Then, in the rest of your code, you could use the constants instead of the numbers:

```
walk(NORTH)
look(EAST)
```

Most of the time, the actual numeric values of these constants are irrelevant (as long as they are unique). All you want to do is differentiate the four directions.

Ruby offers a cleaner alternative. *Symbols* are simply constant names that you don't have to predeclare and that are guaranteed to be unique. A symbol literal starts with a colon and is normally followed by some kind of name:

```
walk(:north)
look(:east)
```

There's no need to assign some kind of value to a symbol—Ruby takes care of that for you. Ruby also guarantees that no matter where it appears in your program, a particular symbol will have the same value. That is, you can write the following:

```
def walk(direction)
  if direction == :north
    # ...
  end
end
```

Symbols are frequently used as keys in hashes. We could write our previous example as this:

```
inst_section = {
  :cello    => 'string',
  :clarinet => 'woodwind',
  :drum     => 'percussion',
  :oboe     => 'woodwind',
  :trumpet  => 'brass',
  :violin   => 'string'
}
inst_section[:oboe]     # =>    "woodwind"
inst_section[:cello]    # =>    "string"
# Note that strings aren't the same as symbols...
inst_section['cello']   # =>    nil
```

In fact, symbols are so frequently used as hash keys that Ruby 1.9 introduces a new syntax—you can use name: value pairs to create a hash if the keys are symbols:

1.9

```
inst_section = {
  cello:    'string',
  clarinet: 'woodwind',
  drum:     'percussion',
  oboe:     'woodwind',
  trumpet:  'brass',
  violin:   'string'
}
puts "An oboe is a #{inst_section[:oboe]}"
```

produces:

```
An oboe is a woodwind
```

Control Structures

Ruby has all the usual control structures, such as if statements and while loops. Java, C, and Perl programmers may well get caught by the lack of braces around the bodies of these statements. Instead, Ruby uses the keyword end to signify the end of a body:

```
if count > 10
  puts "Try again"
elsif tries == 3
  puts "You lose"
```

```
else
  puts "Enter a number"
end
```

Similarly, while statements are terminated with end:

```
while weight < 100 and num_pallets <= 30
  pallet = next_pallet()
  weight += pallet.weight
  num_pallets += 1
end
```

Most statements in Ruby return a value, which means you can use them as conditions. For example, the method gets returns the next line from the standard input stream or nil when end of file is reached. Because Ruby treats nil as a false value in conditions, you could write the following to process the lines in a file:

```
while line = gets
  puts line.downcase
end
```

Here, the assignment statement sets the variable line to either the next line of text or nil, and then the while statement tests the value of the assignment, terminating the loop when it is nil.

Ruby *statement modifiers* are a useful shortcut if the body of an if or while statement is just a single expression. Simply write the expression, followed by if or while and the condition. For example, here's a simple if statement:

```
if radiation > 3000
  puts "Danger, Will Robinson"
end
```

Here it is again, rewritten using a statement modifier:

```
puts "Danger, Will Robinson" if radiation > 3000
```

Similarly, a while loop such as this:

```
square = 2
while square < 1000
  square = square*square
end
```

becomes this more concise version:

```
square = 2
square = square*square  while square < 1000
```

These statement modifiers should seem familiar to Perl programmers.

Regular Expressions

Most of Ruby's built-in types will be familiar to all programmers. A majority of languages have strings, integers, floats, arrays, and so on. However, regular expression support is typically built into only scripting languages, such as Ruby, Perl, and awk. This is a shame, because regular expressions, although cryptic, are a powerful tool for working with text. And having them built in, rather than tacked on through a library interface, makes a big difference.

Entire books have been written about regular expressions (for example, *Mastering Regular Expressions* [Fri02]), so we won't try to cover everything in this short section. Instead, we'll look at just a few examples of regular expressions in action. You'll find full coverage of regular expressions starting on page 99.

A regular expression is simply a way of specifying a *pattern* of characters to be matched in a string. In Ruby, you typically create a regular expression by writing a pattern between slash characters (*/pattern/*). And, Ruby being Ruby, regular expressions are objects and can be manipulated as such.

For example, you could write a pattern that matches a string containing the text *Perl* or the text *Python* using the following regular expression:

```
/Perl|Python/
```

The forward slashes delimit the pattern, which consists of the two things we're matching, separated by a pipe character (|). This pipe character means "either the thing on the right or the thing on the left," in this case either *Perl* or *Python*. You can use parentheses within patterns, just as you can in arithmetic expressions, so you could also have written this pattern like this:

```
/P(erl|ython)/
```

You can also specify *repetition* within patterns. /ab+c/ matches a string containing an *a* followed by one or more *b*'s, followed by a *c*. Change the plus to an asterisk, and /ab*c/ creates a regular expression that matches one *a*, zero or more *b*'s, and one *c*.

You can also match one of a group of characters within a pattern. Some common examples are *character classes* such as \s, which matches a whitespace character (space, tab, newline, and so on); \d, which matches any digit; and \w, which matches any character that may appear in a typical word. A dot (.) matches (almost) any character. A table of these character classes appears on page 107.

We can put all this together to produce some useful regular expressions:

```
/\d\d:\d\d:\d\d/       # a time such as 12:34:56
/Perl.*Python/         # Perl, zero or more other chars, then Python
/Perl Python/          # Perl, a space, and Python
/Perl *Python/         # Perl, zero or more spaces, and Python
/Perl +Python/         # Perl, one or more spaces, and Python
/Perl\s+Python/        # Perl, whitespace characters, then Python
/Ruby (Perl|Python)/   # Ruby, a space, and either Perl or Python
```

Once you have created a pattern, it seems a shame not to use it. The match operator =~ can be used to match a string against a regular expression. If the pattern is found in the string, =~ returns its starting position; otherwise, it returns nil. This means you can use regular expressions as the condition in if and while statements. For example, the following code fragment writes a message if a string contains the text *Perl* or *Python*:

```
if line =~ /Perl|Python/
   puts "Scripting language mentioned: #{line}"
end
```

The part of a string matched by a regular expression can be replaced with different text using one of Ruby's substitution methods:

```
line.sub(/Perl/, 'Ruby')    # replace first 'Perl' with 'Ruby'
line.gsub(/Python/, 'Ruby') # replace every 'Python' with 'Ruby'
```

You can replace every occurrence of *Perl* and *Python* with *Ruby* using this:

```
line.gsub(/Perl|Python/, 'Ruby')
```

We'll have a lot more to say about regular expressions as we go through the book.

Blocks and Iterators

This section briefly describes one of Ruby's particular strengths. We're about to look at *code blocks*, which are chunks of code you can associate with method invocations, almost as if they were parameters. This is an incredibly powerful feature. One of our reviewers commented at this point: "This is pretty interesting and important, so if you weren't paying attention before, you should probably start now." We'd have to agree.

You can use code blocks to implement callbacks (but they're simpler than Java's anonymous inner classes), to pass around chunks of code (but they're more flexible than C's function pointers), and to implement iterators.

Code blocks are just chunks of code between braces or between do...end. This is a code block:

```
{ puts "Hello" }
```

So is this:

```
do
   club.enroll(person)
   person.socialize
end
```

Why are there two kinds of delimiter? It's partly because sometimes one feels more natural to write than another. It's partly too because they have different precedences: the braces bind more tightly than the do/end pairs. In this book, we try to follow what is becoming a Ruby standard and use braces for single-line blocks and do/end for multiline blocks.

All you can do with a block is associate it with a call to a method. You do this by putting the start of the block at the end of the source line containing the method call.

For example, in the following code, the block containing puts "Hi" is associated with the call to the method greet (which we don't show):

```
greet   { puts "Hi" }
```

If the method has parameters, they appear before the block:

```
verbose_greet("Dave", "loyal customer")   { puts "Hi" }
```

A method can then invoke an associated block one or more times using the Ruby yield statement. You can think of yield as being something like a method call that invokes the block associated with the call to the method containing the yield.

The following example shows this in action. We define a method that calls yield twice. We then call this method, putting a block on the same line, after the call (and after any arguments to the method).[3]

```
intro_41.rb
def call_block
  puts "Start of method"
  yield
  yield
  puts "End of method"
end
call_block { puts "In the block" }
```

produces:

```
Start of method
In the block
In the block
End of method
```

The code in the block (puts "In the block") is executed twice, once for each call to yield.

You can provide arguments to the call to yield, and they will be passed to the block. Within the block, you list the names of the parameters to receive these arguments between vertical bars (| params... |). The following example shows a method calling its associated block twice, passing the block two arguments each time:

```
intro_42.rb
def who_says_what
  yield("Dave", "hello")
  yield("Andy", "goodbye")
end
who_says_what {|person, phrase| puts "#{person} says #{phrase}"}
```

produces:

```
Dave says hello
Andy says goodbye
```

---

3.   Some people like to think of the association of a block with a method as a kind of argument passing. This works on one level, but it isn't really the whole story. You may be better off thinking of the block and the method as coroutines, which transfer control back and forth between themselves.

Code blocks are used throughout the Ruby library to implement *iterators*, which are methods that return successive elements from some kind of collection, such as an array:

```
animals = %w( ant bee cat dog elk )    # create an array
animals.each {|animal| puts animal }   # iterate over the contents
```

produces:

```
ant
bee
cat
dog
elk
```

Many of the looping constructs that are built into languages such as C and Java are simply method calls in Ruby, with the methods invoking the associated block zero or more times:

```
intro_44.rb
[ 'cat', 'dog', 'horse' ].each {|name| print name, " " }
5.times {   print "*" }
3.upto(6) {|i|   print i }
('a'..'e').each {|char| print char }
```

produces:

```
cat dog horse *****3456abcde
```

Here we ask an array to call the block once for each of its elements. Then, object 5 calls a block five times. Rather than use for loops, in Ruby we can ask the number 3 to call a block, passing in successive values until it reaches 6. Finally, the range of characters from *a* to *e* invokes a block using the method each.

Reading and 'Riting

Ruby comes with a comprehensive I/O library. However, in most of the examples in this book, we'll stick to a few simple methods. We've already come across two methods that do output: puts writes its arguments with a newline after each; print also writes its arguments but with no newline. Both can be used to write to any I/O object, but by default they write to standard output.

Another output method we use a lot is printf, which prints its arguments under the control of a format string (just like printf in C or Perl):

```
printf("Number: %5.2f,\nString: %s\n", 1.23, "hello")
```

produces:

```
Number:  1.23,
String: hello
```

In this example, the format string "Number: %5.2f,\nString: %s\n" tells printf to substitute in a floating-point number (with a minimum of five characters, two after the decimal point) and a string. Notice the newlines (\n) embedded in the string; each moves the output onto the next line.

You have many ways to read input into your program. Probably the most traditional is to use the routine gets, which returns the next line from your program's standard input stream:

```
line = gets
print line
```

Because gets returns nil when it reaches the end of input, you can use its return value in a loop condition. Notice that here the condition to the while is an assignment: we store whatever gets returns into the variable line and then test to see whether that returned value was nil or false before continuing:

```
while line = gets
  print line
end
```

Command-Line Arguments

When you run a Ruby program from the command line, you can pass in arguments. These are accessible in two different ways.

First, the array ARGV contains each of the arguments passed to the running program. Create a file called cmd_line.rb that contains the following:

```
puts "You gave #{ARGV.size} arguments"
p ARGV
```

When we run it with arguments, we can see that they get passed in:

```
$ ruby cmd_line.rb ant bee cat dog
```

produces:

```
You gave 4 arguments
["ant", "bee", "cat", "dog"]
```

Often, the arguments to a program are the names of files that you want to process. In this case, you can use a second technique: the variable ARGF is a special kind of I/O object that acts like all the contents of all the files whose names are passed on the command line (or standard input if you don't pass any filenames). We'll look at that some more on page 330.

Onward and Upward

That's it. We've finished our lightning-fast tour of some of the basic features of Ruby. We took a look at objects, methods, strings, containers, and regular expressions; saw some simple control structures; and looked at some rather nifty iterators. We hope this chapter has given you enough ammunition to be able to attack the rest of this book.

Time to move on and move up—up to a higher level. Next, we'll be looking at classes and objects, things that are at the same time both the highest-level constructs in Ruby and the essential underpinnings of the entire language.

Chapter 3

Classes, Objects, and Variables

From the examples we've shown so far, you may be wondering about our earlier assertion that Ruby is an object-oriented language. Well, this chapter is where we justify that claim. We're going to be looking at how you create classes and objects in Ruby and at some of the ways in which Ruby is more powerful than most object-oriented languages.

As we saw back on page 13, everything we manipulate in Ruby is an object. And every object in Ruby was generated either directly or indirectly from a class. In this chapter, we'll look in more depth at creating and manipulating those classes.

Let's give ourselves a simple problem to solve. Let's say that we're running a secondhand bookstore. Every week, we do stock control. A gang of clerks uses portable bar-code scanners to record every book on our shelves. Each scanner generates a simple comma-separated value (CSV) file containing one row for each book scanned. The row contains (among other things) the book's ISBN and price. An extract from one of these files looks something like this:

```
"Date","ISBN","Amount"
"2008-04-12","978-1-9343561-0-4",39.45
"2008-04-13","978-1-9343561-6-6",45.67
"2008-04-14","978-1-9343560-7-4",36.95
```

Our job is to take all the CSV files and work out how many of each title we have, as well as the total list price of the books in stock.

Whenever you're designing OO systems, a good first step is to identify the *things* you're dealing with. Typically each type of thing becomes a class in your final program, and the things themselves are instances of these classes.

It seems pretty clear that we'll need something to represent each data reading captured by the scanners. Each instance of this will represent a particular row of data, and the collection of all of these objects will represent all the data we've captured.

Let's call this class BookInStock. (Remember, class names start with an uppercase letter, and method names normally start with a lowercase letter.)

```
class BookInStock
end
```

As we saw in the previous chapter, we can create new instances of this class using new:

```
a_book = BookInStock.new
another_book = BookInStock.new
```

After this code runs, we'd have two distinct objects, both of class BookInStock. But, apart from the fact that they have different identities, these two objects are otherwise the same— there's nothing to distinguish one from the other. And, what's worse, these objects actually don't hold any of the information we need them to hold.

The best way to fix this is to provide the objects with an initialize method. This lets us set the state of each object as it is constructed. We store this state in *instance variables* inside the object. (Remember instance variables? They're the ones that start with an @ sign.) Because each object in Ruby has its own distinct set of instance variables, each object can have its own unique state.

So, here's our updated class definition:

```
tutclasses_4.rb
class BookInStock
  def initialize(isbn, price)
    @isbn  = isbn
    @price = Float(price)
  end
end
```

initialize is a special method in Ruby programs. When you call BookInStock.new to create a new object, Ruby allocates some memory to hold an uninitialized object and then calls that object's initialize method, passing in any parameters that were passed to new. This gives you a chance to write code that sets up your object's state.

For class BookInStock, the initialize method takes two parameters. These parameters act just like local variables within the method, so they follow the local variable naming convention of starting with a lowercase letter. But, as local variables, they would just evaporate once the initialize method returns, so we need to transfer them into instance variables. This is very common behavior in an initialize method—the intent is to have our object set up and usable by the time initialize returns.

This method also illustrates something that often trips up newcomers to Ruby. Notice how we say @isbn = isbn. It's easy to imagine that the two variables here, @isbn and isbn, are somehow related—it looks like they have the same name. But they don't. The former is an instance variable, and the "at" sign is actually part of its name.

Finally, this code illustrates a simple piece of validation. The Float method takes its argument and converts it to a floating-point number,[1] terminating the program with an error if that conversion fails. (Later in the book we'll see how to handle these exceptional situations.) What we're doing here is saying that we want to accept any object for the price parameter as long as that parameter can be converted to a float. We can pass in a float, an integer, and even a string containing the representation of a float, and it will work. Let's try this now. We'll create three objects, each with different initial state. The p method prints out an internal representation of an object. Using it, we can see that in each case our parameters got transferred into the object's state, ending up as instance variables:

```
tutclasses_5.rb
class BookInStock
  def initialize(isbn, price)
    @isbn  = isbn
    @price = Float(price)
  end
end
b1 = BookInStock.new("isbn1", 3)
p b1

b2 = BookInStock.new("isbn2", 3.14)
p b2

b3 = BookInStock.new("isbn3", "5.67")
p b3
```

produces:

```
#<BookInStock:0x0a37f0 @isbn="isbn1", @price=3.0>
#<BookInStock:0x0a3584 @isbn="isbn2", @price=3.14>
#<BookInStock:0x0a3354 @isbn="isbn3", @price=5.67>
```

Why did we use p to write out our objects, rather than puts? Well, let's repeat the code using puts:

```
tutclasses_6.rb
b1 = BookInStock.new("isbn1", 3)
puts b1
b2 = BookInStock.new("isbn2", 3.14)
puts b2
b3 = BookInStock.new("isbn3", 5.67)
puts b3
```

produces:

```
#<BookInStock:0x0a38cc>
#<BookInStock:0x0a3764>
#<BookInStock:0x0a36d8>
```

---

1. Yes, we know. We shouldn't be holding prices in inexact old floats. Ruby has classes that hold fixed-point values exactly, but we want to look at classes, not arithmetic, in this section.

Remember, puts simply writes strings to your program's standard output. When you pass it an object based on a class you wrote, it doesn't really know what to do with it, so it uses a very simple expedient: it writes the name of the object's class, followed by a colon and the object's unique identifier (a hexadecimal number). It puts the whole lot inside #<...>.

Our experience tells us that during development we'll be printing out the contents of a BookInStock object many times, and the default formatting leaves something to be desired. Fortunately, Ruby has a standard message, to_s, that it sends to any object it wants to render as a string. So, when we pass one of our BookInStock objects to puts, the puts method calls to_s in that object to get its string representation. So, let's override the default implementation of to_s to give us a better rendering of our objects:

`tutclasses_7.rb`

```ruby
class BookInStock
  def initialize(isbn, price)
    @isbn  = isbn
    @price = Float(price)
  end
  def to_s
    "ISBN: #{@isbn}, price: #{@price}"
  end
end
b1 = BookInStock.new("isbn1", 3)
puts b1
b2 = BookInStock.new("isbn2", 3.14)
puts b2
b3 = BookInStock.new("isbn3", "5.67")
puts b3
```

produces:

```
ISBN: isbn1, price: 3.0
ISBN: isbn2, price: 3.14
ISBN: isbn3, price: 5.67
```

There's something going on here that's both trivial and profound. See how the values we set into the instance variables @isbn and @price in the initialize method are subsequently available in the to_s method? That shows how instance variables work—they're stored with each object and available to all the instance methods of those objects.

Objects and Attributes

The BookInStock objects we've created so far have an internal state (the ISBN and price). That state is private to those objects—no other object can access an object's instance variables. In general, this is a Good Thing. It means that the object is solely responsible for maintaining its own consistency.

However, an object that is totally secretive is pretty useless—you can create it, but then you can't do anything with it. You'll normally define methods that let you access and manipulate the state of an object, allowing the outside world to interact with the object. These externally visible facets of an object are called its *attributes*.

For our BookInStock objects, the first thing we may need is the ability to find out the ISBN and price (so we can count each distinct book and perform price calculations). One way of doing that is to write accessor methods:

```
tutclasses_8.rb
class BookInStock
  def initialize(isbn, price)
    @isbn  = isbn
    @price = Float(price)
  end
  def isbn
    @isbn
  end
  def price
    @price
  end
  # ..
end
book = BookInStock.new("isbn1", 12.34)
puts "ISBN  = #{book.isbn}"
puts "Price = #{book.price}"
```

produces:

```
ISBN  = isbn1
Price = 12.34
```

Here we've defined two accessor methods to return the values of the two instance variables. The method isbn, for example, returns the value of the instance variable @isbn (because the last thing executed in the method is the expression that simply evaluates the @isbn variable).

Because writing accessor methods is such a common idiom, Ruby provides a convenient shortcut. attr_reader creates these attribute reader methods for you:

```
tutclasses_9.rb
class BookInStock
  attr_reader :isbn, :price
  def initialize(isbn, price)
    @isbn  = isbn
    @price = Float(price)
  end
  # ..
end
book = BookInStock.new("isbn1", 12.34)
puts "ISBN  = #{book.isbn}"
puts "Price = #{book.price}"
```

produces:

```
ISBN  = isbn1
Price = 12.34
```

This is the first time we've used *symbols* in this chapter. As we discussed back on page 20, symbols are just a convenient way of referencing a name. In this code, you can think of

:isbn as meaning the *name* isbn and plain isbn as meaning the *value* of the variable. In this example, we named the accessor methods isbn and price. The corresponding instance variables are @isbn and @price. These accessor methods are identical to the ones we wrote by hand earlier.

There's a common misconception, particularly among people who come from languages such as Java and C#, that the attr_reader declaration somehow declares instance variables. It doesn't. It creates the accessor methods, but the variables themselves don't need to be declared—they just pop into existence when you use them. Ruby completely decouples instance variables and accessor methods, as we'll see in the section *Virtual Attributes* on the next page.

Writable Attributes

Sometimes you need to be able to set an attribute from outside the object. For example, let's assume that we sometimes have to discount the price of some titles after reading in the raw scan data.

In languages such as C# and Java, you'd do this with *setter functions*:

```
class JavaBookInStock {                        // Java code
  private double _price;
  public double getPrice() {
    return _price;
  }
  public void setPrice(double newPrice) {
    _price = newPrice;
  }
}
b = new JavaBookInStock(....);
b.setPrice(calculate_discount(b.getPrice()));
```

In Ruby, the attributes of an object can be accessed as if they were any other variable. We saw this earlier with phrases such as book.isbn. So, it seems natural to be able to assign to these variables when you want to set the value of an attribute. It turns out you do that by creating a Ruby method whose name ends with an equals sign. These methods can be used as the target of assignments:

tutclasses_11.rb

```
class BookInStock
  attr_reader :isbn, :price
  def initialize(isbn, price)
    @isbn  = isbn
    @price = Float(price)
  end
  def price=(new_price)
    @price = new_price
  end
  # ...
end
```

```
book = BookInStock.new("isbn1", 33.80)
puts "ISBN     = #{book.isbn}"
puts "Price    = #{book.price}"
book.price = book.price * 0.75          # discount price
puts "New price = #{book.price}"
```

produces:

```
ISBN      = isbn1
Price     = 33.8
New price = 25.35
```

The assignment book.price = book.price * 0.75 invokes the method price= in the book object, passing it the discounted price as an argument. If you create a method whose name ends with an equals sign, that name can appear on the left side of an assignment.

Again, Ruby provides a shortcut for creating these simple attribute-setting methods. If you want a write-only accessor, you can use the form attr_writer, but that's fairly rare. You're far more likely to want both a reader and a writer for a given attribute, so you'll use the handy-dandy attr_accessor method:

```
tutclasses_12.rb
class BookInStock
  attr_reader    :isbn
  attr_accessor :price
  def initialize(isbn, price)
    @isbn  = isbn
    @price = Float(price)
  end
  # ...
end
book = BookInStock.new("isbn1", 33.80)
puts "ISBN     = #{book.isbn}"
puts "Price    = #{book.price}"
book.price = book.price * 0.75          # discount price
puts "New price = #{book.price}"
```

produces:

```
ISBN      = isbn1
Price     = 33.8
New price = 25.35
```

Virtual Attributes

These attribute-accessing methods do not have to be just simple wrappers around an object's instance variables. For example, you may want to access the price as an exact number of cents, rather than as a floating-point number of dollars.[2]

---

2. We multiply the floating-point price times 100 to get the price in cents but then add 0.5 before converting to an integer. Why? Because floating-point numbers don't always have an exact internal representation. When we

```
tutclasses_13.rb
class BookInStock
  attr_reader    :isbn
  attr_accessor :price
  def initialize(isbn, price)
    @isbn  = isbn
    @price = Float(price)
  end
  def price_in_cents
    Integer(price*100 + 0.5)
  end
  # ...
end
book = BookInStock.new("isbn1", 33.80)
puts "Price          = #{book.price}"
puts "Price in cents = #{book.price_in_cents}"
```

produces:

```
Price          = 33.8
Price in cents = 3380
```

We can take this even further and allow people to assign to our virtual attribute, mapping the value to the instance variable internally:

```
tutclasses_14.rb
class BookInStock
  attr_reader    :isbn
  attr_accessor :price
  def initialize(isbn, price)
    @isbn  = isbn
    @price = Float(price)
  end
  def price_in_cents
    Integer(price*100 + 0.5)
  end
  def price_in_cents=(cents)
    @price = cents / 100.0
  end
  # ...
end
book = BookInStock.new("isbn1", 33.80)
puts "Price          = #{book.price}"
puts "Price in cents = #{book.price_in_cents}"
book.price_in_cents = 1234
```

---

multiply 33.8 times 100, we get 3379.99999999999954525265. The Integer method would truncate this to 3379. Adding 0.5 before calling Integer rounds up the floating-point value, ensuring we get the best integer representation. This is a good example of why you want to use BigDecimal, not Float, in financial calculations.

```
puts "Price          = #{book.price}"
puts "Price in cents = #{book.price_in_cents}"
```

produces:

```
Price          = 33.8
Price in cents = 3380
Price          = 12.34
Price in cents = 1234
```

Here we've used attribute methods to create a virtual instance variable. To the outside world, price_in_cents seems to be an attribute like any other. Internally, though, it has no corresponding instance variable.

This is more than a curiosity. In his landmark book *Object-Oriented Software Construction* [Mey97], Bertrand Meyer calls this the *Uniform Access Principle*. By hiding the difference between instance variables and calculated values, you are shielding the rest of the world from the implementation of your class. You're free to change how things work in the future without impacting the millions of lines of code that use your class. This is a big win.

Attributes, Instance Variables, and Methods

This description of attributes may leave you thinking that they're nothing more than methods —why'd we need to invent a fancy name for them? In a way, that's absolutely right. An attribute *is* just a method. Sometimes an attribute simply returns the value of an instance variable. Sometimes an attribute returns the result of a calculation. And sometimes those funky methods with equals signs at the end of their names are used to update the state of an object. So, the question is, where do attributes stop and regular methods begin? What makes something an attribute and not just a plain old method? Ultimately, that's one of those "angels on a pinhead" questions. Here's a personal take.

When you design a class, you decide what internal state it has and also decide how that state is to appear on the outside (to users of your class). The internal state is held in instance variables. The external state is exposed through methods we're calling *attributes*. And the other actions your class can perform are just regular methods. It really isn't a crucially important distinction, but by calling the external state of an object its *attributes*, you're helping clue people in to how they should view the class you've written.

Classes Working with Other Classes

Our original challenge was to read in data from multiple CSV files and produce various simple reports. So far, all we have is BookInStock, a class that represents the data for one book.

During OO design, you identify external things and make them classes in your code. But there's another source of classes in your designs. There are the classes that correspond to things inside your code itself. For example, we know that the program we're writing will need to consolidate and summarize CSV data feeds. But that's a very passive statement. Let's turn it into a design by asking ourselves *what* does the summarizing and consolidating.

And the answer (in our case) is a *CSV reader*. Let's make it into a class. Here it is in skeletal form:

```ruby
class CsvReader
  def initialize
    # ...
  end

  def read_in_csv_data(csv_file_name)
    # ...
  end

  def total_value_in_stock
    # ...
  end

  def number_of_each_isbn
    # ...
  end
end
```

We'd call it using something like this:

```ruby
reader = CsvReader.new
reader.read_in_csv_data("file1.csv")
reader.read_in_csv_data("file2.csv")
   :           :              :
puts "Total value in stock = #{reader.total_value_in_stock}"
```

We need to be able to handle multiple CSV files, so our reader object needs to accumulate the values from each CSV file it is fed. We'll do that by keeping an array of values in an instance variable. And how shall we represent each book's data? Well, we just finished writing the BookInStock class, so that problem is solved. The only other question is how we parse data in a CSV file. Fortunately, Ruby comes with a good CSV library (described on page 730). Given a CSV file with a header line, we can iterate over the remaining rows and extract values by name:

```ruby
class CsvReader
  def initialize
    @books_in_stock = []
  end

  def read_in_csv_data(csv_file_name)
    CSV.foreach(csv_file_name, headers: true) do |row|
      @books_in_stock << BookInStock.new(row["ISBN"], row["Amount"])
    end
  end
end
```

Just because you're probably wondering what's going on, let's dissect that read_in_csv_data method. On the first line, we tell the CSV library to open the file with the given name. The headers: true option tells the library to parse the first line of the file as the names of the columns.

The library then reads the rest of the file, passing each row in turn to the block (the code between do and end).[3] Inside the block, we extract the data from the ISBN and Amount columns and use that data to create a new BookInStock object. We then append that object to an instance variable called @books_in_stock. And just where does that variable come from? It's an array that we created in the initialize method.

Again, this is the pattern you want to aim for. Your initialize method sets up an environment for your object, leaving it in a usable state. Other methods then use that state.

So, let's turn this from a code fragment into a working program. We're going to organize our source into three files. The first, book_in_stock.rb, will contain the definition of the class BookInStock. The second, csv_reader.rb, is the source for the CsvReader class. Finally, a third file, stock_stats.rb, is the main driver program.

Here's book_in_stock.rb:

book_in_stock.rb
```
class BookInStock
  attr_reader :isbn, :price
  def initialize(isbn, price)
    @isbn  = isbn
    @price = Float(price)
  end
end
```

Here's the csv_reader.rb file. The CsvReader class has two external dependencies: it needs the standard CSV library, and it needs the BookInStock class that's defined in the file book_in_stock.rb. Ruby has a couple of helper methods that let us load external files. In this file we use require to load in the Ruby CSV library and require_relative to load in the book_in_stock class we wrote. (We use require_relative for this because the location of the file we're loading is relative to the file we're loading it from—they're both in the same directory.)

csv_reader.rb
```
require 'csv'
require_relative 'book_in_stock'
class CsvReader
  def initialize
    @books_in_stock = []
  end
  def read_in_csv_data(csv_file_name)
    CSV.foreach(csv_file_name, headers: true) do |row|
      @books_in_stock << BookInStock.new(row["ISBN"], row["Amount"])
    end
  end
```

---

3. If you encounter an error along the lines of 'Float': can't convert nil into Float (TypeError) when you run this code, you've likely got extra spaces at the end of the header line in your CSV data file. The CSV library is pretty strict about the formats it accepts.

```
    # later we'll see how to use inject to sum a collection
    def total_value_in_stock
      sum = 0.0
      @books_in_stock.each {|book| sum += book.price}
      sum
    end
    def number_of_each_isbn
      # ...
    end
  end
```

And finally, here's our main program, in the file stock_stats.rb:

stock_stats.rb

```
require_relative 'csv_reader'
reader = CsvReader.new
ARGV.each do |csv_file_name|
  STDERR.puts "Processing #{csv_file_name}"
  reader.read_in_csv_data(csv_file_name)
end
puts "Total value = #{reader.total_value_in_stock}"
```

Again, this file uses require_relative to bring in the library it needs (in this case, just the csv_reader.rb file). It uses the ARGV variable to access the program's command-line arguments, loading CSV data for each.

We can run this program using the simple CSV data file we showed on page 29:

```
$ ruby stock_stats.rb data.csv
```

produces:

```
Processing data.csv
Total value = 122.07
```

Do we need three source files for this? No. In fact, most Ruby developers would probably start off by sticking all this code into a single file—it would contain both class definitions as well as the driver code. But as your programs grow (and almost all programs grow over time), you'll find that this starts to get cumbersome. You'll also find it harder to write automated tests against the code if it is in a monolithic chunk. Finally, you won't be able to reuse classes if they're all bundled into the final program.

Anyway, let's get back to our discussion of classes.

Access Control

When designing a class interface, it's important to consider just how much of your class you'll be exposing to the outside world. Allow too much access into your class, and you risk increasing the coupling in your application—users of your class will be tempted to rely on details of your class's implementation, rather than on its logical interface. The good news is that the only easy way to change an object's state in Ruby is by calling one of its methods. Control access to the methods, and you've controlled access to the object. A good rule of thumb is never to expose methods that could leave an object in an invalid state.

Ruby gives you three levels of protection:

- *Public methods* can be called by anyone—no access control is enforced. Methods are public by default (except for initialize, which is always private).
- *Protected methods* can be invoked only by objects of the defining class and its subclasses. Access is kept within the family.
- *Private methods* cannot be called with an explicit receiver—the receiver is always the current object, also known as *self*. This means that private methods can be called only in the context of the current object; you can't invoke another object's private methods.

The difference between "protected" and "private" is fairly subtle and is different in Ruby than in most common OO languages. If a method is protected, it may be called by *any* instance of the defining class or its subclasses. If a method is private, it may be called only within the context of the calling object—it is never possible to access another object's private methods directly, even if the object is of the same class as the caller.

Ruby differs from other OO languages in another important way. Access control is determined dynamically, as the program runs, not statically. You will get an access violation only when the code attempts to execute the restricted method.

Specifying Access Control

You specify access levels to methods within class or module definitions using one or more of the three functions public, protected, and private. You can use each function in two different ways.

If used with no arguments, the three functions set the default access control of subsequently defined methods. This is probably familiar behavior if you're a C++ or Java programmer, where you'd use keywords such as public to achieve the same effect:

```
class MyClass
      def method1    # default is 'public'
        #...
      end
    protected        # subsequent methods will be 'protected'
      def method2    # will be 'protected'
        #...
      end
    private          # subsequent methods will be 'private'
      def method3    # will be 'private'
        #...
      end
    public           # subsequent methods will be 'public'
      def method4    # so this will be 'public'
        #...
      end
  end
```

Alternatively, you can set access levels of named methods by listing them as arguments to the access control functions:

tutclasses_23.rb

```ruby
class MyClass
  def method1
  end
  # ... and so on
  public    :method1, :method4
  protected :method2
  private   :method3
end
```

It's time for some examples. Perhaps we're modeling an accounting system where every debit has a corresponding credit. Because we want to ensure that no one can break this rule, we'll make the methods that do the debits and credits private, and we'll define our external interface in terms of transactions.

tutclasses_24.rb

```ruby
class Account
    attr_accessor :balance
    def initialize(balance)
      @balance = balance
    end
end
class Transaction
    def initialize(account_a, account_b)
      @account_a = account_a
      @account_b = account_b
    end
  private
    def debit(account, amount)
      account.balance -= amount
    end
    def credit(account, amount)
      account.balance += amount
    end
  public
    #...
    def transfer(amount)
      debit(@account_a, amount)
      credit(@account_b, amount)
    end
    #...
end
savings = Account.new(100)
checking = Account.new(200)
trans = Transaction.new(checking, savings)
trans.transfer(50)
```

Protected access is used when objects need to access the internal state of other objects of the same class. For example, we may want to allow individual Account objects to compare their cleared balances but to hide those balances from the rest of the world (perhaps because we present them in a different form):

```
tutclasses_25.rb
class Account
  attr_reader :cleared_balance  # accessor method 'cleared_balance'
  protected :cleared_balance    # and make it protected
  def greater_balance_than(other)
    return @cleared_balance > other.cleared_balance
  end
end
```

Because cleared_balance is protected, it's available only within Account objects.

Variables

Now that we've gone to the trouble to create all these objects, let's make sure we don't lose them. Variables are used to keep track of objects; each variable holds a reference to an object.

Let's confirm this with some code:

```
tutclasses_26.rb
person = "Tim"
puts "The object in 'person' is a #{person.class}"
puts "The object has an id of #{person.object_id}"
puts "and a value of '#{person}'"
```

produces:

```
The object in 'person' is a String
The object has an id of 338010
and a value of 'Tim'
```

On the first line, Ruby creates a new String object with the value Tim. A reference to this object is placed in the local variable person. A quick check shows that the variable has indeed taken on the personality of a string, with an object ID, a class, and a value.

So, is a variable an object? In Ruby, the answer is "no." A variable is simply a reference to an object. Objects float around in a big pool somewhere (the heap, most of the time) and are pointed to by variables. Let's make the example slightly more complicated:

```
tutclasses_27.rb
person1 = "Tim"
person2 = person1
person1[0] = 'J'
puts "person1 is #{person1}"
puts "person2 is #{person2}"
```

produces:

```
person1 is Jim
person2 is Jim
```

What happened here? We changed the first character of person1, but both person1 and person2 changed from Tim to Jim.

It all comes back to the fact that variables hold references to objects, not the objects themselves. The assignment of person1 to person2 doesn't create any new objects; it simply copies person1's object reference to person2 so that both person1 and person2 refer to the same object. We show this in Figure 3.1 on the facing page.

Assignment *aliases* objects, potentially giving you multiple variables that reference the same object. But can't this cause problems in your code? It can, but not as often as you'd think (objects in Java, for example, work exactly the same way). For instance, in the example in Figure 3.1, you could avoid aliasing by using the dup method of String, which creates a new String object with identical contents:

tutclasses_28.rb

```
person1 = "Tim"
person2 = person1.dup
person1[0] = "J"
puts "person1 is #{person1}"
puts "person2 is #{person2}"
```

produces:

```
person1 is Jim
person2 is Tim
```

You can also prevent anyone from changing a particular object by freezing it. Attempt to alter a frozen object, and Ruby will raise a RuntimeError exception:

tutclasses_29.rb

```
person1 = "Tim"
person2 = person1
person1.freeze        # prevent modifications to the object
person2[0] = "J"
```

produces:

```
prog.rb:4:in `[]=': can't modify frozen string (RuntimeError)
    from /tmp/prog.rb:4:in `<main>'
```

There's more to say about classes and objects in Ruby. We still have to look at class methods and at concepts such as mixins and inheritance. We'll do that in Chapter 5 on page 71. But, for now, take away the fact that everything you manipulate in Ruby is an object and the fact that objects start life as instances of classes. And one of the most common things we do with objects is create collections of them. But that's the subject of our next chapter.

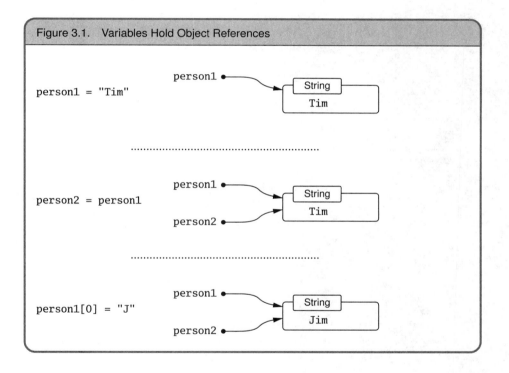

Figure 3.1. Variables Hold Object References

Chapter 4

Containers, Blocks, and Iterators

Most real programs deal with collections of data: the people in a course, the songs in your playlist, the books in the store. Ruby comes with two built-in classes to handle these collections: arrays and hashes.[1] Mastery of these two classes is key to being an effective Ruby programmer. This mastery may take some time, because both classes have large interfaces.

But it isn't just these classes that give Ruby its power when dealing with collections. Ruby also has a block syntax that lets you encapsulate chunks of code. When paired with collections, these blocks become powerful iterator constructs. In this chapter, we'll look at the two collection classes as well as blocks and iterators.

Arrays

The class Array holds a collection of object references. Each object reference occupies a position in the array, identified by a non-negative integer index.

You can create arrays by using literals or by explicitly creating an Array object. A literal array is simply a list of objects between square brackets. (In the code examples that follow, we're often going to show the value of expressions such as a[0] in a comment at the end of the line. If you simply typed this fragment of code into a file and executed it using Ruby, you'd see no output—you'd need to add something like a call to puts to have the values written to the console.)

```
a = [ 3.14159, "pie", 99 ]
a.class    # =>   Array
a.length   # =>   3
a[0]       # =>   3.14159
a[1]       # =>   "pie"
a[2]       # =>   99
a[3]       # =>   nil
```

---

1. Some languages call hashes *associative arrays* or *dictionaries*.

```
b = Array.new
b.class     # =>   Array
b.length    # =>   0
b[0] = "second"
b[1] = "array"
b           # =>   ["second", "array"]
```

Arrays are indexed using the [] operator. As with most Ruby operators, this is actually a method (an instance method of class Array) and hence can be overridden in subclasses. As the example shows, array indices start at zero. Index an array with a non-negative integer, and it returns the object at that position or returns nil if nothing is there. Index an array with a negative integer, and it counts from the end. This indexing scheme is illustrated in more detail in Figure 4.1 on the facing page.

```
a = [ 1, 3, 5, 7, 9 ]
a[-1]    # =>   9
a[-2]    # =>   7
a[-99]   # =>   nil
```

You can also index arrays with a pair of numbers, [start, count]. This returns a new array consisting of references to count objects starting at position start:

```
a = [ 1, 3, 5, 7, 9 ]
a[1, 3]    # =>   [3, 5, 7]
a[3, 1]    # =>   [7]
a[-3, 2]   # =>   [5, 7]
```

Finally, you can index arrays using ranges, in which start and end positions are separated by two or three periods. The two-period form includes the end position, and the three-period form does not:

```
a = [ 1, 3, 5, 7, 9 ]
a[1..3]    # =>   [3, 5, 7]
a[1...3]   # =>   [3, 5]
a[3..3]    # =>   [7]
a[-3..-1]  # =>   [5, 7, 9]
```

The [] operator has a corresponding []= operator, which lets you set elements in the array. If used with a single integer index, the element at that position is replaced by whatever is on the right side of the assignment. Any gaps that result will be filled with nil:

```
a = [ 1, 3, 5, 7, 9 ]   →   [1, 3, 5, 7, 9]
a[1] = 'bat'            →   [1, "bat", 5, 7, 9]
a[-3] = 'cat'          →   [1, "bat", "cat", 7, 9]
a[3] = [ 9, 8 ]        →   [1, "bat", "cat", [9, 8], 9]
a[6] = 99              →   [1, "bat", "cat", [9, 8], 9, nil, 99]
```

If the index to []= is two numbers (a start and a length) or a range, then those elements in the original array are replaced by whatever is on the right side of the assignment. If the length is zero, the right side is inserted into the array before the start position; no elements are removed. If the right side is itself an array, its elements are used in the replacement. The array size is automatically adjusted if the index selects a different number of elements than are available on the right side of the assignment.

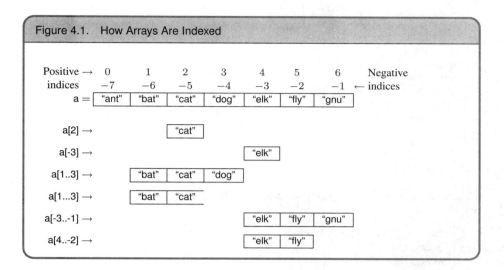

Figure 4.1. How Arrays Are Indexed

```
a = [ 1, 3, 5, 7, 9 ]      →    [1, 3, 5, 7, 9]
a[2, 2] = 'cat'            →    [1, 3, "cat", 9]
a[2, 0] = 'dog'            →    [1, 3, "dog", "cat", 9]
a[1, 1] = [ 9, 8, 7 ]      →    [1, 9, 8, 7, "dog", "cat", 9]
a[0..3] = []               →    ["dog", "cat", 9]
a[5..6] = 99, 98           →    ["dog", "cat", 9, nil, nil, 99, 98]
```

Arrays have a large number of other useful methods. Using them, you can treat arrays as stacks, sets, queues, dequeues, and FIFO queues.

For example, push and pop add and remove elements from the end of an array, so you can use it as a stack:

```
stack = []
stack.push "red"
stack.push "green"
stack.push "blue"
p stack
puts stack.pop
puts stack.pop
puts stack.pop
p stack
```

produces:

```
["red", "green", "blue"]
blue
green
red
[]
```

Similarly, unshift and shift add and remove elements from the head of an array. Combine shift and push, and you have a first-in first-out (FIFO) queue:

```
queue = []
queue.push "red"
queue.push "green"
puts queue.shift
puts queue.shift
```

produces:

```
red
green
```

The first and last methods return the *n* entries at the head or end of an array without removing them:

```
array = [ 1, 2, 3, 4, 5, 6, 7 ]
p array.first(4)
p array.last(4)
```

produces:

```
[1, 2, 3, 4]
[4, 5, 6, 7]
```

A complete list of array methods starts on page 438. It is well worth firing up irb and playing with them.

Hashes

Hashes (sometimes known as *associative arrays*, *maps*, or *dictionaries*) are similar to arrays in that they are indexed collections of object references. However, although you index arrays with integers, you can index a hash with objects of any type: symbols, strings, regular expressions, and so on. When you store a value in a hash, you actually supply two objects—the index, which is normally called the *key*, and the entry to be stored with that key. You can subsequently retrieve the entry by indexing the hash with the same key value that you used to store it.

The example that follows uses hash literals: a list of *key value* pairs between braces:

```
h = { 'dog' => 'canine', 'cat' => 'feline', 'donkey' => 'asinine' }

h.length   # =>   3
h['dog']   # =>   "canine"
h['cow']   = 'bovine'
h[12]      = 'dodecine'
h['cat'] = 99
h          # =>   {"dog"=>"canine", "cat"=>99, "donkey"=>"asinine",
                   "cow"=>"bovine", 12=>"dodecine"}
```

In the previous example, the hash keys were strings. If instead we wanted them to be symbols, we could write the hash literal using either the old syntax with => or the new *key: value* syntax introduced in Ruby 1.9.

```
h = { dog: 'canine', cat: 'feline', donkey: 'asinine' }
# same as...
h = { :dog => 'canine', :cat => 'feline', :donkey => 'asinine' }
```

Compared with arrays, hashes have one significant advantage: they can use any object as an index. And, as of Ruby 1.9, you'll find something that might be surprising: Ruby remembers the order in which you add items to a hash. When you subsequently iterate over the entries, Ruby will return them in that order.

You'll find that hashes are one of the most commonly used data structures in Ruby. A full list of the methods implemented by class Hash starts on page 524.

Word Frequency: Using Hashes and Arrays

Let's round off this section with a simple program that calculates the number of times each word occurs in some text. (So, for example, in this sentence the word *the* occurs two times.)

The problem breaks down into two parts. First, given some text as a string, return a list of words. That sounds like an array. Then, build a count for each distinct word. That sounds like a use for a hash—we can index it with the word and use the corresponding entry to keep a count.

Let's start with the method that splits a string into words:

```
def words_from_string(string)
  string.downcase.scan(/[\w']+/)
end
```

This method uses two very useful String methods: downcase returns a lowercase version of a string, and scan returns an array of substrings that match a given pattern. In this case, the pattern is [\w']+, which matches sequences containing "word characters" and single quotes.

We can play with this method. Notice how the result is an array:

```
p words_from_string("But I didn't inhale, he said (emphatically)")
```

produces:

```
["but", "i", "didn't", "inhale", "he", "said", "emphatically"]
```

Our next task is to calculate word frequencies. To do this, we'll create a hash object indexed by the words in our list. Each entry in this hash stores the number of times that word occurred. Let's say we already have read part of the list, and we have seen the word *the* already. Then we'd have a hash that contained this:

```
{ ...,  "the" => 1, ... }
```

If the variable next_word contained the word *the*, then incrementing the count is as simple as this:

```
counts[next_word] += 1
```

We'd then end up with a hash containing the following:

```
{ ...,  "the" => 2, ... }
```

Our only problem is what to do when we encounter a word for the first time. We'll try to increment the entry for that word, but there won't be one, so our program will fail. There are a number of solutions to this. One is to check to see whether the entry exists before doing the increment:

```
if counts.has_key?(next_word)
  counts[next_word] += 1
else
  counts[next_word] = 1
end
```

However, there's a tidier way. If we create a hash object using Hash.new(0), the parameter (0 in this case) will be used as the hash's default value—it will be the value returned if you look up a key that isn't yet in the hash. Using that, we can write our count_frequency method:

```
def count_frequency(word_list)
  counts = Hash.new(0)
  for word in word_list
    counts[word] += 1
  end
  counts
end

p count_frequency(["sparky", "the", "cat", "sat", "on", "the", "mat"])
```

produces:

```
{"sparky"=>1, "the"=>2, "cat"=>1, "sat"=>1, "on"=>1, "mat"=>1}
```

One little job left. The hash containing the word frequencies is ordered based on the first time it sees each word. It would be better to display the results based on the frequencies of the words. We can do that using the hash's sort_by method. When you use sort_by, you give it a block that tells the sort what to use when making comparisons. In our case, we'll just use the count. The result of the sort is an array containing a set of two-element arrays, each subarray corresponding to a key/entry pair in the original hash. This makes our whole program:

```
tutcontainers_21.rb
def words_from_string(string)
  string.downcase.scan(/[\w']+/)
end

def count_frequency(word_list)
  counts = Hash.new(0)
  for word in word_list
    counts[word] += 1
  end
  counts
end

raw_text  = File.read("para.txt")
word_list = words_from_string(raw_text)
counts    = count_frequency(word_list)
sorted    = counts.sort_by {|word, count| count}
top_five  = sorted.last(5)
```

```
for i in 0...5            # (this is ugly code
  word = top_five[i][0]   #  which we'll fix shortly)
  count = top_five[i][1]
  puts "#{word}:  #{count}"
end
```

produces:

```
that:  2
sounds:  2
like:  2
the:  3
a:  6
```

At this point, a quick test may be in order. To do this, we're going to use a testing framework called Test::Unit that comes with the standard Ruby distributions. We won't describe it fully yet (we do that in the *Unit Testing* chapter starting on page 183). For now, we'll just say that the method assert_equal checks that its two parameters are equal, complaining bitterly if they aren't. We'll use assertions to test our two methods, one method at a time. (That's one reason why we wrote them as separate methods—it makes them testable in isolation.)

Here are some tests for the word_from_string method:

tutcontainers_22.rb

```
require_relative  'words_from_string.rb'
require 'test/unit'
class TestWordsFromString < Test::Unit::TestCase
  def test_empty_string
    assert_equal([], words_from_string(""))
    assert_equal([], words_from_string("      "))
  end
  def test_single_word
    assert_equal(["cat"], words_from_string("cat"))
    assert_equal(["cat"], words_from_string("  cat    "))
  end
  def test_many_words
    assert_equal(["the", "cat", "sat", "on", "the", "mat"],
        words_from_string("the cat sat on the mat"))
  end
  def test_ignores_punctuation
    assert_equal(["the", "cat's", "mat"],
        words_from_string("<the!> cat's, -mat-"))
  end
end
```

produces:

```
Loaded suite /tmp/prog
Started
....
Finished in 0.000509 seconds.

4 tests, 6 assertions, 0 failures, 0 errors, 0 skips
```

The test starts by requiring the source file containing our words_from_string method, along with the unit test framework itself. It then defines a test class. Within that class, any methods whose names start test are automatically run by the testing framework. The results show that four test methods ran, successfully executing six assertions:

`tutcontainers_23.rb`

```ruby
require_relative 'count_frequency.rb'
require 'test/unit'
class TestCountFrequency < Test::Unit::TestCase
  def test_empty_list
    assert_equal({}, count_frequency([]))
  end
  def test_single_word
    assert_equal({"cat" => 1}, count_frequency(["cat"]))
  end
  def test_two_different_words
    assert_equal({"cat" => 1, "sat" => 1},
                 count_frequency(["cat", "sat"]))
  end
  def test_two_words_with_adjacent_repeat
    assert_equal({"cat" => 2, "sat" => 1},
                 count_frequency(["cat", "cat", "sat"]))
  end
  def test_two_words_with_non_adjacent_repeat
    assert_equal({"cat" => 2, "sat" => 1},
                 count_frequency(["cat", "sat", "cat"]))
  end
end
```

produces:

```
Loaded suite /tmp/prog
Started
.....
Finished in 0.000542 seconds.

5 tests, 5 assertions, 0 failures, 0 errors, 0 skips
```

Blocks and Iterators

In our program that wrote out the results of our word frequency analysis, we had the following loop:

```ruby
for i in 0...5
  word = top_five[i][0]
  count = top_five[i][1]
  puts "#{word}:  #{count}"
end
```

This works, and it looks comfortingly familiar: a for loop iterating over an array. What could be more natural?

It turns out there *is* something more natural. In a way, our for loop is somewhat too intimate with the array; it magically knows that we're iterating over five elements, and it retrieves values in turn from the array. To do this, it has to know that the structure it is working with is an array of two-element subarrays. This is a whole lot of coupling.

Instead, we could write this code like this:

```
top_five.each do |word, count|
  puts "#{word}:  #{count}"
end
```

The method each is an *iterator*—a method that invokes a block of code repeatedly. In fact, some Ruby programmers might write this more compactly as this:

```
puts top_five.map { |word, count| "#{word}:  #{count}" }
```

Just how far you take this is a matter of taste. But, however you use them, iterators and code blocks are among the more interesting features of Ruby, so let's spend a while looking into them.

Blocks

A *block* is simply a chunk of code enclosed between either braces or the keywords do and end. The two forms are identical except for precedence, which we'll see in a minute. All things being equal, the current Ruby style seems to favor using braces for blocks that fit on one line and do/end when a block spans multiple lines:

```
some_array.each {|value| puts value * 3 }
sum = 0
other_array.each do |value|
  sum += value
  puts value / sum
end
```

You can think of a block as being somewhat like the body of an anonymous method. Just like a method, the block can take parameters (but, unlike a method, those parameters appear at the start of the block between vertical bars). Both the blocks in the preceding example take a single parameter, value. And, just like a method, the body of a block is not executed when Ruby first sees it. Instead, the block is saved away to be called later.

Blocks can appear in Ruby source code only immediately after the *invocation* of some method. If the method takes parameters, the block appears after these. In a way, you can almost think of the block as being one extra parameter, passed to that method. Let's look at a simple example that sums the squares of the numbers in an array:

```
sum = 0
[1, 2, 3, 4].each do |value|
  square = value * value
  sum   += square
end
puts sum
```

produces:

30

The block is being called by the each method once for each element in the array. The element is passed to the block as the value parameter. But there's something subtle going on, too. Take a look at the sum variable. It's declared outside the block, updated inside the block, and then passed to puts after the each method returns.

This illustrates an important rule: if there's a variable inside a block with the same name as a variable in the same scope outside the block, the two are the same—there's only one variable sum in the preceding program. (You can override this behavior, as we'll see later.)

If, however, a variable appears only inside a block, then that variable is local to the block—in the preceding program, we couldn't have written the value of square at the end of the code, because square is not defined at that point. It is defined only inside the block itself.

Although simple, this behavior can lead to unexpected problems. For example, say our program was dealing with drawing different shapes. We might have this:

```ruby
square = Shape.new(sides: 4) # assume Shape defined elsewhere
#
# .. lots of code
#
sum = 0
[1, 2, 3, 4].each do |value|
  square = value * value
  sum   += square
end
puts sum

square.draw   # BOOM!
```

This code would fail, because the variable square, which originally held a Shape object, will have been overwritten inside the block and will hold a number by the time the each method returns. This problem doesn't bite often, but when it does, it can be very confusing.

1.9 Fortunately, Ruby 1.9 has a couple of answers.

First, parameters to a block are now *always* local to a block, even if they have the same name as locals in the surrounding scope. (You'll get a warning message if you run Ruby with the -w option.)

tutcontainers_30.rb
```ruby
value = "some shape"
[ 1, 2 ].each {|value| puts value }
puts value
```

produces:

```
1
2
some shape
```

Second, you can now define block local variables by putting them after a semicolon in the block's parameter list. So, in our sum-of-squares example, we should have indicated that the square variable was block-local by writing it as follows:

```
tutcontainers_31.rb
square = "some shape"
sum = 0
[1, 2, 3, 4].each do |value; square|
  square = value * value    # this is a different variable
  sum   += square
end
puts sum
puts square
```

produces:

```
30
some shape
```

By making square block-local, values assigned inside the block will not affect the value of the variable with the same name in the outer scope.

Implementing Iterators

A Ruby iterator is simply a method that can invoke a block of code.

We said that a block may appear only in the source adjacent to a method call and that the code in the block is not executed at the time it is encountered. Instead, Ruby remembers the context in which the block appears (the local variables, the current object, and so on) and then enters the method. This is where the magic starts.

Within the method, the block may be invoked, almost as if it were a method itself, using the yield statement. Whenever a yield is executed, it invokes the code in the block. When the block exits, control picks back up immediately after the yield.[2] Let's start with a trivial example:

```
tutcontainers_32.rb
def three_times
  yield
  yield
  yield
end
three_times { puts "Hello" }
```

produces:

```
Hello
Hello
Hello
```

---

2. Programming-language buffs will be pleased to know that the keyword yield was chosen to echo the yield function in Liskov's language CLU, a language that is more than thirty years old and yet contains features that still haven't been widely exploited by the CLU-less.

The block (the code between the braces) is associated with the call to the three_times method. Within this method, yield is called three times in a row. Each time, it invokes the code in the block, and a cheery greeting is printed. What makes blocks interesting, however, is that you can pass parameters to them and receive values from them. For example, we could write a simple function that returns members of the Fibonacci series up to a certain value:[3]

```
tutcontainers_33.rb
def fib_up_to(max)
  i1, i2 = 1, 1          # parallel assignment (i1 = 1 and i2 = 1)
  while i1 <= max
    yield i1
    i1, i2 = i2, i1+i2
  end
end
fib_up_to(1000) {|f| print f, " " }
```

produces:

```
1 1 2 3 5 8 13 21 34 55 89 144 233 377 610 987
```

In this example, the yield statement has a parameter. This value is passed to the associated block. In the definition of the block, the argument list appears between vertical bars. In this instance, the variable f receives the value passed to yield, so the block prints successive members of the series. (This example also shows parallel assignment in action. We'll come back to this on page 134.) Although it is common to pass just one value to a block, this is not a requirement; a block may have any number of arguments.

A block may also return a value to the method. The value of the last expression evaluated in the block is passed back to the method as the value of the yield. This is how the find method used by class Array works.[4] Its implementation would look something like the following:

```
class Array
  def find
    for i in 0...size
      value = self[i]
      return value if yield(value)
    end
    return nil
  end
end

[1, 3, 5, 7, 9].find {|v| v*v > 30 }   # =>   7
```

This passes successive elements of the array to the associated block. If the block returns true (that is, a value other than nil or false), the method returns the corresponding element. If no

---

3.   The basic Fibonacci series is a sequence of integers, starting with two 1s, in which each subsequent term is the sum of the two preceding terms. The series is sometimes used in sorting algorithms and in analyzing natural phenomena.

4.   The find method is actually defined in module Enumerable, which is mixed into class Array.

element matches, the method returns nil. The example shows the benefit of this approach to iterators. The Array class does what it does best, accessing array elements, and leaves the application code to concentrate on its particular requirement (in this case, finding an entry that meets some criteria).

Some iterators are common to many types of Ruby collections. We've looked at find already. Two others are each and collect. each is probably the simplest iterator—all it does is yield successive elements of its collection:

```
[ 1, 3, 5, 7, 9 ].each {|i| puts i }
```

produces:

```
1
3
5
7
9
```

The each iterator has a special place in Ruby; on page 145, we'll describe how it's used as the basis of the language's for loop, and starting on page 80, we'll see how defining an each method can add a whole lot more functionality to your class for free.

Another common iterator is collect (also known as map), which takes each element from the collection and passes it to the block. The results returned by the block are used to construct a new array. The following example uses the succ method, which increments a string value:

```
["H", "A", "L"].collect {|x| x.succ }   # =>   ["I", "B", "M"]
```

Iterators are not limited to accessing existing data in arrays and hashes. As we saw in the Fibonacci example, an iterator can return derived values. This capability is used by Ruby input/output classes, which implement an iterator interface that returns successive lines (or bytes) in an I/O stream:

```
f = File.open("testfile")
f.each do |line|
  puts "The line is: #{line}"
end
f.close
```

produces:

```
The line is: This is line one
The line is: This is line two
The line is: This is line three
The line is: And so on...
```

Sometimes you want to keep track of how many times you've been through the block. The each_with_index is your friend. It calls its block with two parameters: the current element of the iteration and the count (which starts at zero, just like array indices):

```
f = File.open("testfile")
f.each_with_index do |line, index|
  puts "Line #{index} is: #{line}"
end
f.close
```

produces:

```
Line 0 is: This is line one
Line 1 is: This is line two
Line 2 is: This is line three
Line 3 is: And so on...
```

Let's look at just one more useful iterator. The (somewhat obscurely named) inject method (defined in the module Enumerable) lets you accumulate a value across the members of a collection. For example, you can sum all the elements in an array, and find their product, using code such as this:

```
[1,3,5,7].inject(0) {|sum, element| sum+element}      # =>   16
[1,3,5,7].inject(1) {|product, element| product*element}  # =>   105
```

inject works like this: the first time the associated block is called, sum is set to inject's parameter, and element is set to the first element in the collection. The second and subsequent times the block is called, sum is set to the value returned by the block on the previous call. The final value of inject is the value returned by the block the last time it was called. One more thing: if inject is called with no parameter, it uses the first element of the collection as the initial value and starts the iteration with the second value. This means that we could have written the previous examples like this:

```
[1,3,5,7].inject {|sum, element| sum+element}      # =>   16
[1,3,5,7].inject {|product, element| product*element}  # =>   105
```

And, just to add to the mystique of inject, you can also give it the name of the method you want to apply to successive elements of the collection. These examples work because, in Ruby, addition and multiplication are simply methods on numbers, and :+ is the symbol corresponding to the method +:

```
[1,3,5,7].inject(:+)   # =>   16
[1,3,5,7].inject(:*)   # =>   105
```

Enumerators—External Iterators

It's worth spending a paragraph comparing Ruby's approach to iterators to that of languages such as C++ and Java. In the Ruby approach, the basic iterator is internal to the collection— it's simply a method, identical to any other, that happens to call yield whenever it generates a new value. The thing that uses the iterator is just a block of code associated with a call to this method.

In other languages, collections don't contain their own iterators. Instead, they implement methods that generate external helper objects (for example, those based on Java's Iterator interface) that carry the iterator state. In this, as in many other ways, Ruby is a transparent language. When you write a Ruby program, you concentrate on getting the job done, not on building scaffolding to support the language itself.

It's also worth spending another paragraph looking at why Ruby's internal iterators aren't always the best solution. One area where they fall down badly is where you need to treat an iterator as an object in its own right (for example, passing the iterator into a method that needs to access each of the values returned by that iterator). It's also difficult to iterate over two collections in parallel using Ruby's internal iterator scheme.

1.9   Fortunately, Ruby 1.9 comes with a built-in Enumerator class, which implements external iterators in Ruby for just such occasions.

One way to create an Enumerator object is to call the to_enum method (or its synonym, enum_for) on a collection such as an array or a hash:

```
a = [ 1, 3, "cat" ]
h = { dog: "canine", fox: "lupine" }

# Create Enumerators
enum_a = a.to_enum
enum_h = h.to_enum

enum_a.next   # =>   1
enum_h.next   # =>   [:dog, "canine"]
enum_a.next   # =>   3
enum_h.next   # =>   [:fox, "lupine"]
```

Most of the internal iterator methods—the ones that normally yield successive values to a block—will also return an Enumerator object if called without a block:

```
a = [ 1, 3, "cat" ]

enum_a = a.each # create an Enumerator using an internal iterator

enum_a.next   # =>   1
enum_a.next   # =>   3
```

Ruby has a method called loop that does nothing but repeatedly invoke its block. Typically, your code in the block will break out of the loop when some condition occurs. But loop is also smart when you use an Enumerator—when an enumerator object runs out of values inside a loop, the loop will terminate cleanly. The following example shows this in action—the loop ends when the three-element enumerator runs out of values.[5]

```
short_enum = [1, 2, 3].to_enum
long_enum  = ('a'..'z').to_enum

loop do
  puts "#{short_enum.next} - #{long_enum.next}"
end
```

produces:

```
1 - a
2 - b
3 - c
```

---

5.   You can also handle this in your own iterator methods by rescuing the StopIteration exception, but because we haven't talked about exceptions yet, we won't go into details here.

Enumerators Are Objects

Enumerators take something that's normally executable code (the act of iterating) and turn it into an object. This means that you can do things programatically with enumerators that aren't easily done with regular loops.

For example, the Enumerable module defines each_with_index. This invokes its host class's each method, returning successive values along with an index:

```
result = []
[ 'a', 'b', 'c' ].each_with_index {|item, index| result << [item, index] }
result  # =>  [["a", 0], ["b", 1], ["c", 2]]
```

But what if you wanted to iterate and receive an index but use a different method than each to control that iteration? For example, you might want to iterate over the characters in a string. There's no method called each_char_with_index built into the String class.

Enumerators to the rescue. You can use the fact that the each_char method of strings will return an enumerator if you don't give it a block, and you can then call each_with_index on that enumerator:

```
result = []
"cat".each_char.each_with_index {|item, index| result << [item,  index] }
result  # =>  [["c", 0], ["a", 1], ["t", 2]]
```

In fact, this is such a common use of enumerators that Matz has given us with_index, which makes the code read better:

```
result = []
"cat".each_char.with_index {|item, index| result << [item,  index] }
result  # =>  [["c", 0], ["a", 1], ["t", 2]]
```

You can also create the Enumerator object explicitly—in this case we'll create one that will call our string's each_char method. We can call to_a on that enumerator to iterate over it and get the result:

```
enum = "cat".enum_for(:each_char)
enum.to_a  # =>  ["c", "a", "t"]
```

If the method we're using as the basis of our enumerator takes parameters, we can pass them to enum_for:

```
enum_good = (1..10).enum_for(:each_slice, 3)
enum_good.to_a  # =>  [[1, 2, 3], [4, 5, 6], [7, 8, 9], [10]]
```

Enumerators Are Generators and Filters

(This is more advanced material that can be skipped on first reading.) As well as creating enumerators from existing collections, you can create an explicit enumerator, passing it a block. The code in the block will be used when the enumerator object needs to supply a fresh value to your program. However, the block isn't simply executed from top to bottom. Instead, the block is executed in parallel with the rest of your program's code. Execution starts at the top and pauses when the block yields a value to your code. When the code needs the next value, execution resumes at the statement following the yield. This lets you write enumerators that generate infinite sequences (among other things):

```
tutcontainers_50.rb
triangular_numbers = Enumerator.new do |yielder|
  number = 0
  count = 1
  loop do
    number += count
    count += 1
    yielder.yield number
  end
end
5.times { puts triangular_numbers.next }
```

produces:

```
1
3
6
10
15
```

Enumerator objects are also enumerable (that is to say, the methods available to enumerable objects are also available to them). That means we can use enumerable's methods (such as first) on them:

```
triangular_numbers = Enumerator.new do |yielder|
  # ...
end
p triangular_numbers.first(5)
```

produces:

```
[1, 3, 6, 10, 15]
```

You have to be slightly careful with enumerators that can generate infinite sequences. Some of the regular enumerator methods such as count and select will happily try to read the whole enumeration before returning a result. If you want a version of select that works with infinite sequences, you'll need to write it yourself. Here's a version that gets passed an enumerator and a block and returns a new enumerator containing values from the original for which the block returns true. We'll use it to return triangular numbers that are multiples of 10.

```
tutcontainers_52.rb
triangular_numbers = Enumerator.new do |yielder|
  # ... as before
end
def infinite_select(enum, &block)
  Enumerator.new do |yielder|
    enum.each do |value|
      yielder.yield(value) if block.call(value)
    end
  end
end
p infinite_select(triangular_numbers) {|val| val % 10 == 0}.first(5)
```

produces:

```
[10, 120, 190, 210, 300]
```

Here we use the &block notation to pass the block as a parameter to the infinite_select method.

As Brian Candler pointed out in [ruby-core:19679], you can make this more convenient by adding filters such as infinite_select directly to the Enumerator class. Here's an example that returns the first five triangular numbers that are multiples of 10 and that have the digit 3 in them:

```ruby
tutcontainers_53.rb
triangular_numbers = Enumerator.new do |yielder|
  # ... as before
end
class Enumerator
  def infinite_select(&block)
    Enumerator.new do |yielder|
      self.each do |value|
        yielder.yield(value) if block.call(value)
      end
    end
  end
end
p triangular_numbers
    .infinite_select {|val| val % 10 == 0}
    .infinite_select {|val| val.to_s =~ /3/ }
    .first(5)
```

produces:

```
[300, 630, 1830, 3160, 3240]
```

Blocks for Transactions

Although blocks are often used as the target of an iterator, they have other uses. Let's look at a few.

You can use blocks to define a chunk of code that must be run under some kind of transactional control. For example, you'll often open a file, do something with its contents, and then want to ensure that the file is closed when you finish. Although you can do this using conventional linear code, a version using blocks is simpler (and turns out to be less error prone). A naive implementation (ignoring error handling) could look something like the following:

```ruby
tutcontainers_54.rb
class File
  def self.open_and_process(*args)
    f = File.open(*args)
    yield f
    f.close()
  end
end
```

```
File.open_and_process("testfile", "r") do |file|
  while line = file.gets
    puts line
  end
end
```

produces:

```
This is line one
This is line two
This is line three
And so on...
```

open_and_process is a *class method*—it may be called independently of any particular file object. We want it to take the same arguments as the conventional File.open method, but we don't really care what those arguments are. To do this, we specified the arguments as *args, meaning "collect the actual parameters passed to the method into an array named args." We then call File.open, passing it *args as a parameter. This expands the array back into individual parameters. The net result is that open_and_process transparently passes whatever parameters it receives to File.open.

Once the file has been opened, open_and_process calls yield, passing the open file object to the block. When the block returns, the file is closed. In this way, the responsibility for closing an open file has been shifted from the users of file objects back to the file objects themselves.

The technique of having files manage their own life cycle is so useful that the class File supplied with Ruby supports it directly. If File.open has an associated block, then that block will be invoked with a file object, and the file will be closed when the block terminates. This is interesting, because it means that File.open has two different behaviors. When called with a block, it executes the block and closes the file. When called without a block, it returns the file object. This is made possible by the method block_given?, which returns true if a block is associated with the current method. Using this method, you could implement something similar to the standard File.open (again, ignoring error handling) using the following:

```
tutcontainers_55.rb
class File
  def self.my_open(*args)
    result = file = File.new(*args)
    # If there's a block, pass in the file and close
    # the file when it returns
    if block_given?
      result = yield file
      file.close
    end

    return result
  end
end
```

This has one last twist: in the previous examples of using blocks to control resources, we didn't address error handling. If we wanted to implement these methods properly, we'd need to ensure that we closed a file even if the code processing that file somehow aborted. We do this using exception handling, which we talk about later (starting on page 151).

Blocks Can Be Objects

Blocks are like anonymous methods, but there's more to them than that. You can also convert a block into an object, store it in variables, pass it around, and then invoke its code sometime later.

Remember I said that you can think of blocks as being a little like an implicit parameter that's passed to a method? Well, you can also make that parameter explicit. If the last parameter in a method definition is prefixed with an ampersand (such as &action), Ruby looks for a code block whenever that method is called. That code block is converted to an object of class Proc and assigned to the parameter. You can then treat the parameter as any other variable.

Here's an example where we create a Proc object in one instance method and store it in an instance variable. We then invoke the proc from a second instance method.

tutcontainers_56.rb

```
class ProcExample
  def pass_in_block(&action)
    @stored_proc = action
  end
  def use_proc(parameter)
    @stored_proc.call(parameter)
  end
end

eg = ProcExample.new
eg.pass_in_block { |param| puts "The parameter is #{param}" }
eg.use_proc(99)
```

produces:

```
The parameter is 99
```

See how the call method on a proc object invokes the code in the original block?

Many Ruby programs store and later call blocks in this way—it's a great way of implementing callbacks, dispatch tables, and so on.

But, you can go one step further. If a block can be turned into an object by adding an ampersand parameter to a method, what happens if that method then returns the Proc object to the caller?

tutcontainers_57.rb

```
def create_block_object(&block)
  block
end
```

```
bo = create_block_object { |param| puts "You called me with #{param}" }
bo.call 99
bo.call "cat"
```

produces:

```
You called me with 99
You called me with cat
```

In fact, this is so useful that Ruby provides not one but two built-in methods that convert a block to an object.[6] Both lambda and Proc.new take a block and return an object of class Proc. The objects they return differ slightly in how they behave, but we'll hold off talking about that until page 352.

> tutcontainers_58.rb

```
bo = lambda { |param| puts "You called me with #{param}" }
bo.call 99
bo.call "cat"
```

produces:

```
You called me with 99
You called me with cat
```

Blocks Can Be Closures

Remember I said that a block can use local variables from the surrounding scope? So, let's look at a slightly different example of a block doing just that:

> tutcontainers_59.rb

```
def n_times(thing)
  lambda {|n| thing * n }
end

p1 = n_times(23)
p1.call(3)   # =>   69
p1.call(4)   # =>   92
p2 = n_times("Hello ")
p2.call(3)   # =>   "Hello Hello Hello "
```

The method n_times returns a Proc object that references the method's parameter, thing. Even though that parameter is out of scope by the time the block is called, the parameter remains accessible to the block. This is called a *closure*—variables in the surrounding scope that are referenced in a block remain accessible for the life of that block and the life of any Proc object created from that block.

---

6.   There's actually a third, proc, but it is effectively deprecated.

Here's another example, which is a method that returns a Proc object that returns successive powers of 2 when called:

```
tutcontainers_60.rb
def power_proc_generator
  value = 1
  lambda { value += value }
end

power_proc = power_proc_generator

puts power_proc.call
puts power_proc.call
puts power_proc.call
```

produces:

```
2
4
8
```

An Alternative Notation

1.9 Ruby 1.9 has another way of creating Proc objects. Rather than write this:

```
lambda { |params| ... }
```

you can now write the following:[7]

```
->params { ... }
```

The parameters can be enclosed in optional parentheses. For example:

```
tutcontainers_63.rb
proc1 = -> arg { puts "In proc1 with #{arg}" }
proc2 = -> arg1, arg2 { puts "In proc2 with #{arg1} and #{arg2}" }
proc3 = ->(arg1, arg2) { puts "In proc3 with #{arg1} and #{arg2}" }

proc1.call "ant"
proc2.call "bee", "cat"
proc3.call "dog", "elk"
```

produces:

```
In proc1 with ant
In proc2 with bee and cat
In proc3 with dog and elk
```

---

7. Let's start by getting something out of the way. Why ->? For compatibility across all the different source file encodings, Matz is restricted to using pure 7-bit ASCII for Ruby operators, and the choice of available characters is severely limited by the ambiguities inherent in the Ruby syntax. He felt that -> was (kind of) reminiscent of a Greek lambda character λ.

The -> form is more compact than using lambda and seems to be in favor when you want to pass one or more Proc objects to a method:

`tutcontainers_64.rb`

```ruby
def my_if(condition, then_clause, else_clause)
  if condition
    then_clause.call
  else
    else_clause.call
  end
end
5.times do |val|
  my_if val < 3,
        -> { puts "#{val} is small" },
        -> { puts "#{val} is big" }
end
```

produces:

```
0 is small
1 is small
2 is small
3 is big
4 is big
```

One good reason to pass blocks to methods is that you can reevaluate the code in those blocks at any time. Here's a trivial example of reimplementing a while loop using a method. Because the condition is passed as a block, it can be evaluated each time around the loop:

`tutcontainers_65.rb`

```ruby
def my_while(cond, &body)
  while cond.call
    body.call
  end
end
a = 0
my_while -> { a < 3 } do
  puts a
  a += 1
end
```

produces:

```
0
1
2
```

Block Parameter Lists

1.9

Prior to Ruby 1.9, blocks were to some extent the poor cousins of methods when it came to parameter lists. Methods could have splat args, default values, and block parameters, whereas blocks basically had just a list of names (and could accept a trailing splat argument). Now, however, blocks have the same parameter list capabilities as methods.

Blocks written using the old syntax take their parameter lists between vertical bars. Blocks written using the -> syntax take a separate parameter list before the block body. In both cases, the parameter list looks just like the list you can give to methods. It can take default values, splat args (described on page 125), and a block parameter (a trailing argument starting with an ampersand). You can write blocks that are just as versatile as methods.[8]

Here's a block using the original block notation:

`tutcontainers_66.rb`

```
proc1 = lambda do |a, *b, &block|
  puts "a = #{a.inspect}"
  puts "b = #{b.inspect}"
  block.call
end
proc1.call(1, 2, 3, 4) { puts "in block1" }
```

produces:

```
a = 1
b = [2, 3, 4]
in block1
```

And here's one using the new -> notation:

`tutcontainers_67.rb`

```
proc2 = -> a, *b, &block do
  puts "a = #{a.inspect}"
  puts "b = #{b.inspect}"
  block.call
end
proc2.call(1, 2, 3, 4) { puts "in block2" }
```

produces:

```
a = 1
b = [2, 3, 4]
in block2
```

Containers Everywhere

Containers, blocks, and iterators are core concepts in Ruby. The more you write in Ruby, the more you'll find yourself moving away from conventional looping constructs. Instead, you'll write classes that support iteration over their contents. And you'll find that this code is compact, easy to read, and a joy to maintain. If this all seems too weird, don't worry. After a while, it'll start to come naturally. And you'll have plenty of time to practice as you use Ruby libraries and frameworks.

---

8. Actually, they are more versatile, because these blocks are also closures, while methods are not.

## Chapter 5

Sharing Functionality: Inheritance, Modules, and Mixins

One of the accepted principles of good design is the elimination of unnecessary duplication. We work hard to make sure that each concept in our application is expressed just once in our code.[1]

We've already seen how classes help. All the methods in a class are automatically accessible to instances of that class. But there are other, more general types of sharing that we want to do. Maybe we're dealing with an application that ships goods. Many forms of shipping are available, but all forms share some basic functionality (weight calculation, perhaps). We don't want to duplicate the code that implements this functionality across the implementation of each shipping type. Or maybe we have a more generic capability that we want to inject into a number of different classes. For example, an online store may need the ability to calculate sales tax for carts, orders, quotes, and so on. Again, we don't want to duplicate the sales tax code in each of these places.

In this chapter, we'll look at two different (but related) mechanisms for this kind of sharing in Ruby. The first, *class-level inheritance*, is common in object-oriented languages. We'll then look at *mixins*, a technique that is often preferable to inheritance. We'll wind up with a discussion of when to use each.

Inheritance and Messages

In the previous chapter we saw that when puts needs to convert an object to a string, it calls that object's to_s method. But we've also written our own classes that don't explic-

---

1.   Why? Because the world changes. And when you adapt your application to each change, you want to know that you've changed exactly the code you need to change. If each real-world concept is implemented at a single point in the code, this becomes vastly easier.

itly implement to_s. Despite this, objects of these classes respond successfully when we call to_s on them. How this works has to do with inheritance, subclassing, and how Ruby determines what method to run when you send a message to an object.

Inheritance allows you to create a class that is a refinement or specialization of another class. This class is called a *subclass* of the original, and the original is a *superclass* of the subclass. People also talk of *child* and *parent* classes.

The basic mechanism of subclassing is simple. The child inherits all of the capabilities of its parent class—all the parent's instance methods are available in instances of the child.

Let's look at a trivial example and then later build on it. Here's a definition of a parent class and a child class that inherits from it:

`tutmodules_1.rb`

```ruby
class Parent
  def say_hello
    puts "Hello from #{self}"
  end
end
p = Parent.new
p.say_hello
# Subclass the parent...
class Child < Parent
end
c = Child.new
c.say_hello
```

produces:

```
Hello from #<Parent:0x0a40c4>
Hello from #<Child:0x0a3d68>
```

The parent class defines a single instance method, say_hello. We call it by creating a new instance of the class and store a reference to that instance in the variable p.

We then create a subclass using class Child < Parent. The < notation means we're creating a subclass of the thing on the right; the fact that we use less-than presumably signals that the child class is supposed to be a specialization of the parent.

Note that the child class defines no methods, but when we create an instance of it, we can call say_hello. That's because the child inherits all the methods of its parent. Note also that when we output the value of self—the current object—it shows that we're in an instance of class Child, even though the method we're running is defined in the parent.

The superclass method returns the parent of a particular class:

`tutmodules_2.rb`

```ruby
class Parent
end
class Child < Parent
end
puts "The superclass of Child is #{Child.superclass}"
```

produces:

```
The superclass of Child is Parent
```

But what's the superclass of Parent?

```
class Parent
end
puts "The superclass of Parent is #{Parent.superclass}"
```

produces:

```
The superclass of Parent is Object
```

If you don't define an explicit superclass when defining a class, Ruby automatically makes the built-in class Object that class's parent. Let's go further:

```
puts "The superclass of Object is #{Object.superclass}"
```

produces:

```
The superclass of Object is BasicObject
```

1.9 Class BasicObject was introduced in Ruby 1.9. It is used in certain kinds of metaprogramming, acting as a blank canvas. What's its parent?

```
puts "The superclass of BasicObject is #{BasicObject.superclass.inspect}"
```

produces:

```
The superclass of BasicObject is nil
```

So, we've finally reached the end. BasicObject is the root class of our hierarchy of classes. Given any class in any Ruby application, you can ask for its superclass, then the superclass of that class, and so on, and you'll eventually get back to BasicObject.

We've seen that if you call a method in an instance of class Child and that method isn't in Child's class definition, Ruby will look in the parent class. It goes deeper than that, because if the method isn't defined in the parent class, Ruby continues looking in the parent's parent, the parent's parent's parent, and so on, through the ancestors until it runs out of classes.

And this explains our original question. We can work out why to_s is available in just about every Ruby object. to_s is actually defined in class Object. Because Object is an ancestor of every Ruby class (except BasicObject), instances of every Ruby class have a to_s method defined:

```
tutmodules_6.rb
class Person
  def initialize(name)
    @name = name
  end
end
p = Person.new("Michael")
puts p
```

produces:

```
#<Person:0x0a4efc>
```

We saw in the previous chapter that we can override the to_s method:

```
tutmodules_7.rb
class Person
  def initialize(name)
    @name = name
  end
  def to_s
    "Person named #{@name}"
  end
end

p = Person.new("Michael")
puts p
```

produces:

```
Person named Michael
```

Armed with our knowledge of subclassing, we now know there's nothing special about this. The puts method calls to_s on its arguments. In this case, the argument is a Person object. Because class Person defines a to_s method, that method is called. If it hadn't defined a to_s method, then Ruby looks for (and finds) to_s in Person's parent class, Object.

It is common to use subclassing to add application-specific behavior to a standard library or framework class. If you've used Ruby on Rails,[2] you'll have subclassed ActionController when writing your own controller classes. Your controllers get all the behavior of the base controller and add their own specific handlers to individual user actions. If you've used the FXRuby GUI framework,[3] you'll have used subclassing to add your own application-specific behavior to Fox's standard GUI widgets.

Here's a more self-contained example. Ruby comes with a library called GServer that implements basic TCP server functionality. You add your own behavior to it by subclassing the GServer class. Let's use that to write some code that waits for a client to connect on a socket and then returns the last few lines of the system log file. This is an example of something that's actually quite useful in long-running applications—by building in such a server, you can access the internal state of the application while it is running (possibly even remotely).

The GServer class handles all the mechanics of interfacing to TCP sockets. When you create a GServer object, you tell it the port to listen on.[4] Then, when a client connects, the GServer object calls its serve method to handle that connection. Here's the implementation of that serve method in the GServer class:

```
def serve(io)
end
```

---

2. http://www.rubyonrails.com

3. http://www.fxruby.org

4. You can tell it a lot more, as well. We chose to keep it simple here.

As you can see, it does nothing. That's where our own LogServer class comes in:

```
tutmodules_9.rb
require 'gserver'
class LogServer < GServer
  def initialize
    super(12345)
  end

  def serve(client)
    client.puts get_end_of_log_file
  end

private
  def get_end_of_log_file
    File.open("/var/log/system.log") do |log|
      log.seek(-1000, IO::SEEK_END)    # back up 1000 characters from end
      log.gets                         # ignore partial line
      log.read                         # and return rest
    end
  end
end
server = LogServer.new
server.start.join
```

I don't want to focus too much on the details of running the server. Instead, let's look at how inheritance has helped us with this code. First, notice that our LogServer class inherits from GServer. This means that a log server is a kind of GServer, sharing all the GServer functionality. It also means we can add our own specialized behavior.

The first such specialization is the initialize method. We want our LogServer to run on TCP port 12345. That's a parameter that would normally be passed to the GServer constructor. So, within the initialize method of the LogServer, we want to invoke the initialize method of GServer, our parent, passing it the port number. We do that using the Ruby keyword super. When you invoke super, Ruby sends a message to the parent of the current object, asking it to invoke a method of the same name as the method invoking super. It passes this method the parameters that were passed to super.

This is a crucial step and one often forgotten by folks new to OO. When you subclass another class, you are responsible for making sure the initialization required by that class gets run. This means that, unless you know it isn't needed, you'll need to put a call to super somewhere in your subclass's initialize method. (If your subclass doesn't need an initialize method, then there's no need to do anything, because it will be the parent class's initialize method that gets run when your objects get created.)

So, by the time our initialize method finishes, our LogServer object will be a fully fledged TCP server, all without us having to write any protocol-level code. Down at the end of our program, we start the server. The call to join causes our program to wait for the server to exit before itself exiting.

While our server is running, it will receive connections from external clients. These invoke the serve method in the server object. Remember that empty method in class GServer? Well, our LogServer class provides its own implementation. And because it gets found by Ruby first when it's looking for methods to execute, it's our code that gets run whenever GServer accepts a connection. And our code reads the last few lines of the log file and returns them to the client:[5]

```
$ telnet 127.0.0.1 12345
Trying 127.0.0.1...
Connected to localhost.
Escape character is '^]'.
Jul  7 13:39:44 dave com.apple.syncservices.SyncServer[54938]:...
Jul  7 13:39:44 dave com.apple.syncservices.SyncServer[54938]:...
Jul  7 13:39:44 dave com.apple.syncservices.SyncServer[54938]:...
Jul  7 13:42:40 dave login[54768]: DEAD_PROCESS: 54768 ttys001
Jul  7 13:45:34 dave mdworker[54977]: fcntl to turn on F_CHECK...
Jul  7 13:48:44 dave mdworker[54977]: fcntl to turn on F_CHECK...
Connection closed by foreign host.
```

The use of the serve method shows a common idiom when using subclassing. A parent class assumes that it will be subclassed and calls a method that it expects its children to implement. This allows the parent to take on the brunt of the processing but to invoke what are effectively hook methods in subclasses to add application-level functionality. As we'll see at the end of this chapter, just because this idiom is common doesn't make it good design.

So, instead, let's look at *mixins*, a different way of sharing functionality in Ruby code. But, before we look at mixins, we'll need to get familiar with Ruby *modules*.

Modules

Modules are a way of grouping together methods, classes, and constants. Modules give you two major benefits:

- Modules provide a namespace and prevent name clashes.

- Modules support the mixin facility.

Namespaces

As you start to write bigger and bigger Ruby programs, you'll naturally find yourself producing chunks of reusable code—libraries of related routines that are generally applicable. You'll want to break this code into separate files so the contents can be shared among different Ruby programs.

Often this code will be organized into classes, so you'll probably stick a class (or a set of interrelated classes) into a file. However, there are times when you want to group things together that don't naturally form a class.

---

5.   You can also access this server from a web browser by connecting to http://127.0.0.1:12345.

Inheritance and Mixins

Some object-oriented languages (such as C++) support multiple inheritance, where a class can have more than one immediate parent, inheriting functionality from each. Although powerful, this technique can be dangerous, because the inheritance hierarchy can become ambiguous.

Other languages, such as Java and C#, support single inheritance. Here, a class can have only one immediate parent. Although cleaner (and easier to implement), single inheritance also has drawbacks—in the real world objects often inherit attributes from multiple sources (a ball is both a *bouncing thing* and a *spherical thing*, for example).

Ruby offers an interesting and powerful compromise, giving you the simplicity of single inheritance and the power of multiple inheritance. A Ruby class has only one direct parent, so Ruby is a single-inheritance language. However, Ruby classes can include the functionality of any number of *mixins* (a mixin is like a partial class definition). This provides a controlled multiple-inheritance-like capability with none of the drawbacks. We'll explore mixins more beginning on the following page.

An initial approach may be to put all these things into a file and simply load that file into any program that needs it. This is the way the C language works. However, this approach has a problem. Say you write a set of the trigonometry functions sin, cos, and so on. You stuff them all into a file, trig.rb, for future generations to enjoy. Meanwhile, Sally is working on a simulation of good and evil, and she codes a set of her own useful routines, including be_good and sin, and sticks them into moral.rb. Joe, who wants to write a program to find out how many angels can dance on the head of a pin, needs to load both trig.rb and moral.rb into his program. But both define a method called sin. Bad news.

The answer is the module mechanism. Modules define a *namespace*, a sandbox in which your methods and constants can play without having to worry about being stepped on by other methods and constants. The trig functions can go into one module:

```
tutmodules_10.rb
module Trig
  PI = 3.141592654
  def Trig.sin(x)
   # ..
  end
  def Trig.cos(x)
   # ..
  end
end
```

and the good and bad "moral" methods can go into another:

```
tutmodules_11.rb
module Moral
  VERY_BAD = 0
  BAD      = 1
  def Moral.sin(badness)
    # ...
  end
end
```

Module constants are named just like class constants, with an initial uppercase letter.[6] The method definitions look similar, too: module methods are defined just like class methods.

If a third program wants to use these modules, it can simply load the two files (using the Ruby require statement. In order to reference the name sin unambiguously, our code can then qualify the name using the name of the module containing the implementation we want, followed by ::, the scope resolution operator:

```
require 'trig'
require 'moral'

y = Trig.sin(Trig::PI/4)
wrongdoing = Moral.sin(Moral::VERY_BAD)
```

As with class methods, you call a module method by preceding its name with the module's name and a period, and you reference a constant using the module name and two colons.

Mixins

Modules have another, wonderful use. At a stroke, they pretty much eliminate the need for inheritance, providing a facility called a *mixin*.

In the previous section's examples, we defined module methods, methods whose names were prefixed by the module name. If this made you think of class methods, your next thought may well be "What happens if I define instance methods within a module?" Good question. A module can't have instances, because a module isn't a class. However, you can *include* a module within a class definition. When this happens, all the module's instance methods are suddenly available as methods in the class as well. They get *mixed in*. In fact, mixed-in modules effectively behave as superclasses.

---

6. But we will conventionally use all uppercase letters when writing them.

`tutmodules_13.rb`

```ruby
module Debug
  def who_am_i?
    "#{self.class.name} (\##{self.object_id}): #{self.to_s}"
  end
end
class Phonograph
  include Debug
  # ...
end
class EightTrack
  include Debug
  # ...
end
ph = Phonograph.new("West End Blues")
et = EightTrack.new("Surrealistic Pillow")

ph.who_am_i?   # =>   "Phonograph (#330450): West End Blues"
et.who_am_i?   # =>   "EightTrack (#330420): Surrealistic Pillow"
```

By including the Debug module, both the Phonograph and EightTrack classes gain access to the who_am_i? instance method.

We'll make a couple of points about the include statement before we go on. First, it has nothing to do with files. C programmers use a preprocessor directive called #include to insert the contents of one file into another during compilation. The Ruby include statement simply makes a reference to a module. If that module is in a separate file, you must use require (or its less commonly used cousin, load) to drag that file in before using include. Second, a Ruby include does not simply copy the module's instance methods into the class. Instead, it makes a reference from the class to the included module. If multiple classes include that module, they'll all point to the same thing. If you change the definition of a method within a module, even while your program is running, all classes that include that module will exhibit the new behavior.[7]

Mixins give you a wonderfully controlled way of adding functionality to classes. However, their true power comes out when the code in the mixin starts to interact with code in the class that uses it. Let's take the standard Ruby mixin Comparable as an example. The Comparable mixin adds the comparison operators (<, <=, ==, >=, and >), as well as the method between?, to a class. For this to work, Comparable assumes that any class that uses it defines the operator <=>. So, as a class writer, you define one method, <=>, include Comparable, and get six comparison functions for free.

Let's try this with a simple Person class.

---

7.   Of course, we're speaking only of methods here. Instance variables are always per object, for example.

We'll make people comparable based on their names:

```
tutmodules_14.rb
class Person
  include Comparable
  attr_reader :name
  def initialize(name)
    @name = name
  end
  def to_s
    "#{@name}"
  end
  def <=>(other)
    self.name <=> other.name
  end
end
p1 = Person.new("Matz")
p2 = Person.new("Guido")
p3 = Person.new("Larry")
# Compare a couple of names
if p1 > p2
  puts "#{p1.name}'s name > #{p2.name}'s name"
end
# Sort an array of Person objects
puts "Sorted list:"
puts [ p1, p2, p3].sort
```

produces:

```
Matz's name > Guido's name
Sorted list:
Guido
Larry
Matz
```

Note that we included Comparable in our Person class and then defined a <=>. We were then able to perform comparisons (such as p1 > p2) and even sort an array of Person objects.

Iterators and the Enumerable Module

The Ruby collection classes (Array, Hash, and so on) support a large number of operations that do various things with the collection: traverse it, sort it, and so on. You may be thinking, "Gee, it'd sure be nice if *my* class could support all these neat-o features, too!" (If you actually thought that, it's probably time to stop watching reruns of 1960s television shows.)

Well, your classes *can* support all these neat-o features, thanks to the magic of mixins and module Enumerable. All you have to do is write an iterator called each, which returns the elements of your collection in turn. Mix in Enumerable, and suddenly your class supports things such as map, include?, and find_all?. If the objects in your collection implement meaningful ordering semantics using the <=> method, you'll also get methods such as min, max, and sort.

Composing Modules

Enumerable is a standard mixin, implementing a bunch of methods in terms of the host class's each method. One of the methods defined by Enumerable is inject, which we saw back on page 60. This method applies a function or operation to the first two elements in the collection and then applies the operation to the result of this computation and to the third element, and so on, until all elements in the collection have been used.

Because inject is made available by Enumerable, we can use it in any class that includes the Enumerable module and defines the method each. Many built-in classes do this.

tutmodules_15.rb

```
[ 1, 2, 3, 4, 5 ].inject(:+)   # =>   15
( 'a'..'m').inject(:+)         # =>   "abcdefghijklm"
```

We could also define our own class that mixes in Enumerable and hence gets inject support:

tutmodules_16.rb

```
class VowelFinder
  include Enumerable

  def initialize(string)
    @string = string
  end

  def each
    @string.scan(/[aeiou]/) do |vowel|
      yield vowel
    end
  end
end
```

tutmodules_17.rb

```
vf = VowelFinder.new("the quick brown fox jumped")

vf.inject(:+)   # =>   "euiooue"
```

Notice that we've used the same pattern in the call to inject in these examples—we're using it to perform a summation. When applied to numbers, it returns the arithmetic sum; when applied to strings, it concatenates them. We can use a module to encapsulate this functionality too:

tutmodules_18.rb

```
module Summable
  def sum
    inject(:+)
  end
end

class Array
  include Summable
end
```

```
class Range
  include Summable
end
class VowelFinder
  include Summable
end
```

tutmodules_19.rb

```
[ 1, 2, 3, 4, 5 ].sum    # =>    15
('a'..'m').sum           # =>    "abcdefghijklm"

vf = VowelFinder.new("the quick brown fox jumped")
vf.sum                   # =>    "euiooue"
```

Instance Variables in Mixins

People coming to Ruby from C++ often ask, "What happens to instance variables in a mixin? In C++, I have to jump through some hoops to control how variables are shared in a multiple-inheritance hierarchy. How does Ruby handle this?"

Well, for starters, it's not really a fair question. Remember how instance variables work in Ruby: the first mention of an @-prefixed variable creates the instance variable *in the current object,* self.

For a mixin, this means that the module you mix into your client class (the *mixee*?) may create instance variables in the client object and may use attr_reader and friends to define accessors for these instance variables. For instance, the Observable module in the following example adds an instance variable @observer_list to any class that includes it:

```
module Observable
  def observers
    @observer_list ||= []
  end
  def add_observer(obj)
    observers << obj
  end
  def notify_observers
    observers.each {|o| o.update }
  end
end
```

However, this behavior exposes us to a risk. A mixin's instance variables can clash with those of the host class or with those of other mixins. The example that follows shows a class that uses our Observer module but that unluckily also uses an instance variable called @observer_list. At runtime, this program will go wrong in some hard-to-diagnose ways:

```
class TelescopeScheduler
  # other classes can register to get notifications
  # when the schedule changes
  include Observable
```

```
  def initialize
    @observer_list = []  # folks with telescope time
  end
  def add_viewer(viewer)
    @observer_list << viewer
  end
  # ...
end
```

For the most part, mixin modules don't use instance variables directly—they use accessors to retrieve data from the client object. But if you need to create a mixin that has to have its own state, ensure that the instance variables have unique names to distinguish them from any other mixins in the system (perhaps by using the module's name as part of the variable name). Alternatively, the module could use a module-level hash, indexed by the current object ID, to store instance-specific data without using Ruby instance variables:

```
tutmodules_22.rb
module Test
  State = {}
  def state=(value)
    State[object_id] = value
  end
  def state
    State[object_id]
  end
end
```

```
tutmodules_23.rb


class Client
  include Test
end

c1 = Client.new
c2 = Client.new
c1.state = 'cat'
c2.state = 'dog'

c1.state   # =>   "cat"
c2.state   # =>   "dog"
```

A downside of this approach is that the data associated with a particular object will not get automatically deleted if the object is deleted.

Resolving Ambiguous Method Names

One of the other questions folks ask about mixins is, how is method lookup handled? In particular, what happens if methods with the same name are defined in a class, in that class's parent class, and in a mixin included into the class?

The answer is that Ruby looks first in the immediate class of an object, then in the mixins included into that class, and then in superclasses and their mixins. If a class has multiple modules mixed in, the last one included is searched first.

Inheritance, Mixins, and Design

Inheritance and mixins both allow you to write code in one place and effectively inject that code into multiple classes. So, when do you use each?

As is usual with most questions of design, the answer is, to some extent, it depends. However, over the years developers have come up with some pretty clear general guidelines to help us decide.

First, let's look at subclassing. Classes in Ruby are related to the idea of types. It would be natural to say that "cat" is a string and [1,2] is an array. And that's another way of saying that the class of "cat" is String and the class of [1,2] is Array. When we create our own classes, you can think of it as adding new types to the language. And when we subclass either a built-in class or our own class, we're creating a *subtype*.

Now, a lot of research has been done on type theories. One of the more famous results is the *Liskov Substitution Principle*. Formally, this states: "Let q(x) be a property provable about objects x of type T. Then q(y) should be true for objects y of type S where S is a subtype of T." What this means is that you should be able to substitute an object of a child class wherever you use an object of the parent class—the child should honor the parent's contract. There's another way of looking at this: we should be able to say that the child object *is a* kind of the parent. We're used to saying this in English: a car *is a* vehicle, a cat *is an* animal, and so on. This means that a cat should, at the very least, be capable of doing everything we say that an animal can do.

So, when you're looking for subclassing relationships while designing your application, be on the lookout for these *is-a* relationships.

But...here's the bad news. In the real world, there really aren't that many true *is a* relationships. Instead, it's far more common to have *has a* or *uses a* relationships between things. The real world is built using composition, not strict hierarchies.

In the past, we've tended to gloss over that fact when programming. Because inheritance was the only scheme available for sharing code, we got lazy and said things like "My Person class is a subclass of my DatabaseWrapper class."[8] But a person object *is not* a kind of database wrapper object. A person object *uses* a database wrapper to provide persistence services.

Is this just a theoretical issue? No! Inheritance represents an incredibly tight coupling of two components. Change a parent class, and you risk breaking the child class. But, even worse, if code that uses objects of the child class relies on those objects also having methods defined

---

8.   Indeed, the Rails framework makes just this mistake.

in the parent, then all that code will break, too. The parent class's implementation leaks through the child classes and out into the rest of the code. With a decent-sized program, this becomes a serious inhibitor to change.

And that's where we need to move away from inheritance in our designs. Instead, we need to be using *composition* wherever we see a case of A *uses a* B or A *has a* B. Our persisted Person object won't subclass DataWrapper. Instead, it'll construct a reference to a database wrapper object and use that object reference to save and restore itself.

But that can also make code messy. And that's where a combination of mixins and metaprogramming comes to the rescue, because we can say this:

```
class Person
  include Persistable
  # ...
end
```

instead of

```
class Person < DataWrapper
  # ...
end
```

If you're new to object-oriented programming, this discussion probably feels remote and abstract. But as you start to code larger and larger programs, I urge you to think about the issues discussed here. Try to reserve inheritance for the times where it is justified. And try to explore all the cool ways that mixins let you write decoupled, flexible code.

## Chapter 6

Standard Types

So far we've been having fun implementing programs using arrays, hashes, and procs, but we haven't really covered the other basic types in Ruby: numbers, strings, ranges, and regular expressions. Let's spend a few pages on these basic building blocks now.

Numbers

Ruby supports integers and floating-point, rational, and complex numbers. Integers can be any length (up to a maximum determined by the amount of free memory on your system). Integers within a certain range (normally $-2^{30} \ldots 2^{30} - 1$ or $-2^{62} \ldots 2^{62} - 1$) are held internally in binary form and are objects of class Fixnum. Integers outside this range are stored in objects of class Bignum (currently implemented as a variable-length set of short integers). This process is transparent, and Ruby automatically manages the conversion back and forth:

```
num = 81
6.times do
  puts "#{num.class}: #{num}"
  num *= num
end
```

produces:

```
Fixnum: 81
Fixnum: 6561
Fixnum: 43046721
Bignum: 1853020188851841
Bignum: 3433683820292512484657849089281
Bignum: 11790184577738583171520872861412518665678211592275841109096961
```

You write integers using an optional leading sign, an optional base indicator (0 for octal, 0d for decimal [the default], 0x for hex, or 0b for binary), followed by a string of digits in the appropriate base. Underscore characters are ignored in the digit string (some folks use them in place of commas in larger numbers).

```
123456                      => 123456    # Fixnum
0d123456                    => 123456    # Fixnum
123_456                     => 123456    # Fixnum - underscore ignored
-543                        => -543      # Fixnum - negative number
0xaabb                      => 43707     # Fixnum - hexadecimal
0377                        => 255       # Fixnum - octal
-0b10_1010                  => -42       # Fixnum - binary (negated)
123_456_789_123_456_789     => 123456789123456789 # Bignum
```

A numeric literal with a decimal point and/or an exponent is turned into a Float object, corresponding to the native architecture's double data type. You must both precede and follow the decimal point with a digit (if you write 1.0e3 as 1.e3, Ruby will try to invoke the method e3 on the object 1).

1.9 ⟋ As of Ruby 1.9, rational and complex number support is built into the interpreter. Rational numbers are the ratio of two integers—they are fractions—and hence have an exact representation (unlike floats). Complex numbers represent points on the complex plane. They have two components, the real and imaginary parts.

Ruby doesn't have a literal syntax for representing rational and complex numbers. Instead, you create them using explicit calls to the constructor methods Rational and Complex (although, as we'll see, you can use the mathn library to make working with rational numbers easier).

```
Rational(3, 4) * Rational(2, 3)     # =>    (1/2)
Rational("3/4") * Rational("2/3")   # =>    (1/2)

Complex(1, 2) * Complex(3, 4)       # =>    (-5+10i)
Complex("1+2i") * Complex("3+4i")   # =>    (-5+10i)
```

All numbers are objects and respond to a variety of messages (listed in full starting on pages 457 [Bignum], 464 [Complex], 516 [Fixnum], 519 [Float], 534 [Integer], 606 [Numeric], and 651 [Rational]). So, unlike (say) C++, you find the absolute value of a number by writing num.abs, not abs(num).

Finally, we'll offer a warning for Perl users. Strings that contain just digits are *not* automatically converted into numbers when used in expressions. This tends to bite most often when reading numbers from a file. For example, we may want to find the sum of the two numbers on each line for a file such as the following:

```
3 4
5 6
7 8
```

The following code doesn't work:

```
some_file.each do |line|
  v1, v2 = line.split     # split line on spaces
  print v1 + v2, " "
end
```

produces:

```
34 56 78
```

The problem is that the input was read as strings, not numbers. The plus operator concatenates strings, so that's what we see in the output. To fix this, use the Integer method to convert the strings to integers:

```
some_file.each do |line|
  v1, v2 = line.split
  print Integer(v1) + Integer(v2), " "
end
```

produces:

```
7 11 15
```

How Numbers Interact

Most of the time, numbers work the way you'd expect. If you perform some operation between two numbers of the same class, the answer will typically be a number of that same class (although, as we've seen, fixnums can become bignums, and vice versa). If the two numbers are different classes, the result will have the class of the more general one. If you mix integers and floats, the result will be a float; if you mix floats and complex numbers, the result will be complex.

```
1 + 2                  # => 3
1 + 2.0                # => 3.0
1.0 + 2                # => 3.0
1.0 + Complex(1,2)     # => (2.0+2i)
1 + Rational(2,3)      # => (5/3)
1.0 + Rational(2,3)    # => 1.66666666666667
```

The return-type rule still applies when it comes to division. However this often confuses folks, because division between two integers yields an integer result:

```
1.0 / 2   # => 0.5
1 / 2.0   # => 0.5
1 / 2     # => 0
```

If you'd prefer that integer division instead return a fraction (a Rational number), require the mathn library (described on page 758). This will cause arithmetic operations to attempt to find the most *natural* representation for their results. For integer division where the result isn't an integer, a fraction will be returned.

```
22 / 7                    # => 3
Complex::I * Complex::I   # => (-1+0i)

require 'mathn'
22 / 7                    # => (22/7)
Complex::I * Complex::I   # => -1
```

Note that 22/7 is effectively a rational literal once mathn is loaded (albeit one that's calculated at runtime).

Looping Using Numbers

Integers also support several useful iterators. We've seen one already: 6.times in the code example on page 87. Others include upto and downto for iterating up and down between two integers. Class Numeric also provides the more general method step, which is more like a traditional for loop.

```
3.times      { print "X " }
1.upto(5)    {|i| print i, " " }
99.downto(95) {|i| print i, " " }
50.step(80, 5) {|i| print i, " " }
```

produces:

```
X X X 1 2 3 4 5 99 98 97 96 95 50 55 60 65 70 75 80
```

As with other iterators, if you leave the block off, the call returns an Enumerator object:

```
10.downto(7).with_index {|num, index| puts "#{index}: #{num}"}
```

produces:

```
0: 10
1: 9
2: 8
3: 7
```

Strings

Ruby strings are simply sequences of characters.[1] They normally hold printable characters, but that is not a requirement; a string can also hold binary data. Strings are objects of class String.

Strings are often created using string literals—sequences of characters between delimiters. Because binary data is otherwise difficult to represent within program source, you can place various escape sequences in a string literal. Each is replaced with the corresponding binary value as the program is compiled. The type of string delimiter determines the degree of substitution performed. Within single-quoted strings, two consecutive backslashes are replaced by a single backslash, and a backslash followed by a single quote becomes a single quote.

```
'escape using "\\"'  # =>  escape using "\"
'That\'s right'      # =>  That's right
```

Double-quoted strings support a boatload more escape sequences. The most common is probably \n, the newline character. Table 22.2 on page 317 gives the complete list. In addition, you can substitute the value of any Ruby code into a string using the sequence #{ *expr* }. If the code is just a global variable, a class variable, or an instance variable, you can omit the braces.

---

1.   Prior to Ruby 1.9, strings were sequences of 8-bit bytes.

```
"Seconds/day: #{24*60*60}"        # =>    Seconds/day: 86400
"#{'Ho! '*3}Merry Christmas!"     # =>    Ho! Ho! Ho! Merry Christmas!
"This is line #$."                # =>    This is line 3
```

The interpolated code can be one or more statements, not just an expression:

```
puts  "now is #{ def the(a)
                   'the ' + a
                 end
                 the('time')
               } for all good coders..."
```

produces:

```
now is the time for all good coders...
```

You have three more ways to construct string literals: %q, %Q, and *here documents*.

%q and %Q start delimited single- and double-quoted strings (you can think of %q as a thin quote ' and %Q as a thick quote "):

```
%q/general single-quoted string/  # =>    general single-quoted string
%Q!general double-quoted string!  # =>    general double-quoted string
%Q{Seconds/day: #{24*60*60}}      # =>    Seconds/day: 86400
```

In fact, the Q is optional:

```
%!general double-quoted string!   # =>    general double-quoted string
%{Seconds/day: #{24*60*60}}       # =>    Seconds/day: 86400
```

The character following the *q* or *Q* is the delimiter. If it is an opening bracket ([), brace ({), parenthesis ((), or less-than sign (<), the string is read until the matching close symbol is found. Otherwise, the string is read until the next occurrence of the same delimiter. The delimiter can be any nonalphanumeric or nonmultibyte character.

Finally, you can construct a string using a *here document*:

```
string = <<END_OF_STRING
    The body of the string
    is the input lines up to
    one starting with the same
    text that followed the '<<'
END_OF_STRING
```

A here document consists of lines in the source up to but not including the terminating string that you specify after the < < characters. Normally, this terminator must start in the first column. However, if you put a minus sign after the < < characters, you can indent the terminator:

```
string = <<-END_OF_STRING
    The body of the string is the input lines up to
    one starting with the same text that followed the '<<'
    END_OF_STRING
```

You can also have multiple here documents on a single line. Each acts as a separate string. The bodies of the here documents are fetched sequentially from the source lines that follow.

```
print <<-STRING1, <<-STRING2
   Concat
   STRING1
     enate
   STRING2
```

produces:

```
   Concat
     enate
```

Note that Ruby does not strip leading spaces off the contents of the strings in these cases.

Strings and Encodings

1.9

In Ruby 1.9, every string has an associated encoding. The default encoding of a string literal depends on the encoding of the source file that contains it. With no explicit encoding, a source file (and its strings) will be US-ASCII.

```
plain_string = "dog"
puts "Encoding of #{plain_string.inspect} is #{plain_string.encoding}"
```

produces:

```
Encoding of "dog" is US-ASCII
```

If you override the encoding, you'll do that for all strings in the file:

```
#encoding: utf-8
plain_string = "dog"
puts "Encoding of #{plain_string.inspect} is #{plain_string.encoding}"
utf_string = "δog"
puts "Encoding of #{utf_string.inspect} is #{utf_string.encoding}"
```

produces:

```
Encoding of "dog" is UTF-8
Encoding of "δog" is UTF-8
```

We'll have a lot more to say about encoding in Chapter 17 on page 251.

Character Constants

Technically, Ruby does not have a class for characters—characters are simply strings of length one. For historical reasons, character constants can be created by preceding the character (or sequence that represents a character) with a question mark:

```
?a         # => "a"      (printable character)
?\n        # => "\n"     (code for a newline (0x0a))
?\C-a      # => "\x01"   (control a)
?\M-a      # => "\xE1"   (meta sets bit 7)
?\M-\C-a   # => "\x81"   (meta and control a)
?\C-?      # => "\x7F"   (delete character)
```

Do yourself a favor and immediately forget this section. It's far easier to use regular octal and hex escape sequences than to remember these ones. Use "a" rather than ?a, and use "\n" rather than ?\n.

Working with Strings

String is probably the largest built-in Ruby class, with more than 100 standard methods. We won't go through them all here; the library reference has a complete list. Instead, we'll look at some common string idioms—things that are likely to pop up during day-to-day programming.

Maybe we've been given a file containing information on a song playlist. For historical reasons (are there any other kind?), the list of songs is stored as lines in the file. Each line holds the name of the file containing the song, the song's duration, the artist, and the title, all in vertical bar–separated fields. A typical file may start like this:

```
/jazz/j00132.mp3  | 3:45 | Fats      Waller     | Ain't Misbehavin'
/jazz/j00319.mp3  | 2:58 | Louis     Armstrong  | Wonderful World
/bgrass/bg0732.mp3| 4:09 | Strength in Numbers  | Texas Red
         :                     :          :                  :
```

Looking at the data, it's clear that we'll be using some of class String's many methods to extract and clean up the fields before we use them. At a minimum, we'll need to

- break each line into fields,
- convert the running times from mm:ss to seconds, and
- remove those extra spaces from the artists' names.

Our first task is to split each line into fields, and String#split will do the job nicely. In this case, we'll pass split a regular expression, /\s*\|\s*/, that splits the line into tokens wherever split finds a vertical bar, optionally surrounded by spaces. And, because the line read from the file has a trailing newline, we'll use String#chomp to strip it off just before we apply the split. We'll store details of each song in a Struct that contains an attribute for each of the three fields. (A Struct is simply a data structure that contains a given set of attributes—in this case the title, name, and length. See page 687 for the gory details.)

```
tutstdtypes_24.rb
Song = Struct.new(:title, :name, :length)
File.open("songdata") do |song_file|
  songs = []
  song_file.each do |line|
    file, length, name, title = line.chomp.split(/\s*\|\s*/)
    songs << Song.new(title, name, length)
  end
  puts songs[1]
end
```

produces:

```
#<struct Song title="Wonderful World", name="Louis     Armstrong", length="2:58">
```

Unfortunately, whoever created the original file entered the artists' names in columns, so some of them contain extra spaces that we'd better remove before we go much further. We have many ways of doing this, but probably the simplest is String#squeeze, which trims runs of repeated characters. We'll use the squeeze! form of the method, which alters the string in place:

tutstdtypes_25.rb

```
Song = Struct.new(:title, :name, :length)
File.open("songdata") do |song_file|
  songs = []
  song_file.each do |line|
    file, length, name, title = line.chomp.split(/\s*\|\s*/)
    name.squeeze!(" ")
    songs << Song.new(title, name, length)
  end
  puts songs[1]
end
```

produces:

```
#<struct Song title="Wonderful World", name="Louis Armstrong", length="2:58">
```

Finally, we have the minor matter of the time format: the file says 2:58, and we want the number of seconds, 178. We could use split again, this time splitting the time field around the colon character:

```
mins, secs = length.split(/:/)
```

Instead, we'll use a related method. String#scan is similar to split in that it breaks a string into chunks based on a pattern. However, unlike split, with scan you specify the pattern that you want the chunks to match. In this case, we want to match one or more digits for both the minutes and seconds components. The pattern for one or more digits is /\d+/:

tutstdtypes_27.rb

```
Song = Struct.new(:title, :name, :length)
File.open("songdata") do |song_file|
  songs = []
  song_file.each do |line|
    file, length, name, title = line.chomp.split(/\s*\|\s*/)
    name.squeeze!(" ")
    mins, secs = length.scan(/\d+/)
    songs << Song.new(title, name, mins.to_i*60 + secs.to_i)
  end
  puts songs[1]
end
```

produces:

```
#<struct Song title="Wonderful World", name="Louis Armstrong", length=178>
```

We could spend the next 50 pages looking at all the methods in class String. However, let's move on instead to look at a simpler data type: the range.

Ranges

Ranges occur everywhere: January to December, 0 to 9, rare to well done, lines 50 through 67, and so on. If Ruby is to help us model reality, it seems natural for it to support these ranges. In fact, Ruby goes one better: it actually uses ranges to implement three separate features: sequences, conditions, and intervals.

Ranges as Sequences

The first and perhaps most natural use of ranges is to express a sequence. Sequences have a start point, an end point, and a way to produce successive values in the sequence. In Ruby, these sequences are created using the .. and ... range operators. The two-dot form creates an inclusive range, and the three-dot form creates a range that excludes the specified high value:

```
1..10
'a'..'z'
0..."cat".length
```

You can convert a range to an array using the to_a method and convert it to an Enumerator using to_enum:[2]

```
(1..10).to_a          # =>  [1, 2, 3, 4, 5, 6, 7, 8, 9, 10]
('bar'..'bat').to_a   # =>  ["bar", "bas", "bat"]
enum = ('bar'..'bat').to_enum
enum.next             # =>  "bar"
enum.next             # =>  "bas"
```

Ranges have methods that let you iterate over them and test their contents in a variety of ways:

```
digits = 0..9
digits.include?(5)          # =>   true
digits.min                  # =>   0
digits.max                  # =>   9
digits.reject {|i| i < 5 }  # =>   [5, 6, 7, 8, 9]
digits.inject(:+)           # =>   45
```

So far we've shown ranges of numbers and strings. However, as you'd expect from an object-oriented language, Ruby can create ranges based on objects that you define. The only constraints are that the objects must respond to succ by returning the next object in sequence and the objects must be comparable using <=>. Sometimes called the *spaceship operator*, <=>, compares two values, returning −1, 0, or +1 depending on whether the first is less than, equal to, or greater than the second.

---

2. Sometimes people worry that ranges take a lot of memory. That's not an issue: the range 1..100000 is held as a Range object containing references to two Fixnum objects. However, convert a range into an array, and all that memory will get used.

In reality, this isn't something you do very often, so examples tend to be a bit contrived. Here's one—a class that presents numbers that are powers of 2. Because it defines <=> and succ, we can use objects of this class in ranges:

```
tutstdtypes_31.rb
class PowerOfTwo
  attr_reader :value
  def initialize(value)
    @value = value
  end
  def <=>(other)
    @value <=> other.value
  end
  def succ
    PowerOfTwo.new(@value + @value)
  end
  def to_s
    @value.to_s
  end
end

p1 = PowerOfTwo.new(4)
p2 = PowerOfTwo.new(32)

puts (p1..p2).to_a
```

produces:

```
4
8
16
32
```

Ranges as Conditions

As well as representing sequences, ranges can also be used as conditional expressions. Here, they act as a kind of toggle switch—they turn on when the condition in the first part of the range becomes true, and they turn off when the condition in the second part becomes true. For example, the following code fragment prints sets of lines from standard input, where the first line in each set contains the word *start* and the last line contains the word *end*:

```
while line = gets
  puts line if line =~ /start/ .. line =~ /end/
end
```

Behind the scenes, the range keeps track of the state of each of the tests. We'll show some examples of this in the description of loops that starts on page 143 and in the language section on page 336.

Ranges as Intervals

A final use of the versatile range is as an interval test: seeing whether some value falls within the interval represented by the range. We do this using ===, the case equality operator:

```
(1..10)     === 5        # =>    true
(1..10)     === 15       # =>    false
(1..10)     === 3.14159  # =>    true
('a'..'j') === 'c'       # =>    true
('a'..'j') === 'z'       # =>    false
```

This is most often used in case statements:

```
car_age = gets.to_f    # let's assume it's 5.2
case car_age
when 0...1
  puts "Mmm.. new car smell"
when 1...3
  puts "Nice and new"
when 3...6
  puts "Reliable but slightly dinged"
when 6...10
  puts "Can be a struggle"
when 10...30
  puts "Clunker"
else
  puts "Vintage gem"
end
```

produces:

```
Reliable but slightly dinged
```

Note the use of exclusive ranges in the previous example. These are normally the correct choice in case statements. If instead we'd written the following, we'd get the wrong answer because 5.2 does not fall within any of the ranges, so the else clause triggers:

tutstdtypes_35.rb

```
car_age = gets.to_f     # let's assume it's 5.2
case car_age
when 0..0
  puts "Mmm.. new car smell"
when 1..2
  puts "Nice and new"
when 3..5
  puts "Reliable but slightly dinged"
when 6..9
  puts "Can be a struggle"
when 10..29
  puts "Clunker"
else
  puts "Vintage gem"
end
```

produces:

```
Vintage gem
```

Chapter 7

Regular Expressions

We probably spend most of our time in Ruby working with strings, so it seems reasonable for Ruby to have some great tools for working with those strings. As we've seen, the String class itself is no slouch—it has more than 100 methods. But there are still things that the basic String class can't do. For example, we might want to see whether a string contains two or more repeated characters, or we might want to replace every word longer than fifteen characters with its first five characters and an ellipsis. This is when we turn to the power of regular expressions.

Now, before we get too far in, here's a warning: there have been whole books written on regular expressions.[1] There is complexity and subtlety here that rivals that of the rest of Ruby. So if you've never used regular expressions, don't expect to read through this whole chapter the first time. In fact, you'll find two emergency exits in what follows. If you're new to regular expressions, I strongly suggest you read through to the first and then bail out. When some regular expression question next comes up, come back here and maybe read through to the next exit. Then, later, when you're feeling comfortable with regular expressions, you can give the whole chapter a read.

What Regular Expressions Let You Do

A regular expression is a pattern that can be matched against a string. It can be a simple pattern, such as *the string must contain the sequence of letters "cat"*, or the pattern can be complex, such as *the string must start with a protocol identifier, followed by two literal forward slashes, followed by...*, and so on. This is cool in theory. But what makes regular expressions so powerful is what you can do with them in practice:

- You can test a string to see whether it matches a pattern.
- You can extract from a string the sections that match all or part of a pattern.
- You can change the string, replacing parts that match a pattern.

Ruby provides built-in support that makes pattern matching and substitution convenient and concise. In this section, we'll work through the basics of regular expression patterns and

---

1.   Such as *Mastering Regular Expressions: Powerful Techniques for Perl and Other Tools* [Fri02]

see how Ruby supports matching and replacing based on those patterns. In the sections that follow, we'll dig deeper into both the patterns and Ruby's support for them.

Ruby's Regular Expressions

There are many ways of creating a regular expression pattern. By far the most common is to write it between forward slashes. Thus, the pattern /cat/ is a regular expression literal in the same way that "cat" is a string literal.

/cat/ is an example of a simple, but very common, pattern. It matches any string that contains the substring cat. In fact, inside a pattern, all characters except ., |, (,), [,], {, }, +, \, ^, $, *, and ? match themselves. So, at the risk of creating something that sounds like a logic puzzle, here are some patterns and examples of strings they match and don't match:

/cat/   matches "dog and cat", and "catch", but not "Cat" or "c.a.t."
/123/   matches "86512312" and "abc123", but not "1.23"
/t a b/ matches "hit a ball" but not "table"

If you want to match one of the special characters literally in a pattern, precede it with a backslash, so /*/ is a pattern that matches a single asterisk, and /\// is a pattern that matches a forward slash.

Pattern literals are like double-quoted strings. In particular, you can use #{...} expression substitutions in the pattern.

Matching Strings with Patterns

The Ruby operator =~ matches a string against a pattern. It returns the character offset into the string at which the match occurred:

```
/cat/ =~ "dog and cat"   # =>   8
/cat/ =~ "catch"         # =>   0
/cat/ =~ "Cat"           # =>   nil
```

You can put the string first if you prefer:[2]

```
"dog and cat" =~ /cat/   # =>   8
"catch" =~ /cat/         # =>   0
 "Cat" =~ /cat/          # =>   nil
```

Because pattern matching returns nil when it fails and because nil is equivalent to false in Ruby, you can use the result of a pattern match as a condition in statements such as if and while.

```
str = "cat and dog"
if str =~ /cat/
  puts "There's a cat here somewhere"
end
```

---

2.   Some folks say this is inefficient, because the string will end up calling the regular expression code to do the match. These folks are correct in theory but wrong in practice.

produces:

```
There's a cat here somewhere
```

The following code prints lines in testfile that contain on:

```
File.foreach("testfile").with_index do |line, index|
  puts "#{index}: #{line}" if line =~ /on/
end
```

produces:

```
0: This is line one
3: And so on...
```

You can test to see whether a pattern does not match a string using !~:

```
File.foreach("testfile").with_index do |line, index|
  puts "#{index}: #{line}" if line !~ /on/
end
```

produces:

```
1: This is line two
2: This is line three
```

Changing Strings with Patterns

The sub takes a pattern and some replacement text:[3] If it finds a match for the pattern in the string, it replaces the matched substring with the replacement text.

```
str = "Dog and Cat"
new_str = str.sub(/Cat/, "Gerbil")
puts "Let's go to the #{new_str} for a pint."
```

produces:

```
Let's go to the Dog and Gerbil for a pint.
```

The sub method changes only the first match it finds. To replace all matches, use gsub. (The *g* stands for global.)

```
str = "Dog and Cat"
new_str1 = str.sub(/a/, "*")
new_str2 = str.gsub(/a/, "*")
puts "Using sub: #{new_str1}"
puts "Using gsub: #{new_str2}"
```

produces:

```
Using sub: Dog *nd Cat
Using gsub: Dog *nd C*t
```

Both sub and gsub return a new string. (If no substitutions are made, that new string will just be a copy of the original.)

---

3.   Actually, it does more than that, but we won't get to that for a while.

If you want to modify the original string, use the sub! and gsub! forms:

```
str = "now is the time"
str.sub!(/i/, "*")
str.gsub!(/t/, "T")
puts str
```

produces:

```
now *s The Time
```

Unlike sub and gsub, sub! and gsub! return the string only if the pattern was matched. If no match for the pattern is found in the string, they return nil instead. This means it can make sense (depending on your need) to use the ! forms in conditions.

So, at this point you know how to use patterns to look for text in a string and how to substitute different text for those matches. And, for many people, that's enough. So if you're itching to get on to other Ruby topics, now is a good time to move on to the next chapter. At some point, you'll likely need to do something more complex with regular expressions (for example, matching a time by looking for two digits, a colon, and two more digits). You can then come back and read the next section.

Or, you can just stay right here as we dig deeper into patterns, matches, and replacements.

Digging Deeper

Like most things in Ruby, regular expressions are just objects—they're instances of class Regexp. This means you can assign them to variables, pass them to methods, and so on:

```
str = "dog and cat"
pattern = /nd/
pattern =~ str   # =>   5
str =~ pattern   # =>   5
```

You can also create regular expression objects by calling the Regexp class's new method and by using the %r{...} syntax. The %r syntax is particularly useful when creating patterns that contain forward slashes:

```
/mm\/dd/               # =>   /mm\/dd/
Regexp.new("mm/dd")    # =>   /mm\/dd/
%r{mm/dd}              # =>   /mm\/dd/
```

Regular Expression Options

A regular expression may include one or more options that modify the way the pattern matches strings. If you're using literals to create the Regexp object, then the options are one or more characters placed immediately after the terminator. If you're using Regexp.new, the options are constants used as the second parameter of the constructor.

> **Playing with Regular Expressions**
>
> If you're like me, you'll sometimes get confused by regular expressions. You create something that *should* work, but it just doesn't seem to match. That's when I fall back to irb. I'll cut and paste the regular expression into irb and then try to match it against strings. I'll slowly remove portions until I get it to match my target string and add stuff back until it fails. At that point, I'll know what I was doing wrong.

i   *Case insensitive*. The pattern match will ignore the case of letters in the pattern and string. (The old technique of setting $= to make matches case insensitive no longer works.)

o   *Substitute once*. Any #... substitutions in a particular regular expression literal will be performed just once, the first time it is evaluated. Otherwise, the substitutions will be performed every time the literal generates a Regexp object.

m   *Multiline mode*. Normally, "." matches any character except a newline. With the /m option, "." matches any character.

x   *Extended mode*. Complex regular expressions can be difficult to read. The x option allows you to insert spaces and newlines in the pattern to make it more readable. You can also use # to introduce comments.

Another set of options allows you to set the language encoding of the regular expression. If none of these options is specified, the regular expression will have US-ASCII encoding if it contains only 7-bit characters. Otherwise, it will use the default encoding of the source file containing the literal: n: no encoding (ASCII), e: EUC, s: SJIS, and u: UTF-8.

Matching Against Patterns

Once you have a regular expression object, you can match it against a string using the Regexp#match(*string*) method or the match operators =~ (positive match) and !~ (negative match). The match operators are defined for both String and Regexp objects. One operand of the match operator must be a regular expression.

```
name = "Fats Waller"
name =~ /a/                    # =>   1
name =~ /z/                    # =>   nil
/a/ =~ name                    # =>   1
/a/.match(name)                # =>   #<MatchData "a">
Regexp.new("all").match(name)  # =>   #<MatchData "all">
```

The match operators return the character position at which the match occurred, while the match method returns a MatchData object. In all forms, if the match fails, nil is returned.

After a successful match, Ruby sets a whole bunch of magic variables. For example, $& receives the part of the string that was matched by the pattern, $` receives the part of the string that preceded the match, and $' receives the string after the match. However, these particular variables are considered to be fairly ugly, so most Ruby programmers instead use the MatchData object returned from the match method, because it encapsulates all the information Ruby knows about the match. Given a MatchData object, you can call pre_match to return the part of the string before the match, post_match for the string after the match, and index using [0] to get the matched portion.

We can use these methods to write a method, show_regexp, that illustrates where a particular pattern matches:

```
def show_regexp(string, pattern)
  match = pattern.match(string)
  if match
    "#{match.pre_match}->#{match[0]}<-#{match.post_match}"
  else
    "no match"
  end
end
```

```
show_regexp('very interesting', /t/)  # =>   very in->t<-eresting
show_regexp('Fats Waller', /a/)       # =>   F->a<-ts Waller
show_regexp('Fats Waller', /lle/)     # =>   Fats Wa->lle<-r
show_regexp('Fats Waller', /z/)       # =>   no match
```

Deeper Patterns

We said earlier that, within a pattern, all characters match themselves except ., |, (,), [,], {, }, +, \, ^, $, *, and ?. Let's dig a bit deeper into this.

First, always remember that you need to escape any of these characters with a backslash if you want them to be treated as regular characters to match:

```
show_regexp('yes | no', /\|/)      # =>   yes ->|<- no
show_regexp('yes (no)', /\(no\)/)  # =>   yes ->(no)<-
show_regexp('are you sure?', /e\?/)  # =>   are you sur->e?<-
```

Now let's see what some of these characters mean if you use them without escaping them.

Anchors

By default, a regular expression will try to find the first match for the pattern in a string. Match /iss/ against the string "Mississippi," and it will find the substring "iss" starting at position 1 (the second character in the string). But what if you want to force a pattern to match only at the start or end of a string?

The patterns ^ and $ match the beginning and end of a line, respectively. These are often used to *anchor* a pattern match; for example, /^option/ matches the word *option* only if it appears at the start of a line. The sequence \A matches the beginning of a string, and \z and \Z match the end of a string. (Actually, \Z matches the end of a string *unless* the string ends with a \n, in which case it matches just before the \n.)

```
str = "this is\nthe time"
show_regexp(str, /^the/)      # =>   this is\n->the<- time
show_regexp(str, /is$/)       # =>   this ->is<-\nthe time
show_regexp(str, /\Athis/)    # =>   ->this<- is\nthe time
show_regexp(str, /\Athe/)     # =>   no match
```

Similarly, the patterns \b and \B match word boundaries and nonword boundaries, respectively. Word characters are ASCII letters, numbers, and underscores:

```
show_regexp("this is\nthe time", /\bis/)   # =>   this ->is<-\nthe time
show_regexp("this is\nthe time", /\Bis/)   # =>   th->is<- is\nthe time
```

Character Classes

A *character class* is a set of characters between brackets: [*characters*] matches any single character between the brackets. [aeiou] will match a vowel, [,.:;!?] matches some punctuation, and so on. The significance of the special regular expression characters—.|(){+^$*?—is turned off inside the brackets. However, normal string substitution still occurs, so (for example) \b represents a backspace character and \n a newline (see Table 22.2 on page 317). In addition, you can use the abbreviations shown in Table 7.1 on page 107 so that (for example) \s matches any whitespace character, not just a literal space:

```
show_regexp('Price $12.', /[aeiou]/)   # =>   Pr->i<-ce $12.
show_regexp('Price $12.', /[\s]/)      # =>   Price-> <-$12.
show_regexp('Price $12.', /[$.]/)      # =>   Price ->$<-12.
```

Within the brackets, the sequence c_1-c_2 represents all the characters from c_1 to c_2 in the current encoding:

```
a = 'see [The PickAxe-page 123]'
show_regexp(a, /[A-F]/)        # =>   see [The Pick->A<-xe-page 123]
show_regexp(a, /[A-Fa-f]/)     # =>   s->e<-e [The PickAxe-page 123]
show_regexp(a, /[0-9]/)        # =>   see [The PickAxe-page ->1<-23]
show_regexp(a, /[0-9][0-9]/)   # =>   see [The PickAxe-page ->12<-3]
```

You can negate a character class by putting an up arrow or caret (^) immediately after the opening bracket:

```
show_regexp('Price $12.', /[^A-Z]/)       # =>   P->r<-ice $12.
show_regexp('Price $12.', /[^\w]/)        # =>   Price-> <-$12.
show_regexp('Price $12.', /[a-z][^a-z]/)  # =>   Pric->e <-$12.
```

The POSIX character classes in Table 7.2 on page 107 correspond to the ctype(3) macros of the same names. They can also be negated by putting an up arrow (or caret) after the first colon:

```
show_regexp('Price $12.', /[aeiou]/)        # =>   Pr->i<-ce $12.
show_regexp('Price $12.', /[[:digit:]]/)    # =>   Price $->1<-2.
show_regexp('Price $12.', /[[:space:]]/)    # =>   Price-> <-$12.
show_regexp('Price $12.', /[[:^alpha:]]/)   # =>   Price-> <-$12.
show_regexp('Price $12.', /[[:punct:]aeiou]/) # =>  Pr->i<-ce $12.
```

If you want to include the literal characters] and - within a character class, put them at the start or escape them with \:

```
a = 'see [The PickAxe-page 123]'
show_regexp(a, /[]]/)        # =>    see [The PickAxe-page 123->]<-
show_regexp(a, /[0-9\]]/)    # =>    see [The PickAxe-page ->1<-23]
show_regexp(a, /[\d\-]/)     # =>    see [The PickAxe->-<-page 123]
```

Some character classes are used so frequently that Ruby provides abbreviations for them. These abbreviations are listed in Table 7.1 on the next page—they may be used both within brackets and in the body of a pattern.

```
show_regexp('It costs $12.', /\s/)   # =>    It-> <-costs $12.
show_regexp('It costs $12.', /\d/)   # =>    It costs $->1<-2.
```

You can create the intersection of character classes using &&. So, to match all lowercase ASCII letters that aren't vowels, you could use this:

```
str = "now is the time"
str.gsub(/[a-z&&[^aeiou]]/, '*')     # =>    "*o* i* **e *i*e"
```

1.9 The \p construct is new with Ruby 1.9. It gives you an encoding-aware way of matching a character with a particular Unicode property (shown in Table 7.3 on page 108):

```
# encoding: utf-8
string = "δy/δx = 2πx"
show_regexp(string, /\p{Alnum}/)   # =>    δ->y<-/δx = 2πx
show_regexp(string, /\p{Digit}/)   # =>    δy/δx = ->2<-πx
show_regexp(string, /\p{Space}/)   # =>    δy/δx-> <-= 2πx
show_regexp(string, /\p{Greek}/)   # =>    δy/δx = 2->π<-x
show_regexp(string, /\p{Graph}/)   # =>    ->δ<-y/δx = 2πx
```

Finally, a period (.) appearing outside brackets represents any character except a newline (though in multiline mode it matches a newline, too):

```
a = 'It costs $12.'
show_regexp(a, /c.s/)    # =>    It ->cos<-ts $12.
show_regexp(a, /./)      # =>    ->I<-t costs $12.
show_regexp(a, /\./)     # =>    It costs $12->.<-
```

Repetition

When we specified the pattern that split the song list line, /\s*\|\s*/, we said we wanted to match a vertical bar surrounded by an arbitrary amount of whitespace. We now know that the \s sequences match a single whitespace character and \| means a literal vertical bar, so it seems likely that the asterisks somehow mean "an arbitrary amount." In fact, the asterisk is one of a number of modifiers that allow you to match multiple occurrences of a pattern.

If r stands for the immediately preceding regular expression within a pattern, then

$r*$	Matches zero or more occurrences of r.
$r+$	Matches one or more occurrences of r.
$r?$	Matches zero or one occurrence of r.
$r\{m,n\}$	Matches at least m and at most n occurrences of r.
$r\{m,\}$	Matches at least m occurrences of r.
$r\{,n\}$	Matches at most n occurrences of r.
$r\{m\}$	Matches exactly m occurrences of r.

Table 7.1. Character Class Abbreviations

Text in parentheses indicates the Unicode classes. These apply if the regular expression's encoding is one of the Unicode encodings.

Sequence	As [...]	Meaning (Unicode)
\d	[0-9]	Decimal digit character (*Decimal_Number*)
\D	[^0-9]	Any character except a digit
\h	[0-9a-fA-F]	Hexadecimal digit character
\H	[^0-9a-fA-F]	Any character except a hex digit
\s	[\t\r\n\f]	Whitespace character (+ *Line_Separator*)
\S	[^ \t\r\n\f]	Any character except whitespace
\w	[A-Za-z0-9_]	Word character (+ *Connector_Punctuation*, *Letter*, *Mark*, and *Number*)
\W	[^A-Za-z0-9_]	Any character except a word character

Table 7.2. Posix Character Classes

Text in parentheses indicates the Unicode classes. These apply if the regular expression's encoding is one of the Unicode encodings.

POSIX Character Classes (Unicode)	
[:alnum:]	Alphanumeric (*Letter* | *Mark* | *Decimal_Number*)
[:alpha:]	Uppercase or lowercase letter (*Letter* | *Mark*)
[:ascii:]	7-bit character including nonprinting
[:blank:]	Blank and tab (+ *Space_Separator*)
[:cntrl:]	Control characters—at least 0x00–0x1f, 0x7f (*Control* | *Format* | *Unassigned* | *Private_Use* | *Surrogate*)
[:digit:]	Digit (*Decimal_Number*)
[:graph:]	Printable character excluding space (Unicode also excludes *Control, Unassigned,* and *Surrogate*)
[:lower:]	Lowercase letter (*Lowercase_Letter*)
[:print:]	Any printable character (including space)
[:punct:]	Printable character excluding space and alphanumeric. Unicode: (*Connector_Punctuation* | *Dash_Punctuation* | *Close_Punctuation* | *Final_Punctuation* | *Initial_Punctuation* | *Other_Punctuation* | *Open_Punctuation*)
[:space:]	Whitespace (same as \s)
[:upper:]	Uppercase letter (*Uppercase_Letter*)
[:xdigit:]	Hex digit (0–9, a–f, A–F)
[:word:]	Alphanumeric, underscore, and multibyte (*Letter* | *Mark* | *Decimal_Number* | *Connector_Punctuation*)

Table 7.3. Unicode Character Properties

Character Properties	
\p{*name*}	Matches character with named property
\p{^*name*}	Matches any character except named property
\P{*name*}	Matches any character except named property

Property names	
All encodings	Alnum, Alpha, Blank, Cntrl, Digit, Graph, Lower, Print, Punct, Space, Upper, XDigit, Word, ASCII
EUC and SJIS	Hiragana, Katakana
UTF-n	Any, Assigned, C, Cc, Cf, Cn, Co, Cs, L, Ll, Lm, Lo, Lt, Lu, M, Mc, Me, Mn, N, Nd, Nl, No, P, Pc, Pd, Pe, Pf, Pi, Po, Ps, S, Sc, Sk, Sm, So, Z, Zl, Zp, Zs, Arabic, Armenian, Bengali, Bopomofo, Braille, Buginese, Buhid, Canadian_Aboriginal, Cherokee, Common, Coptic, Cypriot, Cyrillic, Deseret, Devanagari, Ethiopic, Georgian, Glagolitic, Gothic, Greek, Gujarati, Gurmukhi, Han, Hangul, Hanunoo, Hebrew, Hiragana, Inherited, Kannada, Katakana, Kharoshthi, Khmer, Lao, Latin, Limbu, Linear_B, Malayalam, Mongolian, Myanmar, New_Tai_Lue, Ogham, Old_Italic, Old_Persian, Oriya, Osmanya, Runic, Shavian, Sinhala, Syloti_Nagri, Syriac, Tagalog, Tagbanwa, Tai_Le, Tamil, Telugu, Thaana, Thai, Tibetan, Tifinagh, Ugaritic, Yi

These repetition constructs have a high precedence—they bind only to the immediately preceding matching construct in the pattern. /ab+/ matches an *a* followed by one or more *b*'s, not a sequence of *ab*'s.

These patterns are called *greedy*, because by default they will match as much of the string as they can. You can alter this behavior, and have them match the minimum, by adding a question mark suffix. The repetition is then called *lazy*—it stops once it has done the minimum amount of work required.

```
a = "The moon is made of cheese"
show_regexp(a, /\w+/)          # =>   ->The<- moon is made of cheese
show_regexp(a, /\s.*\s/)       # =>   The-> moon is made of <-cheese
show_regexp(a, /\s.*?\s/)      # =>   The-> moon <-is made of cheese
show_regexp(a, /[aeiou]{2,99}/)  # =>   The m->oo<-n is made of cheese
show_regexp(a, /mo?o/)         # =>   The ->moo<-n is made of cheese
# here's the lazy version
show_regexp(a, /mo??o/)        # =>   The ->mo<-on is made of cheese
```

(There's an additional modifier, +, that makes them greedy and also stops backtracking, but that will have to wait until the advanced section of the chapter.)

Be very careful when using the * modifier. It matches zero or more occurences. I know that I personally often forget about the zero part. In particular, a pattern that contains just a * repetition will always match, whatever string you pass it. The pattern /a*/ will always match, because every string contains zero or more a's.

```
a = "The moon is made of cheese"
# both of these match an empty substring at the start of the string
show_regexp(a, /m*/)   # =>   -><-The moon is made of cheese
show_regexp(a, /Z*/)   # =>   -><-The moon is made of cheese
```

Alternation

We know that the vertical bar is special, because our line-splitting pattern had to escape it with a backslash. That's because an unescaped vertical bar | matches either the construct that precedes it or the construct that follows it:

```
a = "red ball blue sky"
show_regexp(a, /d|e/)                 # =>   r->e<-d ball blue sky
show_regexp(a, /al|lu/)               # =>   red b->al<-l blue sky
show_regexp(a, /red ball|angry sky/)  # =>   ->red ball<- blue sky
```

There's a trap for the unwary here, because | has a very low precedence. The last example in the previous lines matches *red ball* or *angry sky*, not *red ball sky* or *red angry sky*. To match *red ball sky* or *red angry sky*, you'd need to override the default precedence using grouping.

Grouping

You can use parentheses to group terms within a regular expression. Everything within the group is treated as a single regular expression.

```
# This matches an 'a' followed by one or more 'n's
show_regexp('banana', /an+/)      # =>   b->an<-ana
# This matches the sequence 'an' one or more times
show_regexp('banana', /(an)+/)    # =>   b->anan<-a

a = 'red ball blue sky'
show_regexp(a, /blue|red/)            # =>   ->red<- ball blue sky
show_regexp(a, /(blue|red) \w+/)      # =>   ->red ball<- blue sky
show_regexp(a, /(red|blue) \w+/)      # =>   ->red ball<- blue sky
show_regexp(a, /red|blue \w+/)        # =>   ->red<- ball blue sky

show_regexp(a, /red (ball|angry) sky/)  # =>   no match
a = 'the red angry sky'
show_regexp(a, /red (ball|angry) sky/)  # =>   the ->red angry sky<-
```

Parentheses also collect the results of pattern matching. Ruby counts opening parentheses and for each stores the result of the partial match between it and the corresponding closing parenthesis. You can use this partial match both within the rest of the pattern and in your Ruby program. Within the pattern, the sequence \1 refers to the match of the first group, \2 the second group, and so on. Outside the pattern, the special variables $1, $2, and so on, serve the same purpose.

```
/(\d\d):(\d\d)(..)/ =~ "12:50am"      # =>   0
"Hour is #$1, minute #$2"             # =>   "Hour is 12, minute 50"
/((\d\d):(\d\d))(..)/ =~ "12:50am"    # =>   0
"Time is #$1"                         # =>   "Time is 12:50"
"Hour is #$2, minute #$3"             # =>   "Hour is 12, minute 50"
"AM/PM is #$4"                        # =>   "AM/PM is am"
```

If you're using the MatchData object returned by the match method, you can index into it to get the corresponding subpatterns:

```
md = /(\d\d):(\d\d)(..)/.match("12:50am")
"Hour is #{md[1]}, minute #{md[2]}"   # =>   "Hour is 12, minute 50"
md = /((\d\d):(\d\d))(..)/.match("12:50am")
"Time is #{md[1]}"                     # =>   "Time is 12:50"
"Hour is #{md[2]}, minute #{md[3]}"    # =>   "Hour is 12, minute 50"
"AM/PM is #{md[4]}"                    # =>   "AM/PM is am"
```

The ability to use part of the current match later in that match allows you to look for various forms of repetition:

```
# match duplicated letter
show_regexp('He said "Hello"', /(\w)\1/)   # =>   He said "He->ll<-o"
# match duplicated substrings
show_regexp('Mississippi', /(\w+)\1/)      # =>   M->ississ<-ippi
```

Rather than use numbers, you can also use names to refer to previously matched content. You give a group a name by placing ?<*name*> immediately after the opening parenthesis. You can subsequently refer to this named group using \k<*name*> (or \k'*name*').

```
# match duplicated letter
str = 'He said "Hello"'
show_regexp(str, /(?<char>\w)\k<char>/)   # =>   He said "He->ll<-o"

# match duplicated adjacent substrings
str = 'Mississippi'
show_regexp(str, /(?<seq>\w+)\k<seq>/)    # =>   M->ississ<-ippi
```

The named matches in a regular expression are also available as local variables:[4]

```
/(?<hour>\d\d):(?<min>\d\d)(..)/ =~ "12:50am"   # =>   0
"Hour is #{hour}, minute #{min}"                # =>   "Hour is 12, minute
                                                        50"
```

Once you use named matches in a particular regular expression, Ruby no longer bothers to capture unnamed groups. Thus, in the previous example, you couldn't refer to the last group (which matches am) as $3.

Pattern-Based Substitution

We've already seen how sub and gsub replace the matched part of a string with other text. In those previous examples, the pattern was always fixed text, but the substitution methods work equally well if the pattern contains repetition, alternation, and grouping.

---

4. Note that this works only with literal regular expressions (so you can't, for example, assign a regular expression object to a variable, match the contents of that variable against a string, and expect the local variables to be set).

```
a = "quick brown fox"
a.sub(/[aeiou]/, '*')    # =>   "q*ick brown fox"
a.gsub(/[aeiou]/, '*')   # =>   "q**ck br*wn f*x"
a.sub(/\s\S+/, '')       # =>   "quick fox"
a.gsub(/\s\S+/, '')      # =>   "quick"
```

The substitution methods can take a string or a block. If a block is used, it is passed the matching substring, and the block's value is substituted into the original string.

```
a = "quick brown fox"
a.sub(/^./) {|match| match.upcase }        # =>   "Quick brown fox"
a.gsub(/[aeiou]/) {|vowel| vowel.upcase }  # =>   "qUIck brOwn fOx"
```

Maybe we want to normalize names entered by users into a web application. They may enter DAVE THOMAS, dave thomas, or dAvE tHoMas, and we'd like to store it as Dave Thomas. The following method is a simple first iteration. The pattern that matches the first character of a word is \b\w—look for a word boundary followed by a word character. Combine this with gsub, and we can hack the names:

```
def mixed_case(name)
  name.downcase.gsub(/\b\w/) {|first| first.upcase }
end

mixed_case("DAVE THOMAS")    # =>   "Dave Thomas"
mixed_case("dave thomas")    # =>   "Dave Thomas"
mixed_case("dAvE tHoMas")    # =>   "Dave Thomas"
```

1.9 There's an idiomatic way to write the substitution in Ruby 1.9, but we'll have to wait until Chapter 23 on page 368 to see why it works:

```
def mixed_case(name)
  name.downcase.gsub(/\b\w/, &:upcase)
end

mixed_case("dAvE tHoMas")    # =>   "Dave Thomas"
```

You can also give sub and gsub a hash as the replacement parameter, in which case they will look up matched groups and use the corresponding values as replacement text:

```
replacement = { "cat" => "feline", "dog" => "canine" }
replacement.default = "unknown"

"cat and dog".gsub(/\w+/, replacement)   # =>   "feline unknown canine"
```

Backslash Sequences in the Substitution

Earlier we noted that the sequences \1, \2, and so on, are available in the pattern, standing for the *n*th group matched so far. The same sequences can be used in the second argument of sub and gsub.

```
puts "fred:smith".sub(/(\w+):(\w+)/, '\2, \1')
puts "nercpyitno".gsub(/(.)(.)/, '\2\1')
```

produces:

```
smith, fred
encryption
```

You can also reference named groups:

```
puts "fred:smith".sub(/(?<first>\w+):(?<last>\w+)/, '\k<last>, \k<first>')
puts "nercpyitno".gsub(/(?<c1>.)(?<c2>.)/, '\k<c2>\k<c1>')
```

produces:

```
smith, fred
encryption
```

Additional backslash sequences work in substitution strings: \& (last match), \+ (last matched group), \` (string prior to match), \' (string after match), and \\ (a literal backslash).

It gets confusing if you want to include a literal backslash in a substitution. The obvious thing is to write this:

```
str.gsub(/\\/, '\\\\')
```

Clearly, this code is trying to replace each backslash in str with two. The programmer doubled up the backslashes in the replacement text, knowing that they'd be converted to \\ in syntax analysis. However, when the substitution occurs, the regular expression engine performs another pass through the string, converting \\ to \, so the net effect is to replace each single backslash with another single backslash. You need to write gsub(/\\/, '\\\\\\\\')!

```
str = 'a\b\c'                    # =>   "a\b\c"
str.gsub(/\\/, '\\\\\\\\')       # =>   "a\\b\\c"
```

However, using the fact that \& is replaced by the matched string, you could also write this:

```
str = 'a\b\c'              # =>   "a\b\c"
str.gsub(/\\/, '\&\&')     # =>   "a\\b\\c"
```

If you use the block form of gsub, the string for substitution is analyzed only once (during the syntax pass), and the result is what you intended:

```
str = 'a\b\c'                   # =>   "a\b\c"
str.gsub(/\\/) { '\\\\' }       # =>   "a\\b\\c"
```

At the start of this chapter, we said that it contained two emergency exits. The first was after we discussed basic matching and substitution. This is the second: you now know as much about regular expressions as the vast majority of Ruby developers. Feel free to break away and move on to the next chapter. But if you're feeling brave...

Advanced Regular Expressions

You may never need the information in the rest of this chapter. But, at the same time, knowing some of the real power in the Ruby regular expression implementation might just dig you out of a hole.

Regular Expression Extensions

Ruby uses the Oniguruma regular expression library. This offers a large number of extensions over traditional Unix regular expressions. Most of these extensions are written between the characters (? and). The parentheses that bracket these extensions are groups, but they do not necessarily generate backreferences. Some do not set the values of \1 and $1, and so on.

The sequence (?# *comment*) inserts a comment into the pattern. The content is ignored during pattern matching. As we'll see, commenting complex regular expressions can be as helpful as commenting complex code.

(?:*re*) makes *re* into a group without generating backreferences. This is often useful when you need to group a set of constructs but don't want the group to set the value of $1 or whatever. In the example that follows, both patterns match a date with either colons or slashes between the month, day, and year. The first form stores the separator character (which can be a slash or a colon) in $2 and $4, but the second pattern doesn't store the separator in an external variable.

```
date = "12/25/2008"

date =~ %r{(\d+)(/|:)(\d+)(/|:)(\d+)}
[$1,$2,$3,$4,$5]   # =>   ["12", "/", "25", "/", "2008"]

date =~ %r{(\d+)(?:/|:)(\d+)(?:/|:)(\d+)}
[$1,$2,$3]         # =>   ["12", "25", "2008"]
```

Lookahead and Lookbehind

You'll sometimes want to match a pattern only if the matched subsubtring is preceded by or followed by some other pattern. That is, you want to set some context for your match but don't want to capture that context as part of the match.

For example, you might want to match every word in a string that is followed by a comma, but you don't want the comma to form part of the match. Here you could use the charmingly named *zero-width positive lookahead* extension. (?=*re*) matches *re* at this point but does not consume it—you can look forward for the context of a match without affecting $&. In this example, we'll use scan to pick out the words:

```
str = "red, white, and blue"
str.scan(/[a-z]+(?=,)/)   # =>   ["red", "white"]
```

You can also match before the pattern using (?<=*re*) (*zero-width positive lookbehind*). This lets you look for characters that precede the context of a match without affecting $&. The following example matches the letters *dog* but only if they are preceded by the letters *hot*:

```
show_regexp("seadog hotdog", /(?<=hot)dog/)   # =>   seadog hot->dog<-
```

For the lookbehind extension, *re* either must be a fixed length or consist of a set of fixed length alternatives. That is, (?<=aa) and (?<=aa|bbb) are valid, but (?<=a+b) is not.

Both forms have negated versions, (?!*re*) and (?<!*re*), which are true if the context is not present in the target string.

Controlling Backtracking

Say you're given the problem of searching a string for a sequence of *X*s not followed by an *O*. You know that a string of *X*s can be represented as (X+), and you can use a lookahead to check that it isn't followed by an *O*, so you code up the pattern /(X+)(?!O)/. Let's try it:

```
re = /(X+)(?!O)/

# This one works
re =~ "test XXXY"    # =>    5
$1                   # =>    "XXX"

# But, unfortunately, so does this one
re =~ "test XXXO"    # =>    5
$1                   # =>    "XX"
```

Why did the second match succeed? Well, the regular expression engine saw the X+ in the pattern and happily gobbled up all the *X*s in the string. It then saw the pattern (?!O), saying that it should not now be looking at an *O*. Unfortunately, it is looking at an *O*, so the match doesn't succeed. But the engine doesn't give up. No sir! Instead it says, "Maybe I was wrong to consume every single *X* in the string. Let's try consuming one less and see what happens." This is called *backtracking*—when a match fails, the engine goes back and tries to match a different way. In this case, by backtracking past a single character, it now finds itself looking at the last *X* in the string (the one before the final *O*). And that *X* is not an *O*, so the negative lookahead succeeds, and the pattern matches. Look carefully at the output of the previous program: there are three *X*s in the first match but only two in the second.

But this wasn't the intent of our regexp. Once it finds a sequence of *X*s, those *X*s should be locked away. We don't want one of them being the terminator of the pattern. We can get that behavior by telling Ruby not to backtrack once it finds a string of *X*s. There are a couple of ways of doing this.

The sequence (?>*re*) nests an independent regular expression within the first regular expression. This expression is anchored at the current match position. If it consumes characters, these will no longer be available to the higher-level regular expression. This construct therefore inhibits backtracking.

Let's try it with our previous code:

```
re = /((?>X+))(?!O)/

# This one works
re =~ "test XXXY"          # =>    5
$1                         # =>    "XXX"

# Now this doesn't match
re =~ "test XXXO"          # =>    nil
$1                         # =>    nil

# And this finds the second string of Xs
re =~ "test XXXO XXXXY"    # =>    10
$1                         # =>    "XXXX"
```

You can also control backtracking by using a third form of repetition. We're already seen greedy repetition, such as *re+*, and lazy repetition, *re+?*. The third form is called *possessive*. You code it using a plus sign after the repetition character. It behaves just like greedy repetition, consuming as much of the string as it can. But once consumed, that part of the string can never be reexamined by the pattern—the regular expression engine can't backtrack past a possessive qualifier. This means we could also write our code as this:

```
re = /(X++)(?!0)/

re =~ "test XXXY"          # =>    5
$1                         # =>    "XXX"

re =~ "test XXX0"          # =>    nil
$1                         # =>    nil

re =~ "test XXX0 XXXXY"    # =>    10
$1                         # =>    "XXXX"
```

Backreferences and Named Matches

Within a pattern, the sequences \n, \k'n', and \k<n> all refer to the nth captured subpattern. Thus, the expression /(...)\1/ matches six characters with the first three characters being the same as the last three.

Rather than refer to matches by their number, you can give them names and then refer to those names. A subpattern is named using either of the syntaxes (?<name>...) or (?'name'...). You then refer to these named captures using either \k<name> or \k'name'.

For example, the following shows different ways of matching a time range (in the form hh:mm-hh:mm) where the hour part is the same:

```
same  = "12:15-12:45"
differ = "12:45-13:15"

# use numbered backreference
same   =~ /(\d\d):\d\d-\1:\d\d/    # =>    0
differ =~ /(\d\d):\d\d-\1:\d\d/    # =>    nil


# use named backreference
same   =~ /(?<hour>\d\d):\d\d-\k<hour>:\d\d/    # =>    0
differ =~ /(?<hour>\d\d):\d\d-\k<hour>:\d\d/    # =>    nil
```

Negative backreference numbers refer count backward from the place they're used, so they are relative, not absolute numbers. The following pattern matches four-letter palindromes:[5]

```
"abab" =~ /(.)(.)\k<-1>\k<-2>/    # =>    nil
"abba" =~ /(.)(.)\k<-1>\k<-2>/    # =>    0
```

---

5.   These are words that read the same forward and backward.

You can invoke a named subpattern using \g<name> or \g<number>. Note that this reexecutes the match in the subpattern, in contrast to \k<name>, which matches whatever is matched by the subpattern:

```
re = /(?<color>red|green|blue) \w+ \g<color> \w+/

re =~ "red sun blue moon"    # =>   0
re =~ "red sun white moon"   # =>   nil
```

You can use \g recursively, invoking a subpattern within that pattern. The following code matches a string in which braces are properly nested:

```
re = /
  \A
    (?<brace_expression>
      {
        (
          [^{}]          # anything other than braces
        |
          \g<brace_expression>
        )*
      }
    )
  \Z
/x
```

We use the x option to allow us to write the expression with lots of space, which makes it easier to understand. We also indent it, just as we would indent Ruby code. And we can also use Ruby-style comments to document the tricky stuff. You can read this regular expression as follows: a brace expression is an open brace, then a sequence of zero or more characters or brace expressions, and then a closing brace.

Nested Groups

The ability to invoke subpatterns recursively means that backreferences can get tricky. Ruby solves this by allowing you to refer to a named or numbered group at a particular level of the recursion—simply (!) add a +n or -n to refer to the capture at the given level relative to the current level.

Here's an example from the Oniguruma cheat sheet. It matches palindromes:

```
/\A(?<a>|.|(?:(?<b>.)\g<a>\k<b+0>))\z/
```

That's pretty hard to read, so let's spread it out.

```
palindrome_matcher = /
\A
 (?<palindrome>
                 # nothing, or
  |
    \w           # a single character, or
  |
    (?:          # x <palindrome> x
      (?<some_letter>\w)
      \g<palindrome>
      \k<some_letter+0>
    )
 )
\z
/x

palindrome_matcher.match "madam"    # =>   #<MatchData "madam"
                                           palindrome:"madam"
                                           some_letter:"a">
palindrome_matcher.match "m"        # =>   #<MatchData "m" palindrome:"m"
                                           some_letter:nil>
palindrome_matcher.match "adam"     # =>   nil
```

So, a palindrome is an empty string, a string containing a single character, or a character followed by a palindrome, followed by that same character. The notation \k<some_letter+0> means that the letter matched at the end of the inner palindrome will be the same letter that was at the start of it. Inside the nesting, however, a different letter may wrap the interior palindrome.

Named Subroutines

There's a trick that allows us to write subroutines inside regular expressions. Recall that we can invoke a named group using \g<name>, and we define the group using (?<name>...). Normally, the definition of the group is itself matched as part of executing the pattern. However, if you add the suffix {0} to the group, it means "zero matches of this group," so the group is not executed when first encountered:

```
sentence = %r{
  (?<subject>   cat  | dog  | gerbil   ){0}
  (?<verb>      eats | drinks| generates ){0}
  (?<object>    water | bones | PDFs     ){0}
  (?<adjective> big  | small | smelly   ){0}
  (?<opt_adj>   (\g<adjective>\s)?       ){0}
  The\s\g<opt_adj>\g<subject>\s\g<verb>\s\g<opt_adj>\g<object>
}x
md = sentence.match("The cat drinks water")
puts "The subject is #{md[:subject]} and the verb is #{md[:verb]}"
md = sentence.match("The big dog eats smelly bones")
puts "The last adjective in the second sentence is #{md[:adjective]}"
sentence =~ "The gerbil generates big PDFs"
puts "And the object in the last sentence is #{$~[:object]}"
```

produces:

```
The subject is cat and the verb is drinks
The last adjective in the second sentence is smelly
And the object in the last sentence is PDFs
```

Setting Options

As we saw at the start of this chapter, you can add one or more of the options i (case insensitive), m (multiline), and x (allow spaces) to the end of a regular expression literal. You can also embed these options within the pattern itself.

(?imx)	Turns on the corresponding i, m, or x option. If used inside a group, the effect is limited to that group.
(?-imx)	Turns off the i, m, or x option.
(?imx:*re*)	Turns on the i, m, or x option for *re*.
(?-imx:*re*)	Turns off the i, m, or x option for *re*.

So, that's it. If you've made it this far, consider yourself a regular expression ninja. Get out there and match some strings.

## Chapter 8

More About Methods

So far in this book, we've been defining and using methods without much thought. Now it's time to get into the details.

Defining a Method

As we've seen, a method is defined using the keyword def. Method names should begin with a lowercase letter or underscore,[1] followed by letters, digits, and underscores.

A method name may end with one of ?, !, or =. Methods that return a boolean result (so-called predicate methods) are often named with a trailing ?:

```
1.even?                  # =>   false
2.even?                  # =>   true
1.instance_of?(Fixnum)   # =>   true
```

Methods that are "dangerous," or that modify their receiver, may be named with a trailing exclamation mark, !. These are sometimes called *bang methods*. For instance, String provides both chop and chop! methods. The first one returns a modified string; the second modifies the receiver in place.

Methods that can appear on the left side of an assignment (a feature we discussed on page 34) end with an equals sign (=).

?, !, and = are the only "weird" characters allowed as method name suffixes.

Now that we've specified a name for our new method, we may need to declare some parameters. These are simply a list of local variable names in parentheses. (The parentheses around a method's arguments are optional; our convention is to use them when a method has arguments and omit them when it doesn't.)

---

1.   You won't get an immediate error if you start a method name with an uppercase letter, but when Ruby sees you calling the method, it might guess that it is a constant, not a method invocation, and as a result it may parse the call incorrectly. By convention, methods names starting with an uppercase letter are used for type conversion. The Integer method, for example, converts its parameter to an integer.

```
def my_new_method(arg1, arg2, arg3)     # 3 arguments
  # Code for the method would go here
end
def my_other_new_method                 # No arguments
  # Code for the method would go here
end
```

Ruby lets you specify default values for a method's arguments—values that will be used if the caller doesn't pass them explicitly. You do this using an equals sign (=) followed by a Ruby expression. That expression can include references to previous arguments in the list:

```
def cool_dude(arg1="Miles", arg2="Coltrane", arg3="Roach")
  "#{arg1}, #{arg2}, #{arg3}."
end
```

```
cool_dude                              # =>   "Miles, Coltrane, Roach."
cool_dude("Bart")                      # =>   "Bart, Coltrane, Roach."
cool_dude("Bart", "Elwood")            # =>   "Bart, Elwood, Roach."
cool_dude("Bart", "Elwood", "Linus")   # =>   "Bart, Elwood, Linus."
```

Here's an example where the default argument references a previous argument:

```
def surround(word, pad_width=word.length/2)
  "[" * pad_width  + word +  "]" * pad_width
end
```

```
surround("elephant")   # =>   "[[[[elephant]]]]"
surround("fox")        # =>   "[fox]"
surround("fox", 10)    # =>   "[[[[[[[[[[fox]]]]]]]]]]"
```

The body of a method contains normal Ruby expressions. The return value of a method is the value of the last expression executed or the result of an explicit return expression.

Variable-Length Argument Lists

But what if you want to pass in a variable number of arguments or want to capture multiple arguments into a single parameter? Placing an asterisk before the name of the parameter after the "normal" parameters lets you do just that. This is sometimes called *splatting an argument* (presumably because the asterisk looks somewhat like a bug after hitting the windscreen of a fast moving car).

```
def varargs(arg1, *rest)
  "arg1=#{arg1}.  rest=#{rest.inspect}"
end
```

```
varargs("one")                  # =>   arg1=one.  rest=[]
varargs("one", "two")           # =>   arg1=one.  rest=[two]
varargs "one", "two", "three"   # =>   arg1=one.  rest=[two, three]
```

In this example, the first argument is assigned to the first method parameter as usual. However, the next parameter is prefixed with an asterisk, so all the remaining arguments are bundled into a new Array, which is then assigned to that parameter.

Folks sometimes use a splat to specify arguments that are not used by the method (but that are perhaps used by the corresponding method in a superclass. (Note that in this example we call super with no parameters. This is a special case that means "invoke this method in the superclass, passing it all the parameters that were given to the original method.")

```
class Child < Parent
  def do_something(*not_used)
    # our processing
    super
  end
end
```

In this case, you can also leave off the name of the parameter and just write an asterisk:

```
class Child < Parent
  def do_something(*)
    # our processing
    super
  end
end
```

1.9 In Ruby 1.9, you can put the splat argument anywhere in a method's parameter list, allowing you to write this:

```
def split_apart(first, *splat, last)
  puts "First: #{first.inspect}, splat: #{splat.inspect}, " +
       "last: #{last.inspect}"
end
split_apart(1,2)
split_apart(1,2,3)
split_apart(1,2,3,4)
```

produces:

```
First: 1, splat: [], last: 2
First: 1, splat: [2], last: 3
First: 1, splat: [2, 3], last: 4
```

If you cared only about the first and last parameters, you could define this method using this:

```
def split_apart(first, *, last)
  # ...
end
```

You can have only one splat argument in a method—if you had two, it would be ambiguous. You also can't put arguments with default values after the splat argument. In all cases, the splat argument receives the values left over after assigning to the regular argument.

Methods and Blocks

As we discussed in the section on blocks and iterators beginning on page 54, when a method is called, it may be associated with a block.

Normally, you simply call the block from within the method using yield:

tutmethods_10.rb

```
def double(p1)
  yield(p1*2)
end

double(3) {|val| "I got #{val}" }             # =>   "I got 6"
double("tom") {|val| "Then I got #{val}" }    # =>   "Then I got tomtom"
```

However, if the last parameter in a method definition is prefixed with an ampersand, any associated block is converted to a Proc object, and that object is assigned to the parameter. This allows you to store the block for use later.

tutmethods_11.rb

```
class TaxCalculator
  def initialize(name, &block)
    @name, @block = name, block
  end
  def get_tax(amount)
    "#@name on #{amount} = #{ @block.call(amount) }"
  end
end

tc = TaxCalculator.new("Sales tax") {|amt| amt * 0.075 }

tc.get_tax(100)   # =>   "Sales tax on 100 = 7.5"
tc.get_tax(250)   # =>   "Sales tax on 250 = 18.75"
```

Calling a Method

You call a method by optionally specifying a receiver, giving the name of the method, and optionally passing some parameters and an optional block. Here's a code fragment that shows us calling a method with a receiver, a parameter, and a block:

```
connection.download_mp3("jitterbug") {|p| show_progress(p) }
```

In this example, the object connection is the receiver, download_mp3 is the name of the method, the string "jitterbug" is the parameter, and the stuff between the braces is the associated block. During this method call, Ruby first sets self to the receiver and then invokes the method in that object: For class and module methods, the receiver will be the class or module name.

```
File.size("testfile")   # =>   66
Math.sin(Math::PI/4)    # =>   0.707106781186547
```

If you omit the receiver, it defaults to self, the current object.

```
class InvoiceWriter
  def initialize(order)
    @order = order
  end
```

```
    def write_on(output)
      write_header_on(output)      # called on current object.
      write_body_on(output)        # self is not changed, as
      write_totals_on(output)      # there is no receiver
    end

    def write_header_on(output)
      # ...
    end

    def write_body_on(output)
      # ...
    end

    def write_totals_on(output)
      # ...
    end
  end

  writer = InvoiceWriter.new(my_order)
  writer.write_on(STDOUT)
```

This defaulting mechanism is how Ruby implements private methods. Private methods may *not* be called with a receiver, so they must be methods available in the current object. In the previous example, we'd probably want to make the helper methods private, because they shouldn't be called from outside the InvoiceWriter class:

```
  class InvoiceWriter
    def initialize(order)
      @order = order
    end
    def write_on(output)
      write_header_on(output)
      write_body_on(output)
      write_totals_on(output)
    end

  private

    def write_header_on(output)
      # ...
    end

    def write_body_on(output)
      # ...
    end

    def write_totals_on(output)
      # ...
    end
  end
```

Passing Parameters to a Method

Any parameters follow the method name. If no ambiguity exists, you can omit the parentheses around the argument list when calling a method.[2] However, except in the simplest cases we don't recommend this—some subtle problems can trip you up.[3] Our rule is simple: if you have any doubt, use parentheses.

```
a = obj.hash     # Same as
a = obj.hash()   # this.

obj.some_method "Arg1", arg2, arg3    # Same thing as
obj.some_method("Arg1", arg2, arg3)   # with parentheses.
```

Older Ruby versions compounded the problem by allowing you to put spaces between the method name and the opening parenthesis. This made it hard to parse: is the parenthesis the start of the parameters or the start of an expression? As of Ruby 1.8 you get a warning if you put a space between a method name and an open parenthesis.

Method Return Values

Every called method returns a value (although there's no rule that says you have to use that value). The value of a method is the value of the last statement executed by the method:

```
def meth_one
  "one"
end
meth_one   # =>   "one"

def meth_two(arg)
  case
  when arg > 0  then "positive"
  when arg < 0  then "negative"
  else               "zero"
  end
end

meth_two(23)   # =>   "positive"
meth_two(0)    # =>   "zero"
```

Ruby has a return statement, which exits from the currently executing method. The value of a return is the value of its argument(s). It is idiomatic Ruby to omit the return if it isn't needed, as shown by the previous two examples.

---

2.   Other Ruby documentation sometimes calls these method calls without parentheses *commands*.

3.   In particular, you *must* use parentheses on a method call that is itself a parameter to another method call (unless it is the last parameter).

This next example uses return to exit from a loop inside the method:

```
def meth_three
  100.times do |num|
    square = num*num
    return num, square if square > 1000
  end
end
meth_three   # =>  [32, 1024]
```

As the last case illustrates, if you give return multiple parameters, the method returns them in an array. You can use parallel assignment to collect this return value:

```
num, square = meth_three
num     # =>  32
square  # =>  1024
```

Splat! Expanding Collections in Method Calls

Earlier we saw that if you put an asterisk in front of a parameter in a method definition, multiple arguments in the call to the method will be bundled into an array. Well, the same thing works in reverse.

1.9

When you call a method, you can convert any collection or enumerable object into its constituent elements and pass those elements as individual parameters to the method. Do this by prefixing array arguments with an asterisk:

```
def five(a, b, c, d, e)
  "I was passed #{a} #{b} #{c} #{d} #{e}"
end

five(1, 2, 3, 4, 5 )      # =>  "I was passed 1 2 3 4 5"
five(1, 2, 3, *['a', 'b'])  # =>  "I was passed 1 2 3 a b"
five(*['a', 'b'], 1, 2, 3)  # =>  "I was passed a b 1 2 3"
five(*(10..14))           # =>  "I was passed 10 11 12 13 14"
five(*[1,2], 3, *(4..5))    # =>  "I was passed 1 2 3 4 5"
```

1.9

As of Ruby 1.9, splat arguments can appear anywhere in the parameter list, and you can intermix splat and regular arguments.

Making Blocks More Dynamic

We've already seen how to associate a block with a method call:

```
for_each_bone(aardvark) do |bone|
  # ...
end
```

Normally, this is perfectly good enough—you associate a fixed block of code with a method in the same way you'd have a chunk of code after an if or while statement.

Sometimes, however, you'd like to be more flexible. For example, we may be teaching math skills.[4] The student could ask for an *n*-plus table or an *n*-times table. If the student asked for a 2-times table, we'd output 2, 4, 6, 8, and so on. (This code does not check its inputs for errors.)

```
tutmethods_23.rb
print "(t)imes or (p)lus: "
operator = gets
print "number: "
number = Integer(gets)

if operator =~ /^t/
  puts((1..10).collect {|n| n*number }.join(", "))
else
  puts((1..10).collect {|n| n+number }.join(", "))
end
```

produces:

```
(t)imes or (p)lus: t
number: 2
2, 4, 6, 8, 10, 12, 14, 16, 18, 20
```

This works, but it's ugly, with virtually identical code on each branch of the if statement. It would be nice if we could factor out the block that does the calculation:

```
tutmethods_24.rb
print "(t)imes or (p)lus: "
operator = gets
print "number: "
number = Integer(gets)

if operator =~ /^t/
  calc = lambda {|n| n*number }
else
  calc = lambda {|n| n+number }
end
puts((1..10).collect(&calc).join(", "))
```

produces:

```
(t)imes or (p)lus: t
number: 2
2, 4, 6, 8, 10, 12, 14, 16, 18, 20
```

If the last argument to a method is preceded by an ampersand, Ruby assumes that it is a Proc object. It removes it from the parameter list, converts the Proc object into a block, and associates it with the method.

---

4. Of course, Andy and Dave would have to *learn* math skills first. Conrad Schneiker reminded us that there are three kinds of people: those who can count and those who can't.

Collecting Hash Arguments

Some languages feature *keyword arguments*. Instead of passing a specific number of arguments in a given order, you can invoke the method with the names of the arguments, each with a corresponding value, in any order. Ruby 1.9 does not have keyword arguments, although they might appear in Ruby 2.0. In the meantime, people are using hashes as a way of achieving the same effect. For example, we could consider adding a search facility to an MP3 playlist:

```ruby
class SongList
  def search(name, params)
    # ...
  end
end
list.search(:titles,
            { :genre            => "jazz",
              :duration_less_than => 270
            })
```

The first parameter tells the search what to return. The second parameter is a hash literal containing search parameters. (Note how we used symbols as the keys for this options hash. This has become idiomatic in Ruby libraries and frameworks.) The use of a hash means we can simulate keywords: look for songs with a genre of "jazz" and a duration less than $4\frac{1}{2}$ minutes.

However, this approach is slightly clunky, and that set of braces could easily be mistaken for a block associated with the method. So, Ruby has a shortcut. You can place *key => value* pairs in an argument list, as long as they follow any normal arguments and precede any splat and block arguments. All these pairs will be collected into a single hash and passed as one argument to the method. No braces are needed.

```ruby
list.search(:titles,
            :genre            => 'jazz',
            :duration_less_than => 270)
```

1.9 Option passing is one of the reasons for the new hash literal syntax in Ruby 1.9:

```ruby
list.search(:titles, genre: 'jazz', duration_less_than: 270)
```

A well-written Ruby program will typically contain many methods, each quite small, so it's worth getting familiar with the options available when defining and using Ruby methods. At some point you'll probably want to read the section called *Method Arguments* on page 341 to see exactly how arguments in a method call get mapped to the method's formal parameters when you have combinations of default parameters and splat parameters.

## Chapter 9

Expressions

So far we've been fairly cavalier in our use of expressions in Ruby. After all, a = b + c is pretty standard stuff. You could write a whole heap of Ruby code without reading any of this chapter.

But it wouldn't be as much fun ;-).

One of the first differences with Ruby is that anything that can reasonably return a value does: just about everything is an expression. What does this mean in practice?

Some obvious things include the ability to chain statements together:

```
a = b = c = 0              # =>   0
[ 3, 1, 7, 0 ].sort.reverse   # =>   [7, 3, 1, 0]
```

Perhaps less obvious, things that are normally statements in C or Java are expressions in Ruby. For example, the if and case statements both return the value of the last expression executed:

```
song_type = if song.mp3_type == MP3::Jazz
              if song.written < Date.new(1935, 1, 1)
                Song::TradJazz
              else
                Song::Jazz
              end
            else
              Song::Other
            end

rating = case votes_cast
         when 0...10    then Rating::SkipThisOne
         when 10...50   then Rating::CouldDoBetter
         else               Rating::Rave
         end
```

We'll talk more about if and case starting on page 139.

Operator Expressions

Ruby has the basic set of operators (+, -, *, /, and so on) as well as a few surprises. A complete list of the operators, and their precedences, is given in Table 22.4 on page 333.

In Ruby, many operators are actually implemented as method calls. For example, when you write a*b + c, you're actually asking the object referenced by a to execute the method *, passing in the parameter b. You then ask the object that results from that calculation to execute the + method, passing c as a parameter. This is equivalent to writing the following (perfectly valid) Ruby:

```
a, b, c = 1, 2, 3
a * b + c        # =>   5
(a.*(b)).+(c)    # =>   5
```

Because everything is an object and because you can redefine instance methods, you can always redefine basic arithmetic if you don't like the answers you're getting:

tutexpressions_4.rb

```
class Fixnum
  alias old_plus +   # We can reference the original '+' as 'old_plus'

  def +(other)        # Redefine addition of Fixnums. This is a BAD IDEA!
    old_plus(other).succ
  end
end

1 + 2      # =>   4
a = 3
a += 4     # =>   8
a + a + a  # =>   26
```

More useful is that classes you write can participate in operator expressions just as if they were built-in objects. For example, the left shift operator, <<, is often used to mean *append to receiver*. Arrays support this:

```
a = [ 1, 2, 3 ]
a << 4   # =>   [1, 2, 3, 4]
```

You can add similar support to your classes:

tutexpressions_6.rb

```
class ScoreKeeper
  def initialize
    @total_score = 0
    @count = 0
  end
  def <<(score)
    @total_score += score
    @count += 1
    self
  end
```

```
  def average
    fail "No scores" if @count == 0
    Float(@total_score) / @count
  end
end

scores = ScoreKeeper.new
scores << 10 << 20 << 40
puts "Average = #{scores.average}"
```

produces:

```
Average = 23.3333333333333
```

Note that there's a subtlety in this code—the << method explicitly returns self. It does this to allow the method chaining in the line scores << 10 << 20 << 40. Because each call to << returns the scores object, you can then call << again, passing in a new score.

As well as the obvious operators, such as +, *, and <<, indexing using square brackets is also implemented as a method call. When you write this:

```
some_obj[1,2,3]
```

you're actually calling a method named [] on some_obj, passing it three parameters. You'd define this method using this:

```
class SomeClass
  def [](p1, p2, p3)
    # ...
  end
end
```

Similarly, assignment to an element is implemented using the []= method. This method receives each object passed as an index as its first *n* parameters and the value of the assignment as its last parameter:

```
tutexpressions_9.rb
class SomeClass
  def []=(*params)
    value = params.pop
    puts "Indexed with #{params.join(', ')}"
    puts "value = #{value.inspect}"
  end
end
s = SomeClass.new
s[1] = 2
s['cat', 'dog'] = 'enemies'
```

produces:

```
Indexed with 1
value = 2
Indexed with cat, dog
value = "enemies"
```

Miscellaneous Expressions

As well as the obvious operator expressions and method calls and the (perhaps) less obvious statement expressions (such as if and case), Ruby has a few more things that you can use in expressions.

Command Expansion

If you enclose a string in backquotes (sometimes called *backticks*) or use the delimited form prefixed by %x, it will (by default) be executed as a command by your underlying operating system. The value of the expression is the standard output of that command. Newlines will not be stripped, so it is likely that the value you get back will have a trailing return or linefeed character.

```
`date`                  # =>   "Tue Mar 31 09:57:49 CDT 2009\n"
`ls`.split[34]          # =>   "ext_ruby.tex"
%x{echo "Hello there"}  # =>   "Hello there\n"
```

You can use expression expansion and all the usual escape sequences in the command string:

```
for i in 0..3
  status = `dbmanager status id=#{i}`
  # ...
end
```

The exit status of the command is available in the global variable $?.

Redefining Backquotes

In the description of the command output expression, we said that the string in backquotes would "by default" be executed as a command. In fact, the string is passed to the method called Kernel.` (a single backquote). If you want, you can override this. This example uses $?, which contains the status of the last external process run:

```
tutexpressions_12.rb
alias old_backquote `
def `(cmd)
  result = old_backquote(cmd)
  if $? != 0
    puts "*** Command #{cmd} failed: status = #{$?.exitstatus}"
  end
  result
end
print `ls -l /etc/passwd`
print `ls -l /etc/wibble`
```

produces:

```
-rw-r--r--  1 root  wheel  2888 Sep 23  2007 /etc/passwd
ls: /etc/wibble: No such file or directory
*** Command ls -l /etc/wibble failed: status = 1
```

Assignment

Just about every example we've given so far in this book has featured assignment. Perhaps it's about time we said something about it.

An assignment statement sets the variable or attribute on its left side (the *lvalue*) to refer to the value on the right (the *rvalue*). It then returns that rvalue as the result of the assignment expression. This means you can chain assignments, and you can perform assignments in some unexpected places:

```
a = b = 1 + 2 + 3
a   # =>   6
b   # =>   6
a = (b = 1 + 2) + 3
a   # =>   6
b   # =>   3
File.open(name = gets.chomp)
```

Ruby has two basic forms of assignment. The first assigns an object reference to a variable or constant. This form of assignment is hardwired into the language:

```
instrument = "piano"
MIDDLE_A   = 440
```

The second form of assignment involves having an object attribute or element reference on the left side. These forms are special, because they are implemented by calling methods in the lvalues, which means you can override them.

We've already seen how to define a writable object attribute. Simply define a method name ending in an equals sign. This method receives as its parameter the assignment's rvalue. We've also seen that you can define [] as a method:

tutexpressions_15.rb

```
class ProjectList
  def initialize
    @projects = []
  end
  def projects=(list)
    @projects = list.map(&:upcase)  # store list of names in uppercase
  end
  def [](offset)
    @projects[offset]
  end
end

list = ProjectList.new
list.projects = %w{ strip sand prime sand paint sand paint rub paint }
list[3]   # =>   "SAND"
list[4]   # =>   "PAINT"
```

As this example shows, these attribute-setting methods don't have to correspond with internal instance variables, and you don't need an attribute reader for every attribute writer (or vice versa).

In older Ruby versions, the result of the assignment was the value returned by the attribute-setting method. As of Ruby 1.8, the value of the assignment is *always* the value of the parameter; the return value of the method is discarded. In the code that follows, older versions of Ruby would set a to 99. Now a will be set to 2.

tutexpressions_16.rb

```ruby
class Test
  def val=(val)
    @val = val
    return 99
  end
end

t = Test.new
a = (t.val = 2)
a    # =>   2
```

Parallel Assignment

During your first week in a programming course (or the second semester if it was a party school), you may have had to write code to swap the values in two variables:

```
int a = 1;
int b = 2;
int temp;

temp = a;
a = b;
b = temp;
```

You can do this much more cleanly in Ruby:

```ruby
a = 1
b = 2
a, b = b, a
```

Ruby lets you have a comma-separated list of rvalues (the things on the right of the assignment). Once Ruby sees more than one rvalue in an assignment, the rules of parallel assignment come into play. What follows is a description at the logical level: what happens inside the interpreter is somewhat hairier. Users of older versions of Ruby should note that these rules have changed in Ruby 1.9.

First, all the rvalues are evaluated, left to right, and collected into an array (unless they are already an array). This array will be the eventual value returned by the overall assignment.

Next, the left side (lhs) is inspected. If it contains a single element, the array is assigned to that element.

```
a = 1, 2, 3, 4     # a=[1, 2, 3, 4]
b = [1, 2, 3, 4]   # b=[1, 2, 3, 4]
```

If the lhs contains a comma, Ruby matches values on the rhs against successive elements on the lhs. Excess elements are discarded.

```
a, b = 1, 2, 3, 4   # a=1, b=2
c, = 1, 2, 3, 4     # c=1
```

Splats and Assignment

If Ruby sees any splats on the right side of an assignment (that is, rvalues preceded by an asterisk), each will be expanded inline into its constituent values during the evaluation of the rvalues and before the assignment to lvalues starts:

```
a, b, c, d, e = *(1..2), 3, *[4, 5]   # a=1, b=2, c=3, d=4, e=5
```

Exactly one lvalue may be a splat. This makes it greedy—it will end up being an array, and that array will contain as many of the corresponding rvalues as possible. So, if the splat is the last lvalue, it will soak up any rvalues that are left after assigning to previous lvalues:

```
a, *b = 1, 2, 3   # a=1, b=[2, 3]
a, *b = 1          # a=1, b=[]
```

If the splat is not the last lvalue, then Ruby ensures that the lvalues that follow it will all receive values from rvalues at the end of the right side of the assignment—the splat lvalue will soak up only enough rvalues to leave one for each of the remaining lvalues. (OK, that's a pretty tortuous explanation—some examples will help.)

```
*a, b = 1, 2, 3, 4          # a=[1, 2, 3], b=4
c, *d, e = 1, 2, 3, 4       # c=1, d=[2, 3], e=4
f, *g, h, i, j = 1, 2, 3, 4 # f=1, g=[], h=2, i=3, j=4
```

As with method parameters, you can use a raw asterisk to ignore some rvalues:

```
first, *, last = 1,2,3,4,5,6   # first=1, last=6
```

Nested Assignments

Parallel assignments have one more feature worth mentioning. The left side of an assignment may contain a parenthesized list of terms. Ruby treats these terms as if they were a nested assignment statement. It extracts the corresponding rvalue, assigning it to the parenthesized terms, before continuing with the higher-level assignment.

```
a, (b, c), d = 1,2,3,4      # a=1, b=2, c=nil, d=3
a, (b, c), d = [1,2,3,4]    # a=1, b=2, c=nil, d=3
a, (b, c), d = 1,[2,3],4    # a=1, b=2, c=3, d=4
a, (b, c), d = 1,[2,3,4],5  # a=1, b=2, c=3, d=5
a, (b,*c), d = 1,[2,3,4],5  # a=1, b=2, c=[3, 4], d=5
```

Other Forms of Assignment

In common with many other languages, Ruby has a syntactic shortcut: a = a + 2 may be written as a += 2.

The second form is converted internally to the first. This means that operators you have defined as methods in your own classes work as you'd expect:

tutexpressions_26.rb

```ruby
class Bowdlerize
  def initialize(string)
    @value = string.gsub(/[aeiou]/, '*')
  end
  def +(other)
    Bowdlerize.new(self.to_s + other.to_s)
  end
  def to_s
    @value
  end
end

a = Bowdlerize.new("damn ")    # =>   d*mn
a += "shame"                   # =>   d*mn sh*m*
```

Something you won't find in Ruby are the autoincrement (++) and autodecrement (--) operators of C and Java. Use the += and -= forms instead.

Conditional Execution

Ruby has several different mechanisms for conditional execution of code; most of them should feel familiar, and many have some neat twists. Before we get into them, though, we need to spend a short time looking at boolean expressions.

Boolean Expressions

Ruby has a simple definition of truth. Any value that is not nil or the constant false is true—"cat", 99, 0, and :a_song are all considered true.

In this book, when we want to talk about a general true or false value, we use regular Roman type: true and false. When we want to refer to the actual constants, we write true and false.

The fact that nil is considered to be false is convenient. For example, IO#gets, which returns the next line from a file, returns nil at the end of file, enabling you to write loops such as this:

```ruby
while line = gets
  # process line
end
```

However, C, C++, and Perl programmers sometimes fall into a trap. The number zero is *not* interpreted as a false value. Neither is a zero-length string. This can be a tough habit to break.

And, Or, and Not

Ruby supports all the standard boolean operators. Both the keyword and and the operator && return their first argument if it is false. Otherwise, they evaluate and return their second argument (this is sometimes known as *shortcircuit* evaluation). The only difference in the two forms is precedence (and binds lower than &&).

```
nil   && 99   # =>   nil
false && 99   # =>   false
"cat" && 99   # =>   99
```

Thus, && and and both return a true value only if both of their arguments are true, as expected.

Similarly, both or and || return their first argument unless it is false, in which case they evaluate and return their second argument.

```
nil   || 99   # =>   99
false || 99   # =>   99
"cat" || 99   # =>   "cat"
```

As with and, the only difference between or and || is their precedence. To make life interesting, and and or have the same precedence, but && has a higher precedence than ||.

A common idiom is to use ||= to assign a value to a variable only if that variable isn't already set:

```
var ||= "default value"
```

This is almost, but not quite, the same as var = var || "default value". It differs in that no assignment is made at all if the variable is already set. In pseudocode, this might be written as var = "default value" unless var or as var || var = "default value".

not and ! return the opposite of their operand (false if the operand is true, and true if the operand is false). And, yes, not and ! differ only in precedence.

All these precedence rules are summarized in Table 22.4 on page 333.

defined?

The defined? operator returns nil if its argument (which can be an arbitrary expression) is not defined; otherwise, it returns a description of that argument. If the argument is yield, defined? returns the string "yield" if a code block is associated with the current context.

```
defined? 1         # =>   "expression"
defined? dummy     # =>   nil
defined? printf    # =>   "method"
defined? String    # =>   "constant"
defined? $_        # =>   "global-variable"
defined? Math::PI  # =>   "constant"
defined? a = 1     # =>   "assignment"
defined? 42.abs    # =>   "method"
defined? nil       # =>   "nil"
```

Comparing Objects

In addition to the boolean operators, Ruby objects support comparison using the methods ==, ===, <=>, =~, eql?, and equal? (see Table 9.1 on the facing page). All but <=> are defined in class Object but are often overridden by descendants to provide appropriate semantics. For example, class Array redefines == so that two array objects are equal if they have the same number of elements and the corresponding elements are equal.

1.9 Both == and =~ have negated forms, != and !~. As of Ruby 1.9, the interpreter first looks for methods called != or !~, calling them if found. If not, it will then invoke either == or =~, negating the result.

In the following example, Ruby calls the == method to perform both comparisons:

tutexpressions_32.rb

```
class T
  def ==(other)
    puts "Comparing self == #{other}"
    other == "value"
  end
end
t = T.new
p(t == "value")
p(t != "value")
```

produces:

```
Comparing self == value
true
Comparing self == value
false
```

If instead we explicitly define !=, Ruby calls it instead:

tutexpressions_33.rb

```
class T
  def ==(other)
    puts "Comparing self == #{other}"
    other == "value"
  end
  def !=(other)
    puts "Comparing self != #{other}"
    other != "value"
  end
end
t = T.new
p(t == "value")
p(t != "value")
```

produces:

```
Comparing self == value
true
Comparing self != value
false
```

Table 9.1. Common Comparison Operators

Operator	Meaning
==	Test for equal value.
===	Used to compare each of the items with the target in the when clause of a case statement.
<=>	General comparison operator. Returns −1, 0, or +1, depending on whether its receiver is less than, equal to, or greater than its argument.
<, <=, >=, >	Comparison operators for less than, less than or equal, greater than or equal, and greater than.
=~	Regular expression pattern match.
eql?	True if the receiver and argument have both the same type and equal values. 1 == 1.0 returns true, but 1.eql?(1.0) is false.
equal?	True if the receiver and argument have the same object ID.

You can use a Ruby range as a boolean expression. A range such as exp1..exp2 will evaluate as false until exp1 becomes true. The range will then evaluate as true until exp2 becomes true. Once this happens, the range resets, ready to fire again. We show some examples of this on page 143.

Prior to Ruby 1.8, you could use a bare regular expression as a boolean expression. This is now deprecated. You can still use the ~ operator (described on page 656) to match $_ against a pattern, but this will probably also disappear in the future.

If and Unless Expressions

An if expression in Ruby is pretty similar to if statements in other languages:

```
if artist == "Gillespie" then
  handle = "Dizzy"
elsif artist == "Parker" then
  handle = "Bird"
else
  handle = "unknown"
end
```

The then keyword is optional if you lay out your statements on multiple lines:

```
if song.artist == "Gillespie"
  handle = "Dizzy"
elsif song.artist == "Parker"
  handle = "Bird"
else
  handle = "unknown"
end
```

However, if you want to lay out your code more tightly, you must separate the boolean expression from the following statements with the then keyword:[1]

```
if artist == "Gillespie" then  handle = "Dizzy"
elsif artist == "Parker" then  handle = "Bird"
else  handle = "unknown"
end
```

You can have zero or more elsif clauses and an optional else clause. And notice that there's no e in the middle of elsif.

As we've said before, an if statement is an expression—it returns a value. You don't have to use the value of an if statement, but it can come in handy:

```
handle = if artist == "Gillespie"
           "Dizzy"
         elsif artist == "Parker"
           "Bird"
         else
           "unknown"
         end
```

Ruby also has a negated form of the if statement:

```
unless duration > 180
  listen_intently
end
```

The unless statement does support else, but most people seem to agree that it's clearer to switch to an if statement in these cases.

Finally, for the C fans out there, Ruby also supports the C-style conditional expression:

```
cost = duration > 180 ? 0.35 : 0.25
```

A conditional expression returns the value of either the expression before or the expression after the colon, depending on whether the boolean expression before the question mark is true or false. In the previous example, if the duration is greater than three minutes, the expression returns 0.35. For shorter durations, it returns 0.25. The result is then assigned to cost.

If and Unless Modifiers

Ruby shares a neat feature with Perl. Statement modifiers let you tack conditional statements onto the end of a normal statement:

```
mon, day, year = $1, $2, $3 if date =~ /(\d\d)-(\d\d)-(\d\d)/
puts "a = #{a}" if $DEBUG
print total unless total.zero?
```

---

1. Ruby 1.8 allowed you to use a colon character in place of the then keyword. This is no longer supported.

For an if modifier, the preceding expression will be evaluated only if the condition is true. unless works the other way around:

```
File.foreach("/etc/passwd") do |line|
  next if line =~ /^#/          # Skip comments
  parse(line) unless line =~ /^$/   # Don't parse empty lines
end
```

Because if itself is an expression, you can get really obscure with statements such as this:

```
if artist == "John Coltrane"
  artist = "'Trane"
end unless use_nicknames == "no"
```

This path leads to the gates of madness.

Case Expressions

The Ruby case expression is a powerful beast: a multiway if on steroids. And just to make it even more powerful, it comes in two flavors.

The first form is fairly close to a series of if statements; it lets you list a series of conditions and execute a statement corresponding to the first one that's true:

```
case
when song.name == "Misty"
  puts "Not again!"
when song.duration > 120
  puts "Too long!"
when Time.now.hour > 21
  puts "It's too late"
else
  song.play
end
```

The second form of the case statement is probably more common. You specify a target at the top of the case statement, and each when clause lists one or more comparisons:

```
case command
when "debug"
  dump_debug_info
  dump_symbols
when /p\s+(\w+)/
  dump_variable($1)
when "quit", "exit"
  exit
else
  print "Illegal command: #{command}"
end
```

As with if, case returns the value of the last expression executed, and you can use a then keyword if the expression is on the same line as the condition:[2]

```
kind = case year
       when 1850..1889 then "Blues"
       when 1890..1909 then "Ragtime"
       when 1910..1929 then "New Orleans Jazz"
       when 1930..1939 then "Swing"
       when 1940..1950 then "Bebop"
       else             "Jazz"
       end
```

case operates by comparing the target (the expression after the keyword case) with each of the comparison expressions after the when keywords. This test is done using *comparison === target*. As long as a class defines meaningful semantics for === (and all the built-in classes do), objects of that class can be used in case expressions.

For example, regular expressions define === as a simple pattern match:

```
case line
when /title=(.*)/
  puts "Title is #$1"
when /track=(.*)/
  puts "Track is #$1"
when /artist=(.*)/
  puts "Artist is #$1"
end
```

Ruby classes are instances of class Class. The === operator is defined in Class to test whether the argument is an instance of the receiver or one of its superclasses. So (abandoning the benefits of polymorphism and bringing the gods of refactoring down around your ears), you can test the class of objects:

```
case shape
when Square, Rectangle
  # ...
when Circle
  # ...
when Triangle
  # ...
else
  # ...
end
```

1.9

2.   Ruby 1.8 allowed you to use a colon character in place of the then keyword. As of Ruby 1.9, this is no longer supported.

Loops

Don't tell anyone, but Ruby has pretty primitive built-in looping constructs.

The while loop executes its body zero or more times as long as its condition is true. For example, this common idiom reads until the input is exhausted:

```
while line = gets
  # ...
end
```

The until loop is the opposite; it executes the body *until* the condition becomes true:

```
until play_list.duration > 60
  play_list.add(song_list.pop)
end
```

As with if and unless, you can use both of the loops as statement modifiers:

```
a = 1
a *= 2  while a < 100
a   # =>   128
a -= 10 until a < 100
a   # =>   98
```

On page 139, in the section on boolean expressions, we said that a range can be used as a kind of flip-flop, returning true when some event happens and then staying true until a second event occurs. This facility is normally used within loops. In the example that follows, we read a text file containing the first ten ordinal numbers ("first," "second," and so on) but print only the lines starting with the one that matches "third" and ending with the one that matches "fifth":

```
file = File.open("ordinal")
while line = file.gets
  puts(line)  if line =~ /third/ .. line =~ /fifth/
end
```

produces:

```
third
fourth
fifth
```

You may find folks who come from Perl writing the previous example slightly differently:

```
file = File.open("ordinal")
while file.gets
  print  if ~/third/ .. ~/fifth/
end
```

produces:

```
third
fourth
fifth
```

This uses some behind-the-scenes magic behavior: gets assigns the last line read to the global variable $\_$, the ~ operator does a regular expression match against $\_$, and print with no arguments prints $\_$. This kind of code is falling out of fashion in the Ruby community and may end up being removed from the language.

The start and end of a range used in a boolean expression can themselves be expressions. These are evaluated each time the overall boolean expression is evaluated. For example, the following code uses the fact that the variable $. contains the current input line number to display line numbers 1 through 3 as well as those between a match of /eig/ and /nin/:

```ruby
File.foreach("ordinal") do |line|
  if (($. == 1) || line =~ /eig/) .. (($. == 3) || line =~ /nin/)
    print line
  end
end
```

produces:

```
first
second
third
eighth
ninth
```

You'll come across a wrinkle when you use while and until as statement modifiers. If the statement they are modifying is a begin/end block, the code in the block will always execute at least one time, regardless of the value of the boolean expression:

```ruby
print "Hello\n" while false
begin
  print "Goodbye\n"
end while false
```

produces:

```
Goodbye
```

Iterators

If you read the beginning of the previous section, you may have been discouraged. "Ruby has pretty primitive built-in looping constructs," it said. Don't despair, gentle reader, for we have good news. Ruby doesn't need any sophisticated built-in loops, because all the fun stuff is implemented using Ruby iterators.

For example, Ruby doesn't have a for loop—at least not the kind you'd find in C, C++, and Java. Instead, Ruby uses methods defined in various built-in classes to provide equivalent, but less error-prone, functionality.

Let's look at some examples:

```ruby
3.times do
  print "Ho! "
end
```

produces:

```
Ho! Ho! Ho!
```

It's easy to avoid fence-post and off-by-one errors; this loop will execute three times, period. In addition to times, integers can loop over specific ranges by calling downto and upto, and all numbers can loop using step. For instance, a traditional "for" loop that runs from 0 to 9 (something like i=0; i < 10; i++) is written as follows:

```
0.upto(9) do |x|
  print x, " "
end
```

produces:

```
0 1 2 3 4 5 6 7 8 9
```

A loop from 0 to 12 by 3 can be written as follows:

```
0.step(12, 3) {|x| print x, " " }
```

produces:

```
0 3 6 9 12
```

Similarly, iterating over arrays and other containers is easy if you use their each method:

```
[ 1, 1, 2, 3, 5 ].each {|val| print val, " " }
```

produces:

```
1 1 2 3 5
```

And once a class supports each, the additional methods in the Enumerable module (documented beginning on page 478 and summarized on page 80) become available. For example, the File class provides an each method, which returns each line of a file in turn. Using the grep method in Enumerable, we could iterate over only those lines that end with a d:

```
File.open("ordinal").grep(/d$/) do |line|
  puts line
end
```

produces:

```
second
third
```

Last, and probably least, is the most basic loop of all. Ruby provides a built-in iterator called loop:

```
loop do
  # block ...
end
```

The loop iterator calls the associated block forever (or at least until you break out of the loop, but you'll have to read ahead to find out how to do that).

For ... In

Earlier we said that the only built-in Ruby looping primitives were while and until. What's this for thing, then? Well, for is almost a lump of syntactic sugar.

When you write this:

```
for song in playlist
  song.play
end
```

Ruby translates it into something like this:

```
playlist.each do |song|
  song.play
end
```

The only difference between the for loop and the each form is the scope of local variables that are defined in the body. This is discussed on page 148.

You can use for to iterate over any object that responds to the method each, such as an Array or a Range:

```
for i in ['fee', 'fi', 'fo', 'fum']
  print i, " "
end
for i in 1..3
  print i, " "
end
for i in File.open("ordinal").find_all {|line| line =~ /d$/}
  print i.chomp, " "
end
```

produces:

```
fee fi fo fum 1 2 3 second third
```

As long as your class defines a sensible each method, you can use a for loop to traverse its objects:

```
tutexpressions_64.rb
class Periods
  def each
    yield "Classical"
    yield "Jazz"
    yield "Rock"
  end
end

periods = Periods.new
for genre in periods
  print genre, " "
end
```

produces:

```
Classical Jazz Rock
```

Break, Redo, and Next

The loop control constructs break, redo, and next let you alter the normal flow through a loop or iterator.[3]

break terminates the immediately enclosing loop; control resumes at the statement following the block. redo repeats current iteration of the loop from the start but without reevaluating the condition or fetching the next element (in an iterator). next skips to the end of the loop, effectively starting the next iteration:

```
while line = gets
  next  if line =~ /^\s*#/  # skip comments
  break if line =~ /^END/   # stop at end

  # substitute stuff in backticks and try again
  redo if line.gsub!(/`(.*?)`/) { eval($1) }

  # process line ...
end
```

These keywords can also be used within blocks. Although you can use them with any block, they typically make the most sense when the block is being used for iteration:

```
i=0
loop do
  i += 1
  next if i < 3
  print i
  break if i > 4
end
```

produces:

```
345
```

A value may be passed to break and next. When used in conventional loops, it probably makes sense only to do this with break, where it sets the value returned by the loop. (Any value given to next is effectively lost.) If a conventional loop doesn't execute a break, its value is nil.

```
result = while line = gets
           break(line) if line =~ /answer/
         end

process_answer(result) if result
```

If you want the nitty-gritty details of how break and next work with blocks and procs, take a look at the reference description starting on page 353. If you are looking for a way of exiting from nested blocks or loops, take a look at Kernel.catch, described on pages 357 and 558.

---

3. Prior versions of Ruby also supported the retry keyword as a looping mechanism. This has been removed in Ruby 1.9.

Variable Scope, Loops, and Blocks

The while, until, and for loops are built into the language and do not introduce new scope; previously existing locals can be used in the loop, and any new locals created will be available afterward.

The blocks used by iterators (such as loop and each) are a little different. Normally, the local variables created in these blocks are not accessible outside the block:

```
[ 1, 2, 3 ].each do |x|
  y = x + 1
end
[ x, y ]
```

produces:

```
prog.rb:4:in `<main>': undefined local variable or method `x' for
main:Object (NameError)
```

However, if at the time the block executes a local variable already exists with the same name as that of a variable in the block, the existing local variable will be used in the block. Its value will therefore be available after the block finishes. As the following example shows, this applies to normal variables in the block but not to the block's parameters:

```
x = "initial value"
y = "another value"
[ 1, 2, 3 ].each do |x|
  y = x + 1
end
[ x, y ]   # =>   ["initial value", 4]
```

Note that the assignment to the variable doesn't have to be executed; the Ruby interpreter just needs to have seen that the variable exists on the left side of an assignment:

```
if false
  a = "never used"
end
3.times {|i| a = i }

a   # =>   2
```

Ruby 1.9 introduced the concept of block-local variables. These are listed in the block's parameter list, preceded by a semicolon. Contrast this code, which does not use block-locals:

```
square = "yes"
total = 0
[ 1, 2, 3 ].each do |val|
  square = val * val
  total += square
end
puts "Total = #{total}"
puts "Square = #{square}"
```

produces:

```
Total = 14
Square = 9
```

with the following code, which uses a block-local variable, so square in the outer scope is not affected by a variable of the same name within the block:

```
square = "yes"
total = 0
[ 1, 2, 3 ].each do |val; square|
  square = val * val
  total += square
end
puts "Total = #{total}"
puts "Square = #{square}"
```

produces:

```
Total = 14
Square = yes
```

If you are concerned about the scoping of variables with blocks, turn on Ruby warnings, and declare your block-local variables explicitly.

## Chapter 10

Exceptions,
Catch, and Throw

So far we've been developing code in Pleasantville, a wonderful place where nothing ever, ever goes wrong. Every library call succeeds, users never enter incorrect data, and resources are plentiful and cheap. Well, that's about to change. Welcome to the real world!

In the real world, errors happen. Good programs (and programmers) anticipate them and arrange to handle them gracefully. This isn't always as easy as it may sound. Often the code that detects an error does not have the context to know what to do about it. For example, attempting to open a file that doesn't exist is acceptable in some circumstances and is a fatal error at other times. What's your file-handling module to do?

The traditional approach is to use return codes. The open method could return some specific value to say it failed. This value is then propagated back through the layers of calling routines until someone wants to take responsibility for it. The problem with this approach is that managing all these error codes can be a pain. If a function calls open, then read, and finally close and each can return an error indication, how can the function distinguish these error codes in the value it returns to *its* caller?

To a large extent, *exceptions* solve this problem. Exceptions let you package information about an error into an object. That exception object is then propagated back up the calling stack automatically until the runtime system finds code that explicitly declares that it knows how to handle that type of exception.

The Exception Class

The package that contains the information about an exception is an object of class Exception or one of class Exception's children. Ruby predefines a tidy hierarchy of exceptions, shown in Figure 10.1 on page 153. As we'll see later, this hierarchy makes handling exceptions considerably easier.

When you need to raise an exception, you can use one of the built-in Exception classes, or you can create one of your own. Make your own exceptions subclasses of StandardError or one of its children. If you don't, your exceptions won't be caught by default.

Every Exception has associated with it a message string and a stack backtrace. If you define your own exceptions, you can add extra information.

Handling Exceptions

Here's some simple code that uses the open-uri library to download the contents of a web page and write it to a file, line by line:

```
tutexceptions_1.rb
require 'open-uri'
web_page = open("http://pragprog.com/podcasts")
output = File.open("podcasts.html", "w")
while line = web_page.gets
  output.puts line
end
output.close
```

What happens if we get a fatal error halfway through? We certainly don't want to store an incomplete page to the output file.

Let's add some exception-handling code and see how it helps. To do exception handling, we enclose the code that could raise an exception in a begin/end block and use one or more rescue clauses to tell Ruby the types of exceptions we want to handle. Because we specified Exception in the rescue line, we'll handle all exceptions of class Exception and all of its subclasses (which covers all Ruby exceptions). In the error-handling block, we report the error, close and delete the output file, and then reraise the exception:

```
tutexceptions_2.rb
require 'open-uri'
page = "podcasts"
file_name = "#{page}.html"
web_page = open("http://pragprog.com/#{page}")
output = File.open(file_name, "w")
begin
  while line = web_page.gets
    output.puts line
  end
  output.close
rescue Exception
  STDERR.puts "Failed to download #{page}: #{$!}"
  output.close
  File.delete(file_name)
  raise
end
```

When an exception is raised, and independent of any subsequent exception handling, Ruby places a reference to the associated Exception object into the global variable $! (the exclamation point presumably mirroring our surprise that any of *our* code could cause errors). In the previous example, we used the $! variable to format our error message.

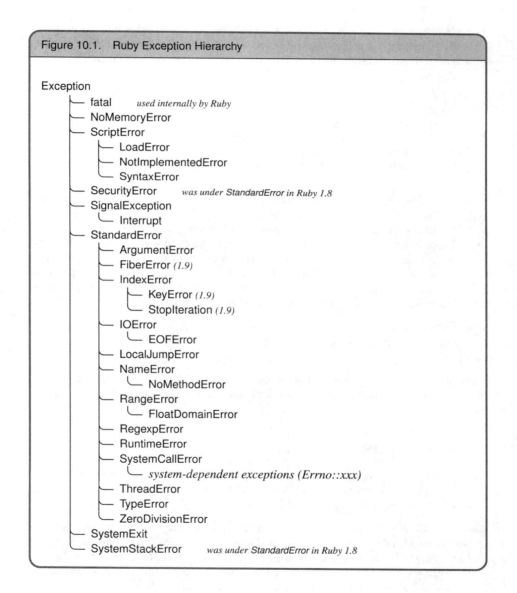

Figure 10.1. Ruby Exception Hierarchy

Exception
    └── fatal   *used internally by Ruby*
    └── NoMemoryError
    └── ScriptError
            └── LoadError
            └── NotImplementedError
            └── SyntaxError
    └── SecurityError   *was under StandardError in Ruby 1.8*
    └── SignalException
            └── Interrupt
    └── StandardError
            └── ArgumentError
            └── FiberError *(1.9)*
            └── IndexError
                    └── KeyError *(1.9)*
                    └── StopIteration *(1.9)*
            └── IOError
                    └── EOFError
            └── LocalJumpError
            └── NameError
                    └── NoMethodError
            └── RangeError
                    └── FloatDomainError
            └── RegexpError
            └── RuntimeError
            └── SystemCallError
                    └── *system-dependent exceptions (Errno::xxx)*
            └── ThreadError
            └── TypeError
            └── ZeroDivisionError
    └── SystemExit
    └── SystemStackError   *was under StandardError in Ruby 1.8*

After closing and deleting the file, we call raise with no parameters, which reraises the exception in $!. This is a useful technique, because it allows you to write code that filters exceptions, passing on those you can't handle to higher levels. It's almost like implementing an inheritance hierarchy for error processing.

You can have multiple rescue clauses in a begin block, and each rescue clause can specify multiple exceptions to catch. At the end of each rescue clause, you can give Ruby the name of a local variable to receive the matched exception. Most people find this more readable than using $! all over the place:

```
begin
  eval string
rescue SyntaxError, NameError => boom
  print "String doesn't compile: " + boom
rescue StandardError => bang
  print "Error running script: " + bang
end
```

How does Ruby decide which rescue clause to execute? It turns out that the processing is pretty similar to that used by the case statement. For each rescue clause in the begin block, Ruby compares the raised exception against each of the parameters in turn. If the raised exception matches a parameter, Ruby executes the body of the rescue and stops looking. The match is made using *parameter*===$!. For most exceptions, this means that the match will succeed if the exception named in the rescue clause is the same as the type of the currently thrown exception or is a superclass of that exception.[1] If you write a rescue clause with no parameter list, the parameter defaults to StandardError.

If no rescue clause matches or if an exception is raised outside a begin/end block, Ruby moves up the stack and looks for an exception handler in the caller, then in the caller's caller, and so on.

Although the parameters to the rescue clause are typically the names of Exception classes, they can actually be arbitrary expressions (including method calls) that return an Exception class.

System Errors

System errors are raised when a call to the operating system returns an error code. On POSIX systems, these errors have names such as EAGAIN and EPERM. (If you're on a Unix box, you could type **man errno** to get a list of these errors.)

Ruby takes these errors and wraps them each in a specific exception object. Each is a subclass of SystemCallError, and each is defined in a module called Errno. This means you'll find exceptions with class names such as Errno::EAGAIN, Errno::EIO, and Errno::EPERM. If you want to get to the underlying system error code, Errno exception objects each have a class constant called (somewhat confusingly) Errno that contains the value.

---

1.   This comparison happens because exceptions are classes, and classes in turn are kinds of Module. The === method is defined for modules, returning true if the class of the operand is the same as or is a descendant of the receiver.

```
Errno::EAGAIN::Errno        # =>    35
Errno::EPERM::Errno         # =>    1
Errno::EIO::Errno           # =>    5
Errno::EWOULDBLOCK::Errno   # =>    35
```

Note that EWOULDBLOCK and EAGAIN have the same error number. This is a feature of the operating system of the computer used to produce this book—the two constants map to the same error number. To deal with this, Ruby arranges things so that Errno::EAGAIN and Errno::EWOULDBLOCK are treated identically in a rescue clause. If you ask to rescue one, you'll rescue either. It does this by redefining SystemCallError#=== so that if two subclasses of SystemCallError are compared, the comparison is done on their error number and not on their position in the hierarchy.

Tidying Up

Sometimes you need to guarantee that some processing is done at the end of a block of code, regardless of whether an exception was raised. For example, you may have a file open on entry to the block, and you need to make sure it gets closed as the block exits.

The ensure clause does just this. ensure goes after the last rescue clause and contains a chunk of code that will always be executed as the block terminates. It doesn't matter if the block exits normally, if it raises and rescues an exception, or if it is terminated by an uncaught exception—the ensure block will get run:

```
f = File.open("testfile")
begin
  # .. process
rescue
  # .. handle error
ensure
  f.close
end
```

Beginners commonly make the mistake of putting the File.open inside the begin block. In this case, that would be incorrect, because open can itself raise an exception. If that were to happen, you wouldn't want to run the code in the ensure block, because there'd be no file to close.

The else clause is a similar, although less useful, construct. If present, it goes after the rescue clauses and before any ensure. The body of an else clause is executed only if no exceptions are raised by the main body of code.

```
f = File.open("testfile")
begin
  # .. process
rescue
  # .. handle error
else
  puts "Congratulations-- no errors!"
ensure
  f.close
end
```

Play It Again

Sometimes you may be able to correct the cause of an exception. In those cases, you can use the retry statement within a rescue clause to repeat the entire begin/end block. Clearly, tremendous scope exists for infinite loops here, so this is a feature to use with caution (and with a finger resting lightly on the interrupt key).

As an example of code that retries on exceptions, take a look at the following, adapted from Minero Aoki's net/smtp.rb library:

```
@esmtp = true
begin
  # First try an extended login. If it fails because the
  # server doesn't support it, fall back to a normal login
  if @esmtp then
    @command.ehlo(helodom)
  else
    @command.helo(helodom)
  end
rescue ProtocolError
  if @esmtp then
    @esmtp = false
    retry
  else
    raise
  end
end
```

This code tries first to connect to an SMTP server using the EHLO command, which is not universally supported. If the connection attempt fails, the code sets the @esmtp variable to false and retries the connection. If this fails a second time, the exception is raised up to the caller.

Raising Exceptions

So far we've been on the defensive, handling exceptions raised by others. It's time to turn the tables and go on the offensive. (Some say your gentle authors are always offensive, but that's a different book.)

You can raise exceptions in your code with the Kernel.raise method (or its somewhat judgmental synonym, Kernel.fail):

```
raise
raise "bad mp3 encoding"
raise InterfaceException, "Keyboard failure", caller
```

The first form simply reraises the current exception (or a RuntimeError if there is no current exception). This is used in exception handlers that need to intercept an exception before passing it on.

The second form creates a new RuntimeError exception, setting its message to the given string. This exception is then raised up the call stack.

The third form uses the first argument to create an exception and then sets the associated message to the second argument and the stack trace to the third argument. Typically the first argument will be either the name of a class in the Exception hierarchy or a reference to an object instance of one of these classes.[2] The stack trace is normally produced using the Kernel.caller method.

Here are some typical examples of raise in action:

```
raise
raise "Missing name" if name.nil?
if i >= names.size
  raise IndexError, "#{i} >= size (#{names.size})"
end
raise ArgumentError, "Name too big", caller
```

In the last example, we remove the current routine from the stack backtrace, which is often useful in library modules. We do this using the caller method, which returns the current stack trace. We can take this further; the following code removes two routines from the backtrace by passing only a subset of the call stack to the new exception:

```
raise ArgumentError, "Name too big", caller[1..-1]
```

Adding Information to Exceptions

You can define your own exceptions to hold any information that you need to pass out from the site of an error. For example, certain types of network errors may be transient depending on the circumstances. If such an error occurs and the circumstances are right, you could set a flag in the exception to tell the handler that it may be worth retrying the operation:

```
class RetryException < RuntimeError
  attr :ok_to_retry
  def initialize(ok_to_retry)
    @ok_to_retry = ok_to_retry
  end
end
```

Somewhere down in the depths of the code, a transient error occurs:

```
def read_data(socket)
  data = socket.read(512)
  if data.nil?
    raise RetryException.new(true), "transient read error"
  end
  # .. normal processing
end
```

---

2.   Technically, this argument can be any object that responds to the message exception by returning an object such that object.kind_of?(Exception) is true.

Higher up the call stack, we handle the exception:

```
begin
  stuff = read_data(socket)
  # .. process stuff
rescue RetryException => detail
  retry if detail.ok_to_retry
  raise
end
```

Catch and Throw

Although the exception mechanism of raise and rescue is great for abandoning execution when things go wrong, it's sometimes nice to be able to jump out of some deeply nested construct during normal processing. This is where catch and throw come in handy. Here's a trivial example—this code reads a list of words one at a time and adds them to an array. When done, it prints the array in reverse order. However, if any of the lines in the file doesn't contain a valid word, we want to abandon the whole process.

```
tutexceptions_14.rb
word_list = File.open("wordlist")
catch (:done)  do
  result = []
  while line = word_list.gets
    word = line.chomp
    throw :done unless word =~ /^\w+$/
    result << word
  end
  puts result.reverse
end
```

catch defines a block that is labeled with the given name (which may be a Symbol or a String). The block is executed normally until a throw is encountered.

When Ruby encounters a throw, it zips back up the call stack looking for a catch block with a matching symbol. When it finds it, Ruby unwinds the stack to that point and terminates the block. So, in the previous example, if the input does not contain correctly formatted lines, the throw will skip to the end of the corresponding catch, not only terminating the while loop but also skipping the code that writes the reversed list. If the throw is called with the optional second parameter, that value is returned as the value of the catch. In this example, our word list incorrectly contains the line "*wow*." Without the second parameter to throw, the corresponding catch returns nil.

```
tutexceptions_15.rb
word_list = File.open("wordlist")
word_in_error = catch(:done)  do
  result = []
  while line = word_list.gets
    word = line.chomp
```

```
      throw(:done, word) unless word =~ /^\w+$/
      result << word
    end
    puts result.reverse
  end
  if word_in_error
    puts "Failed: '#{word_in_error}' found, but a word was expected"
  end
```

produces:

```
Failed: '*wow*' found, but a word was expected
```

The following example uses a throw to terminate interaction with the user if ! is typed in response to any prompt:

tutexceptions_16.rb

```
def prompt_and_get(prompt)
  print prompt
  res = readline.chomp
  throw :quit_requested if res == "!"
  res
end
catch :quit_requested do
  name = prompt_and_get("Name: ")
  age  = prompt_and_get("Age:  ")
  sex  = prompt_and_get("Sex:  ")
  # ..
  # process information
end
```

As this example illustrates, the throw does not have to appear within the static scope of the catch.

## Chapter 11

Basic Input and Output

Ruby provides what at first sight looks like two separate sets of I/O routines. The first is the simple interface—we've been using it pretty much exclusively so far:

```
print "Enter your name: "
name = gets
```

A whole set of I/O-related methods is implemented in the Kernel module—gets, open, print, printf, putc, puts, readline, readlines, and test—that makes it simple and convenient to write straightforward Ruby programs. These methods typically do I/O to standard input and standard output, which makes them useful for writing filters. You'll find them documented starting on page 555.

The second way, which gives you a lot more control, is to use IO objects.

What Is an IO Object?

Ruby defines a single base class, IO, to handle input and output. This base class is subclassed by classes File and BasicSocket to provide more specialized behavior, but the principles are the same. An IO object is a bidirectional channel between a Ruby program and some external resource.[1] An IO object may have more to it than meets the eye, but in the end you still simply write to it and read from it.

In this chapter, we'll be concentrating on class IO and its most commonly used subclass, class File. For more details on using the socket classes for networking, see the section beginning on page 871.

---

1. For those who just have to know the implementation details, this means that a single IO object can sometimes be managing more than one operating system file descriptor. For example, if you open a pair of pipes, a single IO object contains both a read pipe and a write pipe.

Opening and Closing Files

As you may expect, you can create a new file object using File.new:

```
file = File.new("testfile", "r")
# ... process the file
file.close
```

The first parameter is the filename. The second is the mode string, which lets you open the file for reading, writing, or both. (Here we opened testfile for reading with an "r". We could also have used "w" for write or "r+" for read-write. The full list of allowed modes appears on page 538.) You can also optionally specify file permissions when creating a file; see the description of File.new on page 503 for details. After opening the file, we can work with it, writing and/or reading data as needed. Finally, as responsible software citizens, we close the file, ensuring that all buffered data is written and that all related resources are freed.

But here Ruby can make life a little bit easier for you. The method File.open also opens a file. In regular use, it behaves just like File.new. However, if you associate a block with the call, open behaves differently. Instead of returning a new File object, it invokes the block, passing the newly opened File as a parameter. When the block exits, the file is automatically closed.

```
File.open("testfile", "r") do |file|
  # ... process the file
end    # << file automatically closed here
```

This second approach has an added benefit. In the earlier case, if an exception is raised while processing the file, the call to file.close may not happen. Once the file variable goes out of scope, then garbage collection will eventually close it, but this may not happen for a while. Meanwhile, resources are being held open.

This doesn't happen with the block form of File.open. If an exception is raised inside the block, the file is closed before the exception is propagated on to the caller. It's as if the open method looks like the following:

```
class File
  def File.open(*args)
    result = f = File.new(*args)
    if block_given?
      begin
        result = yield f
      ensure
        f.close
      end
    end

    return result
  end
end
```

Reading and Writing Files

The same methods that we've been using for "simple" I/O are available for all file objects. So, gets reads a line from standard input (or from any files specified on the command line when the script was invoked), and file.gets reads a line from the file object *file*.

For example, we could create a program called copy.rb:

```
while line = gets
  puts line
end
```

If we run this program with no arguments, it will read lines from the console and copy them back to the console. Note that each line is echoed once the Return key is pressed. (In this and later examples, we show user input in a bold font.)

```
% ruby copy.rb
These are lines
These are lines
that I am typing
that I am typing
^D
```

We can also pass in one or more filenames on the command line, in which case gets will read from each in turn:

```
% ruby copy.rb testfile
This is line one
This is line two
This is line three
And so on...
```

Finally, we can explicitly open the file and read from it:

```
File.open("testfile") do |file|
  while line = file.gets
    puts line
  end
end
```

produces:

```
This is line one
This is line two
This is line three
And so on...
```

As well as gets, I/O objects enjoy an additional set of access methods, all intended to make our lives easier.

Iterators for Reading

As well as using the usual loops to read data from an IO stream, you can also use various Ruby iterators. IO#each_byte invokes a block with the next 8-bit byte from the IO object (in this case, an object of type File). The chr method converts an integer to the corresponding ASCII character:

```
File.open("testfile") do |file|
  file.each_byte {|ch| print "#{ch.chr}:#{ch} "  }
end
```

produces:

```
T:84 h:104 i:105 s:115   :32 i:105 s:115   :32 l:108 i:105 ...
T:84 h:104 i:105 s:115   :32 i:105 s:115   :32 l:108 i:105 ...
T:84 h:104 i:105 s:115   :32 i:105 s:115   :32 l:108 i:105 ...
A:65 n:110 d:100  :32 s:115 o:111   :32 o:111 n:110 .:46 ...
```

IO#each_line calls the block with each line from the file. In the next example, we'll make the original newlines visible using String#dump so you can see that we're not cheating:

```
File.open("testfile") do |file|
  file.each_line {|line| puts "Got #{line.dump}" }
end
```

produces:

```
Got "This is line one\n"
Got "This is line two\n"
Got "This is line three\n"
Got "And so on...\n"
```

You can pass each_line any sequence of characters as a line separator, and it will break up the input accordingly, returning the line ending at the end of each line of data. That's why you see the \n characters in the output of the previous example. In the next example, we'll use the character e as the line separator:

```
File.open("testfile") do |file|
  file.each_line("e") {|line|  puts "Got #{ line.dump }" }
end
```

produces:

```
Got "This is line"
Got " one"
Got "\nThis is line"
Got " two\nThis is line"
Got " thre"
Got "e"
Got "\nAnd so on...\n"
```

If you combine the idea of an iterator with the autoclosing block feature, you get IO.foreach. This method takes the name of an I/O source, opens it for reading, calls the iterator once for every line in the file, and then closes the file automatically:

```
IO.foreach("testfile") {|line| puts line }
```

produces:

```
This is line one
This is line two
This is line three
And so on...
```

Or, if you prefer, you can retrieve an entire file into a string or into an array of lines:

```
# read into string
str = IO.read("testfile")
str.length    # =>   66
str[0, 30]    # =>   "This is line one\nThis is line "

# read into an array
arr = IO.readlines("testfile")
arr.length    # =>   4
arr[0]        # =>   "This is line one\n"
```

Don't forget that I/O is never certain in an uncertain world—exceptions will be raised on most errors, and you should be ready to rescue them and take appropriate action.

Writing to Files

So far, we've been merrily calling puts and print, passing in any old object and trusting that Ruby will do the right thing (which, of course, it does). But what exactly *is* it doing?

The answer is pretty simple. With a couple of exceptions, every object you pass to puts and print is converted to a string by calling that object's to_s method. If for some reason the to_s method doesn't return a valid string, a string is created containing the object's class name and ID, something like #<ClassName:0x123456>:

```
# Note the "w", which opens the file for writing
File.open("output.txt", "w") do |file|
  file.puts "Hello"
  file.puts "1 + 2 = #{1+2}"
end
# Now read the file in and print its contents to STDOUT
puts File.read("output.txt")
```

produces:

```
Hello
1 + 2 = 3
```

The exceptions are simple, too. The nil object will print as the empty string, and an array passed to puts will be written as if each of its elements in turn were passed separately to puts.

What if you want to write binary data and don't want Ruby messing with it? Well, normally you can simply use IO#print and pass in a string containing the bytes to be written. However, you can get at the low-level input and output routines if you really want—look at the documentation for IO#sysread and IO#syswrite on page 553.

And how do you get the binary data into a string in the first place? The three common ways are to use a literal, poke it in byte by byte, or use Array#pack:

```
str1 = "\001\002\003"    # =>   "\x01\x02\x03"
str2 = ""
str2 << 1 << 2 << 3      # =>   "\x01\x02\x03"
[ 1, 2, 3 ].pack("c*")   # =>   "\x01\x02\x03"
```

But I Miss My C++ iostream

Sometimes there's just no accounting for taste.... However, just as you can append an object to an Array using the << operator, you can also append an object to an output IO stream:

```
endl = "\n"
STDOUT << 99 << " red balloons" << endl
```

produces:

```
99 red balloons
```

Again, the << method uses to_s to convert its arguments to strings before sending them on their merry way.

Although we started off disparaging the poor << operator, there are actually some good reasons for using it. Because other classes (such as String and Array) also implement a << operator with similar semantics, you can quite often write code that appends to something using << without caring whether it is added to an array, a file, or a string. This kind of flexibility also makes unit testing easy. We discuss this idea in greater detail in the chapter on duck typing, starting on page 359.

Doing I/O with Strings

There are often times where you need to work with code that assumes it's reading from or writing to one or more files. But you have a problem: the data isn't in files. Perhaps it's available instead via a SOAP service, or it has been passed to you as command-line parameters. Or maybe you're running unit tests, and you don't want to alter the real file system.

Enter StringIO objects. They behave just like other I/O objects, but they read and write strings, not files. If you open a StringIO object for reading, you supply it with a string. All read operations on the StringIO object then read from this string. Similarly, when you want to write to a StringIO object, you pass it a string to be filled.

```
require 'stringio'

ip = StringIO.new("now is\nthe time\nto learn\nRuby!")
op = StringIO.new("", "w")

ip.each_line do |line|
  op.puts line.reverse
end
op.string   # =>   "\nsi won\n\nemit eht\n\nnrael ot\n!ybuR\n"
```

Talking to Networks

Ruby is fluent in most of the Internet's protocols, both low-level and high-level.

For those who enjoy groveling around at the network level, Ruby comes with a set of classes in the socket library (documented starting on page 871). These classes give you access to TCP, UDP, SOCKS, and Unix domain sockets, as well as any additional socket types supported on your architecture. The library also provides helper classes to make writing servers easier. Here's a simple program that gets information about the "mysql" user on our local machine using the finger protocol:

```
require 'socket'

client = TCPSocket.open('127.0.0.1', 'finger')
client.send("mysql\n", 0)    # 0 means standard packet
puts client.readlines
client.close
```

produces:

```
Login: _mysql                          Name: MySQL Server
Directory: /var/empty                  Shell: /usr/bin/false
Never logged in.
No Mail.
No Plan.
```

At a higher level, the lib/net set of library modules provides handlers for a set of application-level protocols (currently FTP, HTTP, POP, SMTP, and telnet). These are documented starting on page 764. For example, the following program lists the images that are displayed on this book's home page:

```
tutio_18.rb
require 'net/http'

h = Net::HTTP.new('www.pragprog.com', 80)

response = h.get('/titles/ruby3/programming-ruby-3')

if response.message == "OK"
  puts response.body.scan(/<img alt=".*?" src="(.*?)"/m).uniq
end
```

produces:

```
http://assets1.pragprog.com/images/logo.gif?1238449325
http://assets0.pragprog.com/images/login-button.gif?1238449325
http://assets1.pragprog.com/images/covers/190x228/betas/ruby3.jpg?1236205316
http://assets1.pragprog.com/images/covers/40x48/fr_rr.jpg?1184184147
...
```

Although attractively simple, this example could be improved significantly. In particular, it doesn't do much in the way of error handling. It should really report "Not Found" errors (the infamous 404) and should handle redirects (which happen when a web server gives the client an alternative address for the requested page).

We can take this to a higher level still. By bringing the open-uri library into a program, the Kernel.open method suddenly recognizes http:// and ftp:// URLs in the filename. Not just that—it also handles redirects automatically.

`tutio_19.rb`

```ruby
require 'open-uri'
open('http://pragprog.com') do |f|
  puts f.read.scan(/<img alt=".*?" src="(.*?)"/m).uniq
end
```

produces:

```
http://assets1.pragprog.com/images/logo.gif?1238449325
http://assets0.pragprog.com/images/login-button.gif?1238449325
http://assets1.pragprog.com/images/front_page.png?1238449325
http://assets0.pragprog.com/images/covers/75x90/bhgwad.jpg?1236205194
http://assets3.pragprog.com/images/covers/75x90/ltp2.jpg?1236205271
...
```

## Chapter 12

Fibers, Threads, and Processes

Ruby gives you two basic ways to organize your program so that you can run different parts of it apparently "at the same time." Fibers let you suspend execution of one part of your program and run some other part. For more decoupled execution, you can split up cooperating tasks *within* the program, using multiple threads, or you can split up tasks between different programs, using multiple processes. Let's look at each in turn.

Fibers

Ruby 1.9 introduced *fibers* to the language. Although the name suggests some kind of lightweight thread, in reality Ruby's fibers are really just a very simple coroutine mechanism. They allow you to write programs that look like you are manually scheduling threads without incurring any of the complexity inherent in threading. Let's look at a simple example. We'd like to analyze a text file, counting the occurrence of each word. We could do this (without using fibers) in a simple loop:

```
tutthreads_1.rb
counts = Hash.new(0)
File.foreach("testfile") do |line|
  line.scan(/\w+/) do |word|
    word = word.downcase
    counts[word] += 1
  end
end
counts.keys.sort.each {|k| print "#{k}:#{counts[k]} "}
```

produces:

```
and:1 is:3 line:3 on:1 one:1 so:1 this:3 three:1 two:1
```

However, this code is messy because it conflates the concepts of finding words with the counting of the words.

We could fix this by writing a method that reads the file and yields each successive word. But fibers give us a simpler solution:

```
tutthreads_2.rb
words = Fiber.new do
  File.foreach("testfile") do |line|
    line.scan(/\w+/) do |word|
      Fiber.yield word.downcase
    end
  end
end
counts = Hash.new(0)
while word = words.resume
  counts[word] += 1
end
counts.keys.sort.each {|k| print "#{k}:#{counts[k]} "}
```

produces:

```
and:1 is:3 line:3 on:1 one:1 so:1 this:3 three:1 two:1
```

The constructor for the Fiber class takes a block and returns a fiber object. For now, the code in the block is not executed.

Subsequently, we can call resume on the fiber object. This causes the block to start execution. The file is opened, and the scan method starts extracting individual words. However, at this point, Fiber.yield is invoked. This suspends execution of the block—the resume method that we called to run the block returns any value given to Fiber.yield.

Our main program enters the body of the loop and increments the count for the first word returned by the fiber. It then loops back up to the top of the while loop, which again calls words.resume while evaluating the condition. The resume call goes back into the block, continuing just after it left off (at the line after the Fiber.yield call).

When the fiber runs out of words in the file, the block exits. The next time resume is called, it returns nil (because the block has exited). (You'll get a FiberError if you attempt to call resume again after this.)

Fibers are often used to generate values from infinite sequences on demand. Here's a fiber that returns successive integers divisible by 2 and not divisible by 3:

```
tutthreads_3.rb
twos = Fiber.new do
  num = 2
  loop do
    Fiber.yield(num) unless num % 3 == 0
    num += 2
  end
end
10.times { print twos.resume, " " }
```

produces:

```
2 4 8 10 14 16 20 22 26 28
```

Because fibers are just objects, you can pass them around, store them in variables, and so on. Fibers can be resumed only in the thread that created them.

Fibers, Coroutines, and Continuations

The basic fiber support in Ruby is limited—fibers can yield control only back to the code that resumed them. However, Ruby comes with two standard libraries that extend this behavior. The fiber library (described on page 745) adds full coroutine support. Once it is loaded, fibers gain a transfer method, allowing them to transfer control to arbitrary other fibers.

A related but more general mechanism is the *continuation*. A continuation is a way of recording the state of your running program (where it is, the current binding, and so on) and then resuming from that state at some point in the future. You can use continuations to implement coroutines (and other new control structures). Continuations have also been used to store the state of a running web application between requests—a continuation is created when the application sends a response to the browser; then, when the next request arrives from that browser, the continuation is invoked, and the application continues from where it left off. You enable continuations in Ruby by requiring the continuation library, described on page 729.

Multithreading

Often the simplest way to do two things at once is by using *Ruby threads*. Prior to Ruby 1.9, these were implemented as so-called green threads—threads were switched totally within the interpreter. In Ruby 1.9, threading is now performed by the operating system. This is an improvement, but not quite as big an improvement as you might want. Although threads can now take advantage of multiple processors (and multiple cores in a single processor), there's a major catch. Many Ruby extension libraries are not thread safe (because they were written for the old threading model). So, Ruby compromises: it uses native operating system threads but operates only a single thread at a time. You'll never see two threads in the same application running Ruby code truly concurrently. (You will, however, see threads busy doing (say) I/O while another thread executes Ruby code. That's part of the point....)

Creating Ruby Threads

Creating a new thread is pretty straightforward. The code that follows is a simple example. It downloads a set of web pages in parallel. For each URL that it is asked to download, the code creates a separate thread that handles the HTTP transaction.

```
tutthreads_4.rb
require 'net/http'
pages = %w( www.rubycentral.com  slashdot.org  www.google.com )
threads = []
for page_to_fetch in pages
  threads << Thread.new(page_to_fetch) do |url|
```

```
      h = Net::HTTP.new(url, 80)
      print "Fetching: #{url}\n"
      resp = h.get('/')
      print "Got #{url}:  #{resp.message}\n"
    end
  end
threads.each {|thr|  thr.join }
```

produces:

```
Fetching: www.rubycentral.com
Fetching: slashdot.org
Fetching: www.google.com
Got www.google.com:  OK
Got www.rubycentral.com:  OK
Got slashdot.org:  OK
```

Let's look at this code in more detail, because a few subtle things are happening.

New threads are created with the Thread.new call. It is given a block that contains the code to be run in a new thread. In our case, the block uses the net/http library to fetch the top page from each of our nominated sites. Our tracing clearly shows that these fetches are going on in parallel.

When we create the thread, we pass the required URL as a parameter. This parameter is passed to the block as url. Why do we do this, rather than simply using the value of the variable page_to_fetch within the block?

A thread shares all global, instance, and local variables that are in existence at the time the thread starts. As anyone with a kid brother can tell you, sharing isn't always a good thing. In this case, all three threads would share the variable page_to_fetch. The first thread gets started, and page_to_fetch is set to "www.rubycentral.com". In the meantime, the loop creating the threads is still running. The second time around, page_to_fetch gets set to "slashdot.org". If the first thread has not yet finished using the page_to_fetch variable, it will suddenly start using this new value. These kinds of bugs are difficult to track down.

However, local variables created within a thread's block are truly local to that thread—each thread will have its own copy of these variables. In our case, the variable url will be set at the time the thread is created, and each thread will have its own copy of the page address. You can pass any number of arguments into the block via Thread.new.

This code also illustrates a gotcha. Inside the loop, the threads use print to write out the messages, rather than puts. Why? Because behind the scenes, puts splits its work into two chunks: it writes its argument, and then it writes a newline. Between these two, a thread could get scheduled, and the output would be interleaved. Calling print with a single string that already contains the newline gets around the problem.

Manipulating Threads

Another subtlety occurs on the last line in our download program. Why do we call join on each of the threads we created?

When a Ruby program terminates, all threads are killed, regardless of their states. However, you can wait for a particular thread to finish by calling that thread's Thread#join method. The calling thread will block until the given thread is finished. By calling join on each of the requester threads, you can make sure that all three requests have completed before you terminate the main program. If you don't want to block forever, you can give join a timeout parameter—if the timeout expires before the thread terminates, the join call returns nil. Another variant of join, the method Thread#value, returns the value of the last statement executed by the thread.

In addition to join, a few other handy routines are used to manipulate threads. The current thread is always accessible using Thread.current. You can obtain a list of all threads using Thread.list, which returns a list of all Thread objects that are runnable or stopped. To determine the status of a particular thread, you can use Thread#status and Thread#alive?.

In addition, you can adjust the priority of a thread using Thread#priority= . Higher-priority threads will run before lower-priority threads. We'll talk more about thread scheduling, and stopping and starting threads, in just a bit.

Thread Variables

A thread can normally access any variables that are in scope when the thread is created. Variables local to the block containing the thread code are local to the thread and are not shared.

But what if you need per-thread variables that can be accessed by other threads—including the main thread? Class Thread features a special facility that allows thread-local variables to be created and accessed by name. You simply treat the thread object as if it were a Hash, writing to elements using []= and reading them back using []. In the example that follows, each thread records the current value of the variable count in a thread-local variable with the key mycount. To do this, the code uses the string "mycount" when indexing thread objects. (A *race condition*[1] exists in this code, but we haven't talked about synchronization yet, so we'll just quietly ignore it for now.)

```
tutthreads_6.rb
count = 0
threads = []
10.times do |i|
  threads[i] = Thread.new do
    sleep(rand(0.1))
    Thread.current["mycount"] = count
    count += 1
  end
end
threads.each {|t| t.join; print t["mycount"], ", " }
puts "count = #{count}"
```

---

1. A race condition occurs when two or more pieces of code (or hardware) both try to access some shared resource, and the outcome changes depending on the order in which they do so. In the example here, it is possible for one thread to set the value of its mycount variable to count, but before it gets a chance to increment count, the thread gets descheduled and another thread reuses the same value of count. These issues are fixed by synchronizing the access to shared resources (such as the count variable).

produces:

```
7, 0, 8, 6, 5, 4, 1, 9, 3, 2, count = 10
```

The main thread waits for the subthreads to finish and then prints out the value of count captured by each. Just to make it more interesting, we have each thread wait a random time before recording the value.

Threads and Exceptions

What happens if a thread raises an unhandled exception? It depends on the setting of the abort_on_exception flag (documented on pages 696 and 698) and on the setting of the interpreter's *debug* flag (described on page 220).

If abort_on_exception is false and the debug flag is not enabled (the default condition), an unhandled exception simply kills the current thread—all the rest continue to run. In fact, you don't even hear about the exception until you issue a join on the thread that raised it. In the following example, thread 2 blows up and fails to produce any output. However, you can still see the trace from the other threads.

tutthreads_7.rb

```ruby
threads = []
4.times do |number|
  threads << Thread.new(number) do |i|
    raise "Boom!" if i == 2
    print "#{i}\n"
  end
end
sleep 1
```

produces:

```
0
1
3
```

You normally don't use sleep to wait for threads to terminate. Instead, you'll use the join method. If you join to a thread that has raised an exception, then that exception will be raised in the thread that does the joining:

tutthreads_8.rb

```ruby
threads = []
4.times do |number|
  threads << Thread.new(number) do |i|
    raise "Boom!" if i == 2
    print "#{i}\n"
  end
end
threads.each do |t|
  begin
    t.join
  rescue RuntimeError => e
    puts "Failed: #{e.message}"
  end
end
```

produces:

```
0
1
3
Failed: Boom!
```

However, set abort_on_exception to true or use -d to turn on the debug flag, and an unhandled exception kills all running threads. Once thread 2 dies, no more output is produced.

```
tutthreads_9.rb
Thread.abort_on_exception = true
threads = []
4.times do |number|
  threads << Thread.new(number) do |i|
    raise "Boom!" if i == 2
    print "#{i}\n"
  end
end
threads.each {|t| t.join }
```

produces:

```
0
1
3
prog.rb:5:in `block (2 levels) in <main>': Boom! (RuntimeError)
```

Controlling the Thread Scheduler

In a well-designed application, you'll normally just let threads do their thing; building timing dependencies into a multithreaded application is generally considered to be bad form, because it makes the code far more complex and also prevents the thread scheduler from optimizing the execution of your program.

Class Thread provides a number of methods that control the scheduler. Invoking Thread.stop stops the current thread, and invoking Thread#run arranges for a particular thread to be run. Thread.pass deschedules the current thread, allowing others to run, and Thread#join and Thread#value suspend the calling thread until a given thread finishes. These last two are the only low-level thread control methods that the average program should use. In fact, I now consider most of the other low-level thread control methods too dangerous to use correctly in programs I write.[2] Fortunately, Ruby has support for higher-level thread synchronization.

---

2.   And, worse, some of these primitives are unsafe in use. Charles Nutter of JRuby fame has a blog post that illustrates one problem:
http://headius.blogspot.com/2008/02/rubys-threadraise-threadkill-timeoutrb.html

Mutual Exclusion

Let's start by looking at a simple example of a race condition—two threads updating a shared variable:

```
tutthreads_10.rb
def inc(n)
  n + 1
end

sum = 0
threads = (1..10).map do
  Thread.new do
    10_000.times do
      sum = inc(sum)
    end
  end
end

threads.each(&:join)
p sum
```

produces:

```
70583
```

We create 10 threads, and each increments the shared sum variable 10,000 times. And yet, when the threads all finish, the final value in sum is considerably less than 100,000. Clearly we have a race condition. In one thread, we call inc, passing it the current value in sum— let's say that value is 99. It returns the new value 100, which we assign back into sum. But what happens if, during that sequence, another thread gets scheduled? It also passes the value 99 to inc. Let's say the second thread finishes the call to inc first. It assigns 100 back into sum. Then the first thread gets rescheduled and finishes its call to inc. That call returns 100 as well, which gets assigned into sum. So, we had two calls, in two threads, but the overall effect was that sum changed only from 99 to 100. We lost data.

Fortunately, that's easy to fix. We can use the built-in class Mutex to create synchronized regions—areas of code that only one thread may enter at a time.

Some schools coordinate students' access to the bathrooms during class time using a system of bathroom passes. Each room has two passes, one for girls and one for boys. To visit the bathroom, you have to take the appropriate pass with you. If someone else already has that pass, you have to cross your legs and wait for them to return. The bathroom pass controls access to the critical resource—you have to own the pass to use the resource, and only one person can own it at a time.

A mutex is like that bathroom pass. You create a mutex to control access to a resource and then lock it when you want to use that resource. If no one else has it locked, your thread continues to run. If someone else has already locked that particular mutex, your thread suspends until they unlock it.

Here's a version of our counting code that uses a mutex to ensure that only one thread updates the count at a time:

```
tutthreads_11.rb
def inc(n)
  n + 1
end
sum = 0
mutex = Mutex.new
threads = (1..10).map do
  Thread.new do
    10_000.times do
      mutex.lock        ####
      sum = inc(sum)        # one at a time, please
      mutex.unlock      ####
    end
  end
end
threads.each(&:join)
p sum
```

produces:

```
100000
```

This pattern is so common that the Mutex class provides Mutex#synchronize, which locks the mutex, runs the code in a block, then unlocks the mutex. This also ensures that the mutex will get unlocked even if an exception is thrown while it is locked.

```
tutthreads_12.rb
def inc(n)
  n + 1
end
sum = 0
mutex = Mutex.new
threads = (1..10).map do
  Thread.new do
    10_000.times do
      mutex.synchronize do   ####
        sum = inc(sum)          # one at a time, please
      end                    ####
    end
  end
end
threads.each(&:join)
p sum
```

produces:

```
100000
```

There are times when you want to claim a mutex lock if the mutex is currently unlocked, but you don't want to suspend the current thread if it isn't. The Mutex#try_lock method does just that, taking the lock if it can, but returning false if the lock is already taken. The following code illustrates a hypothetical currency converter. The ExchangeRates class caches rates from an online feed, and a background thread updates that cache once an hour. This update takes a minute or so. In the main thread, we interact with our user. However, rather than just go dead if we can't claim the mutex that protects the rate object, we use try_lock and print a status message if the update is in process.

```ruby
rate_mutex = Mutex.new
exchange_rates = ExchangeRates.new
exchange_rates.update_from_online_feed

Thread.new do
  loop do
    sleep 3600
    rate_mutex.synchronize do
      exchange_rates.update_from_online_feed
    end
  end
end

loop do
  print "Enter currency code and amount: "
  line = gets
  if rate_mutex.try_lock
    begin
      puts exchange_rates.convert(line)
    ensure
      rate_mutex.unlock
    end
  else
    puts "Sorry, rates being updated. Try again in a minute"
  end
end
```

If you are holding the lock on a mutex and you want to temporarily unlock it, allowing others to use it, you can call Mutex#sleep. We could use this to rewrite the previous example:

```ruby
rate_mutex = Mutex.new
exchange_rates = ExchangeRates.new
exchange_rates.update_from_online_feed

Thread.new do
  rate_mutex.lock
  loop do
    rate_mutex.sleep 3600
    exchange_rates.update_from_online_feed
  end
end

loop do
  print "Enter currency code and amount: "
  line = gets
  if rate_mutex.try_lock
    begin
      puts exchange_rates.convert(line)
```

```
    ensure
      rate_mutex.unlock
    end
  else
    puts "Sorry, rates being updated. Try again in a minute"
  end
end
```

Queues and Condition Variables

Most of the examples in this chapter use the Mutex class for synchronization. However, another technique is useful, particularly when you need to synchronize work between producers and consumers. The Queue class, located in the thread library, implements a thread-safe queuing mechanism. Multiple threads can add and remove objects from each queue, and each addition and removal is guaranteed to be atomic. For an example, see the description of the thread library on page 808.

A condition variable is a controlled way of communicating an event (or a condition) between two threads. One thread can wait on the condition, and the other can signal it. The thread library extends threads with condition variables. Again, see the library description for an example.

Running Multiple Processes

Sometimes you may want to split a task into several process-sized chunks—maybe to take advantage of all those cores in your shiny new processor. Or perhaps you need to run a separate process that was not written in Ruby. Not a problem: Ruby has a number of methods by which you may spawn and manage separate processes.

Spawning New Processes

You have several ways to spawn a separate process; the easiest is to run some command and wait for it to complete. You may find yourself doing this to run some separate command or retrieve data from the host system. Ruby does this for you with the system and backquote (or backtick) methods:

```
system("tar xzf test.tgz")   # =>   true
result = `date`
result                       # =>   "Tue Mar 31 09:57:54 CDT 2009\n"
```

The method Kernel.system executes the given command in a subprocess; it returns true if the command was found and executed properly. It raises an exception if the command cannot be found. It returns false if the command ran but returned an error. In case of failure, you'll find the subprocess's exit code in the global variable $?.

One problem with system is that the command's output will simply go to the same destination as your program's output, which may not be what you want. To capture the standard output of a subprocess, you can use the backquote characters, as with `date` in the previous example. Remember that you may need to use String#chomp to remove the line-ending characters from the result.

OK, this is fine for simple cases—we can run some other process and get the return status. But many times we need a bit more control than that. We'd like to carry on a conversation with the subprocess, possibly sending it data and possibly getting some back. The method IO.popen does just this. The popen method runs a command as a subprocess and connects that subprocess's standard input and standard output to a Ruby IO object. Write to the IO object, and the subprocess can read it on standard input. Whatever the subprocess writes is available in the Ruby program by reading from the IO object.

For example, on our systems one of the more useful utilities is pig, a program that reads words from standard input and prints them in pig latin (or igpay atinlay). We can use this when our Ruby programs need to send us output that our five-year-olds shouldn't be able to understand:

```
pig = IO.popen("/usr/local/rubybook/bin/pig", "w+")
pig.puts "ice cream after they go to bed"
pig.close_write
puts pig.gets
```

produces:

```
iceway eamcray afterway eythay ogay otay edbay
```

This example illustrates both the apparent simplicity and the more subtle real-world complexities involved in driving subprocesses through pipes. The code certainly looks simple enough: open the pipe, write a phrase, and read back the response. But it turns out that the pig program doesn't flush the output it writes. Our original attempt at this example, which had a pig.puts followed by a pig.gets, hung forever. The pig program processed our input, but its response was never written to the pipe. We had to insert the pig.close_write line. This sends an end-of-file to pig's standard input, and the output we're looking for gets flushed as pig terminates.

popen has one more twist. If the command you pass it is a single minus sign (−), popen will fork a new Ruby interpreter. Both this and the original interpreter will continue running by returning from the popen. The original process will receive an IO object back, and the child will receive nil. This works only on operating systems that support the fork(2) call (and for now this excludes Windows).

tutthreads_17.rb

```
pipe = IO.popen("-","w+")
if pipe
  pipe.puts "Get a job!"
  STDERR.puts "Child says '#{pipe.gets.chomp}'"
else
  STDERR.puts "Dad says '#{gets.chomp}'"
  puts "OK"
end
```

produces:

```
Dad says 'Get a job!'
Child says 'OK'
```

In addition to the popen method, some platforms support the methods Kernel.fork, Kernel.exec, and IO.pipe. The filenaming convention of many IO methods and Kernel.open will also spawn subprocesses if you put a | as the first character of the filename (see the introduction to class IO on page 537 for details). Note that you *cannot* create pipes using File.new; it's just for files.

Independent Children

Sometimes we don't need to be quite so hands-on; we'd like to give the subprocess its assignment and then go on about our business. Sometime later, we'll check to see whether it has finished. For instance, we may want to kick off a long-running external sort:

```
exec("sort testfile > output.txt") if fork.nil?
# The sort is now running in a child process
# carry on processing in the main program
# ... dum di dum ...
# then wait for the sort to finish
Process.wait
```

The call to Kernel.fork returns a process ID in the parent, and nil in the child, so the child process will perform the Kernel.exec call and run sort. Sometime later, we issue a Process.wait call, which waits for the sort to complete (and returns its process ID).

If you'd rather be notified when a child exits (instead of just waiting around), you can set up a signal handler using Kernel.trap (described on page 570). Here we set up a trap on SIGCLD, which is the signal sent on "death of child process":

```
trap("CLD") do
  pid = Process.wait
  puts "Child pid #{pid}: terminated"
end
fork { exec("sort testfile > output.txt") }
# Do other stuff...
```

produces:

```
Child pid 45389: terminated
```

For more information on using and controlling external processes, see the documentation for Kernel.open, IO.popen, and the section on the Process module on page 632.

Blocks and Subprocesses

IO.popen works with a block in pretty much the same way as File.open does. If you pass it a command, such as date, the block will be passed an IO object as a parameter:

tutthreads_20.rb

```
IO.popen("date") {|f| puts "Date is #{f.gets}" }
```

produces:

```
Date is Tue Mar 31 09:57:54 CDT 2009
```

The IO object will be closed automatically when the code block exits, just as it is with File.open.

If you associate a block with Kernel.fork, the code in the block will be run in a Ruby sub-process, and the parent will continue after the block:

`tutthreads_21.rb`

```
fork do
  puts "In child, pid = #$$"
  exit 99
end
pid = Process.wait
puts "Child terminated, pid = #{pid}, status = #{$?.exitstatus}"
```

produces:

```
In child, pid = 45396
Child terminated, pid = 45396, status = 99
```

$? is a global variable that contains information on the termination of a subprocess. See the section on Process::Status beginning on page 641 for more information.

## Chapter 13

Unit Testing

Unit testing is testing that focuses on small chunks (units) of code, typically individual methods or lines within methods. This is in contrast to most other forms of testing, which consider the system as a whole.

Why focus in so tightly? It's because ultimately all software is constructed in layers; code on one layer relies on the correct operation of the code in the layers below. If this underlying code turns out to contain bugs, then all higher layers are potentially affected. This is a big problem. Fred may write some code with a bug one week, and then you may end up calling it, indirectly, two months later. When your code generates incorrect results, it will take you a while to track down the problem in Fred's method. And when you ask Fred why he wrote it that way, the likely answer will be "I don't remember. That was months ago."

If instead Fred had unit tested his code when he wrote it, two things would have happened. First, he'd have found the bug while the code was still fresh in his mind. Second, because the unit test was only looking at the code he'd just written, when the bug *did* appear, he'd only have to look through a handful of lines of code to find it, rather than doing archaeology on the rest of the code base.

Unit testing helps developers write better code. It helps before the code is actually written, because thinking about testing leads you naturally to create better, more decoupled designs. It helps as you're writing the code, because it gives you instant feedback on how accurate your code is. And it helps after you've written code, both because it gives you the ability to check that the code still works and because it helps others understand how to use your code.

Unit testing is a Good Thing.

But why have a chapter on unit testing in the middle of a book on Ruby? Well, it's because unit testing and languages such as Ruby seem to go hand in hand. The flexibility of Ruby makes writing tests easy, and the tests make it easier to verify that your code is working. Once you get into the swing of it, you'll find yourself writing a little code, writing a test or two, verifying that everything is copacetic, and then writing some more code.

Unit testing is also pretty trivial—run a program that calls part of your application's code, get back some results, and then check the results are what you expected.

Let's say we're testing a Roman number class. So far the code is pretty simple: it just lets us create an object representing a certain number and display that object in Roman numerals:

```
unittesting_1.rb
# NOTE:  This code has bugs!
class Roman
  MAX_ROMAN = 4999

  def initialize(value)
    if value <= 0 || value > MAX_ROMAN
      fail "Roman values must be > 0 and <= #{MAX_ROMAN}"
    end
    @value = value
  end

  FACTORS = [["m", 1000], ["cm", 900], ["d",  500], ["cd", 400],
             ["c",  100], ["xc",  90], ["l",   50], ["xl",  40],
             ["x",   10], ["ix",   9], ["v",    5], ["iv",   4],
             ["i",    1]]

  def to_s
    value = @value
    roman = ""
    for code, factor in FACTORS
      count, value = value.divmod(factor)
      roman << code unless count.zero?
    end
    roman
  end
end
```

We could test this code by writing another program, like this:

```
require 'roman'

r = Roman.new(1)
fail "'i' expected" unless r.to_s == "i"

r = Roman.new(9)
fail "'ix' expected" unless r.to_s == "ix"
```

However, as the number of tests in a project grows, this kind of ad hoc approach can start to get complicated to manage. Over the years, various unit testing frameworks have emerged to help structure the testing process. Ruby comes with one preinstalled. In Ruby 1.8, this used to be Nathaniel Talbott's Test::Unit framework. Ruby 1.9 instead comes with Ryan Davis' MiniTest.

MiniTest is largely compatible with Test::Unit but without a lot of bells and whistles (test-case runners, GUI support, and so on). However, because there are areas where it is different and because there are tens of thousands of tests out there that assume the Test::Unit API, Ryan has also added a compatibility layer to MiniTest. For a little bit more information on the differences between the two, see the sidebar on the facing page. In this chapter, we'll be using the Test::Unit wrapper, because it automatically runs tests for us. But we'll also be using some of the new assertions available in MiniTest.

MiniTest::Unit vs. Test::Unit

Folks have been using Test::Unit with Ruby for a good number of years now. However, the core team decided to replace the testing framework that comes as standard with Ruby with something a little leaner. Ryan Davis and Eric Hodel wrote MiniTest::Unit as a partial drop-in replacement for Test::Unit.

Most of the assertions in MiniTest mirror those in Test::Unit::TestCase. The major differences are the absence of assert_not_raises and assert_not_throws and the renaming of all the negative assertions. Whereas in Test::Unit you'd say assert_not_nil(x) and assert_not(x), in MiniTest you'd use refute_nil(x) and refute(x).

MiniTest also drops most of the little-used features of Test::Unit, including test cases, GUI runners, and some assertions.

And, probably most significantly, MiniTest does not automatically invoke the test cases when you execute a file that contains them.

So, you have three basic options with this style of unit testing:

- require 'minitest/unit' and use the MiniTest functionality.

- require 'test/unit' and use Minitest with the Test::Unit compatibility layer. This adds in the assertions in Figure 13.2 on page 204 and reenables the autorun functionality.

- You can install the test-unit gem and get all the original Test::Unit functionality back.

The Testing Framework

The Ruby testing framework is basically three facilities wrapped into a neat package:

- It gives you a way of expressing individual tests.

- It provides a framework for structuring the tests.

- It gives you flexible ways of invoking the tests.

Assertions == Expected Results

Rather than have you write series of individual if statements in your tests, the testing framework provides a set of assertions that achieve the same thing. Although a number of different styles of assertion exist, they all follow basically the same pattern. Each assertion gives you a way of specifying a desired result or outcome and a way of passing in the actual outcome. If the actual doesn't equal the expected, the assertion outputs a nice message and records the fact as a failure.

For example, we could rewrite our previous test of the Roman class using the testing framework. For now, ignore the scaffolding code at the start and end, and just look at the assert_equal methods:

```
unittesting_3.rb
require 'roman'
require 'test/unit'
class TestRoman < MiniTest::Unit::TestCase
  def test_simple
    assert_equal("i",  Roman.new(1).to_s)
    assert_equal("ix", Roman.new(9).to_s)
  end
end
```

produces:

```
Loaded suite /tmp/prog
Started
.
Finished in 0.000413 seconds.

1 tests, 2 assertions, 0 failures, 0 errors, 0 skips
```

The first assertion says that we're expecting the Roman number string representation of 1 to be "i," and the second test says we expect 9 to be "ix." Luckily for us, both expectations are met, and the tracing reports that our tests pass. Let's add a few more tests:

```
unittesting_4.rb
require 'roman'
require 'test/unit'
class TestRoman < Test::Unit::TestCase
  def test_simple
    assert_equal("i",   Roman.new(1).to_s)
    assert_equal("ii",  Roman.new(2).to_s)
    assert_equal("iii", Roman.new(3).to_s)
    assert_equal("iv",  Roman.new(4).to_s)
    assert_equal("ix",  Roman.new(9).to_s)
  end
end
```

produces:

```
Loaded suite /tmp/prog
Started
F
Finished in 0.000591 seconds.

  1) Failure:
<"ii"> expected but was
<"i">.

1 tests, 2 assertions, 1 failures, 0 errors, 0 skips
test_simple(TestRoman) [/tmp/prog.rb:8]:
```

Uh-oh! The second assertion failed. See how the error message uses the fact that the assert knows both the expected and actual values: it expected to get "ii" but instead got "i." Looking at our code, you can see a clear bug in to_s. If the count after dividing by the factor is greater than zero, then we should output that many Roman digits. The existing code outputs just one. The fix is easy:

```
unittesting_5.rb
def to_s
  value = @value
  roman = ""
  for code, factor in FACTORS
    count, value = value.divmod(factor)
    roman << (code * count)
  end
  roman
end
```

Now let's run our tests again:

```
Loaded suite /tmp/prog
Started
.
Finished in 0.000460 seconds.

1 tests, 5 assertions, 0 failures, 0 errors, 0 skips
```

Looking good. We can now go a step further and remove some of that duplication:

```
unittesting_7.rb
require 'roman'
require 'test/unit'
class TestRoman < Test::Unit::TestCase

  NUMBERS = [
    [ 1, "i" ], [ 2, "ii" ], [ 3, "iii" ],
    [ 4, "iv"], [ 5, "v" ], [ 9, "ix"  ]
  ]

  def test_simple
    NUMBERS.each do |arabic, roman|
      r = Roman.new(arabic)
      assert_equal(roman, r.to_s)
    end
  end
end
```

produces:

```
Loaded suite /tmp/prog
Started
.
Finished in 0.000467 seconds.

1 tests, 6 assertions, 0 failures, 0 errors, 0 skips
```

What else can we test? Well, the constructor checks that the number we pass in can be represented as a Roman number, throwing an exception if it can't. Let's test the exception:

`unittesting_8.rb`

```ruby
require 'roman'
require 'test/unit'
class TestRoman < Test::Unit::TestCase
  def test_range
    # no exception for these two...
    Roman.new(1)
    Roman.new(4999)
    # but an exception for these
    assert_raises(RuntimeError) { Roman.new(0) }
    assert_raises(RuntimeError) { Roman.new(5000) }
  end
end
```

produces:

```
Loaded suite /tmp/prog
Started

.
Finished in 0.000607 seconds.

1 tests, 2 assertions, 0 failures, 0 errors, 0 skips
```

We could do a lot more testing on our Roman class, but let's move on to bigger and better things. Before we go, though, we should say that we've only scratched the surface of the set of assertions available inside the testing framework. For example, for every positive assertion, such as assert_equal, there's a negative refutation (in this case refute_equal). Figure 13.2 on page 204 lists the additional assertions you get if you load the Test::Unit shim (which we do in this chapter), and Figure 13.1 on page 203 gives a full list of the MiniTest assertions.

The final parameter to every assertion is a message that will be output before any failure message. This normally isn't needed, because the failure messages are normally pretty reasonable. The one exception is the test refute_nil (or assert_not_nil in Test::Unit), where the message "Expected nil to not be nil" doesn't help much. In that case, you may want to add some annotation of your own. (This code assumes the existence of some kind of User class.)

`unittesting_9.rb`

```ruby
require 'test/unit'
class ATestThatFails < Test::Unit::TestCase
  def test_user_created
    user = User.find(1)
    refute_nil(user, "User with ID=1 should exist")
  end
end
```

produces:

```
Loaded suite /tmp/prog
Started
```

```
F
Finished in 0.000533 seconds.

  1) Failure:
User with ID=1 should exist.
Expected nil to not be nil.

1 tests, 1 assertions, 1 failures, 0 errors, 0 skips
test_user_created(ATestThatFails) [/tmp/prog.rb:10]:
```

Structuring Tests

Earlier we asked you to ignore the scaffolding around our tests. Now it's time to look at it.

You include the testing framework facilities in your unit test with either this:

```
require 'test/unit'
```

or, for raw MiniTest, with this:

```
require 'minitest/unit'
```

Unit tests seem to fall quite naturally into high-level groupings, called *test cases*, and lower-level groupings, the test methods themselves. The test cases generally contain all the tests relating to a particular facility or feature. Our Roman number class is fairly simple, so all the tests for it will probably be in a single test case. Within the test case, you'll probably want to organize your assertions into a number of test methods, where each method contains the assertions for one type of test; one method could check regular number conversions, another could test error handling, and so on.

The classes that represent test cases must be subclasses of Test::Unit::TestCase. The methods that hold the assertions must have names that start with test. This is important: the testing framework uses reflection to find tests to run, and only methods whose names start with test are eligible.

Quite often you'll find all of the test methods within a test case start by setting up a particular scenario. Each test method then probes some aspect of that scenario. Finally, each method may then tidy up after itself. For example, we could be testing a class that extracts jukebox playlists from a database:

```
unittesting_12.rb
require 'test/unit'
require 'dbi'
require 'playlist_builder'
class TestPlaylistBuilder < Test::Unit::TestCase
  def test_empty_playlist
    db = DBI.connect('DBI:mysql:playlists')
    pb = PlaylistBuilder.new(db)
    assert_empty(pb.playlist)
    db.disconnect
  end
```

```ruby
  def test_artist_playlist
    db = DBI.connect('DBI:mysql:playlists')
    pb = PlaylistBuilder.new(db)
    pb.include_artist("krauss")
    refute_empty(pb.playlist, "Playlist shouldn't be empty")
    pb.playlist.each do |entry|
      assert_match(/krauss/i, entry.artist)
    end
    db.disconnect
  end

  def test_title_playlist
    db = DBI.connect('DBI:mysql:playlists')
    pb = PlaylistBuilder.new(db)
    pb.include_title("midnight")
    refute_empty(pb.playlist, "Playlist shouldn't be empty")
    pb.playlist.each do |entry|
      assert_match(/midnight/i, entry.title)
    end
    db.disconnect
  end
  # ...
end
```

produces:

```
Loaded suite /tmp/prog
Started
...
Finished in 0.000610 seconds.

3 tests, 46 assertions, 0 failures, 0 errors, 0 skips
```

Each test starts by connecting to the database and creating a new playlist builder. Each test ends by disconnecting from the database. (The idea of using a real database in unit tests is questionable, because unit tests are supposed to be fast running, context independent, and easy to set up, but it illustrates a point.)

We can extract all this common code into *setup* and *teardown* methods. Within a TestCase class, a method called setup will be run before each and every test method, and a method called teardown will be run after each test method finishes. Let's emphasize that: the setup and teardown methods bracket each test, rather than being run once per test case. Our test would then become this:

```ruby
unittesting_13.rb
require 'test/unit'
require 'dbi'
require 'playlist_builder'

class TestPlaylistBuilder < Test::Unit::TestCase
  def setup
    @db = DBI.connect('DBI:mysql:playlists')
    @pb = PlaylistBuilder.new(@db)
  end
```

```
    def teardown
      @db.disconnect
    end
    def test_empty_playlist
      assert_empty(@pb.playlist)
    end
    def test_artist_playlist
      @pb.include_artist("krauss")
      refute_empty(@pb.playlist, "Playlist shouldn't be empty")
      @pb.playlist.each do |entry|
        assert_match(/krauss/i, entry.artist)
      end
    end
    def test_title_playlist
      @pb.include_title("midnight")
      refute_empty(@pb.playlist, "Playlist shouldn't be empty")
      @pb.playlist.each do |entry|
        assert_match(/midnight/i, entry.title)
      end
    end
    # ...
  end
```

produces:

```
Loaded suite /tmp/prog
Started
...
Finished in 0.000610 seconds.

3 tests, 46 assertions, 0 failures, 0 errors, 0 skips
```

Inside the teardown method, you can detect whether the preceding test succeeded with the passed? method.

Organizing and Running Tests

The test cases we've shown so far are all runnable Test::Unit programs. If, for example, the test case for the Roman class was in a file called test_roman.rb, we could run the tests from the command line using this:

```
% ruby test_roman.rb
Loaded suite test_roman
Started
..
Finished in 0.000649 seconds.

2 tests, 7 assertions, 0 failures, 0 errors, 0 skips
```

Test::Unit is clever enough to run the tests even though there's no main program. It collects all the test case classes and runs each in turn.

If we want, we can ask it to run just a particular test method:

```
% ruby test_roman.rb -n test_range
Loaded suite test_roman
Started
.
Finished in 0.000560 seconds.

1 tests, 2 assertions, 0 failures, 0 errors, 0 skips
```

or tests whose names match a regular expression:

```
% ruby test_roman.rb -n /range/
Loaded suite test_roman
Started
.
Finished in 0.000570 seconds.

1 tests, 2 assertions, 0 failures, 0 errors, 0 skips
```

This last capability is a great way of grouping your tests. Use meaningful names, and you'll be able to run (for example) all the shopping-cart-related tests by simply running tests with names matching /cart/.

Where to Put Tests

Once you get into unit testing, you may well find yourself generating almost as much test code as production code. All of those tests have to live somewhere. The problem is that if you put them alongside your regular production code source files, your directories start to get bloated—effectively you end up with two files for every production source file.

A common solution is to have a test/ directory where you place all your test source files. This directory is then placed parallel to the directory containing the code you're developing. For example, for our Roman numeral class, we may have this:

```
roman
    ├── lib/
    │     ├── roman.rb
    │     └── other files...
    ├── test/
    │     ├── test_roman.rb
    │     └── other tests...
    └── other stuff
```

This works well as a way of organizing files but leaves you with a small problem: how do you tell Ruby where to find the library files to test? For example, if our TestRoman test code was in a test/ subdirectory, how does Ruby know where to find the roman.rb source file, the thing we're trying to test?

An option that *doesn't* work reliably is to build the path into require statements in the test code and run the tests from the `test/` subdirectory:

```
require 'test/unit'
require '../lib/roman'
class TestRoman < Test::Unit::TestCase
  # ...
end
```

Why doesn't it work? Because our `roman.rb` file may itself require other source files in the library we're writing. It'll load them using require (without the leading ../lib/), and because they aren't in Ruby's $LOAD_PATH, they won't be found. Our test just won't run. A second, less immediate problem is that we won't be able to use these same tests to test our classes once installed on a target system, because then they'll be referenced simply using require 'roman'.

A better solution is to assume that your Ruby program is packaged according to the conventions we'll be discussing in Section 16 on page 237. In this arrangement, the top-level directory of your application is assumed to be in Ruby's load path by all other components of the application. Given that, your unit tests can assume that they can find the components they are testing using the path lib/xxx.rb.

Your test code would then be as follows:

```
require 'test/unit'
require 'lib/roman'
class TestRoman < Test::Unit::TestCase
  # ...
end
```

And you'd run it using this:

```
% ruby -I path/to/app path/to/app/test/test_roman.rb
```

The normal case, where you're already in the application's directory, would be as follows:

```
% ruby -I . test/test_roman.rb
```

This would be a good time to investigate using Rake to automate your testing....

Test Suites

After a while, you'll grow a decent collection of test cases for your application. You may well find that these tend to cluster: one group of cases tests a particular set of functions, and another group tests a different set of functions. If so, you can group those test cases together into *test suites*, letting you run them all as a group.

This is easy to do—just create a Ruby file that requires `test/unit` and then requires each of the files holding the test cases you want to group. This way, you build yourself a hierarchy of test material.

- You can run individual tests by name.
- You can run all the tests in a file by running that file.

- You can group a number of files into a test suite and run them as a unit.
- You can group test suites into other test suites.

This gives you the ability to run your unit tests at a level of granularity that you control, testing just one method or testing the entire application.

At this point, it's worthwhile to think about naming conventions. Nathaniel Talbott, the author of Test::Unit, uses the convention that test cases are in files named tc_*xxx* and test suites are in files named ts_*xxx*. Most people seem to use test_ as the test-case filename prefix:

```
# file ts_dbaccess.rb
require 'test/unit'
require 'test_connect'
require 'test_query'
require 'test_update'
require 'test_delete'
```

Now, if you run Ruby on the file ts_dbaccess.rb, you execute the test cases in the four files you've required.

RSpec and Shoulda

The built-in testing framework has a lot going for it. It is simple, and it is compatible in style with frameworks from other languages (such as JUnit for Java and NUnit for C#).

However, there's a growing movement in the Ruby community to use a different style of testing. So-called behavior-driven development encourages people to write tests in terms of your expectations of the program's behavior in a given set of circumstances. In many ways, this is like testing according to the content of *user stories*, a common requirements-gathering technique in agile methodologies. With these testing frameworks, the focus is not on assertions. Instead, you write expectations.

Although both RSpec and Shoulda allow this style of testing, they focus on different things. RSpec is very much concerned with driving the design side of things. You can write and execute specs with RSpec well before you've written a line of application code. These specs, when run, will output the user stories that describe your application. Then, as you fill in the code, the specs mutate into tests that validate that your code meets your expectations.

Shoulda, on the other hand, is really more focused on the testing side. Whereas RSpec is a complete framework, Shoulda works inside Test::Unit—you can even mix Shoulda tests with regular Test::Unit test methods.

Let's start with a simple example of RSpec in action.

Starting to Score Tennis Matches

The scoring system used in lawn tennis originated in the middle ages. As players win successive points, their scores are shown as 15, 30, and 40. The next point is a win unless your opponent also has 40. If you're both tied at 40, then different rules apply—the first player with a clear two-point advantage is the winner.[1]

We're tasked with writing a class that handles this scoring system. Let's use RSpec specifications to drive the process. We install RSpec with gem install rspec. We'll then create our first specification file:

```
unittesting_20.rb
describe "TennisScorer", "basic scoring" do
  it "should start with a score of 0-0"
  it "should be 15-0 if the server wins a point"
  it "should be 0-15 if the receiver wins a point"
  it "should be 15-15 after they both win a point"
  # ...
end
```

This file contains nothing more than a description of an aspect of the tennis scoring class (that we haven't yet written, by the way). It contains a description of the basic scoring system. Inside the description are a set of four expectations (it "should start..." and so on). We can run this specification using the spec command:

```
$ spec ts_spec.rb
```

produces:

```
****

Pending:

TennisScorer basic scoring should start with a score of 0-0 (Not Yet
 Implemented)
ts_spec.rb:2:in `block in <top (required)>'

TennisScorer basic scoring should be 15-0 if the server wins a point
 (Not Yet Implemented)
ts_spec.rb:3:in `block in <top (required)>'

TennisScorer basic scoring should be 0-15 if the receiver wins a point
 (Not Yet Implemented)
ts_spec.rb:4:in `block in <top (required)>'

TennisScorer basic scoring should be 15-15 after they both win a point
 (Not Yet Implemented)
ts_spec.rb:5:in `block in <top (required)>'

Finished in 0.012842 seconds

4 examples, 0 failures, 4 pending
```

---

1. Some say the 0, 15, 30, 40 system is a corruption of the fact that scoring used to be done using the quarters of a clock face. Me, I just think those medieval folks enjoyed a good joke.

That's pretty cool. Executing the tests echoes our expectations back at us, telling us that each has yet to be implemented. Coding, like life, is full of these disappointments. However, unlike life, fixing things is just a few keystrokes away. Let's start by meeting the first expectation—when a game starts, the score should be 0 to 0. We'll start by fleshing out the test:

`unittesting_22.rb`

```
require "tennis_scorer"
describe TennisScorer do
  it "should start with a score of 0-0" do
    ts = TennisScorer.new
    ts.score.should == "0-0"
  end
  it "should be 15-0 if the server wins a point"
  it "should be 0-15 if the receiver wins a point"
  it "should be 15-15 after they both win a point"
end
```

Note that we've assumed we have a class TennisScorer in a file called tennis_scorer.rb. Our first expectation now has a code block associated with it. Inside that block, we create a TennisScorer and then use a funky RSpec syntax to validate that the score starts out at 0 to 0. This particular aspect of RSpec probably generates the most controversy—some people love it, others find it awkward. Either way, ts.score.should == "0-0" is basically the same as an assertion in Test::Unit.

We'll beef up our TennisScorer class, but only enough to let it satify this assertion:

`unittesting_23.rb`

```
class TennisScorer
  def score
    "0-0"
  end
end
```

Well run our spec again:

```
$ spec ts_spec.rb
```

produces:

```
.***

Pending:

TennisScorer should be 15-0 if the server wins a point (Not Yet
  Implemented)
ts_spec.rb:9:in `block in <top (required)>'

TennisScorer should be 0-15 if the receiver wins a point (Not Yet
  Implemented)
ts_spec.rb:10:in `block in <top (required)>'
```

```
TennisScorer should be 15-15 after they both win a point (Not Yet
 Implemented)
ts_spec.rb:11:in `block in <top (required)>'

Finished in 0.012792 seconds

4 examples, 0 failures, 3 pending
```

Note that we now have three pending expectations; the first one has been satisfied.

Let's flesh out the next expectation:

```ruby
require "tennis_scorer"
describe TennisScorer, "basic scoring" do
  it "should start with a score of 0-0" do
    ts = TennisScorer.new
    ts.score.should == "0-0"
  end
  it "should be 15-0 if the server wins a point" do
    ts = TennisScorer.new
    ts.give_point_to(:server)
    ts.score.should == "15-0"
  end


  it "should be 0-15 if the receiver wins a point"
  it "should be 15-15 after they both win a point"
end
```

This won't run, because our TennisScorer class doesn't implement a give_point_to method. Let's rectify that. Our code isn't finished, but it lets the test pass:

```ruby
class TennisScorer
  OPPOSITE_SIDE_OF_NET = {
    :server => :receiver,
    :receiver => :server
  }
  def initialize
    @score = { :server => 0, :receiver => 0 }
  end
  def score
    "#{@score[:server]*15}-#{@score[:receiver]*15}"
  end
  def give_point_to(player)
    other = OPPOSITE_SIDE_OF_NET[player]
    fail "Unknown player #{player}" unless other
    @score[player] += 1
  end
end
```

Again, we'll run the specification:

```
$ spec ts_spec.rb
```

produces:

```
..**

Pending:

TennisScorer basic scoring should be 0-15 if the receiver wins a point
 (Not Yet Implemented)
ts_spec.rb:16:in `block in <top (required)>'

TennisScorer basic scoring should be 15-15 after they both win a point
 (Not Yet Implemented)
ts_spec.rb:17:in `block in <top (required)>'

Finished in 0.01277 seconds

4 examples, 0 failures, 2 pending
```

We're now meeting two of the four initial expectations. But, before we move on, note there's a bit of duplication in the specification: both our expections create a new TennisScorer object. We can fix that by using a before stanza in the specification. This works a bit like the setup method in Test::Unit, allowing us to run code before expecations are executed. Let's use this feature and, at the same time, build out the last two expectations:

unittesting_28.rb

```ruby
require "tennis_scorer"
describe TennisScorer, "basic scoring" do
  before(:each) do
    @ts = TennisScorer.new
  end
  it "should start with a score of 0-0" do
    @ts.score.should == "0-0"
  end
  it "should be 15-0 if the server wins a point" do
    @ts.give_point_to(:server)
    @ts.score.should == "15-0"
  end
  it "should be 0-15 if the receiver wins a point" do
    @ts.give_point_to(:receiver)
    @ts.score.should == "0-15"
  end
  it "should be 15-15 after they both win a point" do
    @ts.give_point_to(:receiver)
    @ts.give_point_to(:server)
    @ts.score.should == "15-15"
  end
end
```

Let's run it:

```
$ spec ts_spec.rb
```

produces:

```
....

Finished in 0.012988 seconds

4 examples, 0 failures
```

We're going to stop here, but I suggest that you might want to take this code and continue to develop it. Write expectations such as these:

> `unittesting_30.rb`

```
it "should be 40-0 after the server wins three points"
it "should be W-L after the server wins four points"
it "should be L-W after the receiver wins four points"
it "should be Deuce after each wins three points"
it "should be A-server after each wins three points and the server
gets one more"
it "should be A-receiver after each wins three points and the receiver
gets one more"
```

and so on. Note that none of these expectations is met by our current implementation.

RSpec has a lot more depth than just the description of expectations. In particular, it has an entire language for describing and running complete user stories. But that's beyond the scope of this book.

Anyone for Shoulda?

RSpec is testing with attitude. On the other hand, Shoulda takes many of the ideas from RSpec and humbly offers them to you for integration into your regular unit tests. For many developers, particularly those with existing Test::Unit tests, this is a good compromise. You get much of the descriptive power of RSpec-style expectations without having to commit to the full framework.

Install Shoulda using this:

```
% gem install thoughtbot-shoulda --source=http://gems.github.com
```

Then, unlike RSpec, write a regular Test::Unit test case. Inside it, though, you can use the Shoulda mini-language to describe your tests.

Let's recast our final RSpec tennis scoring tests using Shoulda:

```
unittesting_31.rb
```

```ruby
require 'rubygems'
require 'test/unit'
require 'shoulda'
require 'tennis_scorer.rb'
class TennisScorerTest < Test::Unit::TestCase
  def assert_score(target)
    assert_equal(target, @ts.score)
  end
  context "Tennis scores" do
    setup do
      @ts = TennisScorer.new
    end
    should "start with a score of 0-0" do
      assert_score("0-0")
    end
    should "be 15-0 if the server wins a point" do
      @ts.give_point_to(:server)
      assert_score("15-0")
    end
    should "be 0-15 if the receiver wins a point" do
      @ts.give_point_to(:receiver)
      assert_score("0-15")
    end
    should "be 15-15 after they both win a point" do
      @ts.give_point_to(:receiver)
      @ts.give_point_to(:server)
      assert_score("15-15")
    end
  end
end
```

```
$ ruby ts_spec.rb
```

produces:

```
Loaded suite ts_shoulda
Started
....
Finished in 0.000622 seconds.

4 tests, 4 assertions, 0 failures, 0 errors, 0 skips
```

Behind the scenes, Shoulda is creating Test::Unit test methods for each should block in your tests. This is why we can use regular test::Unit assertions in Shoulda code. But Shoulda also works hard to maintain the right context for our tests. For example, I can nest contexts and their setup blocks, allowing me to have some initialization that's common to all tests and some that's common to just a subset. We can apply this to our tennis example. We'll write nested contexts and put setup blocks at each level. When Shoulda executes our tests, it runs all the appropriate setup blocks for the should blocks.

`unittesting_33.rb`

```ruby
require 'rubygems'
require 'test/unit'
require 'shoulda'
require 'tennis_scorer.rb'
class TennisScorerTest < Test::Unit::TestCase
  def assert_score(target)
    assert_equal(target, @ts.score)
  end
  context "Tennis scores" do
    setup do
      @ts = TennisScorer.new
    end
    should "start with a score of 0-0" do
      assert_score("0-0")
    end
    context "where the server wins a point" do
      setup do
        @ts.give_point_to(:server)
      end
      should "be 15-0" do
        assert_score("15-0")
      end
      context "and the oponent wins a point" do
        setup do
          @ts.give_point_to(:receiver)
        end
        should "be 15-15" do
          assert_score("15-15")
        end
      end
    end
    should "be 0-15 if the receiver wins a point" do
      @ts.give_point_to(:receiver)
      assert_score("0-15")
    end
  end
end
```

Let's run it:

```
$ ruby ts_spec.rb
```

produces:

```
Loaded suite ts_shoulda_1
Started
....
Finished in 0.000699 seconds.

4 tests, 4 assertions, 0 failures, 0 errors, 0 skips
```

Would I use these nested contexts for this tennis scoring example? I probably wouldn't as it stands, because the linear form is easier to read. But I use them all the time when I have tests where I want to run through a complex and building scenario. This nesting lets me set up an environment, run some tests, then change the environment, run more tests, change it again, run even more tests, and so on. It ends up making tests far more compact and removes a lot of duplication.

Figure 13.1. Testing Framework Assertions

assert | refute(*boolean*, [*message*])
> Fails if *boolean* is (is not) false or nil.

assert_block { *block* }
> Expects the block to return true.

assert_ | refute_empty(*collection*, [*message*])
> Expects empty? on *collection* to return true (false).

assert_ | refute_equal(*expected*, *actual*, [*message*])
> Expects *actual* to equal/not equal *expected*, using ==.

assert_ | refute_in_delta(*expected_float*, *actual_float*, *delta*, [*message*])
> Expects that the actual floating-point value is (is not) within *delta* of the expected value.

assert_ | refute_in_epsilon(*expected_float*, *actual_float*, *epsilon=0.001*, [*message*])
> Calculates a delta value as *epsilon * min(expected, actual)*, then calls the _in_delta test.

assert_ | refute_includes(*collection*, *obj*, [*message*])
> Expects include?(obj) on *collection* to return true (false).

assert_ | refute_instance_of(*klass*, *obj*, [*message*])
> Expects *obj* to be (not to be) a instance of *klass*.

assert_ | refute_kind_of(*klass*, *obj*, [*message*])
> Expects *obj* to be (not to be) a kind of *klass*.

assert_ | refute_match(*regexp*, *string*, [*message*])
> Expects *string* to (not) match *regexp*.

assert_ | refute_nil(*obj*, [*message*])
> Expects *obj* to be (not) nil.

assert_ | refute_operator(*obj1*, *operator*, *obj2*, [*message*])
> Expects the result of sending the message *operator* to *obj1* with parameter *obj2* to be (not to be) true.

assert_raises(*Exception*, ...) { *block* }
> Expects the block to raise one of the listed exceptions.

assert_ | refute_respond_to(*obj*, *message*, [*message*])
> Expects *obj* to respond to (not respond to) *message* (a symbol).

assert_ | refute_same(*expected*, *actual*, [*message*])
> Expects *expected*.equal?(*actual*).

assert_send(*send_array*, [*message*])
> Sends the message in *send_array[1]* to the receiver in *send_array[0]*, passing the rest of *send_array* as arguments. Expects the return value to be true.

assert_throws(*expected_symbol*, [*message*]) { *block* }
> Expects the block to throw the given symbol.

flunk(*message*="Epic Fail!")
> Always fails.

skip(*message*)
> Indicates that a test is deliberately not run.

pass
> Always passes.

Figure 13.2. Additional Test::Unit Assertions

assert_not_equal(*expected*, *actual*, [*message*])
>   Expects *actual* not to equal *expected*, using ==. Like refute_equal.

assert_not_match(*regexp*, *string*, [*message*])
>   Expects *string* not to match *regexp*. Like refute_match.

assert_not_nil(*obj*, [*message*])
>   Expects *obj* not to be nil. Like refute_nil.

assert_not_same(*expected*, *actual*, [*message*])
>   Expects !*expected*.equal?(*actual*). Like refute_same.

assert_nothing_raised(*Exception*, . . .) { *block* }
>   Expects the block not to raise one of the listed exceptions.

assert_nothing_thrown(*expected_symbol*, [*message*]) { *block* }
>   Expects the block not to throw the given symbol.

assert_raise(*Exception*, . . .) { *block* }
>   Synonym for assert_raises.

## Chapter 14

When Trouble Strikes

It's sad to say, but it is possible to write buggy programs using Ruby. Sorry about that.

But not to worry! Ruby has several features that will help debug your programs. We'll look at these features, and then we'll show some common mistakes you can make in Ruby and how to fix them.

Ruby Debugger

Ruby comes with a debugger, which is conveniently built into the base system. You can run the debugger by invoking the interpreter with the -r debug option, along with any other Ruby options and the name of your script:

```
ruby -r debug [ debug-options ] [ programfile ] [ program-arguments ]
```

The debugger supports the usual range of features you'd expect, including the ability to set breakpoints, to step into and step over method calls, and to display stack frames and variables. It can also list the instance methods defined for a particular object or class, and it allows you to list and control separate threads within Ruby. Table 14.1 on page 216 lists all the commands that are available under the debugger.

If your Ruby installation has readline support enabled, you can use cursor keys to move back and forth in command history and use line-editing commands to amend previous input.

To give you an idea of what the Ruby debugger is like, here is a sample session (with user input in bold type):

```
% ruby -r debug t.rb
Debug.rb
Emacs support available.
t.rb:1:def fact(n)
(rdb:1) list 1-9
[1, 9] in t.rb
=> 1  def fact(n)
   2    if n <= 0
   3      1
   4    else
   5      n * fact(n-1)
```

```
    6    end
    7  end
    8
    9  p fact(5)
(rdb:1) b 2
Set breakpoint 1 at t.rb:2
(rdb:1) c
breakpoint 1, fact at t.rb:2
t.rb:2:  if n <= 0
(rdb:1) disp n
  1: n = 5
(rdb:1) del 1
(rdb:1) watch n==1
Set watchpoint 2
(rdb:1) c
watchpoint 2, fact at t.rb:fact
t.rb:1:def fact(n)
1: n = 1
(rdb:1) where
--> #1  t.rb:1:in `fact'
    #2  t.rb:5:in `fact'
    #3  t.rb:5:in `fact'
    #4  t.rb:5:in `fact'
    #5  t.rb:5:in `fact'
    #6  t.rb:9
(rdb:1) del 2
(rdb:1) c
120
```

Interactive Ruby

If you want to play with Ruby, we recommend Interactive Ruby—irb, for short. irb is essentially a Ruby "shell" similar in concept to an operating system shell (complete with job control). It provides an environment where you can "play around" with the language in real time. You launch irb at the command prompt:

```
irb [ irb-options ] [ ruby_script ] [ program-arguments ]
```

irb will display the value of each expression as you complete it. For instance:

```
% irb
irb(main):001:0> a = 1 +
irb(main):002:0* 2 * 3 /
irb(main):003:0* 4 % 5
=> 2
irb(main):004:0> 2+2
=> 4
irb(main):005:0> def test
irb(main):006:1> puts "Hello, world!"
irb(main):007:1> end
=> nil
```

```
irb(main):008:0> test
Hello, world!
=> nil
irb(main):009:0>
```

irb also allows you to create subsessions, each one of which may have its own context. For example, you can create a subsession with the same (top-level) context as the original session or create a subsession in the context of a particular class or instance. The sample session shown in Figure 14.1 on the following page is a bit longer but shows how you can create subsessions and switch between them.

For a full description of all the commands that irb supports, see the reference beginning on page 265.

As with the debugger, if your version of Ruby was built with GNU readline support, you can use Emacs- or vi-style key bindings to edit individual lines or to go back and reexecute or edit a previous line—just like a command shell.

irb is a great learning tool. It's very handy if you want to try an idea quickly and see whether it works.

Editor Support

The Ruby interpreter is designed to read a program in one pass; this means you can pipe an entire program to the interpreter's standard input, and it will work just fine.

We can take advantage of this feature to run Ruby code from inside an editor. In Emacs, for instance, you can select a region of Ruby text and use the command Meta-| to execute Ruby. The Ruby interpreter will use the selected region as standard input, and output will go to a buffer named *Shell Command Output*. This feature has come in quite handy for us while writing this book—just select a few lines of Ruby in the middle of a paragraph, and try it!

You can do something similar in the vi editor using :%!ruby, which *replaces* the program text with its output, or :w_!ruby, which displays the output without affecting the buffer. Other editors have similar features.[1]

Some Ruby developers look for IDE support. Several decent alternatives came to the fore during 2007 and 2008. Arachno Ruby, NetBeans, Ruby in Steel, Idea, and so on, all have their devotees. It's a rapidly changing field, so I'd recommend a quick web search rather than rely on my advice here.

While we are on the subject, this would probably be a good place to mention that a Ruby mode for Emacs is included in the Ruby source distribution as ruby-mode.el in the misc/ subdirectory. Many other editors now include support for Ruby; check your documentation for details.

---

1.   If you use a Mac, take a look at Textmate (http://macromates.com). It isn't free, but it is a great Ruby environment.

Figure 14.1. Sample irb Session

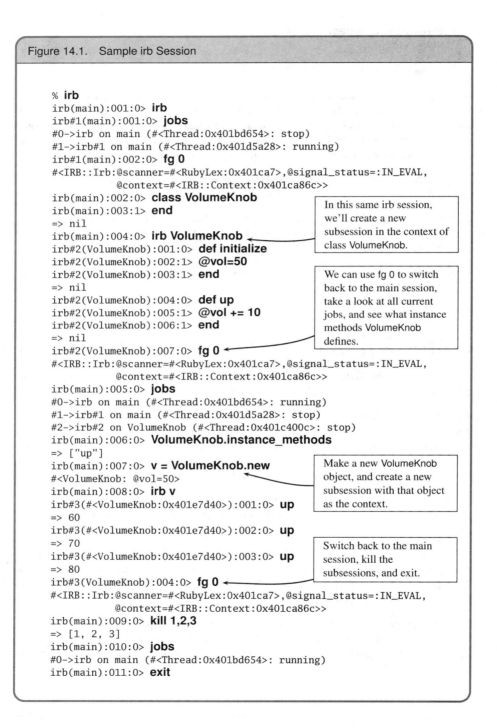

```
% irb
irb(main):001:0> irb
irb#1(main):001:0> jobs
#0->irb on main (#<Thread:0x401bd654>: stop)
#1->irb#1 on main (#<Thread:0x401d5a28>: running)
irb#1(main):002:0> fg 0
#<IRB::Irb:@scanner=#<RubyLex:0x401ca7>,@signal_status=:IN_EVAL,
        @context=#<IRB::Context:0x401ca86c>>
irb(main):002:0> class VolumeKnob
irb(main):003:1> end
=> nil
irb(main):004:0> irb VolumeKnob
irb#2(VolumeKnob):001:0> def initialize
irb#2(VolumeKnob):002:1> @vol=50
irb#2(VolumeKnob):003:1> end
=> nil
irb#2(VolumeKnob):004:0> def up
irb#2(VolumeKnob):005:1> @vol += 10
irb#2(VolumeKnob):006:1> end
=> nil
irb#2(VolumeKnob):007:0> fg 0
#<IRB::Irb:@scanner=#<RubyLex:0x401ca7>,@signal_status=:IN_EVAL,
        @context=#<IRB::Context:0x401ca86c>>
irb(main):005:0> jobs
#0->irb on main (#<Thread:0x401bd654>: running)
#1->irb#1 on main (#<Thread:0x401d5a28>: stop)
#2->irb#2 on VolumeKnob (#<Thread:0x401c400c>: stop)
irb(main):006:0> VolumeKnob.instance_methods
=> ["up"]
irb(main):007:0> v = VolumeKnob.new
#<VolumeKnob: @vol=50>
irb(main):008:0> irb v
irb#3(#<VolumeKnob:0x401e7d40>):001:0> up
=> 60
irb#3(#<VolumeKnob:0x401e7d40>):002:0> up
=> 70
irb#3(#<VolumeKnob:0x401e7d40>):003:0> up
=> 80
irb#3(VolumeKnob):004:0> fg 0
#<IRB::Irb:@scanner=#<RubyLex:0x401ca7>,@signal_status=:IN_EVAL,
        @context=#<IRB::Context:0x401ca86c>>
irb(main):009:0> kill 1,2,3
=> [1, 2, 3]
irb(main):010:0> jobs
#0->irb on main (#<Thread:0x401bd654>: running)
irb(main):011:0> exit
```

In this same irb session, we'll create a new subsession in the context of class VolumeKnob.

We can use fg 0 to switch back to the main session, take a look at all current jobs, and see what instance methods VolumeKnob defines.

Make a new VolumeKnob object, and create a new subsession with that object as the context.

Switch back to the main session, kill the subsessions, and exit.

But It Doesn't Work!

So, you've read through enough of the book, you start to write your very own Ruby program, and it doesn't work. Here's a list of common gotchas and other tips:

- First and foremost, run your scripts with warnings enabled (the -w command-line option).

- If you happen to forget a comma (,) in an argument list—especially to print—you can produce some very odd error messages.

- A parse error at the last line of the source often indicates a missing end keyword, sometimes quite a bit earlier.

- This ugly message:

  ```
  syntax error, unexpected $end, expecting keyword_end
  ```

  means that you have an end missing somewhere in your code. (The $end in the message means end-of-file, so the message simply means that Ruby hit the end of your code before finding all the end keywords it was expecting.) Try running with -w, which will warn when it finds ends that aren't aligned with their opening if/while/class....

- An attribute setter is not being called. Within a class definition, Ruby will parse setter= as an assignment to a local variable, not as a method call. Use the form self.setter= to indicate the method call:

  ```ruby
  class Incorrect
    attr_accessor :one, :two
    def initialize
      one = 1          # incorrect - sets local variable
      self.two = 2
    end
  end

  obj = Incorrect.new
  obj.one   # =>   nil
  obj.two   # =>   2
  ```

- Objects that don't appear to be properly set up may have been victims of an incorrectly spelled initialize method:

  ```ruby
  class Incorrect
    attr_reader :answer
    def initialise       # <-- spelling error
      @answer = 42
    end
  end

  ultimate = Incorrect.new
  ultimate.answer   # =>   nil
  ```

The same kind of thing can happen if you misspell the instance variable name:

```
class Incorrect
  attr_reader :answer
  def initialize
    @anwser = 42        #<-- spelling error
  end
end

ultimate = Incorrect.new
ultimate.answer   # =>   nil
```

1.9

- As of Ruby 1.9, block parameters are no longer in the same scope as local variables. This may cause compatibility problems with older code. Run with the -w flag to spot these issues:

```
entry = "wibble"
[1, 2, 3].each do |entry|
  # do something with entry
end
puts "Last entry = #{entry}"
```

produces:

```
/tmp/prog.rb:2: warning: shadowing outer local variable - entry
Last entry = wibble
```

- Watch out for precedence issues, especially when using {} instead of do/end:

```
def one(arg)
  if block_given?
    "block given to 'one' returns #{yield}"
  else
    arg
  end
end
def two
  if block_given?
    "block given to 'two' returns #{yield}"
  end
end
result1 = one two {
  "three"
}
result2 = one two do
  "three"
end
puts "With braces, result = #{result1}"
puts "With do/end, result = #{result2}"
```

produces:

```
With braces, result = block given to 'two' returns three
With do/end, result = block given to 'one' returns three
```

- Output written to a terminal may be buffered. This means you may not see a message you write immediately. In addition, if you write messages to both STDOUT and STDERR, the output may not appear in the order you were expecting. Always use nonbuffered I/O (set sync=true) for debug messages.

- If numbers don't come out right, perhaps they're strings. Text read from a file will be a String and will not be automatically converted to a number by Ruby. A call to Integer will work wonders (and will throw an exception if the input isn't a well-formed integer). The following is a common mistake Perl programmers make:

```
while line = gets
  num1, num2 = line.split(/,/)
  # ...
end
```

You can rewrite this as follows:

```
while line = gets
  num1, num2 = line.split(/,/)
  num1 = Integer(num1)
  num2 = Integer(num2)
  # ...
end
```

Or, you could convert all the strings using map:

```
while line = gets
  num1, num2 = line.split(/,/).map {|val| Integer(val) }
  # ...
end
```

- Unintended aliasing—if you are using an object as the key of a hash, make sure it doesn't change its hash value (or arrange to call Hash#rehash if it does):

trouble_10.rb

```
arr = [1, 2]
hash = { arr => "value" }
hash[arr]      # =>    "value"
arr[0] = 99
hash[arr]      # =>    nil
hash.rehash    # =>    {[99, 2]=>"value"}
hash[arr]      # =>    "value"
```

- Make sure the class of the object you are using is what you think it is. If in doubt, use puts my_obj.class.

- Make sure your method names start with a lowercase letter and class and constant names start with an uppercase letter.

- If method calls aren't doing what you'd expect, make sure you've put parentheses around the arguments.

- Make sure the open parenthesis of a method's parameter list butts up against the end of the method name with no intervening spaces.

- Use irb and the debugger.

- Use Object#freeze. If you suspect that some unknown portion of code is setting a variable to a bogus value, try freezing the variable. The culprit will then be caught during the attempt to modify the variable.

One major technique makes writing Ruby code both easier and more fun. *Develop your applications incrementally.* Write a few lines of code, and then write tests (perhaps using Test::Unit). Write a few more lines of code, and then exercise them. One of the major benefits of a dynamically typed language is that things don't have to be complete before you use them.

But It's Too Slow!

Ruby is an interpreted, high-level language, and as such it may not perform as fast as a lower-level language such as C. In the following sections, we'll list some basic things you can do to improve performance; also take a look in the index under *Performance* for other pointers.

Typically, slow-running programs have one or two performance graveyards, places where execution time goes to die. Find and improve them, and suddenly your whole program springs back to life. The trick is finding them. The Benchmark module and the Ruby profilers can help.

Benchmark

You can use the Benchmark module, also described on page 722, to time sections of code. For example, we may wonder what the overhead of method invocation is. How to use Benchmark to find out is shown in Figure 14.2 on the next page.

You have to be careful when benchmarking, because oftentimes Ruby programs can run slowly because of the overhead of garbage collection. Because this garbage collection can happen any time during your program's execution, you may find that benchmarking gives misleading results, showing a section of code running slowly when in fact the slowdown was caused because garbage collection happened to trigger while that code was executing. The Benchmark module has the bmbm method that runs the tests twice, once as a rehearsal and once to measure performance, in an attempt to minimize the distortion introduced by garbage collection. The benchmarking process itself is relatively well mannered—it doesn't slow down your program much.

Figure 14.2.   Determining Method Calling Costs Using Benchmark

```
trouble_11.rb

require 'benchmark'
include Benchmark

LOOP_COUNT = 1_000_000

bmbm(12) do |test|
  test.report("inline:")     do
    LOOP_COUNT.times do |x|
      # nothing
    end
  end
  test.report("method:") do
    def method
      # nothing
    end
    LOOP_COUNT.times do |x|
      method
    end
  end
end
```

produces:
```
Rehearsal ---------------------------------------------
inline:       0.080000   0.000000   0.080000 (  0.082863)
method:       0.130000   0.000000   0.130000 (  0.134772)
------------------------------------ total: 0.210000sec

                   user     system      total        real
inline:        0.090000   0.000000   0.090000 (  0.082595)
method:        0.130000   0.000000   0.130000 (  0.135118)
```

The Profiler

Ruby comes with a code profiler (documentation begins on page 783). The profiler shows you the number of times each method in the program is called and the average and cumulative time that Ruby spends in those methods.

You can add profiling to your code using the command-line option -r profile or from within the code using require 'profile'.

For example:

`trouble_12.rb`

```ruby
require 'profile'
count = 0
words = File.open("/usr/share/dict/words")
while word = words.gets
  word = word.chomp!
  if word.length == 12
    count += 1
  end
end
puts "#{count} twelve-character words"
```

The first time we ran this (without profiling) against a dictionary of almost 235,000 words, it took a noticeable time to complete. Wondering if we could improve on this, we added the -r profile command-line option and tried again. Eventually we saw output that looked like the following:

```
20460 twelve-character words
  %   cumulative   self              self    total
 time   seconds   seconds   calls  ms/call ms/call  name
 0.00     0.00      0.00        1    0.00    0.00  File#initialize
 0.00     0.00      0.00        1    0.00    0.00  IO#open
 0.00     0.00      0.00        2    0.00    0.00  IO#write
 0.00     0.00      0.00        1    0.00    0.00  Fixnum#to_s
 0.00     0.00      0.00        1    0.00    0.00  Kernel.puts
16.05     1.25      1.25   234936    0.01    0.01  String#chomp!
20.67     2.86      1.61   234937    0.01    0.01  IO#gets
 0.00     7.79      0.00        1    0.00 7790.00  #toplevel1
```

The first thing to notice is that the timings shown are a lot slower than when the program runs without the profiler. Profiling has a serious overhead, but the assumption is that it applies across the board, and therefore the relative numbers are still meaningful. This particular program clearly spends a lot of time in the loop, which executes almost 235,000 times. Each time, it invokes both gets and chomp!. We could probably improve performance if we could either make the stuff in the loop less expensive or eliminate the loop altogether. One way of doing the latter is to read the word list into one long string and then use a pattern to match and extract all twelve character words:

`trouble_13.rb`

```ruby
words = File.read("/usr/share/dict/words")
count = words.scan(/^............\n/).size
puts "#{count} twelve-character words"
```

Our profile numbers are now a lot better (and the program runs more than five times faster when we take the profiling back out):

```
  %   cumulative   self              self    total
 time   seconds   seconds   calls  ms/call ms/call  name
95.45     0.21      0.21        1  210.00  210.00  String#scan
 4.55     0.22      0.01        1   10.00   10.00  IO#read
 0.00     0.22      0.00        1    0.00    0.00  Fixnum#to_s
```

```
0.00      0.22      0.00        1    0.00      0.00  Array#size
0.00      0.22      0.00        2    0.00      0.00  IO#write
0.00      0.22      0.00        1    0.00      0.00  IO#puts
0.00      0.22      0.00        1    0.00      0.00  Kernel.puts
0.00      0.22      0.00        1    0.00    220.00  #toplevel
20460 twelve-character words
```

Remember to check the code without the profiler afterward, though—sometimes the slow-down the profiler introduces can mask other problems.

Ruby is a wonderfully transparent and expressive language, but it does not relieve the programmer of the need to apply common sense: creating unnecessary objects, performing unneeded work, and creating bloated code will slow down your programs regardless of the language.

Code Execution Coverage

Ruby 1.9.1 comes with experimental support for code coverage analysis—it will track which lines of code were executed in your code. However, the support is currently labeled as *experimental* and is by default disabled in the VM. By the time you read this, it may have settled down. Try doing this:

```
$ ri coverage
```

Of course, there's a good chance it may never make it to production. In that case, feel free to cut out this section of your book and use the words in your next writing project.

Table 14.1. Debugger Commands

b [reak] [file|class:]line	Sets breakpoint at given line in *file* (default current file) or *class*.
b [reak] [file|class:]name	Sets breakpoint at *method* in *file* or *class*.
b [reak]	Displays breakpoints and watchpoints.
wat [ch] expr	Breaks when expression becomes true.
del [ete] [nnn]	Deletes breakpoint *nnn* (default all).
cat [ch] exception	Stops when *exception* is raised.
cat [ch]	Lists current catches.
tr [ace] (on|off) [all]	Toggles execution trace of current or all threads.
disp [lay] expr	Displays value of *nnn* every time debugger gets control.
disp [lay]	Shows current displays.
undisp [lay] [nnn]	Removes display (default all).
c [ont]	Continues execution.
s [tep] nnn=1	Executes next *nnn* lines, stepping into methods.
n [ext] nnn=1	Executes next *nnn* lines, stepping over methods.
fin [ish]	Finishes execution of the current function.
q [uit]	Exits the debugger.
w [here]	Displays current stack frame.
f [rame]	Synonym for where.
l [ist] [start–end]	Lists source lines from start to end.
up nnn=1	Moves up *nnn* levels in the stack frame.
down nnn=1	Moves down *nnn* levels in the stack frame.
v [ar] g [lobal]	Displays global variables.
v [ar] l [ocal]	Displays local variables.
v [ar] i [stance] *obj*	Displays instance variables of *obj*.
v [ar] c [onst] Name	Displays constants in class or module name.
m [ethod] i [nstance] *obj*	Displays instance methods of *obj*.
m [ethod] Name	Displays instance methods of the class or module name.
th [read] l [ist]	Lists all threads.
th [read] [c[ur[rent]]]	Displays status of current thread.
th [read] [c[ur[rent]]] nnn	Makes thread *nnn* current and stops it.
th [read] stop nnn	Makes thread *nnn* current and stops it.
th [read] resume nnn	Resumes thread *nnn*.
th [read] [sw[itch]] nnn	Switches thread context to nnn.
[p] expr	Evaluates *expr* in the current context. *expr* may include assignment to variables and method invocations.
h[elp]	Shows summary of commands.
empty	A null command repeats the last command.

Part II

Ruby in Its Setting

## Chapter 15

Ruby and Its World

It's an unfortunate fact of life that our applications have to deal with the big, bad world. In this chapter, we'll look at how Ruby interacts with its environment. Microsoft Windows users will probably also want to look at platform-specific information beginning on page 303.

Command-Line Arguments

"In the beginning was the command line."[1] Regardless of the system in which Ruby is deployed, whether it be a super high-end scientific graphics workstation or an embedded PDA device, you have to start the Ruby interpreter somehow, and that gives us the opportunity to pass in command-line arguments.

A Ruby command line consists of three parts: options to the Ruby interpreter, optionally the name of a program to run, and optionally a set of arguments for that program:

```
ruby [ options ] [ -- ] [ programfile ] [ arguments ]
```

The Ruby options are terminated by the first word on the command line that doesn't start with a hyphen or by the special flag -- (two hyphens).

If no filename is present on the command line or if the filename is a single hyphen (-), Ruby reads the program source from standard input.

Arguments for the program itself follow the program name. For example, the following:

```
% ruby -w - "Hello World"
```

will enable warnings, read a program from standard input, and pass it the string "Hello World" as an argument.

---

1.   This is the title of a marvelous essay by Neal Stephenson (available online at http://www.spack.org/index. cgi/InTheBeginningWasTheCommandLine).

Command-Line Options

-0[*octal*]

> The 0 flag (the digit zero) specifies the record separator character (\0, if no digit follows). -00 indicates paragraph mode: records are separated by two successive default record separator characters. -0777 reads the entire file at once (as it is an illegal character). Sets $/.

-a

> Autosplit mode when used with -n or -p; equivalent to executing $F = $_.split at the top of each loop iteration.

-C *directory*

> Changes working directory to *directory* before executing.

-c

> Checks syntax only; does not execute the program.

--copyright

> Prints the copyright notice and exits.

-d, --debug

> Sets $DEBUG and $VERBOSE to true. This can be used by your programs to enable additional tracing.

--disable-gems

> Stops Ruby automatically loading RubyGems from require.

-E *encoding*, --encoding *encoding*, --encoding=*encoding*

> Specifies the default character encoding for data read from and written to the outside world. This can be used to set both the external encoding (the encoding to be assumed for file contents) and optionally the default internal encoding (the file contents are transcoded to this when read and transcoded from this when written). The format of the *encoding* parameter is -E external, -E external:internal, or -E :internal. See 17 on page 251 for details. See also -U.

-e '*command*'

> Executes *command* as one line of Ruby source. Several -e's are allowed, and the commands are treated as multiple lines in the same program. If *programfile* is omitted when -e is present, execution stops after the -e commands have been run. Programs run using -e have access to the old behavior of ranges and regular expressions in conditions— ranges of integers compare against the current input line number, and regular expressions match against $_.

-F *pattern*

> Specifies the input field separator ($;) used as the default for split() (affects the -a option).

-h, --help

> Displays a short help screen.

-I *directories*

> Specifies directories to be prepended to $LOAD_PATH ($:). Multiple -I options may be present. Multiple directories may appear following each -I, separated by a colon (:) on Unix-like systems and by a semicolon (;) on DOS/Windows systems.

-i [*extension*]

> Edits ARGV files in place. For each file named in ARGV, anything you write to standard output will be saved back as the contents of that file. A backup copy of the file will be made if *extension* is supplied.

```
% ruby -pi.bak -e "gsub(/Perl/, 'Ruby')" *.txt
```

-l

> Enables automatic line-ending processing; sets $\ to the value of $/ and chops every input line automatically.

-n

> Assumes a while gets; . . . ; end loop around your program. For example, a simple grep command could be implemented as follows:

```
% ruby -n -e "print if /wombat/" *.txt
```

-p

> Places your program code within the loop while gets; . . . ; print; end.

```
% ruby -p -e "$_.downcase!" *.txt
```

-r *library*

> requires the named library or gem before executing.

-S

> Looks for the program file using the RUBYPATH or PATH environment variable.

-s

> Any command-line switches found after the program filename, but before any filename arguments or before a --, are removed from ARGV and set to a global variable named for the switch. In the following example, the effect of this would be to set the variable $opt to "electric":

```
% ruby -s prog -opt=electric ./mydata
```

-T[*level*]

> Sets the safe level, which among other things enables tainting and untrusted checks (see page 425). Sets $SAFE.

-U

> Sets the default internal encoding to UTF-8. See 17 on page 251 for details. See also -E.

-v, --verbose

> Sets $VERBOSE to true, which enables verbose mode. Also prints the version number. In verbose mode, compilation warnings are printed. If no program filename appears on the command line, Ruby exits.

--version

> Displays the Ruby version number and exits.

-w

> Enables verbose mode. Unlike -v, reads program from standard input if no program files are present on the command line. We recommend running your Ruby programs with -w.

-W *level*

> Sets the level of warnings issued. With a *level* or two (or with no level specified), equivalent to -w—additional warnings are given. If *level* is 1, runs at the standard (default) warning level. With -W0, absolutely no warnings are given (including those issued using Kernel.warn).

-X *directory*
> Changes working directory to *directory* before executing. This is the same as -C *directory*.

-x [*directory*]
> Strips off text before #!ruby line and changes working directory to *directory* if given.

-y, --yydebug
> Enables yacc debugging in the parser *(waaay too much information)*.

ARGV

Any command-line arguments after the program filename are available to your Ruby program in the global array ARGV. For instance, assume `test.rb` contains the following program:

```
ARGV.each {|arg| p arg }
```

Invoke it with the following command line:

```
% ruby -w test.rb "Hello World" a1 1.6180
```

It'll generate the following output:

```
"Hello World"
"a1"
"1.6180"
```

There's a gotcha here for all you C programmers—ARGV[0] is the first argument to the program, not the program name. The name of the current program is available in the global variable $0, which is aliased to $PROGRAM_NAME. Notice that all the values in ARGV are strings.

If your program reads from standard input (or uses the special object ARGF, described on page 330), the program arguments in ARGV will be taken to be filenames, and Ruby will read from these files. If your program takes a mixture of arguments and filenames, make sure you empty the nonfilename arguments from the ARGV array before reading from the files.

Program Termination

The method Kernel#exit terminates your program, returning a status value to the operating system. However, unlike some languages, exit doesn't terminate the program immediately. Kernel#exit first raises a SystemExit exception, which you may catch, and then performs a number of cleanup actions, including running any registered at_exit methods and object finalizers. See the reference for Kernel#exit beginning on page 560 for details.

Environment Variables

You can access operating system environment variables using the predefined variable ENV. It responds to the same methods as Hash.[2]

```
ENV['SHELL']    # =>   "/bin/bash"
ENV['HOME']     # =>   "/Users/dave"
ENV['USER']     # =>   "dave"
ENV.keys.size   # =>   36
ENV.keys[0, 4]  # =>   ["MANPATH", "TERM_PROGRAM", "SHELL", "TERM"]
```

The values of some environment variables are read by Ruby when it first starts. These variables modify the behavior of the interpreter, as shown in Table 15.1 on the following page.

Writing to Environment Variables

A Ruby program may write to the ENV object. On most systems, this changes the values of the corresponding environment variables. However, this change is local to the process that makes it and to any subsequently spawned child processes. This inheritance of environment variables is illustrated in the code that follows. A subprocess changes an environment variable, and this change is inherited by a process that it then starts. However, the change is not visible to the original parent. (This just goes to prove that parents never really know what their children are doing.)

1.9 / As of Ruby 1.9, setting an environment variable's value to nil removes the variable from the environment:

```
rubyworld_3.rb
puts "In parent, term = #{ENV['TERM']}"
fork do
  puts "Start of child 1, term = #{ENV['TERM']}"
  ENV['TERM'] = "ansi"
  fork do
    puts "Start of child 2, term = #{ENV['TERM']}"
  end
  Process.wait
  puts "End of child 1, term = #{ENV['TERM']}"
end
Process.wait
puts "Back in parent, term = #{ENV['TERM']}"
```

produces:

```
In parent, term = xterm-color
Start of child 1, term = xterm-color
Start of child 2, term = ansi
End of child 1, term = ansi
Back in parent, term = xterm-color
```

---

2.   ENV is not actually a hash, but if you need to, you can convert it into a Hash using ENV#to_hash.

Table 15.1. Environment Variables Used by Ruby

Variable Name	Description
DLN_LIBRARY_PATH	Specifies the search path for dynamically loaded modules.
HOME	Points to user's home directory. This is used when expanding ~ in file and directory names.
LOGDIR	Specifies the fallback pointer to the user's home directory if $HOME is not set. This is used only by Dir.chdir.
OPENSSL_CONF	Specifies the location of OpenSSL configuration file.
RUBYLIB	Specifies an additional search path for Ruby programs ($SAFE must be 0).
RUBYLIB_PREFIX	(Windows only) Mangles the RUBYLIB search path by adding this prefix to each component.
RUBYOPT	Specifies additional command-line options to Ruby; examined after real command-line options are parsed ($SAFE must be 0).
RUBYPATH	With -S option, specifies the search path for Ruby programs (defaults to PATH).
RUBYSHELL	Specifies shell to use when spawning a process under Windows; if not set, will also check SHELL or COMSPEC.
RUBY_TCL_DLL	Overrides default name for TCL shared library or DLL.
RUBY_TK_DLL	Overrides default name for Tk shared library or DLL. Both this and RUBY_TCL_DLL must be set for either to be used.

Where Ruby Finds Its Libraries

1.9

You use require or load to bring a library into your Ruby program. Some of these libraries are supplied with Ruby, some you may have installed from the Ruby Application Archive, some may have been packaged as RubyGems (of which more later), and some you may have written yourself. How does Ruby find them?

Let's start with the basics. When Ruby is built for your particular machine, it predefines a set of standard directories to hold library stuff. Where these are depends on the machine in question. You can determine this from the command line with something like this:

```
% ruby -e 'puts $:'
```

On my OS X box, this produces the following list (note that I have my Ruby installed in a nonstandard place while I'm writing this book):

```
/usr/local/rubybook/lib/ruby/gems/1.9.0/gems/BlueCloth-1.0.0/lib
/usr/local/rubybook/lib/ruby/gems/1.9.0/gems/BlueCloth-1.0.0/bin
/usr/local/rubybook/lib/ruby/site_ruby/1.9
/usr/local/rubybook/lib/ruby/site_ruby/1.9.0/i686-darwin8.11.1
/usr/local/rubybook/lib/ruby/site_ruby
/usr/local/rubybook/lib/ruby/vendor_ruby/1.9
/usr/local/rubybook/lib/ruby/vendor_ruby/1.9.0/i686-darwin8.11.1
/usr/local/rubybook/lib/ruby/vendor_ruby /usr/local/rubybook/lib/ruby/1.9
/usr/local/rubybook/lib/ruby/1.9.0/i686-darwin8.11.1
```

Let's skip the gems directory for now.

The site_ruby directories are intended to hold modules and extensions that you've added. The architecture-dependent directories (i686-darwin8.11.1 in this case) hold executables and other things specific to this particular machine. All these directories are automatically included in Ruby's search for libraries.

Sometimes this isn't enough. Perhaps you're working on a large project written in Ruby and you and your colleagues have built a substantial library of Ruby code. You want everyone on the team to have access to all this code. You have a couple of options to accomplish this. If your program runs at a safe level of zero (see Chapter 26 beginning on page 425), you can set the environment variable RUBYLIB to a list of one or more directories to be searched.[3] If your program is not *setuid*, you can use the command-line parameter -I to do the same thing.

The Ruby variable $: is an array of places to search for loaded files. As we've seen, this variable is initialized to the list of standard directories, plus any additional ones you specified using RUBYLIB and -I. You can always add directories to this array from within your running program.

RubyGems Integration

1.9

This section is based on the start of the chapter on RubyGems written by Chad Fowler for the second edition of this book.

RubyGems is a standardized packaging and installation framework for Ruby libraries and applications. RubyGems makes it easy to locate, install, upgrade, and uninstall Ruby packages.

Before RubyGems came along, installing a new library involved searching the Web, downloading a package, and attempting to install it—only to find that its dependencies haven't been met. If the library you want is packaged using RubyGems, however, you can now simply ask RubyGems to install it (and all its dependencies). Everything is done for you.

In the RubyGems world, developers bundle their applications and libraries into single files called *gems*. These files conform to a standardized format and typically are stored in repositories on the 'net (but you can also create your own repositories if you want).

The RubyGems system provides a command-line tool, appropriately named gem, for manipulating these gem files. It also provides integration into Ruby so that your programs can access gems as libraries.

Prior to Ruby 1.9, it was your responsibility to install the RubyGems software on your computer. Now, however, Ruby comes with RubyGems baked right in.

---

3.   The separator between entries depends on your platform. For Windows, it's a semicolon; for Unix, it's a colon.

Installing Gems on Your Machine

Your latest project calls for a lot of XML generation. You could just hard-code it, but you've heard great things about Jim Weirich's Builder library, which lets you construct XML directly from Ruby code.

Let's start by seeing whether Builder is available as a gem:

```
% gem query --details --remote --name-matches build
*** REMOTE GEMS ***

AntBuilder (0.4.3)
    Author: JRuby-extras
    Homepage: http://jruby-extras.rubyforge.org/

    AntBuilder: Use ant from JRuby. Only usable within JRuby

builder (2.1.2)
    Author: Jim Weirich
    Homepage: http://onestepback.org

    Builders for MarkUp.

...
```

The --details option displays the description of any gems it finds. The --remote option searches the remote repository. And the --name-matches option says to search the central gem repository for any gem whose name matches the regular expression /build/. (We could have used the short-form options -d, -r, and -n.) The result shows a number of gems have *build* in their name; the one we want is just plain Builder.

The number after the name shows the latest version. You can see a list of all available versions using the --all option. We'll also use the list command, because it lets us match on an exact name:

```
% gem list --details --remote --all builder
*** REMOTE GEMS ***

builder (2.1.2, 2.1.1, 2.0.0, 1.2.4, 1.2.3, 1.2.2, 1.2.1, 1.2.0, 1.1.0,
        1.0.0, 0.1.1, 0.1.0)
    Author: Jim Weirich
    Homepage: http://onestepback.org

    Builders for MarkUp.
```

Because we want to install the most recent one, we don't have to state an explicit version on the install command; the latest is downloaded by default:

```
% gem install builder
Successfully installed builder-2.1.2
1 gem installed
Installing ri documentation for builder-2.1.2...
ERROR:  While generating documentation for builder-2.1.2
```

```
... MESSAGE:    Unhandled special: Special: type=17, text="<!-- HI -->"
... RDOC args: --ri --op /usr/local/rubybook/lib/ruby/gems/1.9.0/...
(continuing with the rest of the installation)
Installing RDoc documentation for builder-2.1.2...
...
```

Several things happened here. First, we see that the latest version of the Builder gem (2.1.2) has been installed. Next we see that RubyGems has determined that Jim has created documentation for his gem, so it sets about extracting it using RDoc. During the extraction, RDoc encounters a construct it can't handle and complains. You'll see this happen every now and then. It's annoying, but you can ignore the message.

If you're running gem install on a Unix platform, you'll need to prefix the command with sudo, because by default the local gems are installed into shared system directories.

During installation, you can add the -t option to the RubyGems install command, causing RubyGems to run the gem's test suite (if one has been created). If the tests fail, the installer will prompt you to either keep or discard the gem. This is a good way to gain a little more confidence that the gem you've just downloaded works on your system the way the author intended.

Let's see what gems we now have installed on our local box:

```
% gem list
*** LOCAL GEMS ***
builder (2.1.2)
```

Reading the Gem Documentation

Being that this is your first time using Builder, you're not exactly sure how to use it. Fortunately, RubyGems installed the documentation for Builder on your local machine. We just have to find it.

As with most things in RubyGems, the documentation for each gem is stored in a central, protected, RubyGems-specific place. This will vary by system and by where you may explicitly choose to install your gems. The most reliable way to find the documents is to ask the gem command where your RubyGems main directory is located:

```
% gem environment gemdir
/usr/local/lib/ruby/gems/1.9.0
```

RubyGems stores generated documentation beneath the doc/ subdirectory of this directory, in this case /usr/local/lib/ruby/gems/1.9.0/doc. Each gem has its own documentation directory. Inside this directory, you'll find the HTML in the subdirectory rdoc/. You can open index.html and view the documentation (the full path is /usr/local/lib/ruby/gems/1.9.0/doc/builder-2.1.2/rdoc/index.html. The result will look something like Figure 15.1 on the following page.

If you find yourself using this path often, you can create a shortcut.

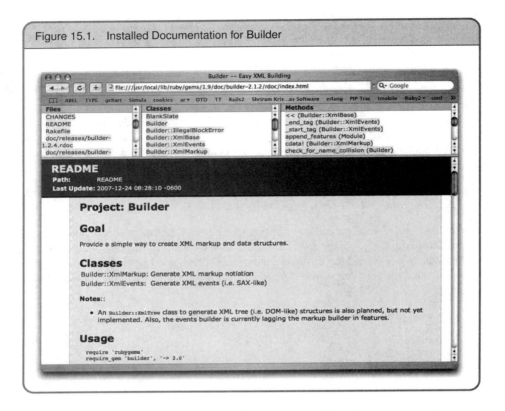

Figure 15.1. Installed Documentation for Builder

Here's one way to do that on Mac OS X boxes:

```
% gemdoc=`gem environment gemdir`/doc
% ls $gemdoc
builder-2.1.2
% open $gemdoc/builder-2.1.2/rdoc/index.html
```

To save time, you could declare $gemdoc in your login shell's profile or .rc file.

The second (and easier) way to view gems' RDoc documentation is to use RubyGems' included gem server utility. To start gem server, simply type this:

```
% gem server
Starting gem server on http://localhost:8808/
```

gem server starts a web server running on whatever computer you run it on. By default, it will start on port 8808 and will serve gems and their documentation from the default RubyGems installation directory. Both the port and the gem directory are overridable via command-line options, using the -p and -d options, respectively.

Once you've started the gem server program, if you are running it on your local computer, you can access the documentation for your installed gems by pointing your web browser to `http://localhost:8808`. There, you will see a list of the gems you have installed with their descriptions and links to their RDoc documentation.

Using a Gem

Once a gem is installed, you use `require` to load it into your own code, just as you would any other Ruby library:[4]

```
rubyworld_5.rb
require 'builder'
xml = Builder::XmlMarkup.new(target: STDOUT, indent: 2)
xml.person(type: "programmer") do
  xml.name do
    xml.first "Dave"
    xml.last "Thomas"
  end
  xml.location "Texas"
  xml.preference("ruby")
end
```

produces:

```
<person type="programmer">
  <name>
    <first>Dave</first>
    <last>Thomas</last>
  </name>
  <location>Texas</location>
  <preference>ruby</preference>
</person>
```

Gems and Versions

Maybe you first started using Builder a few years ago. Back then the interface was a little bit different—with versions prior to Build 1.0, you could say this:

```
xml = Builder::XmlMarkup.new(STDOUT, 2)
xml.person do
  name("Dave Thomas")
  location("Texas")
end
```

Note that the constructor takes positional parameters. Also, in the do block, we can say just name(...) (whereas the current Builder requires xml.name(...)).

---

4.   Prior to Ruby 1.9, before you could use a gem in your code, you first had to load a support library called rubygems. Ruby now integrates that support directly, so this step is no longer needed.

We could go through our old code and update it all to work with the new-style Builder—that's probably the best long-term solution. But we can also let RubyGems handle the issue for us.

When we asked for a listing of the Builder gems in the repository, we saw that multiple versions were available:

```
% gem list -ra builder
*** REMOTE GEMS ***
builder (2.1.2, 2.1.1, 2.0.0, 1.2.4, 1.2.3, 1.2.2, 1.2.1,
1.2.0, 1.1.0, 1.0.0, 0.1.1, 0.1.0)
```

When we installed Builder previously, we didn't specify a version, so RubyGems automatically installed the latest. But we can also get it to install a specific version or a version meeting some given criteria. Let's install the most recent release of Builder whose version number is less than 1:

```
% gem install builder --version '< 1'
Successfully installed builder-0.1.1
1 gem installed
Installing ri documentation for builder-0.1.1...
Installing RDoc documentation for builder-0.1.1...
```

Have we just overwritten the 2.1.2 release of Builder that we'd previously installed? Let's find out by listing our locally installed gems:

```
% gem list builder
*** LOCAL GEMS ***
builder (2.1.2, 0.1.1)
```

Now that we have both versions installed locally, how do we tell our legacy code to use the old one while still having our new code use the latest version? It turns out that require automatically loads the latest version of a gem, so the code from page 229 will work fine. If we want to specify a version number when we load a gem, we have to do a little bit more work, making it explicit that we're using RubyGems:

```
gem 'builder', '< 1.0'
require 'builder'

xml = Builder::XmlMarkup.new(STDOUT, 2)
xml.person do
  name("Dave Thomas")
  location("Texas")
end
```

The magic is the gem line, which says, "When looking for the builder gem, consider only those versions less than 1.0." The subsequent require honors this, so the code loads the correct version of Builder and runs. The '< 1.0' part of the gem line is a version predicate. Table 15.2 on page 232 shows the various predicates that RubyGems supports. You can specify multiple version predicates, so the following is valid:

```
gem 'builder', '> 0.1', '< 0.1.5'
```

Unfortunately, after all this work, there's a problem. Older versions of Builder don't run under 1.9 anyway. You can still run this code in Ruby 1.8, but you'd have to update your code to use the new-style Builder if you want to use Ruby 1.9.

Gems Can Be More Than Libraries

As well as installing libraries that can be used inside your application code, RubyGems can also install utility programs that you can invoke from the command line. Often these utilities are wrappers around the libraries included in the gem. For example, Marcel Molina's AWS:S3 gem is a library that gives you programmatic access to Amazon's S3 storage facility. As well as the library itself, Marcel provided a command-line utility, s3sh, which lets you interact with your S3 assets. When you install the gem, s3sh is automatically loaded into the same bin/ directory that holds the Ruby interpreter.

There's a small problem with these installed utilities. Although gems supports versioning of libraries, it does not version command-line utilities. With these, it's "last one in wins."

The Rake Build Tool

As well as the Builder gem, Jim Weirich wrote an incredibly useful utility program called Rake. Prior to Ruby 1.9, you had to install Rake as a separate gem, but it is now included in the base Ruby installation.

Rake was initially implemented as a Ruby version of Make, the common build utility. However, calling Rake a build utility is to miss its true power. Really, Rake is an automation tool—it's a way of putting all those tasks that you perform in a project into one neat and tidy place.

Let's start with a trivial example. As you edit files, you often accumulate backup files in your working directories. On Unix systems, these files often have the same name as the original files, but with a tilde character appended. On Windows boxes, the files often have a .bak extension.

We could write a trivial Ruby program that deletes these files. For a Unix box, it might look something like this:

```
require 'fileutils'
files = Dir['*~']
FileUtils::rm files, verbose: true
```

The FileUtils module defines methods for manipulating files and directories (see the description on page 746). Our code uses its rm method. We use the Dir class to return a list of filenames matching the given pattern and pass that list to rm.

Let's package this code as a *task*—a chunk of code that Rake can execute for us.

By default, Rake searches the current directory (and its parents) for a file called Rakefile. This file contains definitions for the tasks that Rake can run.

Table 15.2. Version Operators

Both the gem method and the add_dependency attribute in a Gem::Specification accept arguments that specify a version dependency. RubyGems version dependencies are of the form operator major.minor.patch_level. Listed next is a table of all the possible version operators.

Operator	Description
=	Exact version match. Major, minor, and patch level must be identical.
!=	Any version that is not the one specified.
>	Any version that is greater (even at the patch level) than the one specified.
<	Any version that is less than the one specified.
>=	Any version greater than or equal to the specified version.
<=	Any version less than or equal to the specified version.
~>	"Boxed" version operator. Version must be greater than or equal to the specified version *and* less than the specified version after having its minor version number increased by 1. This is to avoid API incompatibilities between minor version releases.

So, put the following code into a file called Rakefile:

```
desc "Remove files whose names end with a tilde"
task :delete_unix_backups do
  files = Dir['*~']
  rm(files, verbose: true) unless files.empty?
end
```

Although it doesn't have an .rb extension, this is actually just a file of Ruby code. Rake defines an environment containing methods such as desc and task and then executes the Rakefile.

The desc method provides a single line of documentation for the task that follows it. The task method defines a Rake task that can be executed from the command line. The parameter is the name of the task (a symbol), and the block that follows is the code to be executed. Here we can just use rm—all the methods in FileUtils are automatically available inside Rake files.

We can invoke this task from the command line:

```
% rake delete_unix_backups
(in /Users/dave/BS2/titles/RUBY3/Book/code/rake)
rm entry~
```

The first line shows us the name of the directory where Rake found the Rakefile (remember that this might be in a directory above our current working directory). The next line is the output of the rm method, in this case showing it deleted the single file entry~.

OK, now let's write a second task in the same Rakefile. This one deletes Windows backup files.

```
desc "Remove files whose names end with a tilde"
task :delete_unix_backups do
  files = Dir['*~']
  rm(files, verbose: true) unless files.empty?
end
desc "Remove files with a .bak extension"
task :delete_windows_backups do
  files = Dir['*.bak']
  rm(files, verbose: true) unless files.empty?
end
```

We can run this with rake delete_windows_backups.

But let's say that our application could be used on both platforms, and we wanted to let our users delete backup files on either. We *could* write a combined task, but Rake gives us a better way—it lets us *compose* tasks. Here, for example, is a new task:

```
desc "Remove Unix and Windows backup files"
task :delete_backups =>
        [ :delete_unix_backups, :delete_windows_backups ] do
  puts "All backups deleted"
end
```

The task's name is delete_backups, and it depends on two other tasks. This isn't some special Rake syntax: we're simply passing the task method a Ruby hash containing a single entry whose key is the task name and whose value is the list of antecedent tasks. What this means is that Rake will execute the two platform-specific tasks before executing the delete_backups task:

```
% rake delete_backups
(in /Users/dave/OldWork/BS2/titles/RUBY3/Book/code/rake)
rm entry~
rm index.bak list.bak
All backups deleted
```

Our current Rakefile contains some duplication between the Unix and Windows deletion tasks. As it is just Ruby code, we can simply define a Ruby method to eliminate this:

```
def delete(pattern)
  files = Dir[pattern]
  rm(files, verbose: true) unless files.empty?
end
desc "Remove files whose names end with a tilde"
task :delete_unix_backups do
  delete "*~"
end
desc "Remove files with a .bak extension"
task :delete_windows_backups do
  delete "*.bak"
end
desc "Remove Unix and Windows backup files"
task :delete_backups => [ :delete_unix_backups, :delete_windows_backups ] do
  puts "All backups deleted"
end
```

If a Rake task is named default, it will be executed if you invoke Rake with no parameters.

You can find the tasks implemented by a Rakefile (or, more accurately, the tasks for which there is a description) using this:

```
% rake -T
(in /Users/dave/BS2/titles/RUBY3/Book/code/rake)
rake delete_backups          # Remove Unix and Windows backup files
rake delete_unix_backups     # Remove files whose names end with a tilde
rake delete_windows_backups  # Remove files with a .bak extension
```

This section only touches on the full power of Rake. It can handle dependencies between files (for example, rebuilding an executable file if one of the source files has changed), it knows about running tests and generating documentation, and it can even package gems for you. Martin Fowler has written a good overview of Rake if you're interested in digging deeper.[5] You might also want to investigate Sake, a tool that makes Rake tasks available no matter what directory you're in.[6]

Build Environment

When Ruby is compiled for a particular architecture, all the relevant settings used to build it (including the architecture of the machine on which it was compiled, compiler options, source code directory, and so on) are written to the module Config within the library file rbconfig.rb. After installation, any Ruby program can use this module to get details on how Ruby was compiled:

```
require 'rbconfig'
include Config
CONFIG["host"]    # =>   "i386-apple-darwin9.6.0"
CONFIG["libdir"]  # =>   "/usr/local/rubybook/lib"
```

Extension libraries use this configuration file in order to compile and link properly on any given architecture. See Chapter 29 beginning on page 825 and the reference for mkmf beginning on page 866 for details.

---

5. http://martinfowler.com/articles/rake.html

6. http://errtheblog.com/posts/60-sake-bomb

## Chapter 16

Namespaces, Source Files, and Distribution

As your programs grow (and they all seem to grow over time), you'll find that you'll need to start organizing your code—simply putting everything into a single huge file becomes unworkable (and makes it hard to reuse chunks of code in other projects). So, we need to find a way to split our project into multiple files and then to knit those files together as our program runs.

There are two major aspects to this organization. The first is internal to your code: how do you prevent different things with the same name from clashing? The second area is related—how do you conveniently organize the source files in your project?

Namespaces

We've already encountered a way that Ruby helps you manage the names of things in your programs. If you define methods or constants in a class, Ruby ensures that their names can be used only in the context of that class (or its objects, in the case of instance methods):

`packaging_1.rb`

```ruby
class Triangle
  SIDES = 3
  def area
    # ..
  end
end
class Square
  SIDES = 4
  def initialize(side_length)
    @side_length = side_length
  end
  def area
    @side_length * @side_length
  end
end
```

```
puts "A triangle has #{Triangle::SIDES} sides"
sq = Square.new(3)
puts "Area of square = #{sq.area}"
```

produces:

```
A triangle has 3 sides
Area of square = 9
```

Both classes define a constant called SIDES and an instance method area, but these things don't get confused. You access the instance method via objects created from the class, and you access the constant by prefixing it with the name of the class followed by a double colon. The double colon (::) is Ruby's namespace resolution operator. The thing to the left must be a class or module, and the thing to the right is a constant defined in that class or module.[1]

So, putting code inside a module or class is a good way of separating it from other code. Ruby's Math module is a good example—it defines constants such as Math::PI and Math::E and methods such as Math.sin and Math.cos. You can access these constants and methods via the Math module object:

```
Math::E              # =>   2.71828182845905
Math.sin(Math::PI/6.0)  # =>   0.5
```

(Modules have another, significant, use—they implement Ruby's *mixin* functionality, which we discussed on page 78).

Ruby has an interesting little secret. The names of classes and modules are themselves just constants.[2] And that means that if you define classes or modules inside other classes and modules, the names of those inner classes follow the same namespacing rules as other constants:

```
module Formatters
  class Html
    # ...
  end
  class Pdf
    # ...
  end
end
html_writer = Formatters::Html.new
```

You can nest classes and modules inside other classes and modules to any depth you want (although it's rare to see them more than three deep).

So, now we know that we can use classes and modules to partition the names used by our programs. The second question to answer is, what do we do with the source code?

---

1.   The thing to the right of the :: can also be a class or module method, but this use is falling out of favor—using a period makes it clearer that it's just a regular old method call.

2.   Remember that we said that most everything in Ruby is an object. Well, classes and modules are, too. The name that you use for a class, such as String, is really just a Ruby constant containing the object representing that class.

Organizing Your Source

This section covers two related issues: how do we split our source code into separate files, and where in the file system do we put those files?

Some languages, such as Java, make this easy. They dictate that each outer-level class should be in its own file, and that file should be named according to the name of the class. Other languages, such as Ruby, have no rules relating source files and their content. In Ruby, you're free to organize your code as you like.

But, in the real world, you'll find that some kind of consistency really helps. It will make it easier for you to navigate your own projects, and it will also help when you read (or incorporate) other people's code.

So, the Ruby community is gradually adopting a kind of de facto standard. In many ways, it follows the spirit of the Java model, but without some of the inconveniences suffered by our Java brethren. Let's start with the basics.

Small Programs

Small, self-contained scripts can be in a single file. However, if you do this, you won't easily be able to write automated tests for your program, because the test code won't be able to load the file containing your source without the program itself running. So, if you want to write a small program that also has automated tests, split that program into a trivial driver that provides the external interface (the command-line part of the code) and one or more files containing the rest. Your tests can then exercise these separate files without actually running the main body of your program.

Let's try this for real. Here's a simple program that finds anagrams in a dictionary. Feed it one or more words, and it gives you the anagrams of each. For example:

```
$  ruby anagram.rb teaching code
Anagrams of teaching: cheating, teaching
Anagrams of code: code, coed
```

If I were typing this program in for casual use, I might just enter it into a single file (perhaps anagram.rb). It would look something like this:

```
packaging_4.rb
#!/usr/bin/env ruby
require 'optparse'
dictionary = "/usr/share/dict/words"
OptionParser.new do |opts|
  opts.banner = "Usage:  anagram [ options ]  word..."
  opts.on("-d", "--dict path", String, "Path to dictionary") do |dict|
    dictionary = dict
  end
  opts.on("-h", "--help", "Show this message") do
    puts opts
    exit
  end
```

```
  begin
    ARGV << "-h" if ARGV.empty?
    opts.parse!(ARGV)
  rescue OptionParser::ParseError => e
    STDERR.puts e.message, "\n", opts
    exit(-1)
  end
end

# convert "wombat" into "abmotw". All anagrams share a signature
def signature_of(word)
  word.unpack("c*").sort.pack("c*")
end

signatures = Hash.new

File.foreach(dictionary) do |line|
  word = line.chomp
  signature = signature_of(word)
  (signatures[signature] ||= []) << word
end

ARGV.each do |word|
  signature = signature_of(word)
  if signatures[signature]
    puts "Anagrams of #{word}: #{signatures[signature].join(', ')}"
  else
    puts "No anagrams of #{word} in #{dictionary}"
  end
end
```

Then someone asks me for a copy, and I start to feel embarassed. It has no tests, and it isn't particularly well packaged.

Looking at the code, there are clearly three sections. The first twenty-five or so lines do option parsing, the next ten or so lines read and convert the dictionary, and the last few lines look up each command-line argument and report the result.

Let's split our file into four parts:

- An option parser
- A class to hold the lookup table for anagrams
- A class that looks up words given on the command line
- A trivial command-line interface

The first three of these are effectively library files, used by the fourth.

Where do we put all these files? The answer is driven by some strong Ruby conventions, first seen in Minero Aoki's setup.rb and later enshrined in the RubyGems system. We'll create a directory for our project containing (for now) three subdirectories:

```
anagram/       <- top-level
    bin/       <- command-line interface goes here
    lib/       <- three library files go here
    test/      <- test files go here
```

Now let's look at the library files. We know we're going to be defining (at least) three classes. Right now, these classes will be used only inside our command-line program, but it's conceivable that other people might want to include one or more of our libraries in their own code. This means that we should be polite and not pollute the top-level Ruby namespace with the names of all our classes and so on. We'll create just one top-level module, Anagram, and then place all our classes inside this module. This means that the full name of (say) our options-parsing class will be Anagram::Options.

This choice informs our decision on where to put the corresponding source files. Because class Options is inside the module Anagram, it makes sense to put the corresponding file options.rb inside a directory named anagram/ in the lib/ directory. This helps people who read your code in the future; when they see a name like A::B::C, they know to look for c.rb in the b/ directory in the a/ directory of your library.

So, we can now flesh out our directory structure with some files:

```
anagram/
    bin/
        anagram        <- command-line interface
    lib/
        anagram/
            finder.rb
            options.rb
            runner.rb
    test/
        ... various test files
```

Let's start with the option parser. Its job is to take an array of command-line options and return to us the path to the dictionary file and the list of words to look up as anagrams. The source, in lib/anagram/options.rb, looks like this:

packaging_5.rb

```ruby
require 'optparse'
module Anagram
  class Options

    DEFAULT_DICTIONARY = "/usr/share/dict/words"

    attr_reader :dictionary
    attr_reader :words_to_find

    def initialize(argv)
      @dictionary = DEFAULT_DICTIONARY
      parse(argv)
      @words_to_find = argv
    end

  private

    def parse(argv)
      OptionParser.new do |opts|
        opts.banner = "Usage:  anagram [ options ]  word..."
        opts.on("-d", "--dict path", String, "Path to dictionary") do |dict|
          @dictionary = dict
        end
```

```
      opts.on("-h", "--help", "Show this message") do
        puts opts
        exit
      end
      begin
        argv = ["-h"] if argv.empty?
        opts.parse!(argv)
      rescue OptionParser::ParseError => e
        STDERR.puts e.message, "\n", opts
        exit(-1)
      end
    end
  end
 end
end
```

Notice how we define the Options class inside a top-level Anagram module.

Let's write some unit tests for this code. This should be relatively easy, because options.rb is self-contained—the only external dependency is to the standard Ruby OptionParser. We'll use the standard Ruby Test::Unit framework, extended using the Shoulda gem.[3] We'll put the source of this test in the file test/test_options.rb:

`packaging_6.rb`

```ruby
require 'test/unit'
require 'shoulda'
require_relative '../lib/anagram/options'
class TestOptions < Test::Unit::TestCase
  context "specifying no dictionary" do
    should "return default" do
      opts = Anagram::Options.new(["someword"])
      assert_equal Anagram::Options::DEFAULT_DICTIONARY, opts.dictionary
    end
  end
  context "specifying a dictionary" do
    should "return it" do
      opts = Anagram::Options.new(["-d", "mydict", "someword"])
      assert_equal "mydict", opts.dictionary
    end
  end
  context "specifying words and no dictionary" do
    should "return the words" do
      opts = Anagram::Options.new(["word1", "word2"])
      assert_equal ["word1", "word2"], opts.words_to_find
    end
  end
  context "specifying words and a dictionary" do
```

---

3. We talk about Shoulda starting on page 194.

```
    should "return the words" do
      opts = Anagram::Options.new(["-d", "mydict", "word1", "word2"])
      assert_equal ["word1", "word2"], opts.words_to_find
    end
  end
end
```

The line to note in this file is as follows:

```
require_relative '../lib/anagram/options'
```

This is where we load in the source of the Options class we just wrote. We use the new Ruby 1.9 feature, require_relative. This is like regular old require, but it always loads from a path relative to the directory of the file that invokes it.

```
$ ruby test/test_options.rb
```

produces:

```
Loaded suite test/test_options
Started
....
Finished in 0.001226 seconds.

4 tests, 4 assertions, 0 failures, 0 errors, 0 skips
```

The finder code (in lib/anagram/finder.rb) is modified slightly from the original version. To make it easier to test, we'll have the default constructor take a list of words, rather than a filename. We'll then provide an additional factory method, from_file, that takes a filename and constructs a new Finder from that file's contents:

`packaging_10.rb`

```
module Anagram
  class Finder
    def self.from_file(file_name)
      new(File.readlines(file_name))
    end
    def initialize(dictionary_words)
      @signatures = Hash.new
      dictionary_words.each do |line|
        word = line.chomp
        signature = Finder.signature_of(word)
        (@signatures[signature] ||= []) << word
      end
    end
    def lookup(word)
      signature = Finder.signature_of(word)
      @signatures[signature]
    end
    def self.signature_of(word)
      word.unpack("c*").sort.pack("c*")
    end
  end
end
```

require_relative and Ruby 1.8

In case you're still running Ruby 1.8, you can still use require_relative. Just put the following code into a file, and then require that file at the top of your program:

```
def require_relative(relative_feature)
  c = caller.first
  fail "Can't parse #{c}" unless c.rindex(/:\d+(:in `.*')?$/)
  file = $`
  if /\A\((.*)\)/ =~ file # eval, etc.
    raise LoadError, "require_relative is called in #{$1}"
  end
  absolute = File.expand_path(relative_feature,
File.dirname(file))
  require absolute
end
```

Again, we embed the Finder class inside the top-level Anagram module. And, again, this code is self-contained, allowing us to write some simple unit tests:

packaging_11.rb

```
require 'test/unit'
require 'shoulda'
require_relative '../lib/anagram/finder'
class TestFinder < Test::Unit::TestCase
  context "signature" do
    { "cat" => "act", "act" => "act", "wombat" => "abmotw" }.each do
      |word, signature|
        should "be #{signature} for #{word}" do
          assert_equal signature, Anagram::Finder.signature_of(word)
      end
    end
  end
  context "lookup" do
    setup do
      @finder = Anagram::Finder.new(["cat", "wombat"])
    end
    should "return word if word given" do
      assert_equal ["cat"], @finder.lookup("cat")
    end
    should "return word if anagram given" do
      assert_equal ["cat"], @finder.lookup("act")
      assert_equal ["cat"], @finder.lookup("tca")
    end
```

```
    should "return nil if no word matches anagram" do
      assert_nil @finder.lookup("wibble")
    end
  end
end
```

These go in lib/test_finder.rb:

```
$ ruby test/test_finder.rb
```

produces:

```
Loaded suite test/test_finder
Started
......
Finished in 0.000776 seconds.

6 tests, 7 assertions, 0 failures, 0 errors, 0 skips
```

So, now we have all the support code in place. We just need to run it. We'll make the command-line interface—the thing the end user actually executes—really thin. It's in a file called bin/anagram (no .rb extension, because that would be unusual in a command). If you're on Windows, you might want to wrap the invocation of this in a .cmd file:

packaging_13.rb

```
#! /usr/local/rubybook/bin/ruby
require 'anagram/runner'

runner = Anagram::Runner.new(ARGV)
runner.run
```

The code that this script invokes (lib/runner.rb) knits our other libraries together:

packaging_14.rb

```
require_relative 'finder'
require_relative 'options'
module Anagram
  class Runner
    def initialize(argv)
      @options = Options.new(argv)
    end
    def run
      finder = Finder.from_file(@options.dictionary)
      @options.words_to_find.each do |word|
        anagrams = finder.lookup(word)
        if anagrams
          puts "Anagrams of #{word}: #{anagrams.join(', ')}"
        else
          puts "No anagrams of #{word} in #{@options.dictionary}"
        end
      end
    end
  end
end
```

In this case, the two libraries finder and options are in the same directory as the runner, so require_relative finds them perfectly.

Now all our files are in place, we can run our program from the command line:

```
$ ruby -I lib bin/anagram teaching code
```

produces:

```
Anagrams of teaching: cheating, teaching
Anagrams of code: code, coed
```

Nothing like a cheating coed teaching code.

Distributing and Installing Your Code

Now that we have our code a little tidier, it would be nice to be able to distribute it to others. We could just zip or tar it up and send them our files, but then they'd have to run the code the way we do, remembering to add the correct -I lib options and so on. They'd also have some problems if they wanted to reuse one of our library files—it would be sitting in some random directory on their hard drive, not in a standard location used by Ruby.

So, we're really looking for a way to take our little application and *install* it in a standard way.

Now Ruby already has a standard installation structure on your computer. When Ruby is installed, it puts its commands (ruby, ri, irb, and so on) into a directory of binary files. It puts its libraries into another directory tree and documentation somewhere else. So, one option would be to write an installation script that you distribute with your code that copies components of your application to the appropriate directories on the system that's installing it.

Using setup.rb

Rather than write this script yourself, you could instead use Minero Aoki's setup.rb. Follow the download link from http://i.loveruby.net/en/projects/setup/, and you'll end up with a gzipped tarball. When you extract the files, you'll find a lot of documentation and other support material. But the key is the file setup.rb that you'll find in the top-level directory. Copy this file into the top-level directory of our new application:

```
anagram/
    bin/
        anagram
    lib/
        anagram/
            finder.rb
            options.rb
            runner.rb
    setup.rb            <- installer
    test/
        ... various test files
```

Perhaps surprisingly, that's all that's needed. The directory structure we chose to use for our application is recognized by setup.rb, so it will automatically copy things into the correct location on our (and other people's) system. (However, before doing this for the first time, you need to be aware of one major hole in setup.rb—it has no uninstall capability. Once you've run it, your application will be installed into the Ruby directory structure. The only way to uninstall is to manually delete your application's files. As we'll see shortly, RubyGems gets around this issue.)

So, installing the application is as simple as this:

```
$ sudo ruby setup.rb
---> bin
<--- bin
...
---> bin
mkdir -p /usr/local/bin/
install anagram /usr/local/bin/
<--- bin
---> lib
mkdir -p /usr/local/lib/ruby/site_ruby/1.9.0/
---> lib/anagram
mkdir -p /usr/local/lib/ruby/site_ruby/1.9.0/anagram
install finder.rb /usr/local/lib/ruby/site_ruby/1.9.0/anagram
install options.rb /usr/local/lib/ruby/site_ruby/1.9.0/anagram
install runner.rb /usr/local/lib/ruby/site_ruby/1.9.0/anagram
<--- lib/anagram
<--- lib
```

At this point, our anagram script is available globally on our system (or on the system of whoever installed it).

setup.rb can do a lot more than we showed here. Take a look at the documentation in the downloaded archive or at `http://i.loveruby.net/en/projects/setup/doc/` for some pointers.

Being a Good Packaging Citizen

So, I've ignored some stuff that you'd want to do before distributing your code to the world. Your distributed directory tree really should have a README file, outlining what it does and probably containing a copyright statement; an INSTALL file, giving installation instructions; and a LICENSE file, giving the license it is distributed under.

You'll probably want to distribute some documentation, too. This would go in a directory called doc/, parallel with the bin and lib directories.

You might also want to distribute native C-language extensions with your library. We talk about creating these in *Extending Ruby* on page 825. These extensions would go into your project's ext/ directory.

Using RubyGems

The RubyGems package management system (which is also just called *Gems*) has become the standard for distributing and managing Ruby code packages. As of Ruby 1.9, it comes bundled with Ruby itself.

RubyGems is also a great way to package your own code. If you want to make your code available to the world, RubyGems is the way to go. Even if you're just sending code to a few friends, or within your company, RubyGems gives you dependency and installation management—one day you'll be grateful for that.

Unlike setup.rb, RubyGems needs to know information about your project that isn't contained in the directory structure. Instead, you have to write a short RubyGems specification: a GemSpec. You can create this in a separate file, but the most convenient way is to use rake (which comes with Ruby 1.9). Using Rake means that the GemSpec will be packaged with a set of tasks that you can use to build your gem. So, let's create the Rakefile in the top-level directory of our application:

packaging_16.rb
```ruby
require 'rake/gempackagetask'
spec = Gem::Specification.new do |s|
    s.name       = "anagram"
    s.summary    = "Find anagrams of words supplied on the command line"
    s.description= File.read(File.join(File.dirname(__FILE__), 'README'))
    s.requirements =
        [ 'An installed dictionary (most Unix systems have one)' ]
    s.version    = "0.0.1"
    s.author     = "Dave Thomas"
    s.email      = "dave@pragprog.com"
    s.homepage   = "http://pragdave.pragprog.com"
    s.platform   = Gem::Platform::RUBY
    s.required_ruby_version = '>=1.9'
    s.files      = Dir['**/**']
    s.executables = [ 'anagram' ]
    s.test_files = Dir["test/test*.rb"]
    s.has_rdoc   = false
end
Rake::GemPackageTask.new(spec).define
```

The first line of this file requires the Rake task definitions for gem packaging. The last line of the file tells Rake to use these definitions. The rest of the file is the GemSpec.

The first line of the spec gives our gem a name. This is important—it will be used as part of the package name, and it will appear as the name of the gem when installed. Although it can be mixed case, I personally find that confusing—do my poor brain a favor and use lowercase for gem names.

The version string is significant, because RubyGems will use it both for package naming and for dependency management. Stick to the *x.y.z* format.[4]

The platform field tells RubyGems that (in this case) our gem is pure Ruby code. It's also possible to package (for example) Windows .exe files inside a gem, in which case you'd use Gem::Platform::Win32.

The next line is also important (and oft-forgotten by package developers). Because we use require_relative, our gem will run only with Ruby 1.9 and later.

We then tell RubyGems which files to include when creating the gem package. Here we've been lazy and included everything. You can be more specific.

The s.executables line tells RubyGems to install the anagram command-line script when the gem gets installed on a user's machine.

To save space, we haven't added RDoc documentation comments to our source files (RDoc is described in Appendix 19 on page 277). The last line of the spec tells RubyGems not to try to extract documentation when the gem is installed.

Obviously I've skipped a lot of details here. A full description of GemSpecs is available online,[5] along with other documents on RubyGems.[6]

Packaging Your RubyGem

Once the Rakefile containing the gem specification is complete, you'll want to create the packaged .gem file for distribution. This is as easy as navigating to the top level of your project and typing this:

```
$ rake gem
(in /Users/dave/code/anagram)
WARNING:  no rubyforge_project specified
WARNING:  RDoc will not be generated (has_rdoc == false)
  Successfully built RubyGem
  Name: anagram
  Version: 0.0.1
  File: anagram-0.0.1.gem
```

You'll find you now have a directory called pkg:

```
$ ls pkg
anagram-0.0.1.gem
```

There's your gem. You can install it:

```
$ sudo gem install pkg/anagram-0.0.1.gem
Successfully installed anagram-0.0.1
1 gem installed
```

---

4. And read http://www.rubygems.org/read/chapter/7 for information on what the numbers mean.

5. http://www.rubygems.org/read/book/4

6. http://www.rubygems.org/

And the check to see it is there:

```
$ gem list anagram -d

*** LOCAL GEMS ***
anagram (0.0.1)
    Author: Dave Thomas
    Homepage: http://pragdave.pragprog.com
    Installed at: /usr/local/lib/ruby/gems/1.9.0

    Find anagrams of words supplied on the command line
```

Now you can send your .gem file to friends and colleagues or share it from a server. Or, you could go one better and share it from a RubyGems server.

If you have RubyGems installed on your local box, you can share them over the network to others. Simply run this:

```
$ gem server
Starting gem server on http://localhost:8808/
```

This starts a server (by default on port 8808, but the --port option overrides that). Other people can connect to your server to list and retrieve RubyGems:

```
$ gem list --remote --source http://dave.local:8808

*** REMOTE GEMS ***

anagram (0.0.1)
builder (2.1.2, 0.1.1)
..
```

This is particularly useful in a corporate environment.

You can speed up the serving of gems by creating a static index—see the help for gem generate_index for details.

Serving Public RubyGems

RubyForge (http://rubyforge.org) has become the main repository for public Ruby libraries and projects. And, if you create a RubyForge project, you can upload your .gem file to the project's download area. Within a few hours, their servers will pick up your gem and add it to their master list. And, at that point, any Ruby user in the world can do this:

```
$ gem search -r anagram

*** REMOTE GEMS ***

anagram (0.0.1)
..
```

and, even better

```
$ gem install anagram
```

GitHub has recently emerged as an alternative place where people are developing and storing RubyGems. You'll find information at http://gems.github.com/. At the time of writing, there are some security concerns related to the naming conventions of GitHub gems,[7] but this will likely be resolved soon.

Adding Even More Automation

The Hoe library[8] helps create a rich set of Rake tasks for RubyGems. Install using gem install hoe. You can then use their sow utility to create an empty project directory, which you populate with code. Hoe provides a number of Rake tasks that will, for example, upload your gem to RubyForge automatically.

Nic Williams has a gem called newgem[9] that extends Hoe even further. After installing the newgem gem, you use the newgem command to create a new project directory structure that contains (among other things) a wonderfully lurid default project website, which it will upload to RubyForge on request.

Some folks like the extra features of these utilities, while others prefer the leaner "roll-your-own" approach. Whatever route you take, taking the time to package your applications and libraries will pay you back many times over.

---

7. http://www.infoq.com/news/2008/08/gems-from-rubyforge-and-github

8. http://seattlerb.rubyforge.org/hoe/

9. http://newgem.rubyforge.org/

## Chapter 17

Character Encoding

1.9

Prior to Ruby 1.9, Ruby programs were basically written using the ASCII character encoding. You could always override this with the -K command-line option, but this led to inconsistencies when manipulating strings and doing file I/O.

Ruby 1.9 changes all this. Ruby now supports the idea of character encodings. And, what's more, these encodings can be applied relatively independently to your program source files, to objects in your running programs, and to the interpretation of I/O streams.

Before delving into the details, let's spend a few minutes thinking about why we need to separate the encodings of source files, variables, and I/O streams. Let's imagine Yui is a developer in Japan who wants to code in her native language. Her editor lets her write code using Shift JIS (which we'll call SJIS from now on), a Japanese character encoding, so she writes her variable names using katakana and kanji characters. But, by default, Ruby assumes that source files are written in ASCII, and the SJIS characters would not be recognized as such. However, by setting the encoding to be used when compiling the source file, Ruby can now parse her program.

She converts her program into a gem, and users around the world try it out. Dan, in the United States, doesn't read Japanese, so the content of her source files makes no sense to him. However, because the source files carry their encoding around with them, there's no problem; his Ruby happily compiles her code. But Dan wants to test her code against a file that contains regular old ASCII characters. That's no problem, because the file encoding is determined by Dan's locale, not by the encoding of the Ruby source. Similarly, Sophie in Paris uses the same library, but her data file is encoded in ISO-8859-1 (which is basically ASCII plus a useful subset of accented European characters in character positions above 127). Again, no problem.

But, back in Japan, Yui has a new feature to add to her library. Users want to create short PDF summaries of the data she reads, but the PDF writing library she's using supports only ISO-8859-1 characters. So, regardless of the encoding of the source code of her program and the encoding of the files she reads, she needs to be able to create strings at runtime with 8859-1 encoding. So, again, we need to be able to decouple the encoding of individual objects from the encoding of everything else.

If this sounds complex, well...it is. But the good news is that the Ruby team spent a long time thinking up ways to make it all relatively easy to use when you're writing code. In this section, we'll look at how to work with the various encodings, and I'll try to list some conventions that will make your code work in the brave new multinational world.

Encodings

At the heart of the Ruby encoding system is the new Encoding class. Objects of class Encoding each represent a different character encoding. The Encoding.list method returns a list of the built-in encodings, and the Encoding.aliases method returns a hash where the keys are aliases and the values are the corresponding base encoding. We can use these two methods to build a table of known encoding names:

```
encoding_1.rb
encodings = {}
Encoding.list.each {|enc| encodings[enc.name] = [enc.name] }
Encoding.aliases.each do |alias_name, base_name|
  fail "#{base_name} #{alias_name}" unless encodings[base_name]
  encodings[base_name] << alias_name
end

names = encodings
        .values
        .sort_by {|base_name, *| base_name.downcase}
        .map do |base_name, *rest|
          if rest.empty?
            base_name
          else
           "#{base_name} (#{rest.join(', ')})"
          end
        end

puts names
```

We can see the output, wrapped into columns, in Figure 17.1 on the next page:

However, that's not the full story. Encodings in Ruby can be dynamically loaded—Ruby actually comes with more encodings than those shown in the output from this code.

Strings, regular expressions, symbols, I/O streams, and program source files are all associated with one of these encoding objects.

Encodings commonly used in Ruby programs include ASCII (7 bit characters), ASCII-8BIT,[1] UTF-8, and Shift JIS.

---

1. There isn't actually a character encoding called ASCII-8BIT. It's a Ruby fantasy, but a useful one. We'll talk about it shortly.

Figure 17.1.   Encodings and Their Aliases

ASCII-8BIT (BINARY)	Big5 (CP950)	CP51932
CP850 (IBM850)	CP852	CP855
CP949	Emacs-Mule	EUC-JP (eucJP)
EUC-KR (eucKR)	EUC-TW (eucTW)	eucJP-ms (euc-jp-ms)
GB12345	GB18030	GB1988
GB2312 (EUC-CN, eucCN)	GBK (CP936)	IBM437 (CP437)
IBM737 (CP737)	IBM775 (CP775)	IBM852
IBM855	IBM857 (CP857)	IBM860 (CP860)
IBM861 (CP861)	IBM862 (CP862)	IBM863 (CP863)
IBM864 (CP864)	IBM865 (CP865)	IBM866 (CP866)
IBM869 (CP869)	ISO-2022-JP (ISO2022-JP)	ISO-2022-JP-2 (ISO2022-JP2)
ISO-8859-1 (ISO8859-1)	ISO-8859-10 (ISO8859-10)	ISO-8859-11 (ISO8859-11)
ISO-8859-13 (ISO8859-13)	ISO-8859-14 (ISO8859-14)	ISO-8859-15 (ISO8859-15)
ISO-8859-16 (ISO8859-16)	ISO-8859-2 (ISO8859-2)	ISO-8859-3 (ISO8859-3)
ISO-8859-4 (ISO8859-4)	ISO-8859-5 (ISO8859-5)	ISO-8859-6 (ISO8859-6)
ISO-8859-7 (ISO8859-7)	ISO-8859-8 (ISO8859-8)	ISO-8859-9 (ISO8859-9)
KOI8-R (CP878)	KOI8-U	macCentEuro
macCroatian	macCyrillic	macGreek
macIceland	MacJapanese (MacJapan)	macRoman
macRomania	macThai	macTurkish
macUkraine	Shift_JIS (SJIS)	stateless-ISO-2022-JP
TIS-620	US-ASCII (ASCII, ANSI_X3.4-1968, 646)	UTF-16BE (UCS-2BE)
UTF-16LE	UTF-32BE (UCS-4BE)	UTF-32LE (UCS-4LE)
UTF-7 (CP65000)	UTF-8 (CP65001, locale, external)	UTF8-MAC (UTF-8-MAC)
Windows-1250 (CP1250)	Windows-1251 (CP1251)	Windows-1252 (CP1252)
Windows-1253 (CP1253)	Windows-1254 (CP1254)	Windows-1255 (CP1255)
Windows-1256 (CP1256)	Windows-1257 (CP1257)	Windows-1258 (CP1258)
Windows-31J (CP932, csWindows31J)	Windows-874 (CP874)	

Source Files

First and foremost, there's a simple rule: if you only ever use 7-bit ASCII characters in your source, then the source file encoding is irrelevant. So, the simplest way to write Ruby source files that just work everywhere is to stick to boring old ASCII.

However, once a source file contains a byte whose top bit is set, you've just left the comfortable world of ASCII and entered the wild and wacky nightmare of character encodings. Here's how it works.

If your source files are not written using 7-bit ASCII, you probably want to tell Ruby about it. Because the encoding is an attribute of the source file, and not anything to do with the environment where the file is used, Ruby has a way of setting the encoding on a file-by-file basis using a new *magic comment*. If the first line of a file[2] is a comment (or the second line if the first line is a #! shebang line), Ruby scans it looking for the string coding:. If it finds it, Ruby then skips any spaces and looks for the (case-insensitive) name of an encoding. Thus, to specify that a source file is in UTF-8 encoding, you can write this:

```
# coding: utf-8
```

As Ruby is just scanning for coding:, you could also write this:

```
# encoding: ascii
```

---

2.   Or a string passed to eval.

Emacs users might like the fact that this also works:

```
#  -*- encoding:  shift_jis -*-
```

(Your favorite editor may also support some kind of flag comment to set a file's encoding.)

If there's a shebang line, the encoding comment must be the second line of the file:

```
#!/usr/local/rubybook/bin/ruby
#  encoding:  utf-8
```

Additionally, Ruby detects any files that start with a UTF-8 byte order mark (BO). If Ruby sees the byte sequence \xEF\xBB\xBF at the start of a source file, it assumes that file is UTF-8 encoded.

The special constant __ENCODING__ returns the encoding of the current source file.

Source Elements That Have Encodings

If nothing overrides the setting, the default encoding for source is US-ASCII. This is basically the same as Ruby 1.8—you write your programs using 7-bit ASCII characters. However, unlike Ruby 1.8, if any characters with the top bit set (that is, with a character code greater than 127) do sneak into your source, Ruby will report an error, probably saying something like "invalid multibyte char." Here's an example where we typed some UTF-8 characters into a Ruby program:

```
π = 3.14159
puts "π = #{π}"
```

produces:

```
prog.rb:1: invalid multibyte char (US-ASCII)
```

The character π actually consists of the two bytes: \xcf \x80. In the default Ruby source encoding of US-ASCII, these characters raise an error because the top bit is set and Ruby doesn't know how to handle them.

We can fix that by setting the encoding:

```
# encoding: utf-8
π = 3.14159
puts "π = #{π}"
```

produces:

```
π = 3.14159
```

Note that Ruby is correctly interpreting π as a single character:

```
# encoding: utf-8
PI = "π"
puts "The size of a string containing π is #{PI.size}"
```

produces:

```
The size of a string containing π is 1
```

Now, let's get perverse. The two-byte sequence "\xcf\x8" represents π in UTF-8 but is not a valid byte sequence in the SJIS encoding. Let's see what happens if we tell Ruby that this same source file is SJIS encoded. (Remember: when we do this, we're not changing the actual bytes in the string—we're just telling Ruby to interpret them with a different set of encoding rules.)

```
# encoding: sjis
PI = "π"
puts "The size of a string containing π is #{PI.size}"
```

produces:

```
puts "The size of a string containing π is #{PI.size}"
       ^
prog.rb:2: invalid multibyte char (Shift_JIS)
prog.rb:3: syntax error, unexpected tCONSTANT, expecting $end
```

This time, Ruby complains because the file contains byte sequences that are illegal in the given encoding. And, to make matters even more confusing, the parser swallowed up the double quote after the π character, presumably while trying to build a valid SJIS character. This led to the second error message, because the word The is now interpreted as program text.

String literals are always encoded using the encoding of the source file that contains them, regardless of the content of the string:

```
# encoding: utf-8
def show_encoding(str)
  puts "'#{str}' (size #{str.size}) is #{str.encoding.name}"
end
show_encoding "cat"    # latin 'c', 'a', 't'
show_encoding "δog"    # greek delta, latin 'o', 'g'
```

produces:

```
'cat' (size 3) is UTF-8
'δog' (size 3) is UTF-8
```

Symbols and regular expression literals that contain only 7-bit characters are encoded using US-ASCII. Otherwise, they will have the encoding of the file that contains them.

```
# encoding: utf-8
def show_encoding(str)
  puts "#{str.inspect} is #{str.encoding.name}"
end
show_encoding :cat
show_encoding :δog
show_encoding /cat/
show_encoding /δog/
```

produces:

```
:cat is US-ASCII
:δog is UTF-8
/cat/ is US-ASCII
/δog/ is UTF-8
```

You can create arbitrary Unicode characters in strings and regular expressions using the \u escape. This has two forms: \uxxxx lets you encode a character using four hex digits, and \u{x... x... x...} lets you specify a variable number of characters, each with a variable number of hex digits:

```
# encoding: utf-8
"Greek pi: \u03c0"              # =>   "Greek pi: π"
"Greek pi: \u{3c0}"            # =>   "Greek pi: π"
"Greek \u{70 69 3a 20 3c0}"   # =>   "Greek pi: π"
```

Literals containing a \u sequence will always be encoded UTF-8, regardless of the source file encoding.

The String#bytes method is a convenient way to inspect the bytes in a string object. Notice that in the following code, the 16-bit codepoint is converted to a two-byte UTF-8 encoding:

```
# encoding: utf-8
"pi: \u03c0".bytes.to_a   # =>   [112, 105, 58, 32, 207, 128]
```

Eight-bit Clean Encodings

Ruby supports a virtual encoding called *ASCII-8BIT*. Despite the *ASCII* in the name, this is really intended to be used on data streams that contain binary data (hence its alias of *BINARY*). However, you can also use this as an encoding for source files. If you do, Ruby interprets all characters with codes below 128 as regular ASCII and all other characters as valid constituents of variable names. This is basically a neat hack, because it allows you to compile a file written in an encoding you don't know—the characters with the high-order bit set will be assumed to be printable.

encoding_15.rb

```
# encoding: ascii-8bit
π = 3.14159
puts "π = #{π}"
puts "Size of 'π' = #{'π'.size}"
```

produces:

```
π = 3.14159
Size of 'π' = 2
```

The last line of output illustrates why ASCII-8BIT is a dangerous encoding for source files. Because it doesn't know to use UTF-8 encoding, the π character looks to Ruby like two separate characters.

Source Encoding Is Per-File

Clearly, a large application will be built from many source files. Some of these files may come from other people (possibly as libraries or gems). In these cases, you may not have control over the encoding used in a file.

Ruby supports this by allowing different encodings in the files that make up a project. Each file starts with the default encoding of US-ASCII. The file's encoding may then be set with either a coding: comment or a UTF-8 BOM.

Here's a file called `iso-8859-1.rb`. Notice the explicit encoding.

```
# -*- encoding: iso-8859-1 -*-
STRING_ISO = "olé"   # \x6f \x6c \xe9
```

And here's its UTF-8 counterpart:

```
# file: utf.rb, encoding: utf-8
STRING_U = "δog"    # \xe2\x88\x82\x6f\x67
```

Now let's require both of these files into a third file. Just for the heck of it, let's declare the third file to have SJIS encoding:

```
# encoding: sjis

require 'iso-8859-1'
require 'utf'

def show_encoding(str)
  puts "'#{str}' (size #{str.size}) is #{str.encoding.name}"
end

show_encoding(STRING_ISO)
show_encoding(STRING_U)
show_encoding("cat")
```

produces:

```
'olé' (size 3) is ISO-8859-1
'δog' (size 3) is UTF-8
'cat' (size 3) is Shift_JIS
```

Notice how each file has an independent encoding. String literals in each retain their own encoding, even when used in a different file. All the encoding directive does is tell Ruby how to interpret the characters in the file and what encoding to use on literal strings and regular expressions containing non-ASCII characters. Ruby will never change the actual bytes in a source file when reading them in.

Transcoding

As we've already seen, strings, symbols, and regular expressions are now labeled with their encoding. You can convert a string from one encoding to another using the String#encode method. For example, we can convert the word *olé* from UTF-8 to ISO-8859-1:

```
# encoding: utf-8
ole_in_utf = "olé"
ole_in_utf.encoding      # =>   #<Encoding:UTF-8>
ole_in_utf.bytes.to_a    # =>   [111, 108, 195, 169]

ole_in_8859 = ole_in_utf.encode("iso-8859-1")
ole_in_8859.encoding     # =>   #<Encoding:ISO-8859-1>
ole_in_8859.bytes.to_a   # =>   [111, 108, 233]
```

You have to be careful when using encode—if the target encoding doesn't contain characters that appear in your source string, Ruby will throw an exception. For example, the π character is available in UTF-8 but not in ISO-8859-1:

```
# encoding: utf-8
pi = "pi = π"
pi.encode("iso-8859-1")
```

produces:

```
prog.rb:3:in `encode': "\xCF\x80" from UTF-8 to ISO-8859-1 (Encoding::UndefinedConversionError)
	from /tmp/prog.rb:3:in `<main>'
```

You can, however, override this behavior, for example supplying a placeholder character to use when no direct translation is possible. (See the description of String#encode on page 669 for more details.)

```
# encoding: utf-8
pi = "pi = π"
puts pi.encode("iso-8859-1", undef: :replace, replace: "??")
```

produces:

```
pi = ??
```

Sometimes you'll have a string containing binary data and you want that data to be interpreted as if it had a particular encoding. You can't use the encode method for this, because you don't want to change the byte contents of the string—you're just changing the encoding associated with those bytes. Use the String#force_encoding method to do this:

encoding_22.rb

```
# encoding: ascii-8bit
str = "\xc3\xa9"      # e-acute in UTF-8
str.encoding      # =>   #<Encoding:ASCII-8BIT>
str.force_encoding("utf-8")
str.bytes.to_a    # =>   [195, 169]
str.encoding      # =>   #<Encoding:UTF-8>
```

Finally, you can use encode (with two parameters) to convert between two encodings if your source string is ASCII-8BIT. This might happen if, for example, you're reading data in binary mode from a file and choose not to encode it at the time you read it. Here we fake that out by creating an ASCII-8BIT string that contains an ISO-8859-1 sequence (our old friend *olé*). We then convert the string to UTF-8. To do this, we have to tell encode the actual encoding of the bytes by passing it a second parameter:

encoding_23.rb

```
# encoding: ascii-8bit
original = "ol\xe9"      # e-acute in ISO-8859-1
original.bytes.to_a   # =>   [111, 108, 233]
original.encoding     # =>   #<Encoding:ASCII-8BIT>
new = original.encode("utf-8", "iso-8859-1")
new.bytes.to_a        # =>   [111, 108, 195, 169]
new.encoding          # =>   #<Encoding:UTF-8>
```

If you're writing programs that will support multiple encodings, you probably want to read the section on *Default Internal Encoding* on page 261—it will greatly simplify your life.

Input and Output Encoding

Playing around with encodings within a program is all very well, but in most code we'll want to read data from and write data to external files. And, often, that data will be in a particular encoding.

Ruby's I/O objects support both encoding and transcoding of data. What does this mean?

Every I/O object has an associated external encoding. This is the encoding of the data being read from or written to the outside world. Through a piece of magic I'll describe on page 261, all Ruby programs run with the concept of a default external encoding. This is the external encoding that will be used by I/O objects unless you override it when you create the object (for example, by opening a file).

Now, your program may want to operate internally in a different encoding. For example, some of my files may be encoded with ISO-8859-1, but I want my Ruby program to work internally using UTF-8. Ruby I/O objects manage this by having an optional associated *internal encoding*. If set, then input will be transcoded from the external to the internal encodings on read operations, and output will be transcoded from internal to external encoding on write operations.

Let's start with the simple cases. On my OS X box, the default external encoding is UTF-8. If I don't override it, all my file I/O will therefore also be in UTF-8. I can query the external encoding of an I/O object using the IO#external_encoding method:

```
f = File.open("/etc/passwd")
puts "File encoding is #{f.external_encoding}"
line = f.gets
puts "Data encoding is #{line.encoding}"
```

produces:

```
File encoding is UTF-8
Data encoding is UTF-8
```

Notice that the data is tagged with a UTF-8 encoding even though it (presumably) contains just 7-bit ASCII characters. Only literals in your Ruby source files have the "change encoding if they contain 8-bit data" rule.

You can force the external encoding associated with an I/O object when you open it—simply add the name of the encoding, preceded by a colon, to the mode string. Note that this in no way changes the data that's read—it simply tags it with the encoding you specify:

```
f = File.open("/etc/passwd", "r:ascii")
puts "File encoding is #{f.external_encoding}"
line = f.gets
puts "Data encoding is #{line.encoding}"
```

produces:

```
File encoding is US-ASCII
Data encoding is US-ASCII
```

You can force Ruby to transcode—change the encoding—of data it reads and writes by putting two encoding names in the mode string, again with a colon before each. For example, the file iso-8859-1.txt contains the word *olé* in ISO-8859-1 encoding. In this encoding, the e-acute character is encoded by the single byte \xe9. I can view this file's contents in hex using the od command-line tool. (Windows users can use the d command in debug to do the same.)

```
% od -t x1 iso-8859-1.txt
0000000    6f  6c  e9  0a
0000004
```

If we try to read it with our default external encoding of UTF-8, we'll encounter a problem:

```
f = File.open("iso-8859-1.txt")
puts f.external_encoding.name
line = f.gets
puts line.encoding
puts line
```

produces:

```
UTF-8
UTF-8
ol?
```

The problem is that the binary sequence for the e-acute isn't the same in ISO-8859-1 and UTF-8. Ruby just assumed the file contained UTF-8 characters, tagging the string it read accordingly.

We can tell the program that the file contains ISO-8859-1:

```
f = File.open("iso-8859-1.txt", "r:iso-8859-1")
puts f.external_encoding.name
line = f.gets
puts line.encoding
puts line
```

produces:

```
ISO-8859-1
ISO-8859-1
ol?
```

This doesn't help us much. The string is now tagged with the correct encoding, but our operating system is still expecting UTF-8 output.

The solution is to map the ISO-8859-1 to UTF-8 on input:

```
f = File.open("iso-8859-1.txt", "r:iso-8859-1:utf-8")
puts f.external_encoding.name
line = f.gets
puts line.encoding
puts line
```

produces:

```
ISO-8859-1
UTF-8
olé
```

If you specify two encoding names when opening an I/O object, the first is the external encoding, and the second is the internal encoding. Data is transcoded from the former to the latter on reading and the opposite way on writing. That's how I created the file containing *olé* in the first place:

% ruby -e 'File.open("iso-8859-1.txt", "w:iso-8859-1:utf-8") { |f| f.puts "olé"}'

Binary Files

In the old days, we Unix users used to make little snide comments about the way that Windows users had to open binary files using a special binary mode. Well, now the Windows folks can get their own back. If you want to open a file containing binary data in Ruby, you must now specify the binary flag, which will automatically select the 8-bit clean ASCII-8BIT encoding. To make things explicit, you can use "binary" as an alias for the encoding:

```
encoding_31.rb
f = File.open("iso-8859-1.txt", "rb")
puts "Implicit encoding is #{f.external_encoding.name}"
f = File.open("iso-8859-1.txt", "rb:binary")
puts "Explicit encoding is #{f.external_encoding.name}"
line = f.gets
puts "String encoding is #{line.encoding.name}"
```

produces:

```
Implicit encoding is ASCII-8BIT
Explicit encoding is ASCII-8BIT
String encoding is ASCII-8BIT
```

Default External Encoding

If you look at the text files on your computer, the chances are that they'll all use the same encoding. In the United States, that'll probably be UTF-8 or ASCII. In Europe, it might be UTF-8 or ISO-8859-x. If you use a Windows box, you may be using a different set of encodings (use the console chcp command to find your current code page). But whatever encoding you use, the chances are good that you'll stick with it for the majority of your work.

On Unix-like boxes, you'll probably find you have the LANG environment variable set. On my OS X box, I have this:

```
% echo $LANG
en_US.UTF-8
```

This says that I'm using the English language in the U.S. territory and my default codeset is UTF-8. On startup, Ruby looks for this environment variable and, if present, sets the default external encoding from the codeset component. Thus, on my box, Ruby 1.9 programs run with a default external encoding of UTF-8. If instead I were in Japan and my LANG variable were set to ja_JP.sjis, my encoding would be set to Shift JIS. We can look at the default external encoding by querying the Encoding class. While we're at it, we'll experiment with different values in the LANG environment variable:

```
% echo $LANG
en_US.UTF-8
% ruby -e 'p Encoding.default_external.name'
"UTF-8"
% LANG=ja_JP.sjis ruby -e 'p Encoding.default_external.name'
"Shift_JIS"
% LANG= ruby -e 'p Encoding.default_external.name'
"US-ASCII"
```

The encoding set from the environment *does not* affect the encoding Ruby uses for source files—it affects only the encoding of data read and written by your programs.

Finally, you can use the -E command-line option (or the long-form --encoding) to set the default external encoding of your I/O objects:

```
% ruby -E utf-8 -e 'p Encoding.default_external.name'
"UTF-8"
% ruby -E sjis -e 'p Encoding.default_external.name'
"Shift_JIS"
% ruby -E sjis:iso-8859-1 -e 'p Encoding.default_internal.name'
"ISO-8859-1"
```

Encoding Compatibility

Before Ruby performs operations involving strings or regular expressions, it first has to check that the operation makes sense. For example, it is valid to perform an equality test between two strings with different encodings, but it is not valid to append one to the other.

The basic steps in this checking are as follows:

1. If the two objects have the same encoding, the operation is valid.

2. If the two objects each contain only 7-bit characters, the operation is permitted regardless of the encodings.

3. If the encodings in the two objects are compatible (which we'll discuss next), the operation is permitted.

4. Otherwise, an exception is raised.

Let's say you have a set of text files containing markup. In some of the files, authors used the sequence \dots to represent an ellipsis. In other files, which have UTF-8 encoding, authors used an actual ellipsis character (\u2026). We want to convert both forms to three periods.

We can start off with a simplistic solution:

```
# encoding: utf-8
while line = gets
  result = line.gsub(/\\dots/, "...")
                .gsub(/…/, "...") # unicode ellipsis
  puts result
end
```

In my environment, the content of files is by default assumed to be UTF-8. Feed our code ASCII files and UTF-encoded files, and it works just fine. But what happens when we feed it a file that contains ISO-8859-1 characters?

```
dots.rb:4:in `gsub': broken UTF-8 string (ArgumentError)
```

Ruby tried to interpret the input text, which is ISO-8859-1 encoded, as UTF-8. Because the byte sequences in the file aren't valid UTF, it failed.

There are three solutions to this problem. The first is to say that it makes no sense to feed files with both ISO-8859 and UTF-8 encoding to the same program without somehow differentiating them. That's perfectly true. This approach means we'll need some command-line options, liberal use of force_encoding, and probably some kind of code to delegate the pattern matching to different sets of patterns depending on the encoding of each file.

A second hack is to simply treat both the data and the program as ASCII-8BIT and perform all the comparisons based on the underlying bytes. This isn't particularly reliable, but it might work in some circumstances.

The third solution is to choose a master encoding and to transcode strings into it before doing the matches. Ruby provides built-in support for this with the default_internal encoding mechanism.

Default Internal Encoding

By default, Ruby performs no automatic transcoding when reading and writing data. However, two command-line options allow you to change this.

We've already seen the -E option, which sets the default encoding applied to the content of external files. When you say -E xxx, the default external encoding is set to xxx.

However, -E takes a second option. In the same way that you can give File#open both an external and an internal encoding, you can also set a default internal encoding using the folllowing option:

-E external:internal

Thus, if all your files are written with ISO-8859-1 encoding but you want your program to have to deal with their content as if it were UTF-8, you can use this:

ruby -E iso-8859-1:utf-8

You can specify just an internal encoding by omitting the external option but leaving the colon:

ruby -E :utf-8

Indeed, because UTF-8 is probably the best of the available transcoding targets, Ruby has the -U command-line option, which sets the internal encoding to UTF-8.

You can query the default internal encoding in your code with the Encoding.default_internal method. This returns nil if no default internal encoding has been set.

One last note before we leave this section: if you compare two strings with different encodings, Ruby does not normalize them. Thus, "é" tagged with a UTF-8 encoding will not compare equal to "é" tagged with ISO-8859-1, because the underlying bytes are different.

Fun with Unicode

As Daniel Berger pointed out,[3] the fact that UTF-8 is now supported in Ruby means that we can do interesting things with our method and variable names:

encoding_36.rb

```
# encoding: utf-8
def Σ(*args)
  args.inject(:+)
end
puts Σ 1, 3, 5, 9
```

produces:

18

Of course, this way can lead to some pretty obscure and hard-to-use code. (For example, is the summation character in the previous code a real summation, \u2211, or a Greek sigma, \u03a3?) Just because we *can* do something doesn't mean we necessarily *should*....

---

3. http://www.oreillynet.com/ruby/blog/2007/10/fun_with_unicode_1.html

## Chapter 18

Interactive Ruby Shell

Back on page 206 we introduced irb, a Ruby module that lets you enter Ruby programs interactively and see the results immediately. This chapter goes into more detail on using and customizing irb.

Command Line

irb is run from the command line:

irb [*irb-options*] [*ruby_script*] [*program arguments*]

The command-line options for irb are listed in Table 18.1 on the following page. Typically, you'll run irb with no options, but if you want to run a script and watch the blow-by-blow description as it runs, you can provide the name of the Ruby script and any options for that script.

Once started, irb displays a prompt and waits for input. In the examples that follow, we'll use irb's default prompt, which shows the current binding, the indent (nesting) level, and the line number.

At a prompt, you can type Ruby code. irb includes a Ruby parser, so it knows when statements are incomplete. When this happens, the prompt will end with an asterisk. You can leave irb by typing **exit** or **quit** or by entering an end-of-file character (unless IGNORE_EOF mode is set).

```
% irb
irb(main):001:0> 1 + 2
=> 3
irb(main):002:0> 3 +
irb(main):003:0* 4
=> 7
irb(main):004:0> quit
%
```

Table 18.1. irb Command-Line Options

Option	Description
--back-trace-limit *n*	Displays backtrace information using the top *n* and last *n* entries. The default value is 16.
--context-mode *n*	See :CONTEXT_MODE on page 271.
-d	Sets $DEBUG to true (same as ruby -d).
-E *enc*	Same as Ruby's -E option.
-f	Suppresses reading ~/.irbrc.
-h, --help	Displays usage information.
-I *path*	Specifies the $LOAD_PATH directory.
--inf-ruby-mode	Sets up irb to run in inf-ruby-mode under Emacs. Same as --prompt inf-ruby --noreadline.
--inspect, --noinspect	Uses/doesn't use Object#inspect to format output (--inspect is the default, unless in math mode).
--irb_debug *n*	Sets internal debug level to *n* (only useful for irb development).
-m	Math mode (fraction and matrix support is available).
--noprompt	Does not display a prompt. Same as --prompt null
--prompt *prompt-mode*	Switches prompt. Predefined prompt modes are null, default, classic, simple, xmp, and inf-ruby.
--prompt-mode *prompt-mode*	Same as --prompt.
-r *module*	Requires *module*. Same as ruby -r.
--readline, --noreadline	Uses/doesn't use readline extension module.
--sample-book-mode	Same as --prompt simple.
--simple-prompt	Same as --prompt simple.
--single-irb	Nested irb sessions will all share the same context.
--tracer	Displays trace for execution of commands.
-U	Same as Ruby's -U option.
-v, --version	Prints the version of irb.

During an irb session, the work you do is accumulated in irb's workspace. Variables you set, methods you define, and classes you create are all remembered and may be used subsequently in that session.

```
irb(main):001:0> def fib_up_to(n)
irb(main):002:1>   f1, f2 = 1, 1
irb(main):003:1>   while f1 <= n
irb(main):004:2>     puts f1
irb(main):005:2>     f1, f2 = f2, f1+f2
irb(main):006:2>   end
irb(main):007:1> end
=> nil
irb(main):008:0> fib_up_to(4)
1
1
2
3
=> nil
```

Notice the nil return values. These are the results of defining the method and then running it—our method printed the Fibonacci numbers but then returned nil.

A great use of irb is experimenting with code you've already written. Perhaps you want to track down a bug, or maybe you just want to play. If you load your program into irb, you can then create instances of the classes it defines and invoke its methods. For example, the file code/fib_up_to.rb contains the following method definition:

```
irb_1.rb
def fib_up_to(max)
  i1, i2 = 1, 1
  while i1 <= max
    yield i1
    i1, i2 = i2, i1+i2
  end
end
```

We can load this into irb and play with the method:

```
% irb
irb(main):001:0> load 'code/fib_up_to.rb'
=> true
irb(main):002:0> result = []
=> []
irb(main):003:0> fib_up_to(20) {|val| result << val}
=> nil
irb(main):004:0> result
=> [1, 1, 2, 3, 5, 8, 13]
```

In this example, we use load, rather than require, to include the file in our session. We do this as a matter of practice: load allows us to load the same file multiple times, so if we find a bug and edit the file, we could reload it into our irb session.

Tab Completion

If your Ruby installation has readline support, then you can use irb's completion facility. Once loaded (and we'll get to how to load it shortly), completion changes the meaning of the [TAB] key when typing expressions at the irb prompt. When you press [TAB] partway through a word, irb will look for possible completions that make sense at that point. If there is only one, irb will fill it in automatically. If there's more than one valid option, irb initially does nothing. However, if you hit [TAB] again, it will display the list of valid completions at that point.

For example, you may be in the middle of an irb session, having just assigned a string object to the variable a:

```
irb(main):002:0> a = "cat"
=> "cat"
```

You now want to try the method String#reverse on this object. You start by typing a.re and then hit [TAB] twice.

```
irb(main):003:0> a.re TAB TAB
a.reject        a.replace       a.respond_to?   a.reverse       a.reverse!
```

irb lists all the methods supported by the object in a whose names start with *re*. We see the one we want, reverse, and enter the next character of its name, *v*, followed by the TAB key:

```
irb(main):003:0> a.rev TAB
irb(main):003:0> a.reverse
=> "tac"
irb(main):004:0>
```

irb responds to the TAB key by expanding the name as far as it can go, in this case completing the word reverse. If we keyed TAB twice at this point, it would show us the current options, reverse and reverse!. However, because reverse is the one we want, we instead hit ENTER, and the line of code is executed.

Tab completion isn't limited to built-in names. If we define a class in irb, then tab completion works when we try to invoke one of its methods:

```
irb(main):004:0> class Test
irb(main):005:1>   def my_method
irb(main):006:2>   end
irb(main):007:1> end
=> nil
irb(main):008:0> t = Test.new
=> #<Test:0x35b724>
irb(main):009:0> t.my TAB
irb(main):009:0> t.my_method
```

Tab completion is implemented as an extension library. On some systems this is loaded by default. On others you'll need to load it when you invoke irb from the command line:

```
% irb -r irb/completion
```

You can also load the completion library when irb is running:

```
irb(main):001:0> require 'irb/completion'
=> true
```

If you use tab completion all the time, it's probably most convenient to put the require command into your .irbrc file:

```
require 'irb/completion'
```

Subsessions

irb supports multiple, concurrent sessions. One is always current; the others lie dormant until activated. Entering the command irb within irb creates a subsession, entering the jobs command lists all sessions, and entering fg activates a particular dormant session. This example also illustrates the -r command-line option, which loads in the given file before irb starts:

```
% irb -r code/fib_up_to.rb
irb(main):001:0> result = []
=> []
```

```
irb(main):002:0> fib_up_to(10) {|val| result << val }
=> nil
irb(main):003:0> result
=> [1, 1, 2, 3, 5, 8]
irb(main):004:0> #  Create a nested irb session
irb(main):005:0* irb
irb#1(main):001:0> result = %w{ cat dog horse }
=> ["cat", "dog", "horse"]
irb#1(main):002:0> result.map {|val| val.upcase }
=> ["CAT", "DOG", "HORSE"]
irb#1(main):003:0> jobs
=> #0->irb on main (#<Thread:0x331740>: stop)
#1->irb#1 on main (#<Thread:0x341694>: running)
irb#1(main):004:0> fg 0
irb(main):006:0> result
=> [1, 1, 2, 3, 5, 8]
irb(main):007:0> fg 1
irb#1(main):005:0> result
=> ["cat", "dog", "horse"]
```

Subsessions and Bindings

If you specify an object when you create a subsession, that object becomes the value of
self in that binding. This is a convenient way to experiment with objects. In the following
example, we create a subsession with the string "wombat" as the default object. Methods
with no receiver will be executed by that object.

```
% irb
irb(main):001:0> self
=> main
irb(main):002:0> irb "wombat"
irb#1(wombat):001:0> self
=> "wombat"
irb#1(wombat):002:0> upcase
=> "WOMBAT"
irb#1(wombat):003:0> size
=> 6
irb#1(wombat):004:0> gsub(/[aeiou]/, '*')
=> "w*mb*t"
irb#1(wombat):005:0> irb_exit
irb(main):003:0> self
=> main
irb(main):004:0> upcase
NameError: undefined local variable or method `upcase' for main:Object
```

Configuration

irb is remarkably configurable. You can set configuration options with command-line options, from within an initialization file, and while you're inside irb itself.

Initialization File

irb uses an initialization file in which you can set commonly used options or execute any required Ruby statements. When irb is run, it will try to load an initialization file from one of the following sources in order: ~/.irbrc, .irbrc, irb.rc, _irbrc, and $irbrc.

Within the initialization file, you may run any arbitrary Ruby code. You can also set configuration values. The list of configuration variables is given starting on the facing page—the values that can be used in an initialization file are the symbols (starting with a colon). You use these symbols to set values into the IRB.conf hash. For example, to make SIMPLE the default prompt mode for all your irb sessions, you could have the following in your initialization file:

```
IRB.conf[:PROMPT_MODE] = :SIMPLE
```

As an interesting twist on configuring irb, you can set IRB.conf[:IRB_RC] to a Proc object. This proc will be invoked whenever the irb context is changed and will receive the configuration for that context as a parameter. You can use this facility to change the configuration dynamically based on the context. For example, the following .irbrc file sets the prompt so that only the main prompt shows the irb level, but continuation prompts and the result still line up:

irb_5.rb
```
IRB.conf[:IRB_RC] = lambda do |conf|
  leader = " " * conf.irb_name.length
  conf.prompt_i = "#{conf.irb_name} --> "
  conf.prompt_s = leader + ' \-" '
  conf.prompt_c = leader + ' \-+ '
  conf.return_format    = leader + " ==> %s\n\n"
  puts "Welcome!"
end
```

An irb session using this .irbrc file looks like the following:

```
% irb
Welcome!
irb --> 1 + 2
    ==> 3

irb --> 2 +
    \-+ 6
    ==> 8
```

Extending irb

Because the things you type into irb are interpreted as Ruby code, you can effectively extend irb by defining new top-level methods. For example, you may want to time how long certain things take. You can use the measure method in the Benchmark library to do this, but it's more convenient to wrap this in a helper method.

Add the following to your `.irbrc` file:

`irb_6.rb`
```ruby
def time(&block)
  require 'benchmark'
  result = nil
  timing = Benchmark.measure do
    result = block.()
  end
  puts "It took: #{timing}"
  result
end
```

The next time you start irb, you'll be able to use this method to get timings:

```
irb(main):001:0> time { 1000000.times { "cat".upcase }}
It took:    0.550000    0.000000    0.550000 (   0.545647)
=> 1000000
irb(main):002:0>
```

Interactive Configuration

Most configuration values are also available while you're running irb. The list starting on the current page shows these values as conf.*xxx*. For example, to change your prompt back to DEFAULT, you could use the following:

```
irb(main):001:0> 1 +
irb(main):002:0* 2
=> 3
irb(main):003:0> conf.prompt_mode = :SIMPLE
=> :SIMPLE
>> 1 +
?> 2
=> 3
```

irb Configuration Options

In the descriptions that follow, a label of the form :XXX signifies a key used in the IRB.conf hash in an initialization file, and conf.xxx signifies a value that can be set interactively. The value in square brackets at the end of the description is the option's default.

:AUTO_INDENT / conf.auto_indent_mode

If true, irb will indent nested structures as you type them. [false]

:BACK_TRACE_LIMIT / conf.back_trace_limit

Displays n initial and n final lines of backtrace. [16]

:CONTEXT_MODE

What binding to use for new workspaces: 0→ proc at the top level, 1→ binding in a loaded, anonymous file, 2→ per thread binding in a loaded file, 3→ binding in a top-level function. [3]

:DEBUG_LEVEL / conf.debug_level

Sets the internal debug level to n. This is useful if you're debugging irb's lexer. [0]

:IGNORE_EOF / conf.ignore_eof

Specifies the behavior of an end of file received on input. If true, it will be ignored; otherwise, irb will quit. [false]

:IGNORE_SIGINT / conf.ignore_sigint

If false, ^C (Ctrl+c) will quit irb. If true, ^C during input will cancel input and return to the top level; during execution, ^C will abort the current operation. [true]

:INSPECT_MODE / conf.inspect_mode

Specifies how values will be displayed: true means use inspect, false uses to_s, and nil uses inspect in nonmath mode and to_s in math mode. [nil]

:IRB_RC

Can be set to a proc object that will be called when an irb session (or subsession) is started. [nil]

conf.last_value

The last value output by irb. [. . .]

:LOAD_MODULES / conf.load_modules

A list of modules loaded via the -r command-line option. [[]]

:MATH_MODE / conf.math_mode

If true, irb runs with the mathn library loaded (see page 758) and does not use inspect to display values. [false]

conf.prompt_c

The prompt for a continuing statement (for example, immediately after an if). [depends]

conf.prompt_i

The standard, top-level prompt. [depends]

:PROMPT_MODE / conf.prompt_mode

The style of prompt to display. [:DEFAULT]

conf.prompt_s

The prompt for a continuing string. [depends]

:PROMPT

See *Configuring the Prompt* on page 274. [{ . . . }]

:RC / conf.rc

If false, do not load an initialization file. [true]

conf.return_format

The format used to display the results of expressions entered interactively. [depends]

:SAVE_HISTORY / conf.save_history

The number of commands to save between irb sessions. [nil]

:SINGLE_IRB

If true, nested irb sessions will all share the same binding; otherwise, a new binding will be created according to the value of :CONTEXT_MODE. [nil]

conf.thread

A read-only reference to the currently executing Thread object. [current thread]

:USE_LOADER / conf.use_loader

Specifies whether irb's own file reader method is used with load/require. [false]

:USE_READLINE / conf.use_readline

irb will use the readline library if available (see page 788) unless this option is set to false, in which case readline will never be used, or nil, in which case readline will not be used in inf-ruby-mode. [depends]

:USE_TRACER / conf.use_tracer

If true, traces the execution of statements. [false]

:VERBOSE / conf.verbose

In theory, switches on additional tracing when true; in practice, almost no extra tracing results. [true]

Commands

At the irb prompt, you can enter any valid Ruby expression and see the results. You can also use any of the following commands to control the irb session:[1]

help *ClassName, string,* **or** *symbol*

1.9

Displays the ri help for the given thing. To get the help for a method name, you'll probably want to pass a string, like this:

```
irb(main):001:0> help "String.encoding"
--------------------------------------------------- String#encoding
 obj.encoding   => encoding
------------------------------------------------------------------
Returns the Encoding object that represents the encoding of obj.
```

exit, quit, irb_exit, irb_quit

Quits this irb session or subsession. If you've used cb to change bindings (see below), exits from this binding mode.

conf, context, irb_context

Displays current configuration. Modifying the configuration is achieved by invoking methods of conf. The list starting on page 271 shows the available conf settings.

1.　For some inexplicable reason, many of these commands have up to nine different aliases. We don't bother to show all of these.

For example, to set the default prompt to something subservient, you could use this:

```
irb(main):001:0> conf.prompt_i = "Yes, Master? "
=> "Yes, Master? "
Yes, Master? 1 + 2
```

cb, irb_change_binding ⟨ *obj* ⟩
Creates and enters a new binding (sometimes called a *workspace*) that has its own scope for local variables. If *obj* is given, it will be used as self in the new binding.

pushb *obj*, **popb**
Pushes and pops the current binding.

bindings
Lists the current bindings.

irb_cwws
Prints the object that's the binding of the current workspace.

irb ⟨ *obj* ⟩
Starts an irb subsession. If *obj* is given, it will be used as self.

jobs, irb_jobs
Lists irb subsessions.

fg *n*, **irb_fg** *n*
Switches into the specified irb subsession. *n* may be any of the following: an irb subsession number, a thread ID, an irb object, or the object that was the value of *self* when a subsession was launched.

kill *n*, **irb_kill** *n*
Kills an irb subsession. *n* may be any of the values as described for irb_fg.

source *filename*
Loads and executes the given file, displaying the source lines.

Configuring the Prompt

You have a lot of flexibility in configuring the prompts that irb uses. Sets of prompts are stored in the prompt hash, IRB.conf[:PROMPT].

For example, to establish a new prompt mode called MY_PROMPT, you could enter the following (either directly at an irb prompt or in the .irbrc file):

```
IRB.conf[:PROMPT][:MY_PROMPT] = { # name of prompt mode
  :PROMPT_I => '-->',            # normal prompt
  :PROMPT_S => '--"',            # prompt for continuing strings
  :PROMPT_C => '--+',            # prompt for continuing statement
  :RETURN => "    ==>%s\n"       # format to return value
}
```

Once you've defined a prompt, you have to tell irb to use it. From the command line, you can use the --prompt option. (Notice how the name of the prompt mode is automatically converted to uppercase, with hyphens changing to underscores.)

```
% irb --prompt my-prompt
```

If you want to use this prompt in all your future irb sessions, you can set it as a configuration value in your .irbrc file:

```
IRB.conf[:PROMPT_MODE] = :MY_PROMPT
```

The symbols PROMPT_I, PROMPT_S, and PROMPT_C specify the format for each of the prompt strings. In a format string, certain % sequences are expanded:

Flag	Description
%N	Current command.
%m	to_s of the main object (self).
%M	inspect of the main object (self).
%l	Delimiter type. In strings that are continued across a line break, %l will display the type of delimiter used to begin the string, so you'll know how to end it. The delimiter will be one of ", ', /,], or `.
%ni	Indent level. The optional number n is used as a width specification to printf, as printf("%nd").
%nn	Current line number (n used as with the indent level).
%%	A literal percent sign.

For instance, the default prompt mode is defined as follows:

```
IRB.conf[:PROMPT][:DEFAULT] = {
      :PROMPT_I => "%N(%m):%03n:%i> ",
      :PROMPT_S => "%N(%m):%03n:%i%l ",
      :PROMPT_C => "%N(%m):%03n:%i* ",
      :RETURN   => "=> %s\n"
}
```

Restrictions

Because of the way irb works, it is slightly incompatible with the standard Ruby interpreter. The problem lies in the determination of local variables.

Normally, Ruby looks for an assignment statement to determine whether something is a variable—if a name hasn't been assigned to, then Ruby assumes that name is a method call:

```
eval "var = 0"
var
```

produces:

```
prog.rb:2:in `<main>': undefined local variable or method `var' for
 main:Object (NameError)
```

In this case, the assignment is there, but it's within a string, so Ruby doesn't take it into account.

irb, on the other hand, executes statements as they are entered:

```
irb(main):001:0> eval "var = 0"
0
irb(main):002:0> var
0
```

In irb, the assignment was executed before the second line was encountered, so var is correctly identified as a local variable.

If you need to match the Ruby behavior more closely, you can place these statements within a begin/end pair:

```
irb(main):001:0> begin
irb(main):002:1*   eval "var = 0"
irb(main):003:1>   var
irb(main):004:1> end
NameError: undefined local variable or method `var'
(irb):3:in `irb_binding'
```

Saving Your Session History

If you have readline support in irb (that is, you can hit the up arrow key and irb recalls the previous command you entered), then you can also configure irb to remember the commands you enter between sessions. Simply add the following to your .irbrc file:

irb_14.rb

```
IRB.conf[:SAVE_HISTORY] = 50      # save last 50 commands
```

Chapter 19

Documenting Ruby

As of version 1.8, Ruby comes bundled with RDoc, a tool that extracts and formats documentation that's embedded in Ruby source code files. This tool is used to document the built-in Ruby classes and modules. An increasing number of libraries and extensions are also documented this way.

RDoc does two jobs. First, it analyzes Ruby and C source files, looking for information to document.[1] Second, it takes this information and converts it into something readable. Out of the box, RDoc produces two kinds of output: HTML and ri. Some HTML-formatted RDoc output in a browser window is shown in Figure 19.1 on the following page. This is the result of feeding RDoc a Ruby source file with no additional documentation—RDoc does a credible job of producing something meaningful. If our source code contains comments, RDoc can use them to spice up the documentation it produces. Typically, the comment before an element is used to document that element, as shown in Figure 19.2 on page 279.

RDoc can also be used to produce documentation that can be read by the ri command-line utility. For example, if we ask RDoc to document the code in Figure 19.2 this way, we can then access the documentation using ri, as shown in Figure 19.3 on page 280. New Ruby distributions have the built-in classes and modules (and some libraries) documented this way. The output produced if you type ri Proc is shown in Figure 19.4 on page 281.

---

1. RDoc can also document Fortran 77 programs.

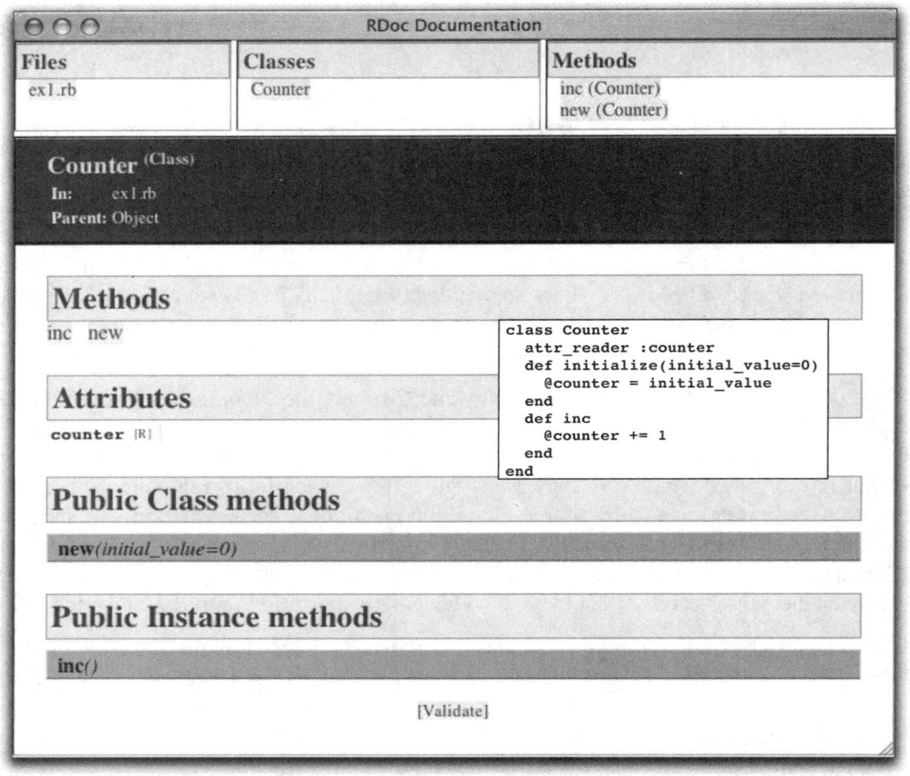

This figure shows some RDoc output in a browser window. The overlaid box shows the source program from which this output was generated. Even though the source contains no internal documentation, RDoc still manages to extract interesting information from it. We have three panes at the top of the screen showing the files, classes, and methods for which we have documentation. For class Counter, RDoc shows us the attributes and methods (including the method signatures). And if we clicked a method signature, RDoc would pop up a window containing the source code for the corresponding method.

Figure 19.1. Browse RDoc Output for Class Counter

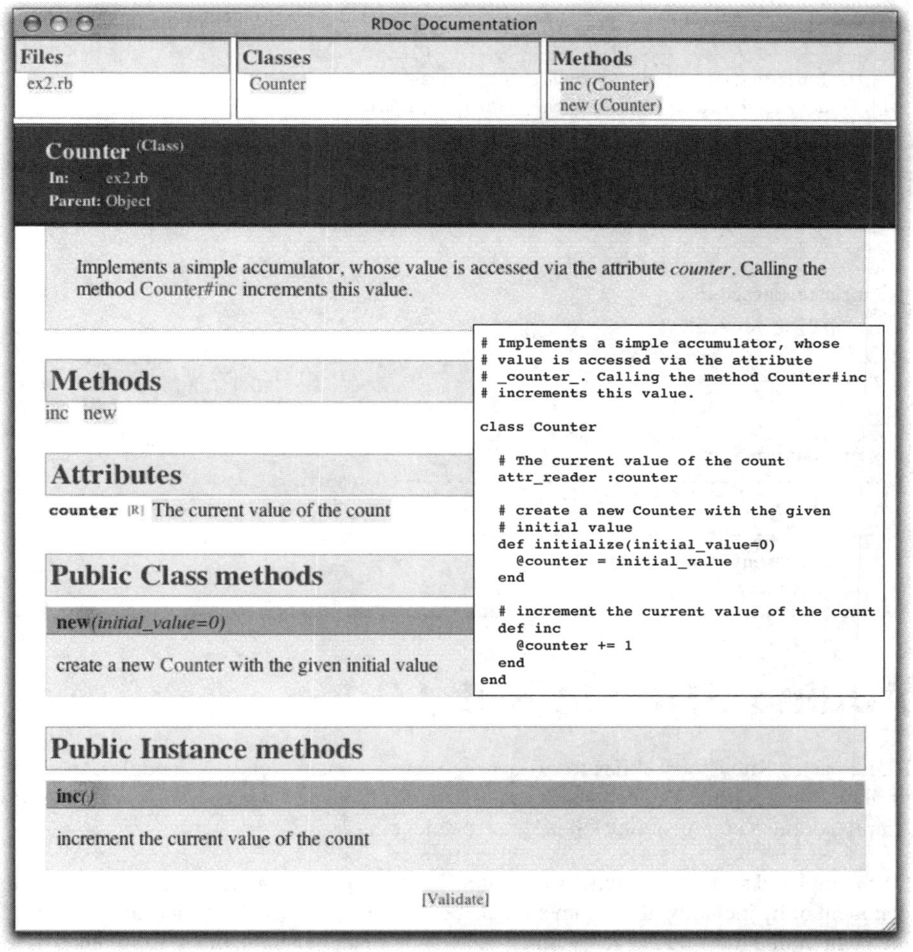

Notice how the comments before each element now appear in the RDoc output, reformatted into HTML. Less obvious is that RDoc has detected hyperlink opportunities in our comments: in the class-level comment, the reference to `Counter#inc` is a hyperlink to the method description, and in the comment for the `new` method, the reference to class `Counter` hyperlinks back to the class documentation. This is a key feature of RDoc: it is designed to be unintrusive in the Ruby source files and to make up for this by trying to be clever when producing output.

Figure 19.2. Browse RDoc Output When Source Has Comments

Figure 19.3. Using ri to Read Documentation

```
% ri Counter
--------------------------------------- Class: Counter
     Implements a simple accumulator, whose value is
     accessed via the attribute counter. Calling the
     method Counter#inc increments this value.
--------------------------------------------------------

Class methods:
     new

Instance methods:
     inc

Attributes:
     counter

% ri Counter.inc
--------------------------------------- Counter#inc
     inc()
--------------------------------------------------------
     increment the current value of the count
```

Adding RDoc to Ruby Code

RDoc parses Ruby source files to extract the major elements (classes, modules, methods, attributes, and so on). You can choose to associate additional documentation with these by simply adding a comment block before the element in the file.

Comment blocks can be written fairly naturally, either by using # on successive lines of the comment or by including the comment in a =begin...=end block. If you use the latter form, the =begin line must be flagged with an rdoc tag to distinguish the block from other styles of documentation.

```
=begin rdoc
Calculate the minimal-cost path though the graph
using Debrinkski's algorithm, with optimized
inverse pruning of isolated leaf nodes.
=end
def calculate_path
  . . .
end
```

Within a documentation comment, paragraphs are lines that share the left margin. Text indented past this margin is formatted verbatim.

Figure 19.4. Documentation for Class `Proc` Generated by RDoc/ri

```
% ri Proc
----------------------------------------- Class: Proc
     Proc objects are blocks of code that have been
     bound to a set of local variables. Once bound,
     the code may be called in different contexts and
     still access those variables.

         def gen_times(factor)
           return Proc.new {|n| n*factor }
         end

         times3 = gen_times(3)
         times5 = gen_times(5)

         times3.call(12)              #=> 36
         times5.call(5)               #=> 25
         times3.call(times5.call(4))  #=> 60


------------------------------------------------------

Class methods:
     new

Instance methods:
     ==, [], arity, binding, call, clone, eql?, hash,
     to_proc, to_s
```

Nonverbatim text can be marked up. To set individual words in italic, bold, or typewriter fonts, you can use _word_, *word*, and +word+, respectively. If you want to do this to multiple words or text containing nonword characters, you can use multiple words, more words, and <tt>yet more words</tt>. Putting a backslash before inline markup stops it being interpreted.

RDoc stops processing comments if it finds a comment line starting #--. This can be used to separate external from internal comments or to stop a comment being associated with a method, class, attribute, or module. Documenting can be turned back on by starting a line with #++:

```
# Extract the age and calculate the
# date of birth.
#--
# FIXME: fails if the birthday falls on
# February 29th, or if the person
# was born before epoch and the installed
# Ruby doesn't support negative time_t
#++
```

```
# The DOB is returned as a Time object.
#--
# But should probably change to use Date.
def get_dob(person)
        ...
end
```

Hyperlinks

Names of classes, source files, and any method names containing an underscore or preceded by a hash character are automatically hyperlinked from comment text to their description.

Hyperlinks to the 'net starting http:, mailto:, ftp:, and www: are recognized. An HTTP URL that references an external image file is converted into an inline <IMG...> tag. Hyperlinks starting link: are assumed to refer to local files whose paths are relative to the --op directory, where output files are stored.

Hyperlinks can also be of the form label[url], in which case the label is used in the displayed text and url is used as the target. If the label contains multiple words, surround it in braces: {two words}[url].

Lists

Lists are typed as indented paragraphs with

- A * or - (for bullet lists)

- A digit followed by a period for numbered lists

- An uppercase or lowercase letter followed by a period for alpha lists

For example, you could produce something like the previous text with this:

```
#  Lists are typed as indented paragraphs with
#  * a * or - (for bullet lists),
#  * a digit followed by a period for
#    numbered lists,
#  * an uppercase or lowercase letter followed
#    by a period for alpha lists.
```

Note how subsequent lines in a list item are indented to line up with the text in the element's first line.

Labeled lists (sometimes called *description lists*) are typed using square brackets for the label:

```
#  [cat]    Small domestic animal
#  [+cat+]  Command to copy standard input
#           to standard output
```

Labeled lists may also be produced by putting a double colon after the label. This sets the result in tabular form so the descriptions all line up in the output.

```
#  cat::    Small domestic animal
#  +cat+:: Command to copy standard input
#          to standard output
```

For both kinds of labeled lists, if the body text starts on the same line as the label, then the start of that text determines the block indent for the rest of the body. The text may also start on the line following the label, indented from the start of the label. This is often preferable if the label is long. Both of the following are valid labeled list entries:

```
#  <tt>--output</tt> <i>name [, name]</i>::
#      specify the name of one or more output files. If multiple
#      files are present, the first is used as the index.
#
#  <tt>--quiet:</tt>:: do not output the names, sizes, byte counts,
#                      index areas, or bit ratios of units as
#                      they are processed.
```

Headings

Headings are entered on lines starting with equals signs. The more equals signs, the higher the level of heading:

```
#  = Level One Heading
#  == Level Two Heading
#  and so on...
```

Rules (horizontal lines) are entered using three or more hyphens:

```
#  and so it goes...
#  ----
#  The next section...
```

Documentation Modifiers

Method parameter lists are extracted and displayed with the method description. If a method calls `yield`, then the parameters passed to `yield` will also be displayed. For example, consider the following code:

```
def fred
  ...
  yield line, address
```

This will get documented as follows:

```
fred() {|line, address| ... }
```

You can override this using a comment containing :yields: ... on the same line as the method definition:

```
def fred        # :yields: index, position
  ...
  yield line, address
```

which will get documented as follows:

```
fred() {|index, position| ... }
```

:yields: is an example of a documentation modifier. These appear immediately after the start of the document element they are modifying.

Other modifiers include the following:

:nodoc: *[all]*
> Don't include this element in the documentation. For classes and modules, the methods, aliases, constants, and attributes directly within the affected class or module will also be omitted from the documentation. By default, though, modules and classes within that class or module will be documented. This is turned off by adding the all modifier. For example, in the following code, only class SM::Input will be documented:

```
module SM  #:nodoc:
  class Input
  end
end
module Markup #:nodoc: all
  class Output
  end
end
```

:doc:
> This forces a method or attribute to be documented even if it wouldn't otherwise be. This is useful if, for example, you want to include documentation of a particular private method.

:notnew:
> (Applicable only to the initialize instance method.) Normally RDoc assumes that the documentation and parameters for #initialize are actually for the corresponding class's new method and so fakes out a new method for the class. The :notnew: modifier stops this. Remember that #initialize is protected, so you won't see the documentation unless you use the -a command-line option.

Other Directives

Comment blocks can contain other directives:

:call-seq: *lines...*
> Text up to the next blank comment line is used as the calling sequence when generating documentation (overriding the parsing of the method parameter list). A line is considered blank even if it starts with #. For this one directive, the leading colon is optional.

:include: *filename*
> This includes the contents of the named file at this point. The file will be searched for in the directories listed by the --include option or in the current directory by default. The contents of the file will be shifted to have the same indentation as the : at the start of the :include: directive.

:title: *text*
> This sets the title for the document. It's equivalent to the --title command-line parameter. (The command-line parameter overrides any :title: directive in the source.)

:main: *name*

> This is equivalent to the --main command-line parameter, setting the initial page displayed for this documentation.

:stopdoc: / :startdoc:

> This stops and starts adding new documentation elements to the current container. For example, if a class has a number of constants that you don't want to document, put a :stopdoc: before the first and a :startdoc: after the last. If you don't specify a :startdoc: by the end of the container, this disables documentation for the entire class or module.

:enddoc:

> This documents nothing further at the current lexical level.

A larger example of a file documented using RDoc is shown in Figure 19.5 on page 289.

Adding RDoc to C Extensions

RDoc understands many of the conventions used when writing extensions to Ruby in C.

If RDoc sees a C function named Init_*Classname*, it treats it as a class definition—any C comment before the Init_ function will be used as the class's documentation.

The Init_ function is normally used to associate C functions with Ruby method names. For example, a Cipher extension may define a Ruby method salt=, implemented by the C function salt_set using a call such as this:

```
rb_define_method(cCipher, "salt=", salt_set, 1);
```

RDoc parses this call, adding the salt= method to the class documentation. RDoc then searches the C source for the C function salt_set. If this function is preceded by a comment block, RDoc uses this for the method's documentation.

This basic scheme works with no effort on your part beyond writing the normal documentation in the comments for functions. However, RDoc cannot discern the calling sequence for the corresponding Ruby method. In this example, the RDoc output will show a single argument with the (somewhat meaningless) name "arg1." You can override this using the call-seq directive in the function's comment. The lines following call-seq (up to a blank line) are used to document the calling sequence of the method:

```
/*
 * call-seq:
 *   cipher.salt = number
 *   cipher.salt = "string"
 *
 * Sets the salt of this cipher to either a binary +number+ or
 * bits in +string+.
 */
static VALUE
salt_set(cipher, salt)
...
```

If a method returns a meaningful value, it should be documented in the call-seq following the characters ->:

```
/*
 * call-seq:
 *    cipher.keylen    -> Fixnum or nil
 */
```

Although RDoc heuristics work well for finding the class and method comments for simple extensions, they don't always work for more complex implementations. In these cases, you can use the directives Document-class: and Document-method: to indicate that a C comment relates to a given class or method, respectively. The modifiers take the name of the Ruby class or method that's being documented:

```
/*
 * Document-method: reset
 *
 * Clear the current buffer and prepare to add new
 * cipher text. Any accumulated output cipher text
 * is also cleared.
 */
```

Finally, it is possible in the Init_xxx function to associate a Ruby method with a C function in a different C source file. RDoc would not find this function without your help: you add a reference to the file containing the function definition by adding a special comment to the rb_define_method call. The following example tells RDoc to look in the file md5.c for the function (and related comment) corresponding to the md5 method:

```
rb_define_method(cCipher, "md5", gen_md5, -1); /* in md5.c */
```

A C source file documented using RDoc is shown in Figure 19.6 on page 290. Note that the bodies of several internal methods have been elided to save space.

Running RDoc

You run RDoc from the command line:

```
% rdoc [options]  [filenames...]
```

Type **rdoc --help** for an up-to-date option summary.

Files are parsed, and the information they contain collected, before any output is produced. This allows cross-references between all files to be resolved. If a name is a directory, it is traversed. If no names are specified, all Ruby files in the current directory (and subdirectories) are processed.

A typical use may be to generate documentation for a package of Ruby source (such as RDoc itself):

```
% rdoc
```

This command generates HTML documentation for all the Ruby and C source files in and below the current directory. These will be stored in a documentation tree starting in the subdirectory doc/.

RDoc uses file extensions to determine how to process each file. Filenames ending .rb and .rbw are assumed to be Ruby source. Filenames ending .c are parsed as C files. All other files are assumed to contain just markup (with or without leading # comment markers). If directory names are passed to RDoc, they are scanned recursively for source files only. To include nonsource files such as READMEs in the documentation process, their names must be given explicitly on the command line.

When writing a Ruby library, you often have some source files that implement the public interface, but the majority are internal and of no interest to the readers of your documentation. In these cases, construct a .document file in each of your project's directories. If RDoc enters a directory containing a .document file, it will process only the files in that directory whose names match one of the lines in that file. Each line in the file can be a filename, a directory name, or a wildcard (a file system "glob" pattern). For example, to include all Ruby files whose names start main, along with the file constants.rb, you could use a .document file containing this:

```
main*.rb
constants.rb
```

Some project standards ask for documentation in a top-level README file. You may find it convenient to write this file in RDoc format and then use the :include: directive to incorporate the README into the documentation for the main class.

Create Documentation for ri

RDoc is also used to create documentation, which will be later displayed using ri.

When you run ri, it by default looks for documentation in three places:[2]

- The *system* documentation directory, which holds the documentation distributed with Ruby and which is created by the Ruby install process

- The *site* directory, which contains sitewide documentation added locally

- The *user* documentation directory, stored under the user's own home directory

You can find these three directories in the following locations:

- $datadir/ri/<ver>/system/...
- $datadir/ri/<ver>/site/...
- ~/.rdoc/....

The variable $datadir is the configured data directory for the installed Ruby. Find your local *datadir* using this:

```
ruby -r rbconfig -e 'p Config::CONFIG["datadir"]'
```

---

2.   You can override the directory location using the --op option to RDoc and subsequently using the --doc-dir option with ri.

To add documentation to ri, you need to tell RDoc which output directory to use. For your own use, it's easiest to use the --ri option, which installs the documentation into ~/.rdoc:

```
% rdoc --ri  file1.rb file2.rb
```

If you want to install sitewide documentation, use the --ri-site option:

```
% rdoc --ri-site  file1.rb file2.rb
```

The --ri-system option is normally used only to install documentation for Ruby's built-in classes and standard libraries. You can regenerate this documentation from the Ruby source distribution (not from the installed libraries themselves):

```
% cd <ruby source base>/lib
% rdoc --ri-system
```

Figure 19.5. Ruby Source File Documented with RDoc

```ruby
# This module encapsulates functionality related to the
# generation of Fibonacci sequences.
#--
# Copyright (c) 2004 Dave Thomas, The Pragmatic Programmers, LLC.
# Licensed under the same terms as Ruby. No warranty is provided.
module Fibonacci

  # Calculate the first _count_ Fibonacci numbers, starting with 1,1.
  #
  # :call-seq:
  #   Fibonacci.sequence(count)              -> array
  #   Fibonacci.sequence(count) {|val| ... }  -> nil
  #
  # If a block is given, supply successive values to the block and
  # return +nil+, otherwise return all values as an array.
  def Fibonacci.sequence(count, &block)
    result, block = setup_optional_block(block)
    generate do |val|
      break if count <= 0
      count -= 1
      block[val]
    end
    result
  end

  # Calculate the Fibonacci numbers up to and including _max_.
  #
  # :call-seq:
  #   Fibonacci.upto(max)              -> array
  #   Fibonacci.upto(max) {|val| ... }  -> nil
  #
  # If a block is given, supply successive values to the
  # block and return +nil+, otherwise return all values as an array.
  def Fibonacci.upto(max, &block)
    result, block = setup_optional_block(block)
    generate do |val|
      break if val > max
      block[val]
    end
    result
  end

  private

  # Yield a sequence of Fibonacci numbers to a block.
  def Fibonacci.generate
    f1, f2 = 1, 1
    loop do
      yield f1
      f1, f2 = f2, f1+f2
    end
  end

  # If a block parameter is given, use it, otherwise accumulate into an
  # array. Return the result value and the block to use.
  def Fibonacci.setup_optional_block(block)
    if block.nil?
      [ result = [], lambda {|val| result << val } ]
    else
      [ nil, block ]
    end
  end
end
```

Figure 19.6.   C Source File Documented with RDoc

```c
#include "ruby.h"
#include "cdjukebox.h"

static VALUE cCDPlayer;
static void cd_free(void *p) { ... }
static VALUE cd_alloc(VALUE klass) { ... }
static void progress(CDJukebox *rec, int percent) { ... }

/* call-seq:
 *     CDPlayer.new(unit)  -> new_cd_player
 *
 * Assign the newly created CDPlayer to a particular unit
 */
static VALUE cd_initialize(VALUE self, VALUE unit) {
  int unit_id;
  CDJukebox *jb;

  Data_Get_Struct(self, CDJukebox, jb);

  unit_id = NUM2INT(unit);
  assign_jukebox(jb, unit_id);

  return self;
}

/* call-seq:
 *   player.seek(int_disc, int_track)  -> nil
 *   player.seek(int_disc, int_track) {|percent| } -> nil
 *
 * Seek to a given part of the track, invoking the block
 * with the percent complete as we go.
 */
static VALUE
cd_seek(VALUE self, VALUE disc, VALUE track) {
  CDJukebox *jb;
  Data_Get_Struct(self, CDJukebox, jb);

  jukebox_seek(jb, NUM2INT(disc), NUM2INT(track), progress);
  return Qnil;
}

/* call-seq:
 *   player.seek_time -> Float
 *
 * Return the average seek time for this unit (in seconds)
 */
static VALUE
cd_seek_time(VALUE self)
{
  double tm;
  CDJukebox *jb;
  Data_Get_Struct(self, CDJukebox, jb);
  tm = get_avg_seek_time(jb);
  return rb_float_new(tm);
}

/* Interface to the Spinzalot[http://spinzalot.cd]
 * CD Player library.
 */

void Init_CDPlayer() {
  cCDPlayer = rb_define_class("CDPlayer", rb_cObject);
  rb_define_alloc_func(cCDPlayer, cd_alloc);
  rb_define_method(cCDPlayer, "initialize", cd_initialize, 1);
  rb_define_method(cCDPlayer, "seek", cd_seek, 2);
  rb_define_method(cCDPlayer, "seek_time", cd_seek_time, 0);
}
```

## Chapter 20

Ruby and the Web

Ruby is no stranger to the Internet. Not only can you write your own SMTP server, FTP daemon, or web server in Ruby, but you can also use Ruby for more usual tasks such as CGI programming or as a replacement for PHP.

Many options are available for using Ruby to implement web applications, and a single chapter can't do them all justice. Instead, we'll try to touch some of the highlights and point you toward libraries and resources that can help.

Let's start with some simple stuff: running Ruby programs as Common Gateway Interface (CGI) programs.

Writing CGI Scripts

You can use Ruby to write CGI scripts quite easily. To have a Ruby script generate HTML output, all you need is something like this:

```
#!/usr/bin/ruby
print "Content-type: text/html\r\n\r\n"
print "<html><body>Hello World! It's #{Time.now}</body></html>\r\n"
```

Put this script in a CGI directory, mark it as executable, and you'll be able to access it via your browser. (If your web server doesn't automatically add headers, you'll need to add the response header yourself, as shown in the following code.)

```
#!/usr/bin/ruby
print "HTTP/1.0 200 OK\r\n"
print "Content-type: text/html\r\n\r\n"
print "<html><body>Hello World! It's #{Time.now}</body></html>\r\n"
```

However, that's hacking around at a pretty low level. You'd need to write your own request parsing, session management, cookie manipulation, output escaping, and so on. Fortunately, options are available to make this easier.

Using cgi.rb

Class CGI provides support for writing CGI scripts. With it, you can manipulate forms, cookies, and the environment; maintain stateful sessions; and so on. It's a fairly large class, but we'll take a quick look at its capabilities here.

Quoting

When dealing with URLs and HTML code, you must be careful to quote certain characters. For instance, a slash character (/) has special meaning in a URL, so it must be "escaped" if it's not part of the path name. That is, any / in the query portion of the URL will be translated to the string %2F and must be translated back to a / for you to use it. Space and ampersand are also special characters. To handle this, CGI provides the routines CGI.escape and CGI.unescape:

```
web_3.rb
require 'cgi'
puts CGI.escape("Nicholas Payton/Trumpet & Flugel Horn")
```

produces:

```
Nicholas+Payton%2FTrumpet+%26+Flugel+Horn
```

More frequently, you may want to escape HTML special characters:

```
web_4.rb
require 'cgi'
puts CGI.escapeHTML("a < 100 && b > 200")
```

produces:

```
a &lt; 100 &amp;&amp; b &gt; 200
```

To get really fancy, you can decide to escape only certain HTML elements within a string:

```
web_5.rb
require 'cgi'
puts CGI.escapeElement('<hr><a href="/mp3">Click Here</a><br>','A')
```

produces:

```
<hr>&lt;a href=&quot;/mp3&quot;&gt;Click Here&lt;/a&gt;<br>
```

Here only the A element is escaped; other elements are left alone. Each of these methods has an "un-" version to restore the original string:

```
web_6.rb
require 'cgi'
puts CGI.unescapeHTML("a &lt; 100 &amp;&amp; b &gt; 200")
```

produces:

```
a < 100 && b > 200
```

Query Parameters

HTTP requests from the browser to your application may contain parameters, either passed as part of the URL or passed as data embedded in the body of the request.

Processing of these parameters is complicated by the fact that a value with a given name may be returned multiple times in the same request. For example, say we're writing a survey to find out why folks like Ruby. The HTML for our form looks like this:

```
<html>
  <head><title>Test Form</title></head>
  <body>
    I like Ruby because:

    <form action="cgi-bin/survey.rb">
      <input type="checkbox" name="reason" value="flexible" />
        It's flexible<br />
      <input type="checkbox" name="reason" value="transparent" />
        It's transparent<br />
      <input type="checkbox" name="reason" value="perlish" />
        It's like Perl<br />
      <input type="checkbox" name="reason" value="fun" />
        It's fun

      <p>
        Your name: <input type="text" name="name">
      </p>

      <input type="submit"/>

    </form>

  </body>
</html>
```

When someone fills in this form, they might check multiple reasons for liking Ruby (as shown in Figure 20.1 on the following page). In this case, the form data corresponding to the name reason will have three values, corresponding to the three checked boxes.

Class CGI gives you access to form data in a couple of ways. First, we can just treat the CGI object as a hash, indexing it with field names and getting back field values.

web_8.rb

```
require 'cgi'
cgi = CGI.new
cgi['name']     # =>   "Dave Thomas"
cgi['reason']   # =>   "flexible"
```

However, this doesn't work well with the reason field, because we see only one of the three values. We can ask to see them all by using the CGI#params method. The value returned by params acts like a hash containing the request parameters. You can both read and write this hash (the latter allows you to modify the data associated with a request). Note that each of the values in the hash is actually an array.

Figure 20.1.   Sample CGI Form

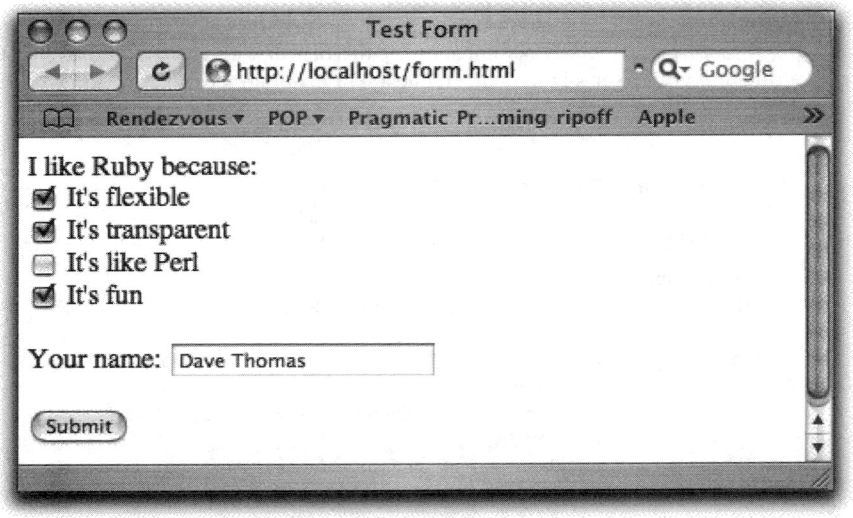

web_9.rb

```
require 'cgi'
cgi = CGI.new
cgi.params              # =>    {"name"=>["Dave Thomas"],
                                 "reason"=>["flexible", "transparent",
                                 "fun"]}
cgi.params['name']      # =>    ["Dave Thomas"]
cgi.params['reason']    # =>    ["flexible", "transparent", "fun"]
cgi.params['name'] = [ cgi['name'].upcase ]
cgi.params              # =>    {"name"=>["DAVE THOMAS"],
                                 "reason"=>["flexible", "transparent",
                                 "fun"]}
```

You can determine whether a particular parameter is present in a request by using
CGI#has_key?:

web_10.rb

```
require 'cgi'
cgi = CGI.new
cgi.has_key?('name')    # =>    true
cgi.has_key?('age')     # =>    false
```

Generating HTML

CGI contains a huge number of methods that can be used to create HTML—one method per element. To enable these methods, you must create a CGI object by calling CGI.new, passing in the required version of HTML. In these examples, we'll use html3.

To make element nesting easier, these methods take their content as code blocks. The code blocks should return a String, which will be used as the content for the element. For this example, we've added some gratuitous newlines to make the output fit on the page:

```
web_11.rb
require 'cgi'
cgi = CGI.new("html3")  # add HTML generation methods
cgi.out do
  cgi.html do
    cgi.head { "\n"+cgi.title { "This Is a Test"} } +
    cgi.body do "\n"+
      cgi.form do"\n"+
        cgi.hr +
        cgi.h1 { "A Form: " } + "\n"+
        cgi.textarea("get_text") +"\n"+
        cgi.br +
        cgi.submit
      end
    end
  end
end
```

produces:

```
Content-Type: text/html
Content-Length: 302

<!DOCTYPE HTML PUBLIC "-//W3C//DTD HTML 3.2 Final//EN"><HTML><HEAD>
<TITLE>This Is a Test</TITLE></HEAD><BODY>
<FORM METHOD="post" ENCTYPE="application/x-www-form-urlencoded">
<HR><H1>A Form: </H1>
<TEXTAREA NAME="get_text" COLS="70" ROWS="10"></TEXTAREA>
<BR><INPUT TYPE="submit"></FORM></BODY></HTML>
```

Although vaguely interesting, this method of generating HTML is fairly laborious and probably isn't used much in practice. Most people seem to write the HTML directly, use a templating system, or use an application framework, such as Rails. Unfortunately, we don't have space here to discuss Rails—take a look at the online documentation at http:/rubyonrails.com—but we can look at templating (including erb, the templating engine used by Rails).

Templating Systems

Templating systems let you separate the presentation and logic of your application. It seems that just about everyone who writes a web application using Ruby at some point also writes a templating system; the RubyGarden wiki lists quite a few,[1] and even this list isn't complete. For now, let's just look at two: Haml and erb/eruby. Also, remember to look at Builder if you need to generate XHTML or XML. (We saw Builder briefly starting on page 226.)

Haml

Haml[2] is a library that generates HTML documents from a template. Unlike many other templating systems, Haml uses indentation to indicate nesting (yup, just like Python). For example, you can represent a <ul> in Haml using this:

```
%ul
  %li item one
  %li item two
```

Install Haml using this:

```
% gem install haml
```

The Haml input syntax is rich and powerful, and the example that follows touches on only a subset of the features. Lines starting % get converted to HTML tags, nested in the output according to their indentation in the input. An equals sign means *substitute in the value of the Ruby code that follows*. A minus sign executes Ruby code but doesn't substitute the value in—our example uses that to look over the reasons when constructing the table.

There are many ways of getting values passed in to the template. In this example, we chose to pass in a hash as the second parameter to render. This results in local variables getting set as the template is expanded, one variable for each key in the hash:

web_13.rb
```
require 'haml'
engine = Haml::Engine.new(%{
%body
  #welcome-box
    %p= greeting
  %p
    As of
    = Time.now
    the reasons you gave were:
  %table
    %tr
      %th Reason
      %th Rank
    - for reason in reasons
      %tr
        %td= reason[:reason_name]
        %td= reason[:rank]
})
```

---

1. http://www.rubygarden.org/ruby?HtmlTemplates

2. http://haml.hamptoncatlin.com//

```
data = {
  :greeting => 'Hello, Dave Thomas',
  :reasons  => [
    { :reason_name => 'flexible',    :rank => '87' },
    { :reason_name => 'transparent', :rank => '76' },
    { :reason_name => 'fun',         :rank => '94' },
  ]
}
puts engine.render(nil, data)
```

produces:

```
<body>
  <div id='welcome-box'>
    <p>Hello, Dave Thomas</p>
  </div>
  <p>
    As of
    2009-03-31 09:58:00 -0500
    the reasons you gave were:
  </p>
  <table>
    <tr>
      <th>Reason</th>
      <th>Rank</th>
    </tr>
    <tr>
      <td>flexible</td>
      <td>87</td>
    </tr>
    <tr>
      <td>transparent</td>
      <td>76</td>
    </tr>
    <tr>
      <td>fun</td>
      <td>94</td>
    </tr>
  </table>
</body>
```

erb and eruby

So far we've looked at using Ruby to create HTML output, but we can turn the problem inside out; we can actually embed Ruby in an HTML document.

A number of packages allow you to embed Ruby statements in some other sort of a document, especially in an HTML page. Generically, this markup is known as "eRuby." Specifically, several different implementations of eRuby exist, including erubis and erb. erubis is available as a gem, while erb is written in pure Ruby and is included with the standard distribution. We'll look at erb here.

Embedding Ruby in HTML is a very powerful concept—it basically gives us the equivalent of a tool such as ASP, JSP, or PHP, but with the full power of Ruby.

Using erb

erb is normally used as a filter. Input text is passed through untouched, with the following exceptions:

Expression	Description
<% *ruby code* %>	This executes the Ruby code between the delimiters.
<%= *ruby expression* %>	This evaluates the Ruby expression and replaces the sequence with the expression's value.
<%# *ruby code* %>	The Ruby code between the delimiters is ignored (useful for testing).
% *line of ruby code*	A line that starts with a percent is assumed to contain just Ruby code.

You can run erb from the command line:

```
erb [ options ] [ document ]
```

If the *document* is omitted, erb will read from standard input. The command-line options for erb are shown in Table 20.1 on the facing page.

Let's look at some simple examples. We'll run the erb executable on the following input:

```
% 99.downto(96) do |number|
<%= number %> bottles of beer...
% end
```

The lines starting with the percent sign simply execute the given Ruby. In this case, it's a loop that iterates the line between them. This middle line contains the sequence <%= number %>, which substitutes in the value of number into the output.

```
% erb f1.erb
```

produces:

```
99 bottles of beer...
98 bottles of beer...
97 bottles of beer...
96 bottles of beer...
```

erb works by rewriting its input as a Ruby script and then executing that script. You can see the Ruby that erb generates using the -n or -x option:

```
% erb -x f1.erb
```

produces:

```
#coding:ASCII-8BIT
_erbout = ''; 99.downto(96) do |number|
_erbout.concat(( number ).to_s); _erbout.concat " bottles of beer...\n"
; end
_erbout.force_encoding(__ENCODING__)
```

Table 20.1. Command-Line Options for erb

Option	Description
-d	Sets $DEBUG to true
-E *ext[:int]*	Sets the default external/internal encodings
-n	Displays resulting Ruby script (with line numbers)
-r *library*	Loads the named *library*
-P	Doesn't do erb processing on lines starting %
-S *level*	Sets the *safe level*
-T *mode*	Sets the *trim mode*
-U	Sets default encoding to UTF-8
-v	Enables verbose mode
-x	Displays resulting Ruby script

Notice how erb builds a string, _erbout, containing both the static strings from the template and the results of executing expressions (in this case the value of number).

Embedding erb in Your Code

So far we've shown erb running as a command-line filter. However, the most common use is to use it as a library in your own code. (This is what Rails does with its .erb templates.)

```
web_17.rb
require 'erb'

SOURCE =
%{<% for number in min..max %>
The number is <%= number %>
<% end %>
}
erb = ERB.new(SOURCE)

min = 4
max = 6
puts erb.result(binding)
```

produces:

```
The number is 4

The number is 5

The number is 6
```

Notice how we can use local variables within the erb template. This works because we pass the current *binding* to the result method. erb can use this binding to make it look as if the template is being evaluated in the context of the calling code.

erb comes with excellent documentation: use ri to read it. One thing that Rails users should know is that in the standard version of erb, you can't use the -%> trick to suppress blank lines. (In the previous example, that's why we have the extra blank lines in the output.) Take a look at the description of trim modes in the documentation of ERB.new for alternatives.

Cookies

Cookies are a way of letting web applications store their state on the user's machine. Frowned upon by some, cookies are still a convenient (if unreliable) way of remembering session information.

The Ruby CGI class handles the loading and saving of cookies for you. You can access the cookies associated with the current request using the CGI#cookies method, and you can set cookies back into the browser by setting the cookie parameter of CGI#out to reference either a single cookie or an array of cookies:

```
#!/usr/bin/ruby
COOKIE_NAME = 'chocolate chip'
require 'cgi'
cgi = CGI.new
values = cgi.cookies[COOKIE_NAME]
if values.empty?
  msg = "It looks as if you haven't visited recently"
else
  msg = "You last visited #{values[0]}"
end
cookie = CGI::Cookie.new(COOKIE_NAME, Time.now.to_s)
cookie.expires = Time.now + 30*24*3600 # 30 days
cgi.out("cookie" => cookie ) { msg }
```

Sessions

Cookies by themselves still need a bit of work to be useful. We really want *sessions:* information that persists between requests from a particular web browser. Sessions are handled by class CGI::Session, which uses cookies but provides a higher-level abstraction.

As with cookies, sessions emulate a hashlike behavior, letting you associate values with keys. Unlike cookies, sessions store the majority of their data on the server, using the browser-resident cookie simply as a way of uniquely identifying the server-side data. Sessions also give you a choice of storage techniques for this data: it can be held in regular files, in a PStore (see the description on page 785), in memory, or even in your own customized store.

Sessions should be closed after use, because this ensures that their data is written out to the store. When you've permanently finished with a session, you should delete it.

```ruby
require 'cgi'
require 'cgi/session'
cgi = CGI.new("html3")
sess = CGI::Session.new(cgi,
                        "session_key" => "rubyweb",
                        "prefix" => "web-session.")
if sess['lastaccess']
  msg = "<p>You were last here #{sess['lastaccess']}.</p>"
else
  msg = "<p>Looks like you haven't been here for a while</p>"
end
count = (sess["accesscount"] || 0).to_i
count += 1
msg << "<p>Number of visits: #{count}</p>"
sess["accesscount"] = count
sess["lastaccess"]  = Time.now.to_s
sess.close
cgi.out {
  cgi.html {
    cgi.body {
      msg
    }
  }
}
```

The code in the previous example used the default storage mechanism for sessions: persistent data was stored in files in your default temporary directory (see Dir.tmpdir). The filenames will all start with web-session. and will end with a hashed version of the session number. See ri CGI::Session for more information.

Choice of Web Servers

So far, we've been running Ruby scripts under the Apache web server. However, Ruby comes bundled with WEBrick, a flexible, pure-Ruby HTTP server toolkit. WEBrick's an extensible plug-in–based framework that lets you write servers to handle HTTP requests and responses. Here's a basic HTTP server that serves documents and directory indexes:

```ruby
#!/usr/bin/ruby
require 'webrick'
include WEBrick
s = HTTPServer.new(
  :Port         => 2000,
  :DocumentRoot => File.join(Dir.pwd, "/html"))
trap("INT") { s.shutdown }
s.start
```

The HTTPServer constructor creates a new web server on port 2000. The code sets the document root to be the html/ subdirectory of the current directory. It then uses Kernel.trap to arrange to shut down tidily on interrupts before starting the server running. If you point your browser at http://localhost:2000, you should see a listing of your html subdirectory.

WEBrick can do far more than serve static content. You can use it just like a Java servlet container. The following code mounts a simple servlet at the location /hello. As requests arrive, the do_GET method is invoked. It uses the response object to display the user agent information and parameters from the request.

```
#!/usr/bin/ruby
require 'webrick'
include WEBrick
s = HTTPServer.new( :Port => 2000 )
class HelloServlet < HTTPServlet::AbstractServlet
  def do_GET(req, res)
    res['Content-Type'] = "text/html"
    res.body = %{
      <html><body>
        <p>Hello. You're calling from a #{req['User-Agent']}</p>
        <p>I see parameters: #{req.query.keys.join(', ')}</p>
      </body></html>
    }
  end
end
s.mount("/hello", HelloServlet)
trap("INT"){ s.shutdown }
s.start
```

More information on WEBrick is available from `http://www.webrick.org`. There you'll find links to a set of useful servlets, including one that lets you write SOAP servers in Ruby.

Frameworks

In reality, CGI is just the start of using Ruby on the Web. Most of the real action these days is with frameworks. Frameworks abstract away all this low-level detail and also help you structure your code into something that is both easy to write and (probably more importantly) easy to maintain.

At the time of writing, Ruby on Rails[3] is the leading web framework for Ruby. It has an incredibly active community and a vast set of plug-ins so the chances are good you'll find a lot of preexisting code to help you kick-start your application. Merb[4] is a lighter-weight alternative. Rails and Merb will merge and become Rails 3. Other alternatives include Camping, Sinatra, and Ramaze.[5] By the time you read this, the list will have grown. And, if you fancy writing your own framework, consider making it independent of the underlying web server by building it on top of Rack.[6]

---

3.   `http://www.rubyonrails.com`

4.   `http://merbivore.com/`

5.   `http://camping.rubyforge.org/files/README.html`, `http://sinatra.rubyforge.org/`, and `http://ramaze.net/`

6.   `http://rack.rubyforge.org/`

## Chapter 21

Ruby and Microsoft Windows

Ruby runs in a number of environments. Some of these are Unix-based, and others are based on the various flavors of Microsoft Windows. Ruby came from people who were Unix-centric, but over the years it has developed a whole lot of useful features in the Windows world, too. In this chapter, we'll look at these features and share some secrets that let you use Ruby effectively under Windows.

Getting Ruby for Windows

Although you could build Ruby for Windows from source, most people simply download the prebuilt binaries from the main Ruby FTP site.[1] Create a directory for your Ruby installation, and download the latest zip file into it. Unzip the file, and you'll end up with a complete, standard Ruby directory tree (\bin, \doc, \lib and so on). Add the bin directory to your path, and Ruby should be available to you. For example, I downloaded the .zip file into the directory C:\ruby19:

```
C:\> mkdir \ruby19
C:\ruby19> cd \ruby19
C:\ruby19> ftp ftp.ruby-lang.org
Connected to carbon.ruby-lang.org.
User (carbon.ruby-lang.org:(none)): ftp
331 Please specify the password.
Password: your email address
230 Login successful.
ftp> cd pub/ruby/binaries/mswin32/unstable
250 Directory successfully changed.
ftp> dir
-rw-r--r-- 1 ... Jul 08  2007 ruby-1.9.0-20070709-i386-mswin32.zip
-rw-r--r-- 1 ... Jul 08  2007 ruby-1.9.0-20070709-x64-mswin64_80.zip
-rw-r--r-- 1 ... Oct 28 15:31 ruby-1.9.1-preview1-i386-mswin32.zip
-rw-r--r-- 1 ... Oct 28 15:31 ruby-1.9.1-preview1-x64-mswin64_80.zip
```

---

1. ftp://ftp.ruby-lang.org/pub/ruby/binaries/mswin32/unstable/

```
ftp> bin
200 Switching to Binary mode.
ftp> get ruby-1.9.1-preview1-i386-mswin32.zip
200 PORT command successful. Consider using PASV.
150 Opening BINARY mode data connection
    for ruby-1.9.1-preview1-i386-mswin32.zip (13535099 bytes).
226 File send OK.
ftp: 13535099 bytes received in 48.06Seconds 280.21Kbytes/sec.
ftp> by
C:\ruby19> unzip.exe ruby-1.9.0-0-i386-mswin32.zip
    :  :
C:\ruby19> PATH=\ruby19\bin;%PATH%
C:\ruby19> ruby -v
ruby 1.9.1 (2008-10-28 revision 19983) [i386-mswin32]
```

Running Ruby Under Windows

You'll find two executables in the Ruby Windows distribution.

ruby.exe is meant to be used at a command prompt (a DOS shell), just as in the Unix version. For applications that read and write to the standard input and output, this is fine. But this also means that any time you run ruby.exe, you'll get a DOS shell even if you don't want one—Windows will create a new command prompt window and display it while Ruby is running. This may not be appropriate behavior if, for example, you double-click a Ruby script that uses a graphical interface (such as Tk) or if you are running a Ruby script as a background task or from inside another program.

In these cases, you will want to use rubyw.exe. It is the same as ruby.exe except that it does not provide standard in, standard out, or standard error and does not launch a DOS shell when run.

You can set up file associations using the assoc and ftype commands so that Ruby will automatically run Ruby when you double-click the name of a Ruby script:

```
C:\> assoc .rb=RubyScript
C:\> ftype RubyScript="C:\ruby1.9\bin\ruby.exe %1 %*
```

Win32API

If you plan on doing Ruby programming that needs to access some Windows 32 API functions directly or that needs to use the entry points in some other DLLs, we've got good news for you—the Win32API library.

As an example, here's some code that's part of a larger Windows application used by our book fulfillment system to download and print invoices and receipts. A web application generates a PDF file, which the Ruby script running on Windows downloads into a local file. The script then uses the print shell command under Windows to print this file.

> ### What About the One-Click Installer?
>
> Ruby 1.8 had a no-assembly-required package called the One-Click Ruby Installer (1CRI). Download it, and it will install Ruby, a bunch of gems, and even a version of the original PickAxe.
>
> However, because this installer packages so many gems and because many of these gems haven't been updated for Ruby 1.9, the team has not released a Ruby 1.9 version of 1CRI at the time of this writing. Check `http://rubyinstaller.rubyforge.org` for the current status.

```
arg   = "ids=#{resp.intl_orders.join(",")}"
fname = "/temp/invoices.pdf"
site = Net::HTTP.new(HOST, PORT)
site.use_ssl = true
http_resp, = site.get2("/ship/receipt?" + arg,
                       'Authorization' => 'Basic ' +
                       ["name:passwd"].pack('m').strip )
File.open(fname, "wb") {|f| f.puts(http_resp.body) }
shell = Win32API.new("shell32","ShellExecute",
                     ['L','P','P','P','P','L'], 'L' )
shell.Call(0, "print", fname, 0,0, SW_SHOWNORMAL)
```

You create a Win32API object that represents a call to a particular DLL entry point by specifying the name of the function, the name of the DLL that contains the function, and the function signature (argument types and return type). In the previous example, the variable shell wraps the Windows function ShellExecute in the shell32 DLL. The second parameter is an array of characters describing the types of the parameters the method takes: 'n' and 'l' represent numbers, 'i' represent integers, 'p' represents pointers to data stored in a string, and 'v' a void type (used for export parameters only). These strings are case-insensitive. So our method takes a number, four string pointers, and a number. The last parameter says that the method returns a number. The resulting object is a proxy to the underlying ShellExecute function, and can be used to make the call to print the file that we downloaded.

Many of the arguments to DLL functions are binary structures of some form. Win32API handles this by using Ruby String objects to pass the binary data back and forth. You will need to pack and unpack these strings as necessary.

Windows Automation

If groveling around in the low-level Windows API doesn't interest you, Windows Automation may—you can use Ruby as a client for Windows Automation thanks to a Ruby extension called WIN32OLE, written by Masaki Suketa. Win32OLE is part of the standard Ruby distribution.

Windows Automation allows an automation controller (a client) to issue commands and queries against an automation server, such as Microsoft Excel, Word, and so on.

You can execute an automation server's method by calling a method of the same name from a WIN32OLE object. For instance, you can create a new WIN32OLE client that launches a fresh copy of Internet Explorer and commands it to visit its home page:

```
require 'win32ole'
ie = WIN32OLE.new('InternetExplorer.Application')
ie.visible = true
ie.gohome
```

You could also make it navigate to a particular page:

```
require 'win32ole'
ie = WIN32OLE.new('InternetExplorer.Application')
ie.visible = true
ie.navigate("http://www.pragprog.com")
```

Methods that aren't known to WIN32OLE (such as visible, gohome, or navigate) are passed on to the WIN32OLE#invoke method, which sends the proper commands to the server.

Getting and Setting Properties

You can set and get *properties* from the server using normal Ruby hash notation. For example, to set the Rotation property in an Excel chart, you could write this:

```
excel = WIN32OLE.new("excel.application")
excelchart = excel.Charts.Add()
...
excelchart['Rotation'] = 45
puts excelchart['Rotation']
```

An OLE object's properties are automatically set up as attributes of the WIN32OLE object. This means you can set a property by assigning to an object attribute:

```
excelchart.rotation = 45
r = excelchart.rotation
```

The following example is a modified version of the sample file excel2.rb (found in the ext/win32/samples directory). It starts Excel, creates a chart, and then rotates it on the screen. Watch out, Pixar!

```
require 'win32ole'
#   -4100 is the value for the Excel constant xl3DColumn.
ChartTypeVal = -4100;
excel = WIN32OLE.new("excel.application")
# Create and rotate the chart
excel['Visible'] = TRUE
excel.Workbooks.Add()
excel.Range("a1")['Value'] = 3
excel.Range("a2")['Value'] = 2
excel.Range("a3")['Value'] = 1
```

```
excel.Range("a1:a3").Select()
excelchart = excel.Charts.Add()
excelchart['Type'] = ChartTypeVal
30.step(180, 5) do |rot|
  excelchart.rotation = rot
  sleep(0.1)
end
excel.ActiveWorkbook.Close(0)
excel.Quit()
```

Named Arguments

Other automation client languages such as Visual Basic have the concept of *named arguments*. Suppose you had a Visual Basic routine with the following signature:

```
Song(artist, title, length):    rem Visual Basic
```

Instead of calling it with all three arguments in the order specified, you could use named arguments:

```
Song title := 'Get It On':    rem Visual Basic
```

This is equivalent to the call Song(nil, 'Get It On', nil).

In Ruby, you can use this feature by passing a hash with the named arguments:

```
Song.new('title' => 'Get It On')
```

for each

Where Visual Basic has a for each statement to iterate over a collection of items in a server, a WIN32OLE object has an each method (which takes a block) to accomplish the same thing:

```
require 'win32ole'
excel = WIN32OLE.new("excel.application")
excel.Workbooks.Add
excel.Range("a1").Value = 10
excel.Range("a2").Value = 20
excel.Range("a3").Value = "=a1+a2"
excel.Range("a1:a3").each do |cell|
  p cell.Value
end
```

Events

Your automation client written in Ruby can register itself to receive events from other programs. This is done using the WIN32OLE_EVENT class.

This example (based on code from the Win32OLE 0.1.1 distribution) shows the use of an event sink that logs the URLs that a user browses to when using Internet Explorer:

```ruby
require 'win32ole'
$urls = []
def navigate(url)
  $urls << url
end
def stop_msg_loop
  puts "IE has exited..."
  throw :done
end
def default_handler(event, *args)
  case event
  when "BeforeNavigate"
    puts "Now Navigating to #{args[0]}..."
  end
end
ie = WIN32OLE.new('InternetExplorer.Application')
ie.visible = TRUE
ie.gohome
ev = WIN32OLE_EVENT.new(ie, 'DWebBrowserEvents')
ev.on_event {|*args| default_handler(*args)}
ev.on_event("NavigateComplete") {|url| navigate(url)}
ev.on_event("Quit") {|*args| stop_msg_loop}
catch(:done) do
  loop do
    WIN32OLE_EVENT.message_loop
  end
end
puts "You Navigated to the following URLs: "
$urls.each_with_index do |url, i|
  puts "(#{i+1}) #{url}"
end
```

Optimizing

As with most (if not all) high-level languages, it can be all too easy to churn out code that is unbearably slow, but that can be easily fixed with a little thought.

With WIN32OLE, you need to be careful with unnecessary dynamic lookups. Where possible, it is better to assign a WIN32OLE object to a variable and then reference elements from it, rather than creating a long chain of "." expressions.

For example, instead of writing this:

```ruby
workbook.Worksheets(1).Range("A1").value = 1
workbook.Worksheets(1).Range("A2").value = 2
workbook.Worksheets(1).Range("A3").value = 4
workbook.Worksheets(1).Range("A4").value = 8
```

we can eliminate the common subexpressions by saving the first part of the expression to a temporary variable and then make calls from that variable:

```
worksheet = workbook.Worksheets(1)
worksheet.Range("A1").value = 1
worksheet.Range("A2").value = 2
worksheet.Range("A3").value = 4
worksheet.Range("A4").value = 8
```

You can also create Ruby stubs for a particular Windows type library. These stubs wrap the OLE object in a Ruby class with one method per entry point. Internally, the stub uses the entry point's number, not name, which speeds access.

Generate the wrapper class using the olegen.rb script in the ext\win32ole\samples directory, giving it the name of the type library to reflect on:

```
C:\> ruby olegen.rb 'NetMeeting 1.1 Type Library' >netmeeting.rb
```

The external methods and events of the type library are written as Ruby methods to the given file. You can then include it in your programs and call the methods directly. Let's try some timings:

```
require 'netmeeting'
require 'benchmark'
include Benchmark
bmbm(10) do |test|
  test.report("Dynamic") do
    nm = WIN32OLE.new('NetMeeting.App.1')
    10000.times { nm.Version }
  end
  test.report("Via proxy") do
    nm = NetMeeting_App_1.new
    10000.times { nm.Version }
  end
end
```

produces:

```
Rehearsal ----------------------------------------
Dynamic      0.600000   0.200000   0.800000 (  1.623000)
Via proxy    0.361000   0.140000   0.501000 (  0.961000)
------------------------------------- total: 1.301000sec

                 user     system      total       real
Dynamic      0.471000   0.110000   0.581000 (  1.522000)
Via proxy    0.470000   0.130000   0.600000 (  0.952000)
```

The proxy version is more than 40 percent faster than the code that does the dynamic lookup.

More Help

If you need to interface Ruby to Windows NT, 2000, or XP, you may want to take a look at Daniel Berger's Win32Utils project (http://rubyforge.org/projects/win32utils/). There you'll find modules for interfacing to the Windows clipboard, event log, scheduler, and so on.

Also, the DL library (described briefly on page 737) allows Ruby programs to invoke methods in dynamically loaded shared objects. On Windows, this means that your Ruby code can load and invoke entry points in a Windows DLL. For example, the following code, taken from the DL source code in the standard Ruby distribution, pops up a message box on a Windows machine and determines which button the user clicked:

`win32_15.rb`

```
require 'dl'
User32 = DL.dlopen("user32")
MB_OKCANCEL = 1
message_box = User32['MessageBoxA', 'ILSSI']
r, rs = message_box.call(0, 'OK?', 'Please Confirm', MB_OKCANCEL)
case r
when 1
  print("OK!\n")
when 2
  print("Cancel!\n")
end
```

This code opens the User32 DLL. It then creates a Ruby object, message_box, that wraps the MessageBoxA entry point. The second paramater, "ILSSI", declares that the method returns an <u>I</u>nteger and takes a <u>L</u>ong, two <u>S</u>trings, and an <u>I</u>nteger as parameters.

The wrapper object is then used to call the message box entry point in the DLL. The return values are the result (in this case, the identifier of the button pressed by the user) and an array of the parameters passed in (which we ignore).

Part III

Ruby Crystallized

## Chapter 22

The Ruby Language

This chapter is a bottom-up look at the Ruby language. Most of what appears here is the syntax and semantics of the language itself—we mostly ignore the built-in classes and modules (these are covered in depth starting on page 433). However, Ruby sometimes implements features in its libraries that in most languages would be part of the basic syntax. We've included these methods here and have tried to flag them with "Library" in the margin.

The contents of this chapter may look familiar—with good reason. We've covered just about all of this in the earlier tutorial chapters. Consider this chapter to be a self-contained reference to the core Ruby language.

Source File Encoding

1.9

Ruby programs are by default written in 7-bit ASCII, also called US-ASCII. If a code set other than 7-bit ASCII is to be used, place a comment containing coding: followed by the name of an encoding on its own on the first line of each source file containing non-ASCII characters. The coding: comment can be on the second line of the file if the first line is a shebang comment. Ruby skips characters in the comment before the word coding:

# coding: utf-8	# -*- encoding: iso-8859-1 -*-	#!/usr/bin/ruby
		# fileencoding: us-ascii
UTF-8 source...	*ISO-8859-1 source...*	*ASCII source...*

Source Layout

Ruby is a line-oriented language. Ruby expressions and statements are terminated at the end of a line unless the parser can determine that the statement is incomplete—for example, if the last token on a line is an operator or comma. A semicolon can be used to separate multiple expressions on a line. You can also put a backslash at the end of a line to continue it onto the next. Comments start with # and run to the end of the physical line. Comments are ignored during syntax analysis.

```
a = 1
b = 2; c = 3
d = 4 + 5 +
    6 + 7          # no '\' needed
e = 8 + 9  \
    + 10           # '\' needed
```

Physical lines between a line starting with =begin and a line starting with =end are ignored by Ruby and may be used to comment out sections of code or to embed documentation.

Ruby reads its program input in a single pass, so you can pipe programs to the Ruby interpreter's standard input stream:

```
echo 'puts "Hello"' | ruby
```

If Ruby comes across a line anywhere in the source containing just "__END__", with no leading or trailing whitespace, it treats that line as the end of the program—any subsequent lines will not be treated as program code. However, these lines can be read into the running program using the global IO object DATA, described on page 331.

BEGIN and END Blocks

Every Ruby source file can declare blocks of code to be run as the file is being loaded (the BEGIN blocks) and after the program has finished executing (the END blocks):

```
BEGIN {
  begin code
}

END {
  end code
}
```

A program may include multiple BEGIN and END blocks. BEGIN blocks are executed in the order they are encountered. END blocks are executed in reverse order.

General Delimited Input

As well as the normal quoting mechanism, alternative forms of literal strings, arrays, regular expressions, and shell commands are specified using a generalized delimited syntax. All these literals start with a percent character, followed by a single character that identifies the literal's type. These characters are summarized in Table 22.1 on the next page; the actual literals are described in the corresponding sections later in this chapter.

Following the type character is a delimiter, which can be any nonalphabetic or nonmultibyte character. If the delimiter is one of the characters (, [, {, or <, the literal consists of the characters up to the matching closing delimiter, taking account of nested delimiter pairs. For all other delimiters, the literal comprises the characters up to the next occurrence of the delimiter character.

Table 22.1. General Delimited Input

Type	Meaning	See Page
%q	Single-quoted string	316
%Q, %	Double-quoted string	316
%w, %W	Array of strings	318
%r	Regular expression pattern	320
%s	A symbol	319
%x	Shell command	332

```
%q/this is a string/
%q-string-
%q(a (nested) string)
```

Delimited strings may continue over multiple lines; the line endings and all spaces at the start of continuation lines will be included in the string:

```
meth = %q{def fred(a)
            a.each {|i| puts i }
          end}
```

The Basic Types

The basic types in Ruby are numbers, strings, arrays, hashes, ranges, symbols, and regular expressions.

Integer and Floating-Point Numbers

Ruby integers are objects of class Fixnum or Bignum. Fixnum objects hold integers that fit within the native machine word minus 1 bit. Whenever a Fixnum exceeds this range, it is automatically converted to a Bignum object, whose range is effectively limited only by available memory. If an operation with a Bignum result has a final value that will fit in a Fixnum, the result will be returned as a Fixnum.

Integers are written using an optional leading sign and an optional base indicator (0 or 0o for octal, 0d for decimal, 0x for hex, or 0b for binary), followed by a string of digits in the appropriate base. Underscore characters are ignored in the digit string.

```
123456                    => 123456    # Fixnum
0d123456                  => 123456    # Fixnum
123_456                   => 123456    # Fixnum - underscore ignored
-543                      => -543      # Fixnum - negative number
0xaabb                    => 43707     # Fixnum - hexadecimal
0377                      => 255       # Fixnum - octal
0o377                     => 255       # Fixnum - octal
-0b10_1010                => -42       # Fixnum - binary (negated)
123_456_789_123_456_789   => 123456789123456789 # Bignum
```

A numeric literal with a decimal point and/or an exponent is turned into a Float object, corresponding to the native architecture's double data type. You must follow the decimal point with a digit; if you write 1.e3, Ruby tries to invoke the method e3 on the Fixnum 1. You must place at least one digit before the decimal point.

```
12.34        # =>   12.34
-0.1234e2    # =>   -12.34
1234e-2      # =>   12.34
```

Rational and Complex Numbers

Classes that support rational numbers (ratios of integers) and complex numbers are built into the Ruby interpreter. However, Ruby provides no language-level support for these numeric types. There are for rational or complex literals, for example. See the descriptions of Complex and Rational on pages 464 and 651 for more information.

Strings

Ruby provides a number of mechanisms for creating literal strings. Each generates objects of type String. The different mechanisms vary in terms of how a string is delimited and how much substitution is done on the literal's content. Literal strings are encoded using the source encoding of the file that contains them.

Single-quoted string literals ('*stuff*' and %q/*stuff*/) undergo the least substitution. Both convert the sequence \\ into a single backslash, and the form with single quotes converts \' into a single quote. All other backslashes appear literally in the string.

```
'hello'                    # =>   hello
'a backslash \'\\\''       # =>   a backslash '\'
%q/simple string/          # =>   simple string
%q(nesting (really) works) # =>   nesting (really) works
%q no_blanks_here ;        # =>   no_blanks_here
```

Double-quoted strings ("*stuff*", %Q/*stuff*/, and %/*stuff*/) undergo additional substitutions, shown in Table 22.2 on the facing page.

```
a  = 123
"\123mile"                 # =>   Smile
"Greek pi: \u03c0"         # =>   Greek pi: π
"Greek \u{70 69 3a 20 3c0}" # =>   Greek pi: π
"Say \"Hello\""            # =>   Say "Hello"
%Q!"I said 'nuts'," I said! # =>   "I said 'nuts'," I said
%Q{Try #{a + 1}, not #{a - 1}} # =>   Try 124, not 122
%<Try #{a + 1}, not #{a - 1}> # =>   Try 124, not 122
"Try #{a + 1}, not #{a - 1}" # =>   Try 124, not 122
%{ #{ a = 1; b = 2; a + b } } # =>   3
```

Last, and probably least (in terms of usage), you can get the string corresponding to an ASCII character by preceding that character with a question mark. You can use the backslash escapes shown in Table 22.2 on the next page.

Table 22.2. Substitutions in Double-Quoted Strings

\a	Bell/alert (0x07)	\nnn	Octal *nnn*
\b	Backspace (0x08)	\xnn	Hex *nn*
\e	Escape (0x1b)	\c*x*	Control-*x*
\f	Formfeed (0x0c)	\C-*x*	Control-*x*
\n	Newline (0x0a)	\M-*x*	Meta-*x*
\r	Return (0x0d)	\M-\C-*x*	Meta-control-*x*
\s	Space (0x20)	*x*	*x*
\t	Tab (0x09)	#{code}	Value of *code*
\v	Vertical tab (0x0b)	\uxxxx	Unicode character
		\u{xx xx xx}	Unicode characters

```
?a          # => "a"       (ASCII character)
?\n         # => "\n"      (newline (0x0a))
?\C-a       # => "\x01"    (control a = 0x65 & 0x9f = 0x01)
?\M-a       # => "\xE1"    (meta sets bit 7)
?\M-\C-a    # => "\x81"    (meta and control a)
?\C-?       # => "\x7F"    (delete character)
```

Strings can continue across multiple input lines, in which case they will contain newline characters. It is also possible to use here documents to express long string literals. Whenever Ruby parses the sequence <<*identifier* or <<*quoted string*, it replaces it with a string literal built from successive logical input lines. It stops building the string when it finds a line that starts with *identifier* or *quoted string*. You can put a minus sign immediately after the << characters, in which case the terminator can be indented from the left margin. If a quoted string was used to specify the terminator, its quoting rules will be applied to the here document; otherwise, double-quoting rules apply.

```
print <<HERE
Double quoted \
here document.
It is #{Time.now}
HERE
print <<-'THERE'
    This is single quoted.
    The above used #{Time.now}
    THERE
```

produces:

```
Double quoted here document.
It is 2009-03-31 09:58:01 -0500
    This is single quoted.
    The above used #{Time.now}
```

Adjacent single- and double-quoted strings in the input are concatenated to form a single String object:

```
'Con' "cat" 'en' "ate"   # =>   "Concatenate"
```

Every time a string literal is used in an assignment or as a parameter, a new String object is created:

```
3.times do
  print 'hello'.object_id, " "
end
```

produces:

```
338430 338370 338330
```

The documentation for class String starts on page 661.

Ranges

Outside the context of a conditional expression, *expr..expr* and *expr...expr* construct Range objects. The two-dot form is an inclusive range; the one with three dots is a range that excludes its last element. See the description of class Range on page 647 for details. Also see the description of conditional expressions on page 336 for other uses of ranges.

Arrays

Literals of class Array are created by placing a comma-separated series of object references between square brackets. A trailing comma is ignored.

```
arr = [ fred, 10, 3.14, "This is a string", barney("pebbles"), ]
```

Arrays of strings can be constructed using the shortcut notations %w and %W. The lower-case form extracts space-separated tokens into successive elements of the array. No substitution is performed on the individual strings. The uppercase version also converts the words to an array but performs all the normal double-quoted string substitutions on each individual word. A space between words can be escaped with a backslash. This is a form of general delimited input, described on pages 314–315.

```
arr = %w( fred wilma barney betty great\ gazoo )
arr   # =>   ["fred", "wilma", "barney", "betty", "great gazoo"]
arr = %w( Hey!\tIt is now -#{Time.now}- )
arr   # =>   ["Hey!\tIt", "is", "now", "-#{Time.now}-"]
arr = %W( Hey!\tIt is now -#{Time.now}- )
arr   # =>   ["Hey! It", "is", "now", "-2009-03-31 09:58:01 -0500-"]
```

Hashes

A literal Ruby Hash is created by placing a list of key/value pairs between braces. Keys and values can be separated by the sequence =>.[1]

```
colors = { "red"   => 0xf00, "green" => 0x0f0, "blue"  => 0x00f }
```

---

1. As of Ruby 1.9, a comma may no longer be used to separate keys and values in hash literals. A comma still appears between each key/value pair.

If the keys are symbols, you can use this alternative notation:

```
colors = { red: 0xf00, green: 0x0f0, blue: 0x00f }
```

The keys and/or values in a particular hash need not have the same type.

Requirements for a Hash Key

Hash keys must respond to the message hash by returning a hash code, and the hash code for a given key must not change. The keys used in hashes must also be comparable using eql?. If eql? returns true for two keys, then those keys must also have the same hash code. This means that certain classes (such as Array and Hash) can't conveniently be used as keys, because their hash values can change based on their contents.

If you keep an external reference to an object that is used as a key and use that reference to alter the object, thus changing its hash code, the hash lookup based on that key may not work. You can force the hash to be reindexed by calling its rehash method.

```
arr = [1, 2, 3]
hash = { arr => 'value' }
hash[arr]    # =>   "value"
arr[1] = 99
hash         # =>   {[1, 99, 3]=>"value"}
hash[arr]    # =>   nil
hash.rehash
hash[arr]    # =>   "value"
```

Because strings are the most frequently used keys and because string contents are often changed, Ruby treats string keys specially. If you use a String object as a hash key, the hash will duplicate the string internally and will use that as its key. The copy will be frozen. Any changes made to the original string will not affect the hash.

If you write your own classes and use instances of them as hash keys, you need to make sure that either (a) the hashes of the key objects don't change once the objects have been created or (b) you remember to call the Hash#rehash method to reindex the hash whenever a key hash *is* changed.

Symbols

A Ruby symbol is an identifier corresponding to a string of characters, often a name. You construct the symbol for a name by preceding the name with a colon, and you can construct the symbol for an arbitrary string by preceding a string literal with a colon. Substitution occurs in double-quoted strings. A particular name or string will always generate the same symbol, regardless of how that name is used within the program. You can also use the %s delimited notation to create a symbol.

```
:Object
:my_variable
:"Ruby rules"
a = "cat"
:'catsup'                    # =>   :catsup
:"#{a}sup"                   # =>   :catsup
:'#{a}sup'                   # =>   :"\#{a}sup"
%s{symbol}                   # =>   :symbol
%s{ symbol with spaces }     # =>   :" symbol with spaces "
```

Other languages call this process *interning* and call symbols *atoms*.

Regular Expressions

This section contains a summary on the Oniguruma regular expression engine used by Ruby. See Chapter 7 on page 99 for a detailed description of regular expressions.

Regular expression literals are objects of type Regexp. They are created explicitly by calling Regexp.new or implicitly by using the literal forms, /*pattern*/ and %r{*pattern*}. The %r construct is a form of general delimited input (described on pages 314–315).

```
/pattern/
/pattern/options
%r{pattern}
%r{pattern}options
Regexp.new( 'pattern' [ , options ] )
```

options is one or more of i (case insensitive), o (substitute once), m (. matches newline), and x (allow spaces and comments). You can additionally override the default encoding of the pattern with n (no encoding-ASCII), e (EUC), s (Shift_JIS), or u (UTF-8).

Regular Expression Patterns

1.9 (This section contains many differences from previous versions of this book. Ruby 1.9 uses the Oniguruma regular expression engine.)[2]

characters	All except ., I, (,), [, \, ^, {, +, $, *, and ? match themselves. To match one of these characters, precede it with a backslash.
\a \cx \e \f \r \t \u*nnnn* \v \x*nn* \n*nn* \C-\M-*x* \C-*x* \M-*x*	Match the character derived according to Table 22.2 on page 317.
^, $	Match the beginning/end of a line.
\A, \z, \Z	Match the beginning/end of the string. \Z ignores trailing \n.
\d, \h	Match any decimal digit (or Unicode *Decimal_Number*), hexadecimal digit ([0-9a-fA-F]).
\s	Matches any whitespace character: tab, newline, vertical tab, form feed, return, and space. For Unicode, add *Line_Separator* codepoints.

---

2.   Some of the information here is based on http://www.geocities.jp/kosako3/oniguruma/doc/RE.txt.

\w	Matches any word character: alphanumerics and underscores. For Unicode, add in the codepoints in *Connector_Punctuation*, *Letter*, *Mark*, and *Number*.
\D,\H, \S, \W	The negated forms of \d, \h, \s, and \w, matching characters that are not digits, hexadecimal digits, whitespace, or word characters.
\b, \B	Match word/nonword boundaries.
\G	The position where a previous repetitive search completed.
\p{*property*}, \P{*property*}, \p{!*property*}	
	Match a character that is in/not in the given property (see Table 7.3 on page 108).
. (period)	Appearing outside brackets, matches any character except a newline. (With the /m option, it matches newline, too).
[*characters*]	Matches a single character from the specified set. See page 105.
re*	Matches zero or more occurrences of *re*.
re+	Matches one or more occurrences of *re*.
re{m,n}	Matches at least "m" and at most "n" occurrences of *re*.
re{m,}	Matches at least "m" occurrences of *re*.
re{,n}	Matches at most "n" occurrences of *re*.
re{m}	Matches exactly "m" occurrences of *re*.
re?	Matches zero or one occurrence of *re*.
	The ?, *, +, and {m,n} modifiers are greedy by default. Append a question mark to make them minimal, and append a plus sign to make them possessive (that is, they are greedy and will not backtrack).
re1|*re2*	Matches either *re1* or *re2*.
(...)	Group regular expressions and introduce extensions.
#{...}	Substitutes expression in the pattern, as with strings. By default, the substitution is performed each time a regular expression literal is evaluated. With the /o option, it is performed just the first time.
\0, \1, \2, ... *n*, \&, \\`, \\', \+	
	Substitute the value matched by the *n*th grouped subexpression or by the entire match, pre- or postmatch, or the highest group.
(?# *comment*)	Inserts a comment into the pattern.
(?:*re*)	Makes *re* into a group without generating backreferences.
(?=*re*), (?!*re*)	Matches if *re* is/is not at this point but does not consume it.
(?<=*re*), (?<!*re*)	
	Matches if *re* is/is not before this point but does not consume it.
(?>*re*)	Matches *re*, but inhibits subsequent backtracking.
(?imx), (?-imx)	Turn on/off the corresponding i, m, or x option. If used inside a group, the effect is limited to that group.
(?imx:*re*), (?-imx:*re*)	
	Turn on/off the i, m, or x option for *re*.

\n, \k'n', and \k<n>
> The nth captured subpattern.

(?<name>...) or (?'name'...)
> Name the string captured by the group.

\k<name> or \k'name'
> The contents of the named group.

\k<name>+n/1 or \k'name'+/-n
> The contents of the named group at the given relative nesting level.

\g<name> or \g<number>
> Invoke the named or numbered group.

Names

Ruby names are used to refer to constants, variables, methods, classes, and modules. The first character of a name helps Ruby to distinguish its intended use. Certain names, listed in Table 22.3 on the next page, are reserved words and should not be used as variable, method, class, or module names.

Method names are described in the section beginning on page 339.

In these descriptions, *Uppercase letter* means *A* though *Z*, and *digit* means *0* through *9*. *lowercase letter* means the characters *a* though *z*, as well as _ , the underscore. In addition, any non-7-bit characters that are valid in the current encoding are considered to be lowercase.[3]

A *name* is an uppercase letter, a lowercase letter, or an underscore, followed by *name characters*: any combination of upper- and lowercase letters, underscores, and digits.

A **local variable name** consists of a lowercase letter followed by name characters. It is conventional to use underscores rather than camelCase to write multiword names, but the interpreter does not enforce this:

```
fred    anObject    _x    three_two_one
```

If the source file encoding is UTF-8, δelta and été are both valid local variable names.

An **instance variable name** starts with an "at" sign (@) followed by a name. It is generally a good idea to use a lowercase letter after the @.

```
@name    @_    @size
```

A **class variable name** starts with two "at" signs (@@) followed by a name.

```
@@name    @@_    @@Size
```

A **constant name** starts with an uppercase letter followed by name characters. Class names and module names are constants and follow the constant naming conventions.

---

3.   Such names will not be usable from other source files with different encoding.

Table 22.3. Reserved Words

__FILE__	and	def	end	in	or	self	unless
__LINE__	begin	defined?	ensure	module	redo	super	until
BEGIN	break	do	false	next	rescue	then	when
END	case	else	for	nil	retry	true	while
alias	class	elsif	if	not	return	undef	yield

By convention, constant object references are normally spelled using uppercase letters and underscores throughout, while class and module names are MixedCase:

```
module Math
  ALMOST_PI = 22.0/7.0
end
class BigBlob
end
```

Global variables, and some special system variables, start with a dollar sign ($) followed by name characters. In addition, Ruby defines a set of two-character global variable names in which the second character is a punctuation character. These predefined variables are listed starting on page 327. Finally, a global variable name can be formed using $- followed by a single letter or underscore. These latter variables typically mirror the setting of the corresponding command-line option (see the table starting on page 329 for details):

```
$params  $PROGRAM  $!  $_  $-a  $-K
```

Variable/Method Ambiguity

When Ruby sees a name such as a in an expression, it needs to determine whether it is a local variable reference or a call to a method with no parameters. To decide which is the case, Ruby uses a heuristic. As Ruby parses a source file, it keeps track of symbols that have been assigned to. It assumes that these symbols are variables. When it subsequently comes across a symbol that could be a variable or a method call, it checks to see whether it has seen a prior assignment to that symbol. If so, it treats the symbol as a variable; otherwise, it treats it as a method call. As a somewhat pathological case of this, consider the following code fragment, submitted by Clemens Hintze:

```
def a
  print "Function 'a' called\n"
  99
end
for i in 1..2
  if i == 2
    print "a=", a, "\n"
  else
    a = 1
    print "a=", a, "\n"
  end
end
```

produces:

```
a=1
Function 'a' called
a=99
```

During the parse, Ruby sees the use of a in the first print statement and, because it hasn't yet seen any assignment to a, assumes that it is a method call. By the time it gets to the second print statement, though, it *has* seen an assignment and so treats a as a variable.

Note that the assignment does not have to be executed—Ruby just has to have seen it. This program does not raise an error.

```
a = 1 if false; a
```

Variables and Constants

Ruby variables and constants hold references to objects. Variables themselves do not have an intrinsic type. Instead, the type of a variable is defined solely by the messages to which the object referenced by the variable responds.[4]

A Ruby *constant* is also a reference to an object. Constants are created when they are first assigned to (normally in a class or module definition). Ruby, unlike less flexible languages, lets you alter the value of a constant, although this will generate a warning message:

```
MY_CONST = 1
MY_CONST = 2   # generates a warning
```

produces:

```
/tmp/prog.rb:2: warning: already initialized constant MY_CONST
```

Note that although constants should not be changed, you can alter the internal states of the objects they reference:[5]

```
MY_CONST = "Tim"
MY_CONST[0] = "J"   # alter string referenced by constant
MY_CONST   # =>   "Jim"
```

Assignment potentially *aliases* objects, creating two references to the same object.

Scope of Constants and Variables

Constants defined within a class or module may be accessed unadorned anywhere within the class or module. Outside the class or module, they may be accessed using the scope operator, :: prefixed by an expression that returns the appropriate class or module object. Constants defined outside any class or module may be accessed unadorned or by using the

---

4. When we say that a variable is not typed, we mean that any given variable can at different times hold references to objects of many different types.

5. You can freeze objects to prevent this.

scope operator :: with no prefix. Constants may not be defined in methods. Constants may be added to existing classes and modules from the outside by using the class or module name and the scope operator before the constant name.

```
OUTER_CONST = 99
class Const
  def get_const
    CONST
  end
  CONST = OUTER_CONST + 1
end

Const.new.get_const   # =>   100
Const::CONST          # =>   100
::OUTER_CONST         # =>   99
Const::NEW_CONST = 123
```

Global variables are available throughout a program. Every reference to a particular global name returns the same object. Referencing an uninitialized global variable returns nil.

Class variables are available throughout a class or module body. Class variables must be initialized before use. A class variable is shared among all instances of a class and is available within the class itself.

```
class Song
  @@count = 0

  def initialize
    @@count += 1
  end
  def Song.get_count
    @@count
  end
end
```

Class variables belong to the innermost enclosing class or module. Class variables used at the top level are defined in Object and behave like global variables. Class variables defined within singleton methods belong to the top level (although this usage is deprecated and generates a warning). In Ruby 1.9, class variables are private to the defining class:

```
class Holder
  @@var = 99
  def Holder.var=(val)
    @@var = val
  end
  def var
    @@var
  end
end
@@var = "top level variable"
a = Holder.new

a.var   # =>   "top level variable"
```

```
Holder.var = 123
a.var   # =>   123

# This references the top-level object
def a.get_var
  @@var
end
a.get_var   # =>   "top level variable"
```

Class variables are inherited by children but are unique across children:

```
class Top
  @@A = 1
  @@B = 1
  def dump
    puts values
  end
  def values
    "#{self.class.name}: @@A = #@@A, @@B = #@@B"
  end
end
class MiddleOne < Top
  @@B = 2
  @@C = 2
  def values
    super + ", C = #@@C"
  end
end
class MiddleTwo < Top
  @@B = 3
  @@C = 3
  def values
    super + ", C = #@@C"
  end
end
class BottomOne < MiddleOne; end
class BottomTwo < MiddleTwo; end

Top.new.dump
MiddleOne.new.dump
MiddleTwo.new.dump
BottomOne.new.dump
BottomTwo.new.dump
```

produces:

```
Top: @@A = 1, @@B = 3
MiddleOne: @@A = 1, @@B = 3, C = 2
MiddleTwo: @@A = 1, @@B = 3, C = 3
BottomOne: @@A = 1, @@B = 3, C = 2
BottomTwo: @@A = 1, @@B = 3, C = 3
```

I recommend against using class variables for this reason.

Instance variables are available within instance methods throughout a class body. Referencing an uninitialized instance variable returns nil. Each instance of a class has a unique set of instance variables. Instance variables are not available to class methods (although classes [and modules] also may have instance variables—see page 376).

Local variables are unique in that their scopes are statically determined but their existence is established dynamically.

A local variable is created dynamically when it is first assigned a value during program execution. However, the scope of a local variable is statically determined to be the immediately enclosing block, method definition, class definition, module definition, or top-level program. Referencing a local variable that is in scope but that has not yet been created generates a NameError exception. Local variables with the same name are different variables if they appear in disjoint scopes.

Method parameters are considered to be variables local to that method.

Block parameters are assigned values when the block is invoked.

If a local variable is first assigned in a block, it is local to the block.

If a block uses a variable that is previously defined in the scope containing the block's definition, then the block will share that variable with the scope. There are two exceptions to this. Block parameters are always local to the block. In addition, variables listed after a semicolon at the end of the block parameter list are also always local to the block.

```
a = 1
b = 2
c = 3
some_method { |b; c| a = b + 1; c = a + 1; d = c + 1 }
```

In this previous example, the variable a inside the block is shared with the surrounding scope. The variables b and c are not shared, because they are listed in the block's parameter list, and the variable d is not shared before it occurs only inside the block.

A block takes on the set of local variables in existence at the time that it is created. This forms part of its binding. Note that although the binding of the variables is fixed at this point, the block will have access to the *current* values of these variables when it executes. The binding preserves these variables even if the original enclosing scope is destroyed.

The bodies of while, until, and for loops are part of the scope that contains them; previously existing locals can be used in the loop, and any new locals created will be available outside the bodies afterward.

Predefined Variables

The following variables are predefined in the Ruby interpreter. In these descriptions, the notation [r/o] indicates that the variables are read-only; an error will be raised if a program attempts to modify a read-only variable. After all, you probably don't want to change the meaning of true halfway through your program (except perhaps if you're a politician). Entries marked [thread] are thread local.

Many global variables look something like Snoopy swearing: $_, $!, $&, and so on. This is for "historical" reasons because most of these variable names come from Perl. If you find memorizing all this punctuation difficult, you may want to take a look at the library file called English, documented on page 739, which gives the commonly used global variables more descriptive names.

In the tables of variables and constants that follow, we show the variable name, the type of the referenced object, and a description.

Exception Information

$!	Exception	The exception object passed to raise. [thread]
$@	Array	The stack backtrace generated by the last exception. See Kernel#caller on page 558 for details. [thread]

Pattern Matching Variables

These variables (except $=) are set to nil after an unsuccessful pattern match.

$&	String	The string matched (following a successful pattern match). This variable is local to the current scope. [r/o, thread]
$+	String	The contents of the highest-numbered group matched following a successful pattern match. Thus, in "cat" =~/(c|a)(t|z)/, $+ will be set to "t." This variable is local to the current scope. [r/o, thread]
$`	String	The string preceding the match in a successful pattern match. This variable is local to the current scope. [r/o, thread]
$'	String	The string following the match in a successful pattern match. This variable is local to the current scope. [r/o, thread]
$1...$n	String	The contents of successive groups matched in a successful pattern match. In "cat" =~/(c|a)(t|z)/, $1 will be set to "a" and $2 to "t." This variable is local to the current scope. [r/o, thread]
$~	MatchData	An object that encapsulates the results of a successful pattern match. The variables $&, $`, $', and $1 to $9 are all derived from $~. Assigning to $~ changes the values of these derived variables. This variable is local to the current scope. [thread]

The variable $=, which previously controlled case-insensitive matches, has been removed from Ruby 1.9.

Input/Output Variables

$/	String	The input record separator (newline by default). This is the value that routines such as Kernel#gets use to determine record boundaries. If set to nil, gets will read the entire file.
$-0	String	Synonym for $/.
$\	String	The string appended to the output of every call to methods such as Kernel#print and IO#write. The default value is nil.
$,	String	The separator string output between the parameters to methods such as Kernel#print and Array#join. Defaults to nil, which adds no text.
$.	Fixnum	The number of the last line read from the current input file.

$;	String	The default separator pattern used by String#split. May be set from the command line using the -F flag.
$<	Object	An object that provides access to the concatenation of the contents of all the files given as command-line arguments or $stdin (in the case where there are no arguments). $< supports methods similar to a File object: binmode, close, closed?, each, each_byte, each_line, eof, eof?, file, filename, fileno, getc, gets, lineno, lineno=, path, pos, pos=, read, readchar, readline, readlines, rewind, seek, skip, tell, to_a, to_i, to_io, to_s, along with the methods in Enumerable. The method file returns a File object for the file currently being read. This may change as $< reads through the files on the command line. [r/o]
$>	IO	The destination of output for Kernel#print and Kernel#printf. The default value is $stdout.
$_	String	The last line read by Kernel#gets or Kernel#readline. Many string-related functions in the Kernel module operate on $_ by default. The variable is local to the current scope. [thread]
$-F	String	Synonym for $;.
$stderr	IO	The current standard error output.
$stdin	IO	The current standard input.
$stdout	IO	The current standard output. Assignment to $stdout is not permitted: use $stdout.reopen instead.

1.9 The variables $defout and $deferr have been removed from Ruby 1.9.

Execution Environment Variables

$0	String	The name of the top-level Ruby program being executed. Typically this will be the program's filename. On some operating systems, assigning to this variable will change the name of the process reported (for example) by the ps(1) command.
$*	Array	An array of strings containing the command-line options from the invocation of the program. Options used by the Ruby interpreter will have been removed. [r/o]
$"	Array	An array containing the filenames of modules loaded by require. [r/o]
$$	Fixnum	The process number of the program being executed. [r/o]
$?	Process::Status	
		The exit status of the last child process to terminate. [r/o, thread]
$:	Array	An array of strings, where each string specifies a directory to be searched for Ruby scripts and binary extensions used by the load and require methods. The initial value is the value of the arguments passed via the -I command-line option, followed by an installation-defined standard library location, followed by the current directory ("."). This variable may be set from within a program to alter the default search path; typically, programs use $: << dir to append dir to the path. [r/o]
$-a	Object	True if the -a option is specified on the command line. [r/o]
__callee__	Symbol	The name of the lexically enclosing method.
$-d	Object	Synonym for $DEBUG.
$DEBUG	Object	Set to true if the -d command-line option is specified.

1.9 (appears at left of __callee__ row)

__ENCODING__

	String	The encoding of the current source file. [r/o]
__FILE__	String	The name of the current source file. [r/o]
$F	Array	The array that receives the split input line if the -a command-line option is used.
$FILENAME	String	The name of the current input file. Equivalent to $<.filename. [r/o]
$-i	String	If in-place edit mode is enabled (perhaps using the -i command-line option), $-i holds the extension used when creating the backup file. If you set a value into $-i, enables in-place edit mode. See page 221.
$-I	Array	Synonym for $:. [r/o]
$-l	Object	Set to true if the -l option (which enables line-end processing) is present on the command line. See page 221. [r/o]
__LINE__	String	The current line number in the source file. [r/o]
$LOAD_PATH	Array	A synonym for $:. [r/o]

$LOADED_FEATURES

	Array	Synonym for $". [r/o]
__method__	Symbol	The name of the lexically enclosing method.

$PROGRAM_NAME

	String	Alias for $0.
$-p	Object	Set to true if the -p option (which puts an implicit while gets ... end loop around your program) is present on the command line. See page 221. [r/o]
$SAFE	Fixnum	The current safe level (see page 426). This variable's value may never be reduced by assignment. [thread]
$VERBOSE	Object	Set to true if the -v, --version, -W, or -w option is specified on the command line. Set to false if no option, or -W1 is given. Set to nil if -W0 was specified. Setting this option to true causes the interpreter and some library routines to report additional information. Setting to nil suppresses all warnings (including the output of Kernel.warn).
$-v	Object	Synonym for $VERBOSE.
$-w	Object	Synonym for $VERBOSE.
$-W	Object	Return the value set by the -W command-line option.

Standard Objects

ARGF	Object	A synonym for $<.
ARGV	Array	A synonym for $*.
ENV	Object	A hash-like object containing the program's environment variables. An instance of class Object, ENV implements the full set of Hash methods. Used to query and set the value of an environment variable, as in ENV["PATH"] and ENV["term"]="ansi".
false	FalseClass	Singleton instance of class FalseClass. [r/o]

nil	NilClass	The singleton instance of class NilClass. The value of uninitialized instance and global variables. [r/o]
self	Object	The receiver (object) of the current method. [r/o]
true	TrueClass	Singleton instance of class TrueClass. [r/o]

Global Constants

The following constants are defined by the Ruby interpreter.

DATA	IO	If the main program file contains the directive _ _END_ _, then the constant DATA will be initialized so that reading from it will return lines following _ _END_ _ from the source file.
FALSE	FalseClass	Constant containing reference to false.
NIL	NilClass	Constant containing reference to nil.
RUBY_COPYRIGHT	String	The interpreter copyright.
RUBY_DESCRIPTION	String	Version number and architecture of the interpreter.
RUBY_ENGINE	String	The name of the Ruby interpreter. Returns ruby for Matz's version. Other interpreters include macruby, ironruby, jruby, and rubinius.
RUBY_PATCHLEVEL	String	The patch level of the interpreter.
RUBY_PLATFORM	String	The identifier of the platform running this program. This string is in the same form as the platform identifier used by the GNU configure utility (which is not a coincidence).
RUBY_RELEASE_DATE	String	The date of this release.
RUBY_REVISION	String	The revision of the interpreter.
RUBY_VERSION	String	The version number of the interpreter.
STDERR	IO	The actual standard error stream for the program. The initial value of $stderr.
STDIN	IO	The actual standard input stream for the program. The initial value of $stdin.
STDOUT	IO	The actual standard output stream for the program. The initial value of $stdout.
SCRIPT_LINES_ _	Hash	If a constant SCRIPT_LINES_ _ is defined and references a Hash, Ruby will store an entry containing the contents of each file it parses, with the file's name as the key and an array of strings as the value. See Kernel.require on page 567 for an example.
TOPLEVEL_BINDING	Binding	A Binding object representing the binding at Ruby's top level—the level where programs are initially executed.
TRUE	TrueClass	A reference to the object true.

The constant _ _FILE_ _ and the variable $0 are often used together to run code only if it appears in the file run directly by the user. For example, library writers often use this to include tests in their libraries that will be run if the library source is run directly, but not if the source is required into another program.

```
# library code
# ...
if __FILE__ == $0
  # tests...
end
```

Expressions

Single terms in an expression may be any of the following.

- **Literal**. Ruby literals are numbers, strings, arrays, hashes, ranges, symbols, and regular expressions. These are described starting on page 315.

- **Shell command**. A shell command is a string enclosed in backquotes or in a general delimited string (page 314) starting with %x. The value of the string is the standard output of running the command represented by the string under the host operating system's standard shell. The execution also sets the $? variable with the command's exit status.

```
filter = "*.c"
files = `ls #{filter}`
files = %x{ls #{filter}}
```

- **Variable reference** or **constant reference**. A variable is referenced by citing its name. Depending on scope (see page 324), a constant is referenced either by citing its name or by qualifying the name, using the name of the class or module containing the constant and the scope operator (::).

```
barney     # variable reference
APP_NAMR   # constant reference
Math::PI   # qualified constant reference
```

- **Method invocation**. The various ways of invoking a method are described starting on page 343.

Operator Expressions

Expressions may be combined using operators. Table 22.4 on the facing page lists the Ruby operators in precedence order. The operators with a ✓ in the Method column are implemented as methods and may be overridden.

More on Assignment

The assignment operator assigns one or more *rvalues* (the *r* stands for "right," because rvalues tend to appear on the right side of assignments) to one or more *lvalues* ("left" values). What is meant by assignment depends on each individual lvalue.

Table 22.4. Ruby Operators (High to Low Precedence)

Method	Operator	Description
✓	[ ] [ ]=	Element reference, element set
✓	**	Exponentiation
✓	! ~ + −	Not, complement, unary plus and minus (method names for the last two are +@ and -@)
✓	* / %	Multiply, divide, and modulo
✓	+ −	Plus and minus
✓	>> <<	Right and left shift (<< is also used as the append operator)
✓	&	"And" (bitwise for integers)
✓	^		Exclusive "or" and regular "or" (bitwise for integers)
✓	<= < > >=	Comparison operators
✓	<=> == === != =~ !~	Equality and pattern match operators
	&&	Logical "and"
	||	Logical "or"
	.. ...	Range (inclusive and exclusive)
	? :	Ternary if-then-else
	= %= /= −= += |= &= >>=	Assignment
	<<= *= &&= ||= **=	
	not	Logical negation
	or and	Logical composition
	if unless while until	Expression modifiers
	begin/end	Block expression

If an lvalue is a variable or constant name, that variable or constant receives a reference to the corresponding rvalue:

```
a = /regexp/
b, c, d = 1, "cat", [ 3, 4, 5 ]
```

If the lvalue is an object attribute, the corresponding attribute setting method will be called in the receiver, passing as a parameter the rvalue:

```
obj = A.new
obj.value = "hello"    # equivalent to obj.value=("hello")
```

If the lvalue is an array element reference, Ruby calls the element assignment operator ([ ]=) in the receiver, passing as parameters any indices that appear between the brackets followed by the rvalue. This is illustrated in the following table.

Element Reference	Actual Method Call
var[ ] = "one"	var.[ ]=("one")
var[1] = "two"	var.[ ]=(1, "two")
var["a", /^cat/] = "three"	var.[ ]=("a", /^cat/, "three")

If you are writing an [ ]= method that accepts a variable number of indices, it might be convenient to define it using this:

```
def []=(*indices, value)
  # ...
end
```

The value of an assignment expression is its rvalue. This is true even if the assignment is to an attribute method that returns something different.

Parallel Assignment

An assignment expression may have one or more lvalues and one or more rvalues. This section explains how Ruby handles assignment with different combinations of arguments:

1. If any rvalue is prefixed with an asterisk and implements to_a, the rvalue is replaced with the elements returned by to_a, with each element forming its own rvalue.

2. If the assignment contains one lvalue and multiple rvalues, the rvalues are converted to an array and assigned to that lvalue.

3. If the assignment contains multiple lvalues and one rvalue, the rvalue is expanded if possible into a set of rvalues as described in (1).

4. Successive rvalues are assigned to the lvalues. This assignment effectively happens in parallel, so that (for example) a,b=b,a swaps the values in a and b.

5. If there are more lvalues than rvalues, the excess will have nil assigned to them.

6. If there are more rvalues than lvalues, the excess will be ignored.

7. At most one lvalue can be prefixed by an asterisk. This lvalue will end up being an array and will contain as many rvalues as possible. If there are lvalues to the right of the starred lvalue, these will be assigned from the trailing rvalues, and whatever rvalues are left will be assigned to the splat lvalue.

8. If an lvalue contains a parenthesized list, the list is treated as a nested assignment statement, and then it is assigned from the corresponding rvalue as described by these rules.

The tutorial has examples starting on page 134. The value of a parallel assignment is its set of rvalues.

Block Expressions

```
begin
  body
end
```

Expressions may be grouped between begin and end. The value of the block expression is the value of the last expression executed.

Block expressions also play a role in exception handling, which is discussed starting on page 355.

Boolean Expressions

Ruby predefines the globals false and nil. Both of these values are treated as being false in a boolean context. All other values are treated as being true. The constant true is available for when you need an explicit "true" value.

And, Or, Not

The and and && operators evaluate their first operand. If false, the expression returns the value of the first operand; otherwise, the expression returns the value of the second operand:

```
expr1   and   expr2
expr1   &&    expr2
```

The or and || operators evaluate their first operand. If true, the expression returns the value of their first operand; otherwise, the expression returns the value of the second operand:

```
expr1   or    expr2
expr1   ||    expr2
```

The not and ! operators evaluate their operand. If true, the expression returns false. If false, the expression returns true. For historical reasons, a string, regexp, or range may not appear as the single argument to not or !.

The word forms of these operators (and, or, and not) have a lower precedence than the corresponding symbol forms (&&, ||, and !). See Table 22.4 on page 333 for details.

defined?

The defined? keyword returns nil if its argument, which can be an arbitrary expression, is not defined. Otherwise, it returns a description of that argument. For examples, see page 137 in the tutorial.

Comparison Operators

The Ruby syntax defines the comparison operators ==, ===, <=>, <, <=, >, >=, =~. All of these operators are implemented as methods. By convention, the language also uses the standard methods eql? and equal? (see Table 9.1 on page 139). Although the operators have intuitive meaning, it is up to the classes that implement them to produce meaningful comparison semantics. The library reference starting on page 433 describes the comparison semantics for the built-in classes. The module Comparable provides support for implementing the operators ==, <, <=, >, and >=, as well as the method between? in terms of <=>. The operator === is used in case expressions, described on page 337.

Both == and =~ have negated forms, != and !~. If an object defines these methods, Ruby will call them. Otherwise, a != b is mapped to !(a == b), and a !~ b is mapped to !(a =~ b).

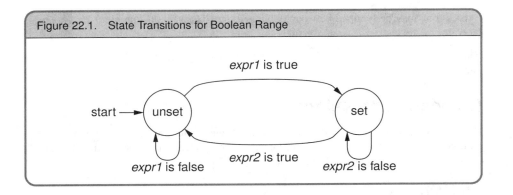

Figure 22.1. State Transitions for Boolean Range

Ranges in Boolean Expressions

```
if    expr1 .. expr2
while  expr1 ... expr2
```

A range used in a boolean expression acts as a flip-flop. It has two states, set and unset, and is initially unset. On each call, the range executes a transition in the state machine shown in Figure 22.1. The range expression returns true if the state machine is in the set state at the end of the call, and false otherwise.

The two-dot form of a range behaves slightly differently than the three-dot form. When the two-dot form first makes the transition from unset to set, it immediately evaluates the end condition and makes the transition accordingly. This means that if *expr1* and *expr2* both evaluate to true on the same call, the two-dot form will finish the call in the unset state. However, it still returns true for this call.

The three-dot form does not evaluate the end condition immediately upon entering the set state.

The difference is illustrated by the following code:

```
a = (11..20).collect {|i| (i%4 == 0)..(i%3 == 0) ? i : nil}
a  # =>   [nil, 12, nil, nil, nil, 16, 17, 18, nil, 20]

a = (11..20).collect {|i| (i%4 == 0)...(i%3 == 0) ? i : nil}
a  # =>   [nil, 12, 13, 14, 15, 16, 17, 18, nil, 20]
```

Regular Expressions in Boolean Expressions

1.9 / In versions of Ruby prior to 1.8, a single regular expression in boolean expression was matched against the current value of the variable $_. This behavior is now supported only if the condition appears in a command-line -e parameter:

```
$ ruby -ne 'print if /one/' testfile
```

In regular code, the use of implicit operands and $_ is being slowly phased out, so it is better to use an explicit match against a variable. If a match against $_ is required, use this:

```
if ~/re/ ...      or       if $_ =~ /re/ ...
```

if and unless Expressions

```
if boolean-expression [ then ]
  body
[ elsif boolean-expression [ then ]
  body , ... ]
[ else
  body ]
end

unless boolean-expression [ then ]
  body
[ else
  body ]
end
```

The then keyword separates the body from the condition.[6] It is not required if the body starts on a new line. The value of an if or unless expression is the value of the last expression evaluated in whichever body is executed.

if and unless Modifiers

```
expression if      boolean-expression
expression unless boolean-expression
```

This evaluates *expression* only if *boolean-expression* is true (for if) or false (for unless).

Ternary Operator

```
boolean-expression ? expr1 : expr2
```

This returns *expr1* if *boolean expression* is true and *expr2* otherwise.

case Expressions

Ruby has two forms of case statement. The first allows a series of conditions to be evaluated, executing code corresponding to the first condition that is true:

```
case
when condition [, condition ]... [ then ]
    body
when condition [, condition ]... [ then ]
    body
  ...
[ else
    body ]
end
```

---

6. Prior to Ruby 1.9, you could use a colon instead of then. This is no longer supported.

The second form of a case expression takes a target expression following the case keyword. It searches for a match by starting at the first (top left) comparison, performing *comparison === target*:

```
case target
when comparison [, comparison ]... [ then ]
    body
when comparison [, comparison ]... [ then ]
    body
  ...
[ else
    body  ]
end
```

A comparison can be an array reference preceded by an asterisk, in which case it is expanded into that array's elements before the tests are performed on each. When a comparison returns true, the search stops, and the body associated with the comparison is executed (no break is required). case then returns the value of the last expression executed. If no *comparison* matches, this happens: if an else clause is present, its body will be executed; otherwise, case silently returns nil.

The then keyword separates the when comparisons from the bodies and is not needed if the body starts on a new line.

1.9 | As an optimization in Matz's Ruby 1.9, comparisons with literal strings and numbers do not use ===.

Loops

```
while boolean-expression [ do ]
    body
end
```

This executes *body* zero or more times as long as *boolean-expression* is true.

```
until boolean-expression [ do ]
    body
end
```

This executes *body* zero or more times as long as *boolean-expression* is false.

In both forms, the do separates *boolean-expression* from the *body* and can be omitted when the body starts on a new line:

```
for name [, name ]... in expression [ do ]
    body
end
```

The for loop is executed as if it were the following each loop, except that local variables defined in the body of the for loop will be available outside the loop, and those defined within an iterator block will not.

```
expression.each do | name [, name ]... |
    body
end
```

loop, which iterates its associated block, is not a language construct—it is a method in   *Library*
module Kernel.

```
loop do
  print "Input: "
  break unless line = gets
  process(line)
end
```

while and until Modifiers

> *expression* while *boolean-expression*
> *expression* until *boolean-expression*

If *expression* is anything other than a begin/end block, executes *expression* zero or more
times while *boolean-expression* is true (for while) or false (for until).

If *expression* is a begin/end block, the block will always be executed at least one time.

break, redo, next, and retry

break, redo, next, and retry alter the normal flow through a while, until, for, or iterator controlled loop.

break terminates the immediately enclosing loop—control resumes at the statement following the block. redo repeats the loop from the start but without reevaluating the condition or
fetching the next element (in an iterator). The next keyword skips to the end of the loop,
effectively starting the next iteration. retry restarts the loop, reevaluating the condition.

break and next may optionally take one or more arguments. If used within a block, the given
argument(s) are returned as the value of the yield. If used within a while, until, or for loop,
the value given to break is returned as the value of the statement, and the value given to next
is silently ignored. If break is never called or if it is called with no value, the loop returns
nil.

```
match = while line = gets
          next if line =~ /^#/
          break line if line =~ /ruby/
        end

match = for line in ARGF.readlines
          next if line =~ /^#/
          break line if line =~ /ruby/
        end
```

Method Definition

```
def defname [ ( [ arg [ =val ], ... ] [ , &blockarg ] ) ]
  body
end
```

defname is both the name of the method and optionally the context in which it is valid.

> *defname* ← *methodname*
> *constant*.*methodname*
> (*expr*).*methodname*

A *methodname* is either a redefinable operator (see Table 22.4 on page 333) or a name. If *methodname* is a name, it should start with a lowercase letter (or underscore) optionally followed by uppercase and lowercase letters, underscores, and digits. A *methodname* may optionally end with a question mark (?), exclamation point (!), or equals sign (=). The question mark and exclamation point are simply part of the name. The equals sign is also part of the name but additionally signals that this method may be used as an lvalue (described on page 34).

A method definition using an unadorned method name within a class or module definition creates an instance method. An instance method may be invoked only by sending its name to a receiver that is an instance of the class that defined it (or one of that class's subclasses).

Outside a class or module definition, a definition with an unadorned method name is added as a private method to class Object and hence may be called in any context without an explicit receiver.

A definition using a method name of the form *constant*.*methodname* or the more general (*expr*).*methodname* creates a method associated with the object that is the value of the constant or expression; the method will be callable only by supplying the object referenced by the expression as a receiver. This style of definition creates per object or *singleton methods*.

```
class MyClass
  def MyClass.method        # definition
  end
end

MyClass.method              # call

obj = Object.new
def obj.method              # definition
end

obj.method                  # call

def (1.class).fred          # receiver may be an expression
end

Fixnum.fred                 # call
```

Method definitions may not contain class or module definitions. They may contain nested instance or singleton method definitions. The internal method is defined when the enclosing method is executed. The internal method does *not* act as a closure in the context of the nested method—it is self-contained.

```ruby
def toggle
  def toggle
    "subsequent times"
  end
  "first time"
end

toggle    # =>    "first time"
toggle    # =>    "subsequent times"
toggle    # =>    "subsequent times"
```

The body of a method acts as if it were a begin/end block, in that it may contain exception handling statements (rescue, else, and ensure).

Method Arguments

A method definition may have zero or more regular arguments and an optional block argument. Arguments are separated by commas, and the argument list may be enclosed in parentheses.

A regular argument is a local variable name, optionally followed by an equals sign and an expression giving a default value. The expression is evaluated at the time the method is called. The expressions are evaluated from left to right. An expression may reference a parameter that precedes it in the argument list.

```ruby
def options(a=99, b=a+1)
  [ a, b ]
end
options          # =>   [99, 100]
options 1        # =>   [1, 2]
options 2, 4     # =>   [2, 4]
```

1.9

In Ruby 1.9, arguments without default values may appear after arguments with defaults. When such a method is called, Ruby will use the default values only if fewer parameters are passed to the method call than the total number of arguments.

```ruby
def mixed(a, b=50, c=b+10, d)
  [ a, b, c, d ]
end
mixed 1, 2        # =>   [1, 50, 60, 2]
mixed 1, 2, 3     # =>   [1, 2, 12, 3]
mixed 1, 2, 3, 4  # =>   [1, 2, 3, 4]
```

As with parallel assignment, one of the arguments may start with an asterisk. If the method call specifies any parameters in excess of the regular argument count, all these extra parameters will be collected into this newly created array.

```ruby
def varargs(a, *b)
  [ a, b ]
end
varargs 1          # =>   [1, []]
varargs 1, 2       # =>   [1, [2]]
varargs 1, 2, 3    # =>   [1, [2, 3]]
```

In Ruby 1.9, this argument need not be the last in the argument list. See the description of parallel assignment to see how values are assigned to this parameter.

```
def splat(a, *b, c)
  [ a, b, c ]
end
splat 1, 2        # =>  [1, [], 2]
splat 1, 2, 3     # =>  [1, [2], 3]
splat 1, 2, 3, 4  # =>  [1, [2, 3], 4]
```

If an array argument follows arguments with default values, parameters will first be used to override the defaults. The remainder will then be used to populate the array.

```
def mixed(a, b=99, *c)
  [ a, b, c]
end
mixed 1           # =>  [1, 99, []]
mixed 1, 2        # =>  [1, 2, []]
mixed 1, 2, 3     # =>  [1, 2, [3]]
mixed 1, 2, 3, 4  # =>  [1, 2, [3, 4]]
```

The optional block argument must be the last in the list. Whenever the method is called, Ruby checks for an associated block. If a block is present, it is converted to an object of class Proc and assigned to the block argument. If no block is present, the argument is set to nil.

```
def example(&block)
  puts block.inspect
end

example
example { "a block" }
```

produces:

```
nil
#<Proc:0x0a5064@/tmp/prog.rb:6>
```

Undefining a Method

The keyword undef allows you to undefine a method.

```
undef name | symbol  [ , ... ]
```

An undefined method still exists—it is simply marked as being undefined. If you undefine a method in a child class and then call that method on an instance of that child class, Ruby will immediately raise a NoMethodError—it will not look for the method in the child's parents.

Invoking a Method

```
[ receiver.  ] name [  parameters  ] [  block  ]
[ receiver:: ] name [  parameters  ] [  block  ]

parameters  ←  ( [ param, ... ] [ , hashlist ] [ *array ] [ &a_proc ] )

   block    ←   { blockbody }
                do blockbody end
```

The parentheses around the parameters may be omitted if it is otherwise unambiguous.

1.9 Initial parameters are assigned to the actual arguments of the method. Following these parameters may be a list of *key => value* or *key: value* pairs. These pairs are collected into a single new Hash object and passed as a single parameter.

1.9 Any parameter may be a single parameter prefixed with an asterisk. If a starred parameter supports the to_a method, that method is called, and the resulting array is expanded inline to provide parameters to the method call. If a starred argument does not support to_a, it is simply passed through unaltered.

```
def regular(a, b, *c)
  "a=#{a}, b=#{b}, c=#{c}"
end
regular 1, 2, 3, 4                  # =>   a=1, b=2, c=[3, 4]
regular(1, 2, 3, 4)                 # =>   a=1, b=2, c=[3, 4]
regular(1, *[2, 3, 4])              # =>   a=1, b=2, c=[3, 4]
regular(1, *[2, 3], 4)              # =>   a=1, b=2, c=[3, 4]
regular(1, *[2, 3], *4)             # =>   a=1, b=2, c=[3, 4]
regular(*[], 1, *[], *[2, 3], *[], 4)  # =>   a=1, b=2, c=[3, 4]
```

A block may be associated with a method call using either a literal block (which must start on the same source line as the last line of the method call) or a parameter containing a reference to a Proc or Method object prefixed with an ampersand character.

```
def some_method
  yield
end
some_method { }
some_method do
end
a_proc = lambda { 99 }
some_method(&a_proc)
```

Ruby arranges for the value of Kernel.block_given? to reflect the availability of a block associated with the call, regardless of the presence of a block argument. A block argument will be set to nil if no block is specified on the call to a method.

```
def other_method(&block)
  puts "block_given = #{block_given?}, block = #{block.inspect}"
end
other_method { }
other_method
```

produces:

```
block_given = true, block = #<Proc:0x0a4f88@/tmp/prog.rb:4>
block_given = false, block = nil
```

A method is called by passing its name to a receiver. If no receiver is specified, self is assumed. The receiver checks for the method definition in its own class and then sequentially in its ancestor classes. The instance methods of included modules act as if they were in anonymous superclasses of the class that includes them. If the method is not found, Ruby invokes the method method_missing in the receiver. The default behavior defined in Kernel.method_missing is to report an error and terminate the program.

When a receiver is explicitly specified in a method invocation, it may be separated from the method name using either a period (.) or two colons (::). The only difference between these two forms occurs if the method name starts with an uppercase letter. In this case, Ruby will assume that a receiver::Thing method call is actually an attempt to access a constant called Thing in the receiver *unless* the method invocation has a parameter list between parentheses. Using :: to indicate a method call is mildly deprecated.

```
Foo.Bar()       # method call
Foo.Bar         # method call
Foo::Bar()      # method call
Foo::Bar        # constant access
```

The return value of a method is the value of the last expression executed.

```
def odd_or_even(val)
  if val.odd?
    "odd"
  else
    "even"
  end
end

odd_or_even(26)   # =>   "even"
odd_or_even(27)   # =>   "odd"
```

A return expression immediately exits a method.

```
return [ expr, ... ]
```

The value of a return is nil if it is called with no parameters, the value of its parameter if it is called with one parameter, or an array containing all of its parameters if it is called with more than one parameter.

super

```
super  [ ( [ param, ... ] [ *array ] )  ]  [ block ]
```

Within the body of a method, a call to super acts just like a call to that original method, except that the search for a method body starts in the superclass of the object that was found to contain the original method. If no parameters (and no parentheses) are passed to super, the original method's parameters will be passed; otherwise, the parameters to super will be passed.

Operator Methods

> *expr1 operator*
> *operator expr1*
> *expr1 operator expr2*

If the operator in an operator expression corresponds to a redefinable method (see Table 22.4 on page 333), Ruby will execute the operator expression as if it had been written like this:

> (*expr1*).*operator*( )   or
> (*expr1*).*operator*(*expr2*)

Attribute Assignment

> *receiver*.*attrname* = *rvalue*

When the form *receiver.attrname* appears as an lvalue, Ruby invokes a method named *attrname=* in the receiver, passing *rvalue* as a single parameter. The value returned by this assignment is always *rvalue*—the return value of the method *attrname=* is discarded. If you want to access the return value (in the unlikely event that it isn't the *rvalue* anyway), send an explicit message to the method.

```
class Demo
  attr_reader :attr
  def attr=(val)
    @attr = val
    "return value"
  end
end

d = Demo.new

# In all these cases, @attr is set to 99
d.attr = 99          # =>   99
d.attr=(99)          # =>   99
d.send(:attr=, 99)   # =>   "return value"
d.attr               # =>   99
```

Element Reference Operator

> *receiver*[*expr* [, *expr*]...]
> *receiver*[*expr* [, *expr*]...] = *rvalue*

When used as an rvalue, element reference invokes the method [ ] in the receiver, passing as parameters the expressions between the brackets.

When used as an lvalue, element reference invokes the method [ ]= in the receiver, passing as parameters the expressions between the brackets, followed by the *rvalue* being assigned.

Aliasing

```
alias new_name old_name
```

This creates a new name that refers to an existing method, operator, global variable, or regular expression backreference ($&, $`, $', and $+). Local variables, instance variables, class variables, and constants may not be aliased. The parameters to alias may be names or symbols.

```
class Fixnum
  alias plus +
end
1.plus(3)          # =>   4

alias $prematch $`
"string" =~ /i/    # =>   3
$prematch          # =>   "str"

alias :cmd :`
cmd "date"         # =>   "Tue Mar 31 09:58:01 CDT 2009\n"
```

When a method is aliased, the new name refers to a copy of the original method's body. If the method is subsequently redefined, the aliased name will still invoke the original implementation.

```
def meth
  "original method"
end
alias original meth
def meth
  "new and improved"
end
meth       # =>   "new and improved"
original   # =>   "original method"
```

Class Definition

```
class [ scope:: ] classname [ < superexpr ]
  body
end

class << obj
  body
end
```

A Ruby class definition creates or extends an object of class Class by executing the code in *body*. In the first form, a named class is created or extended. The resulting Class object is assigned to a constant named *classname* (keep reading for scoping rules). This name should start with an uppercase letter. In the second form, an anonymous (singleton) class is associated with the specific object.

If present, *superexpr* should be an expression that evaluates to a Class object that will be the superclass of the class being defined. If omitted, it defaults to class Object.

Within *body*, most Ruby expressions are executed as the definition is read. However:

- Method definitions will register the methods in a table in the class object.

- Nested class and module definitions will be stored in constants within the class, not as global constants. These nested classes and modules can be accessed from outside the defining class using :: to qualify their names.

```
module NameSpace
  class Example
    CONST = 123
  end
end
obj = NameSpace::Example.new
a = NameSpace::Example::CONST
```

- The Module#include method will add the named modules as anonymous superclasses of the class being defined.

The *classname* in a class definition may be prefixed by the names of existing classes or modules using the scope operator (::). This syntax inserts the new definition into the namespace of the prefixing module(s) and/or class(es) but does not interpret the definition in the scope of these outer classes. A *classname* with a leading scope operator places that class or module in the top-level scope.

In the following example, class C is inserted into module A's namespace but is not interpreted in the context of A. As a result, the reference to CONST resolves to the top-level constant of that name, not A's version. We also have to fully qualify the singleton method name, because C on its own is not a known constant in the context of A::C.

```
CONST = "outer"

module A
  CONST = "inner"   # This is A::CONST
end

module A
  class B
    def B.get_const
      CONST
    end
  end
end

A::B.get_const   # =>    "inner"
```

```
class A::C
  def (A::C).get_const
    CONST
  end
end

A::C.get_const   # =>   "outer"
```

It is worth emphasizing that a class definition is executable code. Many of the directives used in class definitions (such as attr and include) are actually simply private instance methods of class Module (documented starting on page 596). The value of a class definition is the value of the last executed statement.

Chapter 24, which begins on page 373, describes in more detail how Class objects interact with the rest of the environment.

Creating Objects from Classes

obj = *classexpr*.new [([*args*, ...])]

Class Class defines the instance method Class#new, which creates an object of the class of the receiver (*classexpr* in the syntax example). This is done by calling the method *classexpr*.allocate. You can override this method, but your implementation must return an object of the correct class. It then invokes initialize in the newly created object and passes it any arguments originally passed to new.

If a class definition overrides the class method new without calling super, no objects of that class can be created, and calls to new will silently return nil.

Like any other method, initialize should call super if it wants to ensure that parent classes have been properly initialized. This is not necessary when the parent is Object, because class Object does no instance-specific initialization.

Class Attribute Declarations

Library

Class attribute declarations are not part of the Ruby syntax; they are simply methods defined in class Module that create accessor methods automatically.

```
class name
  attr attribute   [ , writable ]
  attr_reader      attribute [, attribute ]...
  attr_writer      attribute [, attribute ]...
  attr_accessor    attribute [, attribute ]...
end
```

Module Definitions

```
module name
  body
end
```

A module is basically a class that cannot be instantiated. Like a class, its body is executed during definition, and the resulting Module object is stored in a constant. A module may contain class and instance methods and may define constants and class variables. As with classes, module methods are invoked using the Module object as a receiver, and constants are accessed using the :: scope resolution operator. The name in a module definition may optionally be preceded by the names of enclosing class(es) and/or module(s).

```
CONST = "outer"
module Mod
  CONST = 1
  def Mod.method1      # module method
    CONST + 1
  end
end
module Mod::Inner
  def (Mod::Inner).method2
    CONST + " scope"
  end
end
Mod::CONST              # =>   1
Mod.method1            # =>   2
Mod::Inner::method2    # =>   "outer scope"
```

Mixins: Including Modules

```
class|module name
  include expr
end
```

A module may be included within the definition of another module or class using the include method. The module or class definition containing the include gains access to the constants, class variables, and instance methods of the module it includes.

Library

If a module is included within a class definition, the module's constants, class variables, and instance methods made available via an anonymous (and inaccessible) superclass for that class. Objects of the class will respond to messages sent to the module's instance methods. Calls to methods not defined in the class will be passed to the module(s) mixed into the class before being passed to any parent class. A module may choose to define an initialize method, which will be called upon the creation of an object of a class that mixes in the module if either (a) the class does not define its own initialize method or (b) the class's initialize method invokes super.

A module may also be included at the top level, in which case the module's constants, class variables, and instance methods become available at the top level.

Module Functions

Although include is useful for providing mixin functionality, it is also a way of bringing the constants, class variables, and instance methods of a module into another namespace. However, functionality defined in an instance method will not be available as a module method.

```
module Math
  def sin(x)
    #
  end
end
# Only way to access Math.sin is...
include Math
sin(1)
```

Library The method Module#module_function solves this problem by taking one or more module instance methods and copying their definitions into corresponding module methods.

```
module Math
  def sin(x)
    #
  end
  module_function :sin
end
Math.sin(1)
include Math
sin(1)
```

The instance method and module method are two different methods: the method definition is copied by module_function, not aliased.

You can also use module_function with no parameters, in which case all subsequent methods will be module methods.

Access Control

Ruby defines three levels of protection for module and class constants and methods:

- **Public**. Accessible to anyone.
- **Protected**. Can be invoked only by objects of the defining class and its subclasses.
- **Private**. Can be called only in functional form (that is, with an implicit self as the receiver). Private methods therefore can be called in the defining class and by that class's descendents and ancestors, but only within the same object. See the discussion starting on page 40 for examples.

```
private    [ symbol, ... ]
protected  [ symbol, ... ]
public     [ symbol, ... ]
```

Library Each function can be used in two different ways:

- If used with no arguments, the three functions set the default access control of subsequently defined methods.
- With arguments, the functions set the access control of the named methods and constants.

Access control is enforced when a method is invoked.

Blocks, Closures, and Proc Objects

A code block is a set of Ruby statements and expressions between braces or a do/end pair. The block may start with an argument list between vertical bars. A code block may appear only immediately after a method invocation. The start of the block (the brace or the do) must be on the same logical line as the end of the invocation.

```
invocation  do  | a1, a2, ... |
end

invocation  {   | a1, a2, ... |
}
```

Braces have a high precedence; do has a low precedence. If the method invocation has parameters that are not enclosed in parentheses, the brace form of a block will bind to the last parameter, not to the overall invocation. The do form will bind to the invocation.

Within the body of the invoked method, the code block may be called using the yield keyword. Parameters passed to the yield will be assigned to arguments in the block. A warning will be generated if yield passes multiple parameters to a block that takes just one. The return value of the yield is the value of the last expression evaluated in the block or the value passed to a next statement executed in the block.

A block is a *closure*; it remembers the context in which it was defined, and it uses that context whenever it is called. The context includes the value of *self*, the constants, class variables, local variables, and any captured block.

```
class BlockExample
  CONST = 0
  @@a = 3
  def return_closure
    a = 1
    @a = 2
    lambda { [ CONST, a, @a, @@a, yield ] }
  end
  def change_values
    @a += 1
    @@a += 1
  end
end

eg = BlockExample.new
block = eg.return_closure { "original" }

block.call  # =>   [0, 1, 2, 3, "original"]
eg.change_values
block.call  # =>   [0, 1, 3, 4, "original"]
```

Here, the return_closure method returns a lambda that encapsulates access to the local variable a, instance variable @a, class variable @@a, and constant CONST. We call the block outside the scope of the object that contains these values, and they are still available via the closure. If we then call the object to change some of the values, the values accessed via the closure also change.

Block Arguments

_{1.9} As of Ruby 1.9, block argument lists are more like method argument lists:

- You can specify default values.

- You can specify splat (starred) arguments.

- The last argument can be prefixed with an ampersand, in which case it will collect any block passed when the original block is called.

These changes make it possible to use Module#define_method to create methods based on blocks that have similar capabilities to methods created using def.

Proc Objects

Ruby's blocks are chunks of code attached to a method. They operate in the context in which they were defined. Blocks are not objects, but they can be converted into objects of class Proc. There are four ways of converting a block into a Proc object.

- By passing a block to a method whose last parameter is prefixed with an ampersand. That parameter will receive the block as a Proc object.

```
def meth1(p1, p2, &block)
  puts block.inspect
end
meth1(1,2) { "a block" }
meth1(3,4)
```

produces:

```
#<Proc:0x0a4f4c@/tmp/prog.rb:4>
nil
```

Library

- By calling Proc.new, again associating it with a block.[7]

```
block = Proc.new { "a block" }
block   # =>   #<Proc:0x0a53c0@/tmp/prog.rb:1>
```

Library

- By calling the method Kernel.lambda, associating a block with the call.

```
block = lambda { "a block" }
block   # =>   #<Proc:0x0a53e8@/tmp/prog.rb:1 (lambda)>
```

_{1.9}

- As of Ruby 1.9, using the -> syntax.

```
lam = ->(p1, p2) { p1 + p2 }
lam.call(4, 3)   # =>   7
```

Note that there cannot be a space between > and the opening parenthesis.

_{1.9} 7.   There's also a built-in Kernel.proc method. In Ruby 1.8, this was equivalent to lambda. In Ruby 1.9, it is the same as Proc.new. Don't use proc in new code.

The first two styles of Proc object are identical in use. We'll call these objects *raw procs*. The third and fourth styles, generated by lambda and ->, add some functionality to the Proc object, as we'll see in a minute. We'll call these objects *lambdas*.

Calling a Proc

You can call a proc by invoking its methods call, yield, or []. The three forms are identical. Each takes arguments that can be passed to the proc, just as if it were a regular method call. If the proc you're invoking is a lambda, Ruby will check that the supplied arguments match .the expected parameters.

You can also invoke a proc using the syntax name.(*args...*). This is mapped internally into a.call(...).

Procs, break, and next

Within both raw procs and lambdas, executing next causes the block to exit. The value of the block is the value (or values) passed to next, or nil if no values are passed.

```
def meth
  res = yield
  "The block returns #{res}"
end

meth { next 99 }   # =>   "The block returns 99"

pr = Proc.new { next 99 }
pr.call            # =>   99

pr = lambda { next 99 }
pr.call            # =>   99

pr = ->() { next 99 }
pr.call            # =>   99
```

Within a raw proc, a break terminates the method that invoked the block. The return value of the method is any parameters passed to the break.

Return and Blocks

A return from inside a *block* that's still in scope acts as a return from that scope. A return from a block whose original context is not longer valid raises an exception (LocalJumpError or ThreadError depending on the context). The following example illustrates the first case:

```
def meth1
  (1..10).each do |val|
    return val          # returns from meth1
  end
end
meth1  # =>   1
```

This example shows a return failing because the context of its block no longer exists:

```
def meth2(&b)
  b
end
res = meth2 { return }
res.call
```

produces:

```
prog.rb:5:in `block in <main>': unexpected return (LocalJumpError)
from /tmp/prog.rb:6:in `call'
from /tmp/prog.rb:6:in `<main>'
```

And here's a return failing because the block is created in one thread and called in another:

```
def meth3
  yield
end
t = Thread.new do
  meth3 { return }
end
t.join
```

produces:

```
prog.rb:6:in `block (2 levels) in <main>': unexpected return (LocalJumpError)
from /tmp/prog.rb:2:in `meth3'
from /tmp/prog.rb:6:in `block in <main>'
```

The situation with Proc objects is slightly more complicated. If you use Proc.new to create a proc from a block, that proc acts like a block, and the previous rules apply:

```
def meth4
  p = Proc.new { return 99 }
  p.call
  puts "Never get here"
end

meth4    # =>   99
```

If the Proc object is created using Kernel.lambda, it behaves more like a free-standing method body: a return simply returns from the block to the caller of the block:

```
def meth5
  p = lambda { return 99 }
  res = p.call
  "The block returned #{res}"
end

meth5    # =>    "The block returned 99"
```

Because of this, if you use Module#define_method, you'll probably want to pass it a proc created using lambda, not Proc.new, because return will work as expected in the former and will generate a LocalJumpError in the latter.

Exceptions

Ruby exceptions are objects of class Exception and its descendents (a full list of the built-in exceptioons is given in Figure 27.1 on page 493).

Raising Exceptions

The Kernel.raise method raises an exception: *Library*

```
raise
raise string
raise thing [ , string [ stack trace ] ]
```

The first form reraises the exception in $! or a new RuntimeError if $! is nil.

The second form creates a new RuntimeError exception, setting its message to the given string.

The third form creates an exception object by invoking the method exception on its first argument. It then sets this exception's message and backtrace to its second and third arguments.

Class Exception and objects of class Exception contain a factory method called exception, so an exception class name or instance can be used as the first parameter to raise.

When an exception is raised, Ruby places a reference to the Exception object in the global variable $!.

Handling Exceptions

Exceptions may be handled in the following ways:

- Within the scope of a begin/end block:

```
begin
   code...
   code...
[ rescue  [ parm, ... ] [ => var ] [ then ]
   error handling code... , ... ]
[ else
   no exception code... ]
[ ensure
   always executed code... ]
   end
```

- Within the body of a method:

```
def method and args
   code...
   code...
[ rescue  [ parm, ... ] [ => var ] [ then ]
   error handling code... , ... ]
[ else
   no exception code... ]
```

```
[ ensure
    always executed code... ]
  end
```

- After the execution of a single statement:

```
statement [ rescue statement, ... ]
```

A block or method may have multiple rescue clauses, and each rescue clause may specify zero or more exception parameters. A rescue clause with no parameter is treated as if it had a parameter of StandardError. This means that some lower-level exceptions will not be caught by a parameterless rescue class. If you want to rescue every exception, use this:

```
rescue Exception => e
```

When an exception is raised, Ruby scans the call stack until it finds an enclosing begin/end block, method body, or statement with a rescue modifier. For each rescue clause in that block, Ruby compares the raised exception against each of the rescue clause's parameters in turn; each parameter is tested using *parameter*===$!. If the raised exception matches a rescue parameter, Ruby executes the body of the rescue and stops looking. If a matching rescue clause ends with => and a variable name, the variable is set to $!.

Although the parameters to the rescue clause are typically the names of Exception classes, they can actually be arbitrary expressions (including method calls) that return an appropriate class.

If no rescue clause matches the raised exception, Ruby moves up the stack looking for a higher-level begin/end block that matches. If an exception propagates to the top level of the main thread without being rescued, the program terminates with a message.

If an else clause is present, its body is executed if no exceptions were raised in *code*. Exceptions raised during the execution of the else clause are not captured by rescue clauses in the same block as the else.

If an ensure clause is present, its body is always executed as the block is exited (even if an uncaught exception is in the process of being propagated).

Within a rescue clause, raise with no parameters will reraise the exception in $!.

Rescue Statement Modifier

A statement may have an optional rescue modifier followed by another statement (and by extension another rescue modifier, and so on). The rescue modifier takes no exception parameter and rescues StandardError and its children.

If an exception is raised to the left of a rescue modifier, the statement on the left is abandoned, and the value of the overall line is the value of the statement on the right:

```
values = [ "1", "2.3", /pattern/ ]

result = values.map {|v| Integer(v) rescue Float(v) rescue String(v) }

result   # =>   [1, 2.3, "(?-mix:pattern)"]
```

Retrying a Block

The retry statement can be used within a rescue clause to restart the enclosing begin/end block from the beginning.

Catch and Throw

The method Kernel.catch executes its associated block:

Library

```
catch ( symbol | string )  do
  block...
end
```

The method Kernel.throw interrupts the normal processing of statements:

Library

```
throw( symbol | string [ , obj ] )
```

When a throw is executed, Ruby searches up the call stack for the first catch block with a matching symbol or string. If it is found, the search stops, and execution resumes past the end of the catch's block. If the throw was passed a second parameter, that value is returned as the value of the catch. Ruby honors the ensure clauses of any block expressions it traverses while looking for a corresponding catch.

If no catch block matches the throw, Ruby raises a NameError exception at the location of the throw.

## Chapter 23

Duck Typing

You'll have noticed that in Ruby we don't declare the types of variables or methods—everything is just some kind of object.

Now, it seems like folks react to this in two ways. Some like this kind of flexibility and feel comfortable writing code with dynamically typed variables and methods. If you're one of those people, you might want to skip to the section called "Classes Aren't Types" on the next page. Some, though, get nervous when they think about all those objects floating around unconstrained. If you've come to Ruby from a language such as C# or Java, where you're used to giving all your variables and methods a type, you may feel that Ruby is just too sloppy to use to write "real" applications.

It isn't.

We'd like to spend a couple of paragraphs trying to convince you that the lack of static typing is not a problem when it comes to writing reliable applications. We're not trying to criticize other languages here. Instead, we'd just like to contrast approaches.

The reality is that the static type systems in most mainstream languages don't really help that much in terms of program security. If Java's type system were reliable, for example, it wouldn't need to implement ClassCastException. The exception is necessary, though, because there is runtime type uncertainty in Java (as there is in C++, C#, and others). Static typing can be good for optimizing code, and it can help IDEs do clever things with tooltip help, but we haven't seen much evidence that it promotes more reliable code.

On the other hand, once you use Ruby for a while, you realize that dynamically typed variables actually add to your productivity in many ways. You'll also be surprised to discover that your fears about the type chaos were unfounded. Large, long-running, Ruby programs run significant applications and just don't throw any type-related errors. Why is this?

Partly, it's a question of common sense. If you coded in Java (pre–Java 1.5), all your containers were effectively untyped: everything in a container was just an Object, and you cast it to the required type when you extracted an element. And yet you probably never saw a ClassCastException when you ran these programs. The structure of the code just didn't permit it. You put Person objects in, and you later took Person objects out. You just don't write programs that would work in another way.

Well, it's the same in Ruby. If you use a variable for some purpose, chances are very good that you'll be using it for the same purpose when you access it again three lines later. The kind of chaos that *could* happen just doesn't happen.

On top of that, folks who code Ruby a lot tend to adopt a certain style of coding. They write lots of short methods and tend to test as they go along. The short methods mean that the scope of most variables is limited; there just isn't that much time for things to go wrong with their type. And the testing catches the silly errors when they happen; typos and the like just don't get a chance to propagate through the code.

The upshot is that the "safety" in "type safety" is often illusory and that coding in a more dynamic language such as Ruby is both safe and productive. So, if you're nervous about the lack of static typing in Ruby, we suggest you try to put those concerns on the back burner for a little while and give Ruby a try. We think you'll be surprised at how rarely you see errors because of type issues and at how much more productive you feel once you start to exploit the power of dynamic typing.

Classes Aren't Types

The issue of types is actually somewhat deeper than an ongoing debate between strong typing advocates and the hippie-freak dynamic typing crowd. The real issue is the question, what is a type in the first place?

If you've been coding in conventional typed languages, you've probably been taught that the *type* of an object is its *class*—all objects are instances of some class, and that class is the object's type. The class defines the operations (methods) the object can support, along with the state (instance variables) on which those methods operate. Let's look at some Java code:

```
Customer  c;
c = database.findCustomer("dave");    /* Java */
```

This fragment declares the variable c to be of type Customer and sets it to reference the customer object for Dave that we've created from some database record. So, the type of the object in c is Customer, right?

Maybe. However, even in Java, the issue is slightly deeper. Java supports the concept of *interfaces*, which are a kind of emasculated abstract base class. A Java class can be declared as implementing multiple interfaces. Using this facility, you may have defined your classes as follows:

```
public interface Customer {
   long  getID();
   Calendar getDateOfLastContact();
   // ...
}
public class Person
   implements Customer {
   public long getID() { ... }
   public Calendar getDateOfLastContact() { ... }
   // ...
}
```

So, even in Java, the class is not always the type—sometimes the type is a subset of the class, and sometimes objects implement multiple types.

In Ruby, the class is never (OK, almost never) the type. Instead, the type of an object is defined more by what that object can do. In Ruby, we call this *duck typing*. If an object walks like a duck and talks like a duck, then the interpreter is happy to treat it as if it were a duck.

Let's look at an example. Perhaps we've written a method to write our customer's name to the end of an open file:

```
ducktyping_3.rb
class Customer
  def initialize(first_name, last_name)
    @first_name = first_name
    @last_name  = last_name
  end
  def append_name_to_file(file)
    file << @first_name << " " << @last_name
  end
end
```

Being good programmers, we'll write a unit test for this. Be warned, though—it's messy (and we'll improve on it shortly):

```
ducktyping_4.rb
require 'test/unit'
require 'addcust'
class TestAddCustomer < Test::Unit::TestCase
  def test_add
    c = Customer.new("Ima", "Customer")
    f = File.open("tmpfile", "w") do |f|
      c.append_name_to_file(f)
    end
    f = File.open("tmpfile") do |f|
      assert_equal("Ima Customer", f.gets)
    end
  ensure
    File.delete("tmpfile") if File.exist?("tmpfile")
  end
end
```

produces:

```
Finished in 0.060073 seconds.
1 tests, 1 assertions, 0 failures, 0 errors, 0 skips
```

We have to do all that work to create a file to write to, then reopen it, and read in the contents to verify the correct string was written. We also have to delete the file when we've finished (but only if it exists).

Instead, though, we could rely on duck typing. All we need is something that walks like a file and talks like a file that we can pass in to the method under test. And all that means *in this circumstance* is that we need an object that responds to the << method by appending something. Do we have something that does this? How about a humble String?

ducktyping_5.rb
```ruby
require 'test/unit'
require 'addcust'
class TestAddCustomer < Test::Unit::TestCase
  def test_add
    c = Customer.new("Ima", "Customer")
    f = ""
    c.append_name_to_file(f)
    assert_equal("Ima Customer", f)
  end
end
```

produces:
```
Finished in 0.000353 seconds.
1 tests, 1 assertions, 0 failures, 0 errors, 0 skips
```

The method under test thinks it's writing to a file, but instead it's just appending to a string. At the end, we can then just test that the content is correct.

We didn't have to use a string—for the object we're testing here, an array would work just as well:

ducktyping_6.rb
```ruby
require 'test/unit'
require 'addcust'
class TestAddCustomer < Test::Unit::TestCase
  def test_add
    c = Customer.new("Ima", "Customer")
    f = []
    c.append_name_to_file(f)
    assert_equal(["Ima", " ", "Customer"], f)
  end
end
```

produces:
```
Finished in 0.000358 seconds.
1 tests, 1 assertions, 0 failures, 0 errors, 0 skips
```

Indeed, this form may be more convenient if we wanted to check that the correct individual things were inserted.

So, duck typing is convenient for testing, but what about in the body of applications themselves? Well, it turns out that the same thing that made the tests easy in the previous example also makes it easy to write flexible application code.

In fact, Dave had an interesting experience where duck typing dug him (and a client) out of a hole. He'd written a large Ruby-based web application that (among other things) kept a database table full of details of participants in a competition. The system provided a comma-separated value (CSV) download capability, allowing administrators to import this information into their local spreadsheets.

Just before competition time, the phone starts ringing. The download, which had been working fine up to this point, was now taking so long that requests were timing out. The pressure was intense, because the administrators had to use this information to build schedules and send out mailings.

A little experimentation showed that the problem was in the routine that took the results of the database query and generated the CSV download. The code looked something like this:

```ruby
def csv_from_row(op, row)
  res = ""
  until row.empty?
    entry = row.shift.to_s
    if /[,"]/ =~ entry
      entry = entry.gsub(/"/, '""')
      res << '"' << entry << '"'
    else
      res << entry
    end
    res << "," unless row.empty?
  end
  op << res << CRLF
end

result = ""
query.each_row {|row|  csv_from_row(result, row)}
http.write result
```

When this code ran against moderate-size data sets, it performed fine. But at a certain input size, it suddenly slowed right down. The culprit? Garbage collection. The approach was generating thousands of intermediate strings and building one big result string, one line at a time. As the big string grew, it needed more space, and garbage collection was invoked, which necessitated scanning and removing all the intermediate strings.

The answer was simple and surprisingly effective. Rather than build the result string as it went along, the code was changed to store each CSV row as an element in an array. This meant that the intermediate lines were still referenced and hence were no longer garbage. It also meant that we were no longer building an ever-growing string that forced garbage collection. Thanks to duck typing, the change was trivial:

```ruby
def csv_from_row(op, row)
  # as before
end
result = []
query.each_row {|row|  csv_from_row(result, row)}
http.write result.join
```

All that changed is that we passed an array into the csv_from_row method. Because it (implicitly) used duck typing, the method itself was not modified; it continued to append the data it generated to its parameter, not caring what type that parameter was. After the method returned its result, we joined all those individual lines into one big string. This one change reduced the time to run from more than three minutes to a few seconds.

Coding like a Duck

If you want to write your programs using the duck typing philosophy, you really need to remember only one thing: an object's type is determined by what it can do, not by its class. (In fact, older versions of Ruby had a method Object#type that returned the class of an object. That has been removed in Ruby 1.9—the name type was misleading.)

What does this mean in practice? At one level, it simply means that there's often little value testing the class of an object.

For example, you may be writing a routine to add song information to a string. If you come from a C# or Java background, you may be tempted to write this:

```ruby
def append_song(result, song)
  # test we're given the right parameters
  unless result.kind_of?(String)
    fail TypeError.new("String expected")
  end
  unless song.kind_of?(Song)
    fail TypeError.new("Song expected")
  end

  result << song.title << " (" << song.artist << ")"
end

result = ""
append_song(result, song)   # =>   "I Got Rhythm (Gene Kelly)"
```

Embrace Ruby's duck typing, and you'd write something far simpler:

```ruby
def append_song(result, song)
  result << song.title << " (" << song.artist << ")"
end

result = ""
append_song(result, song)   # =>   "I Got Rhythm (Gene Kelly)"
```

You don't need to check the type of the arguments. If they support << (in the case of *result*) or title and artist (in the case of *song*), everything will just work. If they don't, your method will throw an exception anyway (just as it would have done if you'd checked the types). But without the check, your method is suddenly a lot more flexible. You could pass it an array, a string, a file, or any other object that appends using <<, and it would just work.

Now sometimes you may want more than this style of *laissez-faire* programming. You may have good reasons to check that a parameter can do what you need. Will you get thrown out of the duck typing club if you check the parameter against a class? No, you won't.[1] But you may want to consider checking based on the object's capabilities, rather than its class:

`ducktyping_11.rb`

```
def append_song(result, song)
  # test we're given the right parameters
  unless result.respond_to?(:<<)
    fail TypeError.new("'result' needs `<<' capability")
  end
  unless song.respond_to?(:artist) && song.respond_to?(:title)
    fail TypeError.new("'song' needs 'artist' and 'title'")
  end

  result << song.title << " (" << song.artist << ")"
end

result = ""
append_song(result, song)   # =>   "I Got Rhythm (Gene Kelly)"
```

However, before going down this path, make sure you're getting a real benefit—it's a lot of extra code to write and to maintain.

Standard Protocols and Coercions

Although not technically part of the language, the interpreter and standard library use various protocols to handle issues that other languages would deal with using types.

Some objects have more than one natural representation. For example, you may be writing a class to represent Roman numbers (I, II, III, IV, V, and so on). This class is not necessarily a subclass of Integer, because its objects are representations of numbers, not numbers in their own right. At the same time, they do have an integer-like quality. It would be nice to be able to use objects of our Roman number class wherever Ruby was expecting to see an integer.

To do this, Ruby has the concept of *conversion protocols*—an object may elect to have itself converted to an object of another class. Ruby has three standard ways of doing this.

We've already come across the first. Methods such as to_s and to_i convert their receiver into strings and integers. These conversion methods are not particularly strict. If an object has some kind of decent representation as a string, for example, it will probably have a to_s method. Our Roman class would probably implement to_s in order to return the string representation of a number (VII, for instance).

The second form of conversion function uses methods with names such as to_str and to_int. These are strict conversion functions. You implement them only if your object can naturally be used every place a string or an integer could be used. For example, our Roman number

---

1. The duck typing club doesn't check to see whether you're a member anyway....

objects have a clear representation as an integer and so should implement to_int. When it comes to stringiness, however, we have to think a bit harder.

Roman numbers clearly have a string representation, but are they strings? Should we be able to use them wherever we can use a string itself? No, probably not. Logically, they're a representation of a number. You can represent them as strings, but they aren't plug-compatible with strings. For this reason, a Roman number won't implement to_str—it isn't really a string. Just to drive this home: Roman numerals can be converted to strings using to_s, but they aren't inherently strings, so they don't implement to_str.

To see how this works in practice, let's look at opening a file. The first parameter to File.new can be either an existing file descriptor (represented by an integer) or a filename to open. However, Ruby doesn't simply look at the first parameter and check whether its type is Fixnum or String. Instead, it gives the object passed in the opportunity to represent itself as a number or a string. If it were written in Ruby, it may look something like this:

```
ducktyping_12.rb
class File
  def File.new(file, *args)
    if file.respond_to?(:to_int)
      IO.new(file.to_int, *args)
    else
      name = file.to_str
      # call operating system to open file 'name'
    end
  end
end
```

So, let's see what happens if we want to pass a file descriptor integer stored as a Roman number into File.new. Because our class implements to_int, the first respond_to? test will succeed. We'll pass an integer representation of our number to IO.open, and the file descriptor will be returned, all wrapped up in a new IO object.

A small number of strict conversion functions are built into the standard library.

to_ary → Array

This is used when interpreter needs a parameter to a method to be an array, and when expanding parameters and assignments containing the *xyz syntax.

```
ducktyping_13.rb
class OneTwo
  def to_ary
    [ 1, 2 ]
  end
end

ot = OneTwo.new
puts ot
```

produces:

```
1
2
```

to_a → Array

1.9

This is used when interpreter needs to convert an object into an array for parameter passing or multiple assignment.

> ducktyping_14.rb

```
class OneTwo
  def to_a
    [ 1, 2 ]
  end
end
ot = OneTwo.new
a, b = *ot
puts "a = #{a}, b = #{b}"
printf("%d -- %d\n", *ot)
```

produces:

```
a = 1, b = 2
1 -- 2
```

to_enum → Enumerator

1.9

This converts an object (presumably a collection) to an enumerator. It's never called internally by the interpreter.

to_hash → Hash

This is used when the interpreter expects to see Hash. (The only known use is the second parameter to Hash#replace.)

to_int → Integer

This is used when the interpreter expects to see an integer value (such as a file descriptor or as a parameter to Kernel.Integer).

to_io → IO

This is used when the interpreter is expecting I/O objects (for example, as parameters to IO#reopen or IO.select).

to_open → IO

This is called (if defined) on the first parameter to IO.open.

to_path → String

1.9

This is called by the interpreter when it is looking for a filename (for example, by File#open).

to_proc → Proc

This is used to convert an object prefixed with an ampersand in a method call.

```
class OneTwo
  def to_proc
    proc { "one-two" }
  end
end
def silly
  yield
end
```

```
ducktyping_16.rb
```

```
ot = OneTwo.new
silly(&ot)   # =>   "one-two"
```

to_regexp → **Regexp**

This is invoked by Regexp#try_convert to convert its argument to a regular expression.

to_str → **String**

This is used pretty much any place the interpreter is looking for a String value.

```
ducktyping_17.rb
```

```
class OneTwo
  def to_str
    "one-two"
  end
end
ot = OneTwo.new
puts("count: " + ot)
File.open(ot) rescue puts $!.message
```

produces:

```
count: one-two
No such file or directory - one-two
```

to_sym → **Symbol**

This expresses the receiver as a symbol. This is used by the interpreter when compiling instruction sequences, but it's probably not useful in user code.

One last point is that classes such as Integer and Fixnum implement the to_int method, and String implements to_str. That way you can call the strict conversion functions polymorphically:

```
# it doesn't matter if obj is a Fixnum or a
# Roman number, the conversion still succeeds
num = obj.to_int
```

The Symbol.to_proc Trick

Ruby 1.9 implements the to_proc for objects of class symbol. Say you want to convert an array of strings to uppercase. You could write this:

```
names = %{ant bee cat}
result = names.map {|name| name.upcase}
```

That's fairly concise, right? Return a new array where each element is the corresponding element in the original, converted to uppercase. But, as of Ruby 1.9, you can instead write this:

```
names = %{ant bee cat}
result = names.map(&:upcase)
```

Now that's concise: apply the upcase method to each element of names.

So, how does it work? It relies on Ruby's type coercions. Let's start at the top.

When you say names.map(&xxx), you're telling Ruby to pass the Proc object in xxx to the map method as a block. If xxx isn't already a Proc object, Ruby tries to coerce it into one by sending it a to_proc message.

Now :upcase isn't a Proc object—it's a symbol. So when Ruby sees names.map(&:upcase), the first thing it does is try to convert the symbol :upcase into a Proc by calling to_proc. And, by an incredible coincidence, Ruby implements just such a method. If it was written in Ruby, it would look something like this:

```
def to_proc
  proc { |obj, *args| obj.send(self, *args) }
end
```

This method creates a Proc, which, when called on an object, sends that object the symbol itself. So, when names.map(&:upcase) starts to iterate over the strings in names, it'll call the block, passing in the first name and invoking its upcase method.

It's an incredibly elegant use of coercion and of closures. However, it comes at a price. The use of dynamic method invocations mean that the version of our code that uses &:upcase is about half as fast as the more explicitly coded block. This doesn't worry me personally unless I happen to be in a performance-critical section of my code.

Numeric Coercion

Back on page 365 we said there were three types of conversion performed by the interpreter. We covered loose and strict conversion. The third is numeric coercion.

Here's the problem. When you write 1+2, Ruby knows to call the + on the object 1 (a Fixnum), passing it the Fixnum 2 as a parameter. However, when you write 1+2.3, the same + method now receives a Float parameter. How can it know what to do (particularly because checking the classes of your parameters is against the spirit of duck typing)?

The answer lies in Ruby's coercion protocol, based on the method coerce. The basic operation of coerce is simple. It takes two numbers (one as its receiver, the other as a parameter). It returns a two-element array containing representations of these two numbers (but with the parameter first, followed by the receiver). The coerce method guarantees that these two objects will have the same class and therefore that they can be added (or multiplied, compared, or whatever).

```
1.coerce(2)        # =>  [2, 1]
1.coerce(2.3)      # =>  [2.3, 1.0]
(4.5).coerce(2.3)  # =>  [2.3, 4.5]
(4.5).coerce(2)    # =>  [2.0, 4.5]
```

The trick is that the receiver calls the coerce method of its parameter to generate this array. This technique, called *double dispatch*, allows a method to change its behavior based not only on its class but also on the class of its parameter. In this case, we're letting the parameter decide exactly *what* classes of objects should get added (or multiplied, divided, and so on).

Let's say that we're writing a new class that's intended to take part in arithmetic. To participate in coercion, we need to implement a coerce method. This takes some other kind of number as a parameter and returns an array containing two objects of the same class, whose values are equivalent to its parameter and itself.

For our Roman number class, it's fairly easy. Internally, each Roman number object holds its real value as a Fixnum in an instance variable, @value. The coerce method checks to see whether the class of its parameter is also an Integer. If so, it returns its parameter and its internal value. If not, it first converts both to floating point.

```
ducktyping_23.rb
```

```ruby
class Roman
  def initialize(value)
    @value = value
  end

  def coerce(other)
    if  Integer === other
      [ other, @value ]
    else
      [ Float(other), Float(@value) ]
    end
  end

  # .. other Roman stuff
end

iv = Roman.new(4)
xi = Roman.new(11)

3 * iv    # =>   12
1.1 * xi  # =>   12.1
```

Of course, class Roman as implemented doesn't know how to do addition. You couldn't have written xi+3 in the previous example, because Roman doesn't have a + method. And that's probably as it should be. But let's go wild and implement addition for Roman numbers:

```
ducktyping_24.rb
```

```ruby
class Roman
  MAX_ROMAN = 4999

  attr_reader :value
  protected :value

  def initialize(value)
    if value <= 0 || value > MAX_ROMAN
      fail "Roman values must be > 0 and <= #{MAX_ROMAN}"
    end
    @value = value
  end
```

```ruby
    def coerce(other)
      if  Integer === other
        [ other, @value ]
      else
        [ Float(other), Float(@value) ]
      end
    end

    def +(other)
      if Roman === other
        other = other.value
      end
      if Fixnum === other && (other + @value) < MAX_ROMAN
        Roman.new(@value + other)
      else
        x, y = other.coerce(@value)
        x + y
      end
    end

    FACTORS = [["m", 1000], ["cm", 900], ["d",  500], ["cd", 400],
              ["c",  100], ["xc",  90], ["l",   50], ["xl",  40],
              ["x",   10], ["ix",   9], ["v",    5], ["iv",   4],
              ["i",    1]]

    def to_s
      value = @value
      roman = ""
      for code, factor in FACTORS
        count, value = value.divmod(factor)
        roman << (code * count)
      end
      roman
    end
  end
```

ducktyping_25.rb

```ruby
iv = Roman.new(4)
xi = Roman.new(11)

iv + 3          # =>   vii
iv + 3 + 4      # =>   xi
iv + 3.14159    # =>   7.14159
xi + 4900       # =>   mmmmcmxi
xi + 4990       # =>   5001
```

Finally, be careful with coerce—try always to coerce into a more general type, or you may end up generating coercion loops. This is a situation where A tries to coerce to B, and B tries to coerce back to A.

Walk the Walk, Talk the Talk

Duck typing can generate controversy. Every now and then a thread flares on the mailing lists or someone blogs for or against the concept. Many of the contributors to these discussions have some fairly extreme positions.

Ultimately, though, duck typing isn't a set of rules; it's just a style of programming. Design your programs to balance paranoia and flexibility. If you feel the need to constrain the types of objects that the users of a method pass in, ask yourself why. Try to determine what could go wrong if you were expecting a String and instead get an Array. Sometimes, the difference is crucially important. Often, though, it isn't. Try erring on the more permissive side for a while, and see whether bad things happen. If not, perhaps duck typing isn't just for the birds.

## Chapter 24

Metaprogramming

The Jacquard loom, invented more than 200 years ago, was the first device controlled using punched cards—rows of holes in each card were used to control the pattern woven into the cloth. But imagine if instead of churning out fabric, the loom could punch more cards, and those cards could be fed back into the mechanism. The machine could be used to create new programming that it could then execute. And that would be metaprogramming—writing code that writes code.

Programming is all about building layers of abstractions. As you solve problems, you're building bridges from the unrelenting and mechanical world of silicon to the more ambiguous and fluid world we inhabit. Some programming languages—such as C—are close to the machine. The distance from C code to the application domain can be large. Other languages—Ruby, perhaps—provide higher-level abstractions and hence let you start coding closer to the target domain. For this reason, most people consider a higher-level language to be a better starting place for application development (although they'll argue about the choice of language).

But when you metaprogram, you are no longer limited to the set of abstractions built in to your programming language. Instead, you can create new abstractions that are integrated into the host language. In effect, you're creating a new, domain-specific programming language—one that's designed to let you express the concepts you need to solve your particular problem.

Ruby makes metaprogramming easy. As a result, most advanced Ruby programmers will use metaprogramming techniques to simplify their code. This chapter shows how they do it. It isn't intended to be an exhaustive survey of metaprogramming techniques. Instead, we'll look at the underlying Ruby principles that make metaprogramming possible. From there you'll be able to invent your own metaprogramming idioms.

Objects and Classes

Classes and objects are obviously central to Ruby, but at first sight they can be a little confusing. There seem to be a lot of concepts: classes, objects, class objects, instance methods, class methods, singleton classes, and virtual classes. In reality, however, Ruby has just a single underlying class and object structure.

A Ruby object has three components: a set of flags, some instance variables, and an associated class.

A Ruby class is itself an object of class Class. It contains all the things an object has plus a set of method definitions and a reference to a superclass (which is itself another class).

And, basically, that's it. From here, you could work out the details of metaprogramming for yourself. But, as always, the devil lurks in the details, so let's dig a little deeper.

self and Method Calling

Ruby has the concept of the *current object*. This current object is referenced by the built-in, read-only variable self. self has two significant roles in a running Ruby program.

First, self controls how Ruby finds instance variables. We already said that every object carries around a set of instance variables. When you access an instance variable, Ruby looks for it in the object referenced by self.

Second, self plays a vital role in method calling. In Ruby, each method call is made on some object. This object is called the *receiver* of the call. When you make a method call such as items.size, the object referenced by the variable items is the receiver and size is the method to invoke.

If you make a method call such as puts "hi", there's no explicit receiver. In this case, Ruby uses the current object, self, as the receiver. It goes to self's class and looks up the method (in this case, puts). If it can't find the method in the class, it looks in the class's superclass and then in that class's superclass, stopping when it runs out of superclasses (which will happen after it has looked in BasicObject).[1]

When you make a method call with an explicit receiver (for example, invoking items.size), the process is surprisingly similar. The only change—but it's a vitally important one—is the fact that self is changed for the duration of the call. Before starting the method lookup process, Ruby sets self to the receiver (the object referenced by items in this case). Then, after the call returns, Ruby restores the value that self had before the call.

Let's see how this works in practice. Here's a simple program:

```
classes_1.rb
class Test
  def one
    @var = 99
    two
  end
```

---

1. If it can't find the method after exhausting the object's class hierarchy, Ruby looks for a method called method_missing on the original receiver, starting back at the class of self and then looking up the superclass chain.

```
  def two
    puts @var
  end
end
t = Test.new
t.one
```

produces:

```
99
```

The call to Test.new on the second-to-last line creates a new object of class Test, assigning that object to the variable t. Then, on the next line, we call the method t.one. To execute this call, Ruby sets self to t and then looks in t's class for the method one. Ruby finds the method defined on line 2 and calls it.

Inside the method, we set the instance variable @var to 99. This instance variable will be associated with the current object. What is that object? Well, the call to t.one set self to t, so within the one method, self will be that particular instance of class Test.

On the next line, the one calls the two. Because there's no explicit receiver, self is not changed. When Ruby looks for the method two, it looks in Test, the class of t.

The method two references an instance variable @var. Again, Ruby looks for this variable in the current object and finds the same variable that was set by the method one.

The call to puts at the end of two works the same way. Again, because there's no explicit receiver, self will be unchanged. Ruby looks for the puts method in the class of the current object but can't find it. It then looks in Test's superclass, class Object. Again, it doesn't find puts. However, Object mixes in the module Kernel. We'll talk more about this later, for now we can say that mixed-in modules act as if they were superclasses. The kernel module *does* define puts, so the method is found and executed.

After two and one return, Ruby resets self to the value it had before the original call to t.one.

This explanation may seem labored, but understanding it is vital to mastering metaprogramming in Ruby.

`self` and Class Definitions

We've seen that calling a method with an explicit receiver changes self. Perhaps surprisingly, self is also changed by a class definition. This is a consequence of the fact that class definitions are actually executable code in Ruby—if we can execute code, we need to have a current object. A simple test shows what this object is:

```
class Test
  puts "In the definition of class Test"
  puts "self = #{self}"
  puts "Class of self = #{self.class}"
end
```

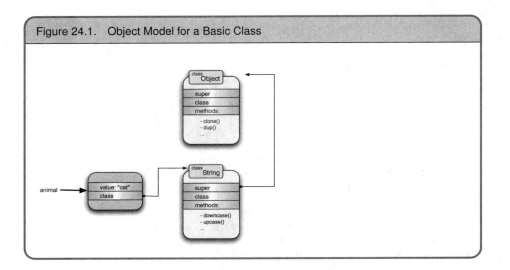

Figure 24.1. Object Model for a Basic Class

produces:

```
In the definition of class Test
self = Test
Class of self = Class
```

Inside a class definition, self is set to the class object of the class being defined. This means that instance variables set in a class definition will be available to class methods (because self will be the same when the variables are defined and when the methods execute):

```
classes_3.rb
class Test
  @var = 99
  def self.value_of_var
    @var
  end
end
puts Test.value_of_var
```

produces:

```
99
```

The fact that self is set to the class during a class definition turns out to be a dramatically elegant decision, but to see why, we'll first need to have a look at singletons.

Singletons

Ruby lets you define methods that are specific to a particular object. These are called *singleton methods*. For example, let's start with a simple string object:

```
animal = "cat"
puts animal.upcase
```

produces:

```
CAT
```

This results in the object structure shown in Figure 24.1 on the preceding page. The animal variable points to an object containing (among other things) the value of the string ("cat") and a pointer to the object's class, String.

When we call animal.upcase, Ruby goes to the object referenced by the animal variable and then looks up the method upcase in the class object referenced from the animal object. Our animal is a string and so has the methods of class String available.

Now let's make it more interesting by defining a singleton method on the string referenced from animal:

```
def animal.speak
  puts "The #{self} says miaow"
end
animal.speak
puts animal.upcase
```

produces:

```
The cat says miaow
CAT
```

We've already seen how the call to animal.speak works when we looked at how methods are invoked. Ruby sets self to the string object "cat" referenced by animal and then looks for a method speak in that object's class. Surprisingly, it finds it. It's initially surprising because the class of "cat" is String, and String doesn't have a speak method. So, does Ruby have some kind of special-case magic for these methods that are defined on individual objects?

Thankfully, the answer is "no." Ruby's object model is remarkably consistent. When we defined the singleton method for the "cat" object, Ruby created a new anonymous class and defined the speak method in that class. This anonymous class is sometimes called a *singleton class* and other times an *eigenclass*. I prefer the former, because it ties in to the idea of singleton methods.

Ruby makes this singleton class the class of the "cat" object and makes String (which was the original class of "cat") the superclass of the singleton class. This is shown in Figure 24.2 on the following page.

Now let's follow the call to animal.speak. Ruby goes to the object referenced by animal and then looks in its class for the method speak. The class of the animal object is the newly created singleton class, and it contains the method we need.

What happens if we instead call animal.upcase? The processing starts the same way: Ruby looks for the method upcase in the singleton class but fails to find it there. It then follows the normal processing rules and starts looking up the chain of superclasses. The superclass of the singleton is String, and Ruby finds the upcase method there. Notice that there is no special-case processing here—Ruby method calls always work the same way.

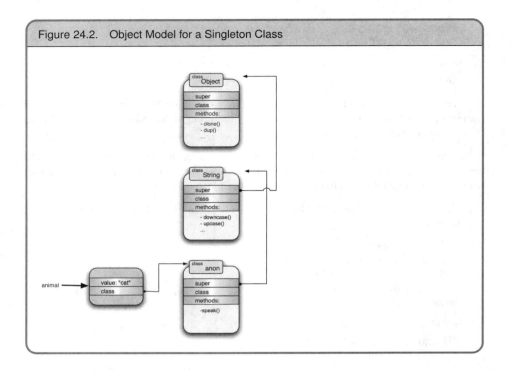

Figure 24.2.   Object Model for a Singleton Class

Singletons and Classes

Earlier, we said that inside a class definition, self is set to the class object being defined. It turns out that this is the basis for one of the more elegant aspects of Ruby's object model.

Recall that we can define class methods in Ruby using either of the forms def self.xxx or def ClassName.xxx:

```
classes_6.rb
class Dave
  def self.class_method_one
    puts "Class method one"
  end
  def Dave.class_method_two
    puts "Class method two"
  end
end
Dave.class_method_one
Dave.class_method_two
```

produces:

```
Class method one
Class method two
```

Now we know why the two forms are identical: inside the class definition, self is set to Dave.

But now that we've looked at singleton methods, we also know that, in reality, there are no such thing as class methods in Ruby. Both of the previous definitions define singleton methods on the class object. As with all other singleton methods, we can then call them via the object (in this case, the class Dave).

Before we created the two singleton methods in class Dave, the class pointer in the class object pointed to class Class. (That's a confusing sentence. Another way of saying it is "Dave is a class, so the class of Dave is class Class," but that's pretty confusing, too.) The situation looks like Figure 24.3 on the next page.

The object diagram for class Dave after the methods are defined is shown in Figure 24.4 on page 381. Do you see how the singleton class is created, just as it was for the *animal* example? The class is inserted as the class of Dave, and the original class of Dave is made this new class's parent.

We can now tie together the two uses of self, the current object. We talked about how instance variables are looked up in self, and we talked about how singleton methods defined on self become class methods. Let's use these facts to access instance variables for class objects:

```
classes_7.rb
class Test
  @var = 99
  def self.var
    @var
  end
  def self.var=(value)
    @var = value
  end
end
puts "Original value = #{Test.var}"
Test.var = "cat"
puts "New value = #{Test.var}"
```

produces:

```
Original value = 99
New value = cat
```

Newcomers to Ruby commonly make the mistake of setting instance variables inline in the class definition (as we did with @var in the previous code) and then attempting to access these variables from instance methods. As the code illustrates, this won't work, because instance variables defined in the class body are associated with the class object, not with instances of the class.

Another Way to Access the Singleton Class

We've seen how you can create methods in an object's singleton class by adding the object reference to the method definition using something like def animal.speak.

You can do the same using Ruby's class << an_object notation:

Figure 24.3. Basic Class Definition

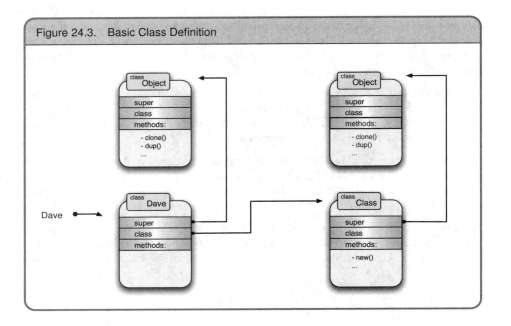

```
classes_8.rb
animal = "dog"
class << animal
  def speak
    puts "The #{self} says WOOF!"
  end
end
animal.speak
```

produces:

```
The dog says WOOF!
```

Inside this kind of class definition, self is set to the singleton class for the given object (animal in this case). Because class definitions return the value of the last statement executed in the class body, we can use this fact to get the singleton class object:

```
classes_9.rb
animal = "dog"
def animal.speak
  puts "The #{self} says WOOF!"
end
singleton = class << animal
  def lie
    puts "The #{self} lies down"
  end
  self      # << return singleton class object
end
```

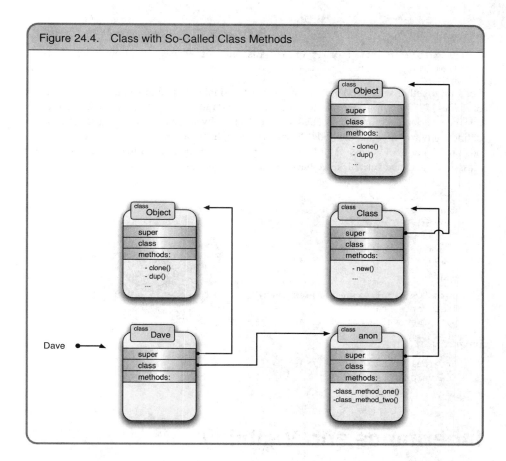

Figure 24.4. Class with So-Called Class Methods

```
animal.speak
animal.lie
puts "Singleton class object is #{singleton}"
puts "It defines methods #{singleton.instance_methods - 'cat'.methods}"
```

produces:

```
The dog says WOOF!
The dog lies down
Singleton class object is #<Class:#<String:0x0a36d8>>
It defines methods [:speak, :lie]
```

Note the notation that Ruby uses to denote a singleton class: #<Class:#<String:...>>.

Ruby goes to some trouble to stop you from using singleton classes outside the context of their original object. For example, you can't create a new instance of a singleton class:

`classes_10.rb`
```
singleton = class << "cat"; self; end
singleton.new
```

produces:

```
prog.rb:2:in `new': can't create instance of singleton class (TypeError)
from /tmp/prog.rb:2:in `<main>'
```

Let's tie together what we know about instance variables, self, and singleton classes. Back on page 379, we wrote class-level accessor methods to let us get and set the value of an instance variable defined in a class object. But Ruby already has attr_accessor, which defines getter and setter methods. Normally, though, these are defined as instance methods and hence will access values stored in instances of a class. To make them work with class-level instance variables, we have to invoke attr_accessor in the singleton class:

```
classes_11.rb
class Test
  @var = 99
  class << self
    attr_accessor :var
  end
end

puts "Original value = #{Test.var}"
Test.var = "cat"
puts "New value = #{Test.var}"
```

produces:

```
Original value = 99
New value = cat
```

Inheritance and Visibility

There's a wrinkle to when it comes to method definition and class inheritance, but it's fairly obscure. Within a class definition, you can change the visibility of a method in an ancestor class.

For example, you can do something like this:

```
classes_12.rb
class Base
  def a_method
    puts "Got here"
  end
  private :a_method
end

class Derived1 < Base
  public :a_method
end

class Derived2 < Base
end
```

In this example, you would be able to invoke a_method in instances of class Derived1 but not via instances of Base or Derived2.

So, how does Ruby pull off this feat of having one method with two different visibilities? Simply put, it cheats.

If a subclass changes the visibility of a method in a parent, Ruby effectively inserts a hidden proxy method in the subclass that invokes the original method using super. It then sets the visibility of that proxy to whatever you requested. This means that the following code:

```
class Derived1 < Base
  public :a_method
end
```

is effectively the same as this:

```
class Derived1 < Base
  def a_method(*)
    super
  end
  public :a_method
end
```

The call to super can access the parent's method regardless of its visibility, so the rewrite allows the subclass to override its parent's visibility rules. Pretty scary, eh?

Modules and Mixins

You know that when you include a module into a Ruby class, the instance methods in that module become available as instance methods of the class.

```
classes_15.rb
module Logger
  def log(msg)
    STDERR.puts Time.now.strftime("%H:%M:%S: ") + "#{self} (#{msg})"
  end
end
class Song
  include Logger
end
class Album
  include Logger
end
s = Song.new
s.log("created")
```

produces:

```
09:58:03: #<Song:0x0a323c> (created)
```

Ruby implements include very simply: the module that you include is effectively added as a superclass of the class being defined. It's as if the module was the parent of the class that it is mixed in to. And that would be the end of the description except for one small wrinkle. Because the module is injected into the chain of superclasses, it must itself hold a link to the original parent class. If it didn't, there'd be no way of traversing the superclass chain to look up methods. However, you can mix the same module into many different classes, and those classes could potentially have totally different superclass chains. If there were just one module object that we mixed in to all these classes, there'd be no way of keeping track of the different superclasses for each.

To get around this, Ruby uses a clever trick. When you include a module in class Example, Ruby constructs a new class object, makes it the superclass of Example, and then sets the superclass of the new class to be the original superclass of Example. It then references the module from this new class object in such a way that when you look a method up in this class, it actually looks it up in the module, as shown in Figure 24.5 on the facing page.

A nice side effect of this arrangement is that if you change a module after including it in a class, those changes are reflected in the class (and the class's objects). In this way, modules behave just like classes.

```
classes_16.rb
module Mod
  def greeting
    "Hello"
  end
end
class Example
  include Mod
end
ex = Example.new
puts "Before change, greeting is #{ex.greeting}"
module Mod
  def greeting
    "Hi"
  end
end
puts "After change, greeting is #{ex.greeting}"
```

produces:

```
Before change, greeting is Hello
After change, greeting is Hi
```

If a module itself includes other modules, a chain of proxy classes will be added to any class that includes that module, one proxy for each module that is directly or indirectly included.

Finally, Ruby will include a module only once in an inheritance chain—including a module that is already included by one of your superclasses is a no-op.

extend

The include method effectively adds a module as a superclass of self. It is used inside a class definition to make the instance methods in the module available to instances of the class.

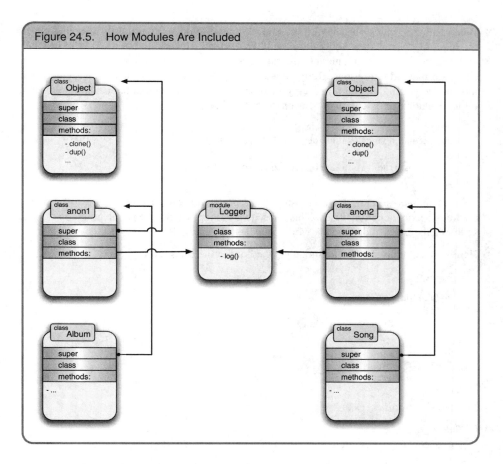

Figure 24.5.   How Modules Are Included

However, it is sometimes useful to add the instance methods to a particular object. You do this using Object#extend. For example:

```
classes_17.rb
module Humor
  def tickle
    "#{self} says hee, hee!"
  end
end

obj = "Grouchy"
obj.extend Humor
puts obj.tickle
```

produces:

```
Grouchy says hee, hee!
```

Stop for a second to think about how this might be implemented....

When Ruby executes obj.tickle in this code example, it does the usual trick of looking in the class of obj for a method called tickle. For extend to work, it has to add the instance methods in the Humor module into the superclass chain for the class of obj. So, just as with singleton method definitions, Ruby creates a singleton class for obj and then includes the module Humor in that class. In fact, just to prove that this is all that happens, here's the C implementation of extend in the current Ruby 1.9 interpreter:

```
void
rb_extend_object(VALUE obj, VALUE module)
{
    rb_include_module(rb_singleton_class(obj), module);
}
```

There is an interesting trick with extend. If you use it within a class definition, the module's methods become class methods. This is because calling extend is equivalent to self.extend, so the methods are added to self, which in a class definition is the class itself.

Here's an example of adding a module's methods at the class level:

classes_19.rb

```
module Humor
  def tickle
    "#{self} says hee, hee!"
  end
end
class Grouchy
  extend  Humor
end
puts Grouchy.tickle
```

produces:

```
Grouchy says hee, hee!
```

Later, on page 389, we'll see how to use extend to add macro-style methods to a class.

Metaprogramming Class-Level Macros

If you've used Ruby for any time at all, the chances are good that you've used attr_accessor, the method that defines reader and writer methods for instance variables:

```
class Song
  attr_accessor :duration
end
```

If you've written a Ruby on Rails application, you've probably used has_many:

```
class Album < ActiveRecord::Base
  has_many :tracks
end
```

These are both examples of class-level methods that generate code behind the scenes. Because of the way they expand into something bigger, folks sometimes call these kinds of methods *macros*.

Let's create a trivial example and then build it up into something realistic. We'll start by implementing a simple method that adds logging capabilities to instances of a class. We previously did this using a module—this time we'll do it using a class-level method. Here's the first iteration:

classes_22.rb

```
class Example
  def self.add_logging
    def log(msg)
      STDERR.puts Time.now.strftime("%H:%M:%S: ") + "#{self} (#{msg})"
    end
  end
  add_logging
end
ex = Example.new
ex.log("hello")
```

produces:

```
09:58:03: #<Example:0x0a39a8> (hello)
```

Clearly, this is a silly piece of code. But bear with me—it'll get better. And we can still learn some stuff from it. First, notice that add_logging is a class-method—it is defined in the class object's singleton class. That means that we can call it later in the class definition without an explicit receiver, because self is set to the class object inside a class definition.

Then, notice that the add_logging method contains a nested method definition. This inner definition will get executed only when we call the add_logging method. The result is that log will be defined as an instance method of class Example.

Let's take one more step. We can define the add_logging method in one class and then use it in a subclass. This works because the singleton class hierarchy parallels the regular class hierarchy. As a result, class methods in a parent class are also available in the child class:

classes_23.rb

```
class Logger
  def self.add_logging
    def log(msg)
      STDERR.puts Time.now.strftime("%H:%M:%S: ") + "#{self} (#{msg})"
    end
  end
end
class Example < Logger
  add_logging
end
ex = Example.new
ex.log("hello")
```

produces:

```
09:58:03: #<Example:0x0a34d0> (hello)
```

Think back to the two examples at the start of this section. Both work this way. attr_accessor is a class method defined in class Module and so is available in all module and class definitions. has_many is a class method defined in the Base class within the Rails ActiveRecord module and so is available to all classes that subclass ActiveRecord::Base.

This example is still not particularly compelling; it would still be easier to add the log method directly as an instance method of our Logger class. But what happens if we want to construct a different version of the log method for each class that uses it? For example, let's add the capability to add a short class-specific identifying string to the start of each log message. We want to be able to say something like this:

```
classes_24.rb
class Song < Logger
  add_logging "Song"
end
class Album < Logger
  add_logging "CD"
end
```

To do this, let's define the log method on the fly. We can no longer use a straightforward def ... end-style definition. Instead, we'll use define_method, one of the cornerstones of metaprogramming. define_method takes the name of a method and a block, defining a method with the given name and with the block as the method body. Any arguments in the block definition become parameters to the method being defined.

```
classes_25.rb
class Logger
  def self.add_logging(id_string)
    define_method(:log) do |msg|
      now = Time.now.strftime("%H:%M:%S")
      STDERR.puts "#{now}-#{id_string}: #{self} (#{msg})"
    end
  end
end
class Song < Logger
  add_logging "Tune"
end
class Album < Logger
  add_logging "CD"
end
song = Song.new
song.log("rock on")
```

produces:

```
09:58:03-Tune: #<Song:0x0a20e4> (rock on)
```

There's an important subtlety in this code. Notice that the body of the log method contains this line:

```
STDERR.puts "#{now}-#{id_string}: #{self} (#{msg})"
```

The value now is a local variable, and msg is the parameter to the block. But id_string is the parameter to the enclosing add_logging method. It's accessible inside the block because block definitions create closures, allowing the context in which the block is defined to be carried forward and used when the block is used. In this case, we're taking a value from a class-level method and using it in an instance method we're defining. This is a common pattern when creating these kinds of class-level macros.

As well as passing parameters from the class method into the body of the method being defined, we can also use the parameter to determine the name of the method or methods to create. Here's an example that creates a new kind of attr_accessor that logs all assignments to a given instance variable:

`classes_27.rb`

```ruby
class AttrLogger
  def self.attr_logger(name)
    attr_reader name
    define_method("#{name}=") do |val|
      puts "Assigning #{val.inspect} to #{name}"
      instance_variable_set("@#{name}", val)
    end
  end
end

class Example < AttrLogger
  attr_logger :value
end

ex = Example.new
ex.value = 123
puts "Value is #{ex.value}"
ex.value = "cat"
puts "Value is now #{ex.value}"
```

produces:

```
Assigning 123 to value
Value is 123
Assigning "cat" to value
Value is now cat
```

Again, we use the fact that the block defining the method body is a closure, accessing the name of the attribute in the log message string. Notice we also make use of the fact that attr_reader is simply a class method—we can call it inside our class method to define the reader method for our attribute. Note another common bit of metaprogramming—we use instance_variable_set to set the value of an instance variable (duh). There's a corresponding _get method that fetches the value of a named instance variable.

Class Macros and Modules

Sometimes it is perfectly acceptable to define class macros in one class and then use these macro methods in subclasses of this class. Other times, though, it isn't appropriate to use subclassing, either because we already have to subclass some other class or because our design aesthetic rebels against making something like a song a subclass of a logger.

In these cases, you can use a module to hold your metaprogramming implementation. As we've seen, using extend inside a class definition will add the methods in a module as class methods to the class being defined:

`classes_28.rb`

```ruby
module AttrLogger
  def attr_logger(name)
    attr_reader name
    define_method("#{name}=") do |val|
      puts "Assigning #{val.inspect} to #{name}"
      instance_variable_set("@#{name}", val)
    end
  end
end

class Example
  extend AttrLogger
  attr_logger :value
end

ex = Example.new
ex.value = 123
puts "Value is #{ex.value}"
ex.value = "cat"
puts "Value is now #{ex.value}"
```

produces:

```
Assigning 123 to value
Value is 123
Assigning "cat" to value
Value is now cat
```

Things get a little trickier if you want to add both class methods and instance methods into the class being defined. Here's one technique, used extensively in the implementation of the Rails framework. It makes use of a Ruby hook method, included, which is called automatically by Ruby when you include a module into a class. It is passed the class object of the class being defined.

`classes_29.rb`

```ruby
module GeneralLogger
  # Instance method to be added to any class that includes us
  def log(msg)
    puts Time.now.strftime("%H:%M: ") + msg
  end

  # module containing class methods to be added
  module ClassMethods
    def attr_logger(name)
      attr_reader name
      define_method("#{name}=") do |val|
        log "Assigning #{val.inspect} to #{name}"
        instance_variable_set("@#{name}", val)
      end
```

```
      end
    end
    # extend host class with class methods when we're included
    def self.included(host_class)
      host_class.extend(ClassMethods)
    end
  end
  class Example
    include GeneralLogger
    attr_logger :value
  end
  ex = Example.new
  ex.log("New example created")
  ex.value = 123
  puts "Value is #{ex.value}"
  ex.value = "cat"
  puts "Value is #{ex.value}"
```

produces:

```
  09:58: New example created
  09:58: Assigning 123 to value
  Value is 123
  09:58: Assigning "cat" to value
  Value is cat
```

Notice how the included callback is used to extend the host class with the methods defined in the inner module ClassMethods.

Now, as an exercise, try executing the previous example in your head. For each line of code, work out the value of self. Master this, and you've pretty much mastered this style of metaprogramming in Ruby.

Two Other Forms of Class Definition

Just in case you thought we'd exhausted the ways of defining Ruby classes, let's look at two other options.

Subclassing Expressions

The first form is really nothing new—it's simply a generalization of the regular class definition syntax. You know that you can write this:

```
  class Parent
    ...
  end
  class Child < Parent
    ...
  end
```

What you might not know is that the thing to the right of the < needn't be just a class name; it can be any expression that returns a class object. In this code example, we have the constant Parent. A constant is a simple form of expression, and in this case the constant Parent holds the class object of the first class we defined.

Ruby comes with a class called Struct, which allows you to define classes that contain just data attributes. For example, you could write this:

```
classes_31.rb
Person = Struct.new(:name, :address, :likes)
dave = Person.new('Dave', 'TX')
dave.likes = "Programming Languages"
puts dave
```

produces:

```
#<struct Person name="Dave", address="TX", likes="Programming Languages">
```

The return value from Struct.new(...) is a class object. By assigning it to the constant Person, we can thereafter use Person as if it were any other class.

But say we wanted to change the to_s method of our structure.

We could do it by opening up the class and writing the method:

```
classes_32.rb
Person = Struct.new(:name, :address, :likes)
class Person
  def to_s
    "#{self.name} lives in #{self.address} and likes #{self.likes}"
  end
end
```

However, we can do this more elegantly (although at the cost of an additional class object) by writing this:

```
classes_33.rb
class Person < Struct.new(:name, :address, :likes)
  def to_s
    "#{self.name} lives in #{self.address} and likes #{self.likes}"
  end
end
dave = Person.new('Dave', 'Texas')
dave.likes = "Programming Languages"
puts dave
```

produces:

```
Dave lives in Texas and likes Programming Languages
```

Creating Singleton Classes

Let's look at some Ruby code:

```
class Example
end
ex = Example.new
```

When we call Example.new, we're invoking the method new on the class object Example. This is just a regular method call—Ruby looks for the method new in the class of the object (and the class of Example is Class) and invokes it. It turns out that we can also invoke Class#new directly:

```
some_class = Class.new
puts some_class.class
```

produces:

```
Class
```

If you pass Class.new a block, that block is used as the body of the class:

```
classes_36.rb
some_class = Class.new do
  def self.class_method
    puts "In class method"
  end
  def instance_method
    puts "In instance method"
  end
end

some_class.class_method
obj = some_class.new
obj.instance_method
```

produces:

```
In class method
In instance method
```

By default, these classes will be direct descendents of Object. You can give them a different parent by passing the parent's class as a parameter:

```
classes_37.rb
some_class = Class.new(String) do
  def vowel_movement
    tr 'aeiou', '*'
  end
end
obj = some_class.new("now is the time")
puts obj.vowel_movement
```

produces:

```
n*w *s th* t*m*
```

How Classes Get Their Names

You may have noticed that the classes created by Class.new have no name. However, all is not lost. If you assign the class object for a class with no name to a constant, Ruby will automatically name the class after the constant:

```
some_class = Class.new
obj = some_class.new
puts "Initial name is #{some_class.name}"
SomeClass = some_class
puts "Then the name is #{some_class.name}"
puts "also works via the object: #{obj.class.name}"
```

produces:

```
Initial name is
Then the name is SomeClass
also works via the object: SomeClass
```

We can use these dynamically constructed classes to extend Ruby in interesting ways. For example, here's a simple reimplementation of the Ruby Struct class:

classes_39.rb

```ruby
def MyStruct(*keys)
  Class.new do
    attr_accessor *keys
    def initialize(hash)
      hash.each do |key, value|
        instance_variable_set("@#{key}", value)
      end
    end
  end
end
Person = MyStruct :name, :address, :likes
dave = Person.new(name: "dave", address: "TX", likes: "Stilton")
chad = Person.new(name: "chad", likes: "Jazz")
chad.address = "CO"
puts "Dave's name is #{dave.name}"
puts "Chad lives in #{chad.address}"
```

produces:

```
Dave's name is dave
Chad lives in CO
```

instance_eval and class_eval

The methods Object#instance_eval, Object#class_eval, and Object#module_eval let you set self to be some arbitrary object, evaluate the code in a block with, and then reset self:

```
"cat".instance_eval do
  puts "Upper case = #{upcase}"
  puts "Length is #{self.length}"
end
```

produces:

```
Upper case = CAT
Length is 3
```

Both forms also take a string (but see the sidebar on the following page for some notes on the dangers of evaluating strings):

```
"cat".instance_eval('puts "Upper=#{upcase}, length=#{self.length}"')
```

produces:

```
Upper=CAT, length=3
```

class_eval and instance_eval both set self for the duration of the block. However, they differ in the way they set up the environment for method definition. class_eval sets things up as if you were in the body of a class definition, so method definitions will define instance methods:

```
class MyClass
end
MyClass.class_eval do
  def instance_method
    puts "In an instance method"
  end
end
obj = MyClass.new
obj.instance_method
```

produces:

```
In an instance method
```

In contrast, instance_eval acts as if you were working inside the singleton class of self. Therefore, any methods you define will become class methods.

```
class MyClass
end
MyClass.instance_eval do
  def class_method
    puts "In a class method"
  end
end
MyClass.class_method
```

produces:

```
In a class method
```

> ### `eval` Is Soo Last Year
>
> You may have noticed that we've been doing a fair amount of metaprogramming—accessing instance variables, defining methods, and creating classes—and we haven't yet used eval. This is deliberate. In the old days of Ruby, the language lacked many of these metaprogramming facilities, and eval was the only way of achieving these effects. But eval comes with a couple of downsides.
>
> First, it is slow—calling eval effectively compiles the code in the string before executing it. But, even worse, eval can be dangerous. If there's any chance that external data—stuff that comes from outside your application—can wind up inside the parameter to eval, then you have a security hole, because that external data may end up containing arbitrary code that your application will blindly execute.
>
> eval is now considered a method of last resort.

It might be helpful to remember that, when defining methods, class_eval and instance_eval have precisely the wrong names: class_eval defines instance methods, and instance_eval defines class methods. Go figure.

1.9 Ruby 1.9 introduces variants of these methods. Object#instance_exec, Module#class_exec, and Module#module_exec behave identically to their _eval counterparts but take only a block (that is, they do not take a string). Any arguments given to the methods are passed in as block parameters. This is an important feature. Previously it was impossible to pass a local or instance variable into a block given to one of the _eval methods—because self is changed by the call, these variables go out of scope. With the _exec form, you can now pass them in:

```
classes_44.rb
animal = "cat"
"dog".instance_exec(animal) do |other|
  puts "#{other} and #{self}"
end
```

produces:

```
cat and dog
```

`instance_eval` and Constants

1.9 Ruby 1.9 has changed the way Ruby looks up constants when executing a block using instance_eval and class_eval. Previously, constants were looked up in the lexical scope in which there were referenced. In Ruby 1.9, they are now looked up in the scope in which instance_eval is called. This (artificial) example shows the output produced by Ruby 1.9:

```
classes_45.rb
module One
  CONST = "Defined in One"
  def self.eval_block(&block)
    instance_eval(&block)
  end
end

module Two
  CONST = "Defined in Two"
  def self.call_eval_block
    One.eval_block do
      puts CONST
    end
  end
end

Two.call_eval_block
```

produces:

```
Defined in One
```

In Ruby 1.8, this same code would print Defined in Two.

instance_eval and Domain-Specific Languages

It turns out that instance_eval has a pivotal role to play in a certain type of domain-specific language (DSL). For example, we might be writing a simple DSL for turtle graphics.[2] To draw a set of three 5x5 squares, we might write this:[3]

```
3.times do
  forward(8)
  pen_down
  4.times do
    forward(4)
    left
  end
  pen_up
end
```

Clearly, pen_down, forward, left, and pen_up can be implemented as Ruby methods. However, to call them without a receiver like this, either we have to be within a class that defines them (or is a child of such a class) or we have to make the methods global. instance_eval to the rescue. We can define a class Turtle that defines the various methods we need as instance methods. We'll also define a walk method, which will execute our turtle DSL, and a draw method to draw the resulting picture:

---

2.   In turtle graphics systems, you imagine you have a turtle you can command to move forward n squares, turn left, and turn right. You can also make the turtle raise and lower a pen. If the pen is lowered, a line will be drawn tracing the turtle's subsequent movements. Very few of these turtles exist in the wild, so we tend to simulate them inside computers.

3.   Yes, the forward(4) is correct in this code. The initial point is always drawn.

```
class Turtle
  def left; ... end
  def right; ... end
  def forward(n); ... end
  def pen_up; .. end
  def pen_down; ... end
  def walk(...); end
  def draw; ... end
end
```

If we implement walk correctly, we can then write this:

```
turtle = Turtle.new
turtle.walk do
  3.times do
    forward(8)
    pen_down
    4.times do
      forward(4)
      left
    end
    pen_up
  end
end
turtle.draw
```

So, what is the correct implementation of walk? Well, we clearly have to use instance_eval, because we want the DSL commands in the block to call the methods in the turtle object. We also have to arrange to pass the block given to the walk method to be evaluated by that instance_eval call. Our implementation looks like this:

```
def walk(&block)
  instance_eval(&block)
end
```

Notice how we captured the block into a variable and then expanded that variable back into a block in the call to instance_eval.

A complete listing of the turtle program starts on page 407.

Is this a good use of instance_eval? It depends on the circumstances. The benefit is that the code inside the block looks simple—you don't have to make the receiver explicit:

```
4.times do
  turtle.forward(4)
  turtle.left
end
```

There's a drawback, though. Inside the block, scope isn't what you think it is, so this code wouldn't work:

```
@size = 4
turtle.walk do
  4.times do
    turtle.forward(@size)
```

```
        turtle.left
    end
  end
end
```

Instance variables are looked up in self, and self in the block isn't the same as self in the code that sets the instance variable @size. Because of this, most people are moving away from this style of CFinstance_evaled block.

Hook Methods

In the section starting on page 389, we defined a method called included in our General-Logger module. When this module was included in a class, Ruby automatically invoked this included method, allowing our module to add class methods to the host class.

included is an example of a *hook method* (sometimes called a *callback*). A hook method is a method that you write but that Ruby calls from within the interpreter when some particular event occurs. The interpreter looks for these methods by name—if you define a method in the right context with an appropriate name, Ruby will call it when the corresponding event happens.

The methods that can be invoked from within the interpreter are shown in Table 24.1 on the next page. We won't discuss all of them in this chapter—instead, we'll show just a few examples of use. The reference section of this book describes the individual methods, and the *Duck Typing* chapter on page 359 discusses the coercion methods in more detail.

The inherited Hook

If a class defines a class method called inherited, Ruby will call it whenever that class is subclassed (that is, whenever any class inherits from the original).

This hook is often used in situations where a base class needs to keep track of its children. For example, an online store might offer a variety of shipping options. Each might be represented by a separate class, and each of these classes could be a subclass of a single Shipping class. This parent class could keep track of all the various shipping options by recording every class that subclasses it. When it comes time to display the shipping options to the user, the application could call the base class, asking it for a list of its children:

classes_52.rb

```
class Shipping      # Base class
  @children = []    # this variable is in the class, not instances
  def self.inherited(child)
    @children << child
  end
  def self.shipping_options(weight, international)
    @children.select {|child| child.can_ship(weight, international)}
  end
end
```

Table 24.1. Ruby Hook Methods

Method-related hooks

method_added, method_missing, method_removed, method_undefined, single-ton_method_added, singleton_method_removed, singleton_method_undefined

Class and module-related hooks

append_features, const_missing, extend_object, extended, included, inherited, initial-ize_copy

Object marshaling hooks

marshal_dump, marshal_load

Coercion hooks

coerce, induced_from, to_*xxx*

```ruby
class MediaMail < Shipping
  def self.can_ship(weight, international)
    !international
  end
end
class FlatRatePriorityEnvelope < Shipping
  def self.can_ship(weight, international)
    weight < 64 && !international
  end
end
class InternationalFlatRateBox < Shipping
  def self.can_ship(weight, international)
    weight < 9*16 && international
  end
end
puts "Shipping 16oz domestic"
puts Shipping.shipping_options(16, false)

puts "\nShipping 90oz domestic"
puts Shipping.shipping_options(90, false)

puts "\nShipping 16oz international"
puts Shipping.shipping_options(16, true)
```

produces:

```
Shipping 16oz domestic
MediaMail
FlatRatePriorityEnvelope

Shipping 90oz domestic
MediaMail

Shipping 16oz international
InternationalFlatRateBox
```

Command interpreters are another common user of this pattern: the base class keeps a track of available commands, each of which is implemented in a subclass.

The method_missing Hook

Earlier, we saw how Ruby executes a method call by looking for the method, first in the object's class, then in its superclass, then in that class's superclass, and so on. If the method call has an explicit receiver, then private methods are skipped in this search. If the method is not found by the time we run out of superclasses (because BasicObject has no superclass), then Ruby tries to invoke the hook method method_missing on the original object. Again, the same process is followed—Ruby first looks in the object's class, then in its superclass, and so on. However, Ruby predefines its own version of method_missing in class BasicObject, so typically the search stops there. The built-in method_missing basically raises an exception (either a NoMethodError or a NameError depending on the circumstances).

The key here is that method_missing is simply a Ruby method. We can override it in our own classes to handle calls to otherwise undefined methods in an application-specific way.

method_missing has a simple signature, but many people get it wrong:

```
def method_missing(name, *args, &block)  # ...
```

The name argument receives the name of the method that couldn't be found. It is passed as a symbol. The args argument is an array of the arguments that were passed in the original call. And the oft-forgotten block argument will receive any block passed to the original method.

```
classes_54.rb
def method_missing(name, *args, &block)
  puts "Called #{name} with #{args.inspect} and #{block}"
end

wibble
wobble 1, 2
wurble(3, 4) { stuff }
```

produces:

```
Called wibble with [] and
Called wobble with [1, 2] and
Called wurble with [3, 4] and #<Proc:0x0a3d68@/tmp/prog.rb:7>
```

Before we get too deep into the details, I'll offer a tip about etiquette. There are two main ways that people use method_missing. The first intercepts every use of an undefined method and handles it. The second is more subtle; it intercepts all calls but handles only some of them. In the latter case, it is important to forward on the call to a superclass if you decide not to handle it in your method_missing implementation:

```
classes_55.rb
class MyClass < OtherClass
  def method_missing(name, *args, &block)
    if <some condition>
      # handle call
    else
      super    # otherwise pass it on
    end
  end
end
```

If you fail to pass on calls that you don't handle, your application will silently ignore calls to unknown methods in your class.

Let's show a couple of uses of method_missing.

method_missing to Simulate Accessors

The OpenStruct class is distributed with Ruby. It allows you to write objects with attributes that are created dynamically by assignment. (We describe it in more detail on page 778.) For example, you could write this:

classes_56.rb

```ruby
require 'ostruct'
obj = OpenStruct.new(name: "Dave")
obj.address = "Texas"
obj.likes   = "Programming"
puts "#{obj.name} lives in #{obj.address} and likes #{obj.likes}"
```

produces:

```
Dave lives in Texas and likes Programming
```

Let's use method_missing to write our own version of OpenStruct:

classes_57.rb

```ruby
class MyOpenStruct < BasicObject
  def initialize(initial_values = {})
    @values = initial_values
  end
  def _singleton_class
    class << self
      self
    end
  end
  def method_missing(name, *args, &block)
    if name[-1] == "="
      base_name = name[0..-2].intern
      _singleton_class.instance_exec(name) do |name|
        define_method(name) do |value|
          @values[base_name] = value
        end
      end
      @values[base_name] = args[0]
    else
      _singleton_class.instance_exec(name) do |name|
        define_method(name) do
          @values[name]
        end
      end
      @values[name]
    end
  end
end
```

```
obj = MyOpenStruct.new(name: "Dave")
obj.address = "Texas"
obj.likes   = "Programming"
puts "#{obj.name} lives in #{obj.address} and likes #{obj.likes}"
```

produces:

```
Dave lives in Texas and likes Programming
```

1.9

Notice how we base our class on BasicObject, a class introduced in Ruby 1.9. BasicObject is the root of Ruby's object hierarchy and contains only a minimal number of methods:

```
p BasicObject.instance_methods
```

produces:

```
[:==, :equal?, :!, :!=, :instance_eval, :instance_exec, :__send__]
```

This is good, because it means that our MyOpenStruct class will be able to have attributes such as display or class. If instead we'd based MyOpenStruct on class Object, then these names, along with 47 others, would have been predefined and hence wouldn't trigger method_missing.

Notice also another common pattern inside method_missing. The first time we reference or assign to an attribute of our object, we access or update the @values hash appropriately. But we also define the method that the caller was trying to access. This means that the next time this attribute is used, it will use the method and not invoke method_missing. This may or may no be worth the trouble, depending on the access patterns to your object.

Also notice how we had to jump through some hoops to define the method. We want to define the method only for the current object. This means we have to put the method into the object's singleton class. We can do that using instance_exec and define_method. But that means we have to use the class << self trick to get the object's singleton class. Through an interesting implementation subtlety, define_method will always define an instance method, independent of whether it is invoked via instance_exec or class_exec.

However, this code reveals a dark underbelly of using method_missing and BasicObject. Consider this:

```
obj = MyOpenStruct.new(name: "Dave")
obj.address = "Texas"
o1 = obj.dup
o1.name = "Mike"
o1.address = "Colorado"
```

produces:

```
prog.rb:5:in `<main>': undefined method `name=' for nil:NilClass (NoMethodError)
```

The dup method is not defined by BasicObject; it appears in class Object. So when we called dup, it was picked up by our method_missing handler, and we just returned nil (because we don't have yet have an attribute called dup). We could fix this so that it at least reports an error:

```
def method_missing(name, *args, &block)
  if name[-1] == "="
    # as before...
  else
    super unless @values.has_key? name
    # as before...
  end
end
```

This class now reports an error if we call dup (or any other method) on it. However, we still can't dup or clone it (or inspect, convert to a string, and so on). Although BasicObject seems like a natural fit for method_missing, you may find it to be more trouble than it's worth.

method_missing as a Filter

As the previous example showed, method_missing has some drawbacks if you use it to intercept all calls. It is probably better to use it to recognize certain patterns of call, passing on those it doesn't recognize to its parent class to handle.

An example of this is the dynamic finder facility in the Ruby on Rails ActiveRecord module. Active Record is the object-relational library in Rails—it allows you to access relational databases as if they were object stores. One particular feature allows you to find rows that match the criteria of having given values in certain columns. For example, if an Active Record class called Book was mapping a relational table called books and the books table included columns called title and author, you could write this:

```
pickaxe = Book.find_by_title("Programming Ruby")
daves_books = Book.find_all_by_author("Dave Thomas")
```

Active Record does not predefine all these potential finder methods. Instead, it uses our old friend method_missing. Inside that method, it looks for calls to undefined methods that match the pattern /^find_(all_)?by_(.*)/. [4] If the method being invoked does not match this pattern or if the field(s) in the method name don't correspond to columns in the database table, Active Record calls super so that a genuine method_missing report will be generated.

One Last Example

Let's bring together all of the metaprogramming topics we've discussed in a final example by writing a module that allows us to trace the execution of methods in any class that mixes the module in. This would let us write:

```
require 'code/trace_calls'
class Example
  def one(arg)
    puts "One called with #{arg}"
  end
end
```

---

4. It also looks for /^find_or_(initialize|create)_by_(.*)/.

```
ex1 = Example.new
ex1.one("Hello")        # no tracing from this call
class Example
  include TraceCalls
  def two(arg1, arg2)
    arg1 + arg2
  end
end
ex1.one("Goodbye")     # but we see tracing from these two
puts ex1.two(4, 5)
```

produces:

```
One called with Hello
==> calling one with ["Goodbye"]
One called with Goodbye
<== one returned nil
==> calling two with [4, 5]
<== two returned 9
9
```

We can see immediately that there's a subtlety here. When we mix the TraceCalls module into a class, it has to add tracing to any existing instance methods in that class. It also has to arrange to add tracing to any methods we subsequently add.

Let's start with the full listing of the TraceCalls module:

```
trace_calls.rb
```

```
module TraceCalls
  def self.included(klass)
    klass.instance_methods(false).each do |existing_method|
      wrap(klass, existing_method)
    end
    def klass.method_added(method)  # note: nested definition
      unless @trace_calls_internal
        @trace_calls_internal = true
        TraceCalls.wrap(self, method)
        @trace_calls_internal = false
      end
    end
  end
  def self.wrap(klass, method)
    klass.instance_eval do
      method_object = instance_method(method)
      define_method(method) do |*args, &block|
        puts "==> calling #{method} with #{args.inspect}"
        result = method_object.bind(self).call(*args, &block)
        puts "<== #{method} returned #{result.inspect}"
        result
      end
    end
  end
end
```

When we include this module in a class, the included hook method gets invoked. It first uses the instance_methods reflection method to find all the existing instance methods in the host class (the false parameter limits the list to methods in the class itself, and not in its superclasses). For each existing method, the module calls a helper method, wrap, to add some tracing code to it. We'll talk about wrap shortly.

Next, the included method uses another hook, method_added. This is called by Ruby whenever a method is defined in the receiver. Note that we define this method in the class passed to the included method. This means that the method will be called when methods are added to this host class and not to the module. This is what allows us to include TraceCalls at the top of a class and then add methods to that class—all those method definitions will be handled by method_added.

Now look at the code inside the method_added method. We have to deal with a potential problem here. As you'll see when we look at the wrap method, we add tracing to a method by creating a new version of the method that calls the old. Inside method_added, we call the wrap function to add this tracing. But inside wrap, we'll define a new method to handle this wrapping, and that definition will invoke method_added again, and then we'd call wrap again, and so on, until the stack gets exhausted. To prevent this, we use an instance variable and do the wrapping only if we're not already doing it.

The wrap method takes a class object and the name of a method to wrap. It finds the original definition of that method (using instance_method) and saves it. It then redefines this method. This new method outputs some tracing and then calls the original, passing in the parameters and block from the wrapper.[5] Note how we call the method by binding the method object to the current instance and then invoking that bound method.

The key to understanding this code, and most metaprogramming code, is to follow the basic principles we worked out at the start of this chapter—how self changes as methods are called and classes are defined and how methods are called by looking for them in the class of the receiver. If you get stuck, do what I do and draw little boxes and arrows. I find it useful to stick with the convention I used in this chapter: class links go to the right, and superclass links go up. Given an object, a method call is then a question of finding the receiver object, going right once, and then following the superclass chain up as far as you need to go.

Top-Level Execution Environment

Finally, there's one small detail we have to cover to complete the metaprogramming environment. Many times in this book we've claimed that everything in Ruby is an object. However, we've used one thing time and time again that appears to contradict this—the top-level Ruby execution environment:

```
puts "Hello, World"
```

---

5. The ability of a block to take a block parameter was added in Ruby 1.9.

Not an object in sight. We may as well be writing some variant of Fortran or BASIC. But dig deeper, and you'll come across objects and classes lurking in even the simplest code.

We know that the literal "Hello, World" generates a Ruby String, so that's one object. We also know that the bare method call to puts is effectively the same as self.puts. But what is self?

```
self.class   # =>   Object
```

At the top level, we're executing code in the context of some predefined object. When we define methods, we're actually creating (private) instance methods for class Object. This is fairly subtle; as they are in class Object, these methods are available everywhere. And because we're in the context of Object, we can use all of Object's methods (including those mixed in from Kernel) in function form. This explains why we can call Kernel methods such as puts at the top level (and indeed throughout Ruby); it's because these methods are part of every object. Top-level instance variables also belong to this top-level object.

Metaprogramming is one of Ruby's sharpest tools. Don't be afraid to use it to raise up the level at which you program. But, at the same time, use it only when necessary—overly metaprogrammed applications can become pretty obscure pretty quickly.

The Turtle Graphics Program

`classes_66.rb`

```ruby
class Turtle
  # directions: 0 = E, 1 = S, 2 = W, 3 = N
  # axis: 0 = x, 1 = y
  def initialize
    @board = Hash.new(" ")
    @x = @y = 0
    @direction = 0
    pen_up
  end
  def pen_up
    @pen_down = false
  end
  def pen_down
    @pen_down = true
    mark_current_location
  end
  def forward(n=1)
    n.times { move }
  end
  def left
    @direction -= 1
    @direction = 3 if @direction < 0
  end
  def right
    @direction += 1
    @direction = 0 if @direction > 3
  end
```

```ruby
      def walk(&block)
        instance_eval(&block)
      end
      def draw
        min_x, max_x = @board.keys.map{|x,y| x}.minmax
        min_y, max_y = @board.keys.map{|x,y| y}.minmax
        min_y.upto(max_y) do |y|
          min_x.upto(max_x) do |x|
            print @board[[x,y]]
          end
          puts
        end
      end
      private
      def move
        increment = @direction > 1 ? -1 : 1
        if @direction.even?
          @x += increment
        else
          @y += increment
        end
        mark_current_location
      end
      def mark_current_location
        @board[[@x,@y]] = "#" if @pen_down
      end
    end
    turtle = Turtle.new
    turtle.walk do
      3.times do
        forward(8)
        pen_down
        4.times do
          forward(4)
          left
        end
        pen_up
      end
    end
    turtle.draw
```

produces:

```
#####   #####   #####
#   #   #   #   #   #
#   #   #   #   #   #
#   #   #   #   #   #
#####   #####   #####
```

## Chapter 25

Reflection, ObjectSpace, and Distributed Ruby

One of the advantages of dynamic languages such as Ruby is the ability to *introspect*—to examine aspects of a program from within the program itself. This process is also called *reflection.*

When you introspect, you think about your thoughts and feelings. This is interesting, because you're using thought to analyze thought. It's the same when programs use introspection—a program can discover the following information about itself:

- What objects it contains
- Its class hierarchy
- The attributes and methods of objects
- Information on methods

Armed with this information, we can look at particular objects and decide which of their methods to call at runtime—even if the class of the object didn't exist when we first wrote the code. We can also start doing clever things, perhaps modifying the program while it's running. Later in this chapter we'll look at distributed Ruby and marshaling, two reflection-based technologies that let us send objects around the world and through time.

Looking at Objects

Have you ever craved the ability to traverse *all* the living objects in your program? We have! Ruby lets you perform this trick with ObjectSpace.each_object. We can use it to do all sorts of neat tricks.

For example, to iterate over all objects of type Float, you'd write the following:

```
a = 102.7
b = 95.1
ObjectSpace.each_object(Float) {|x| p x }
```

produces:

```
95.1
102.7
2.71828182845905
3.14159265358979
2.22044604925031e-16
1.79769313486232e+308
2.2250738585072e-308
```

Hey, where did all those extra numbers come from? We didn't define them in our program. Well, the Math module defines constants for e and π, and if you look on pages 519 and 579, you'll see that the Float class defines constants for the maximum and minimum float, as well as epsilon, the smallest distinguishable difference between two floats. Since we are examining *all* living objects in the system, these turn up as well.

Let's try the same example with different values. This time, they're objects of type Fixnum:

```
a = 102
b = 95
ObjectSpace.each_object(Fixnum) {|x| p x }
```

(Produces no output.)

Neither of the Fixnum objects we created showed up. That's because ObjectSpace doesn't know about objects with immediate values: Fixnum, Symbol, true, false, and nil.

Looking Inside Objects

Once you've found an interesting object, you may be tempted to find out just what it can do. Unlike static languages, where a variable's type determines its class, and hence the methods it supports, Ruby supports liberated objects. You really cannot tell exactly what an object can do until you look under its hood.[1] We talk about this in the *Duck Typing* chapter starting on page 359.

For instance, we can get a list of all the methods to which an object will respond (these include methods in an object's class and that class's ancestors):

```
r = 1..10 # Create a Range object
list = r.methods
list.length   # =>   101
list[0..3]    # =>   [:==, :===, :eql?, :hash]
```

We can check to see whether an object responds to a particular method:

```
r.respond_to?("frozen?")    # =>   true
r.respond_to?(:has_key?)    # =>   false
"me".respond_to?("==")      # =>   true
```

---

1. Or under its bonnet, for objects created to the east of the Atlantic.

We can determine our object's class and its unique object ID and test its relationship to other classes:

```
num = 1
num.object_id            # =>    3
num.class                # =>    Fixnum
num.kind_of? Fixnum      # =>    true
num.kind_of? Numeric     # =>    true
num.instance_of? Fixnum  # =>    true
num.instance_of? Numeric # =>    false
```

Looking at Classes

Knowing about objects is one part of reflection, but to get the whole picture, you also need to be able to look at classes—the methods and constants that they contain.

Looking at the class hierarchy is easy. You can get the parent of any particular class using Class#superclass. For classes *and* modules, Module#ancestors lists both superclasses and mixed-in modules:

```
klass = Fixnum
begin
  print klass
  klass = klass.superclass
  print " < " if klass
end while klass
puts
p Fixnum.ancestors
```

produces:

```
Fixnum < Integer < Numeric < Object < BasicObject
[Fixnum, Integer, Numeric, Comparable, Object, Kernel, BasicObject]
```

If you want to build a complete class hierarchy, just run that code for every class in the system. We can use ObjectSpace to iterate over all Class objects:

```
ObjectSpace.each_object(Class) do |klass|
   # ...
end
```

Looking Inside Classes

We can find out a bit more about the methods and constants in a particular object. Instead of just checking to see whether the object responds to a given message, we can ask for methods by access level, and we can ask for just singleton methods.

1.9 We can also take a look at the object's constants, local, and instance variables:

```ruby
class Demo
  @@var = 99
  CONST = 1.23

  private
    def private_method
    end
  protected
    def protected_method
    end
  public
    def public_method
      @inst = 1
      i = 1
      j = 2
      local_variables
    end

  def Demo.class_method
  end
end

Demo.private_instance_methods(false)      # =>   [:private_method]
Demo.protected_instance_methods(false)    # =>   [:protected_method]
Demo.public_instance_methods(false)       # =>   [:public_method]
Demo.singleton_methods(false)             # =>   [:class_method]
Demo.class_variables                      # =>   [:@@var]
Demo.constants(false)                     # =>   [:CONST]

demo = Demo.new
demo.instance_variables                   # =>   []
# Get 'public_method' to return its local variables
# and set an instance variable
demo.public_method                        # =>   [:i, :j]
demo.instance_variables                   # =>   [:@inst]
```

You may be wondering what all the false parameters were in the previous code. As of Ruby 1.8, these reflection methods will by default recurse into parent classes, their parents, and so on, up the ancestor chain. Passing in false stops this kind of prying.

Given a list of method names, we may now be tempted to try calling them. Fortunately, that's easy with Ruby.

Calling Methods Dynamically

The Object#send method lets you tell an object to invoke a method by name. It works on any object.

```
"John Coltrane".send(:length)            # =>   13
"Miles Davis".send("sub", /iles/, '.')   # =>   "M. Davis"
```

Another way of invoking methods dynamically uses Method objects. A Method object is like a Proc object: it represents a chunk of code and a context in which it executes. In this case, the code is the body of the method, and the context is the object that created the method. Once we have our Method object, we can execute it sometime later by sending it the message call:

```
trane = "John Coltrane".method(:length)
miles = "Miles Davis".method("sub")

trane.call                # =>   13
miles.call(/iles/, '.')   # =>   "M. Davis"
```

You can pass the Method object around as you would any other object, and when you invoke Method#call, the method is run just as if you had invoked it on the original object. It's like having a C-style function pointer but in a fully object-oriented style.

You can use Method objects where you could use proc objects. For example, they work with iterators:

```
def double(a)
  2*a
end

method_object = method(:double)

[ 1, 3, 5, 7 ].map(&method_object)   # =>   [2, 6, 10, 14]
```

Method objects are bound to one particular object. You can create *unbound* methods (of class UnboundMethod) and then subsequently bind them to one or more objects. The binding creates a new Method object. As with aliases, unbound methods are references to the definition of the method at the time they are created:

```
unbound_length = String.instance_method(:length)
class String
  def length
    99
  end
end
str = "cat"
str.length              # =>   99
bound_length = unbound_length.bind(str)
bound_length.call   # =>   3
```

As good things come in threes, here's yet another way to invoke methods dynamically. The eval method (and its variations such as class_eval, module_eval, and instance_eval) will parse and execute an arbitrary string of legal Ruby source code.

```
trane = %q{"John Coltrane".length}
miles = %q{"Miles Davis".sub(/iles/, '.')}

eval trane   # =>   13
eval miles   # =>   "M. Davis"
```

When using eval, it can be helpful to state explicitly the context in which the expression should be evaluated, rather than using the current context. You can obtain a context by calling Kernel#binding at the desired point:

```
def get_a_binding
  val = 123
  binding
end

val = "cat"

the_binding = get_a_binding
eval("val", the_binding)    # =>   123
eval("val")                 # =>   "cat"
```

The first eval evaluates val in the context of the binding *as it was* when the method get_a_binding was executing. In this binding, the variable val had a value of 123. The second eval evaluates val in the top-level binding, where it has the value "cat".

Performance Considerations

As we've seen in this section, Ruby gives us several ways to invoke an arbitrary method of some object: Object#send, Method#call, and the various flavors of eval.

You may prefer to use any one of these techniques depending on your needs, but be aware that eval is significantly slower than the others (or, for optimistic readers, send and call are significantly faster than eval):

`ospace_15.rb`

```
require 'benchmark'
include Benchmark
test = "Stormy Weather"
m = test.method(:length)
n = 100000
bm(12) {|x|
  x.report("call") { n.times { m.call } }
  x.report("send") { n.times { test.send(:length) } }
  x.report("eval") { n.times { eval "test.length" } }
}
```

produces:

	user	system	total	real
call	0.020000	0.000000	0.020000	(0.022580)
send	0.010000	0.000000	0.010000	(0.016217)
eval	0.760000	0.000000	0.760000	(0.755715)

System Hooks

A *hook* is a technique that lets you trap some Ruby event, such as object creation. Let's take a look at some common Ruby hook techniques.

Hooking Method Calls

The simplest hook technique in Ruby is to intercept calls to methods in system classes. Perhaps you want to log all the operating system commands your program executes. Simply rename the method Kernel.system and substitute it with one of your own that both logs the command and calls the original Kernel method:

```
module Kernel
  alias_method :old_system, :system
  def system(*args)
    result = old_system(*args)
    puts "system(#{args.join(', ')}) returned #{result.inspect}"
    result
  end
end

system("date")
system("kangaroo", "-hop 10", "skippy")
```

produces:

```
Tue Mar 31 09:58:04 CDT 2009
system(date) returned true
system(kangaroo, -hop 10, skippy) returned nil
```

The problem with this technique is that you're relying on there not being an existing method called old_system. A better alternative is to make use of method objects, which are effectively anonymous:

```
module Kernel
  old_system_method = instance_method(:system)
  define_method(:system) do |*args|
    result = old_system_method.bind(self).call(*args)
    puts "system(#{args.join(', ')}) returned #{result.inspect}"
    result
  end
end

system("date")
system("kangaroo", "-hop 10", "skippy")
```

produces:

```
Tue Mar 31 09:58:05 CDT 2009
system(date) returned true
system(kangaroo, -hop 10, skippy) returned nil
```

Object Creation Hooks

Ruby lets you get involved when objects are created. If you can be present when every object is born, you can do all sorts of interesting things: you can wrap them, add methods to them, remove methods from them, and add them to containers to implement persistence—you name it. We'll show a simple example here. We'll add a timestamp to every object as it's created. First, we'll add a timestamp attribute to every object in the system. We can do this by hacking class Object itself:

```
class Object
  attr_accessor :timestamp
end
```

Then, we need to hook object creation to add this timestamp. One way to do this is to do our method renaming trick on Class#new, the method that's called to allocate space for a new object. The technique isn't perfect—some built-in objects, such as literal strings, are constructed without calling new—but it'll work just fine for objects we write.

```
class Class
  old_new = instance_method :new
  define_method :new do |*args, &block|
    result = old_new.bind(self).call(*args, &block)
    result.timestamp = Time.now
    result
  end
end
```

Finally, we can run a test. We'll create a couple of objects a few milliseconds apart and check their timestamps:

```
class Test
end

obj1 = Test.new
sleep(0.002)
obj2 = Test.new

obj1.timestamp.to_f   # =>   1238511485.08061
obj2.timestamp.to_f   # =>   1238511485.08265
```

Tracing Your Program's Execution

While we're having fun reflecting on all the objects and classes in our programs, let's not forget about the humble statements that make our code actually do things. It turns out that Ruby lets us look at these statements, too.

First, you can watch the interpreter as it executes code. set_trace_func executes a proc with all sorts of juicy debugging information whenever a new source line is executed, methods are called, objects are created, and so on.

You'll find a full description on page 567, but here's a taste:

```
ospace_21.rb
class Test
  def test
    a = 1
    b = 2
  end
end

set_trace_func lambda {|event, file, line, id, binding, classname|
  printf "%8s %s:%-2d %-15s %-15s\n", event, file, line, classname, id
}
t = Test.new
t.test
```

produces:

```
c-return prog.rb:10 Kernel          set_trace_func
    line prog.rb:11
  c-call prog.rb:11 Class           new
  c-call prog.rb:11 BasicObject     initialize
c-return prog.rb:11 BasicObject     initialize
c-return prog.rb:11 Class           new
    line prog.rb:12
    call prog.rb:2  Test            test
    line prog.rb:3  Test            test
    line prog.rb:4  Test            test
  return prog.rb:2  Test            test
```

The method trace_var (described on page 570) lets you add a hook to a global variable; whenever an assignment is made to the global, your proc is invoked.

How Did We Get Here?

That's a fair question...one we ask ourselves regularly. Mental lapses aside, in Ruby at least you can find out exactly "how you got there" by using the method caller, which returns an Array of String objects representing the current call stack:

```
def cat_a
  puts caller
end
def cat_b
  cat_a
end
def cat_c
  cat_b
end
cat_c
```

produces:

```
/tmp/prog.rb:5:in `cat_b'
/tmp/prog.rb:8:in `cat_c'
/tmp/prog.rb:10:in `<main>'
```

Once you've figured out how you got there, where you go next is up to you.

Source Code

Ruby executes programs from plain old files. You can look at these files to examine the source code that makes up your program using one of a number of techniques.

The special variable __FILE__ contains the name of the current source file. This leads to a fairly short (if cheating) Quine—a program that outputs its own source code:

```
print File.read(__FILE__)
```

produces:

```
print File.read(__FILE__)
```

As we saw in the previous section, the method Kernel.caller returns the call stack as a list. Each entry in this list starts off with a filename, a colon, and a line number in that file. You can parse this information to display source. In the following example, we have a main program, main.rb, that calls a method in a separate file, sub.rb. That method in turns invokes a block, where we traverse the call stack and write out the source lines involved. Notice the use of a hash of file contents, indexed by the filename.

Here's the code that dumps out the call stack, including source information:

```
def dump_call_stack
  file_contents = {}
  puts "File            Line  Source Line"
  puts "--------------+----+------------"
  caller.each do |position|
    next unless position =~ /\A(.*?):(\d+)/
    file = $1
    line = Integer($2)
    file_contents[file] ||= File.readlines(file)
    printf("%-15s:%3d - %s", File.basename(file), line,
           file_contents[file][line-1].lstrip)
  end
end
```

The (trivial) file sub.rb contains a single method:

```
def sub_method(v1, v2)
  main_method(v1*3, v2*6)
end
```

And here's the main program, which invokes the stack dumper after being called back by the submethod:

```
require 'sub'
require 'stack_dumper'
def main_method(arg1, arg2)
  dump_call_stack
end
sub_method(123, "cat")
```

produces:

```
File             Line  Source Line
---------------+----+------------
main.rb        :  5 - dump_call_stack
sub.rb         :  2 - main_method(v1*3, v2*6)
main.rb        :  8 - sub_method(123, "cat")
```

The SCRIPT_LINES__ constant is closely related to this technique. If a program initializes a constant called SCRIPT_LINES__ with a hash, that hash will receive a new entry for every file subsequently loaded into the interpreter using require or load. The entry's key is the name of the file, and the value is the source of the file as an array of strings.

Behind the Curtain: The Ruby VM

1.9

Ruby 1.9 comes with a new virtual machine, called YARV. As well as being faster than the old interpreter, YARV exposes some of its state via Ruby classes.

If you'd like to know what Ruby is doing with all that code you're writing, you can ask YARV to show you the intermediate code that it is executing. You can ask it to compile the Ruby code in a string or in a file and then disassemble it and even run it.[2] Here's a trivial example:

```
code = RubyVM::InstructionSequence.compile('a = 1; puts 1 + a')
puts code.disassemble
```

produces:

```
== disasm: <RubyVM::InstructionSequence:<compiled>@<compiled>>==========
local table (size: 2, argc: 0 [opts: 0, rest: -1, post: 0, block: -1] s1)
[ 2] a
0000 trace            1                                               (   1)
0002 putobject        1
0004 setlocal         a
0006 trace            1
0008 putnil
0009 putobject        1
0011 getlocal         a
0013 opt_plus
0014 send             :puts, 1, nil, 8, <ic>
0020 leave
```

Maybe you want to know how Ruby handles #{ } substitutions in strings:

```
code = RubyVM::InstructionSequence.compile('a = 1; puts "a = #{a}."')
puts code.disassemble
```

---

2. People often ask if they can dump the opcodes out and later reload them. The answer is no—the interpreter has the code to do this, but it is disabled because there is not yet an intermediate code verifier for YARV.

produces:

```
== disasm: <RubyVM::InstructionSequence:<compiled>@<compiled>>==========
local table (size: 2, argc: 0 [opts: 0, rest: -1, post: 0, block: -1] s1)
[ 2] a
0000 trace            1                                          (   1)
0002 putobject        1
0004 setlocal         a
0006 trace            1
0008 putnil
0009 putobject        "a = "
0011 getlocal         a
0013 tostring
0014 putstring        "."
0016 concatstrings    3
0018 send             :puts, 1, nil, 8, <ic>
0024 leave
```

For a full list of the opcodes, print out RubyVM::INSTRUCTION_NAMES.

Marshaling and Distributed Ruby

Ruby features the ability to *serialize* objects, letting you store them somewhere and reconstitute them when needed. You can use this facility, for instance, to save a tree of objects that represent some portion of application state—a document, a CAD drawing, a piece of music, and so on.

Ruby calls this kind of serialization *marshaling* (think of railroad marshaling yards where individual cars are assembled in sequence into a complete train, which is then dispatched somewhere). Saving an object and some or all of its components is done using the method Marshal.dump. Typically, you will dump an entire object tree starting with some given object. Later, you can reconstitute the object using Marshal.load.

Here's a short example. We have a class Chord that holds a collection of musical notes. We'd like to save away a particularly wonderful chord so we can e-mail it to a couple of hundred of our closest friends. They can then load it into their copy of Ruby and savor it too. Let's start with the classes for Note and Chord:

```ruby
class Note < Struct.new(:value)
  def to_s
    value.to_s
  end
end
class Chord
  def initialize(arr)
    @arr = arr
  end
  def play
    @arr.join('-')
  end
end
```

Now we'll create our masterpiece and use Marshal.dump to save a serialized version to disk:

```
c = Chord.new( [ Note.new("G"),
                 Note.new("Bb"),
                 Note.new("Db"),
                 Note.new("E") ] )
File.open("posterity", "w+") do |f|
  Marshal.dump(c, f)
end
```

Finally, our grandchildren read it in and are transported by our creation's beauty:

```
chord =   Marshal.load(File.open("posterity"))

chord.play   # =>   "G-Bb-Db-E"
```

Custom Serialization Strategy

Not all objects can be dumped: bindings, procedure objects, instances of class IO, and singleton objects cannot be saved outside the running Ruby environment (a TypeError will be raised if you try). Even if your object doesn't contain one of these problematic objects, you may want to take control of object serialization yourself.

Marshal provides the hooks you need. In the objects that require custom serialization, simply implement two instance methods: one called marshal_dump, which writes the object out to a string, and one called marshal_load, which reads a string that you had previously created and uses it to initialize a newly allocated object. (In earlier Ruby versions you'd use methods called _dump and _load, but the new versions play better with Ruby 1.8's new allocation scheme.) The instance method marshal_dump should return an object representing the state to be dumped. When the object is subsequently reconstituted using Marshal.load, the method marshal_load will be called with this object and will use it to set the state of its receiver—it will be run in the context of an allocated but not initialized object of the class being loaded.

For instance, here is a sample class that defines its own serialization. For whatever reasons, Special doesn't want to save one of its internal data members, @volatile. The author has decided to serialize the two other instance variables in an array.

```
class Special
  def initialize(valuable, volatile, precious)
    @valuable = valuable
    @volatile = volatile
    @precious = precious
  end
  def marshal_dump
    [ @valuable, @precious ]
  end
  def marshal_load(variables)
    @valuable = variables[0]
    @precious = variables[1]
    @volatile = "unknown"
  end
```

```
    def to_s
      "#@valuable #@volatile #@precious"
    end
end
obj = Special.new("Hello", "there", "World")
puts "Before: obj = #{obj}"
data = Marshal.dump(obj)
obj = Marshal.load(data)
puts "After: obj = #{obj}"
```

produces:

```
Before: obj = Hello there World
After: obj = Hello unknown World
```

For more details, see the reference section on Marshal beginning on page 574.

YAML for Marshaling

The Marshal module is built into the interpreter and uses a binary format to store objects externally. Although fast, this binary format has one major disadvantage: if the interpreter changes significantly, the marshal binary format may also change, and old dumped files may no longer be loadable.

An alternative is to use a less fussy external format, preferably one using text rather than binary files. One option, supplied as a standard library, is YAML.[3]

We can adapt our previous marshal example to use YAML. Rather than implement specific loading and dumping methods to control the marshal process, we simply define the method to_yaml_properties, which returns a list of instance variables to be saved:

```
require 'yaml'
class Special
  def initialize(valuable, volatile, precious)
    @valuable = valuable
    @volatile = volatile
    @precious = precious
  end
  def to_yaml_properties
    %w{ @precious @valuable }
  end
  def to_s
    "#@valuable #@volatile #@precious"
  end
end
```

---

3.   http://www.yaml.org. YAML stands for YAML Ain't Markup Language, but that hardly seems important.

```
obj = Special.new("Hello", "there", "World")

puts "Before: obj = #{obj}"
data = YAML.dump(obj)
obj = YAML.load(data)
puts "After: obj = #{obj}"
```

produces:

```
Before: obj = Hello there World
After: obj = Hello  World
```

We can have a look at what YAML creates as the serialized form of the object—it's pretty simple:

```
obj = Special.new("Hello", "there", "World")
puts YAML.dump(obj)
```

produces:

```
--- !ruby/object:Special
precious: World
valuable: Hello
```

Distributed Ruby

Since we can serialize an object or a set of objects into a form suitable for out-of-process storage, we can use this capability for the *transmission* of objects from one process to another. Couple this capability with the power of networking, and *voilà*—you have a distributed object system. To save you the trouble of having to write the code, we suggest using Masatoshi Seki's Distributed Ruby library (drb), which is now available as a standard Ruby library.

Using drb, a Ruby process may act as a server, as a client, or as both. A drb server acts as a source of objects, while a client is a user of those objects. To the client, it appears that the objects are local, but in reality the code is still being executed remotely.

A server starts a service by associating an object with a given port. Threads are created internally to handle incoming requests on that port, so remember to join the drb thread before exiting your program:

```
require 'drb'

class TestServer
  def add(*args)
    args.inject {|n,v| n + v}
  end
end

server = TestServer.new
DRb.start_service('druby://localhost:9000', server)
DRb.thread.join   # Don't exit just yet!
```

A simple drb client simply creates a local drb object and associates it with the object on the remote server; the local object is a proxy:

```
require 'drb'
DRb.start_service()
obj = DRbObject.new(nil, 'druby://localhost:9000')
# Now use obj
puts "Sum is: #{obj.add(1, 2, 3)}"
```

The client connects to the server and calls the method add, which uses the magic of inject to sum its arguments. It returns the result, which the client prints out:

```
Sum is: 6
```

The initial nil argument to DRbObject indicates that we want to attach to a new distributed object. We could also use an existing object.

Ho hum, you say. This sounds like Java's RMI, or CORBA, or whatever. Yes, it is a functional distributed object mechanism—but it is written in just a few hundred lines of Ruby code. No C, nothing fancy, just plain old Ruby code. Of course, it has no naming service or trader service, or anything like you'd see in CORBA, but it is simple and reasonably fast. On my 2.5GHz Power Mac system, this sample code runs at about 1,300 remote message calls per second. And if you do need naming services, DRb has a ring server that might fit the bill.

And, if you like the look of Sun's JavaSpaces, the basis of the JINI architecture, you'll be interested to know that drb is distributed with a short module that does the same kind of thing. JavaSpaces is based on a technology called Linda. To prove that its Japanese author has a sense of humor, Ruby's version of Linda is known as *Rinda*.

Compile Time? Runtime? Anytime!

The important thing to remember about Ruby is that there isn't a big difference between "compile time" and "runtime." It's all the same. You can add code to a running process. You can redefine methods on the fly, change their scope from public to private, and so on. You can even alter basic types, such as Class and Object.

Once you get used to this flexibility, it is hard to go back to a static language such as C++ or even to a half-static language such as Java.

But then, why would you want to do that?

## Chapter 26

Locking Ruby in the Safe

Walter Webcoder has a great idea for a portal site: the Web Arithmetic Page. Surrounded by all sorts of cool mathematical links and banner ads that will make him rich is a simple web form containing a text field and a button. Users type an arithmetic expression into the field, click the button, and the answer is displayed. All the world's calculators become obsolete overnight; Walter cashes in and retires to devote his life to his collection of car license plate numbers.

Implementing the calculator is easy, thinks Walter. He accesses the contents of the form field using Ruby's CGI library and uses the eval method to evaluate the string as an expression:

```
taint_1.rb
require 'cgi'

cgi = CGI.new("html4")

# Fetch the value of the form field "expression"
expr = cgi["expression"].to_s

begin
  result = eval(expr)
rescue Exception => detail
  # handle bad expressions
end

# display result back to user...
```

Roughly seven seconds after Walter puts the application online, a twelve-year-old from Waxahachie with glandular problems and no real life types system("rm *") into the form, and like his computer's files, Walter's dreams come tumbling down.

Walter learned an important lesson: *All external data is dangerous. Don't let it close to interfaces that can modify your system.* In this case, the content of the form field was the external data, and the call to eval was the security breach.

Fortunately, Ruby provides support for reducing this risk. All information from the outside world can be marked as *tainted*. When running in a safe mode, potentially dangerous methods will raise a SecurityError if passed a tainted object.

Safe Levels

The variable $SAFE determines Ruby's level of paranoia. Table 26.1 on page 429 gives more details of the checks performed at each safe level.

$SAFE	Constraints
0	No checking of the use of externally supplied (tainted) data is performed. This is Ruby's default mode.
≥ 1	Ruby disallows the use of tainted data by potentially dangerous operations.
≥ 2	Ruby prohibits the loading of program files from globally writable locations.
≥ 3	All newly created objects are considered tainted and untrusted.
≥ 4	Ruby effectively partitions the running program in two. Nontrusted objects may not be modified.

The default value of $SAFE is zero under most circumstances. However, if a Ruby script is run *setuid* or *setgid*[1] or if it run under mod_ruby, its safe level is automatically set to 1. The safe level may also be set by using the -T command-line option and by assigning to $SAFE within the program. It is not possible to lower the value of $SAFE by assignment.

The current value of $SAFE is inherited when new threads are created. However, within each thread, the value of $SAFE may be changed without affecting the value in other threads. This facility may be used to implement secure "sandboxes," areas where external code may run safely without risk to the rest of your application or system. Do this by wrapping code that you load from a file in its own, anonymous module. This will protect your program's namespace from any unintended alteration.

```
taint_2.rb
File.open(filename,"w") do |f|
   f.print ...   # write untrusted program into file.
end
Thread.start do
   $SAFE = 4
   load(filename, true)
end
```

With a $SAFE level of 4, you can load *only* wrapped files. See the description of Kernel.load on page 562 for details.

This concept is used by Clemens Wyss on Ruby CHannel (http://www.ruby.ch). On this site, you can run the code from the first edition of this book. You can also type Ruby code into a window and execute it. And yet he doesn't lose sleep at night, because his site runs your code in a sandbox.

---

1.   A Unix script may be flagged to be run under a different user or group ID than the person running it. This allows the script to have privileges that the user does not have; the script can access resources that the user would otherwise be prohibited from using. These scripts are called *setuid* or *setgid*.

You can find a listing of the source of this sandbox at `http://www.approximity.com/cgi-bin/rubybuch_wiki/wpage.rb?nd=214`.

The safe level in effect when a Proc object is created is stored with that object. The safe level may be set during the execution of a proc object without affecting the safe level of the code that invoked tha proc. A proc may not be passed to a method if it is tainted and the current safe level is greater than that in effect when the block was created.

Tainted Objects

Any Ruby object derived from some external source (for example, a string read from a file or an environment variable) is automatically marked as being tainted. If your program uses a tainted object to derive a new object, then that new object will also be tainted, as shown in the following code. Any object with external data somewhere in its past will be tainted. This tainting process is performed regardless of the current safe level. You can see whether an object is tainted using Object#tainted?.

```
# internal data                           # external data
# =============                           # =============

x1 = "a string"                           y1 = ENV["HOME"]
x1.tainted?        # =>    false          y1.tainted?        # =>    true

x2 = x1[2, 4]                             y2 = y1[2, 4]
x2.tainted?        # =>    false          y2.tainted?        # =>    true

x1 =~ /([a-z])/    # =>    0             y1 =~ /([a-z])/    # =>    2
$1.tainted?        # =>    false          $1.tainted?        # =>    true
```

You can force any object to become tainted by invoking its taint method. If the safe level is less than 3, you can remove the taint from an object by invoking untaint.[2] This is not something to do lightly.

Trusted Objects

1.9 Ruby 1.9 adds *trust*, a new dimension to the concept of safety. All objects are marked as being *trusted* or *untrusted*. In addition, running code can be trusted or not. And, when you're running untrusted code, objects that you create are untrusted, and the only objects that you can modify are those that are marked untrusted. What this in effect means is that you can create a sandbox to execute untrusted code, and code in that sandbox cannot affect objects outside that sandbox.

---

2.   You can also use some devious tricks to do this without using untaint. We'll leave it up to your darker side to find them.

Let's get more specific. Objects created while Ruby's safe level is less than 3 are trusted. However, objects created while the safe level is 3 or 4 will be untrusted. Code running at safe levels 3 and 4 is also considered to be untrusted. Because untrusted code can modify only untrusted objects, code at safe levels 3 and 4 will not be able to modify objects created at a lower safe level.

taint_5.rb

```
dog = "dog is trusted"
cat = lambda { $SAFE = 3; "cat is untrusted" }.call
puts "dog.untrusted? = #{dog.untrusted?}"
puts "cat.untrusted? = #{cat.untrusted?}"
# running at safe level 1, these operations will succeed
puts dog.upcase!
puts cat.upcase!

# running at safe level 4, we can modify the cat
lambda { $SAFE = 4; cat.downcase! }.call
puts "cat is now '#{cat}'"
# but we can't modify the dog
lambda { $SAFE = 4; dog.downcase! }.call
puts "so we never get here"
```

produces:

```
dog.untrusted? =  false
cat.untrusted? =  true
DOG IS TRUSTED
CAT IS UNTRUSTED
cat is now 'cat is untrusted'
prog.rb:17:in `downcase!': Insecure: can't modify string (SecurityError)
from /tmp/prog.rb:17:in `block in <main>'
from /tmp/prog.rb:17:in `call'
from /tmp/prog.rb:17:in `<main>'
```

You can set and unset the trusted status of an object using Object#untrust and Object#trust (but you have to be at below safe level 4 to call untrust and below safe level 3 to call trust). The method Object#untrusted? returns true if an object is untrusted.

Table 26.1. Definition of the Safe Levels

$SAFE >= 1

- The environment variables RUBYLIB and RUBYOPT are not processed, and the current directory is not added to the path.
- The command-line options -e, -i, -l, -r, -s, -S, and -x are not allowed.
- Can't start processes from $PATH if any directory in it is world-writable.
- Can't manipulate or chroot to a directory whose name is a tainted string.
- Can't glob tainted strings.
- Can't eval tainted strings.
- Can't load or require a file whose name is a tainted string (unless the load is wrapped).
- Can't manipulate or query the status of a file or pipe whose name is a tainted string.
- Can't execute a system command or exec a program from a tainted string.
- Can't pass trap a tainted string.

$SAFE >= 2

- Can't change, make, or remove directories, or use chroot.
- Can't load a file from a world-writable directory.
- Can't load a file from a tainted filename starting with ~.
- Can't use File#chmod, File#chown, File#lstat, File.stat, File#truncate, File.umask, File#flock, IO#ioctl, IO#stat, Kernel#fork, Kernel#syscall, Kernel#trap. Process.setpgid, Process.setsid, Process.setpriority, or Process.egid=.
- Can't handle signals using trap.

$SAFE >= 3

- All objects are tainted when they are created.
- Can't untaint objects.
- Can't add trust to an object.
- Objects are created untrusted.

$SAFE >= 4

- Can't modify a nontainted array, hash, or string.
- Can't modify a global variable.
- Can't access instance variables of nontainted objects.
- Can't change an environment variable.
- Can't close or reopen nontainted files.
- Can't freeze nontainted objects.
- Can't change visibility of methods (private/public/protected).
- Can't make an alias in a nontainted class or module.
- Can't get metainformation (such as method or variable lists).
- Can't define, redefine, remove, or undef a method in a nontainted class or module.
- Can't modify Object.
- Can't remove instance variables or constants from nontainted objects.
- Can't manipulate threads, terminate a thread other than the current thread, or set abort_on_exception.
- Can't have thread local variables.
- Can't raise an exception in a thread with a lower $SAFE value.
- Can't move threads between ThreadGroups.
- Can't invoke exit, exit!, or abort.
- Can load only wrapped files and can't include modules in untainted classes and modules.
- Can't convert symbol identifiers to object references.
- Can't write to files or pipes.
- Can't use autoload.
- Can't taint objects.
- Can't untrust an object.

1.9

Part IV

Ruby Library Reference

Chapter 27

Built-in Classes and Modules

This chapter documents the classes and modules built into the standard Ruby language. They are available to every Ruby program automatically; no require is required. This section does not contain the various predefined variables and constants; these are listed starting on page 327.

In the descriptions starting on page 438, we show sample invocations for each method:

---
new   String.new(*some_string*) → *new_string*

This description shows a class method that is called as String.new. The italic parameter indicates that a single string is passed in, and the arrow indicates that another string is returned from the method. Because this return value has a different name than that of the parameter, it represents a different object.

When we illustrate instance methods, we show a sample call with a dummy object name in italics as the receiver:

---
each   *str*.each(*sep=$/*) {| *record* | *block* } → *str*

The parameter to String#each is shown to have a default value; call each with no parameter, and the value of $/ will be used. This method is an iterator, so the call is followed by a block. String#each returns its receiver, so the receiver's name (*str* in this case) appears again after the arrow.

Some methods have optional parameters. We show these parameters between angle brackets, $\langle xxx \rangle$. (Additionally, we use the notation $\langle xxx \rangle^*$ to indicate zero or more occurrences of *xxx* and use $\langle xxx \rangle^+$ to indicate one or more occurrences of *xxx*.)

---
index   self.index(*str* $\langle$, *offset* $\rangle$) → *pos* or nil
---

Finally, for methods that can be called in several different forms, we list each form on a separate line.

Alphabetical Listing

Standard classes are listed alphabetically, followed by the standard modules. Within each, we list the class (or module) methods, followed by its instance methods.

Summary of Built-in Classes

Array (page 438): *Class:* [ ], new, try_convert. *Instance:* &, *, +, −, <<, <=>, ==, [ ], [ ]=, |, assoc, at, clear, combination, collect!, compact, compact!, concat, count, cycle, delete, delete_at, delete_if, each, each_index, empty?, eql?, fetch, fill, find_index, flatten, flatten!, frozen?, index, insert, join, last, length, map!, pack, permutation, pop, product, push, rassoc, reject!, replace, reverse, reverse!, reverse_each, rindex, sample, shift, shuffle, shuffle!, size, slice, slice!, sort!, to_a, to_ary, to_s, transpose, uniq, uniq!, unshift, values_at.

BasicObject (page 454): *Instance:* !, ==, !=, equal?, instance_eval, instance_exec, method_missing, __send__.

Bignum (page 457): *Instance:* Arithmetic operations, Bit operations, <=>, ==, [ ], abs, div, divmod, eql?, fdiv, magnitude, modulo, remainder, size, to_f, to_s.

Binding (page 460): *Instance:* eval.

Class (page 461): *Class:* inherited, new. *Instance:* allocate, new, superclass.

Complex (page 464): *Class:* polar, rect, rectangular. *Instance:* Arithmetic operations, ==, abs, abs2, angle, arg, conj, conjugate, denominator, eql?, fdiv, imag, imaginary, magnitude, numerator, phase, polar, quo, rect, rectangular, real, real?, to_f, to_i, to_r.

Dir (page 469): *Class:* [ ], chdir, chroot, delete, entries, exist?, exists?, foreach, getwd, glob, mkdir, new, open, pwd, rmdir, unlink. *Instance:* close, each, path, pos, pos=, read, rewind, seek, tell.

Encoding (page 474): *Class:* aliases, compatible?, default_external, default_external=, default_internal, default_internal=, find, list, locale_charmap, name_list. *Instance:* dummy?, name, names.

Enumerator (page 487): *Class:* new. *Instance:* each, each_with_index, each_with_object, next, rewind, with_index, with_object.

Exception (page 492): *Class:* exception, new. *Instance:* backtrace, exception, message, set_backtrace, status, success?, to_s.

FalseClass (page 495): *Instance:* &, ^, |.

Fiber (page 496): *Class:* new, yield. *Instance:* resume.

File (page 497): *Class:* absolute_path, atime, basename, blockdev?, chardev?, chmod, chown, ctime, delete, directory?, dirname, executable?, executable_real?, exist?, exists?, expand_path, extname, file?, fnmatch, fnmatch?, ftype, grpowned?, identical?, join, lchmod, lchown, link, lstat, mtime, new, owned?, path, pipe?, readable?, readable_real?, readlink, rename, setgid?, setuid?, size, size?, socket?, split, stat, sticky?, symlink, symlink?, truncate, umask, unlink, utime, world_readable?, world_writable?, writable?, writable_real?, zero?. *Instance:* atime, chmod, chown, ctime, flock, lchmod, lchown, lstat, mtime, path, to_path, truncate.

File::Stat (page 509): *Instance:* <=>, atime, blksize, blockdev?, blocks, chardev?, ctime, dev, dev_major, dev_minor, directory?, executable?, executable_real?, file?, ftype, gid, grpowned?, ino, mode, mtime, nlink, owned?, pipe?, rdev, rdev_major, rdev_minor, readable?, readable_real?, setgid?, setuid?, size, size?, socket?, sticky?, symlink?, uid, world_readable?, world_writable?, writable?, writable_real?, zero?.

Fixnum (page 516): *Class:* . *Instance:* Arithmetic operations, Bit operations, Comparisons, <=>, [ ], abs, div, even?, divmod, fdiv, magnitude, modulo, odd?, size, succ, to_f, to_s, zero?.

Float (page 519): *Instance:* Arithmetic operations, Comparisons, <=>, ==, abs, ceil, divmod, eql?, fdiv, finite?, floor, infinite?, magnitude, modulo, nan?, quo, round, to_f, to_i, to_int, to_r, to_s, truncate, zero?.

Hash (page 524): *Class:* [ ], new, try_convert. *Instance:* ==, [ ], [ ]=, assoc, clear, compare_by_identity, compare_by_identity?, default, default=, default_proc, default_proc=, delete, delete_if, each, each_key, each_pair, each_value, empty?, fetch, flatten, has_key?, has_value?, include?, index, invert, key, key?, keys, length, member?, merge, merge!, rassoc, rehash, reject, reject!, replace, select, shift, size, sort, store, to_a, to_hash, to_s, update, value?, values, values_at.

Integer (page 534): *Instance:* ceil, chr, denominator, downto, even?, floor, gcd, gcdlcm, integer?, lcm, next, numerator, odd?, ord, pred, round, succ, times, to_i, to_int, to_r, truncate, upto.

IO (page 537): *Class:* binread, copy_stream, for_fd, foreach, new, open, pipe, popen, read, readlines, select, sysopen, try_convert. *Instance:* <<, binmode, binmode?, bytes, chars, close, close_on_exec?, close_on_exec=, close_read, close_write, closed?, each, each_byte, each_char, each_line, eof, eof?, external_encoding, fcntl, fileno, flush, fsync, getbyte, getc, gets, internal_encoding, ioctl, isatty, lineno, lineno=, lines, pid, pos, pos=, print, printf, putc, puts, read, readbyte, readchar, readline, readlines, readpartial, read_nonblock, reopen, rewind, seek, set_encoding, stat, sync, sync=, sysread, sysseek, syswrite, tell, to_i, to_io, tty?, ungetbyte, ungetc, write, write_nonblock.

MatchData (page 576): *Instance:* [ ], begin, captures, end, length, names, offset, post_match, pre_match, regexp, size, string, to_a, to_s, values_at.

Method (page 582): *Instance:* [ ], ==, arity, call, eql?, name, owner, receiver, source_location, to_proc, unbind.

Module (page 585): *Class:* constants, nesting, new. *Instance:* <, <=, >, >=, <=>, ===, ancestors, autoload, autoload?, class_eval, class_exec, class_variable_defined?, class_variable_get, class_variable_set, class_variables, const_defined?, const_get, const_missing, const_set, constants, include?, included_modules, instance_method, instance_methods, method_defined?, module_eval, module_exec, name, private_class_method, private_instance_methods, private_method_defined?, protected_instance_methods, protected_method_defined?, public_class_method, public_instance_method, public_instance_methods, public_method_defined?, remove_class_variable. *Private:* alias_method, append_features, attr, attr_accessor, attr_reader, attr_writer, define_method, extend_object, extended, include, included, method_added, method_removed, method_undefined, module_function, private, protected, public, remove_const, remove_method, undef_method.

Mutex (page 603): *Instance:* lock, locked?, sleep, synchronize, try_lock, unlock.

NilClass (page 604): *Instance:* &, ^, |, nil?, to_a, to_c, to_f, to_i, to_r, to_s.

Numeric (page 606): *Instance:* +@, -@, <=>, abs, abs2, angle, arg, ceil, coerce, conj, conjugate, denominator, div, divmod, eql?, fdiv, floor, imag, imaginary, integer?, magnitude, modulo, nonzero?, numerator, phase, polar, quo, real, real?, rect, rectangular, remainder, round, step, to_c, to_int, truncate, zero?.

Object (page 613): *Instance:* ===, =~, !~, class, clone, define_singleton_method, display, dup, enum_for, eql?, extend, freeze, frozen?, hash, __id__, initialize_copy, inspect, instance_of?, instance_variable_defined?, instance_variable_get, instance_variable_set, instance_variables, is_a?, kind_of?, method, methods, nil?, object_id, private_methods, protected_methods, public_method, public_methods, public_send, respond_to?, send, singleton_methods, taint, tainted?, tap, to_enum, to_s, trust, untaint, untrust, untrusted?. *Private:* initialize, remove_instance_variable, singleton_method_added, singleton_method_removed, singleton_method_undefined.

Proc (page 628): *Class:* new. *Instance:* [ ], ==, ===, arity, call, curry, lambda?, source_location, to_proc, to_s, yield.

Process::Status (page 641): *Instance:* ==, &, >>, coredump?, exited?, exitstatus, pid, signaled?, stopped?, success?, stopsig, termsig, to_i, to_s.

Range (page 647): *Class:* new. *Instance:* ==, ===, begin, cover?, each, end, eql?, exclude_end?, first, include?, last, max, member?, min, step.

Rational (page 651): *Instance:* Arithmetic operations, Comparisons, <=>, ==, ceil, denominator, div, fdiv, floor, numerator, quo, round, to_f, to_i, to_r, truncate.

Regexp (page 654): *Class:* compile, escape, last_match, new, quote, try_convert, union. *Instance:* ==, ===, =~, ~, casefold?, encoding, fixed_encoding?, match, named_captures, names, options, source, to_s.

String (page 661): *Class:* new, try_convert. *Instance:* %, *, +, <<, <=>, ==, =~, [ ], [ ]=, ascii_only?, bytes, bytesize, capitalize, capitalize!, casecmp, center, chars, chr, clear, chomp, chomp!, chop, chop!, codepoints, concat, count, crypt, delete, delete!, downcase, downcase!, dump, each_byte, each_char, each_codepoint, each_line, empty?, encode, encode!, encoding, end_with?, eql?, force_encoding, getbyte, gsub, gsub!, hex, include?, index, insert, intern, length, lines, ljust, lstrip, lstrip!, match, next, next!, oct, ord, partition, replace, reverse, reverse!, rindex, rjust, rpartition, rstrip, rstrip!, scan, setbyte, size, slice, slice!, split, squeeze, squeeze!, start_with?, strip, strip!, sub, sub!, succ, succ!, sum, swapcase, swapcase!, to_c, to_f, to_i, to_r, to_s, to_str, to_sym, tr, tr!, tr_s, tr_s!, unpack, upcase, upcase!, upto, valid_encoding?.

Struct (page 687): *Class:* new, new, [ ], members. *Instance:* ==, [ ], [ ]=, each, each_pair, length, members, size, to_a, values, values_at.

Struct::Tms (page 691)

Symbol (page 692): *Class:* all_symbols. *Instance:* <=>, ==, =~, [ ], capitalize, casecmp, downcase, empty?, encoding, id2name, inspect, intern, length, match, next, size, slice, succ, swapcase, to_proc, to_s, to_sym, upcase.

Thread (page 696): *Class:* abort_on_exception, abort_on_exception=, current, exclusive, exit, fork, kill, list, main, new, pass, start, stop. *Instance:* [ ], [ ]=, abort_on_exception, abort_on_exception=, alive?, exit, group, join, keys, key?, kill, priority, priority=, raise, run, safe_level, status, stop?, terminate, value, wakeup.

ThreadGroup (page 703): *Class:* new. *Instance:* add, enclose, enclosed?, list.

Time (page 705): *Class:* at, gm, local, mktime, new, now, utc. *Instance:* +, −, <=>, asctime, ctime, day, dst?, getgm, getlocal, getutc, gmt?, gmtime, gmt_offset, gmtoff, hour, isdst, localtime, mday, min, mon, month, nsec, sec, strftime, succ, to_a, to_f, to_i, to_s, tv_nsec, tv_sec, tv_usec, usec, utc, utc?, utc_offset, wday, yday, year, zone.

TrueClass (page 714): *Instance:* &, ^, |.

UnboundMethod (page 715): *Instance:* arity, bind, name, owner, source_location.

Summary of Built-in Modules

Comparable (page 463): *Instance:* Comparisons, between?.

Enumerable (page 478): *Instance:* all?, any?, collect, count, cycle, detect, drop, drop_while, each_cons, each_slice, each_with_index, each_with_object, entries, find, find_all, find_index, first, grep, group_by, include?, inject, map, max, max_by, member?, min, min_by, minmax, minmax_by, none?, one?, partition, reduce, reject, reverse_each, select, sort, sort_by, take, take_while, to_a, zip.

Errno (page 491)

FileTest (page 515)

GC (page 523): *Class:* count, disable, enable, start, stress, stress=. *Instance:* garbage_collect.

Kernel (page 555): *Class:* __callee__, __method__, Array, Complex, Float, Integer, Rational, String, ` (backquote), abort, at_exit, autoload, autoload?, binding, block_given?, caller, catch, chomp, chop, eval, exec, exit, exit!, fail, fork, format, gem, gets, global_variables, gsub, iterator?, lambda, load, local_variables, loop, open, p, print, printf, proc, putc, puts, raise, rand, readline, readlines, require, require_relative, select, set_trace_func, sleep, spawn, sprintf, srand, sub, syscall, system, test, throw, trace_var, trap, untrace_var, warn.

Marshal (page 574): *Class:* dump, load, restore.

Math (page 579): *Class:* acos, acosh, asin, asinh, atan, atanh, atan2, cbrt, cos, cosh, erf, erfc, exp, frexp, gamma, hypot, ldexp, lgamma, log, log10, log2, sin, sinh, sqrt, tan, tanh.

ObjectSpace (page 626): *Class:* _id2ref, count_objects, define_finalizer, each_object, garbage_collect, undefine_finalizer.

Process (page 632): *Class:* abort, daemon, detach, egid, egid=, euid, euid=, exec, exit, exit!, fork, getpgid, getpgrp, getpriority, getrlimit, gid, gid=, groups, groups=, initgroups, kill, maxgroups, maxgroups=, pid, ppid, setpgid, setpgrp, setpriority, setrlimit, setsid, spawn, times, uid, uid=, wait, waitall, wait2, waitpid, waitpid2.

Process::GID (page 639): *Class:* change_privilege, eid, eid=, grant_privilege, re_exchange, re_exchangeable?, rid, sid_available?, switch.

Process::Sys (page 644): *Class:* getegid, geteuid, getgid, getuid, issetugid, setegid, seteuid, setgid, setregid, setresgid, setresuid, setreuid, setrgid, setruid, setuid.

Process::UID (page 646): *Class:* change_privilege, eid, eid=, grant_privilege, re_exchange, re_exchangeable?, rid, sid_available?, switch.

Signal (page 659): *Class:* list, trap.

Class
Array < Object

Relies on: each, <=>

Arrays are ordered, integer-indexed collections of any object. Array indexing starts at 0, as in C or Java. A negative index is assumed to be relative to the end of the array; that is, an index of −1 indicates the last element of the array, −2 is the next to last element in the array, and so on.

Mixes in

Enumerable:

```
all?, any?, collect, count, cycle, detect, drop, drop_while, each_cons,
each_slice, each_with_index, entries, find, find_all, find_index, first, grep,
group_by, include?, inject, map, max, max_by, member?, min, min_by, minmax,
minmax_by, none?, one?, partition, reduce, reject, select, sort, sort_by,
take, take_while, to_a, zip
```

Class methods

[ ]   Array[⟨ obj ⟩*] → *an_array*

Returns a new array populated with the given objects. Equivalent to the operator form Array.[](...).

```
Array.[]( 1, 'a', /^A/ )   # =>   [1, "a", /^A/]
Array[ 1, 'a', /^A/ ]      # =>   [1, "a", /^A/]
[ 1, 'a', /^A/ ]           # =>   [1, "a", /^A/]
```

new   Array.new → *an_array*
Array.new (*size=0, obj=nil*) → *an_array*
Array.new(*array*) → *an_array*
Array.new(*size*) {| *i* | *block* } → *an_array*

Returns a new array. In the first form, the new array is empty. In the second it is created with *size* copies of *obj* (that is, *size* references to the same *obj*). The third form creates a copy of the array passed as a parameter (the array is generated by calling to_ary on the parameter). In the last form, an array of the given size is created. Each element in this array is calculated by passing the element's index to the given block and storing the return value.

```
Array.new            # =>   []
Array.new(2)         # =>   [nil, nil]
Array.new(5, "A")    # =>   ["A", "A", "A", "A", "A"]

# only one instance of the default object is created
a = Array.new(2, Hash.new)
a[0]['cat'] = 'feline'
a   # =>   [{"cat"=>"feline"}, {"cat"=>"feline"}]
a[1]['cat'] = 'Felix'
a   # =>   [{"cat"=>"Felix"}, {"cat"=>"Felix"}]
```

```
a = Array.new(2) { Hash.new }  # Multiple instances
a[0]['cat'] = 'feline'
a   # =>   [{"cat"=>"feline"}, {}]

squares = Array.new(5) {|i| i*i}
squares  # =>  [0, 1, 4, 9, 16]

copy = Array.new(squares)      # initialized by copying
squares[5] = 25
squares  # =>   [0, 1, 4, 9, 16, 25]
copy     # =>   [0, 1, 4, 9, 16]
```

---

try_convert   Array.try_convert(*obj*) → *an_array* or nil

1.9 If *obj* is not already an array, attempts to convert it to one by calling its to_ary method.
Returns nil if no conversion could be made.

```
class Stooges
  def to_ary
    [ "Larry", "Curly", "Moe" ]
  end
end
Array.try_convert(Stooges.new)   # =>   ["Larry", "Curly", "Moe"]
Array.try_convert("Shemp")       # =>   nil
```

Instance methods

&   *enum* & *other_array* → *an_array*

Set Intersection—Returns a new array containing elements common to the two arrays, with
no duplicates. The rules for comparing elements are the same as for hash keys. If you need
setlike behavior, see the library class Set on page 799.

```
[ 1, 1, 3, 5 ] & [ 1, 2, 3 ]   # =>   [1, 3]
```

---

*   *enum* * *int* → *an_array*
                                                    enum * *str* → *a_string*

Repetition—With an argument that responds to to_str, equivalent to *enum*.join(*str*). Otherwise, returns a new array built by concatenating *int* copies of *enum*.

```
[ 1, 2, 3 ] * 3    # =>   [1, 2, 3, 1, 2, 3, 1, 2, 3]
[ 1, 2, 3 ] * "--"  # =>   "1--2--3"
```

+   *enum* + *other_array* → *an_array*

Concatenation—Returns a new array built by concatenating the two arrays together to produce a third array.

```
[ 1, 2, 3 ] + [ 4, 5 ]   # =>   [1, 2, 3, 4, 5]
```

−   *enum* - *other_array* → *an_array*

Array Difference—Returns a new array that is a copy of the original array, removing any items that also appear in *other_array*. If you need setlike behavior, see the library class Set on page 799.

```
[ 1, 1, 2, 2, 3, 3, 4, 5 ] - [ 1, 2, 4 ]   # =>   [3, 3, 5]
```

<<   *enum << obj → enum*

Append—Pushes the given object on to the end of this array. This expression returns the array itself, so several appends may be chained together. See also Array#push.

```
[ 1, 2 ] << "c" << "d" << [ 3, 4 ]   # =>   [1, 2, "c", "d", [3, 4]]
```

<=>   *enum <=> other_array → −1, 0, +1*

Comparison—Returns an integer −1, 0, or +1 if this array is less than, equal to, or greater than *other_array*. Each object in each array is compared (using <=>). If any value isn't equal, then that inequality is the return value. If all the values found are equal, then the return is based on a comparison of the array lengths. Thus, two arrays are "equal" according to Array#<=> if and only if they have the same length and the value of each element is equal to the value of the corresponding element in the other array.

```
[ "a", "a", "c" ]    <=> [ "a", "b", "c" ]   # =>   -1
[ 1, 2, 3, 4, 5, 6 ] <=> [ 1, 2 ]            # =>   1
```

==   *enum == obj →* true or false

Equality—Two arrays are equal if they contain the same number of elements and if each element is equal to (according to Object#==) the corresponding element in the other array. If *obj* is not an array, attempt to convert it using to_ary and return *obj==enum*.

```
[ "a", "c" ]    == [ "a", "c", 7 ]   # =>   false
[ "a", "c", 7 ] == [ "a", "c", 7 ]   # =>   true
[ "a", "c", 7 ] == [ "a", "d", "f" ] # =>   false
```

[ ]   *enum[int] → obj* or nil
enum[start, length] → an_array or nil
enum[range] → an_array or nil

Element Reference—Returns the element at index *int*, returns a subarray starting at index *start* and continuing for *length* elements, or returns a subarray specified by *range*. Negative indices count backward from the end of the array (−1 is the last element). Returns nil if the index of the first element selected is greater than the array size. If the start index equals the array size and a *length* or *range* parameter is given, an empty array is returned. Equivalent to Array#slice.

```
a = [ "a", "b", "c", "d", "e" ]
a[2] + a[0] + a[1]   # =>   "cab"
a[6]                 # =>   nil
a[1, 2]              # =>   ["b", "c"]
a[1..3]              # =>   ["b", "c", "d"]
a[4..7]              # =>   ["e"]
a[6..10]             # =>   nil
a[-3, 3]             # =>   ["c", "d", "e"]
```

```
# special cases
a[5]      # =>   nil
a[5, 1]   # =>   []
a[5..10]  # =>   []
```

[ ]=
$$enum[int] = obj \rightarrow obj$$
$$enum[start, length] = obj \rightarrow obj$$
$$enum[range] = obj \rightarrow obj$$

Element Assignment—Sets the element at index *int*, replaces a subarray starting at index *start* and continuing for *length* elements, or replaces a subarray specified by *range*. If *int* is greater than the current capacity of the array, the array grows automatically. A negative *int* will count backward from the end of the array. Inserts elements if *length* is zero. If *obj* is an array, the form with the single index will insert that array into *enum*, and the forms with a length or with a range will replace the given elements in *enum* with the array contents. An IndexError is raised if a negative index points past the beginning of the array. (Prior to Ruby 1.9, assigning nil with the second and third forms of element assignment could delete the corresponding array elements; now it simply assigns nil to them.) See also Array#push and Array#unshift.

```
a = Array.new              # =>   []
a[4] = "4";            a  # =>   [nil, nil, nil, nil, "4"]
a[0] = [ 1, 2, 3 ];    a  # =>   [[1, 2, 3], nil, nil, nil, "4"]
a[0, 3] = [ 'a', 'b', 'c' ]; a # => ["a", "b", "c", nil, "4"]
a[1..2] = [ 1, 2 ];    a  # =>   ["a", 1, 2, nil, "4"]
a[0, 2] = "?";         a  # =>   ["?", 2, nil, "4"]
a[0..2] = "A", "B", "C"; a # =>  ["A", "B", "C", "4"]
a[-1]  = "Z";          a  # =>   ["A", "B", "C", "Z"]
a[1..-1] = nil;        a  # =>   ["A", nil]
```

|
$$enum \mid other\_array \rightarrow an\_array$$

Set Union—Returns a new array by joining this array with *other_array*, removing duplicates. The rules for comparing elements are the same as for hash keys. If you need setlike behavior, see the library class Set on page 799.

```
[ "a", "b", "c" ] | [ "c", "d", "a" ]  # =>  ["a", "b", "c", "d"]
```

---

assoc
$$enum.assoc(\ obj\ ) \rightarrow an\_array \text{ or nil}$$

Searches through an array whose elements are also arrays comparing *obj* with the first element of each contained array using *obj*.== . Returns the first contained array that matches (that is, the first *assoc*iated array) or nil if no match is found. See also Array#rassoc.

```
s1 = [ "colors", "red", "blue", "green" ]
s2 = [ "letters", "a", "b", "c" ]
s3 = "foo"
a  = [ s1, s2, s3 ]
a.assoc("letters")  # =>   ["letters", "a", "b", "c"]
a.assoc("foo")      # =>   nil
```

Array

at *enum*.at(*int*) → *obj* or nil

Returns the element at index *int*. A negative index counts from the end of *enum*. Returns nil if the index is out of range. See also Array#[].

```
a = [ "a", "b", "c", "d", "e" ]
a.at(0)    # =>    "a"
a.at(-1)   # =>    "e"
```

clear *enum*.clear → *enum*

Removes all elements from *enum*.

```
a = [ "a", "b", "c", "d", "e" ]
a.clear   # =>   []
```

combination *enum*.combination(*size*) → *enumerator*
enum.combination(*size*) {| *array* | *block* } → *enum*

1.9 Constructs all combinations of the elements of *enum* of length *size*. If called with a block, passes each combination to that block; otherwise, returns an enumerator object. An empty result is generated if no combinations of the given length exist. See also Array#permutation.

```
a = [ "a", "b", "c" ]
a.combination(1).to_a  # =>    [["a"], ["b"], ["c"]]
a.combination(2).to_a  # =>    [["a", "b"], ["a", "c"], ["b", "c"]]
a.combination(3).to_a  # =>    [["a", "b", "c"]]
a.combination(4).to_a  # =>    []
```

collect! *enum*.collect! {| *obj* | *block* } → *enum*

Invokes *block* once for each element of *enum*, replacing the element with the value returned by *block*. See also Enumerable#collect.

```
a = [ "a", "b", "c", "d" ]
a.collect! {|x| x + "!" }  # =>   ["a!", "b!", "c!", "d!"]
a                          # =>   ["a!", "b!", "c!", "d!"]
```

compact *enum*.compact → *an_array*

Returns a copy of *enum* with all nil elements removed.

```
[ "a", nil, "b", nil, "c", nil ].compact   # =>   ["a", "b", "c"]
```

compact! *enum*.compact! → *enum* or nil

Removes nil elements from *enum*. Returns nil if no changes were made.

```
[ "a", nil, "b", nil, "c" ].compact!   # =>   ["a", "b", "c"]
[ "a", "b", "c" ].compact!             # =>   nil
```

concat *enum*.concat(*other_array*) → *enum*

Appends the elements in *other_array* to *enum*.

```
[ "a", "b" ].concat( ["c", "d"] )   # =>   ["a", "b", "c", "d"]
```

count

enum.count(*obj*) → *int*

enum.count {| *obj* | *block* } → *int*

1.9

Returns the count of objects in *enum* that equal *obj* or for which the block returns a true value. Returns an Enumerator if neither an argument nor a block is given (which seems strange...). Shadows the corresponding method in Enumerable.

```
[1, 2, 3, 4].count(3)              # =>   1
[1, 2, 3, 4].count {|obj| obj > 2 }  # =>   2
```

---

cycle

enum.cycle {| *obj* | *block* } → nil or *enumerator*

enum.cycle(*times*) {| *obj* | *block* } → nil or *enumerator*

1.9

Returns nil if *enum* has no elements; otherwise, passes the elements, one at a time to the block. When it reaches the end, it repeats. The number of times it repeats is set by the parameter. If the parameter is missing, cycles forever. Equivalent to *enum*.to_a.cycle. See Array#cycle. Returns an Enumerator object if no block is given.

```
[1,2,3].cycle(3)        # =>   #<Enumerator:0x0a4fec>
[1,2,3].cycle(3).to_a   # =>   [1, 2, 3, 1, 2, 3, 1, 2, 3]

columns = [ 1, 2, 3 ]
data = %w{ a b c d e f g h }

columns.cycle do |column_number|
  print data.shift, "\t"
  break if data.empty?
  puts if column_number == columns.last
end
puts
```

produces:

```
a b c
d e f
g h
```

---

delete

enum.delete(*obj*) → *obj* or nil

enum.delete(*obj*) { *block* } → *obj* or nil

Deletes items from *enum* that are equal to *obj*. If the item is not found, returns nil. If the optional code block is given, returns the result of *block* if the item is not found.

```
a = [ "a", "b", "b", "b", "c" ]
a.delete("b")                   # =>   "b"
a                               # =>   ["a", "c"]
a.delete("z")                   # =>   nil
a.delete("z") { "not found" }   # =>   "not found"
```

---

delete_at

enum.delete_at(*index*) → *obj* or nil

Deletes the element at the specified index, returning that element or nil if the index is out of range. See also Array#slice!.

```
a = %w( ant bat cat dog )
a.delete_at(2)    # =>   "cat"
a                 # =>   ["ant", "bat", "dog"]
a.delete_at(99)   # =>   nil
```

delete_if   *enum*.delete_if { | *item* | *block* } → *enum*

Deletes every element of *enum* for which *block* evaluates to true.

```
a = [ "a", "b", "c" ]
a.delete_if {|x| x >= "b" }  # =>   ["a"]
```

each   *enum*.each { | *item* | *block* } → *enum*

Calls *block* once for each element in *enum*, passing that element as a parameter.

```
a = [ "a", "b", "c" ]
a.each {|x| print x, " -- " }
```

produces:

```
a -- b -- c --
```

each_index   *enum*.each_index { | *index* | *block* } → *enum*

Same as Array#each but passes the index of the element instead of the element itself.

```
a = [ "a", "b", "c" ]
a.each_index {|x| print x, " -- " }
```

produces:

```
0 -- 1 -- 2 --
```

empty?   *enum*.empty? → true or false

Returns true if *enum* array contains no elements.

```
[].empty?              # =>   true
[ 1, 2, 3 ].empty?     # =>   false
```

eql?   *enum*.eql?(*other*) → true or false

Returns true if *enum* and *other* are the same object or if *other* is an object of class Array with the same length and content as *enum*. Elements in the arrays are compared using Object#eql?. See also Array#<=>.

```
[ "a", "b", "c" ].eql?(["a", "b", "c"])   # =>   true
[ "a", "b", "c" ].eql?(["a", "b"])        # =>   false
[ "a", "b", "c" ].eql?(["b", "c", "d"])   # =>   false
```

fetch   *enum*.fetch(*index*) → *obj*
                                          enum.fetch(*index*, *default*) → *obj*
                                      enum.fetch(*index*) { | *i* | *block* } → *obj*

Tries to return the element at position *index*. If the index lies outside the array, the first form throws an IndexError exception, the second form returns *default*, and the third form returns the value of invoking the block, passing in the index. Negative values of *index* count from the end of the array.

```
a = [ 11, 22, 33, 44 ]
a.fetch(1)              # =>   22
a.fetch(-1)             # =>   44
a.fetch(-1, 'cat')      # =>   44
a.fetch(4, 'cat')       # =>   "cat"
a.fetch(4) {|i| i*i }   # =>   16
```

fill

> *enum*.fill(*obj*) → *enum*
> *enum*.fill(*obj*, *start* ⟨ , *length* ⟩) → *enum*
> *enum*.fill(*obj*, *range*) → *enum*
> *enum*.fill { | *i* | *block* } → *enum*
> *enum*.fill(*start* ⟨ , *length* ⟩) { | *i* | *block* } → *enum*
> *enum*.fill(*range*) { | *i* | *block* } → *enum*

The first three forms set the selected elements of *enum* (which may be the entire array) to *obj*. A *start* of nil is equivalent to zero. A *length* of nil is equivalent to *enum*.length. The last three forms fill the array with the value of the block. The block is passed the absolute index of each element to be filled.

```
a = [ "a", "b", "c", "d" ]
a.fill("x")             # =>   ["x", "x", "x", "x"]
a.fill("z", 2, 2)       # =>   ["x", "x", "z", "z"]
a.fill("y", 0..1)       # =>   ["y", "y", "z", "z"]
a.fill {|i| i*i}        # =>   [0, 1, 4, 9]
a.fill(-3) {|i| i+100}  # =>   [0, 101, 102, 103]
```

find_index

> *enum*.find_index(*obj*) → *int* or nil
> *enum*.find_index { | *item* | *block* } → *int* or nil

1.9

Returns the index of the first object in *enum* that is == to *obj* or for which the block returns a true value. Returns nil if no match is found. See also Enumerable#select and Array#rindex.

```
a = [ "a", "b", "c", "b" ]
a.find_index("b")             # =>   1
a.find_index("z")             # =>   nil
a.find_index {|item| item > "a"}   # =>   1
```

flatten

> *enum*.flatten(*level* = -1) → *an_array*

1.9

Returns a new array that is a one-dimensional flattening of this array (recursively). That is, for every element that is an array, extracts its elements into the new array. The level parameter controls how deeply the flattening occurs. If less than zero, all subarrays are expanded. If zero, no flattening takes place. If greater than zero, only that depth of subarray is expanded.

```
s = [ 1, 2, 3 ]          # =>   [1, 2, 3]
t = [ 4, 5, 6, [7, 8] ]  # =>   [4, 5, 6, [7, 8]]
a = [ s, t, 9, 10 ]      # =>   [[1, 2, 3], [4, 5, 6, [7, 8]], 9, 10]
a.flatten(0)             # =>   [[1, 2, 3], [4, 5, 6, [7, 8]], 9, 10]
a.flatten                # =>   [1, 2, 3, 4, 5, 6, 7, 8, 9, 10]
a.flatten(1)             # =>   [1, 2, 3, 4, 5, 6, [7, 8], 9, 10]
a.flatten(2)             # =>   [1, 2, 3, 4, 5, 6, 7, 8, 9, 10]
```

flatten!

enum.flatten!(*level* = -1) → *enum* or nil

1.9 Same as Array#flatten but modifies the receiver in place. Returns nil if no modifications were made (i.e., *enum* contains no subarrays).

```
a = [ 1, 2, [3, [4, 5] ] ]
a.flatten!  # =>   [1, 2, 3, 4, 5]
a.flatten!  # =>   nil
a           # =>   [1, 2, 3, 4, 5]
```

frozen?

enum.frozen?! → true or false

1.9 Returns true if *enum* is frozen or if it is in the middle of being sorted.

index

enum.index(*obj*) → *int* or nil

enum.index {| *item* | *block* } → *int* or nil

1.9 Synonym for Array#find_index.

insert

enum.insert(*index*, ⟨ *obj* ⟩⁺) → *enum*

If *index* is not negative, inserts the given values before the element with the given index. If *index* is negative, adds the values after the element with the given index (counting from the end).

```
a = %w{ a b c d }
a.insert(2, 99)        # =>   ["a", "b", 99, "c", "d"]
a.insert(-2, 1, 2, 3)  # =>   ["a", "b", 99, "c", 1, 2, 3, "d"]
a.insert(-1, "e")      # =>   ["a", "b", 99, "c", 1, 2, 3, "d", "e"]
```

join

enum.join(*separator*=$,) → *str*

Returns a string created by converting each each element of the array to a string and concatenating them, separated each by *separator*.

```
[ "a", "b", "c" ].join       # =>   "abc"
[ "a", "b", "c" ].join("-")  # =>   "a-b-c"
```

last

enum.last → *obj* or nil

enum.last(*count*) → *an_array*

Returns the last element, or last *count* elements, of *enum*. If the array is empty, the first form returns nil, and the second returns an empty array. (first is defined by Enumerable.)

```
[ "w", "x", "y", "z" ].last     # =>   "z"
[ "w", "x", "y", "z" ].last(1)  # =>   ["z"]
[ "w", "x", "y", "z" ].last(3)  # =>   ["x", "y", "z"]
```

Table 27.1. Template Characters for Array#pack

Directive	Meaning
@	Move to absolute position
A	Sequence of bytes (space padded, count is width)
a	Sequence of bytes (null padded, count is width)
B	Bit string (descending bit order)
b	Bit string (ascending bit order)
C	Unsigned byte
c	Byte
D, d	Double-precision float, native format
E	Double-precision float, little-endian byte order
e	Single-precision float, little-endian byte order
F, f	Single-precision float, native format
G	Double-precision float, network (big-endian) byte order
g	Single-precision float, network (big-endian) byte order
H	Hex string (high nibble first)
h	Hex string (low nibble first)
I	Unsigned integer
i	Integer
L	Unsigned long
l	Long
M	Quoted printable, MIME encoding (see RFC2045)
m	Base64-encoded string; by default adds linefeeds every 60 characters; "m0" suppresses linefeeds
N	Long, network (big-endian) byte order
n	Short, network (big-endian) byte order
P	Pointer to a structure (fixed-length string)
p	Pointer to a null-terminated string
Q, q	64-bit number
S	Unsigned short
s	Short
U	UTF-8
u	UU-encoded string
V	Long, little-endian byte order
v	Short, little-endian byte order
w	BER-compressed integer[1]
X	Back up a byte
x	Null byte
Z	Same as "a," except a null byte is appended if the * modifier is given

[1] The octets of a BER-compressed integer represent an unsigned integer in base 128, most significant digit first, with as few digits as possible. Bit eight (the high bit) is set on each byte except the last (*Self-Describing Binary Data Representation*, MacLeod).

1.9

1.9

1.9

1.9

Array

---

length *enum*.length → *int*

Returns the number of elements in *enum*.

```
[ 1, nil, 3, nil, 5 ].length   # =>   5
```

---

map! *enum*.map! { | *obj* | *block* } → *enum*

Synonym for Array#collect!.

---

pack *enum*.pack (*template*) → *binary_string*

Packs the contents of *enum* into a binary sequence according to the directives in *template* (see Table 27.1 on the previous page). Directives A, a, and Z may be followed by a count, which gives the width of the resulting field. The remaining directives also may take a count, indicating the number of array elements to convert. If the count is an asterisk (*), all remaining array elements will be converted. Any of the directives sSiIlL may be followed by an underscore (_) or bang (!) to use the underlying platform's native size for the specified type; otherwise, they use a platform-independent size. Spaces are ignored in the template string. Comments starting with # to the next newline or end of string are also ignored. See also String#unpack on page 684.

```
a = [ "a", "b", "c" ]
n = [ 65, 66, 67 ]
a.pack("A3A3A3")   # =>   "a␣␣b␣␣c␣␣"
a.pack("a3a3a3")   # =>   "a\x00\x00b\x00\x00c\x00\x00"
n.pack("ccc")      # =>   "ABC"
```

---

permutation *enum*.permutation(*size*) → *enumerator*
enum.permutation(*size*) { | *array* | *block* } → *enum*

Constructs all permutations of the elements of *enum* of length *size*. If called with a block, passes each permutation to that block; otherwise, returns an enumerator object. An empty result is generated if no permutations of the given length exist. See also Array#combination.

```
words = {}
File.readlines("/usr/share/dict/words").map(&:chomp).each do |word|
  words[word.downcase] = 1
end

%w{ c a m e l }.permutation(5) do |letters|
  anagram = letters.join
  puts anagram if words[anagram]
end
```

produces:

```
camel
clame
cleam
macle
```

pop

enum.pop(⟨ n ⟩[*]) → obj or nil

1.9

Removes the last element (or the last *n* elements) from *enum*. Returns whatever is removed or nil if the array is empty.

```
a = %w{ f r a b j o u s }
a.pop      # =>  "s"
a          # =>  ["f", "r", "a", "b", "j", "o", "u"]
a.pop(3)   # =>  ["j", "o", "u"]
a          # =>  ["f", "r", "a", "b"]
```

product

enum.product(⟨ arrays ⟩[*]) → result_array

1.9

Generates all combinations of selecting an element each from *enum* and from any arrays passed as arguments. The number of elements in the result is the product of the lengths of *enum* and the lengths of the arguments (so if any of these arrays is empty, the result will be an empty array). Each element in the result is an array containing *n* + 1 elements, where *n* is the number of arguments.

```
[1, 2].product([3, 4])       # =>  [[1, 3], [1, 4], [2, 3], [2, 4]]
[1, 2].product([3, 4], [5])  # =>  [[1, 3, 5], [1, 4, 5], [2, 3, 5], [2,
                                       4, 5]]
[1, 2].product               # =>  [[1], [2]]
```

push

enum.push(⟨ obj ⟩[*]) → enum

Appends the given argument(s) to *enum*.

```
a = [ "a", "b", "c" ]
a.push("d", "e", "f")  # =>  ["a", "b", "c", "d", "e", "f"]
```

rassoc

enum.rassoc(key) → an_array or nil

Searches through the array whose elements are also arrays. Compares *key* with the second element of each contained array using ==. Returns the first contained array that matches. See also Array#assoc.

```
a = [ [ 1, "one"], [2, "two"], [3, "three"], ["ii", "two"] ]
a.rassoc("two")    # =>  [2, "two"]
a.rassoc("four")   # =>  nil
```

reject!

enum.reject! { block } item → enum or nil

Equivalent to Array#delete_if but returns nil if no changes were made. Also see Enumerable#reject.

replace

enum.replace(other_array) → enum

Replaces the contents of *enum* with the contents of *other_array*, truncating or expanding if necessary.

```
a = [ "a", "b", "c", "d", "e" ]
a.replace([ "x", "y", "z" ])   # =>  ["x", "y", "z"]
a                              # =>  ["x", "y", "z"]
```

reverse

enum.reverse → *an_array*

Returns a new array using *enum*'s elements in reverse order.

```
[ "a", "b", "c" ].reverse   # =>   ["c", "b", "a"]
[ 1 ].reverse               # =>   [1]
```

reverse!

enum.reverse! → *enum*

Reverses *enum* in place.

```
a = [ "a", "b", "c" ]
a.reverse!      # =>   ["c", "b", "a"]
a               # =>   ["c", "b", "a"]
[ 1 ].reverse!  # =>   [1]
```

reverse_each

enum.reverse_each {| *item* | *block* } → *enum*

Same as Array#each but traverses *enum* in reverse order.

```
a = [ "a", "b", "c" ]
a.reverse_each {|x| print x, " " }
```

produces:

```
c b a
```

rindex

enum.rindex(*obj*) → *int* or nil

enum.rindex {| *item* | *block* } → *int* or nil

1.9 Returns the index of the last object in *enum* that is == to *obj* or for which the block returns a true value. Returns nil if no match is found. See also Enumerable#select and Array#index.

```
a = [ "a", "b", "e", "b", "d" ]
a.rindex("b")                      # =>   3
a.rindex("z")                      # =>   nil
a.rindex {|item| item =~ /[aeiou]/}  # =>   2
```

sample

enum.sample(*n*=1) → *an_array* or nil

1.9 Returns min(*n*, *enum*.size) random elements from *enum* or nil if *enum* is empty and no argument is given.

```
a = [ "a", "b", "c", "d" ]
a.sample      # =>   "c"
a.sample(3)   # =>   ["c", "a", "d"]
a.sample(6)   # =>   ["d", "c", "b", "a"]
b = []
b.sample      # =>   nil
```

shift

enum.shift(n = 1) → *obj* or nil

1.9 Returns the first *n* elements (or the first element with no argument) of *enum* and removes it (shifting all other elements down by one). Returns nil if the array is empty.

```
args = [ "-m", "-q", "-v", "filename" ]
args.shift        # =>   "-m"
args.shift(2)     # =>   ["-q", "-v"]
args              # =>   ["filename"]
```

shuffle

enum.shuffle → *an_array*

1.9 Returns an array containing the elements of *enum* in random order.

```
[ 1, 2, 3, 4, 5 ].shuffle   # =>   [3, 4, 5, 1, 2]
```

shuffle!

enum.shuffle! → *enum*

1.9 Randomizes the order of the elements of *enum*.

size

enum.size → *int*

Synonym for Array#length.

slice

enum.slice(*int*) → *obj*
enum.slice(*start*, *length*) → *an_array*
enum.slice(*range*) → *an_array*

Synonym for Array#[ ].

```
a = [ "a", "b", "c", "d", "e" ]
a.slice(2) + a.slice(0) + a.slice(1)   # =>   "cab"
a.slice(6)                             # =>   nil
a.slice(1, 2)                          # =>   ["b", "c"]
a.slice(1..3)                          # =>   ["b", "c", "d"]
a.slice(4..7)                          # =>   ["e"]
a.slice(6..10)                         # =>   nil
a.slice(-3, 3)                         # =>   ["c", "d", "e"]
# special cases
a.slice(5)                             # =>   nil
a.slice(5, 1)                          # =>   []
a.slice(5..10)                         # =>   []
```

slice!

enum.slice!(*int*) → *obj* or nil
enum.slice!(*start*, *length*) → *an_array* or nil
enum.slice!(*range*) → *an_array* or nil

Deletes the element(s) given by an index (optionally with a length) or by a range. Returns the deleted object, subarray, or nil if the index is out of range.

```
a = [ "a", "b", "c" ]
a.slice!(1)     # =>   "b"
a               # =>   ["a", "c"]
a.slice!(-1)    # =>   "c"
a               # =>   ["a"]
a.slice!(100)   # =>   nil
a               # =>   ["a"]
```

Array

sort!

$enum.\text{sort!} \rightarrow enum$
$enum.\text{sort!} \{\,|\,a,b\,|\ block\,\} \rightarrow enum$

Sorts *enum* in place (see Enumerable#sort). *enum* is effectively frozen while a sort is in progress.

```
a = [ "d", "a", "e", "c", "b" ]
a.sort!  # =>  ["a", "b", "c", "d", "e"]
a        # =>  ["a", "b", "c", "d", "e"]
```

to_a

$enum.\text{to\_a} \rightarrow enum$
$array\_subclass.\text{to\_a} \rightarrow array$

If *enum* is an array, returns *enum*. If *enum* is a subclass of Array, invokes to_ary and uses the result to create a new array object.

to_ary

$enum.\text{to\_ary} \rightarrow enum$

Returns *enum*.

to_s

$enum.\text{to\_s} \rightarrow str$

1.9

Returns a string representation of *enum*. (Prior to Ruby 1.9, this representation was the same as *enum*.join. Now it is the array as a literal.)

```
[ 1, 3, 5, 7, 9 ].to_s  # =>  "[1, 3, 5, 7, 9]"
```

transpose

$enum.\text{transpose} \rightarrow an\_array$

Assumes that *enum* is an array of arrays and transposes the rows and columns.

```
a = [[1,2], [3,4], [5,6]]
a.transpose  # =>  [[1, 3, 5], [2, 4, 6]]
```

uniq

$enum.\text{uniq} \rightarrow an\_array$

Returns a new array by removing duplicate values in *enum*, where duplicates are detected by comparing using eql? and hash.

```
a = [ "a", "a", "b", "b", "c" ]
a.uniq  # =>  ["a", "b", "c"]
```

uniq!

$enum.\text{uniq!} \rightarrow enum$ or nil

Same as Array#uniq but modifies the receiver in place. Returns nil if no changes are made (that is, no duplicates are found).

```
a = [ "a", "a", "b", "b", "c" ]
a.uniq!  # =>  ["a", "b", "c"]
b = [ "a", "b", "c" ]
b.uniq!  # =>  nil
```

unshift

$enum.\text{unshift}(\ \langle\,obj\,\rangle^{+}\ ) \rightarrow enum$

Prepends object(s) to *enum*.

```
a = [ "b", "c", "d" ]
a.unshift("a")    # =>  ["a", "b", "c", "d"]
a.unshift(1, 2)   # =>  [1, 2, "a", "b", "c", "d"]
```

---

values_at   *enum*.values_at(⟨ *selector* ⟩*) → *an_array*

Returns an array containing the elements in *enum* corresponding to the given selector(s). The selectors may be either integer indices or ranges.

```
a = %w{ a b c d e f }
a.values_at(1, 3, 5)        # =>   ["b", "d", "f"]
a.values_at(1, 3, 5, 7)     # =>   ["b", "d", "f", nil]
a.values_at(-1, -3, -5, -7) # =>   ["f", "d", "b", nil]
a.values_at(1..3, 2...5)    # =>   ["b", "c", "d", "c", "d", "e"]
```

Class
BasicObject

1.9

BasicObject is the root of Ruby's class hierarchy. It deliberately has just a few methods, allowing it to be conveniently used as the basis for a number of metaprogramming techniques.

If you write code in a direct descendent of BasicObject, you will not have unqualified access to the methods in Kernel, which normally get mixed in to Object. This example illustrates how to invoke Kernel methods explicitly:

```ruby
class SimpleBuilder < BasicObject
  def __puts_at_indent__(string)
    ::Kernel.puts " " * @indent + string
  end
  def method_missing(name, *args, &block)
    @indent ||= 0
    __puts_at_indent__("<#{name}>")
    @indent += 2
    __puts_at_indent__(args.join) unless args.empty?
    yield if ::Kernel.block_given?
    @indent -= 2
    __puts_at_indent__("</#{name}>")
  end
end
r = SimpleBuilder.new
r.person do
  r.name "Dave"
  r.address do
    r.street "123 Main"
    r.city   "Pleasantville"
  end
end
```

produces:

```
<person>
  <name>
    Dave
  </name>
  <address>
    <street>
      123 Main
    </street>
    <city>
      Pleasantville
    </city>
  </address>
</person>
```

Instance methods

!
! ! *obj* → true or false

Returns false unless *obj* is false. It is defined in BasicObject so ! is defined for all objects in Ruby.

==
== *obj* == *other_obj* → true or false

Equality—At the BasicObject level, == returns true only if *obj* and *other_obj* are the same object. Typically, this method is overridden in descendent classes to provide class-specific meaning.

!=
!= *obj* != *other* → true or false

Returns the opposite of BasicObject#==.

equal?
equal? *obj*.equal?(*other_obj*) → true or false

Alias for BasicObject#==.

instance_eval
instance_eval *obj*.instance_eval(*string* ⟨ , *file* ⟨ , *line* ⟩ ⟩) → *other_obj*
obj.instance_eval { *block* } → *other_obj*

Evaluates a string containing Ruby source code, or the given block, within the context of the receiver (*obj*). To set the context, the variable self is set to *obj* while the code is executing, giving the code access to *obj*'s instance variables. In the version of instance_eval that takes a String, the optional second and third parameters supply a filename and starting line number that are used when reporting compilation errors.

```ruby
class Klass
  def initialize
    @secret = 99
  end
end
k = Klass.new
k.instance_eval { @secret }   # =>   99
```

When metaprogramming, instance_eval is often used to execute the methods in a block in the context of the caller:

```ruby
class Recorder < BasicObject
  attr_reader :__calls__
  def method_missing(name, *args, &block)
    @__calls__ ||= []
    @__calls__ << [ name, args ]
  end
  def record(&block)
    instance_eval(&block)
  end
end
```

```
r = Recorder.new
r.record do
  disable "safety"
  pull    "control rod", dir: "out"
  run
end
p r.__calls__
```

produces:

```
[[:disable, ["safety"]], [:pull, ["control rod", {:dir=>"out"}]], [:run, []]]
```

---

instance_exec   *obj*.instance_exec(⟨ args ⟩* {| *args* | *block* } → *other_obj*)

1.9

Executes the block with self set to *obj*, passing *args* as parameters to the block.

```
class Dummy < BasicObject
  def initialize
    @iv = 33
  end
  def double_and_call(value, &block)
    instance_exec(value*2, &block)
  end
end
d = Dummy.new
d.double_and_call(22) do |param|
  ::Kernel::puts "Parameter = #{param}"
  ::Kernel::puts "@iv = #{@iv}"
end
```

produces:

```
Parameter = 44
@iv = 33
```

---

method_missing   *obj*.method_missing(*symbol* ⟨ , *args* ⟩) → *other_obj*

Invoked by Ruby when *obj* is sent a message it cannot handle. *symbol* is the symbol for the method called, and *args* are any arguments that were passed to it. method_missing can be used to implement proxies, delegators, and forwarders. It can also be used to simulate the existence of methods in the receiver, as the example at the start of this section shows.

__send__   *obj*.__send__(*symbol* ⟨ , *args* ⟩* ⟨ , &*block* ⟩) → *other_obj*

Invokes the method identified by *symbol*, passing it any arguments and block.

```
class Klass < BasicObject
  def hello(*args)
    "Hello " + args.join(' ')
  end
end
k = Klass.new
k.__send__ :hello, "gentle", "readers"  # =>  "Hello gentle readers"
```

Class

Bignum < Integer

Bignum objects hold integers outside the range of Fixnum. Bignum objects are created automatically when integer calculations would otherwise overflow a Fixnum. When a calculation involving Bignum objects returns a result that will fit in a Fixnum, the result is automatically converted.

For the purposes of the bitwise operations and [ ], a Bignum is treated as if it were an infinite-length bitstring with 2's complement representation.

While Fixnum values are immediate, Bignum objects are not—assignment and parameter passing work with references to objects, not the objects themselves.

Instance methods

Arithmetic operations

Performs various arithmetic operations on *big*.

big	+	*number*	Addition
big	−	*number*	Subtraction
big	*	*number*	Multiplication
big	/	*number*	Division
big	%	*number*	Modulo
big	**	*number*	Exponentiation
big	-@		Unary minus

Bit operations

Performs various operations on the binary representations of the Bignum.

~ *big*			Invert bits
big	|	*number*	Bitwise OR
big	&	*number*	Bitwise AND
big	^	*number*	Bitwise EXCLUSIVE OR
big	<<	*number*	Left-shift *number* bits
big	>>	*number*	Right-shift *number* bits (with sign extension)

<=> $big <=> number \rightarrow -1, 0, +1$

Comparison—Returns -1, 0, or $+1$ depending on whether *big* is less than, equal to, or greater than *number*. This is the basis for the tests in Comparable.

== $big == obj \rightarrow$ true or false

Returns true only if *obj* has the same value as *big*. Contrast this with Bignum#eql?, which requires *obj* to be a Bignum.

```
68719476736 == 68719476736.0   # =>   true
```

B ignum

[ ] $big[\,n\,] \rightarrow 0, 1$

Bit Reference—Returns the *n*th bit in the (assumed) binary representation of *big*, where *big*[0] is the least significant bit.

```
a = 9**15
```
```
50.downto(0) do |n|
  print a[n]
end
```

produces:

000101110110100000111000011110010100111100010111001

abs $big.\text{abs} \rightarrow bignum$

Returns the absolute value of *big*.

```
1234567890987654321.abs   # =>   1234567890987654321
-1234567890987654321.abs  # =>   1234567890987654321
```

div $big.\text{div}(\ number\ ) \rightarrow other\_number$

Synonym for Bignum#/.

```
-1234567890987654321.div(13731)       # =>   -89910996357706
-1234567890987654321.div(13731.0)     # =>   -89910996357705
-1234567890987654321.div(-987654321)  # =>   1249999989
```

divmod $big.\text{divmod}(\ number\ ) \rightarrow array$

See Numeric#divmod on page 608.

eql? $big.\text{eql?}(\ obj\ ) \rightarrow$ true or false

Returns true only if *obj* is a Bignum with the same value as *big*. Contrast this with Bignum#==, which performs type conversions.

```
68719476736.eql? 68719476736    # =>   true
68719476736   ==  68719476736   # =>   true
68719476736.eql? 68719476736.0  # =>   false
68719476736   ==  68719476736.0 # =>   true
```

fdiv $big.\text{fdiv}(\ number\ ) \rightarrow float$

1.9   Returns the floating-point result of dividing *big* by *number*. Alias for Bignum#quo.

```
-1234567890987654321.fdiv(13731)       # =>   -89910996357705.5
-1234567890987654321.fdiv(13731.0)     # =>   -89910996357705.5
-1234567890987654321.fdiv(-987654321)  # =>   1249999989.60938
```

magnitude $big.\text{magnitude} \rightarrow bignum$

1.9   Returns the magnitude of *big*(the distance of *big* from the origin of the number line. Synonym for Bignum#abs. See also Complex#magnitude.

---

modulo   *big*.modulo(*number*) → *number*

Synonym for Bignum#%.

---

remainder   *big*.remainder(*number*) → *other_number*

Returns the remainder after dividing *big* by *number*.

```
-1234567890987654321.remainder(13731)     # =>   -6966
-1234567890987654321.remainder(13731.24)  # =>   -9906.22531493148
```

---

size   *big*.size → *integer*

Returns the number of bytes in the machine representation of *big*.

```
(256**10 - 1).size   # =>   12
(256**20 - 1).size   # =>   20
(256**40 - 1).size   # =>   40
```

---

to_f   *big*.to_f → *float*

Converts *big* to a Float. If *big* doesn't fit in a Float, the result is infinity.

---

to_s   *big*.to_s(*base=10*) → *str*

Returns a string containing the representation of *big* radix *base* (2 to 36).

```
12345654321.to_s          # =>   "12345654321"
12345654321.to_s(2)       # =>   "1011011111110110111011110000110001"
12345654321.to_s(8)       # =>   "133766736061"
12345654321.to_s(16)      # =>   "2dfdbbc31"
12345654321.to_s(26)      # =>   "1dp1pc6d"
78546939656932.to_s(36)   # =>   "rubyrules"
```

B inding

Binding < Object

Objects of class Binding encapsulate the execution context at some particular place in the code and retain this context for future use. The variables, methods, value of self, and possibly an iterator block accessible in this context are all retained. Binding objects can be created using Kernel#binding and are made available to the callback of Kernel#set_trace_func.

These binding objects can be passed as the second argument of the Kernel#eval method, establishing an environment for the evaluation.

```ruby
class Demo
  def initialize(n)
    @secret = n
  end
  def get_binding
    return binding()
  end
end

k1 = Demo.new(99)
b1 = k1.get_binding
k2 = Demo.new(-3)
b2 = k2.get_binding

# Pass to eval...
eval("@secret", b1)   # =>   99
# Or eval via binding...
b2.eval("@secret")    # =>   -3

eval("@secret")       # =>   nil
```

Instance methods

eval   *bind*.eval(*string* ⟨ , *file* ⟨ , *line* ⟩ ⟩) → *obj*

1.9   Evaluates the Ruby code in *string* using the context of *bind*. Equivalent to calling Kernel#eval with a second argument of *bind*. See the start of this section for an example.

Class

Class < Module

Classes in Ruby are first-class objects—each is an instance of class Class.

When a new class is defined (typically using class *Name* ... end), an object of type Class is created and assigned to a constant (*Name*, in this case). When Name.new is called to create a new object, the new instance method in Class is run by default, which in turn invokes allocate to allocate memory for the object, before finally calling the new object's initialize method.

Class methods

inherited   *cls*.inherited(*sub_class*)

Invoked by Ruby when a subclass of *cls* is created. The new subclass is passed as a parameter.

```
class Top
  def self.inherited(sub)
    puts "New subclass: #{sub}"
  end
end
class Middle < Top
end
class Bottom < Middle
end
```

produces:

```
New subclass: Middle
New subclass: Bottom
```

new   Class.new(*super_class*=Object) ⟨ { *block* } ⟩ → *cls*

Creates a new anonymous (unnamed) class with the given superclass (or Object if no parameter is given). If called with a block, that block is used as the body of the class. Within the block, self is set to the class instance.

```
name = "Dave"
FriendlyClass = Class.new do
  define_method :hello do
    "Hello, #{name}"
  end
end
f = FriendlyClass.new
f.hello   # =>   "Hello, Dave"
```

Instance methods

allocate

cls.allocate $\rightarrow$ obj

Allocates space for a new object of cls's class. The returned object must be an instance of cls. Calling new is basically the same as calling the class method allocate to create an object, followed by calling initialize on that new object. You cannot override allocate in normal programs; Ruby invokes it without going through conventional method dispatch.

```
class MyClass
  def self.another_new(*args)
    o = allocate
    o.send(:initialize, *args)
    o
  end
  def initialize(a, b, c)
    @a, @b, @c = a, b, c
  end
end

mc = MyClass.another_new(4, 5, 6)
mc.inspect   # =>   "#<MyClass:0x0a34f8 @a=4, @b=5, @c=6>"
```

new

cls.new(⟨ $args$ ⟩*) $\rightarrow$ obj

Calls allocate to create a new object of cls's class and then invokes the newly created object's initialize method, passing it $args$.

superclass

cls.superclass $\rightarrow$ $super\_class$ or nil

Returns the superclass of cls or returns nil.

```
Class.superclass   # =>   Module
Object.superclass  # =>   BasicObject
```

Module
Comparable

Relies on: <=>

The Comparable mixin is used by classes whose objects may be ordered. The class must define the <=> operator, which compares the receiver against another object, returning −1, 0, or +1 depending on whether the receiver is less than, equal to, or greater than the other object. Comparable uses <=> to implement the conventional comparison operators (<, <=, ==, >=, and >) and the method between?.

```
class CompareOnSize
  include Comparable
  attr :str
  def <=>(other)
    str.length <=> other.str.length
  end
  def initialize(str)
    @str = str
  end
end

s1 = CompareOnSize.new("Z")
s2 = CompareOnSize.new([1,2])
s3 = CompareOnSize.new("XXX")

s1 < s2              # =>    true
s2.between?(s1, s3)  # =>    true
s3.between?(s1, s2)  # =>    false
[ s3, s2, s1 ].sort  # =>    ["Z", [1, 2], "XXX"]
```

Instance methods

Comparisons

$obj < other\_object \rightarrow$ true or false
$obj <= other\_object \rightarrow$ true or false
$obj == other\_object \rightarrow$ true or false
$obj >= other\_object \rightarrow$ true or false
$obj > other\_object \rightarrow$ true or false

Compares two objects based on the receiver's <=> method.

between?

obj.between?(min, max) $\rightarrow$ true or false

Returns false if *obj* <=> *min* is less than zero or if *obj* <=> *max* is greater than zero; returns true otherwise.

```
3.between?(1, 5)            # =>    true
6.between?(1, 5)            # =>    false
'cat'.between?('ant', 'dog')   # =>    true
'gnu'.between?('ant', 'dog')   # =>    false
```

C omplex

Class — Complex < Numeric

Represents complex numbers, represented internally as numbers with a real and imaginary part, both of which can be any scalar number. Note that scalar comparison operations (<=>, <, and so on) are not defined on complex numbers (which would argue that Complex should not be a subclass of Numeric, but that ship has sailed). Also see the standard library, somewhat confusingly named complex, on page 728, for a way add complex number support to standard math functions, as well as the mathn library on page 758 for a way of integrating complex numbers into regular arithmetic (so that the square root of −1 returns Complex::I).

```
v1 = Complex(2,3)                            # =>   (2+3i)
v2 = Complex("0+2i")   # Alternative constructor  # =>   (0+2i)
v1 + v2                                      # =>   (2+5i)
v1 * v2                                      # =>   (-6+4i)
v2**2                                        # =>   (-4+0i)
v2**2 == -4                                  # =>   true

# Euler's theorem
include Math
E**(PI*Complex::I)   # =>   (-1.0+1.22464679914735e-16i)
```

Class constants

I   The imaginary unit.

Class methods

polar   Complex.polar(*magnitude, angle*) → *complex*

Returns the complex number represented by the given polar coordinates.

```
Complex.polar(1.23, 0.5)      # =>   1.07942655112516+0.589693412483171i
Complex.polar(1, Math::PI/2)  # =>   6.12323399573677e-17+1.0i
```

rect   Complex.rect(*read, imag*) → *complex*

Returns the complex number represented by the given real and imaginary parts.

```
Complex.rect(1.23, 0.5)   # =>   1.23+0.5i
```

rectangular   Complex.rectangular(*read, imag*) → *complex*

Synonym for Complex.rect.

Instance methods

Arithmetic operations

Performs various arithmetic operations on *complex*.

complex	+	*numeric*	Addition
complex	–	*numeric*	Subtraction
complex	*	*numeric*	Multiplication
complex	/	*numeric*	Division
complex	**	*numeric*	Exponentiation
complex	-@		Unary minus
complex	-+		Unary plus

==

complex == *other* → true or false

Returns true if *complex* does equals *other*, converting *other* to a complex number if necessary.

```
Complex::I == Complex(0,1)   # =>   true
Complex::I == Complex(1,0)   # =>   false
Complex(1,0) == 1            # =>   true
Complex(1,0) == "1"          # =>   false
```

abs

complex.abs → *number*

Returns the absolute value (magnitude) of *complex*.

```
Complex::I.abs    # =>   1.0
Complex(1,1).abs  # =>   1.4142135623731
```

abs2

complex.abs2 → *number*

Returns the square of the absolute value (magnitude) of *complex*.

```
Complex::I.abs2   # =>   1
Complex(1,1).abs2 # =>   2
```

angle

complex.angle → *number*

Returns the angle between the x-axis and a line from the origin to *complex*. By convention, Complex(0,0).angle is 0.

```
Complex(1, 0).angle   # =>   0.0
Complex(1, 1).angle   # =>   0.785398163397448
Complex(0, 1).angle   # =>   1.5707963267949
```

arg

complex.arg → *number*

Synonym for Complex#angle.

conj

complex.conj → *a_complex*

Synonym for Complex#conjugate.

conjugate
complex.conjugate → *a_complex*

Returns the conjugate of *complex* (the reflection of *complex* around the x-axis).

```
Complex::I.conjugate      # =>   (0-1i)
Complex(1,1).conjugate    # =>   (1-1i)
```

denominator
complex.denominator → *number*

Returns the lowest common multiple of the denominators of the real and imaginary parts of *complex*.

```
Complex("1/3+1/4i").denominator   # =>   12
Complex(-2, 4).denominator        # =>   1
```

eql?
complex.eql(*other*) → true or false

Returns true only if *other* is a complex number with real and imaginary parts eql? to *complex*'s.

```
Complex(1, 0).eql?(Complex(1,0))      # =>   true
Complex(1, 0).eql?(Complex(1.0, 0))   # =>   false
Complex(1, 0).eql?(1)                 # =>   false
Complex(1, 0) == Complex(1,0)         # =>   true
Complex(1, 0) == Complex(1.0, 0)      # =>   true
Complex(1, 0) == 1                    # =>   true
```

fdiv
complex.fdiv(*other*) → *a_complex*

Returns *complex* / *other* after converting the real and imaginary parts of *complex* to floats. (Contrast with Complex#quo.)

```
c1 = Complex(1, 2)
c2 = Complex(2, 2)
c1 /c2        # =>   ((3/4)+(1/4)*i)
c1.fdiv(c2)   # =>   (0.75+0.25i)
```

imag
complex.imag → *number*

Returns the imaginary part of *complex*.

```
Complex(2, -3).imag   # =>   -3
```

imaginary
complex.imaginary → *number*

Synonym for Complex#imag.

magnitude
complex.magnitude → *int* or *float*

Returns the magnitude of *complex*(the distance of *complex* from the origin of the number line. The positive square root of $real^2 + imag^2$.

```
Complex(3, 4).magnitude   # =>   5.0
Complex::I.magnitude      # =>   1.0
```

numerator

$complex$.numerator → $a\_complex$

If cd is $complex$.denominator and re and im are the real and imaginary parts of $complex$, $complex$.numerator is as follows:

$$re.numerator \times \frac{cd}{re.denominator} + im.numerator \times \frac{cd}{im.denominator}i$$

phase

$complex$.phase → [$magnitude, angle$]

Returns the phase angle of $complex$ (the angle between the positive x-axis and the line from the origin to $(real, imag)$), measured in radians.

```
Complex(3, 4).phase   # =>   0.927295218001612
Complex(-3, 4).phase  # =>   2.21429743558818
```

polar

$complex$.polar → [$magnitude, angle$]

Returns $complex$ as polar coordinates.

```
Complex(1,1).polar    # =>   [1.4142135623731, 0.785398163397448]
Complex(-2,-3).polar  # =>   [3.60555127546399, -2.15879893034246]
```

quo

$complex$.quo($other$) → $a\_complex$

Returns $complex$ / $other$ after converting the real and imaginary parts of $complex$ to rational numbers. (Contrast with Complex#fdiv.)

```
c1 = Complex(1, 2)
c2 = Complex(2, 2)
c1 /c2       # =>   ((3/4)+(1/4)*i)
c1.quo(c2)   # =>   ((3/4)+(1/4)*i)
```

rect

$complex$.rect → [$complex$.real, $complex$.imag]

Returns an array containing the real and imaginary components of $complex$.

```
Complex::I.rect   # =>   [0, 1]
```

rectangular

$complex$.rectangular → [$complex$.real, $complex$.imag]

Synonym for Complex#rect.

real

$complex$.real → $number$

Returns the real part of $complex$.

```
Complex(2, 3).real   # =>   2
```

real?

$complex$.real? → $false$

Complex numbers are never real numbers (even if their imaginary part is zero).

```
Complex(1, 1).real?   # =>   false
Complex(1, 0).real?   # =>   false
```

---

to_f *complex*.to_f → *float*

Returns the real part of *complex* as a float, raising an exception if the imaginary part is not zero.

```
Complex(2, 0).to_f   # =>   2.0
```

---

to_i *complex*.to_i → *float*

Returns the real part of *complex* as an integer, raising an exception if the imaginary part is not zero.

```
Complex(2.2, 0).to_i   # =>   2
```

---

to_r *complex*.to_r → *float*

Returns the real part of *complex* as a rational number, raising an exception if the imaginary part is not zero.

```
Complex(2.5, 0).to_r   # =>   (5/2)
```

Class
Dir < Object

Objects of class Dir are directory streams representing directories in the underlying file system. They provide a variety of ways to list directories and their contents. See also File, page 497.

The directory used in these examples contains the two regular files (config.h and main.rb), the parent directory (..), and the directory itself (.).

Mixes in

Enumerable:

all?, any?, collect, count, cycle, detect, drop, drop_while, each_cons, each_slice, each_with_index, entries, find, find_all, find_index, first, grep, group_by, include?, inject, map, max, max_by, member?, min, min_by, minmax, minmax_by, none?, one?, partition, reduce, reject, select, sort, sort_by, take, take_while, to_a, zip

Class methods

[ ]   Dir[*glob_pattern*] → *array*

Equivalent to calling Dir.glob(*glob_pattern,* 0).

chdir   Dir.chdir(⟨ *dir* ⟩) → 0
Dir.chdir(⟨ *dir* ⟩) {| path | *block* } → *obj*

Changes the current working directory of the process to the given string. When called without an argument, changes the directory to the value of the environment variable HOME or LOGDIR. Raises a SystemCallError (probably Errno::ENOENT) if the target directory does not exist.

If a block is given, it is passed the name of the new current directory, and the block is executed with that as the current directory. The original working directory is restored when the block exits. The return value of chdir is the value of the block. chdir blocks can be nested, but in a multithreaded program an error will be raised if a thread attempts to open a chdir block while another thread has one open. This is because the underlying operating system only understands the concept of a single current working directory at any one time.

```
Dir.chdir("/var/log")
puts Dir.pwd
Dir.chdir("/tmp") do
  puts Dir.pwd
  Dir.chdir("/usr") do
    puts Dir.pwd
  end
  puts Dir.pwd
end
puts Dir.pwd
```

produces:

```
/var/log
/tmp
/usr
/tmp
/var/log
```

---

chroot   Dir.chroot(*dirname*) → 0

Changes this process's idea of the file system root. Only a privileged process may make this call. Not available on all platforms. On Unix systems, see chroot(2) for more information.

```
Dir.chdir("/production/secure/root")
Dir.chroot("/production/secure/root")    → 0
Dir.pwd                                  → "/"
```

---

delete   Dir.delete(*dirname*) → 0

Deletes the named directory. Raises a subclass of SystemCallError if the directory isn't empty.

---

entries   Dir.entries(*dirname*) → *array*

Returns an array containing all of the filenames in the given directory. Will raise a System-CallError if the named directory doesn't exist.

```
Dir.entries("testdir")   # =>   [".", "..", "config.h", "main.rb"]
```

---

exist?   Dir.exist?(*path*) → true or false

Returns true if *path* exists and is a directory. Alias for File.directory?.

```
Dir.exist?("/tmp")   # =>    true
Dir.exist?("/temp")  # =>    false
```

---

exists?   Dir.exists?(*path*) → true or false

Alias for Dir.exist?.

---

foreach   Dir.foreach(*dirname*) {| *filename* | *block* } → nil

Calls the block once for each entry in the named directory, passing the filename of each entry as a parameter to the block.

```
Dir.foreach("testdir") {|x| puts "Got #{x}" }
```

produces:

```
Got .
Got ..
Got config.h
Got main.rb
```

getwd   Dir.getwd → *dirname*

Returns a string containing the canonical path to the current working directory of this process. Note that on some operating systems this name may not be the name you gave to Dir.chdir. On OS X, for example, /tmp is a symlink.

```
Dir.chdir("/tmp")   # =>   0
Dir.getwd           # =>   "/private/tmp"
```

glob   Dir.glob(*glob_pattern*, ⟨ *flags* ⟩) → *array*
Dir.glob(*glob_pattern*, ⟨ *flags* ⟩) {| *filename* | *block* } → false

Returns the filenames found by expanding the pattern given in *glob_pattern*, either as elements in *array* or as parameters to the block. Note that this pattern is not a regexp (it's closer to a shell glob). See File.fnmatch on page 500 for the meaning of the *flags* parameter. Case sensitivity depends on your system (so File::FNM_CASEFOLD is ignored). Metacharacters in the pattern are as follows:

*	Any sequence of characters in a filename: * will match all files, c* will match all files beginning with *c*, 'c will match all files ending with *c*, and *c* will match all files that have *c* in their name.
**	Matches zero or more directories (so **/fred) matches a file named *fred* in or below the current directory).
?	Matches any one character in a filename.
[*chars*]	Matches any one of *chars*. If the first character in *chars* is ^, matches any character not in the remaining set.
{*patt*,...}	Matches one of the patterns specified between braces. These patterns may contain other metacharacters.
\	Removes any special significance in the next character.

```
Dir.chdir("testdir")                  # =>   0
Dir["config.?"]                       # =>   ["config.h"]
Dir.glob("config.?")                  # =>   ["config.h"]
Dir.glob("*.[a-z][a-z]")              # =>   ["main.rb"]
Dir.glob("*.[^r]*")                   # =>   ["config.h"]
Dir.glob("*.{rb,h}")                  # =>   ["main.rb", "config.h"]
Dir.glob("*")                         # =>   ["config.h", "main.rb"]
Dir.glob("*", File::FNM_DOTMATCH)     # =>   [".", "..", "config.h",
                                              "main.rb"]

Dir.chdir("..")                       # =>   0
Dir.glob("code/**/fib*.rb")           # =>   ["code/fib_up_to.rb",
                                              "code/fiber.rb",
                                              "code/rdoc/fib_example.rb"]
Dir.glob("**/rdoc/fib*.rb")           # =>   ["code/rdoc/fib_example.rb"]
```

mkdir   Dir.mkdir(*dirname* ⟨ , *permissions* ⟩) → 0

Makes a new directory named *dirname*, with permissions specified by the optional parameter *permissions*. The permissions may be modified by the value of File.umask and are ignored on Windows. Raises a SystemCallError if the directory cannot be created. See also the discussion of permissions on page 497.

---

new   Dir.new(*dirname* ⟨ , :encoding => *enc* ⟩) → *dir*

1.9

Returns a new directory object for the named directory. The optional hash parameter lets you specify the encoding used by filenames. If not given, it defaults to the file system local on the current machine.

---

open   Dir.open(*dirname* ⟨ , :encoding => *enc* ⟩) → *dir*
Dir.open(*dirname* ⟨ , :encoding => *enc* ⟩) {| *dir* | *block* } → *obj*

With no block, open is a synonym for Dir.new. If a block is present, it is passed *dir* as a parameter. The directory is closed at the end of the block, and Dir.open returns the value of the block.

---

pwd   Dir.pwd → *dirname*

Synonym for Dir.getwd.

---

rmdir   Dir.rmdir(*dirname*) → 0

Synonym for Dir.delete.

---

unlink   Dir.unlink(*dirname*) → 0

Synonym for Dir.delete.

Instance methods

---

close   *dir*.close → nil

Closes the directory stream. Any further attempts to access *dir* will raise an IOError.

```
d = Dir.new("testdir")
d.close   # =>   nil
```

---

each   *dir*.each {| *filename* | *block* } → *dir*

Calls the block once for each entry in this directory, passing the filename of each entry as a parameter to the block.

```
d = Dir.new("testdir")
d.each  {|name| puts "Got #{name}" }
```

produces:

```
Got .
Got ..
Got config.h
Got main.rb
```

---

path   *dir*.path → dirname

Returns the path parameter passed to *dir*'s constructor.

```
d = Dir.new("..")
d.path   # =>   ".."
```

pos $\hspace{8cm}$ *dir*.pos → *int*

Synonym for Dir#tell.

pos= $\hspace{7cm}$ *dir*.pos(*int*) → *int*

Synonym for Dir#seek but returns the position parameter.

```
d = Dir.new("testdir")   # =>   #<Dir:testdir>
d.read                   # =>   "."
i = d.pos                # =>   1
d.read                   # =>   ".."
d.pos = i                # =>   1
d.read                   # =>   ".."
```

read $\hspace{6cm}$ *dir*.read → *filename* or nil

Reads the next entry from *dir* and returns it as a string. Returns nil at the end of the stream.

```
d = Dir.new("testdir")
d.read   # =>   "."
d.read   # =>   ".."
d.read   # =>   "config.h"
```

rewind $\hspace{7cm}$ *dir*.rewind → *dir*

Repositions *dir* to the first entry.

```
d = Dir.new("testdir")
d.read     # =>   "."
d.rewind   # =>   #<Dir:testdir>
d.read     # =>   "."
```

seek $\hspace{7cm}$ *dir*.seek(*int*) → *dir*

Seeks to a particular location in *dir*. *int* must be a value returned by Dir#tell (it is not necessarily a simple index into the entries).

```
d = Dir.new("testdir")   # =>   #<Dir:testdir>
d.read                   # =>   "."
i = d.tell               # =>   1
d.read                   # =>   ".."
d.seek(i)                # =>   #<Dir:testdir>
d.read                   # =>   ".."
```

tell $\hspace{8cm}$ *dir*.tell → *int*

Returns the current position in *dir*. See also Dir#seek.

```
d = Dir.new("testdir")
d.tell   # =>   0
d.read   # =>   "."
d.tell   # =>   1
```

Class	
Encoding <	Object

An encoding describes how to map the binary data in the internal representation of strings into characters. Ruby has support for a large number of encodings built in—others can be loaded dynamically at runtime.

Encodings are identified by name (*UTF-** or *ISO-8859-1*, for example). They are represented by encoding objects. The Encoding class contains predefined constants for these encoding objects. Often there are multiple objects for the same encoding. For example, the constants Encoding::IBM860 and Encoding::CP860 are both representations of the encoding named *IBM860*. In Table 27.2 on the facing page, we can see the names of the encodings are in the first column and the names on the constants in the Encoding class for the corresponding encoding object(s). An entry such as ISO-8859-1 – 11 indicates that there are 11 separate encodings (with the obvious names).

Encodings are used when opening files, creating strings, and so on. The methods that accept an encoding as a parameter will take either an encoding name or an encoding object. Use of the object is marginally faster.

Chapter 17 on page 251 is devoted to a discussion of encodings.

Class methods

---
aliases Encoding.aliases → *hash*

Returns a hash whose keys are aliases for encodings and whose values are the corresponding base encoding names.

```
Encoding.aliases["BINARY"]   # =>   "ASCII-8BIT"
```

---
compatible? Encoding.compatible?(*str1, str2*) → *enc* or nil

---

Determines whether two strings have compatible encodings (meaning, for example, that you could concatenate them). Returns the encoding of the string that would result from the concatenation or nil if the strings are not compatible.

```
# encoding: utf-8
ascii1 = "ant"
ascii2 = "bee"
iso    = "\xee"
iso.force_encoding(Encoding::ISO_8859_1)
utf    = "δog"

Encoding.compatible?(ascii1, ascii2)   # =>   #<Encoding:UTF-8>
Encoding.compatible?(ascii1, iso)      # =>   #<Encoding:ISO-8859-1>
Encoding.compatible?(ascii1, utf)      # =>   #<Encoding:UTF-8>
Encoding.compatible?(iso,    utf)      # =>   nil
```

---
default_external Encoding.default_external → *enc*

Returns the default external encoding, used when reading and writing data from I/O streams.

```
Encoding.default_external   # =>   #<Encoding:UTF-8>
```

Table 27.2. Encoding Names and Class Names

Encoding name	Encoding::*xxx* class name(s)
ASCII-8BIT	ASCII_8BIT, BINARY
Big5	Big5, BIG5, CP950
CP51932	CP51932
CP850	CP850, IBM850
CP852	CP852
CP855	CP855
CP949	CP949
Emacs-Mule	Emacs_Mule, EMACS_MULE
EUC-JP	EUC_JP, EucJP, EUCJP
EUC-KR	EUC_KR, EucKR, EUCKR
EUC-TW	EUC_TW, EucTW, EUCTW
eucJP-ms	EucJP_ms, EUCJP_MS, EUC_JP_MS
GB12345	GB12345
GB18030	GB18030
GB1988	GB1988
GB2312	EUC_CN, EucCN, EUCCN
GBK	GBK, CP936
IBM437	IBM437, CP437
IBM737	IBM737, CP737
IBM775	IBM775, CP775
IBM852	IBM852
IBM855	IBM855
IBM857	IBM857, CP857
IBM860 – 6	IBM860 – 6, CP8600 – 6
IBM869	IBM869, CP869
ISO-2022-JP	ISO_2022_JP, ISO2022_JP
ISO-2022-JP-2	ISO_2022_JP_2, ISO2022_JP2
ISO-8859-1 – 11	ISO8859_1 – 11
ISO-8859-13 – 16	ISO8859_13 – 16
KOI8-R	KOI8_R, CP878
KOI8-U	KOI8_U
macCentEuro	MacCentEuro, MACCENTEURO
macCroatian	MacCroatian, MACCROATIAN
macCyrillic	MacCyrillic, MACCYRILLIC
macGreek	MacGreek, MACGREEK
macIceland	MacIceland, MACICELAND
MacJapanese	MacJapanese, MACJAPANESE, MacJapan, MACJAPAN
macRoman	MacRoman, MACROMAN
macRomania	MacRomania, MACROMANIA
macThai	MacThai, MACTHAI
macTurkish	MacTurkish, MACTURKISH
macUkraine	MacUkraine, MACUKRAINE
Shift_JIS	Shift_JIS, SHIFT_JIS, SJIS
stateless-ISO-2022-JP	Stateless_ISO_2022_JP, STATELESS_ISO_2022_JP
TIS-620	TIS_620
US-ASCII	US_ASCII, ASCII, ANSI_X3_4_1968
UTF-16BE	UTF_16BE, UCS_2BE
UTF-16LE	UTF_16LE
UTF-32BE	UTF_32BE, UCS_4BE
UTF-32LE	UTF_32LE, UCS_4LE
UTF-7	UTF_7, CP65000
UTF-8	UTF_8, CP65001
UTF8-MAC	UTF8_MAC, UTF_8_MAC
Windows-1250 – 1258	Windows_1250 – 1258, WINDOWS_1250 – 1258, CP1250 – 1258
Windows-31J	Windows_31J, WINDOWS_31J, CP932, CsWindows31J, CSWINDOWS31J
Windows-874	Windows_874, WINDOWS_874, CP874

default_external=   Encoding.default_external = *enc*

Sets the default external encoding.

---

default_internal   Encoding.default_internal → *enc* or nil

Returns the default internal encoding, used when transcoding data read and written. Returns nil if no default encoding is set.

---

default_internal=   Encoding.default_internal = *enc*

Sets the default internal encoding.

```
Encoding.default_internal = 'utf-8'
Encoding.default_internal   # =>   #<Encoding:UTF-8>
```

---

find   Encoding.find(*name*) → *enc*

Returns the encoding object for the given encoding name or throws an ArgumentError.

```
Encoding.find("Shift_JIS")   # =>   #<Encoding:Shift_JIS>
```

---

list   Encoding.list → *array*

Returns a list of the encoding objects loaded into the current interpreter.

---

locale_charmap   Encoding.locale_charmap → *name*

Returns the name of the charmap of the current locale. This is normally set externally, often in an environment variable or other operating-system context.

```
ENV["LANG"]                  # =>   "en_US.UTF-8"
Encoding.locale_charmap      # =>   "UTF-8"
```

---

name_list   Encoding.name_list → *array*

Returns a list of the names of loaded encodings.

```
Encoding.name_list.sort.first(5)   # =>   ["646", "ANSI_X3.4-1968",
                                           "ASCII", "ASCII-8BIT", "BINARY"]
```

Instance methods

dummy?   *enc*.dummy? → true or false

Dummy encodings are placeholders for encodings that cannot be handled properly by the current mechanism of Ruby M17N, often because they are stateful.

```
Encoding::UTF_7.dummy?   # =>   true
Encoding::UTF_8.dummy?   # =>   false
```

---

name   *enc*.name → *string*

Returns the name of *enc*.

```
Encoding::UTF_8.name     # =>   "UTF-8"
Encoding::CP65001.name   # =>   "UTF-8"
```

names enc.names $\rightarrow$ [$\langle\,string\,\rangle^+$]

Returns the name of *enc*, along with the names of *enc*'s aliases.

```
Encoding::UTF_8.names     # =>   ["UTF-8", "CP65001", "locale",
                                  "external"]
Encoding::CP65001.names   # =>   ["UTF-8", "CP65001", "locale",
                                  "external"]
Encoding::ASCII.names     # =>   ["US-ASCII", "ASCII", "ANSI_X3.4-1968",
                                  "646"]
```

E
numerable

Module
Enumerable

Relies on: each, <=>

The Enumerable mixin provides collection classes with traversal and searching methods and with the ability to sort. The class must provide a method each, which yields successive members of the collection. If Enumerable#max, #min, #sort, or #sort_by is used, the objects in the collection must also implement a meaningful <=> operator, because these methods rely on an ordering between members of the collection.

1.9 Ruby 1.9 adds a substantial number of methods to this module, as well as changing the semantics of many others. Even experienced Ruby programmers should probably read this section carefully.

Instance methods

all? *enum*.all? ⟨ {| *obj* | *block* } ⟩ → true or false

Passes each element of the collection to the given block. The method returns true if the block never returns false or nil. If the block is not given, Ruby adds an implicit block of {|obj| obj} (that is all? will return true only if none of the collection members is false or nil.)

```
%w{ ant bear cat}.all? {|word| word.length >= 3}   # =>   true
%w{ ant bear cat}.all? {|word| word.length >= 4}   # =>   false
[ nil, true, 99 ].all?                             # =>   false
```

any? *enum*.any? ⟨ {| *obj* | *block* } ⟩ → true or false

Passes each element of the collection to the given block. The method returns true if the block ever returns a value other than false or nil. If the block is not given, Ruby adds an implicit block of {|obj| obj} (that is, any? will return true if at least one of the collection members is not false or nil). See also Enumerable#none? and Enumerable#one?.

```
%w{ ant bear cat}.any? {|word| word.length >= 3}   # =>   true
%w{ ant bear cat}.any? {|word| word.length >= 4}   # =>   true
[ nil, true, 99 ].any?                             # =>   true
```

collect *enum*.collect {| *obj* | *block* } → *array* or *enumerator*

Returns a new array containing the results of running *block* once for every element in *enum*. Returns an Enumerator object if no block is given.

```
(1..4).collect {|i| i*i }   # =>   [1, 4, 9, 16]
(1..4).collect { "cat"  }   # =>   ["cat", "cat", "cat", "cat"]
(1..4).collect(&:even?)     # =>   [false, true, false, true]
```

count *enum*.count(*obj*) → *int*
enum.count {| *obj* | *block* } → *int*

1.9 Returns the count of objects in *enum* that equal *obj* or for which the block returns a true value. Returns the count of all elements in *enum* if neither a block nor an argument is given.

```
(1..4).count                  # =>   4
(1..4).count(3)               # =>   1
(1..4).count {|obj| obj > 2 } # =>   2
```

cycle

enum.cycle { | *obj* | *block* } → nil or *enumerator*
enum.cycle(*times*) { | *obj* | *block* } → nil or *enumerator*

1.9

Returns nil if *enum* has no elements; otherwise, passes the elements, one at a time to the block. When it reaches the end, it repeats. The number of times it repeats is set by the parameter. If the parameter is missing, cycles forever. Equivalent to *enum*.to_a.cycle. See also Array#cycle. Returns an Enumerator object if no block is given.

```
('a'..'c').cycle(2)      # =>   #<Enumerator:0x0a503c>
('a'..'c').cycle(2).to_a # =>   ["a", "b", "c", "a", "b", "c"]
```

detect

enum.detect(*ifnone* = nil) { | *obj* | *block* } → *obj* or nil or *enumerator*

Passes each entry in *enum* to *block*. Returns the first for which *block* is not false. Returns nil if no object matches unless the proc *ifnone* is given, in which case it is called and its result is returned. Returns an Enumerator object if no block is given.

```
(1..10).detect  {|i| i % 5 == 0 and i % 7 == 0 }  # =>   nil
(1..100).detect {|i| i % 5 == 0 and i % 7 == 0 }  # =>   35
sorry = lambda { "not found" }
(1..10).detect(sorry) {|i| i > 50}                # =>   "not found"
```

drop

enum.drop(*n*) → *an_array*

1.9

Returns an array containing all but the first *n* elements of *enum*.

```
[ 1, 1, 2, 3, 5, 8, 13 ].drop(4)   # =>   [5, 8, 13]
[ 1, 1, 2, 3, 5, 8, 13 ].drop(99)  # =>   []
```

drop_while

enum.drop_while { | *item* | *block* } → *an_array* or *enumerator*

1.9

Passes elements in turn to the block until the block does not return a true value. Starting with that element, copies the remainder to an array and returns it. Returns an Enumerator object if no block is given.

```
[ 1, 1, 2, 3, 5, 8, 13 ].drop_while {|item| item < 6 }  # =>   [8, 13]
```

each_cons

enum.each_cons(*length*) [{ | *array* | *block* }] → nil or *enumerator*

1.9

Passes to the block each consecutive subarray of size *length* from self. Returns an Enumerator object if no block is given.

```
(1..4).each_cons(2) {|array| p array }
```

produces:

```
[1, 2]
[2, 3]
[3, 4]
```

Enumerable

---

each_slice   *enum*.each_slice(*length*) [{| *array* | *block* }] → nil or *enumerator*

1.9   Divides *enum* into slices of size *length*, passing each in turn to the block. Returns an Enumerator object if no block is given.

```
(1..10).each_slice(4) {|array| p array }
```
produces:
```
[1, 2, 3, 4]
[5, 6, 7, 8]
[9, 10]
```

---

each_with_index   *enum*.each_with_index(⟨ args ⟩*) {| *obj, index* | *block* }
                                                                    → *enum* or *enumerator*

1.9   Calls *block*, passing in successive items from *enum* and the corresponding index. If any arguments are given, they are passed to each during the iteration. Returns an Enumerator object if no block is given.

```
%w(cat dog wombat).each_with_index do |item, index|
  puts "#{item} is at position #{index}"
end
```
produces:
```
cat is at position 0
dog is at position 1
wombat is at position 2
```

---

each_with_object   *enum*.each_with_object(*memo*) → *memo* or *enumerator*

1.9   Calls *block* with two arguments, the item and the memo object, for each item in *enum*. Returns an Enumerator object if no block is given.

```
hash = %w(cat dog wombat).each_with_object({}) do |item, memo|
  memo[item] = item.upcase.reverse
end
hash   # =>   {"cat"=>"TAC", "dog"=>"GOD", "wombat"=>"TABMOW"}
```

---

entries   *enum*.entries → *array*

Synonym for Enumerable#to_a.

---

find   *enum*.find(*ifnone* = nil) {| *obj* | *block* } → *obj* or nil

Synonym for Enumerable#detect.

---

find_all   *enum*.find_all {| *obj* | *block* } → *array* or *enumerator*

Returns an array containing all elements of *enum* for which *block* is not false (see also Enumerable#reject). Returns an Enumerator object if no block is given.

```
(1..10).find_all {|i|  i % 3 == 0 }   # =>   [3, 6, 9]
```

---

find_index   *enum*.find_index {| *obj* | *block* } → *int* or nil or *enumerator*

1.9   Returns the index of the first item for which the given block returns a true value or returns or nil if the block only ever returns false. *block* is not false (see also Enumerable#reject). Returns an Enumerator object if no block is given.

```
%w{ant bat cat dog}.find_index {|item|  item =~ /g/ }  # =>  3
%w{ant bat cat dog}.find_index {|item|  item =~ /h/ }  # =>  nil
```

first

enum.first → *an_object* or nil
enum.first(*n*) → *an_array*

1.9 With no parameters, returns the first item of *enum* or nil. With a parameter, returns the first *n* items of *enum*.

```
%w{ant bat cat dog}.find_index.first     # =>  "ant"
%w{ant bat cat dog}.find_index.first(2)  # =>  ["ant", "bat"]
```

grep

enum.grep(*pattern*) → *array*
enum.grep(*pattern*) {| *obj* | *block* } → *array*

Returns an array of every element in *enum* for which pattern === element. If the optional *block* is supplied, each matching element is passed to it, and the block's result is stored in the output array.

```
(1..100).grep 38..44                      # =>  [38, 39, 40, 41, 42, 43, 44]
c = IO.constants
c.grep(/SEEK/)                            # =>  [:SEEK_SET, :SEEK_CUR,
                                          #      :SEEK_END]
res = c.grep(/SEEK/) {|v| IO.const_get(v) }
res                                       # =>  [0, 1, 2]
[ 123, 9**11, 12.34 ].grep(Integer)       # =>  [123, 31381059609]
```

group_by

enum.group_by {| *item* | *block* } → *hash* or *enumerator*

1.9 Partitions *enum* by calling the block for each item and using the result returned by the block to group the items into buckets. Returns a hash where the keys are the objects returned by the block, and the values for a key are those items for which the block returned that object. Returns an Enumerator object if no block is given.

```
p (1..5).group_by {|item| item.even? ? "even" : "odd" }
```

produces:

```
{"odd"=>[1, 3, 5], "even"=>[2, 4]}
```

include?

enum.include?(*obj*) → true or false

Returns true if any member of *enum* equals *obj*. Equality is tested using ==.

```
IO.constants.include? :SEEK_SET        # =>  true
IO.constants.include? :SEEK_NO_FURTHER # =>  false
```

inject

enum.inject(*initial*) {| memo, obj | *block* } → *obj*
enum.inject(*initial*, *sym*) → *obj*
enum.inject {| memo, obj | *block* } → *obj*
enum.inject(*sym*) → *obj*

1.9 Combines the items in *enum* by iterating over them. For each item, passes an accumulator object (called *memo* in the examples) and the item itself to the block, or invokes memo.send(sym, obj). At each step, *memo* is set to the value returned by the block on the previous step. The value returned by inject is the final value returned by the block. The first two forms let you supply an initial value for *memo*. The second two forms use the first element of the collection as the initial value (and skip that element while iterating). Some languages call this operation foldl or reduce. Ruby supports the latter as an alias for inject.

```
# Sum some numbers. These forms do the same thing
(5..10).inject(0) {|sum, n| sum + n }         # =>   45
(5..10).inject {|sum, n| sum + n }            # =>   45
(5..10).inject(0, :+)                          # =>   45
(5..10).inject(:+)                             # =>   45

# Multiply some numbers
(5..10).inject(1) {|product, n| product * n } # =>   151200

# find the longest word
longest_word = %w{ cat sheep bear }.inject do |memo, word|
  memo.length > word.length ? memo : word
end
longest_word                                   # =>   "sheep"

# find the length of the longest word
longest_length = %w{ cat sheep bear }.inject(0) do |memo, word|
  memo >= word.length ? memo : word.length
end
longest_length                                 # =>   5
```

---

map   *enum*.map { | *obj* | *block* } → *array*

Synonym for Enumerable#collect.

---

max   *enum*.max → *obj*
                                               enum.max { | *a,b* | *block* } → *obj*

Returns the object in *enum* with the maximum value. The first form assumes all objects implement <=>; the second uses the block to return *a* <=> *b*.

```
a = %w(albatross dog horse)
a.max                              # =>   "horse"
a.max {|a,b| a.length <=> b.length } # =>   "albatross"
```

---

max_by   *enum*.max_by { | *item* | *block* } → *obj* or *enumerator*

1.9   Passes each item in the collection to the block. Returns the item corresponding to the largest value returned by the block. Returns an Enumerator object if no block is given.

```
a = %w(albatross dog horse fox)
a.max_by {|item| item.length }   # =>   "albatross"
a.max_by {|item| item.reverse }  # =>   "fox"
```

---

member?   *enum*.member?(*obj*) → true or false

Synonym for Enumerable#include?.

min

enum.min → *obj*

enum.min { | *a,b* | *block* } → *obj*

Returns the object in *enum* with the minimum value. The first form assumes all objects implement Comparable; the second uses the block to return *a* <=> *b*.

```
a = %w(albatross dog horse)
a.min                               # =>    "albatross"
a.min {|a,b| a.length <=> b.length }   # =>    "dog"
```

min_by

enum.min_by { | *a,b* | *block* } → *obj* or *enumerator*

1.9 Passes each item in the collection to the block. Returns the item corresponding to the smallest value returned by the block. Returns an Enumerator object if no block is given.

```
a = %w(albatross dog horse fox)
a.min_by {|item| item.length }   # =>    "dog"
a.min_by {|item| item.reverse }  # =>    "horse"
```

minmax

enum.minmax → [*min, max*]

enum.minmax { | *a,b* | *block* } → [*min, max*]

1.9 Compares the elements of self using either <=> of the given block, returning the minimum and maximum values.

```
a = %w(albatross dog horse)
a.minmax                             # =>    ["albatross", "horse"]
a.minmax {|a,b| a.length <=> b.length }   # =>    ["dog", "albatross"]
```

minmax_by

enum.minmax_by { | *a,b* | *block* } → [*min, max*] or *enumerator*

1.9 Passes each item in the collection to the block. Returns the items corresponding to the smallest and largest values returned by the block. Returns an Enumerator object if no block is given.

```
a = %w(albatross dog horse fox)
a.minmax_by {|item| item.length }   # =>    ["dog", "albatross"]
a.minmax_by {|item| item.reverse }  # =>    ["horse", "fox"]
```

none?

enum.none? ⟨ { | *obj* | *block* } ⟩ → true or false

1.9 Passes each element of the collection to the given block. The method returns true if the block never returns a value other than false or nil. If the block is not given, Ruby adds an implicit block of {|obj| obj} (that is, any? will return true if at least one of the collection members is not false or nil). See also Enumerable#any? and Enumerable#one?.

```
%w{ ant bear cat}.none? {|word| word.length >= 3}   # =>    false
%w{ ant bear cat}.none? {|word| word.length > 3}    # =>    false
[ nil, true, 99 ].none?                             # =>    false
```

one?

enum.one? ⟨ { | *obj* | *block* } ⟩ → true or false

1.9 Passes each element of the collection to the given block. The method returns true if the block returns true exactly one time. If the block is not given, Ruby adds an implicit block of

{|obj| obj} (that is, any? will return true if at least one of the collection members is not false or nil). See also Enumerable#any? and Enumerable#none?.

```
%w{ ant bear cat}.one? {|word| word.length >= 3}   # =>   false
%w{ ant bear cat}.one? {|word| word.length >= 4}   # =>   true
[ nil, nil, 99 ].one?                              # =>   true
```

---

partition   *enum*.partition {| *obj* | *block* } → [*true_array, false_array*] or *enumerator*

Returns two arrays, the first containing the elements of *enum* for which the block evaluates to true, the second containing the rest. Returns an Enumerator object if no block is given.

```
(1..6).partition {|i| (i&1).zero?}   # =>   [[2, 4, 6], [1, 3, 5]]
```

---

reduce   *enum*.reduce(*initial*) {| memo, obj | *block* } → *obj*
                                                    enum.reduce(*initial, sym*) → *obj*
                                                    enum.reduce {| memo, obj | *block* } → *obj*
                                                    enum.reduce(*sym*) → *obj*

1.9 Synonym for Enumerable#inject.

---

reject   *enum*.reject {| *obj* | *block* } → *array* or *enumerator*

Returns an array containing the elements of *enum* for which *block* is false (see also Enumerable#find_all). Returns an Enumerator object if no block is given.

```
(1..10).reject {|i|  i % 3 == 0 }   # =>   [1, 2, 4, 5, 7, 8, 10]
```

---

reverse_each   *enum*.reverse_each ⟨ {| *obj* | *block* } ⟩ → *enum*

Invokes the block with the elements of *enum* in reverse order. Creates an intermediate array internally, so this might be expensive on large collections. Returns an Enumerator object if no block is given.

```
(1..5).reverse_each {|i|  print i, " " }
```

produces:

```
5 4 3 2 1
```

---

select   *enum*.select {| *obj* | *block* } → *array*

Synonym for Enumerable#find_all.

---

sort   *enum*.sort → *array*
                                                    enum.sort {| *a, b* | *block* } → *array*

Returns an array containing the items in *enum* sorted, either according to their own <=> method or by using the results of the supplied block. The block should return −1, 0, or +1 depending on the comparison between *a* and *b*. See also Enumerable#sort_by.

```
%w(rhea kea flea).sort      # =>   ["flea", "kea", "rhea"]

(1..10).sort {|a,b| b <=> a}   # =>   [10, 9, 8, 7, 6, 5, 4, 3, 2, 1]
```

sort_by
enum.sort_by { | *obj* | *block* } → *array*

Sorts *enum* using keys generated by mapping the values in *enum* through the given block, using the result of that block for element comparison.

```
sorted = %w{ apple pear fig }.sort_by {|word| word.length}

sorted  # =>   ["fig", "pear", "apple"]
```

Internally, sort_by generates an array of tuples containing the original collection element and the mapped value. This makes sort_by fairly expensive when the keysets are simple.

```
require 'benchmark'
include Benchmark
a = (1..100000).map {rand(100000)}
bm(10) do |b|
  b.report("Sort")    { a.sort }
  b.report("Sort by") { a.sort_by {|a| a} }
end
```

produces:

```
               user      system      total          real
Sort        0.030000    0.000000    0.030000 (   0.029595)
Sort by     0.130000    0.000000    0.130000 (   0.132719)
```

However, in cases where comparing the keys is a nontrivial operation, the algorithm used by sort_by is considerably faster.[1]

sort_by can also be useful for multilevel sorts. One trick, which relies on the fact that arrays are compared element by element, is to have the block return an array of each of the comparison keys. For example, to sort a list of words first on their length and then alphabetically, you could write the following:

```
words = %w{ puma cat bass ant aardvark gnu fish }
sorted = words.sort_by {|w| [w.length, w] }
sorted  # =>   ["ant", "cat", "gnu", "bass", "fish", "puma", "aardvark"]
```

Returns an Enumerator object if no block is given.

take
enum.take(*n*) → *array*

1.9

Returns an array containing the first *n* items from *enum*.

```
(1..7).take(3)                     # =>   [1, 2, 3]
{ 'a'=>1, 'b'=>2, 'c'=>3 }.take(2) # =>   [["a", 1], ["b", 2]]
```

take_while
enum.take_while { | *item* | *block* } → *array* or *enumerator*

1.9

Passes successive items to the block, adding them to the result array until the block returns false or nil. Returns an Enumerator object if no block is given.

1.　It caches the sort keys before the sort. Perl users often call this approach a Schwartzian Transform, named after Randal Schwartz.

E numerable

```
(1..7).take_while {|item| item < 3 }     # =>   [1, 2]
[ 2, 4, 6, 9, 11, 16 ].take_while(&:even?)  # =>   [2, 4, 6]
```

---

to_a   *enum*.to_a(*args) → *array*

1.9   Returns an array containing the items in *enum*. This is done using the each method. Any arguments passed to to_a are passed to each.

```
(1..7).to_a                # =>   [1, 2, 3, 4, 5, 6, 7]
{ 'a'=>1, 'b'=>2, 'c'=>3 }.to_a  # =>   [["a", 1], ["b", 2], ["c", 3]]
```

---

zip   *enum*.zip(⟨ *arg* ⟩⁺) → *array*

enum.zip(⟨ *arg* ⟩⁺) {| *arr* | *block* } → nil

Converts any arguments to arrays and then merges elements of *enum* with corresponding elements from each argument. The result is an array containing the same number of elements as *enum*. Each element is a *n*-element array, where *n* is one more than the count of arguments. If the size of any argument is less than the number of elements in *enum*, nil values are supplied. If a block given, it is invoked for each output array; otherwise, an array of arrays is returned.

```
a = [ 4, 5, 6 ]
b = [ 7, 8, 9 ]

(1..3).zip(a, b)   # =>   [[1, 4, 7], [2, 5, 8], [3, 6, 9]]
[1, 2].zip([3])    # =>   [[1, 3], [2, nil]]
(1..3).zip         # =>   [[1], [2], [3]]
```

Class

Enumerator < Object

1.9   Relies on: each, <=>

Enumerator allows you to capture the concept of an enumeration as an object. This allows you to store enumerations in variables, pass them as parameters, and so on.

Some of the methods in the Enumerable module can return an Enumerator object.

```
enum = (1..10).take_while {|num| num % 5 != 0 }
enum.class    # =>    Array
enum.to_a     # =>    [1, 2, 3, 4]
```

You can also create enumerators with the method Kernel#to_enum (or via its alias, Kernel#enum_for). By default, these methods look for an each method in the object you're enumerating, but this can be overridden by passing them the name of a method (and possibly parameters to be used) that invokes a block for each item to be enumerated.

```
str = "quick brown fox"
case what_to_process       # set elsewhere to :by_word
when :by_bytes
  enum = str.to_enum(:each_byte)
when :by_word
  enum = str.to_enum(:scan, /\w+/)
end
enum.each {|item| p item}
```

produces:

```
"quick"
"brown"
"fox"
```

Mixes in

Enumerable:

> all?, any?, collect, count, cycle, detect, drop, drop_while, each_cons, each_slice, each_with_index, entries, find, find_all, find_index, first, grep, group_by, include?, inject, map, max, max_by, member?, min, min_by, minmax, minmax_by, none?, one?, partition, reduce, reject, select, sort, sort_by, take, take_while, to_a, zip

Class methods

new   Enumerator.new {| *yielder* | *block* } → *enum*
               Enumerator.new(*obj*, *method*=:*each*, ⟨ *args* ⟩*) → *enum*

The second form constructs an enumerator based on the block. The block is passed an object of class Enumerator::Yielder. You can use the << or yield methods of this yielder to supply values to be returned by the enumerator. This process is performed lazily (similar to the way that fibers can be used to generate sequences).

```
def multiples_of(n)
  Enumerator.new do |yielder|
```

```
    number = 0
    loop do
      yielder.yield number
      number += n
    end
  end
end
twos = multiples_of(2)
threes = multiples_of(3)
5.times do
  puts "#{twos.next} #{threes.next}"
end
```

produces:

```
0 0
2 3
4 6
6 9
8 12
```

The second form builds an enumerator based on the given method of *obj*. Any additional arguments are passed to this method. The method then yields successive values to a block—these values are picked up and used by the new enumerator. You should avoid this form in favor of the equivalent to_enum call.

```
enum_poor = Enumerator.new(1..10, :each_slice, 3)
enum_poor.to_a   # =>   [[1, 2, 3], [4, 5, 6], [7, 8, 9], [10]]

enum_good = (1..10).enum_for(:each_slice, 3)
enum_good.to_a   # =>   [[1, 2, 3], [4, 5, 6], [7, 8, 9], [10]]
```

Instance methods

each   *enum*.each { | *item, ...* | *block* } →

Calls the block for each item in the enumeration. This does not create an intermediate array. Instead, the original iterating method (the one used when creating the enumerator) is called passing it the block passed to this method. The block receives as many parameters as the original method passes.

```
def dump_enum(enum)
  enum.each { |item| p item }
end
enum = (1..10).enum_for(:each_slice, 3)
dump_enum(enum)
```

produces:

```
[1, 2, 3]
[4, 5, 6]
[7, 8, 9]
[10]
```

Note that because Enumerator defines each and includes Enumerable, all the enumerable methods are available too.

```
enum = "quick brown fox".enum_for(:scan, /\w+/)
enum.minmax   # =>   ["brown", "quick"]
```

each_with_index   *enum*.each_with_index {| *item, ..., index* | *block* } →

Same as each but appends an index argument when calling the block. Returns a new Enumerator if no block is given.

```
enum = (1..10).enum_for(:each_slice, 3)
enum.each_with_index do |subarray, index|
  puts "#{index}: #{subarray}"
end
```

produces:

```
0: [1, 2, 3]
1: [4, 5, 6]
2: [7, 8, 9]
3: [10]
```

each_with_object
                 enum.each_with_object(*memo*) {| *item, memo* | *block* } → *memo* or *enumerator*

1.9   Calls *block* for each item in *enum*, passing it the item and the parameter passed initially to each_with_object. Returns an Enumerator object if no block is given.

```
animals = %w(cat dog wombat).to_enum
hash = animals.each_with_object({}) do |item, memo|
  memo[item] = item.upcase.reverse
end
hash   # =>   {"cat"=>"TAC", "dog"=>"GOD", "wombat"=>"TABMOW"}
```

next   *enum*.next →

Returns the next item in the enumeration. Raises StopIteration if you call it past the last item. Internally this is implemented using fibers and so cannot be called across threads.

```
array = [ 1, 2, 3, 4 ]
e1 = array.to_enum
e2 = array.to_enum
e1.next   # =>   1
e1.next   # =>   2
e2.next   # =>   1
```

If the underlying method called by the enumerator has side effects (such as moving your position while reading a file), those side effects will be triggered. For this reason, next breaks the abstraction provided by Enumerator.

```
f = File.open("testfile")
enum1 = f.to_enum(:each_byte)
enum2 = f.to_enum
enum1.next   # =>   84
enum1.next   # =>   104
enum2.next   # =>   "is is line one\n"
f.gets       # =>   "This is line two\n"
enum2.next   # =>   "This is line three\n"
```

rewind   *enum*.rewind → *enum*

Resets the sequence of values to be returned by next.

```
array = [ 1, 2, 3, 4 ]
e1 = array.to_enum
e2 = array.to_enum
e1.next   # =>   1
e1.next   # =>   2
e2.next   # =>   1
e1.rewind
e1.next   # =>   1
e2.next   # =>   2
```

Has no effect if the underlying method of the enumerator has side effects and therefore cannot be rewound.

```
enum = File.open("testfile").to_enum
enum.next   # =>   "This is line one\n"
enum.next   # =>   "This is line two\n"
enum.rewind
enum.next   # =>   "This is line one\n"
```

with_index   *enum*.with_index {| *item, ..., index* | *block* } →

Synonym for each_with_index.

with_object   *enum*.with_object(*memo*) {| *item, memo* | *block* } → *memo* or *enumerator*

1.9   Synonym for each_with_object.

Module
Errno

Ruby exception objects are subclasses of Exception. However, operating systems typically report errors using plain integers. Module Errno is created dynamically to map these operating system errors to Ruby classes, with each error number generating its own subclass of SystemCallError. As the subclass is created in module Errno, its name will start Errno::.

```
Exception
    StandardError
        SystemCallError
            Errno::xxx
```

The names of the Errno:: classes depend on the environment in which Ruby runs. On a typical Unix or Windows platform, you'll find Ruby has Errno classes such as Errno::EACCES, Errno::EAGAIN, Errno::EINTR, and so on.

The integer operating system error number corresponding to a particular error is available as the class constant Errno::*error*::Errno.

```
Errno::EACCES::Errno   # =>   13
Errno::EAGAIN::Errno   # =>   35
Errno::EINTR::Errno    # =>   4
```

The full list of operating system errors on your particular platform is available as the constants of Errno. Any user-defined exceptions in this module (including subclasses of existing exceptions) must also define an Errno constant.

```
Errno.constants   # =>   E2BIG, EACCES, EADDRINUSE, EADDRNOTAVAIL, EADV,
                         EAFNOSUPPORT, EAGAIN, ...
```

1.9   As of Ruby 1.8, exceptions are matched in rescue clauses using Module#===. The === method is overridden for class SystemCallError to compare based on the Errno value. Thus, if two distinct Errno classes have the same underlying Errno value, they will be treated as the same exception by a rescue clause.

Exception   <   Object

Class

Descendents of class Exception are used to communicate between raise methods and rescue statements in begin/end blocks. Exception objects carry information about the exception—its type (the exception's class name), an optional descriptive string, and optional traceback information.

The standard library defines the exceptions shown in Figure 27.1 on the facing page. Note that Ruby 1.9 has changed the hierarchy slightly: SecurityError is no longer a subclass of StandardError and so will not be rescued implicitly. See also the description of Errno on the previous page.

Class methods

exception   Exception.exception(⟨ *message* ⟩) → *exc*

Creates and returns a new exception object, optionally setting the message to *message*.

new   Exception.new(⟨ *message* ⟩) → *exc*

Creates and returns a new exception object, optionally setting the message to *message*.

Instance methods

backtrace   *exc*.backtrace → *array*

Returns any backtrace associated with the exception. The backtrace is an array of strings, each containing either *filename:line: in 'method'* or *filename:line*.

```
def a
  raise "boom"
end
def b
  a()
end
begin
  b()
rescue => detail
  print detail.backtrace.join("\n")
end
```

produces:

```
/tmp/prog.rb:2:in `a'
/tmp/prog.rb:6:in `b'
/tmp/prog.rb:10:in `<main>'
```

exception   *exc*.exception(⟨ *message* ⟩) → *exc* or *exception*

With no argument, returns the receiver. Otherwise, creates a new exception object of the same class as the receiver but with a different message.

Exception

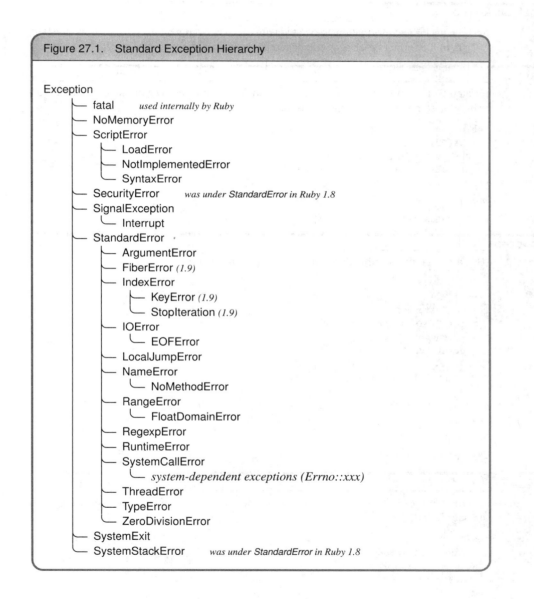

Figure 27.1. Standard Exception Hierarchy

Exception
├── fatal   *used internally by Ruby*
├── NoMemoryError
├── ScriptError
│   ├── LoadError
│   ├── NotImplementedError
│   └── SyntaxError
├── SecurityError   *was under StandardError in Ruby 1.8*
├── SignalException
│   └── Interrupt
├── StandardError
│   ├── ArgumentError
│   ├── FiberError *(1.9)*
│   ├── IndexError
│   │   ├── KeyError *(1.9)*
│   │   └── StopIteration *(1.9)*
│   ├── IOError
│   │   └── EOFError
│   ├── LocalJumpError
│   ├── NameError
│   │   └── NoMethodError
│   ├── RangeError
│   │   └── FloatDomainError
│   ├── RegexpError
│   ├── RuntimeError
│   ├── SystemCallError
│   │   └── *system-dependent exceptions (Errno::xxx)*
│   ├── ThreadError
│   ├── TypeError
│   └── ZeroDivisionError
├── SystemExit
└── SystemStackError   *was under StandardError in Ruby 1.8*

---

message   *exc*.message → *msg*

Returns the message associated with this exception.

---

set_backtrace   *exc*.set_backtrace(*array*) → *array*

Sets the backtrace information associated with *exc*. The argument must be an array of String objects in the format described in Exception#backtrace.

---

status   *exc*.status → status

1.9 (SystemExit only) Returns the exit status associated with this SystemExit exception. Normally this status is set using the Kernel#exit.

```
begin
  exit(99)
rescue SystemExit => e
  puts "Exit status is: #{e.status}"
end
```

produces:

```
Exit status is: 99
```

---

success?   *exc*.success? → true or false

1.9 (SystemExit only) Returns true is the exit status if nil or zero.

```
begin
  exit(99)
rescue SystemExit => e
  print "This program "
  if e.success?
    print "did"
  else
    print "did not"
  end
  puts " succeed"
end
```

produces:

```
This program did not succeed
```

---

to_s   *exc*.to_s → *msg*

Returns the message associated with this exception (or the name of the exception if no message is set).

```
begin
  raise "The message"
rescue Exception => e
  puts e.to_s
end
```

produces:

```
The message
```

Class

FalseClass < Object

The global value false is the only instance of class FalseClass and represents a logically false value in boolean expressions. The class provides operators allowing false to participate correctly in logical expressions.

Instance methods

&   false & *obj* → false

And—Returns false. *obj* is always evaluated because it is the argument to a method call—no short-circuit evaluation is performed in this case. In other words, the following code, which uses &&, will not invoke the lookup method.

```
def lookup(val)
  puts "Looking up #{val}"
  return true
end
false && lookup("cat")
```

However, this code, using &, will:

```
false & lookup("cat")
```

produces:

```
Looking up cat
```

^   false ^ *obj* → true or false

Exclusive Or—If *obj* is nil or false, returns false; otherwise, returns true.

| false | *obj* → true or false

Or—Returns false if *obj* is nil or false; true otherwise.

Class
Fiber < Object

1.9

A fiber is a lightweight asymetrical coroutine. Code in a fiber is created in a suspended state. It runs when resumed and can suspend itself (passing a value back to the code that resumed it). There is a full description of fibers on page 169.

```
fibs = Fiber.new do
  n1 = n2 = 1
  loop do
    Fiber.yield n1
    n1, n2 = n2, n1+n2
  end
end
10.times { print fibs.resume, ' ' }
```

produces:

```
1 1 2 3 5 8 13 21 34 55
```

Class methods

new
Fiber.new { *block* } → *fiber*

Uses the block as a new, suspended fiber.

yield
Fiber.yield(⟨ val ⟩*) → *obj*

Suspends execution of the current fiber. Any parameters will be returned as the value of the resume call that awoke the fiber. Similarly, any values passed to resume will become the return value of the subsequent yield.

```
f = Fiber.new do
  num = 1
  loop do
    num += Fiber.yield(num)
  end
end
square = 1
10.times do
  square = f.resume(square)
  print square, ' '
end
```

produces:

```
1 2 4 8 16 32 64 128 256 512
```

Instance methods

resume
fiber.resume(⟨ ( )*val)) → *obj*

Resumes *fiber*. See Fiber.yield for a discussion and example of parameter passing.

Class

File < IO

A File is an abstraction of any file object accessible by the program and is closely associated with class IO, page 537. File includes the methods of module FileTest as class methods, allowing you to write (for example) File.exist?("foo").

In this section, *permission bits* are a platform-specific set of bits that indicate permissions of a file. On Unix-based systems, permissions are viewed as a set of three octets, for the owner, the group, and the rest of the world. For each of these entities, permissions may be set to read, write, or execute the file.

Owner			Group			Other		
r	w	x	r	w	x	r	w	x
4	2	1	4	2	1	4	2	1

The permission bits 0644 (in octal) would thus be interpreted as read/write for owner and read-only for group and other. Higher-order bits may also be used to indicate the type of file (plain, directory, pipe, socket, and so on) and various other special features. If the permissions are for a directory, the meaning of the execute bit changes; when set, the directory can be searched.

Each file has three associated times. The *atime* is the time the file was last accessed. The *ctime* is the time that the file status (not necessarily the file contents) were last changed. Finally, the *mtime* is the time the file's data was last modified. In Ruby, all these times are returned as Time objects.

On non-POSIX operating systems, there may be only the ability to make a file read-only or read/write. In this case, the remaining permission bits will be synthesized to resemble typical values. For instance, on Windows the default permission bits are 0644, which means read/write for owner and read-only for all others. The only change that can be made is to make the file read-only, which is reported as 0444.

See also Pathname on page 779 and IO on page 537.

Class methods

absolute_path File.absolute_path(*filename* ⟨ , *dirstring* ⟩) → *filename*

1.9

Converts a path name to an absolute path name. Relative paths are referenced from the current working directory of the process unless *dirstring* is given, in which case it will be used as the starting point. Path names starting with ~ are not expanded, in contrast with File#expand_path.

```
puts File.absolute_path("bin")
puts File.absolute_path("../../bin", "/tmp/x")
```

produces:

```
/Users/dave/BS2/titles/RUBY3/Book/bin
/bin
```

F ile

atime   File.atime(*filename*) → *time*

Returns a Time object containing the last access time for the named file, or returns epoch if
the file has not been accessed.

```
File.atime("testfile")  # =>  2009-03-31 09:58:10 -0500
```

basename   File.basename(*filename* ⟨ , *suffix* ⟩) → *string*

Returns the last component of the filename given in *filename*. If *suffix* is given and is present
at the end of *filename*, it is removed. Any extension can be removed by giving an extension
of .*.

```
File.basename("/home/gumby/work/ruby.rb")          # =>   "ruby.rb"
File.basename("/home/gumby/work/ruby.rb", ".rb")   # =>   "ruby"
File.basename("/home/gumby/work/ruby.rb", ".*")    # =>   "ruby"
```

blockdev?   File.blockdev?(*filename*) → true or false

Returns true if the named file is a block device and returns false if it isn't or if the operating
system doesn't support this feature.

```
File.blockdev?("testfile")  # =>  false
```

chardev?   File.chardev?(*filename*) → true or false

Returns true if the named file is a character device and returns false if it isn't or if the
operating system doesn't support this feature.

```
File.chardev?("/dev/tty")  # =>  true
```

chmod   File.chmod(*permission* ⟨ , *filename* ⟩⁺) → *int*

Changes permission bits on the named file(s) to the bit pattern represented by *permission*.
Actual effects are operating system dependent (see the beginning of this section). On Unix
systems, see chmod(2) for details. Returns the number of files processed.

```
File.chmod(0644, "testfile", "out")  # =>  2
```

chown   File.chown(*owner, group* ⟨ , *filename* ⟩⁺) → *int*

Changes the owner and/or group of the named file(s) to the given numeric owner and group
IDs. Only a process with superuser privileges may change the owner of a file. The current
owner of a file may change the file's group to any group to which the owner belongs. A nil
or −1 owner or group ID is ignored. Returns the number of files processed.

```
File.chown(nil, 100, "testfile")
```

ctime   File.ctime(*filename*) → *time*

Returns a Time object containing the time that the file status associated with the named file
was changed.

```
File.ctime("testfile")  # =>  2009-03-31 09:58:11 -0500
```

delete   File.delete(⟨ *filename* ⟩⁺) → *int*

Deletes the named file(s). Returns the number of files processed. See also Dir.rmdir.

```
File.open("testrm", "w+") {}
File.delete("testrm")  # =>  1
```

directory?   File.directory?(*path*) → true or false

Returns true if the named file is a directory; returns false otherwise.

```
File.directory?(".")  # =>  true
```

dirname   File.dirname(*filename*) → *filename*

Returns all components of the filename given in *filename* except the last one.

```
File.dirname("/home/gumby/work/ruby.rb")  # =>  "/home/gumby/work"
File.dirname("ruby.rb")                   # =>  "."
```

executable?   File.executable?(*filename*) → true or false

Returns true if the named file is executable. The tests are made using the effective owner of the process.

```
File.executable?("testfile")  # =>  false
```

executable_real?   File.executable_real?(*filename*) → true or false

Same as File#executable? but tests using the real owner of the process.

exist?   File.exist?(*filename*) → true or false

Returns true if the named file or directory exists.

```
File.exist?("testfile")  # =>  true
```

exists?   File.exists? (*filename*) → true or false

Synonym for File.exist?.

expand_path   File.expand_path(*filename* ⟨ , *dirstring* ⟩) → *filename*

Converts a path name to an absolute path name. Relative paths are referenced from the current working directory of the process unless *dirstring* is given, in which case it will be used as the starting point. The given path name may start with a ~, which expands to the process owner's home directory (the environment variable HOME must be set correctly). *~user* expands to the named user's home directory. See also File#absolute_path.

```
File.expand_path("~/bin")               # =>  "/Users/dave/bin"
File.expand_path("../../bin", "/tmp/x") # =>  "/bin"
```

extname   File.extname(*path*) → *string*

Returns the extension (the portion of filename in *path* after the period).

```
File.extname("test.rb")        # =>   ".rb"
File.extname("a/b/d/test.rb")  # =>   ".rb"
File.extname("test")           # =>   ""
```

---

file?   File.file?(*filename*) → true or false

Returns true if the named file is a regular file (not a device file, directory, pipe, socket, and
so on).

```
File.file?("testfile")  # =>   true
File.file?(".")         # =>   false
```

---

fnmatch   File.fnmatch(*glob_pattern*, *path*, ⟨ *flags* ⟩) → true or false

1.9   Returns true if *path* matches against *glob_pattern*. (As of Ruby 1.9, File.fnmatch is an alias
for Dir.fnmatch.) The pattern is not a regular expression; instead, it follows rules similar to
shell filename globbing. A *glob_pattern* may contain the following metacharacters.

*	Matches zero or more characters in a file or directory name.
**	Matches zero or more characters, ignoring name boundaries. Most often used to scan subdirectories recursively.
?	Matches any single character.
[*charset*]	Matches any character from the given set of characters. A range of characters is written as *from-to*. The set may be negated with an initial caret (^).
\	Escapes any special meaning of the next character.

flags is a bitwise OR of the FNM_xxx parameters listed on the next page. See also Dir.glob
on page 471.

```
File.fnmatch('cat',      'cat')         # =>   true
File.fnmatch('cat',      'category')    # =>   false
File.fnmatch('c?t',      'cat')         # =>   true
File.fnmatch('c\?t',     'cat')         # =>   false

File.fnmatch('c??t',     'cat')                         # =>   false
File.fnmatch('c*',       'cats')                        # =>   true
File.fnmatch('c/**/t',   'c/a/b/c/t')                   # =>   true
File.fnmatch('c**t',     'c/a/b/c/t')                   # =>   true
File.fnmatch('c**t',     'cat')                         # =>   true
File.fnmatch('**.txt',   'notes.txt')                   # =>   true
File.fnmatch('**.txt',   'some/dir/tree/notes.txt')     # =>   true
File.fnmatch('c*t',      'cat')                         # =>   true
File.fnmatch('c\at',     'cat')                         # =>   true
File.fnmatch('c\at',     'cat', File::FNM_NOESCAPE)     # =>   false
File.fnmatch('a?b',      'a/b')                         # =>   true
File.fnmatch('a?b',      'a/b', File::FNM_PATHNAME)     # =>   false
```

Table 27.3. Match-Mode Constants

FNM_NOESCAPE	Backslash does not escape special characters in globs, and a backslash in the pattern must match a backslash in the filename.
FNM_PATHNAME	Forward slashes in the filename are treated as separating parts of a path and so must be explicitly matched in the pattern.
FNM_DOTMATCH	If this option is not specified, filenames containing leading periods must be matched by an explicit period in the pattern. A leading period is one at the start of the filename or (if FNM_PATHNAME is specified) following a slash.
FNM_CASEFOLD	Filename matches are case insensitive

```
File.fnmatch('*',    '.profile')                            # =>   false
File.fnmatch('*',    '.profile', File::FNM_DOTMATCH)        # =>   true
File.fnmatch('*',    'dave/.profile')                       # =>   true
File.fnmatch('*',    'dave/.profile', File::FNM_DOTMATCH)   # =>   true
File.fnmatch('*',    'dave/.profile', File::FNM_PATHNAME)   # =>   false
File.fnmatch('*/*', 'dave/.profile', File::FNM_PATHNAME)    # =>   false
STRICT = File::FNM_PATHNAME | File::FNM_DOTMATCH
File.fnmatch('*/*', 'dave/.profile', STRICT)                # =>   true
```

fnmatch?   File.fnmatch?(*glob_pattern, path,* ⟨ *flags* ⟩) → (true or false)

Synonym for File#fnmatch.

ftype   File.ftype(*filename*) → *filetype*

Identifies the type of the named file. The return string is one of file, directory, characterSpecial, blockSpecial, fifo, link, socket, or unknown.

```
File.ftype("testfile")     # =>   "file"
File.ftype("/dev/tty")     # =>   "characterSpecial"
system("mkfifo wibble")    # =>   true
File.ftype("wibble")       # =>   "fifo"
```

grpowned?   File.grpowned?(*filename*) → true or false

Returns true if the effective group ID of the process is the same as the group ID of the named file. On Windows, returns false.

```
File.grpowned?("/etc/passwd")   # =>   false
```

identical?   File.identical?(*name1, name2*) → true or false

Returns true only if *name1* and *name2* refer to the same file. Two separate files with the same content are not considered to be identical.

```
File.identical?("testfile", "./code/../testfile")   # =>   true
File.symlink("testfile", "wibble")
File.identical?("testfile", "wibble")               # =>   true
File.link("testfile", "wobble")
File.identical?("testfile", "wobble")               # =>   true
File.identical?("wibble", "wobble")                 # =>   true
```

join

File.join(⟨ *string* ⟩⁺) → *filename*

Returns a new string formed by joining the strings using File::SEPARATOR. The various separators are listed in Table 27.4 on the next page.

```
File.join("usr", "mail", "gumby")   # =>   "usr/mail/gumby"
```

lchmod

File.lchmod(*permission*, ⟨ *filename* ⟩⁺) → 0

Equivalent to File.chmod but does not follow symbolic links (so it will change the permissions associated with the link, not the file referenced by the link). Often not available.

lchown

File.lchown(*owner*, *group*, ⟨ *filename* ⟩⁺) → 0

Equivalent to File.chown but does not follow symbolic links (so it will change the owner associated with the link, not the file referenced by the link). Often not available.

link

File.link(*oldname*, *newname*) → 0

Creates a new name for an existing file using a hard link. Will not overwrite *newname* if it already exists (in which case link raises a subclass of SystemCallError). Not available on all platforms.

```
File.link("testfile", "testfile.2")   # =>   0
f = File.open("testfile.2")
f.gets                                 # =>   "This is line one\n"
File.delete("testfile.2")
```

lstat

File.lstat(*filename*) → *stat*

Returns status information for *file* as an object of type File::Stat. Same as IO#stat (see page 552), but does not follow the last symbolic link. Instead, reports on the link itself.

```
File.symlink("testfile", "link2test")   # =>   0
File.stat("testfile").size              # =>   66
File.lstat("link2test").size            # =>   8
File.stat("link2test").size             # =>   66
```

mtime

File.mtime(*filename*) → *time*

Returns a Time object containing the modification time for the named file.

```
File.mtime("testfile")   # =>   2009-03-31 09:09:07 -0500
File.mtime("/tmp")       # =>   2009-03-31 09:54:58 -0500
```

Table 27.4. Path Separator Constants (Platform-Specific)

ALT_SEPARATOR	Alternate path separator (\ on Windows, nil otherwise).
PATH_SEPARATOR	Separator for filenames in a search path (such as : or ;).
SEPARATOR	Separator for directory components in a filename (such as \ or /).
Separator	Alias for SEPARATOR.

new

File.new(*filename, modestring*="r") → *file*
File.new(*filename* ⟨ , *modenum* ⟨ , *permission* ⟩ ⟩) → *file*
File.new(*fd* ⟨ , *modenum* ⟨ , *permission* ⟩ ⟩) → *file*

1.9

Opens the file named by *filename* according to *modestring* (the default is "r") and returns a new File object. The *modestring* is described in Table 27.7 on page 538—it contains both information on the way the file is to be opened and optionally on the encodings to be associated with the file data. The file mode may optionally be specified as a Fixnum by *or*-ing together the flags described in Table 27.5 on page 505. Optional permission bits may be given in *permission*. These mode and permission bits are platform dependent; on Unix systems, see open(2) for details. If the first parameter is an integer (or can be converted to an integer using to_int, it is assumed to be the file descriptor or an already-open file. In that case, the call is passed to IO.new for processing. See also IO.open on page 505 for a block form of File.new.

```
# open for reading, default external encoding
f = File.new("testfile", "r")

# open for reading, assume contents are utf-8
f = File.new("testfile", "r:utf-8")

# open for read/write. external utf-8 data will be converted to iso-8859-1
# when read, and converted from 8859-1 to utf-8 on writing
f = File.new("newfile",  "w+:utf-8:iso-8859-1")

# same as specifying "w+"
f = File.new("newfile", File::CREAT|File::TRUNC|File::RDWR, 0644)
```

owned?

File.owned?(*filename*) → true or false

Returns true if the effective user ID of the process is the same as the owner of the named file.

```
File.owned?("/etc/passwd")  # =>   false
```

path

File.path(*obj*) → *string*

1.9

Returns the path of *obj*. If *obj* responds to to_path, its value is returned. Otherwise, attempt to convert *obj* to a string and return that value.

```
File.path("testfile")           # =>   "testfile"
File.path("/tmp/../tmp/xxx")     # =>   "/tmp/../tmp/xxx"
f = File.open("/tmp/../tmp/xxx")
File.path(f)                     # =>   "/tmp/../tmp/xxx"
```

---

pipe?   File.pipe?(*filename*) → true or false

Returns true if the OS supports pipes and the named file is one; false otherwise.

```
File.pipe?("testfile")   # =>   false
```

---

readable?   File.readable?(*filename*) → true or false

Returns true if the named file is readable by the effective user ID of this process.

```
File.readable?("testfile")   # =>   true
```

---

readable_real?   File.readable_real?(*filename*) → true or false

Returns true if the named file is readable by the real user ID of this process.

```
File.readable_real?("testfile")   # =>   true
```

---

readlink   File.readlink(*filename*) → *filename*

Returns the given symbolic link as a string. Not available on all platforms.

```
File.symlink("testfile", "link2test")   # =>   0
File.readlink("link2test")              # =>   "testfile"
```

---

rename   File.rename(*oldname, newname*) → 0

Renames the given file or directory to the new name. Raises a SystemCallError if the file cannot be renamed.

```
File.rename("afile", "afile.bak")   # =>   0
```

---

setgid?   File.setgid?(*filename*) → true or false

Returns true if the named file's set-group-id permission bit is set and returns false if it isn't or if the operating system doesn't support this feature.

```
File.setgid?("/usr/sbin/lpc")   # =>   false
```

---

setuid?   File.setuid?(*filename*) → true or false

Returns true if the named file's set-user-id permission bit is set and returns false if it isn't or if the operating system doesn't support this feature.

```
File.setuid?("/bin/su")   # =>   false
```

---

size   File.size(*filename*) → *int*

Returns the size of the file in bytes.

```
File.size("testfile")   # =>   66
```

---

size?   File.size?(*filename*) → *int* or nil

Returns nil if the named file is of zero length; otherwise, returns the size. Usable as a condition in tests.

```
File.size?("testfile")    # =>   66
File.size?("/dev/zero")   # =>   nil
```

Table 27.5. Open-Mode Constants

File::APPEND	Opens the file in append mode; all writes will occur at end of file.
File::CREAT	Creates the file on open if it does not exist.
File::EXCL	When used with File::CREAT, opens will fail if the file exists.
File::NOCTTY	When opening a terminal device (see IO#isatty on page 548), does not allow it to become the controlling terminal.
File::NONBLOCK	Opens the file in nonblocking mode.
File::RDONLY	Opens for reading only.
File::RDWR	Opens for reading and writing.
File::TRUNC	Opens the file and truncates it to zero length if the file exists.
File::WRONLY	Opens for writing only.

---

socket?   File.socket?(*filename*) → true or false

Returns true if the named file is a socket and returns false if it isn't or if the operating system doesn't support this feature.

---

split   File.split(*filename*) → *array*

Splits the given string into a directory and a file component and returns them in a two-element array. See also File.dirname and File.basename.

```
File.split("/home/gumby/.profile")   # =>   ["/home/gumby", ".profile"]
File.split("ruby.rb")                # =>   [".", "ruby.rb"]
```

---

stat   File.stat(*filename*) → *stat*

Returns a File::Stat object for the named file (see File::Stat, page 509).

```
stat = File.stat("testfile")
stat.mtime  # =>   2009-03-31 09:09:07 -0500
stat.ftype  # =>   "file"
```

---

sticky?   File.sticky?(*filename*) → true or false

Returns true if the named file has its sticky bit set and returns false if it doesn't or if the operating system doesn't support this feature.

---

symlink   File.symlink(*oldname*, *newname*) → 0 or nil

Creates a symbolic link called *newname* for the file *oldname*. Returns nil on all platforms that do not support symbolic links.

```
File.symlink("testfile", "link2test")   # =>   0
```

---

symlink?   File.symlink?(*filename*) → true or false

Returns true if the named file is a symbolic link and returns false if it isn't or if the operating system doesn't support this feature.

```
File.symlink("testfile", "link2test")   # =>   0
File.symlink?("link2test")              # =>   true
```

truncate   File.truncate(*filename*, *int*) → 0

Truncates the file *filename* to be at most *int* bytes long. Not available on all platforms.

```
f = File.new("out", "w")
f.write("1234567890")    # =>   10
f.close                  # =>   nil
File.truncate("out", 5)  # =>   0
File.size("out")         # =>   5
```

umask   File.umask(⟨ *int* ⟩) → *int*

Returns the current umask value for this process. If the optional argument is given, sets the umask to that value and returns the previous value. Umask values are *excluded* from the default permissions; so a umask of 0222 would make a file read-only for everyone. See also the discussion of permissions on page 497.

```
File.umask(0006)  # =>   18
File.umask        # =>   6
```

unlink   File.unlink(⟨ *filename* ⟩⁺) → *int*

Synonym for File.delete. See also Dir.rmdir.

```
File.open("testrm", "w+") {}  # =>   nil
File.unlink("testrm")         # =>   1
```

utime   File.utime(*accesstime*, *modtime* ⟨ , *filename* ⟩⁺) → *int*

Changes the access and modification times on a number of files. The times must be instances of class Time or integers representing the number of seconds since epoch. Returns the number of files processed. Not available on all platforms.

```
File.utime(0, 0, "testfile")         # =>   1
File.mtime("testfile")               # =>   1969-12-31 18:00:00 -0600
File.utime(0, Time.now, "testfile")  # =>   1
File.mtime("testfile")               # =>   2009-03-31 09:58:11 -0500
```

world_readable?   File.world_readable?(*filename*) → *perm_int* or nil

If *filename* is readable by others, returns an integer representing the file permission bits of *filename*. Returns nil otherwise. The meaning of the bits is platform dependent; on Unix systems, see stat(2).

```
File.world_readable?("/etc/passwd")            # =>   420
File.world_readable?("/etc/passwd").to_s(8)    # =>   "644"
```

world_writable?   File.world_writable?(*filename*) → *perm_int* or nil

If *filename* is writable by others, returns an integer representing the file permission bits of *filename*. Returns nil otherwise. The meaning of the bits is platform dependent; on Unix systems, see stat(2).

```
File.world_writable?("/etc/passwd")      # =>   nil
File.world_writable?("/tmp")             # =>   511
File.world_writable?("/tmp").to_s(8)     # =>   "777"
```

writable?   File.writable?(*filename*) → true or false

Returns true if the named file is writable by the effective user ID of this process.

```
File.writable?("/etc/passwd")    # =>    false
File.writable?("testfile")       # =>    true
```

writable_real?   File.writable_real?(*filename*) → true or false

Returns true if the named file is writable by the real user ID of this process.

zero?   File.zero?(*filename*) → true or false

Returns true if the named file is of zero length and returns false otherwise.

```
File.zero?("testfile")   # =>    false
File.open("zerosize", "w") {}
File.zero?("zerosize")   # =>    true
```

Instance methods

atime   *file*.atime → *time*

Returns a Time object containing the last access time for *file*, or returns epoch if the file has not been accessed.

```
File.new("testfile").atime   # =>   1969-12-31 18:00:00 -0600
```

chmod   *file*.chmod(*permission*) → 0

Changes permission bits on *file* to the bit pattern represented by *permission*. Actual effects are platform dependent; on Unix systems, see chmod(2) for details. Follows symbolic links. See the discussion of permissions on page 497. Also see File#lchmod.

```
f = File.new("out", "w");
f.chmod(0644)   # =>   0
```

chown   *file*.chown(*owner, group*) → 0

Changes the owner and group of *file* to the given numeric owner and group IDs. Only a process with superuser privileges may change the owner of a file. The current owner of a file may change the file's group to any group to which the owner belongs. A nil or −1 owner or group id is ignored. Follows symbolic links. See also File#lchown.

```
File.new("testfile").chown(502, 1000)
```

ctime   *file*.ctime → *time*

Returns a Time object containing the time that the file status associated with *file* was changed.

```
File.new("testfile").ctime   # =>   2009-03-31 09:58:11 -0500
```

flock   *file*.flock (*locking_constant*) → 0 or false

Locks or unlocks a file according to *locking_constant* (a logical *or* of the values shown in Table 27.6 on the facing page). Returns false if File::LOCK_NB is specified and the operation would otherwise have blocked. Not available on all platforms.

```
File.new("testfile").flock(File::LOCK_UN)   # =>   0
```

lchmod   *file*.lchmod(*permission*) → 0

Equivalent to File#chmod but does not follow symbolic links (so it will change the permissions associated with the link, not the file referenced by the link). Often not available.

lchown   *file*.lchown(*owner*, *group*) → 0

Equivalent to File#chown but does not follow symbolic links (so it will change the owner associated with the link, not the file referenced by the link). Often not available.

lstat   *file*.lstat → *stat*

Same as IO#stat but does not follow the last symbolic link. Instead, reports on the link itself.

```
File.symlink("testfile", "link2test")   # =>   0
File.stat("testfile").size              # =>   66
f = File.new("link2test")
f.lstat.size                            # =>   8
f.stat.size                             # =>   66
```

mtime   *file*.mtime → *time*

Returns a Time object containing the modification time for *file*.

```
File.new("testfile").mtime   # =>   2009-03-31 09:58:11 -0500
```

path   *file*.path → *filename*

Returns the path name used to create *file* as a string. Does not normalize the name.

```
File.new("testfile").path               # =>   "testfile"
File.new("/tmp/../tmp/xxx", "w").path   # =>   "/tmp/../tmp/xxx"
```

to_path   *file*.to_path → *filename*

Alias for File#path.

truncate   *file*.truncate(*int*) → 0

Truncates *file* to at most *int* bytes. The file must be opened for writing. Not available on all platforms.

```
f = File.new("out", "w")
f.syswrite("1234567890")   # =>   10
f.truncate(5)              # =>   0
f.close()                  # =>   nil
File.size("out")           # =>   5
```

Table 27.6. Lock-Mode Constants

LOCK_EX	Exclusive lock. Only one process may hold an exclusive lock for a given file at a time.
LOCK_NB	Don't block when locking. May be combined with other lock options using logical *or*.
LOCK_SH	Shared lock. Multiple processes may each hold a shared lock for a given file at the same time.
LOCK_UN	Unlock.

Class **File::Stat** < Object

Objects of class File::Stat encapsulate common status information for File objects. The information is recorded at the moment the File::Stat object is created; changes made to the file after that point will not be reflected. File::Stat objects are returned by IO#stat, File.stat, File#lstat, and File.lstat. Many of these methods may return platform-specific values, and not all values are meaningful on all systems. See also Kernel#test on page 570.

Mixes in

Comparable:

    <, <=, ==, >=, >, between?

Instance methods

<=>
                                                      statfile <=> *other_stat* → −1, 0, 1

Compares File::Stat objects by comparing their respective modification times.

```
f1 = File.new("f1", "w")
sleep 1
f2 = File.new("f2", "w")
f1.stat <=> f2.stat   # =>   -1
# Methods in Comparable are also available
f1.stat > f2.stat     # =>   false
f1.stat < f2.stat     # =>   true
```

atime
                                                              statfile.atime → *time*

Returns a Time object containing the last access time for *statfile*, or returns epoch if the file has not been accessed.

```
File.stat("testfile").atime       # =>   1969-12-31 18:00:00 -0600
File.stat("testfile").atime.to_i  # =>   0
```

blksize
                                                           statfile.blksize → *int*

Returns the native file system's block size. Will return nil on platforms that don't support this information.

```
File.stat("testfile").blksize  # =>   4096
```

blockdev?   *statfile*.blockdev? → true or false

Returns true if the file is a block device and returns false if it isn't or if the operating system doesn't support this feature.

```
File.stat("testfile").blockdev?    # =>    false
File.stat("/dev/disk0").blockdev?  # =>    true
```

blocks   *statfile*.blocks → *int*

Returns the number of native file system blocks allocated for this file or returns nil if the operating system doesn't support this feature.

```
File.stat("testfile").blocks   # =>    8
```

chardev?   *statfile*.chardev? → true or false

Returns true if the file is a character device and returns false if it isn't or if the operating system doesn't support this feature.

```
File.stat("/dev/tty").chardev?     # =>    true
File.stat("testfile").chardev?     # =>    false
```

ctime   *statfile*.ctime → *time*

Returns a Time object containing the time that the file status associated with *statfile* was changed.

```
File.stat("testfile").ctime    # =>    2009-03-31 09:58:11 -0500
```

dev   *statfile*.dev → *int*

Returns an integer representing the device on which *statfile* resides. The bits in the device integer will often encode major and minor device information.

```
File.stat("testfile").dev            # =>    234881032
"%x" % File.stat("testfile").dev     # =>    "e000008"
```

dev_major   *statfile*.dev_major → *int*

Returns the major part of File::Stat#dev or nil if the operating system doesn't support this feature.

```
File.stat("testfile").dev_major    # =>    14
```

dev_minor   *statfile*.dev_minor → *int*

Returns the minor part of File::Stat#dev or nil if the operating system doesn't support this feature.

```
File.stat("testfile").dev_minor    # =>    8
```

directory?   *statfile*.directory? → true or false

Returns true if *statfile* is a directory and returns false otherwise.

```
File.stat("testfile").directory?    # =>    false
File.stat(".").directory?           # =>    true
```

executable?   *statfile*.executable? → true or false

Returns true if *statfile* is executable or if the operating system doesn't distinguish executable files from nonexecutable files. The tests are made using the effective owner of the process.

```
File.stat("testfile").executable?   # =>    false
```

executable_real?   *statfile*.executable_real? → true or false

Same as executable? but tests using the real owner of the process.

file?   *statfile*.file? → true or false

Returns true if *statfile* is a regular file (not a device file, pipe, socket, and so on).

```
File.stat("testfile").file?   # =>    true
```

ftype   *statfile*.ftype → *type_string*

Identifies the type of *statfile*. The return string is one of the following: file, directory, characterSpecial, blockSpecial, fifo, link, socket, or unknown.

```
File.stat("/dev/tty").ftype   # =>    "characterSpecial"
```

gid   *statfile*.gid → *int*

Returns the numeric group ID of the owner of *statfile*.

```
File.stat("testfile").gid   # =>    501
```

grpowned?   *statfile*.grpowned? → true or false

Returns true if the effective group ID of the process is the same as the group ID of *statfile*. On Windows, returns false.

```
File.stat("testfile").grpowned?     # =>    true
File.stat("/etc/passwd").grpowned?  # =>    false
```

ino   *statfile*.ino → *int*

Returns the inode number for *statfile*.

```
File.stat("testfile").ino   # =>    1707345
```

mode   *statfile*.mode → *int*

Returns an integer representing the permission bits of *statfile*. The meaning of the bits is platform dependent; on Unix systems, see stat(2).

```
File.chmod(0644, "testfile")        # =>    1
File.stat("testfile").mode.to_s(8)  # =>    "100644"
```

mtime   *statfile*.mtime → *time*

Returns a Time object containing the modification time for *statfile*.

```
File.stat("testfile").mtime   # =>   2009-03-31 09:58:11 -0500
```

nlink   *statfile*.nlink → *int*

Returns the number of hard links to *statfile*.

```
File.stat("testfile").nlink          # =>   1
File.link("testfile", "testfile.bak")  # =>   0
File.stat("testfile").nlink          # =>   2
```

owned?   *statfile*.owned? → true or false

Returns true if the effective user ID of the process is the same as the owner of *statfile*.

```
File.stat("testfile").owned?     # =>   true
File.stat("/etc/passwd").owned?  # =>   false
```

pipe?   *statfile*.pipe? → true or false

Returns true if the operating system supports pipes and *statfile* is a pipe.

rdev   *statfile*.rdev → *int*

Returns an integer representing the device type on which *statfile* (which should be a special file) resides. Returns nil if the operating system doesn't support this feature.

```
File.stat("/dev/disk0s1").rdev  # =>   234881026
File.stat("/dev/tty").rdev      # =>   33554432
```

rdev_major   *statfile*.rdev_major → *int*

Returns the major part of File::Stat#rdev or nil if the operating system doesn't support this feature.

```
File.stat("/dev/disk0s1").rdev_major  # =>   14
File.stat("/dev/tty").rdev_major      # =>   2
```

rdev_minor   *statfile*.rdev_minor → *int*

Returns the minor part of File::Stat#rdev or nil if the operating system doesn't support this feature.

```
File.stat("/dev/disk0s1").rdev_minor  # =>   2
File.stat("/dev/tty").rdev_minor      # =>   0
```

readable?   *statfile*.readable? → true or false

Returns true if *statfile* is readable by the effective user ID of this process.

```
File.stat("testfile").readable?  # =>   true
```

readable_real?   *statfile*.readable_real? → true or false

Returns true if *statfile* is readable by the real user ID of this process.

```
File.stat("testfile").readable_real?      # =>    true
File.stat("/etc/passwd").readable_real?   # =>    true
```

setgid?   *statfile*.setgid? → true or false

Returns true if *statfile* has the set-group-id permission bit set and returns false if it doesn't or if the operating system doesn't support this feature.

```
File.stat("testfile").setgid?             # =>    false
File.stat("/usr/sbin/postdrop").setgid?   # =>    true
```

setuid?   *statfile*.setuid? → true or false

Returns true if *statfile* has the set-user-id permission bit set and returns false if it doesn't or if the operating system doesn't support this feature.

```
File.stat("testfile").setuid?     # =>    false
File.stat("/usr/bin/su").setuid?  # =>    true
```

size   *statfile*.size → *int*

Returns the size of *statfile* in bytes.

```
File.stat("/dev/zero").size  # =>    0
File.stat("testfile").size   # =>    66
```

size?   *statfile*.size? → *int* or nil

Returns nil if *statfile* is a zero-length file; otherwise, returns the file size. Usable as a condition in tests.

```
File.stat("/dev/zero").size?  # =>    nil
File.stat("testfile").size?   # =>    66
```

socket?   *statfile*.socket? → true or false

Returns true if *statfile* is a socket and returns false if it isn't or if the operating system doesn't support this feature.

```
File.stat("testfile").socket?  # =>    false
```

sticky?   *statfile*.sticky? → true or false

Returns true if *statfile* has its sticky bit set and returns false if it doesn't or if the operating system doesn't support this feature.

```
File.stat("testfile").sticky?  # =>    false
```

symlink?   *statfile*.symlink? → true or false

Returns true if *statfile* is a symbolic link; returns false if it isn't or if the operating system doesn't support this feature. Because File.stat automatically follows symbolic links, symlink? will always be false for an object returned by File.stat.

```
File.symlink("testfile", "alink")   # =>   0
File.stat("alink").symlink?         # =>   false
File.lstat("alink").symlink?        # =>   true
```

---

uid   *statfile*.uid → *int*

Returns the numeric user ID of the owner of *statfile*.

```
File.stat("testfile").uid   # =>   501
```

---

world_readable?   File.world_readable?(*filename*) → *perm_int* or nil

1.9 If *filename* is readable by others, returns an integer representing the file permission bits of *filename*. Returns nil otherwise. The meaning of the bits is platform dependent; on Unix systems, see stat(2).

```
File.world_readable?("/etc/passwd")          # =>   420
File.world_readable?("/etc/passwd").to_s(8)  # =>   "644"
```

---

world_writable?   File.world_writable?(*filename*) → *perm_int* or nil

1.9 If *filename* is writable by others, returns an integer representing the file permission bits of *filename*. Returns nil otherwise. The meaning of the bits is platform dependent; on Unix systems, see stat(2).

```
File.world_writable?("/etc/passwd")         # =>   nil
File.world_writable?("/tmp")                # =>   511
File.world_writable?("/tmp").to_s(8)        # =>   "777"
```

---

writable?   *statfile*.writable? → true or false

Returns true if *statfile* is writable by the effective user ID of this process.

```
File.stat("testfile").writable?   # =>   true
```

---

writable_real?   *statfile*.writable_real? → true or false

Returns true if *statfile* is writable by the real user ID of this process.

```
File.stat("testfile").writable_real?   # =>   true
```

---

zero?   *statfile*.zero? → true or false

Returns true if *statfile* is a zero-length file; returns false otherwise.

```
File.stat("testfile").zero?   # =>   false
```

Module

FileTest

FileTest implements file test operations similar to those used in File::Stat. The methods in FileTest are duplicated in class File. Rather than repeat the documentation here, we list the names of the methods and refer you to the documentation for File starting on page 497. FileTest appears to be a somewhat vestigial module.

The FileTest methods are as follows:

blockdev?, chardev?, directory?, executable?, executable_real?, exist?, exists?, file?, grpowned?, identical?, owned?, pipe?, readable?, readable_real?, setgid?, setuid?, size, size?, socket?, sticky?, symlink?, world_readable?, world_writable?, writable?, writable_real?, zero?

1.9

F ileTest

Class		
Fixnum	<	Integer

A Fixnum holds Integer values that can be represented in a native machine word (minus 1 bit). If any operation on a Fixnum exceeds this range, the value is automatically converted to a Bignum.

Fixnum objects have immediate value. This means that when they are assigned or passed as parameters, the actual object is passed, rather than a reference to that object. Assignment does not alias Fixnum objects. Because there is effectively only one Fixnum object instance for any given integer value, you cannot, for example, add a singleton method to a Fixnum.

Instance methods

Arithmetic operations

Performs various arithmetic operations on *fix*.

fix	+	*numeric*	Addition
fix	–	*numeric*	Subtraction
fix	*	*numeric*	Multiplication
fix	/	*numeric*	Division
fix	%	*numeric*	Modulo
fix	**	*numeric*	Exponentiation
fix	-@		Unary minus

Bit operations

Performs various operations on the binary representations of the Fixnum.

~ *fix*			Invert bits
fix	|	*numeric*	Bitwise OR
fix	&	*numeric*	Bitwise AND
fix	^	*numeric*	Bitwise EXCLUSIVE OR
fix	<<	*numeric*	Left-shift *numeric* bits
fix	>>	*numeric*	Right-shift *numeric* bits (with sign extension)

Comparisons

Compares *fix* to other numbers. Fixnum.

<, <=, ==, >=, and >.

<=>   *fix* <=> *numeric* → −1, 0, +1

Comparison—Returns −1, 0, or +1 depending on whether *fix* is less than, equal to, or greater than *numeric*. Although Fixnum's grandparent, mixes in Comparable, Fixnum does not use that module for performing comparisons, instead implementing the comparison operators explicitly.

```
42 <=> 13   # =>   1
13 <=> 42   # =>  -1
-1 <=> -1   # =>   0
```

[ ]
$fix[\ n\ ] \rightarrow 0, 1$

Bit Reference—Returns the *n*th bit in the binary representation of *fix*, where *fix*[0] is the least significant bit.

```
a = 0b11001100101010
30.downto(0) {|n| print a[n] }
```

produces:

0000000000000000011001100101010

abs
$fix.abs \rightarrow int$

Returns the absolute value of *fix*.

```
-12345.abs   # =>   12345
12345.abs    # =>   12345
```

div
$fix.div(\ numeric\ ) \rightarrow integer$

1.9   Division that always produces an integral result. Not affected by the mathn library (unlike Fixnum#/).

```
654321.div(13731)      # =>   47
654321.div(13731.34)   # =>   47
```

even?
$fix.even? \rightarrow$ true or false

1.9   Returns true is *fix* is even.

```
1.even?   # =>   false
2.even?   # =>   true
```

divmod
$fix.divmod(\ numeric\ ) \rightarrow array$

See Numeric#divmod on page 608.

fdiv
$fix.fdiv(\ numeric\ ) \rightarrow float$

1.9   Returns the floating-point result of dividing *fix* by *numeric*.

```
63.fdiv(9)             # =>   7.0
654321.fdiv(13731)     # =>   47.6528293642124
654321.fdiv(13731.24)  # =>   47.6519964693647
```

magnitude
$fix.magnitude \rightarrow int$

1.9   Returns the magnitude of *fix* (the distance of *fix* from the origin of the number line). Synonym for Fixnum#abs. See also Complex#magnitude.

modulo
$fix.modulo(\ numeric\ ) \rightarrow numeric$

Synonym for Fixnum#%.

```
654321.modulo(13731)     # =>   8964
654321.modulo(13731.24)  # =>   8952.72000000001
```

F ixnum

odd?

fix.odd? → true or false

1.9

Returns true if *fix* is odd.

```
1.odd?   # =>   true
2.odd?   # =>   false
```

size

fix.size → int

Returns the number of *bytes* in the machine representation of a Fixnum.

```
1.size            # =>   4
-1.size           # =>   4
2147483647.size   # =>   4
```

succ

fix.succ → int

1.9

Returns *fix* + 1.

```
1.succ   # =>   2
-1.succ  # =>   0
```

to_f

fix.to_f → float

Converts *fix* to a Float.

to_s

fix.to_s(base=10) → string

Returns a string containing the representation of *fix* radix *base* (2 to 36).

```
12345.to_s                          # =>   "12345"
12345.to_s(2)                       # =>   "11000000111001"
12345.to_s(8)                       # =>   "30071"
12345.to_s(10)                      # =>   "12345"
12345.to_s(16)                      # =>   "3039"
12345.to_s(36)                      # =>   "9ix"
848237232330358117454971171.to_s(36)  # =>   "anotherrubyhacker"
```

zero?

fix.zero? → true or false

Returns true if *fix* is zero.

```
42.zero?  # =>   false
0.zero?   # =>   true
```

Class
Float < Numeric

Float objects represent real numbers using the native architecture's double-precision floating-point representation.

Class constants

DIG	Precision of Float (in decimal digits)
EPSILON	The smallest Float such that $1.0+$ EPSILON $\neq 1.0$
MANT_DIG	The number of mantissa digits (base RADIX)
MAX	The largest Float
MAX_10_EXP	The maximum integer x such that 10^x is a finite Float
MAX_EXP	The maximum integer x such that $\text{FLT\_RADIX}^{(x-1)}$ is a finite Float
MIN	The smallest Float
MIN_10_EXP	The minimum integer x such that 10^x is a finite Float
MIN_EXP	The minimum integer x such that $\text{FLT\_RADIX}^{(x-1)}$ is a finite Float
RADIX	The radix of floating-point representations
ROUNDS	The rounding mode for floating-point operations; possible values include

-1	if the mode is indeterminate
0	if rounding is toward zero
1	if rounding is to nearest representable value
2	if rounding is toward $+\infty$
3	if rounding is toward $-\infty$

Instance methods

Arithmetic operations

Performs various arithmetic operations on *flt*.

flt	+	*numeric*	Addition
flt	−	*numeric*	Subtraction
flt	*	*numeric*	Multiplication
flt	/	*numeric*	Division
flt	%	*numeric*	Modulo
flt	**	*numeric*	Exponentiation
flt	-@		Unary minus

Comparisons

Compares *flt* to other numbers.

<, <=, ==, >=, >.

<=>   *flt* <=> *numeric* → −1, 0, +1

Returns -1, 0, or $+1$ depending on whether *flt* is less than, equal to, or greater than *numeric*.

F loat

==   *flt* == *obj* → true or false

Returns true only if *obj* has the same value as *flt*. Contrast this with Float#eql?, which requires *obj* to be a Float.

```
1.0 == 1.0        # =>   true
(1.0).eql?(1.0)   # =>   true
1.0 == 1          # =>   true
(1.0).eql?(1)     # =>   false
```

---

abs   *flt*.abs → *numeric*

Returns the absolute value of *flt*.

```
(-34.56).abs  # =>   34.56
-34.56.abs    # =>   34.56
```

---

ceil   *flt*.ceil → *int*

Returns the smallest Integer greater than or equal to *flt*.

```
1.2.ceil      # =>   2
2.0.ceil      # =>   2
(-1.2).ceil   # =>   -1
(-2.0).ceil   # =>   -2
```

---

divmod   *flt*.divmod(*numeric*) → *array*

See Numeric#divmod on page 608.

---

eql?   *flt*.eql?(*obj*) → true or false

Returns true only if *obj* is a Float with the same value as *flt*. Contrast this with Float#==, which performs type conversions.

```
1.0.eql?(1)   # =>   false
1.0 == 1      # =>   true
```

---

fdiv   *flt*.fdiv(*number*) → *float*

1.9   Returns the floating-point result of dividing *flt* by *number*. Alias for Float#quo.

```
63.0.fdiv(9)         # =>   7.0
1234.56.fdiv(3.45)   # =>   357.84347826087
```

---

finite?   *flt*.finite? → true or false

Returns true if *flt* is a valid IEEE floating-point number (it is not infinite, and nan? is false).

```
(42.0).finite?      # =>   true
(1.0/0.0).finite?   # =>   false
```

floor   *flt*.floor → *int*

Returns the largest integer less than or equal to *flt*.

```
1.2.floor       # =>   1
2.0.floor       # =>   2
(-1.2).floor    # =>   -2
(-2.0).floor    # =>   -2
```

infinite?   *flt*.infinite? → nil, −1, +1

Returns nil, −1, or +1 depending on whether *flt* is finite, −∞, or +∞.

```
(0.0).infinite?      # =>   nil
(-1.0/0.0).infinite? # =>   -1
(+1.0/0.0).infinite? # =>   1
```

magnitude   *flt*.magnitude → *float*

1.9 Returns the magnitude of *flt* (the distance of *flt* from the origin of the number line). Synonym for Float#abs. See also Complex#magnitude.

modulo   *flt*.modulo(*numeric*) → *numeric*

Synonym for Float#%.

```
6543.21.modulo(137)     # =>   104.21
6543.21.modulo(137.24)  # =>   92.9299999999996
```

nan?   *flt*.nan? → true or false

Returns true if *flt* is an invalid IEEE floating-point number.

```
(-1.0).nan?     # =>   false
(0.0/0.0).nan?  # =>   true
```

quo   *flt*.quo(*number*) → *float*

1.9 Returns the floating-point result of dividing *flt* by *number*.

```
63.0.quo(9)        # =>   7.0
1234.56.quo(3.45)  # =>   357.84347826087
```

round   *flt*.round(*digits*=0) → *numeric*

1.9 Rounds *flt* to the nearest integer if the parameter is omitted or zero or rounds to the given number of digits.

```
1.5.round       # =>   2
(-1.5).round    # =>   -2
3.14159.round   # =>   3
3.14159.round(4)# =>   3.1416
3.14159.round(2)# =>   3.14
```

to_f   *flt*.to_f → *flt*

Returns *flt*.

Float

---

to_i   *flt*.to_i → *int*

Returns *flt* truncated to an Integer.

```
1.5.to_i      # =>   1
(-1.5).to_i   # =>   -1
```

---

to_int   *flt*.to_int → *int*

Synonym for Float#to_i.

---

to_r   *flt*.to_r → *number*

1.9

Converts *flt* to a rational number.

```
1.5.to_r      # =>   3/2
(1.0/3).to_r  # =>   6004799503160661/18014398509481984
```

---

to_s   *flt*.to_s → *string*

Returns a string containing a representation of *flt*. As well as a fixed or exponential form of the number, the call may return NaN, Infinity, and -Infinity.

---

truncate   *flt*.truncate → *int*

Synonym for Float#to_i.

---

zero?   *flt*.zero? → true or false

Returns true if *flt* is 0.0.

Module **GC**

The GC module provides an interface to Ruby's mark and sweep garbage collection mechanism. Some of the underlying methods are also available via the ObjectSpace module, described beginning on page 626.

Module methods

count
GC.count → int

1.9 Returns a count of the number of times GC has run in the current process.

```
GC.count   # =>   1
res = ""
10_000.times { res += "wibble" }
GC.count   # =>   38
```

disable
GC.disable → true or false

Disables garbage collection, returning true if garbage collection was already disabled.

```
GC.disable   # =>   false
GC.disable   # =>   true
```

enable
GC.enable → true or false

Enables garbage collection, returning true if garbage collection was disabled.

```
GC.disable   # =>   false
GC.enable   # =>   true
GC.enable   # =>   false
```

start
GC.start → nil

Initiates garbage collection, unless manually disabled.

```
GC.start   # =>   nil
```

stress
GC.stress → true or false

1.9 Returns the current value of the stress flag (see GC.stress=).

stress=
GC.stress = bool → bool

1.9 Ruby will normally run garbage collection periodically. Setting the stress flag to true forces garbage collection to occur every time Ruby allocates a new object. This is typically used only for testing extensions (and Ruby itself).

```
GC.stress = true
```

Instance methods

garbage_collect
garbage_collect → nil

Equivalent to GC.start.

```
include GC
garbage_collect   # =>   nil
```

Class

Hash   <   Object

Relies on: each, <=>

A Hash is a collection of key/value pairs. It is similar to an Array, except that indexing is done via arbitrary keys of any object type, not an integer index. The order in which keys and/or values are returned by the various iterators over hash contents may seem arbitrary and will generally not be in insertion order.

Hashes have a *default value*. This value is returned when an attempt is made to access keys that do not exist in the hash. By default, this value is nil.

Mixes in

Enumerable:

```
all?, any?, collect, count, cycle, detect, drop, drop_while, each_cons,
each_slice, each_with_index, entries, find, find_all, find_index, first, grep,
group_by, include?, inject, map, max, max_by, member?, min, min_by, minmax,
minmax_by, none?, one?, partition, reduce, reject, select, sort, sort_by,
take, take_while, to_a, zip
```

Class methods

[ ]   Hash[⟨ *key => value* ⟩*] → *hsh*

Creates a new hash populated with the given objects. Equivalent to creating a hash using the literal { *key=>value*, ... }. Keys and values occur in pairs, so there must be an even number of arguments.

```
Hash["a", 100, "b", 200]       # =>   {"a"=>100, "b"=>200}
Hash["a" => 100, "b" => 200]   # =>   {"a"=>100, "b"=>200}
{ "a" => 100, "b" => 200 }     # =>   {"a"=>100, "b"=>200}
```

new   Hash.new → *hsh*
                                                  Hash.new(*obj*) → *hsh*
                        Hash.new {| *hash, key* | *block* } → *hsh*

Returns a new, empty hash. If this hash is subsequently accessed by a key that doesn't correspond to a hash entry, the value returned depends on the style of new used to create the hash. In the first form, the access returns nil. If *obj* is specified, this single object will be used for all *default values*. If a block is specified, it will be called with the hash object and the key, and it should return the default value. It is the block's responsibility to store the value in the hash if required.

```
h = Hash.new("Go Fish")
h["a"] = 100
h["b"] = 200
h["a"]            # =>   100
h["c"]            # =>   "Go Fish"
# The following alters the single default object
h["c"].upcase!    # =>   "GO FISH"
h["d"]            # =>   "GO FISH"
h.keys            # =>   ["a", "b"]

# While this creates a new default object each time
h = Hash.new {|hash, key| hash[key] = "Go Fish: #{key}" }
h["c"]            # =>   "Go Fish: c"
h["c"].upcase!    # =>   "GO FISH: C"
h["d"]            # =>   "Go Fish: d"
h.keys            # =>   ["c", "d"]
```

---

try_convert   Hash.try_convert(*obj*) → *a_hash* or nil

1.9

If *obj* is not already a hash, attempts to convert it to one by calling its to_hash method. Returns nil if no conversion could be made.

```
class ConfigFile
  def initialize(name)
    @content = File.read(name)
  end
  def to_hash
    result = {}
    @content.scan(/^(\w+):\s*(.*)/) do |name, value|
      result[name] = value
    end
    result
  end
end
config = ConfigFile.new("some_config")
Hash.try_convert(config)   # =>    {"user_name"=>"dave",
                                    "password"=>"wibble"}
```

Instance methods

==   *hsh* == *obj* → true or false

Equality—Two hashes are equal if they have the same default value, they contain the same number of keys, and the value corresponding to each key in the first hash is equal (using ==) to the value for the same key in the second. If *obj* is not a hash, attempts to convert it using to_hash and returns *obj* == *hsh*.

```
h1 = { "a" => 1, "c" => 2 }
h2 = { 7 => 35, "c" => 2, "a" => 1 }
h3 = { "a" => 1, "c" => 2, 7 => 35 }
h4 = { "a" => 1, "d" => 2, "f" => 35 }
h1 == h2   # =>   false
h2 == h3   # =>   true
h3 == h4   # =>   false
```

H ash

[ ]   *hsh*[*key*] → *value*

Element Reference—Retrieves the *value* stored for *key*. If not found, returns the default value (see Hash.new for details).

```
h = { "a" => 100, "b" => 200 }
h["a"]   # =>   100
h["c"]   # =>   nil
```

[ ]=   *hsh*[*key*] = *value* → *value*

Element Assignment—Associates the value given by *value* with the key given by *key*. *key* should not have its value changed while it is in use as a key (a String passed as a key will be duplicated and frozen).

```
h = { "a" => 100, "b" => 200 }
h["a"] = 9
h["c"] = 4
h   # =>   {"a"=>9, "b"=>200, "c"=>4}
```

---

assoc   *hsh*.assoc(*key* → [*key, val]* or nil

1.9

Returns the two element array [*key*, *hsh*[*key*]] or nil if *key* does not reference an entry in the hash.

```
h = { "a" => 100, "b" => 200 }   # =>   {"a"=>100, "b"=>200}
h.assoc("a")                     # =>   ["a", 100]
h.assoc("c")                     # =>   nil
```

---

clear   *hsh*.clear → *hsh*

Removes all key/value pairs from *hsh*.

```
h = { "a" => 100, "b" => 200 }   # =>   {"a"=>100, "b"=>200}
h.clear                          # =>   {}
```

---

compare_by_identity   *hsh*.compare_by_identity → *hsh*

1.9

Hashes normally compare key values using eql?, which returns true if two objects have the same *value*. If you call compare_by_identity, keys will instead be considered to be equal only if they are the same object. Note that when strings are used as keys, they are automatically duplicated, so you will never be able to retrieve a string-keyed entry if keys are compared using identity.

```
key = "key"
h = { key => 100, 99 => "ninety nine" }
h[key]     # =>   100
h["key"]   # =>   100
h[99]      # =>   "ninety nine"
h.compare_by_identity
h[key]     # =>   nil
h["key"]   # =>   nil
h[99]      # =>   "ninety nine"
```

compare_by_identity?

1.9 *hsh*.compare_by_identity? → true or false

Returns true if *hsh* compares keys by identity.

default

hsh.default(*key*=nil) → *obj*

Returns the default value, the value that would be returned by *hsh*[*key*] if *key* did not exist in *hsh*. See also Hash.new and Hash#default=.

```
h = Hash.new                        # =>   {}
h.default                           # =>   nil
h.default(2)                        # =>   nil

h = Hash.new("cat")                 # =>   {}
h.default                           # =>   "cat"
h.default(2)                        # =>   "cat"

h = Hash.new {|h,k| h[k] = k.to_i*10}  # =>   {}
h.default                           # =>   nil
h.default(2)                        # =>   20
```

default=

hsh.default = *obj* → *hsh*

1.9 Sets the default value, the value returned for a key that does not exist in the hash. Use Hash#default_proc= to set the proc to be called to calculate a default.

```
h = { "a" => 100, "b" => 200 }
h.default = "Go fish"
h["a"]     # =>   100
h["z"]     # =>   "Go fish"
# This doesn't do what you might hope... (but see default_proc=)
h.default = lambda do |hash, key|
  hash[key] = key + key
end
h[2]       # =>   #<Proc:0x0a300c@/tmp/prog.rb:7 (lambda)>
h["cat"]   # =>   #<Proc:0x0a300c@/tmp/prog.rb:7 (lambda)>
```

default_proc

hsh.default_proc → *obj* or nil

If Hash.new was invoked with a block, returns that block; otherwise, returns nil.

```
h = Hash.new {|h,k| h[k] = k*k }   # =>   {}
p = h.default_proc                 # =>   #<Proc:0x0a3b24@/tmp/prog.rb:1>
a = []                             # =>   []
p.call(a, 2)
a                                  # =>   [nil, nil, 4]
```

default_proc=

hsh.default_proc = *proc* → *proc* or nil

1.9 Sets the proc to be called to calculate values to be returned when an array is accessed with a key it does not contain.

```
h = { "a" => 100, "b" => 200 }
h.default = "Go fish"
h["a"]      # =>    100
h["z"]      # =>    "Go fish"
h.default_proc = lambda do |hash, key|
  hash[key] = key + key
end
h[2]        # =>    4
h["cat"]    # =>    "catcat"
```

---

delete   *hsh*.delete(*key*) → *value*

hsh.delete(*key*) { | *key* | *block* } → *value*

Deletes from *hsh* the entry whose key is to *key*, returning the corresponding value. If the key is not found, returns nil. If the optional code block is given and the key is not found, passes it the key and returns the result of *block*.

```
h = { "a" => 100, "b" => 200 }
h.delete("a")                         # =>    100
h.delete("z")                         # =>    nil
h.delete("z") {|el| "#{el} not found" }   # =>    "z not found"
```

---

delete_if   *hsh*.delete_if ⟨ { | *key, value* | *block* } ⟩ → *hsh* or *enumerator*

Deletes every key/value pair from *hsh* for which *block* is true. Returns an Enumerator object if no block is given.

```
h = { "a" => 100, "b" => 200, "c" => 300 }
h.delete_if {|key, value| key >= "b" }   # =>    {"a"=>100}
```

---

each   *hsh*.each { | *key, value* | *block* } → *hsh*

Calls *block* once for each key in *hsh*, passing the key and value as parameters.

```
h = { "a" => 100, "b" => 200 }
h.each {|key, value| puts "#{key} is #{value}" }
```

produces:

```
a is 100
b is 200
```

---

each_key   *hsh*.each_key { | *key* | *block* } → *hsh*

Calls *block* once for each key in *hsh*, passing the key as a parameter.

```
h = { "a" => 100, "b" => 200 }
h.each_key {|key| puts key }
```

produces:

```
a
b
```

---

each_pair   *hsh*.each_pair { | *key, value* | *block* } → *hsh*

Synonym for Hash#each.

each_value
hsh.each_value { | value | block } → hsh

Calls *block* once for each key in *hsh*, passing the value as a parameter.

```
h = { "a" => 100, "b" => 200 }
h.each_value {|value| puts value }
```

produces:

```
100
200
```

empty?
hsh.empty? → true or false

Returns true if *hsh* contains no key/value pairs.

```
{}.empty?   # =>   true
```

fetch
hsh.fetch(key ⟨ , default ⟩) → obj
hsh.fetch(key) { | key | block } → obj

Returns a value from the hash for the given key. If the key can't be found, several options exist. With no other arguments, it will raise an IndexError exception; if *default* is given, then that will be returned; if the optional code block is specified, then that will be run and its result returned. fetch does not evaluate any default values supplied when the hash was created—it looks only for keys in the hash.

```
h = { "a" => 100, "b" => 200 }
h.fetch("a")                       # =>   100
h.fetch("z", "go fish")            # =>   "go fish"
h.fetch("z") {|el| "go fish, #{el}"}   # =>   "go fish, z"
```

The following example shows that an exception is raised if the key is not found and a default value is not supplied:

```
h = { "a" => 100, "b" => 200 }
h.fetch("z")
```

produces:

```
prog.rb:2:in `fetch': key not found (KeyError)
from /tmp/prog.rb:2:in `<main>'
```

flatten
hsh.flatten(depth = 1) → an_array

1.9 Converts *hsh* to an array and then invokes Array#flatten! on the result.

```
h = { feline: [ "felix", "tom" ], equine: "ed" }
h.flatten      # =>   [:feline, ["felix", "tom"], :equine, "ed"]
h.flatten(1)   # =>   [:feline, ["felix", "tom"], :equine, "ed"]
h.flatten(2)   # =>   [:feline, "felix", "tom", :equine, "ed"]
```

has_key?
hsh.has_key?(key) → true or false

Returns true if the given key is present in *hsh*.

```
h = { "a" => 100, "b" => 200 }
h.has_key?("a")   # =>   true
h.has_key?("z")   # =>   false
```

has_value?

hsh.has_value?(*value*) → true or false

Returns true if the given value is present for some key in *hsh*.

```
h = { "a" => 100, "b" => 200 }
h.has_value?(100)   # =>   true
h.has_value?(999)   # =>   false
```

include?

hsh.include?(*key*) → true or false

Synonym for Hash#has_key?.

index

hsh.index(*value*) → *key*

1.9   Deprecated—use Hash#key instead.

invert

hsh.invert → *other_hash*

Returns a new hash created by using *hsh*'s values as keys and using the keys as values. If *hsh* has duplicate values, the result will contain only one of them as a key—which one is not predictable.

```
h = { "n" => 100, "m" => 100, "y" => 300, "d" => 200, "a" => 0 }
h.invert   # =>   {100=>"m", 300=>"y", 200=>"d", 0=>"a"}
```

key

hsh.key(*value*) → *key* or nil

1.9   Returns the key of the first hash entry whose value is *value*.

```
h = { a: 100, b: 200, c: 100 }
h.key(100)   # =>   :a
h.key(200)   # =>   :b
h.key(300)   # =>   nil
```

key?

hsh.key?(*key*) → true or false

Synonym for Hash#has_key?.

keys

hsh.keys → *array*

Returns a new array populated with the keys from this hash. See also Hash#values.

```
h = { "a" => 100, "b" => 200, "c" => 300, "d" => 400 }
h.keys   # =>   ["a", "b", "c", "d"]
```

length

hsh.length → *fixnum*

Returns the number of key/value pairs in the hash.

```
h = { "d" => 100, "a" => 200, "v" => 300, "e" => 400 }
h.length        # =>   4
h.delete("a")   # =>   200
h.length        # =>   3
```

member?

hsh.member?(*key*) → true or false

Synonym for Hash#has_key?.

merge

hsh.merge(*other_hash*) → *result_hash*

hsh.merge(*other_hash*) {| key, old_val, new_val | *block* } → *result_hash*

Returns a new hash containing the contents of *other_hash* and the contents of *hsh*. With no block parameter, overwrites entries in *hsh* with duplicate keys with those from *other_hash*. If a block is specified, it is called with each duplicate key and the values from the two hashes. The value returned by the block is stored in the new hash.

```
h1 = { "a" => 100, "b" => 200 }
h2 = { "b" => 254, "c" => 300 }
h1.merge(h2)             # =>   {"a"=>100, "b"=>254, "c"=>300}
h1.merge(h2) {|k,o,n| o} # =>   {"a"=>100, "b"=>200, "c"=>300}
h1                       # =>   {"a"=>100, "b"=>200}
```

merge!

hsh.merge!(*other_hash*) → *hsh*

hsh.merge!(*other_hash*) {| key, old_val, new_val | *block* } → *hsh*

Like Hash#merge but changes the contents of *hsh*.

```
h1 = { "a" => 100, "b" => 200 }
h2 = { "b" => 254, "c" => 300 }
h1.merge!(h2)             # =>   {"a"=>100, "b"=>254, "c"=>300}
h1 = { "a" => 100, "b" => 200 }
h1.merge!(h2) {|k,o,n| o} # =>   {"a"=>100, "b"=>200, "c"=>300}
h1                        # =>   {"a"=>100, "b"=>200, "c"=>300}
```

rassoc

hsh.rassoc(*key* → [*key, val]* or nil

1.9

Searches *hsh* for the first element whose value is *key*, returning the key and value as a two-element array. Returns nil if the value does not occur in the hash.

```
h = { "a" => 100, "b" => 200, "c" => 100 }  # =>   {"a"=>100, "b"=>200,
                                                    "c"=>100}
h.rassoc(100)                                # =>   ["a", 100]
h.rassoc(200)                                # =>   ["b", 200]
```

rehash

hsh.rehash → *hsh*

Rebuilds the hash based on the current hash values for each key. If values of key objects have changed since they were inserted, this method will reindex *hsh*. If Hash#rehash is called while an iterator is traversing the hash, an IndexError will be raised in the iterator.

```
a = [ "a", "b" ]
c = [ "c", "d" ]
h = { a => 100, c => 300 }
h[a]      # =>   100
a[0] = "z"
h[a]      # =>   nil
h.rehash  # =>   {["z", "b"]=>100, ["c", "d"]=>300}
h[a]      # =>   100
```

reject   *hsh*.reject {| *key, value* | *block* } → *hash*

Same as Hash#delete_if but works on (and returns) a copy of *hsh*. This is equivalent to *hsh*.dup.delete_if.

reject!   *hsh*.reject! ⟨ {| *key, value* | *block* } ⟩ → *hsh* or *enumerator*

Equivalent to Hash#delete_if but returns nil if no changes were made. Returns an Enumerator object if no block is given.

replace   *hsh*.replace(*other_hash*) → *hsh*

Replaces the contents of *hsh* with the contents of *other_hash*.

```
h = { "a" => 100, "b" => 200 }
h.replace({ "c" => 300, "d" => 400 })   # =>   {"c"=>300, "d"=>400}
```

select   *hsh*.select {| *key, value* | *block* } → *array*

1.9 Returns a new hash consisting of [key, value] pairs for which the block returns true. Also see Hash#values_at. (This behavior differs from Ruby 1.8, which returns an array of arrays.)

```
h = { "a" => 100, "b" => 200, "c" => 300 }
h.select {|k,v| k > "a"}   # =>   {"b"=>200, "c"=>300}
h.select {|k,v| v < 200}   # =>   {"a"=>100}
```

shift   *hsh*.shift → *array* or nil

Removes a key/value pair from *hsh* and returns it as the two-item array [*key, value*]. If the hash is empty, returns the default value, calls the default proc (with a key value of nil), or returns nil.

```
h = { 1 => "a", 2 => "b", 3 => "c" }
h.shift   # =>   [1, "a"]
h         # =>   {2=>"b", 3=>"c"}
```

size   *hsh*.size → *fixnum*

Synonym for Hash#length.

sort   *hsh*.sort → *array*
                                                    hsh.sort {| *a, b* | *block* } → *array*

Converts *hsh* to a nested array of [*key, value*] arrays and sorts it, using Array#sort.

```
h = { "a" => 20, "b" => 30, "c" => 10  }
h.sort                   # =>   [["a", 20], ["b", 30], ["c", 10]]
h.sort {|a,b| a[1]<=>b[1]}   # =>   [["c", 10], ["a", 20], ["b", 30]]
```

store   *hsh*.store(*key, value*) → *value*

Synonym for Element Assignment (Hash#[]=).

to_a   *hsh*.to_a → *array*

Converts *hsh* to a nested array of [*key, value*] arrays.

```
h = { "c" => 300, "a" => 100, "d" => 400, "c" => 300  }
h.to_a   # =>   [["c", 300], ["a", 100], ["d", 400]]
```

to_hash   *hsh*.to_hash → *hsh*

See page 365.

to_s   *hsh*.to_s → *string*

Converts *hsh* to a string by converting the hash to an array of [*key, value*] pairs and then converting that array to a string using Array#join with the default separator.

```
h = { "c" => 300, "a" => 100, "d" => 400, "c" => 300  }
h.to_s   # =>   "{\"c\"=>300, \"a\"=>100, \"d\"=>400}"
```

update   *hsh*.update(*other_hash*) → *hsh*
                                 hsh.update(*other_hash*) {| key, old_val, new_val | *block* } → *hsh*

Synonym for Hash#merge!.

value?   *hsh*.value?(*value*) → true or false

Synonym for Hash#has_value?.

values   *hsh*.values → *array*

Returns an array populated with the values from *hsh*. See also Hash#keys.

```
h = { "a" => 100, "b" => 200, "c" => 300 }
h.values   # =>   [100, 200, 300]
```

values_at   *hsh*.values_at(⟨ *key* ⟩[+]) → *array*

Returns an array consisting of values for the given key(s). Will insert the *default value* for keys that are not found.

```
h = { "a" => 100, "b" => 200, "c" => 300 }
h.values_at("a", "c")        # =>   [100, 300]
h.values_at("a", "c", "z")   # =>   [100, 300, nil]
h.default = "cat"
h.values_at("a", "c", "z")   # =>   [100, 300, "cat"]
```

Class

Integer < Numeric

Subclasses: Bignum, Fixnum

Integer is the basis for the two concrete classes that hold whole numbers, Bignum and Fixnum. (If you've come here looking for the iterator step, it's on page 612.)

Instance methods

ceil

int.ceil → *integer*

Synonym for Integer#to_i.

chr

int.chr → *string*

Returns a string containing the ASCII character represented by the receiver's value.

```
65.chr    # =>   "A"
?a.chr    # =>   "a"
230.chr   # =>   "\xE6"
```

denominator

int.denominator → *integer*

1.9   Converts the denominator of the rational representation of *int*.

```
1.denominator      # =>   1
1.5.denominator    # =>   2
num = 1.0/3
num.to_r           # =>   (6004799503160661/18014398509481984)
num.denominator    # =>   18014398509481984
```

downto

int.downto(*integer*) {| i | *block* } → *int*

Iterates *block*, passing decreasing values from *int* down to and including *integer*.

```
5.downto(1) {|n| print n, ".. " }
print "  Liftoff!\n"
```

produces:

```
5.. 4.. 3.. 2.. 1..   Liftoff!
```

even?

int.even? → true or false

1.9   Returns true if *int* is even.

```
1.even?  # =>   false
2.even?  # =>   true
```

floor

int.floor → *integer*

Returns the largest integer less than or equal to *int*. Equivalent to Integer#to_i.

```
1.floor      # =>   1
(-1).floor   # =>   -1
```

gcd

int.gcd(*other_integer*) → *integer*

1.9 Returns the greatest common denominator of *int* and *other_integer*.

```
10.gcd(15)   # =>   5
10.gcd(16)   # =>   2
10.gcd(17)   # =>   1
```

gcdlcm

int.gcdlcm(*other_integer*) → [*gcd, lcm*]

1.9 Returns both the GCD and LCM of *int* and *other_integer*.

```
10.gcdlcm(15)   # =>   [5, 30]
10.gcdlcm(16)   # =>   [2, 80]
10.gcdlcm(17)   # =>   [1, 170]
```

integer?

int.integer? → true

Always returns true.

lcm

int.lcm(*other_integer*) → *integer*

1.9 Returns the lowest common multiple of *int* and *other_integer*.

```
10.lcm(15)   # =>   30
10.lcm(20)   # =>   20
10.lcm(-2)   # =>   10
```

next

int.next → *integer*

Returns the Integer equal to *int* + 1.

```
1.next      # =>   2
(-1).next   # =>   0
```

numerator

int.numerator → *integer*

1.9 Converts the numerator of the rational representation of *int*.

```
1.numerator     # =>   1
1.5.numerator   # =>   3
num = 1.0/3
num.to_r        # =>   (6004799503160661/18014398509481984)
num.numerator   # =>   6004799503160661
```

odd?

int.odd? → true or false

1.9 Returns true is *int* is odd.

```
1.odd?   # =>   true
2.odd?   # =>   false
```

ord

int.ord → *int*

1.9 The ord method was added to assist in the migration from Ruby 1.8 to 1.9. It allows ?A.ord to return 65. If ?A returns a string, ord will be called on that string and return 65; if ?A returns an integer, then Numeric#ord is called, which is basically a no-op.

Integer

---

pred
int.pred $\rightarrow$ *integer*

1.9 Returns $int - 1$.

---

round
int.round $\rightarrow$ *integer*

Synonym for Integer#to_i.

---

succ
int.succ $\rightarrow$ *integer*

Synonym for Integer#next.

---

times
int.times { | i | *block* } $\rightarrow$ *int*

Iterates block int times, passing in values from zero to $int -1$.

```
5.times do |i|
  print i, " "
end
```
produces:
```
0 1 2 3 4
```

---

to_i
int.to_i $\rightarrow$ *int*

Returns int.

---

to_int
int.to_int $\rightarrow$ *integer*

Synonym for Integer#to_i.

---

to_r
int.to_r $\rightarrow$ *number*

1.9 Converts int to a rational number.

```
1.to_r    # =>    1/1
-1.to_r   # =>    -1/1
```

---

truncate
int.truncate $\rightarrow$ *integer*

Synonym for Integer#to_i.

---

upto
int.upto(*integer*) { | i | *block* } $\rightarrow$ *int*

Iterates *block*, passing in integer values from int up to and including *integer*.

```
5.upto(10) {|i| print i, " " }
```
produces:
```
5 6 7 8 9 10
```

IO < Object

Subclasses: File

Class IO is the basis for all input and output in Ruby. An I/O stream may be *duplexed* (that is, bidirectional) and so may use more than one native operating system stream.

Many of the examples in this section use class File, the only standard subclass of IO. The two classes are closely associated.

As used in this section, *portname* may take any of the following forms:

- A plain string represents a filename suitable for the underlying operating system.

- A string starting with | indicates a subprocess. The remainder of the string following the | is invoked as a process with appropriate input/output channels connected to it.

- A string equal to |- will create another Ruby instance as a subprocess.

The IO class uses the Unix abstraction of *file descriptors* (fds), small integers that represent open files. Conventionally, standard input has an fd of 0, standard output an fd of 1, and standard error an fd of 2.

Ruby will convert pathnames between different operating system conventions if possible. For instance, on a Windows system the filename /gumby/ruby/test.rb will be opened as \gumby\ruby\test.rb. When specifying a Windows-style filename in a double-quoted Ruby string, remember to escape the backslashes.

```
"c:\\gumby\\ruby\\test.rb"
```

Our examples here will use the Unix-style forward slashes; File::SEPARATOR can be used to get the platform-specific separator character.

I/O ports may be opened in any one of several different modes, which are shown in this section as *mode*. This mode string must be one of the values listed in Table 27.7 on the next page. As of Ruby 1.9, the mode may also contain information on the external and internal encoding of the data associated with the port. If an external encoding is specified, Ruby assumes that the data it received from the operating system uses that encoding. If no internal encoding is given, strings read from the port will have this encoding. If an internal encoding is given, data will be transcoded from the external to the internal encoding, and strings will have that encoding. The reverse happens on output.

The file mode may optionally be specified as a Fixnum by *or*-ing together the flags described in Table 27.5 on page 505. (Yes, it is bad coupling that the IO class uses constants defined in a child.)

Mixes in

Enumerable:

```
all?, any?, collect, count, cycle, detect, drop, drop_while, each_cons,
each_slice, each_with_index, entries, find, find_all, find_index, first, grep,
group_by, include?, inject, map, max, max_by, member?, min, min_by, minmax,
minmax_by, none?, one?, partition, reduce, reject, select, sort, sort_by,
take, take_while, to_a, zip
```

Table 27.7. Mode Strings

Modes can be represented as an integer formed by or-ing together values from Table 27.7. They are more commonly represented as a string. Mode strings have the form "file-mode[:external-encoding[:internal-encoding]]". The file-mode portion is one of the options listed in the following table. The two encodings are the names (or aliases) of encodings supported by your interpreter. See Chapter 17 on page 251 for more information.

Mode	Meaning
r	Read-only, starts at beginning of file (default mode).
r+	Read/write, starts at beginning of file.
w	Write-only, truncates an existing file to zero length or creates a new file for writing.
w+	Read/write, truncates existing file to zero length or creates a new file for reading and writing.
a	Write-only, starts at end of file if file exists; otherwise, creates a new file for writing.
a+	Read/write, starts at end of file if file exists; otherwise, creates a new file for reading and writing.
b	Binary file mode (may appear with any of the key letters listed earlier). As of Ruby 1.9, this modifier should be supplied on all ports opened in binary mode (on Unix as well as on DOS/Windows). To read a file in binary mode and receive the data as a stream of bytes, use the modestring "rb:ascii-8bit".

Class methods

binread

$\qquad$ IO.binread((name) $\langle$, *length* $\langle$, offset $\rangle$ $\rangle$) → *string*

Opens *name* with mode rb:ASCII-8BIT, reads *length* bytes starting at *offset*, and then closes the file. The bytes are returned in a string with ASCII-8BIT encoding. *offset* defaults to 0, and *length* defaults to the number of bytes between *offset* and the end of the file.

```
IO.binread("testfile", 20)        # =>    "This is line one\nThi"
IO.binread("testfile", 20, 20)    # =>    "s is line two\nThis i"
str = IO.binread("testfile")
str.encoding                      # =>    #<Encoding:ASCII-8BIT>
str1 = IO.read("testfile")
str1.encoding                     # =>    #<Encoding:UTF-8>
```

copy_stream

$\qquad$ IO.copy_stream(*from, to* $\langle$, *max_length* $\langle$, offset $\rangle$ $\rangle$) → *integer*

Copies *from* to *to*. These may be specified as either filenames or as open IO streams. You may optionally specify a maximum length to copy and a byte offset to start the copy from. Returns the number of bytes copied.

```
IO.copy_stream("testfile", "newfile", 10, 10)
ip = File.open("/etc/passwd")
op = File.open("extract", "w")
op.puts "First 20 characters of /etc/passwd"
IO.copy_stream(ip, op, 20)
```

```
op.puts "\nEnd of extract"
op.close
puts File.readlines("extract")
```

produces:

```
First 20 characters of /etc/passwd
##
# User Database
#
End of extract
```

---

for_fd   IO.for_fd(*int*, *mode*) → *io*

Synonym for IO.new.

---

foreach   *io*.foreach(*portname*, *separator*=$/ ⟨ , *options* ⟩) {| *line* | *block* } → nil
                           io.foreach(*portname*, *limit* ⟨ , *options* ⟩) {| *line* | *block* } → nil
               io.foreach(*portname*, *separator*, *limit* ⟨ , *options* ⟩) {| *line* | *block* } → nil

<u>1.9</u>   Executes the block for every line in the named I/O port, where lines are separated by *separator*. If *separator* is nil, the entire file is passed as a single string. If the *limit* argument is present and positive, at most that many characters will be returned in each iteration. If only the *limit* argument is given and that argument is negative, then encodings will be ignored while looking for the record separator, which increases performance.

```
IO.foreach("testfile") {|x| puts "GOT: #{x}" }
```

produces:

```
GOT: This is line one
GOT: This is line two
GOT: This is line three
GOT: And so on...
```

<u>1.9</u>   *options* is an optional hash used to pass parameters to the underlying open call used by read. It may contain one or more of

key	Value(s)
encoding:	The encoding for the string, either as "external" or "external:internal"
mode:	The mode string to be passed to open
open_args:	An array containing the arguments to be passed to open; other options are ignored if this one is present

```
IO.foreach("testfile", nil, mode: "rb", encoding: "ascii-8bit") do |content|
  puts content.encoding
end
IO.foreach("testfile", nil, open_args: ["r:iso-8859-1"]) do |content|
  puts content.encoding
end
```

produces:

```
ASCII-8BIT
ISO-8859-1
```

---

new IO.new(*int, mode*) → *io*

Returns a new IO object (a stream) for the given integer file descriptor and mode. See also IO#fileno and IO.for_fd.

```
a = IO.new(2, "w")      # '2' is standard error
STDERR.puts "Hello"
a.puts "World"
```

produces:

```
Hello
World
```

---

open IO.open(⟨ args ⟩+) → *io*
IO.open(⟨ args ⟩+) {| *io* | *block* } → *obj*

IO.open creates a new IO object, passing *args* to that object's initialize method. If no block is given, simply returns that object. If a block is given, passes the IO object to the block. When the block exits (even via exception or program termination), the *io* object will be closed. If the block is present, IO.open returns the value of the block. The rough implementation is as follows:

```
class IO
  def open(*args)
    file = return_value = self.new(*args)
    begin
      return_value = yield(file)
    ensure
      file.close
    end if block_given?
    return_value
  end
end
```

Note that subclasses of IO such as File can use open even though their constructors take different parameters. Calling File.open(...) will invoke File's constructor, not IO's.

```
IO.open(1, "w") do |io|
  io.puts "Writing to stdout"
end
```

produces:

```
Writing to stdout
```

```
File.open("testfile", mode: "r", encoding: "utf-8") do |f|
  puts f.read
end
```

produces:

```
This is line one
This is line two
This is line three
And so on...
```

pipe   IO.pipe → [*read_file, write_file*]

Creates a pair of pipe endpoints (connected to each other) and returns them as a two-element array of IO objects. *write_file* is automatically placed into sync mode. Not available on all platforms.

In the following example, the two processes close the ends of the pipe that they are not using. This is not just a cosmetic nicety. The read end of a pipe will not generate an end-of-file condition if any writers have the pipe still open. In the case of the parent process, the rd.read will never return if it does not first issue a wr.close.

```
rd, wr = IO.pipe
if fork
  wr.close
  puts "Parent got: <#{rd.read}>"
  rd.close
  Process.wait
else
  rd.close
  puts "Sending message to parent"
  wr.write "Hi Dad"
  wr.close
end
```

produces:

```
Sending message to parent
Parent got: <Hi Dad>
```

popen   IO.popen(*cmd, mode="r"*) → *io*
                                   IO.popen(*cmd, mode="r"*) {| *io* | *block* } → *obj*

Runs the specified command string as a subprocess; the subprocess's standard input and output will be connected to the returned IO object. The parameter *cmd* may be a string or (in Ruby 1.9) an array of strings. In the latter case, the array is used as the argv parameter for the new process, and no special shell processing is performed on the strings. In addition, if the array starts with a hash, it will be used to set environment variables in the subprocess, and if it ends with a hash, the hash will be used to set execution options for the subprocess. See Kernel.spawn for details. If *cmd* is a string, it will be subject to shell expansion. If the *cmd* string starts with a minus sign (–) and the operating system supports fork(2), then the current Ruby process is forked. The default mode for the new file object is r, but *mode* may be set to any of the modes in Table 27.7 on page 538.

If a block is given, Ruby will run the command as a child connected to Ruby with a pipe. Ruby's end of the pipe will be passed as a parameter to the block. In this case, IO.popen returns the value of the block.

If a block is given with a *cmd_string* of "–", the block will be run in two separate processes: once in the parent and once in a child. The parent process will be passed the pipe object as a parameter to the block, the child version of the block will be passed nil, and the child's standard in and standard out will be connected to the parent through the pipe. Not available on all platforms. Also see the Open3 library on page 774 and Kernel#exec on page 559.

```
pipe = IO.popen("uname")
p(pipe.readlines)
puts "Parent is #{Process.pid}"
IO.popen("date") {|pipe| puts pipe.gets }
IO.popen("-") {|pipe| STDERR.puts "#{Process.pid} is here, pipe=#{pipe}" }
```

produces:

```
["Darwin\n"]
Parent is 46759
Tue Mar 31 09:58:16 CDT 2009
46759 is here, pipe=#<IO:0x0a2eb8>
46762 is here, pipe=
```

Here's an example that uses the Ruby 1.9 options to merge standard error and standard output into a single stream. Note that buffering means that the error output comes back ahead of the standard output.

```
pipe = IO.popen([ "bc", { STDERR => STDOUT }], "r+" )
pipe.puts '1 + 3; bad_function()'
pipe.close_write
puts pipe.readlines
```

produces:

```
Runtime error (func=(main), adr=8): Function bad_function not defined.
4
```

---

read　　　　　　　　　　IO.read(*portname*, ⟨ *length*=$/ ⟨ , *offset* ⟩ ⟩ ⟨ , *options* ⟩) → *string*

1.9

Opens the file, optionally seeks to the given offset, and then returns *length* bytes (defaulting to the rest of the file). read ensures the file is closed before returning.

options is an optional hash used to pass parameters to the underlying open call used by read. See IO.foreach for details.

```
IO.read("testfile")        # =>   "This is line one\nThis is line
                                  two\nThis is line three\nAnd so
                                  on...\n"
IO.read("testfile", 20)    # =>   "This is line one\nThi"
IO.read("testfile", 20, 10) # =>   "ne one\nThis is line "
```

---

readlines　　　　　　　　IO.readlines(*portname*, *separator*=$/ ⟨ , *options* ⟩) → *array*
　　　　　　　　　　　　　　IO.readlines(*portname*, *limit* ⟨ , *options* ⟩) → *array*
　　　　　　　　　　　IO.readlines(*portname*, *separator*, *limit* ⟨ , *options* ⟩) → *array*

1.9

Reads the entire file specified by *portname* as individual lines and returns those lines in an array. Lines are separated by *separator*. If *separator* is nil, the entire file is passed as a single string. If the *limit* argument is present and positive, at most that many characters will be returned in each iteration. If only the *limit* argument is given and that argument is negative, then encodings will be ignored while looking for the record separator, which increases performance. *options* is an optional hash used to pass parameters to the underlying open call used by read. See IO.foreach for details.

```
a = IO.readlines("testfile")
a[0]   # =>   "This is line one\n"
```

| **select** | IO.select(*read_array* ⟨ , *write_array* ⟨ , *error_array* ⟨ , *timeout* ⟩ ⟩ ⟩) → *array* or nil |

See Kernel#select on page 567.

| **sysopen** | IO.sysopen(*path*, ⟨ *mode* ⟨ , *perm* ⟩ ⟩) → *int* |

Opens the given path, returning the underlying file descriptor as a Fixnum.

```
IO.sysopen("testfile")   # =>   4
```

| **try_convert** | IO.try_convert(*obj*) → *an_io* or nil |

1.9   If *obj* is not already an I/O object, attempt to convert it to one by calling its to_io method. Returns nil if no conversion could be made.

```
class SillyIOObject
  def to_io
    STDOUT
  end
end
IO.try_convert(SillyIOObject.new)   # =>   #<IO:<STDOUT>>
IO.try_convert("Shemp")             # =>   nil
```

Instance methods

| **<<** | *io* << *obj* → *io* |

String Output—Writes *obj* to *io*. *obj* will be converted to a string using to_s.

```
STDOUT << "Hello " << "world!\n"
```

produces:

```
Hello world!
```

| **binmode** | *io*.binmode → *io* |

1.9   Puts *io* into binary mode. It is more common to use the "b" modifier in the mode string to set binary mode when you open a file. Binary mode is required when reading or writing files containing bit sequences that are not valid in the encoding of the file. Once a stream is in binary mode, it cannot be reset to nonbinary mode.

| **binmode?** | *io*.binmode? → true or false |

1.9   Returns true if *io* is in binary mode.

```
f = File.open("/etc/passwd")
f.binmode?   # =>   false
f = File.open("/etc/passwd", "rb:binary")
f.binmode?   # =>   true
```

| **bytes** | *io*.bytes → *enumerator* |

1.9   Returns an enumerator that iterates over the bytes (not characters) in *io*, returning each as an integer. See also IO#getbyte.

```
file = File.open("testfile")
enum = file.bytes
enum.first(10)   # =>  [84, 104, 105, 115, 32, 105, 115, 32, 108, 105]
```

---

chars   *io*.chars → *enumerator*

1.9   Returns an enumerator that allows iteration over the characters in *io*.

```
file = File.open("testfile")
enum = file.chars
enum.first(7)   # =>  ["T", "h", "i", "s", " ", "i", "s"]
```

---

close   *io*.close → nil

Closes *io* and flushes any pending writes to the operating system. The stream is unavailable for any further data operations; an IOError is raised if such an attempt is made. I/O streams are automatically closed when they are claimed by the garbage collector.

---

close_on_exec?   *io*.close_on_exec? → true or false

1.9   Returns the state of the *close on exec* flag for *io*. Raises NotImplemented if not available.

---

close_on_exec=   *io*.close_on_exec = true or false → nil

1.9   Sets the *close on exec* flag for *io*. Raises NotImplemented if not available. I/O objects with this flag set will be closed across exec() calls.

---

close_read   *io*.close_read → nil

Closes the read end of a duplex I/O stream (in other words, one that contains both a read and a write stream, such as a pipe). Raises an IOError if the stream is not duplexed.

```
f = IO.popen("/bin/sh","r+")
f.close_read
f.readlines
```

produces:

```
prog.rb:3:in `readlines': not opened for reading (IOError)
        from /tmp/prog.rb:3:in `<main>'
```

---

close_write   *io*.close_write → nil

Closes the write end of a duplex I/O stream (in other words, one that contains both a read and a write stream, such as a pipe). Will raise an IOError if the stream is not duplexed.

```
f = IO.popen("/bin/sh","r+")
f.close_write
f.print "nowhere"
```

produces:

```
prog.rb:3:in `write': not opened for writing (IOError)
        from /tmp/prog.rb:3:in `print'
        from /tmp/prog.rb:3:in `<main>'
```

O

closed?

Returns true if *io* is completely closed (for duplex streams, both reader and writer) and returns false otherwise.

```
f = File.new("testfile")
f.close           # =>   nil
f.closed?         # =>   true
f = IO.popen("/bin/sh","r+")
f.close_write     # =>   nil
f.closed?         # =>   false
f.close_read      # =>   nil
f.closed?         # =>   true
```

each

io.each(*separator*=$/) {| *line* | *block* } → *io*
io.each(*limit*) {| *line* | *block* } → *io*
io.each(*separator*, *limit*) {| *line* | *block* } → *io*
io.each(*args*..) → *enum*

1.9

Executes the block for every line in *io*, where lines are separated by *separator*. If *separator* is nil, the entire file is passed as a single string. If the *limit* argument is present and positive, at most that many characters will be returned in each iteration. If only the *limit* argument is given and that argument is negative, then encodings will be ignored while looking for the record separator, which increases performance.

Returns an enumerator if no block is given.

```
f = File.new("testfile")
f.each {|line| puts "#{f.lineno}: #{line}" }
```

produces:

```
1: This is line one
2: This is line two
3: This is line three
4: And so on...
```

each_byte

1.9

Calls the given block once for each byte (a Fixnum in the range 0 to 255) in *io*, passing the byte as an argument. The stream must be opened for reading or an IOerror will be raised. Returns an enumerator if no block is given.

```
f = File.new("testfile")
checksum = 0
f.each_byte {|x| checksum ^= x }   # =>   #<File:testfile>
checksum                           # =>   12
```

each_char

1.9

Calls the given block passing it each character (a string of length 1) in *io*. The stream must be opened for reading or an IOerror will be raised. Returns an enumerator if no block is given.

```
f = File.new("testfile")
result = []
f.each_char {|ch| result << ch}    # =>    #<File:testfile>
result[0, 10]                      # =>    ["T", "h", "i", "s", " ", "i",
                                           "s", " ", "l", "i"]
```

---

each_line   *io*.each_line(...) {| *line* | *block* } → *io*

Synonym for IO#each.

---

eof   *io*.eof → true or false

Returns true if *io* is at end of file. The stream must be opened for reading or an IOError will
be raised.

```
f = File.open("testfile")
f.eof   # =>    false
dummy = f.readlines
f.eof   # =>    true
```

---

eof?   *io*.eof? → true or false

Synonym for IO#eof.

---

external_encoding   *io*.external_encoding → *encoding*

1.9

Returns the encoding object representing the external encoding of this I/O object.

```
io = File.open("testfile", "r:utf-8:iso-8859-1")
io.external_encoding   # =>    #<Encoding:UTF-8>
io.internal_encoding   # =>    #<Encoding:ISO-8859-1>
```

---

fcntl   *io*.fcntl(*cmd, arg*) → *int*

Provides a mechanism for issuing low-level commands to control or query file-oriented I/O
streams. Commands (which are integers), arguments, and the result are platform dependent.
If *arg* is a number, its value is passed directly. If it is a string, it is interpreted as a binary
sequence of bytes. On Unix platforms, see fcntl(2) for details. The Fcntl module provides
symbolic names for the first argument (see page 744). Not implemented on all platforms.

---

fileno   *io*.fileno → *int*

Returns an integer representing the numeric file descriptor for *io*.

```
STDIN.fileno    # =>    0
STDOUT.fileno   # =>    1
```

---

flush   *io*.flush → *io*

Flushes any buffered data within *io* to the underlying operating system (note that this is
Ruby internal buffering only; the OS may buffer the data as well).

```
STDOUT.print "no newline"
STDOUT.flush
```

produces:

```
no newline
```

fsync

io.fsync → 0 or nil

Immediately writes all buffered data in *io* to disk. Returns nil if the underlying operating system does not support *fsync(2)*. Note that fsync differs from using IO#sync=. The latter ensures that data is flushed from Ruby's buffers but does not guarantee that the underlying operating system actually writes it to disk.

getbyte

io.getbyte → *fixnum* or nil

1.9 Returns the next 8-bit byte (as opposed to an encoded character) from *IO* or returns nil at end of file. See also IO#bytes.

```
file = File.open("testfile")
file.getbyte   # =>   84
file.getbyte   # =>   104
```

getc

io.getc → *string* or nil

1.9 Gets the next character from *io*. Returns nil if called at end of file.

```
f = File.new("testfile")
f.getc   # =>   "T"
f.getc   # =>   "h"
```

gets

io.gets(*separator=$/*) → *string* or nil
io.gets(*limit*) → *string* or nil
io.gets(*separator, limit*) → *string* or nil

1.9 Reads the next "line" from the I/O stream; lines are separated by *separator*. A separator of nil reads the entire contents, and a zero-length separator reads the input a paragraph at a time (two or more successive newlines in the input separate paragraphs). If *separator* is nil, the entire file is passed as a single string. If the *limit* argument is present and positive, at most that many characters will be returned in each iteration. If only the *limit* argument is given and that argument is negative, then encodings will be ignored while looking for the record separator, which increases performance. The line read in will be returned and also assigned to $_ (although the setting of $_ is considered ugly—it may be removed in future). Returns nil if called at end of file.

```
file = File.new("testfile")
file.gets              # =>   "This is line one\n"
$_                     # =>   "This is line one\n"
file.gets(10)          # =>   "This is li"
file.gets("line")      # =>   "ne two\nThis is line"
file.gets("line", 4)   # =>   " thr"
```

internal_encoding

io.internal_encoding → *encoding*

1.9 Returns the encoding object representing the internal encoding of this I/O object.

```
io = File.open("testfile", "r:utf-8:iso-8859-1")
io.external_encoding   # =>   #<Encoding:UTF-8>
io.internal_encoding   # =>   #<Encoding:ISO-8859-1>
```

---

ioctl   *io*.ioctl(*cmd, arg*) → *int*

Provides a mechanism for issuing low-level commands to control or query I/O devices. The command (which is an integer), arguments, and results are platform dependent. If *arg* is a number, its value is passed directly. If it is a string, it is interpreted as a binary sequence of bytes. On Unix platforms, see ioctl(2) for details. Not implemented on all platforms.

---

isatty   *io*.isatty → true or false

Returns true if *io* is associated with a terminal device (tty) and returns false otherwise.

```
File.new("testfile").isatty   # =>   false
File.new("/dev/tty").isatty   # =>   true
```

---

lineno   *io*.lineno → *int*

Returns the current line number in *io*. The stream must be opened for reading. lineno counts the number of times gets is called, rather than the number of newlines encountered. The two values will differ if gets is called with a separator other than newline. See also the $. variable.

```
f = File.new("testfile")
f.lineno   # =>   0
f.gets     # =>   "This is line one\n"
f.lineno   # =>   1
f.gets     # =>   "This is line two\n"
f.lineno   # =>   2
```

---

lineno=   *io*.lineno = *int* → *int*

Manually sets the current line number to the given value. $. is updated only on the next read.

```
f = File.new("testfile")
f.gets                      # =>   "This is line one\n"
$.                          # =>   1
f.lineno = 1000
f.lineno                    # =>   1000
$. # lineno of last read    # =>   1
f.gets                      # =>   "This is line two\n"
$. # lineno of last read    # =>   1001
```

---

lines   *io*.lines(*separator=$/*) → *enumerator*
           io.lines(*limit*) → *enumerator*
           io.lines(*separator, limit*) → *enumerator*

1.9

Returns an enumerator which allows iteration over the lines in *io*, where lines are terminated by *separator*. If *separator* is nil, the entire file is passed as a single string. If the *limit* argument is present and positive, at most that many characters will be returned in each iteration. If only the *limit* argument is given and that argument is negative, then encodings will be ignored while looking for the record separator, which increases performance.

---

pid   *io*.pid → *int*

Returns the process ID of a child process associated with *io*. This will be set by IO.popen.

```
pipe = IO.popen("-")
if pipe
  STDERR.puts "In parent, child pid is #{pipe.pid}"
else
  STDERR.puts "In child, pid is #{$$}"
end
```

produces:

```
In parent, child pid is 46821
In child, pid is 46821
```

---

pos   *io*.pos → *int*

Returns the current offset (in bytes) of *io*.

```
f = File.new("testfile")
f.pos    # =>   0
f.gets   # =>   "This is line one\n"
f.pos    # =>   17
```

---

pos=   *io*.pos = *int* → 0

Seeks to the given position (in bytes) in *io*.

```
f = File.new("testfile")
f.pos = 17
f.gets   # =>   "This is line two\n"
```

---

print   *io*.print(⟨ *obj*=$_ ⟩*) → nil

Writes the given object(s) to *io*. The stream must be opened for writing. If the output record separator ($\) is not nil, it will be appended to the output. If no arguments are given, prints $_. Objects that aren't strings will be converted by calling their to_s method. Returns nil.

```
STDOUT.print("This is ", 100, " percent.\n")
```

produces:

```
This is 100 percent.
```

---

printf   *io*.printf(*format* ⟨ , *obj* ⟩*) → nil

Formats and writes to *io*, converting parameters under control of the format string. See Kernel#sprintf on page 568 for details.

---

putc   *io*.putc(*obj*) → *obj*

Writes the given character (the first byte from String or a Fixnum) on *io*. Note that this is not encoding safe, because the byte may be just part of a multibyte sequence.

```
STDOUT.putc "ABC"
STDOUT.putc 65
```

produces:

```
AA
```

puts   *io*.puts(⟨ *obj* ⟩*) → nil

Writes the given objects to *io* as with IO#print. Writes a newline after any that do not already end with a newline sequence. If called with an array argument, writes each element on a new line. If called without arguments, outputs a single newline.

```
STDOUT.puts("this", "is", "a", "test")
```

produces:

```
this
is
a
test
```

read   *io*.read(⟨ *int* ⟨ , *buffer* ⟩ ⟩) → *string* or nil

Reads at most *int* bytes from the I/O stream or to the end of file if *int* is omitted. Returns nil if called at end of file. If *buffer* (a String) is provided, it is resized accordingly, and input is read directly into it.

```
f = File.new("testfile")
f.read(16)        # =>   "This is line one"
str = "cat"
f.read(10, str)   # =>   "\nThis is l"
str               # =>   "\nThis is l"
```

readbyte   *io*.getbyte → *fixnum*

_{1.9} Returns the next 8-byte byte (as opposed to an encoded character) from *IO*, raising EOFError at end of file. See also IO#bytes.

readchar   *io*.readchar → *string*

Reads a character as with IO#getc but raises an EOFError on end of file.

readline   *io*.readline(*separator*=$/) → *string* or nil
                                                      io.readline(*limit*) → *string* or nil
                                          io.readline(*separator*, *limit*) → *string* or nil

_{1.9} Reads a line as with IO#gets, but raises an EOFError on end of file.

readlines   *io*.readlines(*separator*=$/) → *array*
                                                      io.readlines(*limit*) → *array*
                                          io.readlines(*separator*, *limit*) → *array*

_{1.9} Returns all of the lines in *io* as an array. Lines are separated by the optional *separator*. If *separator* is nil, the entire file is passed as a single string. If the *limit* argument is present and positive, at most that many characters will be returned in each iteration. If only the *limit* argument is given and that argument is negative, then encodings will be ignored while looking for the record separator, which increases performance.

```
f = File.new("testfile")
f.readlines            # =>    ["This is line one\n", "This is line two\n",
                               "This is line three\n", "And so on...\n"]
f = File.new("testfile")
f.readlines("line")    # =>    ["This is line", " one\nThis is line", "
                               two\nThis is line", " three\nAnd so on...\n"]
f = File.new("testfile")
f.readlines(10)        # =>    ["This is li", "ne one\n", "This is li", "ne
                               two\n", "This is li", "ne three\n", "And so
                               on.", "..\n"]
```

---

readpartial   *io*.readpartial(*limit, result=""*) → *result*

1.9

Data read from files and devices is normally buffered. When reading line by line (for example using IO#gets), Ruby will read many lines at a time into an internal buffer and then return lines from that buffer. This buffering is normally transparent—Ruby will refill the buffer automatically when required. However, when reading from a device or pipe (as opposed to a file), you sometimes want to read whatever is in the buffer, reading from the device or pipe only if the buffer is empty when the read starts. This is what readpartial does. If any data is available in local buffers, it will be returned immediately. readpartial will read from the device or pipe (potentially blocking) only if the buffer is empty. Raises EOFError when it reached EOF. See also IO#read_nonblock.

The following example comes from the internal documentation, with thanks to the anonymous author:

```
r, w = IO.pipe           #                  buffer          pipe content
w << "abc"               #                   ""             "abc".
r.readpartial(4096)      #=> "abc"           ""             ""
r.readpartial(4096)      # blocks because buffer and pipe is empty.

r, w = IO.pipe           #                  buffer          pipe content
w << "abc"               #                   ""             "abc"
w.close                  #                   ""             "abc" EOF
r.readpartial(4096)      #=> "abc"           ""             EOF
r.readpartial(4096)      # raises EOFError

r, w = IO.pipe           #                  buffer          pipe content
w << "abc\ndef\n"        #                   ""             "abc\ndef\n"
r.gets                   #=> "abc\n"         "def\n"        ""
w << "ghi\n"             #                   "def\n"        "ghi\n"
r.readpartial(4096)      #=> "def\n"         ""             "ghi\n"
r.readpartial(4096)      #=> "ghi\n"         ""             ""
```

---

read_nonblock   *io*.readpartial(*limit, result=""*) → *result*

1.9

Effectively the same as IO#readpartial, except in cases where no buffered data is available. In this case, it puts *io* into nonblocking mode before attempting to read data. This means that the call may return EAGAIN and EINTR errors, which should be handled by the caller.

---

reopen   *io*.reopen(*other_io*) → *io*
                                                        io.reopen(*path*, *mode*) → *io*

Reassociates *io* with the I/O stream given in *other_io* or to a new stream opened on *path*.
This may dynamically change the actual class of this stream.

```
f1 = File.new("testfile")
f2 = File.new("testfile")
f2.readlines[0]   # =>   "This is line one\n"
f2.reopen(f1)     # =>   #<File:testfile>
f2.readlines[0]   # =>   "This is line one\n"
```

---

rewind   *io*.rewind → 0

Positions *io* to the beginning of input, resetting lineno to zero.

```
f = File.new("testfile")
f.readline  # =>   "This is line one\n"
f.rewind    # =>   0
f.lineno    # =>   0
f.readline  # =>   "This is line one\n"
```

---

seek   *io*.seek(*int*, *whence*=SEEK_SET) → 0

Seeks to a given offset *int* in the stream according to the value of *whence*.

IO::SEEK_CUR	Seeks to *int* plus current position
IO::SEEK_END	Seeks to *int* plus end of stream (you probably want a negative value for *int*)
IO::SEEK_SET	Seeks to the absolute location given by *int*

```
f = File.new("testfile")
f.seek(-13, IO::SEEK_END)   # =>   0
f.readline                  # =>   "And so on...\n"
```

---

set_encoding   *io*.set_encoding(*external*, *internal*=*external*) → *io*
                                       io.set_encoding(*"external-name:internal-name"*) → *io*

Sets the external and internal encodings for *io*. In the first form, encodings can be specified
by name (using strings) or as encoding objects. In the second form, the external and internal
encoding names are separated by a colon in a string.

```
f = File.new("testfile")
f.internal_encoding                         # =>   nil
f.external_encoding                         # =>   #<Encoding:UTF-8>
f.set_encoding("ascii-8bit:iso-8859-1")     # =>   #<File:testfile>
f.internal_encoding                         # =>   #<Encoding:ISO-8859-1>
f.external_encoding                         # =>   #<Encoding:ASCII-8BIT>
```

---

stat   *io*.stat → *stat*

Returns status information for *io* as an object of type File::Stat.

```
f = File.new("testfile")
s = f.stat
"%o" % s.mode    # =>    "100644"
s.blksize        # =>    4096
s.atime          # =>    2009-03-31 09:58:16 -0500
```

sync   *io*.sync → true or false

Returns the current "sync mode" of *io*. When sync mode is true, all output is immediately flushed to the underlying operating system and is not buffered by Ruby. See also IO#fsync.

sync=   *io*.sync = *bool* → true or false

Sets the "sync mode" to true or false. When sync mode is true, all output is immediately flushed to the underlying operating system and is not buffered internally. Returns the new state. See also IO#fsync.

```
f = File.new("testfile")
f.sync = true
```

sysread   *io*.sysread(*int* ⟨ , *buffer* ⟩) → *string*

Reads *int* bytes from *io* using a low-level read and returns them as a string. If *buffer* (a String) is provided, input is read directly in to it. Do not mix with other methods that read from *io*, or you may get unpredictable results. Raises SystemCallError on error and EOFError at end of file.

```
f = File.new("testfile")
f.sysread(16)        # =>    "This is line one"
str = "cat"
f.sysread(10, str)   # =>    "\nThis is l"
str                  # =>    "\nThis is l"
```

sysseek   *io*.sysseek(*offset*, *whence*=SEEK_SET) → *int*

Seeks to a given *offset* in the stream according to the value of *whence* (see IO#seek for values of *whence*). Returns the new offset into the file.

```
f = File.new("testfile")
f.sysseek(-13, IO::SEEK_END)    # =>    53
f.sysread(10)                   # =>    "And so on."
```

syswrite   *io*.syswrite(*string*) → *int*

Writes the given string to *io* using a low-level write. Returns the number of bytes written. Do not mix with other methods that write to *io*, or you may get unpredictable results. Raises SystemCallError on error.

```
f = File.new("out", "w")
f.syswrite("ABCDEF")    # =>    6
```

tell   *io*.tell → *int*

Synonym for IO#pos.

---

to_i io.to_i → int

Synonym for IO#fileno.

---

to_io io.to_io → io

Returns io.

---

tty? io.tty? → true or false

Synonym for IO#isatty.

---

ungetbyte io.ungetbyte($string$ or int) → nil

1.9 Pushes back one or more bytes onto io, such that a subsequent buffered read will return them. Has no effect with unbuffered reads (such as IO#sysread).

```
f = File.new("testfile")   # =>   #<File:testfile>
c = f.getbyte             # =>   84
f.ungetbyte(c)            # =>   nil
f.getbyte                 # =>   84
f.ungetbyte("cat")        # =>   nil
f.getbyte                 # =>   99
f.getbyte                 # =>   97
```

---

ungetc io.ungetc($string$) → nil

Pushes back one or more characters onto io, such that a subsequent buffered read will return them. Has no effect with unbuffered reads (such as IO#sysread).

```
# encoding: utf-8
f = File.new("testfile")   # =>   #<File:testfile>
c = f.getc                # =>   "T"
f.ungetc(c)               # =>   nil
f.getc                    # =>   "T"
f.ungetc("δog")           # =>   nil
f.getc                    # =>   "δ"
f.getc                    # =>   "o"
```

---

write io.write($string$) → int

Writes the given string to io. The stream must be opened for writing. If the argument is not a string, it will be converted to a string using to_s. Returns the number of bytes written.

```
count = STDOUT.write( "This is a test\n" )
puts "That was #{count} bytes of data"
```

produces:

```
This is a test
That was 15 bytes of data
```

---

write_nonblock io.write_nonblock($string$) → int

Writes the given string to io after setting io into nonblocking mode. The stream must be opened for writing. If the argument is not a string, it will be converted to a string using to_s. Returns the number of bytes written. Your application should expect to receive errors typical of nonblocking I/O (including EAGAIN and EINTR).

Module
Kernel

The Kernel module is included by class Object, so its methods are available in every Ruby object. The Kernel instance methods are documented in class Object beginning on page 613. This section documents the private methods. These methods are called without a receiver and thus can be called in functional form.

Module methods

__callee__
__callee__ → *symbol* or nil

1.9 Returns the name of the current method or nil outside the context of a method.

```
def fred
  puts "I'm in #{__callee__.inspect}"
end
fred
puts "Then in #{__callee__.inspect}"
```

produces:

```
I'm in :fred
Then in nil
```

__method__
__method__ → *symbol* or nil

1.9 Synonym for __callee__.

Array
Array(*arg*) → *array*

1.9 Returns *arg* as an Array. First tries to call *arg*.to_ary, then *arg*.to_a. If both fail, creates a single element array containing *arg* (or an empty array if *arg* is nil).

```
Array(1..5)   # =>   [1, 2, 3, 4, 5]
```

Complex
Complex(*real*, *imag*=0) → *complex*

1.9 Returns the complex number with the given real and imaginary parts.

```
Complex(1)          # =>   1+0i
Complex("1")        # =>   1+0i
Complex("1", "3/2") # =>   1+3/2i
Complex("3+2i")     # =>   3+2i
```

Float
Float(*arg*) → *float*

Returns *arg* converted to a float. Numeric types are converted directly; the rest are converted using *arg*.to_f. Converting nil generates a TypeError.

```
Float(1)          # =>   1.0
Float("123.456")  # =>   123.456
```

Integer
Integer(*arg*) → *int*

Converts *arg* to a Fixnum or Bignum. Numeric types are converted directly (floating-point numbers are truncated). If *arg* is a String, leading radix indicators (0, 0b, and 0x) are honored. Others are converted using to_int and to_i. This behavior is different from that of String#to_i. Converting nil generates a TypeError.

```
Integer(123.999)    # =>   123
Integer("0x1a")     # =>   26
Integer(Time.new)   # =>   1238511509
```

Rational   Rational(*numerator, denominator*=1) → *complex*

Returns the rational number with the given representation.

```
Rational(1)            # =>   1/1
Rational("1")          # =>   1/1
Rational("1", "2")     # =>   1/2
Rational(1, 0.5)       # =>   2/1
Rational("3/2")        # =>   3/2
Rational("3/2", "4/5") # =>   15/8
```

String   String(*arg*) → *string*

Converts *arg* to a String by calling its to_s method.

```
String(self)        # =>    "main"
String(self.class)  # =>    "Object"
String(123456)      # =>    "123456"
```

` (backquote)                                            `*cmd*` → *string*

Returns the standard output of running *cmd* in a subshell. The built-in syntax %x{...} described on page 132 uses this method. Sets $? to the process status.

```
`date`                 # =>    "Tue Mar 31 09:58:29 CDT 2009\n"
`ls testdir`.split[1]  # =>    "main.rb"
`echo oops && exit 99` # =>    "oops\n"
$?.exitstatus          # =>    99
```

abort   abort
                                                                 abort(*msg*)

Terminates execution immediately with an exit code of 1. The optional String parameter is written to standard error before the program terminates.

at_exit   at_exit { *block* } → *proc*

Converts *block* to a Proc object (and therefore binds it at the point of call) and registers it for execution when the program exits. If multiple handlers are registered, they are executed in reverse order of registration.

```
def do_at_exit(str1)
  at_exit { print str1 }
end
at_exit { puts "cruel world" }
do_at_exit("goodbye ")
exit
```

produces:

```
goodbye cruel world
```

---

autoload

autoload(*name*, *file_name*) → nil

Registers *file_name* to be loaded (using Kernel.require) the first time that the module *name* (which may be a String or a symbol) is accessed.

```
autoload(:MyModule, "/usr/local/lib/modules/my_module.rb")
```

Module.autoload lets you define namespace-specific autoload hooks:

```
module X
 autoload :XXX, "xxx.rb"
end
```

Note that xxx.rb should define a class in the correct namespace. That is, in this example xxx.rb should contain the following:

```
class X::XXX
  # ...
end
```

---

autoload?

autoload?(*name*) → *file_name* or nil

Returns the name of the file that will be autoloaded when the string or symbol *name* is referenced in the top-level context or returns nil if there is no associated autoload.

```
autoload(:Fred, "module_fred")    # =>   nil
autoload?(:Fred)                   # =>   "module_fred"
autoload?(:Wilma)                  # =>   nil
```

---

binding

binding → *a_binding*

Returns a Binding object, describing the variable and method bindings at the point of call. This object can be used when calling eval to execute the evaluated command in this environment. Also see the description of class Binding beginning on page 460.

```
def get_binding(param)
  return binding
end
b = get_binding("hello")
eval("param", b)   # =>   "hello"
```

---

block_given?

block_given? → true or false

Returns true if yield would execute a block in the current context.

```
def try
  if block_given?
    yield
  else
    "no block"
  end
end
try                 # =>   "no block"
try { "hello" }     # =>   "hello"
block = lambda { "proc object" }
try(&block)         # =>   "proc object"
```

---

caller   caller(⟨ *int* ⟩) → *array*

Returns the current execution stack—an array containing strings in the form *file:line* or *file:line: in 'method'*. The optional *int* parameter determines the number of initial stack entries to omit from the result.

```
def a(skip)
  caller(skip)
end
def b(skip)
  a(skip)
end
def c(skip)
  b(skip)
end
c(0)  # =>   ["/tmp/prog.rb:2:in `a'", "/tmp/prog.rb:5:in `b'",
      #      "/tmp/prog.rb:8:in `c'", "/tmp/prog.rb:10:in `<main>'"]
c(1)  # =>   ["/tmp/prog.rb:5:in `b'", "/tmp/prog.rb:8:in `c'",
      #      "/tmp/prog.rb:11:in `<main>'"]
c(2)  # =>   ["/tmp/prog.rb:8:in `c'", "/tmp/prog.rb:12:in `<main>'"]
c(3)  # =>   ["/tmp/prog.rb:13:in `<main>'"]
```

---

catch   catch(*object*=Object.new) { *block* } → obj

_1.9_ catch executes its block. If a throw is encountered, Ruby searches up its stack for a catch block with a parameter identical to the throw's parameter. If found, that block is terminated, and catch returns the value given as the second parameter to throw. If throw is not called, the block terminates normally, and the value of catch is the value of the last expression evaluated. catch expressions may be nested, and the throw call need not be in lexical scope.

_1.9_ Prior to Ruby 1.9 the parameters to catch and throw had to be symbols—they can now be any object. When using literals, it probably makes sense to use only immediate objects.

```
def routine(n)
  print n, ' '
  throw :done if n <= 0
  routine(n-1)
end
catch(:done) { routine(4) }
```

produces:

```
4 3 2 1 0
```

chomp

chomp(⟨ *rs* ⟩) → $_ or *string*

Equivalent to $_ = $_.chomp(*rs*), except no assignment is made if chomp doesn't change $_. See String#chomp on page 666. Available only with the -n or -p command-line options are present.

chop

chop → *string*

(Almost) equivalent to ($_.dup).chop!, except that if chop would perform no action, $_ is unchanged and nil is not returned. See String#chop! on page 667. Available only with the -n or -p command-line options are present.

eval

eval(*string* ⟨ , *binding* ⟨ , *file* ⟨ , *line* ⟩ ⟩ ⟩) → *obj*

Evaluates the Ruby expression(s) in *string*. If *binding* is given, the evaluation is performed in its context. The binding must be a Binding object. If the optional *file* and *line* parameters are present, they will be used when reporting syntax errors.

```
def get_binding(str)
  return binding
end
str = "hello"
eval "str + ' Fred'"                    # =>   "hello Fred"
eval "str + ' Fred'", get_binding("bye")  # =>   "bye Fred"
```

Local variables assigned within an eval are available after the eval only if they were defined at the outer scope before the eval executed. In this way, eval has the same scoping rules as blocks.

```
a = 1
eval "a = 98; b = 99"
puts a
puts b
```

produces:

```
98
prog.rb:4:in `<main>': undefined local variable or method `b' for
  main:Object (NameError)
```

exec

exec(⟨ env, ⟩ *command* ⟨ , *args* ⟩*, ⟨ options ⟩)

Replaces the current process by running the given external command. If exec is given a single argument, that argument is taken as a line that is subject to shell expansion before being executed. If *command* contains a newline or any of the characters *?{}[]<>()~\&|\$;'`", or under Windows if *command* looks like a shell-internal command (for example dir), *command* is run under a shell. On Unix system, Ruby does this by prepending sh -c. Under Windows, it uses the name of a shell in either RUBYSHELL or COMSPEC.

If multiple arguments are given, the second and subsequent arguments are passed as parameters to *command* with no shell expansion. If the first argument is a two-element array, the first element is the command to be executed, and the second argument is used as the argv[0] value, which may show up in process listings. In MSDOS environments, the command is executed in a subshell; otherwise, one of the exec(2) system calls is used, so the running command may inherit some of the environment of the original program (including open file descriptors). Raises SystemCallError if the *command* couldn't execute (typically Errno::ENOENT).

```
exec "echo *"        # echoes list of files in current directory
# never get here
exec "echo", "*"     # echoes an asterisk
# never get here
```

env, if present, is a hash that adds to the environment variables in the subshell. An entry with a nil value clears the corresponding environment variable. The keys must be strings. *options*, if present, is a hash that controls the setup of the subshell. The possible keys and their meanings are listed in Table 27.8 on page 571. See also Kernel.spawn and Kernel.system.

---

exit   exit(true | false | *status*=1)

Initiates the termination of the Ruby script. If called in the scope of an exception handler, raises a SystemExit exception. This exception may be caught. Otherwise, exits the process using exit(2). The optional parameter is used to return a status code to the invoking environment. With an argument of true, exits with a status of zero. With an argument that is false (or no argument), exits with a status of 1; otherwise, exits with the given status. The default exit value is 1.

```
fork { exit 99 }
Process.wait
puts "Child exits with status: #{$?.exitstatus}"
 begin
   exit
   puts "never get here"
 rescue SystemExit
   puts "rescued a SystemExit exception"
 end
 puts "after begin block"
```

produces:

```
Child exits with status: 99
rescued a SystemExit exception
after begin block
```

Just prior to termination, Ruby executes any at_exit functions and runs any object finalizers (see ObjectSpace beginning on page 626).

```
at_exit { puts "at_exit function" }
ObjectSpace.define_finalizer("xxx",  lambda { |obj| puts "in finalizer" })
exit
```

produces:

```
at_exit function
in finalizer
```

exit!   exit!(true | false | *status*=1)

Similar to Kernel.exit, but exception handling, at_exit functions, and finalizers are bypassed.

---

fail   fail
fail(*message*)
fail(*exception* ⟨ , *message* ⟨ , *array* ⟩ ⟩)

Synonym for Kernel.raise.

---

fork   fork ⟨ { *block* } ⟩ → *int* or nil

Creates a subprocess. If a block is specified, that block is run in the subprocess, and the subprocess terminates with a status of zero. Otherwise, the fork call returns twice, once in the parent, returning the process ID of the child, and once in the child, returning nil. The child process can exit using Kernel.exit! to avoid running any at_exit functions. The parent process should use Process.wait to collect the termination statuses of its children or use Process.detach to register disinterest in their status; otherwise, the operating system may accumulate zombie processes.

```
fork do
  3.times {|i| puts "Child: #{i}" }
end
3.times {|i| puts "Parent: #{i}" }
Process.wait
```

produces:

```
Parent: 0
Child: 0
Child: 1
Child: 2
Parent: 1
Parent: 2
```

---

format   format(*format_string* ⟨ , *arg* ⟩*) → *string*

Synonym for Kernel.sprintf.

---

gem   gem(*gem_name* ⟨ , *version* ⟩) → true or false

_1.9_   Adds the given gem to the applications include path, so that subsequent requires will search. Defaults to the latest version of the gem if no version information is given. See section *Gems and Versions* on page 229 for more information and examples.

---

gets   gets(*separator*=$/) → *string* or nil

Returns (and assigns to $_) the next line from the list of files in ARGV (or $*) or from standard input if no files are present on the command line. Returns nil at end of file. The optional argument specifies the record separator. The separator is included with the contents of each record. A separator of nil reads the entire contents, and a zero-length separator reads the input one paragraph at a time, where paragraphs are divided by two consecutive newlines. If multiple filenames are present in ARGV, gets(nil) will read the contents one file at a time.

```
ARGV << "testfile"
print while gets
```

produces:

```
This is line one
This is line two
This is line three
And so on...
```

The style of programming using $_ as an implicit parameter is gradually losing favor in the Ruby community.

---

global_variables   global_variables → *array*

Returns an array of the names of global variables.

```
global_variables.grep /std/   # =>   [:$stdin, :$stdout, :$stderr]
```

---

gsub   gsub(*pattern, replacement*) → *string*
                                               gsub(*pattern*) { *block* } → *string*

1.9   Equivalent to $_.gsub(...), except that $_ will be updated if substitution occurs. Available only with the -n or -p command-line options are present.

---

iterator?   iterator? → true or false

Deprecated synonym for Kernel.block_given?.

---

lambda   lambda { *block* } → *proc*

Creates a new procedure object from the given block. See page 352 for an explanation of the difference between procedure objects created using lambda and those created using Proc.new. Note that lambda is now preferred over proc.

```
prc = lambda { "hello" }
prc.call   # =>   "hello"
```

---

load   load(*file_name, wrap*=false) → true

Loads and executes the Ruby program in the file *file_name*. If the filename does not resolve to an absolute path, the file is searched for in the library directories listed in $:. If the optional *wrap* parameter is true, the loaded script will be executed under an anonymous module, protecting the calling program's global namespace. In no circumstance will any local variables in the loaded file be propagated to the loading environment.

local_variables   local_variables → *array*

Returns the names of the current local variables.

```ruby
fred = 1
for i in 1..10
  # ...
end
local_variables  # =>   [:fred, :i]
```

Note that local variables are associated with bindings.

```ruby
def fred
  a = 1
  b = 2
  binding
end
freds_binding = fred
eval("local_variables", freds_binding)  # =>   [:a, :b]
```

loop   loop ⟨ { *block* } ⟩

Repeatedly executes the block.

```ruby
loop do
  print "Type something: "
  line = gets
  break if line.nil?  || line =~ /^[qQ]/
  # ...
end
```

1.9 ⟋   loop silently rescues the StopIteration exception, which works well with external iterators.

```ruby
enum1 = [1, 2, 3].to_enum
enum2 = [10, 20].to_enum
loop do
  puts enum1.next + enum2.next
end
```

produces:

```
11
22
```

open   open(*name* ⟨ , *mode* ⟨ , *permission* ⟩ ⟩) → *io* or nil
                                                 open(*name* ⟨ , *mode* ⟨ , *permission* ⟩ ⟩) { | *io* | *block* } → *obj*

1.9 ⟋   Creates an IO object connected to the given stream, file, or subprocess.

If *name* does not start with a pipe character (|), treats it as the name of a file to open using the specified mode defaulting to "r" (see the table of valid modes on page 538). If a file is being created, its initial permissions may be set using the third parameter, which is an integer. If this third parameter is present, the file will be opened using the low-level open(2) rather than fopen(3) call.

If a block is specified, it will be invoked with the IO object as a parameter, which will be automatically closed when the block terminates. The call returns the value of the block in this case.

If *name* starts with a pipe character, a subprocess is created, connected to the caller by a pair of pipes. The returned IO object may be used to write to the standard input and read from the standard output of this subprocess. If the command following the | is a single minus sign, Ruby forks, and this subprocess is connected to the parent. In the subprocess, the open call returns nil. If the command is not "–", the subprocess runs the command. If a block is associated with an open("|–") call, that block will be run twice—once in the parent and once in the child. The block parameter will be an IO object in the parent and nil in the child. The parent's IO object will be connected to the child's STDIN and STDOUT. The subprocess will be terminated at the end of the block.

```
open("testfile", "r:iso-8859-1") do |f|
  print f.gets
end
```

produces:

```
This is line one
```

Open a subprocess, and read its output:

```
cmd = open("|date")
print cmd.gets
cmd.close
```

produces:

```
Tue Mar 31 09:58:31 CDT 2009
```

Open a subprocess running the same Ruby program:

```
f = open("|-", "w+")
if f.nil?
  puts "in Child"
  exit
else
  puts "Got: #{f.gets}"
end
```

produces:

```
Got: in Child
```

Open a subprocess using a block to receive the I/O object:

```
open("|-") do |f|
  if f.nil?
    puts "in Child"
  else
    puts "Got: #{f.gets}"
  end
end
```

produces:

```
Got: in Child
```

p   p(⟨ *obj* ⟩⁺) → *obj*

1.9

For each object, writes *obj*.inspect followed by the current output record separator to the program's standard output. Also see the PrettyPrint library on page 781.

```
Info = Struct.new(:name, :state)
p Info['dave', 'TX']
```

produces:

```
#<struct Info name="dave", state="TX">
```

print   print(⟨ *obj* ⟩*) → nil

Prints each object in turn to STDOUT. If the output field separator ($,) is not nil, its contents will appear between each field. If the output record separator ($\) is not nil, it will be appended to the output. If no arguments are given, prints $_. Objects that aren't strings will be converted by calling their to_s method.

```
print "cat", [1,2,3], 99, "\n"
$, = ", "
$\ = "\n"
print "cat", [1,2,3], 99
```

produces:

```
cat[1, 2, 3]99
cat, [1, 2, 3], 99,
```

printf   printf(*io*, *format* ⟨ , *obj* ⟩*) → nil
                    printf(*format* ⟨ , *obj* ⟩*) → nil

Equivalent to

> *io*.write sprintf(*format*, *obj* ...)

or

> STDOUT.write sprintf(*format*, *obj* ...)

proc   proc { *block* } → *a_proc*

Creates a new procedure object from the given block. Mildly deprecated in favor of Kernel#lambda.

```
prc = proc {|name| "Goodbye, #{name}" }
prc.call('Dave')   # =>   "Goodbye, Dave"
```

putc   putc(*obj*) → *obj*

1.9

Equivalent to STDOUT.putc(*obj*). If *obj* is a string, output its first byte as a character; otherwise, attempts to convert *obj* to an integer and outputs the corresponding character code.

```
putc 65
putc 66.123
putc "CAT"
putc 12        # newline
```

produces:

```
ABC
```

Kernel

---

puts puts(⟨ *arg* ⟩*) → nil

Equivalent to STDOUT.puts(*arg*...).

---

raise raise
raise(message)
raise(exception ⟨ , message ⟨ , array ⟩ ⟩)

With no arguments, raises the exception in $! or raises a RuntimeError if $! is nil. With a single String argument (or an argument that responds to to_str), raises a RuntimeError with the string as a message. Otherwise, the first parameter should be the name of an Exception class (or an object that returns an Exception when its exception method is called). The optional second parameter sets the message associated with the exception, and the third parameter is an array of callback information. Exceptions are caught by the rescue clause of begin. . . end blocks.

```
raise "Failed to create socket"
raise ArgumentError, "No parameters", caller
```

---

rand rand(max=0) → number

Converts *max* to an integer using $max_1 = max$.to_i.abs. If the result is zero, returns a pseudorandom floating-point number greater than or equal to 0.0 and less than 1.0. Otherwise, returns a pseudorandom integer greater than or equal to zero and less than max_1. Kernel.srand may be used to ensure repeatable sequences of random numbers between different runs of the program. Ruby currently uses a modified Mersenne Twister with a period of $2^{19937} - 1$.

```
srand 1234                # =>    213170800215535175859315805189367326543
[ rand, rand ]            # =>    [0.191519450378892, 0.622108771039832]
[ rand(10), rand(1000) ]  # =>    [4, 664]
srand 1234                # =>    1234
[ rand, rand ]            # =>    [0.191519450378892, 0.622108771039832]
```

---

readline readline(⟨ separator=$/ ⟩) → string

Equivalent to Kernel.gets, except readline raises EOFError at end of file.

---

readlines readlines(⟨ separator=$/ ⟩) → array

Returns an array containing the lines returned by calling Kernel.gets(*separator*) until the end of file.

---

require require(library_name) → true or false

Ruby tries to load *library_name*, returning true if successful. If the filename does not resolve to an absolute path, it will be searched for in the directories listed in $:. If the file has the extension .rb, it is loaded as a source file; if the extension is .so, .o, or .dll,[2] Ruby loads the shared library as a Ruby extension. Otherwise, Ruby tries adding .rb, .so, and so on, to

---

2.   Or whatever the default shared library extension is on the current platform.

the name. The name of the loaded feature is added to the array in $". A feature will not be loaded if its name already appears in $".[3] require returns true if the feature was successfully loaded.

```
require 'my-library.rb'
require 'db-driver'
```

require_relative   require_relative(*library_path*) → true or false

1.9 Requires a library whose path is relative to the file containing the call. Thus, if the file /usr/local/mylib/bin contains the file myprog.rb and that program contains the following line:

```
require_relative "../lib/mylib"
```

Ruby will look for mylib in /usr/local/mylib/lib.

require_relative cannot be called interactively in irb.

select   select(*read_array* ⟨ , *write_array* ⟨ , *error_array* ⟨ , *timeout* ⟩ ⟩ ⟩) → *array* or nil

Performs a low-level select call, which waits for data to become available from input/output devices. The first three parameters are arrays of IO objects or nil. The last is a timeout in seconds, which should be an Integer or a Float. The call waits for data to become available for any of the IO objects in *read_array*, for buffers to have cleared sufficiently to enable writing to any of the devices in *write_array*, or for an error to occur on the devices in *error_array*. If one or more of these conditions are met, the call returns a three-element array containing arrays of the IO objects that were ready. Otherwise, if there is no change in status for *timeout* seconds, the call returns nil. If all parameters are nil, the current thread sleeps forever.

```
select( [STDIN], nil, nil, 1.5 )   # =>   [[#<IO:<STDIN>>], [], []]
```

set_trace_func   set_trace_func(*proc*) → *proc*
set_trace_func(nil) → nil

Establishes *proc* as the handler for tracing or disables tracing if the parameter is nil. *proc* takes up to six parameters: an event name, a filename, a line number, an object ID, a binding, and the name of a class. *proc* is invoked whenever an event occurs. Events are c-call (calls a C-language routine), c-return (returns from a C-language routine), call (calls a Ruby method), class (starts a class or module definition), end (finishes a class or module definition), line (executes code on a new line), raise (raises an exception), and return (returns from a Ruby method). Tracing is disabled within the context of *proc*.

See the example starting on page 416 for more information.

sleep   sleep(*numeric*=0) → *fixnum*

Suspends the current thread for *numeric* seconds (which may be a Float with fractional seconds). Returns the actual number of seconds slept (rounded), which may be less than that

---

3. As of Ruby 1.9 this name is converted to an absolute path, so that require 'a';require './a' will load a.rb just once.

asked for if the thread was interrupted by a SIGALRM or if another thread calls Thread#run. An argument of zero causes sleep to sleep forever.

```
Time.now    # =>   2009-03-31 09:58:32 -0500
sleep 1.9   # =>   1
Time.now    # =>   2009-03-31 09:58:33 -0500
```

---

spawn   spawn(⟨ env, ⟩ *command* ⟨ , *args* ⟩*, ⟨ options ⟩) → *pid*

1.9

Executes *command* in a subshell, returning immediately. (Compare with Kernel.system, which waits for the command to complete before returning to the caller.) Returns the process ID for the subprocess running the command. The arguments are processed in the same way as for Kernel.exec on page 559. Raises SystemCallError if the *command* couldn't execute (typically Errno::ENOENT).

```
pid = spawn("echo hello")
puts "Back in main program"
rc, status = Process::waitpid2(pid)
puts "Status = #{status}"
```

produces:

```
Back in main program
hello
Status = pid 47937 exit 0
```

env, if present, is a hash that adds to the environment variables in the subshell. An entry with a nil value clears the corresponding environment variable. The keys must be strings.

```
pid = spawn({"FRED" => "caveman"}, "echo FRED = $FRED")
Process::waitpid2(pid)
```

produces:

```
FRED = caveman
```

options, if present, is a hash that controls the setup of the subshell. The possible keys and their meanings are listed in Table 27.8 on page 571.

```
reader, writer = IO.pipe
pid = spawn("echo '4*a(1)' | bc -l", [ STDERR, STDOUT ] => writer)
writer.close
Process::waitpid2(pid)
reader.gets   # =>   "3.14159265358979323844\n"
```

---

sprintf   sprintf(*format_string* ⟨ , *arguments* ⟩*) → *string*

Returns the string resulting from applying *format_string* to any additional arguments. Within the format string, any characters other than format sequences are copied to the result.

1.9

A format sequence consists of a percent sign; followed by optional flags, width, and precision indicators, and an optional name; and then terminated with a field type character. The field type controls how the corresponding sprintf argument is to be interpreted, and the flags modify that interpretation. The flag characters are shown in Table 27.9 on page 572, and the field type characters are listed in Table 27.10.

The field width is an optional integer, followed optionally by a period and a precision. The width specifies the minimum number of characters that will be written to the result for this field. For numeric fields, the precision controls the number of decimal places displayed. As of Ruby 1.9, number zero is converted to a zero-length string if a precision of 0 is given. For string fields, the precision determines the maximum number of characters to be copied from the string. (Thus, the format sequence %10.10s will always contribute exactly ten characters to the result.)

```
sprintf("%d %04x", 123, 123)              # =>   "123_007b"
sprintf("%08b '%4s'", 123, 123)           # =>   "01111011_'_123'"
sprintf("%1$*2$s %2$d %1$s", "hello", 8)  # =>   "___hello_8_hello"
sprintf("%1$*2$s %2$d", "hello", -8)      # =>   "hello____-8"
sprintf("%+g:% g:%-g", 1.23, 1.23, 1.23)  # =>   "+1.23:_1.23:1.23"
```

In Ruby 1.9, you can pass a hash as the second argument and insert values from this hash into the string. The notation <name> can be used between a percent sign and a field-type character, in which case the name will be used to look up a value in the hash, and that value will be formatted according to the field specification. The notation {name} is equivalent to <name>s, substituting the corresponding value as a string. You can use width and other flag characters between the opening percent sign and the {.

```
sprintf("%<number>d %04<number>x", number: 123)   # =>   "123_007b"
sprintf("%08<number>b '%5{number}'", number: 123) # =>   "01111011_'__123'"
sprintf("%6{k}: %{v}", k: "Dave", v: "Ruby")      # =>   "__Dave:_Ruby"
```

---

srand   srand(⟨ *number* ⟩) → *old_seed*

Seeds the pseudorandom number generator to the value of *number*.to_i. If *number* is omitted or zero, seeds the generator using a system random number generator if available; otherwise, seeds it using a combination of the time, the process ID, and a sequence number. (This is also the behavior if Kernel.rand is called without previously calling srand, but without the sequence.) By setting the seed to a known value, scripts that use rand can be made deterministic during testing. The previous seed value is returned. Also see Kernel.rand on page 566.

---

sub   sub(*pattern*, *replacement*) → $_
                                                   sub(*pattern*) { *block* } → $_

Equivalent to $_.sub(*args*), except that $_ will be updated if substitution occurs. Available only with the -n or -p command-line options are present.

---

syscall   syscall(*fixnum* ⟨ , *args* ⟩*) → *int*

Calls the operating system function identified by *fixnum*. The arguments must be either String objects or Integer objects that fit within a native long. Up to nine parameters may be passed. The function identified by *fixnum* is system dependent. On some Unix systems, the numbers may be obtained from a header file called syscall.h.

```
syscall 4, 1, "hello\n", 6   # '4' is write(2) on our system
```

produces:

```
hello
```

system   system(⟨ env, ⟩ *command* ⟨ , *args* ⟩*, ⟨ options ⟩) → true or false or nil

Executes *command* in a subshell, returning true if the command was found and ran success-fully, false is the command exited with a nonzero exit status, and nil if the command failed to execute. An error status is available in $?. The arguments are processed in the same way as for Kernel.exec on page 559. *env*, if present, is a hash that adds to the environment variables in the subshell. An entry with a nil value clears the corresponding environment variable. The keys must be strings. *options*, if present, is a hash that controls the setup of the sub-shell. The possible keys and their meanings are listed in Table 27.8 on the facing page. See also Kernel.spawn.

```
system("echo *")
system("echo", "*")
system({"WILMA" => "shopper"}, "echo $WILMA")
```

produces:

```
config.h main.rb
*
shopper
```

test   test(*cmd*, *file1* ⟨ , *file2* ⟩) → *obj*

Uses the integer *cmd* to perform various tests on *file1* (Table 27.11 on page 573) or on *file1* and *file2* (Table 27.12).

throw   throw(*symbol* ⟨ , *obj* ⟩)

Transfers control to the end of the active catch block waiting for *symbol*. Raises NameError if there is no catch block for the symbol. The optional second parameter supplies a return value for the catch block, which otherwise defaults to nil. For examples, see Kernel.catch on page 558.

trace_var   trace_var(*symbol*, *cmd*) → nil
          trace_var(*symbol*) {| *val* | *block* } → nil

Controls tracing of assignments to global variables. The parameter *symbol* identifies the variable (as either a string name or a symbol identifier). *cmd* (which may be a string or a Proc object) or the block is executed whenever the variable is assigned and receives the variable's new value as a parameter. Only explicit assignments are traced. Also see Kernel.untrace_var.

```
trace_var :$dave, lambda {|v| puts "$dave is now '#{v}'" }
$dave = "hello"
$dave.sub!(/ello/, "i")
$dave += " Dave"
```

produces:

```
$dave is now 'hello'
$dave is now 'hi Dave'
```

trap   trap(*signal*, *proc*) → *obj*
          trap(*signal*) { *block* } → *obj*

See the Signal module on page 659.

---

untrace_var untrace_var(*symbol* ⟨ , *cmd* ⟩) → *array* or nil

Removes tracing for the specified command on the given global variable and returns nil. If no command is specified, removes all tracing for that variable and returns an array containing the commands actually removed.

---

warn warn *msg*

Writes the given message to STDERR (unless $VERBOSE is nil, perhaps because the -W0 command-line option was given).

```
warn "Danger, Will Robinson!"
```

produces:

```
Danger, Will Robinson!
```

Table 27.8. Options to Spawn and System

Option	Effect on new process
:pgroup => true | 0 | *int*	If true or 0, the new process will be a process group leader. Otherwise, the process will belong to group *int*.
:rlimit_*xxx* => val | [cur, max]	Sets a resource limit. See Process.getrlimit for information on the available limits.
:unsetenv_others => true	Clears all environment variables; then sets only those passed in the *env* parameter.
:chdir => *dir*	Changes to directory *dir* before running the process.
:umask => *int*	Specifies the umask for the process.
fd_desc => *stream*	Sets the process's standard input, output, or error to *stream*. See the description that follows this table for information.
:close_others => true | false	By default, all file descriptors apart from 0, 1, and 2 are closed. You can specify false to leave them open.
io_obj => :close	Explicitly closes the file descriptor corresponding to *io_obj* in the child process.

The *fd_desc* parameter identifies an I/O stream to be opened or assigned in the child process. It can be one of :in, STDIN, or 0 to represent standard input; :out, STDOUT, or 1 to represent standard output; or :err, STDERR, or 2 to represent standard error. It can also be an array containing one or more of these, in which case all fds in the array will be opened on the same stream.

The *stream* parameter can be the following:

- One of :in, STDIN, or 0 to represent the current standard input; :out, STDOUT, or 1 to represent the current standard output; or :err, STDERR, or 2 to represent the current standard error.
- A string representing the name of a file or device.
- An array. The first element is the name of a file or device, the optional second element is the mode, and the optional third element the permission. See the description of File#new on page 503 for details.

Kernel

Table 27.9. sprintf Flag Characters

Flag	Applies To	Meaning
␣ (space)	bdEefGgiouXx	Leaves a space at the start of positive numbers.
digit$	all	Specifies the absolute argument number for this field. Absolute and relative argument numbers cannot both be used in a sprintf string.
#	beEfgGoxX	Uses an alternative format. For the conversions b, o, X, and x, prefixes the result with b, 0, 0X, 0x, respectively. For E, e, f, G, and g, forces a decimal point to be added, even if no digits follow. For G and g, does not remove trailing zeros.
+	bdEefGgiouXx	Adds a leading plus sign to positive numbers.
-	all	Left-justifies the result of this conversion.
0 (zero)	bdEefGgiouXx	Pads with zeros, not spaces.
*	all	Uses the next argument as the field width. If negative, left-justifies the result. If the asterisk is followed by a number and a dollar sign, uses the indicated argument as the width.

Table 27.10. sprintf Field Types

Field	Conversion
B	Converts argument as a binary number (0B0101 if # modifier used).
b	Converts argument as a binary number (0b0101 if # modifier used).
c	Argument is the numeric code for a single character.
d	Converts argument as a decimal number.
E	Equivalent to e but uses an uppercase E to indicate the exponent.
e	Converts floating point-argument into exponential notation with one digit before the decimal point. The precision determines the number of fractional digits (defaulting to six).
f	Converts floating-point argument as [␣-]ddd.ddd, where the precision determines the number of digits after the decimal point.
G	Equivalent to g but uses an uppercase E in exponent form.
g	Converts a floating-point number using exponential form if the exponent is less than -4 or greater than or equal to the precision, or in d.dddd form otherwise.
i	Identical to d.
o	Converts argument as an octal number.
p	The value of *argument.inspect*.
s	Argument is a string to be substituted. If the format sequence contains a precision, at most that many characters will be copied.
u	Treats argument as an unsigned decimal number.
X	Converts argument as a hexadecimal number using uppercase letters. Negative numbers will be displayed with two leading periods (representing an infinite string of leading FFs).
x	Converts argument as a hexadecimal number. Negative numbers will be displayed with two leading periods (representing an infinite string of leading FFs.)

Table 27.11. File Tests with a Single Argument

Flag	Description	Returns
?A	Last access time for *file1*	Time
?b	True if *file1* is a block device	true or false
?c	True if *file1* is a character device	true or false
?C	Last change time for *file1*	Time
?d	True if *file1* exists and is a directory	true or false
?e	True if *file1* exists	true or false
?f	True if *file1* exists and is a regular file	true or false
?g	True if *file1* has the setgid bit set (false under NT)	true or false
?G	True if *file1* exists and has a group ownership equal to the caller's group	true or false
?k	True if *file1* exists and has the sticky bit set	true or false
?l	True if *file1* exists and is a symbolic link	true or false
?M	Last modification time for *file1*	Time
?o	True if *file1* exists and is owned by the caller's effective UID	true or false
?O	True if *file1* exists and is owned by the caller's real UID	true or false
?p	True if *file1* exists and is a fifo	true or false
?r	True if *file1* is readable by the effective UID/GID of the caller	true or false
?R	True if *file1* is readable by the real UID/GID of the caller	true or false
?s	If *file1* has nonzero size, returns the size; otherwise, returns nil	Integer or nil
?S	True if *file1* exists and is a socket	true or false
?u	True if *file1* has the setuid bit set	true or false
?w	True if *file1* exists and is writable by the effective UID/ GID	true or false
?W	True if *file1* exists and is writable by the real UID/GID	true or false
?x	True if *file1* exists and is executable by the effective UID/GID	true or false
?X	True if *file1* exists and is executable by the real UID/GID	true or false
?z	True if *file1* exists and has a zero length	true or false

Table 27.12. File Tests with Two Arguments

Flag	Description
?-	True if *file1* is a hard link to *file2*
?=	True if the modification times of *file1* and *file2* are equal
?<	True if the modification time of *file1* is prior to that of *file2*
?>	True if the modification time of *file1* is after that of *file2*

Marshal

The marshaling library converts collections of Ruby objects into a byte stream, allowing them to be stored outside the currently active script. This data may subsequently be read and the original objects reconstituted. Marshaling is described starting on page 420. Also see the YAML library on page 822.

Marshaled data has major and minor version numbers stored along with the object information. In normal use, marshaling can load only data written with the same major version number and an equal or lower minor version number. If Ruby's "verbose" flag is set (normally using -d, -v, -w, or --verbose), the major and minor numbers must match exactly. Marshal versioning is independent of Ruby's version numbers. You can extract the version by reading the first two bytes of marshaled data.

```
RUBY_VERSION                                  # =>  "1.9.1"
[ Marshal::MAJOR_VERSION, Marshal::MINOR_VERSION ]  # =>  [4, 8]
str = Marshal.dump("thing")
str.bytes.first(2)                            # =>  [4, 8]
```

Some objects cannot be dumped: if the objects to be dumped include bindings, procedure or method objects, instances of class IO, or singleton objects, or if you try to dump anonymous classes or modules, a TypeError will be raised.

If your class has special serialization needs (for example, if you want to serialize in some specific format) or if it contains objects that would otherwise not be serializable, you can implement your own serialization strategy using the instance methods marshal_dump and marshal_load: If an object to be marshaled responds to marshal_dump, that method is called instead of _dump. marshal_dump can return an object of any class (not just a String). A class that implements marshal_dump must also implement marshal_load, which is called as an instance method of a newly allocated object and passed the object originally created by marshal_dump.

The following code uses this to store a Time object in the serialized version of an object. When loaded, this object is passed to marshal_load, which converts this time to a printable form, storing the result in an instance variable.

```
class TimedDump
  attr_reader :when_dumped
  attr_accessor :other_data
  def marshal_dump
    [ Time.now, @other_data ]
  end
  def marshal_load(marshal_data)
    @when_dumped = marshal_data[0].strftime("%I:%M%p")
    @other_data  = marshal_data[1]
  end
end

t = TimedDump.new
t.other_data = "wibble"
t.when_dumped        # =>  nil

str = Marshal.dump(t)

newt = Marshal.load(str)
newt.when_dumped     # =>  "09:58AM"
```

Module constants

MAJOR_VERSION   Major part of marshal format version number.
MINOR_VERSION   Minor part of marshal format version number.

Module methods

dump   dump(*obj* ⟨ , *io* ⟩ , *limit*=–1) → *io*

Serializes *obj* and all descendent objects. If *io* is specified, the serialized data will be written to it; otherwise, the data will be returned as a String. If *limit* is specified, the traversal of subobjects will be limited to that depth. If *limit* is negative, no checking of depth will be performed.

```
class Klass
  def initialize(str)
    @str = str
  end
  def say_hello
    @str
  end
end
o = Klass.new("hello\n")
data = Marshal.dump(o)
obj = Marshal.load(data)
obj.say_hello   # =>   "hello\n"
```

load   load(*from* ⟨ , *proc* ⟩) → *obj*

Returns the result of converting the serialized data in *from* into a Ruby object (possibly with associated subordinate objects). *from* may be either an instance of IO or an object that responds to to_str. If *proc* is specified, it will be passed each object as it is deserialized.

restore   restore(*from* ⟨ , *proc* ⟩) → *obj*

A synonym for Marshal.load.

Marshal

Class **MatchData** < Object

All pattern matches set the special variable $~ to a MatchData containing information about the match. The methods Regexp#match and Regexp.last_match also return a MatchData object. The object encapsulates all the results of a pattern match, results normally accessed through the special variables $&, $', $`, $1, $2, and so on (see the list on page 328).

Instance methods

[ ]

match[*i*] → *string*
match[*name*] → *string*
match[*start*, *length*] → *array*
match[*range*] → *array*

1.9

Match Reference—MatchData acts as an array and/or hash and may be accessed using the normal indexing techniques. Numeric indices return the captures at the corresponding position in the regular expression (starting at 1). Symbol indices return the corresponding named capture. *match*[0] is equivalent to the special variable $& and returns the entire matched string. See also MatchData#select and MatchData#values_at.

```
m = /(.)(.)(\d+)(\d)/.match("THX1138.")
m[0]                    # =>   "HX1138"
m[1, 2]                 # =>   ["H", "X"]
m[1..3]                 # =>   ["H", "X", "113"]
m[-3, 2]                # =>   ["X", "113"]
m = /..(?<digit_prefix>\d+)\d/.match("THX1138.")
m[:digit_prefix]    # =>   "113"
```

begin

match.begin(*n*) → *int*
match.begin(*name*) → *int*

1.9

Returns the offset in the original string of the start of the *n*th capture or the named capture.

```
m = /(.)(.)(\d+)(\d)/.match("THX1138.")
m.begin(0)                  # =>   1
m.begin(2)                  # =>   2
m = /..(?<digit_prefix>\d+)\d/.match("THX1138.")
m.begin(:digit_prefix)   # =>   3
```

captures

match.captures → *array*

Returns the array of all the matching groups. Compare to MatchData#to_a, which returns both the complete matched string and all the matching groups.

```
m = /(.)(.)(\d+)(\d)/.match("THX1138.")
m.captures   # =>   ["H", "X", "113", "8"]
```

captures is useful when extracting parts of a match in an assignment.

```
f1, f2, f3 = /(.)(.)(\d+)(\d)/.match("THX1138.").captures
f1   # =>   "H"
f2   # =>   "X"
f3   # =>   "113"
```

end

1.9 Returns the offset in the original string of the end of the *n*th capture or the named capture.

```
m = /(.)(.)(\d+)(\d)/.match("THX1138.")
m.end(0)                 # =>   7
m.end(2)                 # =>   3
m = /..(?<digit_prefix>\d+)\d/.match("THX1138.")
m.end(:digit_prefix)   # =>   6
```

length

Returns the number of elements in the match array.

```
m = /(.)(.)(\d+)(\d)/.match("THX1138.")
m.length   # =>   5
m.size     # =>   5
```

names

1.9 Returns the list of named captures in the regular expression that created *match*.

```
m = /(?<prefix>[A-Z]+)(?<hyphen>-?)(?<digits>\d+)/.match("THX1138.")
m.names       # =>   ["prefix", "hyphen", "digits"]
m.captures    # =>   ["THX", "", "1138"]
m[:prefix]    # =>   "THX"
```

offset

1.9 Returns a two-element array containing the beginning and ending offsets of the *n*th or named capture.

```
m = /(.)(.)(\d+)(\d)/.match("THX1138.")
m.offset(0)                 # =>   [1, 7]
m.offset(4)                 # =>   [6, 7]
m = /..(?<digit_prefix>\d+)\d/.match("THX1138.")
m.offset(:digit_prefix)   # =>   [3, 6]
```

post_match

Returns the portion of the original string after the current match. Equivalent to the special variable $'.

```
m = /(.)(.)(\d+)(\d)/.match("THX1138: The Movie")
m.post_match   # =>   ": The Movie"
```

pre_match

Returns the portion of the original string before the current match. Equivalent to the special variable $`.

```
m = /(.)(.)(\d+)(\d)/.match("THX1138.")
m.pre_match   # =>   "T"
```

regexp   *match*.regexp → *a_regexp*

1.9   Returns the regexp object for the regular expression that created *match*.

```
m = /(.)(.)(\d+)(\d)/.match("THX1138: The Movie")
m.regexp   # =>   /(.)(.)(\d+)(\d)/
```

size   *match*.size → *int*

A synonym for MatchData#length.

string   *match*.string → *string*

Returns a frozen copy of the string passed in to match.

```
m = /(.)(.)(\d+)(\d)/.match("THX1138.")
m.string   # =>   "THX1138."
```

to_a   *match*.to_a → *array*

Returns the array of matches. Unlike MatchData#captures, returns the full string matched.

```
m = /(.)(.)(\d+)(\d)/.match("THX1138.")
m.to_a   # =>   ["HX1138", "H", "X", "113", "8"]
```

to_s   *match*.to_s → *string*

Returns the entire matched string.

```
m = /(.)(.)(\d+)(\d)/.match("THX1138.")
m.to_s   # =>   "HX1138"
```

values_at   *match*.values_at(⟨ *index* ⟩*) → *array*

Synonym for MatchData#select.

Module Math

The Math module contains module methods for basic trigonometric and transcendental functions. See class Float on page 519 for a list of constants that define Ruby's floating-point accuracy.

Module constants

E   An approximation of e (base of natural logarithms)

PI   An approximation of π

Module methods

acos $Math.acos(\ x\ ) \rightarrow float$

Computes the arc cosine of x. Returns $0..\pi$.

acosh $Math.acosh(\ x\ ) \rightarrow float$

Computes the inverse hyperbolic cosine of x.

asin $Math.asin(\ x\ ) \rightarrow float$

Computes the arc sine of x. Returns $-\frac{\pi}{2}..\frac{\pi}{2}$.

asinh $Math.asinh(\ x\ ) \rightarrow float$

Computes the inverse hyperbolic sine of x.

atan $Math.atan(\ x\ ) \rightarrow float$

Computes the arc tangent of x. Returns $-\frac{\pi}{2}..\frac{\pi}{2}$.

atanh $Math.atanh(\ x\ ) \rightarrow float$

Computes the inverse hyperbolic tangent of x.

atan2 $Math.atan2(\ y,\ x\ ) \rightarrow float$

Computes the arc tangent given y and x. Returns $-\pi..\pi$.

cbrt $Math.cbrt(\ numeric\ ) \rightarrow float$

1.9   Returns the cube root of *numeric*.

cos $Math.cos(\ x\ ) \rightarrow float$

Computes the cosine of x (expressed in radians). Returns $-1..1$.

cosh $Math.cosh(\ x\ ) \rightarrow float$

Computes the hyperbolic cosine of x (expressed in radians).

Math

---

erf $\qquad\qquad\qquad\qquad\qquad\qquad\qquad$ Math.erf(x) → *float*

Returns the error function of x.

$$erf(x) = \frac{2}{\sqrt{\pi}} \int_0^x e^{-t^2} dt$$

---

erfc $\qquad\qquad\qquad\qquad\qquad\qquad\qquad$ Math.erfc(x) → *float*

Returns the complementary error function of x.

$$erfc(x) = 1 - \frac{2}{\sqrt{\pi}} \int_0^x e^{-t^2} dt$$

---

exp $\qquad\qquad\qquad\qquad\qquad\qquad\qquad\qquad$ Math.exp(x) → *float*

Returns e^x.

---

frexp $\qquad\qquad\qquad\qquad$ Math.frexp(*numeric*) → [*fraction, exponent*]

Returns a two-element array containing the normalized fraction (a Float) and exponent (a Fixnum) of *numeric*.

```
fraction, exponent = Math.frexp(1234)   # =>   [0.6025390625, 11]
fraction * 2**exponent                  # =>   1234.0
```

---

gamma $\qquad\qquad\qquad\qquad\qquad\qquad\qquad$ Math.gamma(x) → *float*

1.9 ╱ Returns the gamma function Γx. For integral x, the Γx approximates $factorial(x-1)$.

```
Math.gamma(2)      # =>   1.0
Math.gamma(3)      # =>   2.0
Math.gamma(4)      # =>   6.0
Math.gamma(10.34)  # =>   784993.609149316
```

---

hypot $\qquad\qquad\qquad\qquad\qquad\qquad\qquad$ Math.hypot(x, y) → *float*

Returns $\sqrt{x^2 + y^2}$, the hypotenuse of a right-angled triangle with sides x and y.

```
Math.hypot(3, 4)   # =>   5.0
```

---

ldexp $\qquad\qquad\qquad\qquad\qquad\qquad$ Math.ldexp(*float, integer*) → *float*

Returns the value of *float* $\times 2^{integer}$.

```
fraction, exponent = Math.frexp(1234)
Math.ldexp(fraction, exponent)   # =>   1234.0
```

---

lgamma $\qquad\qquad\qquad\qquad\qquad\qquad$ Math.lgamma(x) → [*float, sign*

1.9 ╱ The first element of the returned array is the natural logarithm of the absolute value of the gamma function of x. The second value is -1 is the gamma function returned a negative number, $+1$ otherwise.

log   Math.log(*numeric*) → *float*

Returns the natural logarithm of *numeric*.

log10   Math.log10(*numeric*) → *float*

Returns the base 10 logarithm of *numeric*.

log2   Math.log2(*numeric*) → *float*

1.9   Returns the base 2 logarithm of *numeric*.

sin   Math.sin(*numeric*) → *float*

Computes the sine of *numeric* (expressed in radians). Returns −1..1.

sinh   Math.sinh(*float*) → *float*

Computes the hyperbolic sine of *numeric* (expressed in radians).

sqrt   Math.sqrt(*float*) → *float*

Returns the non-negative square root of *numeric*. Raises ArgError if *numeric* is less than zero.

tan   Math.tan(*float*) → *float*

Returns the tangent of *numeric* (expressed in radians).

tanh   Math.tanh(*float*) → *float*

Computes the hyperbolic tangent of *numeric* (expressed in radians).

Math

Class

Method < Object

Method objects are created by Object#method. They are associated with a particular object (not just with a class). They may be used to invoke the method within the object and as a block associated with an iterator. They may also be unbound from one object (creating an UnboundMethod) and bound to another.

```
def square(n)
  n*n
end
meth  = self.method(:square)

meth.call(9)               # =>   81
[ 1, 2, 3 ].collect(&meth) # =>   [1, 4, 9]
```

Instance methods

[ ]
meth[⟨ *args* ⟩*] → *object*

Synonym for Method.call.

==
meth== *other* → true or false

Returns true if *meth* is the same method as *other*.

```
def fred()
  puts "Hello"
end

alias bert fred   # =>   nil

m1 = method(:fred)
m2 = method(:bert)
m1 == m2          # =>   true
```

arity
meth.arity → *fixnum*

Returns an indication of the number of arguments accepted by a method. See Figure 27.2 on the next page. See also Method#parameters.

call
meth.call(⟨ *args* ⟩*) → *object*

Invokes the *meth* with the specified arguments, returning the method's return value.

```
m = 12.method("+")
m.call(3)   # =>   15
m.call(20)  # =>   32
```

eql?
meth.eql?(*other*) → true or false

Returns true if *meth* is the same method as *other*.

> ### Figure 27.2.   Method#arity in Action
>
> Method#arity returns a non-negative integer for methods that take a fixed number of arguments. For Ruby methods that take a variable number of arguments, returns $-n-1$, where n is the number of required arguments. For methods written in C, returns -1 if the call takes a variable number of arguments.
>
> ```ruby
> class C
>   def one;    end
>   def two(a); end
>   def three(*a);  end
>   def four(a, b); end
>   def five(a, b, *c);    end
>   def six(a, b, *c, &d); end
> end
> c = C.new
> c.method(:one).arity    # =>   0
> c.method(:two).arity    # =>   1
> c.method(:three).arity  # =>   -1
> c.method(:four).arity   # =>   2
> c.method(:five).arity   # =>   -3
> c.method(:six).arity    # =>   -3
>
> "cat".method(:size).arity      # =>   0
> "cat".method(:replace).arity   # =>   1
> "cat".method(:squeeze).arity   # =>   -1
> "cat".method(:count).arity     # =>   -1
> ```

```ruby
def fred()
  puts "Hello"
end

alias bert fred   # =>   nil

m1 = method(:fred)
m2 = method(:bert)
m1.eql?(m2)       # =>   true
```

---

name   *meth*.name → *string*

1.9 Returns the name of the method *meth*.

```ruby
method = "cat".method(:upcase)
method.name   # =>   :upcase
```

---

owner   *meth*.owner → *module*

1.9 Returns the class or module in which *meth* is defined.

```ruby
method = "cat".method(:upcase)
method.owner   # =>   String
```

receiver   *meth*.receiver → *obj*

Returns the object on which *meth* is defined.

```
method = "cat".method(:upcase)
method.receiver   # =>   "cat"
```

source_location   *meth*.source_location → [*filename*, *lineno*] or nil

Returns the source filename and line number where *meth* was defined or nil if self was not defined in Ruby source.

```
internal_method = "cat".method(:upcase)
internal_method.source_location   # =>   nil

require 'set'
set = Set.new
ruby_method = set.method(:clear)
ruby_method.source_location       # =>   ["/usr/lib/ruby/1.9.1/set.rb",
                                          114]
```

to_proc   *meth*.to_proc → *prc*

Returns a Proc object corresponding to this method. Because to_proc is called by the interpreter when passing block arguments, method objects may be used following an ampersand to pass a block to another method call. See the example at the start of this section.

unbind   *meth*.unbind → unbound_method

Dissociates *meth* from its current receiver. The resulting UnboundMethod can subsequently be bound to a new object of the same class (see UnboundMethod on page 715).

Class

Module   <   Object

Subclasses: Class

A Module is a collection of methods and constants. The methods in a module may be instance methods or module methods. Instance methods appear as methods in a class when the module is included; module methods do not. Conversely, module methods may be called without creating an encapsulating object, and instance methods may not. See also Module#module_function on page 600.

In the descriptions that follow, the parameter *symbol* refers to a symbol, which is either a quoted string or a Symbol (such as :name).

```ruby
module Mod
  include Math
  CONST = 1
  def meth
    #  ...
  end
end
Mod.class              # =>   Module
Mod.constants          # =>   [:CONST, :PI, :E]
Mod.instance_methods   # =>   [:meth]
```

Class methods

constants   Module.constants → *array*

Module.constants(*include_parents*) → *array*

1.9   With no argument returns a list of the top-level constants in the interpreter. With one argument, returns the constants defined in class Module (and its parents if the argument is true). This somewhat obscure interface is because Module is a kind of Class, and Class is a subclass of Module. The first form of call is a true call to the class method constants, while the second form actually proxies to the instance method form (see Module#constants later in this section).

```ruby
module Mixin
  CONST_MIXIN = 1
end
class Module
  include Mixin
  SPURIOUS_CONSTANT = 2
end
Module.constants.sort[1..5]            # =>   [:ARGV, :ArgumentError,
                                       #      :Array, :BasicObject,
                                       #      :Bignum]

Module.constants.include? :CONST_MIXIN # =>   false
Module.constants(false)                # =>   [:SPURIOUS_CONSTANT]
Module.constants(true)                 # =>   [:SPURIOUS_CONSTANT,
                                       #      :CONST_MIXIN]
```

nesting   Module.nesting → *array*

Returns the list of Modules nested at the point of call.

```
module M1
  module M2
    nest = Module.nesting
    p nest
    p nest[0].name
  end
end
```

produces:

```
[M1::M2, M1]
"M1::M2"
```

new   Module.new → *mod*
       Module.new { | *mod* | *block* } → *mod*

Creates a new anonymous module. If a block is given, it is passed the module object, and the block is evaluated in the context of this module using module_eval.

```
Fred = Module.new do
  def meth1
    "hello"
  end
  def meth2
    "bye"
  end
end
a = "my string"
a.extend(Fred)    # =>   "my string"
a.meth1           # =>   "hello"
a.meth2           # =>   "bye"
```

Instance methods

<, <=, >, >=   *mod relop module* → true or false

Hierarchy Query—One module is considered *greater than* another if it is included in (or is a parent class of) the other module. The other operators are defined accordingly. If there is no relationship between the modules, all operators return false.

```
module Mixin
end

module Parent
  include Mixin
end

module Unrelated
end
```

```
Parent > Mixin        # =>    false
Parent < Mixin        # =>    true
Parent <= Parent      # =>    true
Parent < Unrelated    # =>    nil
Parent > Unrelated    # =>    nil
```

<=>   *mod <=> other_mod* → −1, 0, +1

Comparison—Returns −1 if *mod* includes *other_mod*, 0 if *mod* is the same module as *other_mod*, and +1 if *mod* is included by *other_mod* or if *mod* has no relationship with *other_mod*.

===   *mod === obj* → true or false

Case Equality—Returns true if *obj* is an instance of *mod* or one of *mod*'s descendents. Of limited use for modules but can be used in case statements to test objects by class.

---

ancestors   *mod*.ancestors → *array*

Returns a list of modules included in *mod* (including *mod* itself).

```
module Mod
  include Math
  include Comparable
end

Mod.ancestors    # =>    [Mod, Comparable, Math]
Math.ancestors   # =>    [Math]
```

---

autoload   *mod*.autoload(*name*, *file_name*) → nil

Registers *file_name* to be loaded (using Kernel.require) the first time that module *name* (which may be a String or a Symbol) is accessed in the namespace of *mod*. Note that the autoloaded file is evaluated in the top-level context. In this example, module_b.rb contains the following:

```
module A::B     # in module_b.rb
  def doit
    puts "In Module A::B"
  end
  module_function :doit
end
```

Other code can then include this module automatically.

```
module A
  autoload(:B, "module_b")
end

A::B.doit            # autoloads "module_b"
```

produces:

```
In Module A::B
```

autoload?

mod.autoload?(*name*) → *file_name* or nil

Returns the name of the file that will be autoloaded when the string or symbol *name* is referenced in the context of *mod* or returns nil if there is no associated autoload.

```
module A
  autoload(:B, "module_b")
end
A.autoload?(:B)   # =>   "module_b"
A.autoload?(:C)   # =>   nil
```

class_eval

mod.class_eval(*string* ⟨ , *file_name* ⟨ , *line_number* ⟩ ⟩) → *obj*

mod.class_eval { *block* } → *obj*

Synonym for Module.module_eval.

class_exec

mod.class_exec(⟨ args ⟩⁺) {| *args* | *block* } → *obj*

1.9 Synonym for Module.module_exec.

class_variable_defined?

mod.class_variable_defined?(*name*) → true or false

1.9 Returns true if the named class variable is defined in *mod*. The two @ signs are a required part of the name.

```
class One
  @@var1 = "wibble"
end
One.class_variable_defined?(:@@var1)   # =>   true
One.class_variable_defined?(:@@var2)   # =>   false
```

class_variable_get

mod.class_variable_get(*name*) → *obj*

1.9 Returns the value of the named class variable. The two @ signs must appear in the name.

```
class One
  @@var1 = "wibble"
end
One.class_variable_get(:@@var1)    # =>   "wibble"
One.class_variable_get("@@var1")   # =>   "wibble"
```

class_variable_set

mod.class_variable_set(*name*, *value*) → *value*

1.9 Returns the value of the named class variable. The two @ signs must appear in the name.

```
class One
  @@var1 = "wibble"
end
One.class_variable_set(:@@var1, 99)   # =>   99
One.class_variable_get("@@var1")      # =>   99
```

class_variables

mod.class_variables → *array*

1.9 Returns an array of the names of class variables in *mod*. (As of Ruby 1.9 class variables are no longer shared with child classes, so this listing is restricted to the class variables defined in *mod*.)

```
class One
  @@var1 = 1
end
class Two < One
  @@var2 = 2
end
One.class_variables  # =>  [:@@var1]
Two.class_variables  # =>  [:@@var2]
```

---

const_defined?   *mod*.const_defined?(*symbol* ⟨ *search_parents*=true ⟩) → true or false

Returns true if a constant with the given name is defined by *mod* or the parents of *mod* (if the second parameter is true).

```
Math.const_defined? "PI"  # =>  true
```

---

const_get   *mod*.const_get(*symbol*) → *obj*

Returns the value of the named constant in *mod*.

```
Math.const_get :PI  # =>  3.14159265358979
```

---

const_missing   const_missing(*symbol*) → *obj*

Invoked when a reference is made to an undefined constant in *mod*. It is passed a symbol for the undefined constant and returns a value to be used for that constant. The following code is very poor style. If a reference is made to an undefined constant, it attempts to load a file whose name is the lowercase version of the constant (thus, class Fred is assumed to be in file fred.rb). If found, it returns the value of the loaded class. It therefore implements a perverse kind of autoload facility.

```
def Object.const_missing(name)
  @looked_for ||= {}
  str_name = name.to_s
  raise "Class not found: #{name}" if @looked_for[str_name]
  @looked_for[str_name] = 1
  file = str_name.downcase
  require file
  klass = const_get(name)
  return klass if klass
  raise "Class not found: #{name}"
end
```

---

const_set   *mod*.const_set(*symbol, obj*) → *obj*

Sets the named constant to the given object, returning that object. Creates a new constant if no constant with the given name previously existed.

```
Math.const_set("HIGH_SCHOOL_PI", 22.0/7.0)  # =>  3.14285714285714
Math::HIGH_SCHOOL_PI - Math::PI             # =>  0.00126448926734968
```

---

constants   *mod*.constants(*include_parents* = true) → *array*

1.9

Returns an array of the names of the constants accessible in *mod*. If the parameter is true, this includes the names of constants in any included modules.

```
IO.constants(false)       # =>   [:SEEK_SET, :SEEK_CUR, :SEEK_END]
# Now include stuff defined in module File::Constants
IO.constants(true)[1,6]   # =>   [:SEEK_CUR, :SEEK_END, :LOCK_SH,
                                  :LOCK_EX, :LOCK_UN, :LOCK_NB]
```

---

include?   *mod*.include?(*other_mod*) → true or false

Returns true if *other_mod* is included in *mod* or one of *mod*'s ancestors.

```
module A
end

class B
  include A
end

class C < B
end

B.include?(A)   # =>   true
C.include?(A)   # =>   true
A.include?(A)   # =>   false
```

---

included_modules   *mod*.included_modules → *array*

Returns the list of modules included in *mod*.

```
module Mixin
end

module Outer
  include Mixin
end

Mixin.included_modules   # =>   []
Outer.included_modules   # =>   [Mixin]
```

---

instance_method   *mod*.instance_method(*symbol*) → *unbound_method*

Returns an UnboundMethod representing the given instance method in *mod*.

```
class Interpreter
  def do_a() print "there, "; end
  def do_d() print "Hello ";  end
  def do_e() print "!\n";     end
  def do_v() print "Dave";    end
  Dispatcher = {
    'a' => instance_method(:do_a),
    'd' => instance_method(:do_d),
```

```
    'e' => instance_method(:do_e),
    'v' => instance_method(:do_v)
  }

  def interpret(string)
    string.each_char {|ch| Dispatcher[ch].bind(self).call }
  end
end

interpreter = Interpreter.new
interpreter.interpret('dave')
```

produces:

```
Hello there, Dave!
```

---

instance_methods   *mod*.instance_methods(*inc_super*=true) → *array*

Returns an array containing the names of public and protected instance methods in the receiver. For a module, these are the public methods; for a class, they are the instance (not singleton) methods. With no argument or with an argument that is true, the methods in *mod* and *mod*'s superclasses are returned. When called with a module as a receiver or with a parameter that is false, the instance methods in *mod* are returned. (The parameter defaults to false in versions of Ruby prior to January 2004.)

```
module A
  def method1()
  end
end

class B
  def method2()
  end
end

class C < B
  def method3()
  end
end

A.instance_methods           # =>    [:method1]
B.instance_methods(false)    # =>    [:method2]
C.instance_methods(false)    # =>    [:method3]
C.instance_methods(true).length  # =>    54
```

---

method_defined?   *mod*.method_defined?(*symbol*) → true or false

Returns true if the named method is defined by *mod* (or its included modules and, if *mod* is a class, its ancestors). Public and protected methods are matched.

```
module A
  def method1()  end
end
class B
  def method2()  end
end
class C < B
  include A
  def method3()  end
end

A.method_defined? :method1    # =>    true
C.method_defined? "method1"   # =>    true
C.method_defined? "method2"   # =>    true
C.method_defined? "method3"   # =>    true
C.method_defined? "method4"   # =>    false
```

---

module_eval   *mod*.class_eval(*string* ⟨ , *file_name* ⟨ , *line_number* ⟩ ⟩) → *obj*
                               mod.module_eval { *block* } → *obj*

Evaluates the string or block in the context of *mod*. This can be used to add methods to a class. module_eval returns the result of evaluating its argument. The optional *file_name* and *line_number* parameters set the text for error messages.

```
class Thing
end
a = %q{def hello() "Hello there!" end}
Thing.module_eval(a)
puts Thing.new.hello()
Thing.module_eval("invalid code", "dummy", 123)
```

produces:

```
Hello there!
dummy:123:in `<main>': undefined local variable
    or method `code' for Thing:Class
```

---

module_exec   *mod*.module_exec(⟨ args ⟩⁺) {| *args* | *block* } → *obj*

1.9   Behaves the same as the block form for Module#module_eval, except any parameters passed to the method are in turn passed to the block. This gives you a way of passing in values that would otherwise not be in scope in the block (because *self* is changed).

```
class Thing
end
name  = :new_instance_variable
Thing.module_exec(name) do |iv_name|
  attr_accessor iv_name
end
t = Thing.new
t.new_instance_variable = "wibble"
p t
```

produces:

```
#<Thing:0x0a4268 @new_instance_variable="wibble">
```

name
mod.name → string

Returns the name of the module mod.

private_class_method
mod.private_class_method(⟨ symbol ⟩⁺) → nil

Makes existing class methods private. Often used to hide the default constructor new.

```
class SimpleSingleton  # Not thread safe
  private_class_method :new
  def SimpleSingleton.create(*args, &block)
    @me = new(*args, &block) if ! @me
    @me
  end
end
```

private_instance_methods
mod.private_instance_methods(inc_super=true) → array

Returns a list of the private instance methods defined in mod. If the optional parameter is true, the methods of any ancestors are included. (The parameter defaults to false in versions of Ruby prior to January 2004.)

```
module Mod
  def method1()  end
  private :method1
  def method2()  end
end
Mod.instance_methods          # =>   [:method2]
Mod.private_instance_methods  # =>   [:method1]
```

private_method_defined?
mod.private_method_defined?(symbol) → true or false

Returns true if the named private method is defined by mod (or its included modules and, if mod is a class, its ancestors).

```
module A
  def method1()  end
end
class B
  private
  def method2()  end
end
class C < B
  include A
  def method3()  end
end

A.method_defined? :method1           # =>   true
C.private_method_defined? "method1"  # =>   false
C.private_method_defined? "method2"  # =>   true
C.method_defined? "method2"          # =>   false
```

protected_instance_methods   *mod*.protected_instance_methods(*inc_super*=true) → *array*

Returns a list of the protected instance methods defined in *mod*. If the optional parameter is true, the methods of any ancestors are included. (The parameter defaults to false in versions of Ruby prior to January 2004.)

protected_method_defined?   *mod*.protected_method_defined?(*symbol*) → true or false

Returns true if the named protected method is defined by *mod* (or its included modules and, if *mod* is a class, its ancestors).

```
module A
  def method1()  end
end
class B
  protected
  def method2()  end
end
class C < B
  include A
  def method3()  end
end

A.method_defined? :method1            # =>    true
C.protected_method_defined? "method1"  # =>    false
C.protected_method_defined? "method2"  # =>    true
C.method_defined? "method2"            # =>    true
```

public_class_method   *mod*.public_class_method(⟨ *symbol* ⟩⁺) → nil

Makes a list of existing class methods public.

public_instance_method   *mod*.public_instance_method(*symbol*) → *unbound_method*

Returns an UnboundMethod representing the given public instance method in *mod*. See also Module#instance_method, which ignores scope.

```
class Test
  def method_a; end
private
  def method_b; end
end
puts "method_a is #{Test.public_instance_method(:method_a)}"
puts "method_b is #{Test.public_instance_method(:method_b)}"
```

produces:

```
method_a is #<UnboundMethod: Test#method_a>
prog.rb:7:in `public_instance_method': undefined private method `method_b' for
class `Test' (NameError)
from /tmp/prog.rb:7:in `<main>'
```

public_instance_methods

mod.public_instance_methods(*inc_super*=true) → *array*

Returns a list of the public instance methods defined in *mod*. If the optional parameter is true, the methods of any ancestors are included. (The parameter defaults to false in versions of Ruby prior to January 2004.)

public_method_defined?

mod.public_method_defined?(*symbol*) → true or false

Returns true if the named public method is defined by *mod* (or its included modules and, if *mod* is a class, its ancestors).

```
module A
  def method1()  end
end
class B
  protected
  def method2()  end
end
class C < B
  include A
  def method3()  end
end

A.method_defined? :method1          # =>   true
C.public_method_defined? "method1"  # =>   true
C.public_method_defined? "method2"  # =>   false
C.method_defined? "method2"         # =>   true
```

remove_class_variable

remove_class_variable(*symbol*) → *obj*

1.9 Removes the definition of the *symbol*, returning that variable's value. Prior to Ruby 1.9, this method was private.

```
class Dummy
  @@var = 99
end
Dummy.class_eval { p defined? @@var }
puts Dummy.remove_class_variable(:@@var)
Dummy.class_eval { p defined? @@var }
```

produces:

```
"class variable"
99
nil
```

Private instance methods

alias_method
alias_method(new_id, old_id) → mod

Makes *new_id* a new copy of the method *old_id*. This can be used to retain access to methods that are overridden.

```
module Mod
  alias_method :orig_exit, :exit
  def exit(code=0)
    puts "Exiting with code #{code}"
    orig_exit(code)
  end
end
include Mod
exit(99)
```

produces:

```
Exiting with code 99
```

append_features
append_features(other_mod) → mod

When this module is included in another, Ruby calls append_features in this module, passing it the receiving module in *other_mod*. Ruby's default implementation is to add the constants, methods, and module variables of this module to *other_mod* if this module has not already been added to *other_mod* or one of its ancestors. Prior to Ruby 1.8, user code often redefined append_features, added its own functionality, and then invoked super to handle the real include. Now you should instead implement the method Module#included, described on page 599.

attr
attr(⟨ symbol ⟩⁺) → nil

1.9 An alias for Module#attr_reader as of Ruby 1.9.

attr_accessor
attr_accessor(⟨ symbol ⟩⁺) → nil

Creates a reader and a writer method for each symbol passed as an argument. These methods provide access to the underlying instance variables of the name name (with a leading @ sign).

```
class Test
  attr_accessor :name, :likes
  def initialize(name, likes)
    @name = name
    @likes = likes
  end
end
d = Test.new("Dave", "Ruby")
d.name = "Chad"
d.name   # =>   "Chad"
d.likes  # =>   "Ruby"
```

attr_reader

Creates instance variables and corresponding methods that return the value of each instance variable.

```
class Test
  attr_reader :name, :likes
  def initialize(name, likes)
    @name = name
    @likes = likes
  end
end
d = Test.new("Dave", "Ruby")
d.name    # =>   "Dave"
d.likes   # =>   "Ruby"
```

attr_writer

attr_writer(⟨ *symbol* ⟩⁺) → nil

Creates an accessor method to allow assignment to the attribute *symbol*.id2name.

```
class Test
  attr_writer :name, :likes
  def initialize(name, likes)
    @name = name
    @likes = likes
  end
end
d = Test.new("Dave", "Ruby")
d.name = "Chad"
d   # =>   #<Test:0x0a3c28 @name="Chad", @likes="Ruby">
```

define_method

define_method(*symbol, method*) → *method*
define_method(*symbol*) { *block* } → *proc*

Defines an instance method in the receiver. The *method* parameter can be a Proc or Method object. If a block is specified, it is used as the method body. This block is evaluated using instance_eval. This is tricky to demonstrate because define_method is private. (This is why we resort to the send hack in this example.) See also Object#define_singleton_method.

```
class A
  def fred
    puts "In Fred"
  end
  def create_method(name, &block)
    self.class.send(:define_method, name, &block)
  end
  define_method(:wilma) { puts "Charge it!" }
end
class B < A
  define_method(:barney, instance_method(:fred))
end
b = B.new
b.barney
b.wilma
```

```
b.create_method(:betty) { p self }
b.betty
```

produces:

```
In Fred
Charge it!
#<B:0x0a2454>
```

1.9 Note that it is possible to define methods with names that are not valid if you were to use the def keyword. This methods can not be invoked directly.

```
class Silly
  define_method("Oh !@!#^!") { puts "As Snoopy says" }
end
Silly.new.send("Oh !@!#^!")
```

produces:

```
As Snoopy says
```

---

extend_object   extend_object(*obj*) → *obj*

Extends the specified object by adding this module's constants and methods (which are added as singleton methods). This is the callback method used by Object#extend.

```
module Picky
  def Picky.extend_object(o)
    if String === o
      puts "Can't add Picky to a String"
    else
      puts "Picky added to #{o.class}"
      super
    end
  end
end
(s = Array.new).extend Picky   # Call Object.extend
(s = "quick brown fox").extend Picky
```

produces:

```
Picky added to Array
Can't add Picky to a String
```

---

extended   extended(*other_mod*)

Callback invoked whenever the receiver is used to extend an object. The object is passed as a parameter. This should be used in preference to Module#extend_object if your code wants to perform some action when a module is used to extend an object.

```
module A
  def A.extended(obj)
    puts "#{self} extending '#{obj}'"
  end
end
"cat".extend(A)
```

produces:

```
A extending 'cat'
```

include include(⟨ *other_mod* ⟩+) → *mod*

Invokes Module.append_features (documented on page 596) on each parameter (in reverse order). Equivalent to the following code:

```
def include(*modules)
  modules.reverse_each do |mod|
    mod.append_features(self)
    mod.included(self)
  end
end
```

included included(*other_mod*)

Callback invoked whenever the receiver is included in another module or class. This should be used in preference to Module#append_features if your code wants to perform some action when a module is included in another.

```
module A
  def A.included(mod)
    puts "#{self} included in #{mod}"
  end
end
module Enumerable
  include A
end
```

produces:

```
A included in Enumerable
```

method_added method_added(*symbol*)

Invoked as a callback whenever a method is added to the receiver.

```
module Chatty
  def Chatty.method_added(id)
    puts "Adding #{id.id2name}"
  end
  def one()   end
end
module Chatty
  def two()   end
end
```

produces:

```
Adding one
Adding two
```

method_removed method_removed(*symbol*)

Invoked as a callback whenever a method is removed from the receiver.

```
module Chatty
  def Chatty.method_removed(id)
    puts "Removing #{id.id2name}"
```

```
    end
    def one()    end
  end
  module Chatty
    remove_method(:one)
  end
```

produces:

```
Removing one
```

---

method_undefined   method_undefined(*symbol*)

Invoked as a callback whenever a method is undefined in the receiver.

```
module Chatty
  def Chatty.method_undefined(id)
    puts "Undefining #{id.id2name}"
  end
  def one()    end
end
module Chatty
  undef_method(:one)
end
```

produces:

```
Undefining one
```

---

module_function   module_function(⟨ *symbol* ⟩*) → *mod*

Creates module functions for the named methods. These functions may be called with the module as a receiver and are available as instance methods to classes that mix in the module. Module functions are copies of the original and so may be changed independently. The instance-method versions are made private. If used with no arguments, subsequently defined methods become module functions.

```
module Mod
  def one
    "This is one"
  end
  module_function :one
end
class Cls
  include Mod
  def call_one
    one
  end
end
```

```
Mod.one      # =>   "This is one"
c = Cls.new
c.call_one   # =>   "This is one"
module Mod
  def one
    "This is the new one"
  end
end
Mod.one      # =>   "This is one"
c.call_one   # =>   "This is the new one"
```

---

private   private(⟨ *symbol* ⟩*) → *mod*

With no arguments, sets the default visibility for subsequently defined methods to private.
With arguments, sets the named methods to have private visibility. See "Access Control"
starting on page 350.

```
module Mod
  def a()  end
  def b()  end
  private
  def c()  end
  private :a
end
Mod.private_instance_methods  # =>   [:a, :c]
```

---

protected   protected(⟨ *symbol* ⟩*) → *mod*

With no arguments, sets the default visibility for subsequently defined methods to protected.
With arguments, sets the named methods to have protected visibility. See "Access Control"
starting on page 350.

---

public   public(⟨ *symbol* ⟩*) → *mod*

With no arguments, sets the default visibility for subsequently defined methods to public.
With arguments, sets the named methods to have public visibility. See "Access Control"
starting on page 350.

---

remove_const   remove_const(*symbol*) → *obj*

Removes the definition of the given constant, returning that constant's value. Predefined
classes and singleton objects (such as *true*) cannot be removed.

---

remove_method   remove_method(*symbol*) → *mod*

Removes the method identified by *symbol* from the current class. For an example, see Mod-
ule.undef_method.

---

undef_method   undef_method(⟨ *symbol* ⟩+) → *mod*

Prevents the current class from responding to calls to the named method(s). Contrast this
with remove_method, which deletes the method from the particular class; Ruby will still
search superclasses and mixed-in modules for a possible receiver.

```ruby
class Parent
  def hello
    puts "In parent"
  end
end
class Child < Parent
  def hello
    puts "In child"
  end
end
c = Child.new
c.hello
class Child
  remove_method :hello  # remove from child, still in parent
end
c.hello
class Child
  undef_method :hello   # prevent any calls to 'hello'
end
c.hello
```

produces:

```
In child
In parent
prog.rb:23:in `<main>': undefined method `hello' for #<Child:0x0a3048>
(NoMethodError)
```

Class

Mutex < Object

A mutex is a semaphore object that can be used to synchronize access to resources shared across threads. We discuss mutexes (and other synchronization mechanisms) starting on page 176. Because the code examples tend to be long, I haven't duplicated them in this library description.

Instance methods

lock   *mutex*.lock → *mutex*

Takes a lock on *mutex*. Suspends if *mutex* is already locked by another thread and raises a ThreadError if the mutex is already locked by the calling thread.

locked?   *mutex*.locked? → true or false

Returns the current locked state of *mutex*.

sleep   *mutex*.sleep(*time* | nil) → *seconds_slept*

Releases the current thread's lock on *mutex*, sleeps for *time* seconds (or forever if nil is passed), and then regains the lock. Returns the number of seconds actually slept.

synchronize   *mutex*.synchronize { *block* } → *obj*

Locks *mutex*, executes the block, and then unlocks *mutex*. Returns the value returned by the block.

try_lock   *mutex*.try_lock → true or false

If *mutex* is not currently locked, locks it and returns true. Otherwise, returns false. (That is, try_lock is like lock, but it will never wait for a mutex to become available.)

unlock   *mutex*.unlock → *mutex*

Unlock *mutex*, which must be locked by the current thread.

> **Class**
> ## NilClass < Object

The class of the singleton object nil.

Instance methods

&   nil & *obj* → false

And—Returns false. Because *obj* is an argument to a method call, it is always evaluated; there is no short-circuit evaluation in this case.

```
nil && puts("logical and")
nil &  puts("and")
```

produces:

and

---

^   nil ^ *obj* → true or false

Exclusive Or—Returns false if *obj* is nil or false, and returns true otherwise.

| nil | *obj* → true or false

Or—Returns false if *obj* is nil or false and returns true otherwise.

```
nil | false   # =>   false
nil | 99      # =>   true
```

---

nil?   nil.nil? → true

Always returns true.

---

to_a   nil.to_a → []

Always returns an empty array.

```
nil.to_a   # =>   []
```

---

to_c   nil.to_c → Complex(0,0)

1.9   Always returns the origin of the complex plane.

```
nil.to_c   # =>   (0+0i)
```

---

to_f   nil.to_f → 0.0

Always returns zero.

```
nil.to_f   # =>   0.0
```

---

to_i   nil.to_i → 0

Always returns zero.

```
nil.to_i   # =>   0
```

to_r

1.9

Always returns zero as a rational number.

```
nil.to_r   # =>   (0/1)
```

to_s

Always returns the empty string.

```
nil.to_s   # =>   ""
```

Class	
Numeric	< Object

Subclasses: Float, Integer

Numeric is the fundamental base type for the abstract class Integer and the concrete number classes Bignum, Complex, Float, Fixnum, and Rational. Many methods in Numeric are over-ridden in child classes, and Numeric takes some liberties by calling methods in these child classes. A complete list of the methods defined in all five classes is shown in Table 27.13 on page 609.

Mixes in

Comparable:
    <, <=, ==, >=, >, between?

Instance methods

+@	$+num \rightarrow num$

Unary Plus—Returns the receiver's value.

-@	$-num \rightarrow numeric$

Unary Minus—Returns the receiver's value, negated.

<=>	$num <=> other \rightarrow 0 \text{ or nil}$

Returns zero if *num* equals *other* and returns nil otherwise.

abs	$num.abs \rightarrow numeric$

Returns the absolute value of *num*.

```
12.abs       # =>   12
(-34.56).abs # =>   34.56
-34.56.abs   # =>   34.56
```

abs2	$num.abs2 \rightarrow numeric$

Returns the square of (the absolute value of) *num*.

```
12.abs2       # =>   144
(-34.56).abs2 # =>   1194.3936
-34.56.abs2   # =>   1194.3936
```

angle	$num.angle \rightarrow numeric$

For noncomplex numbers, returns π for negative numbers, 0 otherwise. See Complex for more details.

arg	$num.arg \rightarrow numeric$

Synonym for Numeric#angle.

ceil

$num.\text{ceil} \rightarrow int$

Returns the smallest Integer greater than or equal to *num*. Class Numeric achieves this by converting itself to a Float and then invoking Float#ceil.

```
1.ceil       # =>   1
1.2.ceil     # =>   2
(-1.2).ceil  # =>   -1
(-1.0).ceil  # =>   -1
```

coerce

$num.\text{coerce}(\ numeric\ ) \rightarrow array$

coerce is both an instance method of Numeric and part of a type conversion protocol. When a number is asked to perform an operation and it is passed a parameter of a class different from its own, it must first coerce both itself and that parameter into a common class so that the operation makes sense. For example, in the expression $1 + 2.5$, the Fixnum 1 must be converted to a Float to make it compatible with 2.5. This conversion is performed by coerce. For all numeric objects, coerce is straightforward: if *numeric* is the same type as *num*, returns an array containing *numeric* and *num*. Otherwise, returns an array with both *numeric* and *num* represented as Float objects.

```
1.coerce(2.5)   # =>   [2.5, 1.0]
1.2.coerce(3)   # =>   [3.0, 1.2]
1.coerce(2)     # =>   [2, 1]
```

If a numeric object is asked to operate on a non-numeric, it tries to invoke coerce on that other object. For example, if you write this:

```
1 + "2"
```

Ruby will effectively execute the code as follows:

```
n1, n2 = "2".coerce(1)
n2 + n1
```

In the more general case, this won't work, because most non-numerics don't define a coerce method. However, you can use this (if you feel so inclined) to implement part of Perl's automatic conversion of strings to numbers in expressions.

```
class String
  def coerce(other)
    case other
    when Integer
      begin
        return other, Integer(self)
      rescue
        return Float(other), Float(self)
      end
    when Float
      return other, Float(self)
    else super
    end
  end
end
```

```
1   + "2"    # =>   3
1   - "2.3"  # =>   -1.3
1.2 + "2.3"  # =>   3.5
1.5 - "2"    # =>   -0.5
```

coerce is discussed further on page 369.

___

conj num.conj $\rightarrow$ num

1.9 Synonym for Numeric#conjugate.

___

conjugate num.conjugate $\rightarrow$ num

1.9 Returns the complex conjugate of *num*. For noncomplex numbers, returns *num*.

___

denominator num.denominator $\rightarrow$ *integer*

1.9 Returns the denominator of the rational representation of *num*.

```
1.denominator      # =>   1
1.5.denominator    # =>   2
num = 1.0/3
num.to_r           # =>   (6004799503160661/18014398509481984)
num.denominator    # =>   18014398509481984
```

___

div num.div(*numeric*) $\rightarrow$ *int*

Uses / to perform division and then converts the result to an integer. Numeric does not define the / operator; this is left to subclasses.

___

divmod num.divmod(*numeric*) $\rightarrow$ *array*

Returns an array containing the quotient and modulus obtained by dividing *num* by *numeric*. If q,r = x.divmod(y), $q = floor(float(x)/float(y))$ and $x = q \times y + r$. The quotient is rounded toward $-\infty$. See Table 27.14 on page 610 for examples.

___

eql? num.eql?(*numeric*) $\rightarrow$ true or false

Returns true if *num* and *numeric* are the same type and have equal values.

```
1 == 1.0           # =>   true
1.eql?(1.0)        # =>   false
(1.0).eql?(1.0)    # =>   true
```

___

fdiv num.fdiv(*numeric*) $\rightarrow$ *numeric*

1.9 Synonym for Numeric#quo.

___

floor num.floor $\rightarrow$ *int*

Returns the largest integer less than or equal to *num*. Numeric implements this by converting *int* to a Float and invoking Float#floor.

```
1.floor      # =>   1
(-1).floor   # =>   -1
```

Table 27.13: Methods defined in class Numeric and its subclasses. A ✓ means that the method is defined in the corresponding class.

	Numeric	Integer	Fixnum	Bignum	Float
%	–	–	✓	✓	✓
&	–	–	✓	✓	–
*	–	–	✓	✓	✓
**	–	–	✓	✓	✓
+	–	–	✓	✓	✓
+@	✓	–	–	–	–
-	–	–	✓	✓	✓
-@	✓	–	✓	✓	✓
/	–	–	✓	✓	✓
<	–	–	✓	–	✓
<<	–	–	✓	✓	–
<=	–	–	✓	–	✓
<=>	✓	–	✓	✓	✓
==	–	–	✓	✓	✓
>	–	–	✓	–	✓
>=	–	–	✓	–	✓
>>	–	–	✓	✓	–
[]	–	–	✓	✓	–
^	–	–	✓	✓	–
abs	✓	–	✓	✓	✓
abs2	✓	–	–	–	–
angle	✓	–	–	–	–
arg	✓	–	–	–	–
ceil	✓	✓	–	–	✓
chr	–	✓	–	–	–
coerce	✓	–	–	✓	✓
conj	✓	–	–	–	–
conjugate	✓	–	–	–	–
denominator	✓	✓	–	–	–
div	✓	–	✓	✓	–
divmod	✓	–	✓	✓	✓
downto	–	✓	–	–	–
eql?	✓	–	–	✓	✓
even?	–	✓	✓	✓	–
fdiv	✓	–	✓	✓	✓
finite?	–	–	–	–	✓
floor	✓	✓	–	–	✓
gcd	–	✓	–	–	–
gcdlcm	–	✓	–	–	–
hash	–	–	–	✓	✓
imag	✓	–	–	–	–
imaginary	✓	–	–	–	–
infinite?	–	–	–	–	✓
integer?	✓	✓	–	–	–
lcm	–	✓	–	–	–
magnitude	✓	–	✓	✓	✓
modulo	✓	–	✓	✓	✓
nan?	–	–	–	–	✓
next	–	✓	–	–	–
nonzero?	✓	–	–	–	–
numerator	✓	✓	–	–	–
odd?	–	✓	✓	✓	–
ord	–	✓	–	–	–
phase	✓	–	–	–	–
polar	✓	–	–	–	–
pred	–	✓	–	–	–
quo	✓	–	–	–	✓
real	✓	–	–	–	–
real?	✓	–	–	–	–
rect	✓	–	–	–	–
rectangular	✓	–	–	–	–
remainder	✓	–	–	✓	–
round	✓	✓	–	–	✓
singleton_method_added	✓	–	–	–	–
size	–	–	✓	✓	–
step	✓	–	–	–	–
succ	–	✓	✓	–	–
times	–	✓	–	–	–
to_c	✓	–	–	–	–
to_f	–	–	✓	✓	✓
to_i	–	✓	–	–	✓
to_int	✓	✓	–	–	✓
to_r	–	✓	–	–	✓
to_s	–	–	✓	✓	✓
truncate	✓	✓	–	–	✓
upto	–	✓	–	–	–
zero?	✓	–	✓	–	✓
|	–	–	✓	✓	–
~	–	–	✓	–	–

Table 27.14. Difference between modulo and remainder. The modulo operator ("%") always has the sign of the divisor whereas remainder has the sign of the dividend.

a	b	a.divmod(b)	a / b	a.modulo(b)	a.remainder(b)
13	4	3, 1	3	1	1
13	−4	−4, −3	−4	−3	1
−13	4	−4, 3	−4	3	−1
−13	−4	3, −1	3	−1	−1
11.5	4	2, 3.5	2.875	3.5	3.5
11.5	−4	−3, −0.5	−2.875	−0.5	3.5
−11.5	4	−3, 0.5	−2.875	0.5	−3.5
−11.5	−4	2, −3.5	2.875	−3.5	−3.5

imag   *num*.imag → 0

1.9 Synonym for Numeric#imaginary.

imaginary   *num*.image → 0

1.9 Returns the imaginary part of *num*. Always 0 unless *num* is a complex number.

```
1.imaginary   # =>   0
```

integer?   *num*.integer? → true or false

Returns true if *num* is an Integer (including Fixnum and Bignum).

magnitude   *num*.magnitude → *int* or *float*

1.9 Returns the magnitude of *num*(the distance of *num* from the origin of the number line. See also Complex#magnitude.

```
3.magnitude      # =>   3
-3.0.magnitude   # =>   3.0
```

modulo   *num*.modulo(*numeric*) → *numeric*

Equivalent to *num*.divmod(*numeric*)[1].

nonzero?   *num*.nonzero? → *num* or nil

Returns *num* if *num* is not zero and returns nil otherwise. This behavior is useful when chaining comparisons.

```
a = %w( z Bb bB bb BB a aA Aa AA A )
b = a.sort {|a,b| (a.downcase <=> b.downcase).nonzero? || a <=> b }
b   # =>   ["A", "a", "AA", "Aa", "aA", "BB", "Bb", "bB", "bb", "z"]
```

numerator
num.numerator → *integer*

Returns the numerator of the rational representation of *num*.

```
1.numerator     # =>   1
1.5.numerator   # =>   3
num = 1.0/3
num.to_r        # =>   (6004799503160661/18014398509481984)
num.numerator   # =>   6004799503160661
```

phase
num.phase → [*magnitude, angle*]

Returns the phase angle of *num*. See Complex for more information. For noncomplex numbers, returns 0 if *num* is nonnegative, π otherwise.

```
123.polar   # =>   [123, 0]
```

polar
num.polar → [*magnitude, angle*]

Returns *num* in polar form. See Complex for more information. For noncomplex numbers, returns [*num*,0].

```
123.polar   # =>   [123, 0]
```

quo
num.quo(*numeric*) → *numeric*

Equivalent to Numeric#/ but overridden in subclasses. The intent of quo is to return the most accurate result of division (in context). Thus, 1.quo(2) will equal the rational number $\frac{1}{2}$, while 1/2 equals 0.

real
num.real → *num*

Returns the real part of *num*. Always *num* unless *num* is a complex number.

```
1.real     # =>   1
1.5.real   # =>   1.5
```

real?
num.real? → true

All the built-in numeric classes except Complex represent scalar types and hence respond true to real?.

```
1.real?            # =>   true
1.0.real?          # =>   true
Complex(1,0).real? # =>   false
```

rect
num.rect → [*num*, 0]

Returns an array containing the real and imaginary components of *num*. See also Complex#rect.

```
1.5.rect   # =>   [1.5, 0]
```

rectangular
num.rectangular → [*num*, 0]

Synonym for Numeric#rect.

remainder   *num*.remainder(*numeric*) → *numeric*

If *num* and *numeric* have different signs, returns *mod−numeric*; otherwise, returns *mod*. In both cases, *mod* is the value *num*.modulo(*numeric*). The differences between remainder and modulo (%) are shown in Table 27.14 on page 610.

round   *num*.round → *int*

Rounds *num* to the nearest integer. Numeric implements this by converting *int* to a Float and invoking Float#round.

step   *num*.step(*end_num*, *step*) {| i | *block* } → *num*

Invokes *block* with the sequence of numbers starting at *num*, incremented by *step* on each call. The loop finishes when the value to be passed to the block is greater than *end_num* (if *step* is positive) or less than *end_num* (if *step* is negative). If all the arguments are integers, the loop operates using an integer counter. If any of the arguments are floating-point numbers, all are converted to floats, and the loop is executed $\lfloor n + n * \epsilon \rfloor + 1$ times, where $n = (end\_num - num)/step$. Otherwise, the loop starts at *num*, uses either the < or > operator to compare the counter against *end_num*, and increments itself using the + operator.

```
1.step(10, 2) {|i| print i, " " }
Math::E.step(Math::PI, 0.2) {|f| print f, " " }
```
produces:
```
1 3 5 7 9
2.71828182845905 2.91828182845905 3.11828182845905
```

to_c   *num*.to_c → *complex*

1.9

Returns *num* as a complex number.

```
123.to_c   # =>   123+0i
```

to_int   *num*.to_int → *int*

Invokes the child class's to_i method to convert *num* to an integer.

truncate   *num*.truncate → *int*

Returns *num* truncated to an integer. Numeric implements this by converting its value to a float and invoking Float#truncate.

zero?   *num*.zero? → true or false

Returns true if *num* has a zero value.

Class
Object

Subclasses: Array, Binding, Continuation, Data (used internally by the interpreter), Dir, Exception, FalseClass, File::Stat, Hash, IO, MatchData, Method, Module, NilClass, Numeric, Proc, Process::Status, Range, Regexp, String, Struct, Symbol, Thread, Thread-Group, Time, TrueClass, UnboundMethod

Object is the parent class of all classes in Ruby. Its methods are therefore available to all objects unless explicitly overridden.

Object mixes in the Kernel module, making the built-in kernel functions globally accessible. Although the instance methods of Object are defined by the Kernel module, we have chosen to document them here for clarity.

In the descriptions that follow, the parameter *symbol* refers to a symbol, which is either a quoted string or a Symbol (such as :name).

Instance methods

===   *obj* === *other_obj* → true or false

Case Equality—A synonym for Object#== but typically overridden by descendents to provide meaningful semantics in case statements.

=~   *obj* =~ *other_obj* → nil

Pattern Match—Overridden by descendents (notably Regexp and String) to provide meaningful pattern-match semantics.

!~   *obj* =~ *other_obj* → !(*obj*=~ *other_obj*)

1.9   Opposite of =~.

class   *obj*.class → *klass*

Returns the class object of *obj*. This method must always be called with an explicit receiver, because class is also a reserved word in Ruby.

```
1.class      # =>   Fixnum
self.class   # =>   Object
```

clone   *obj*.clone → *other_obj*

Produces a shallow copy of *obj*—the instance variables of *obj* are copied, but not the objects they reference. Copies the frozen and tainted state of *obj*. See also the discussion under Object#dup.

```
class Klass
  attr_accessor :str
end
s1 = Klass.new       # =>   #<Klass:0x0a2f1c>
s1.str = "Hello"     # =>   "Hello"
s2 = s1.clone        # =>   #<Klass:0x0a2cb0 @str="Hello">
s2.str[1,4] = "i"    # =>   "i"
s1.inspect           # =>   "#<Klass:0x0a2f1c @str=\"Hi\">"
s2.inspect           # =>   "#<Klass:0x0a2cb0 @str=\"Hi\">"
```

---

define_singleton_method *obj*.define_singleton_method(*symbol, method*) → *method*
obj.define_method(*symbol*) { *block* } → *proc*

1.9

Defines a singleton method in the receiver. The *method* parameter can be a Proc or Method object. If a block is specified, it is used as the method body. This block is evaluated using instance_eval. See also Module#define_method.

```
a = "cat"
a.define_singleton_method(:speak) do
  puts "miaow"
end
a.speak
```

produces:

```
miaow
```

define_singleton_method is also useful with Module#class_eval:

```
class Test
end
Test.class_eval do
  define_method(:one) { puts "instance method" }
  define_singleton_method(:two) { puts "class method" }
end
t = Test.new
t.one
Test.two
```

produces:

```
instance method
class method
```

---

display *obj*.display(*port=$>*) → nil

Prints *obj* on the given port (default $>). Equivalent to the following:

```
def display(port=$>)
  port.write self
end
```

For example:

```
1.display
"cat".display
[ 4, 5, 6 ].display
puts
```

produces:

```
lcat[4, 5, 6]
```

---

dup   *obj*.dup → *other_obj*

Produces a shallow copy of *obj*—the instance variables of *obj* are copied, but not the objects they reference. dup copies the tainted state of *obj*. See also the discussion under Object#clone. In general, clone and dup may have different semantics in descendent classes. Although clone is used to duplicate an object, including its internal state, dup typically uses the class of the descendent object to create the new instance.

---

enum_for   *obj*.enum_for(*using*=:each, ⟨ args ⟩⁺ → *enumerator*

1.9   Synonym for Object#to_enum.

---

eql?   *obj*.eql?(*other_obj*) → true or false

Returns true if *obj* and *other_obj* have the same value. Used by Hash to test members for equality. For objects of class Object, eql? is synonymous with ==. Subclasses normally continue this tradition, but there are exceptions. Numeric types, for example, perform type conversion across ==, but not across eql?. This means that

```
1 == 1.0    # =>   true
1.eql? 1.0  # =>   false
```

---

extend   *obj*.extend(⟨ *mod* ⟩⁺) → *obj*

Adds to *obj* the instance methods from each module given as a parameter. See also Module#extend_object.

```
module Mod
  def hello
    "Hello from Mod.\n"
  end
end

class Klass
  def hello
    "Hello from Klass.\n"
  end
end

k = Klass.new
k.hello          # =>   "Hello from Klass.\n"
k.extend(Mod)    # =>   #<Klass:0x0a3200>
k.hello          # =>   "Hello from Mod.\n"
```

Writing *obj*.extend(Mod) is basically the same as the following:

```
class <<obj
  include Mod
end
```

freeze _obj_.freeze → _obj_

Prevents further modifications to _obj_. A RuntimeError will be raised if modification is attempted. You cannot unfreeze a frozen object. See also Object#frozen?.

```
a = [ "a", "b", "c" ]
a.freeze
a << "z"
```

produces:

```
prog.rb:3:in `<main>': can't modify frozen array (RuntimeError)
```

frozen? _obj_.frozen? → true or false

Returns the freeze status of _obj_.

```
a = [ "a", "b", "c" ]
a.freeze    # =>   ["a", "b", "c"]
a.frozen?   # =>   true
```

hash _obj_.hash → _fixnum_

Generates a Fixnum hash value for this object. This function must have the property that a.eql?(b) implies a.hash == b.hash. The hash value is used by class Hash. Any hash value that exceeds the capacity of a Fixnum will be truncated before being used. For instances of class Object, the hash is also the object_id. This will not always be the case for subclasses.

__id__ _obj_.__id__ → _fixnum_

1.9 Synonym for Object#object_id.

initialize_copy _obj_.initialize_copy(_other_) → _other_obj_ or _obj_

Part of the protocol used by Object#dup and Object#clone, initialize_copy is invoked as a callback, which should copy across any state information that dup and clone cannot copy themselves. For example, in the following code, a and b reference two instances of the container class, but each instance shares a single string object:

```
class Container
  attr_accessor :content
end
a = Container.new
a.content = "cat"
b = a.dup
a.content[1..-1] = "anary"
a.content    # =>   "canary"
b.content    # =>   "canary"
```

The next example uses initialize_copy to create a new string in the duplicated object.

```
class Container
  attr_accessor :content
  def initialize_copy(other)
    @content = String.new(other.content)
  end
end
a = Container.new
a.content = "cat"
b = a.dup
a.content[1..-1] = "anary"
a.content   # =>   "canary"
b.content   # =>   "cat"
```

---

inspect   *obj*.inspect → *string*

Returns a string containing a human-readable representation of *obj*. For objects classes written in Ruby, displays the values of instance variables along with the class name if any instance variables exist. In other cases, uses the to_s method to generate the string. Often this is overridden in child classes to provide class-specific information.

```
[ 1, 2, 3..4, 'five' ].inspect   # =>   [1, 2, 3..4, "five"]
Time.new.inspect                 # =>   2009-03-31 09:58:19 -0500
class Demo
  def initialize
    @a, @b = 1, 2
  end
end
Demo.new.inspect                 # =>   #<Demo:0x0a33a4 @a=1, @b=2>
```

---

instance_of?   *obj*.instance_of?(*klass*) → true or false

Returns true if *obj* is an instance of the given class. See also Object#kind_of?.

---

instance_variable_defined?   *obj*.instance_variable_defined?(*name*) → true or false

Returns true if the named variable is defined. Note that a common idiom, testing to see whether @fred is nil, is incorrect in two ways: first the variable could be defined but set to nil, and second it will generate a warning if debug mode is enabled.

```
class Fred
  def initialize(p1, p2)
    @a, @b = p1, p2
  end
end
fred = Fred.new('cat', 99)
fred.instance_variable_defined?(:@a)    # =>   true
fred.instance_variable_defined?("@b")   # =>   true
fred.instance_variable_defined?(:@c)    # =>   false
```

---

instance_variable_get   *obj*.instance_variable_get(*symbol*) → *other_obj*

Returns the value of the given instance variable (or throws a NameError exception). The @ part of the variable name should be included for regular instance variables.

```
class Fred
  def initialize(p1, p2)
    @a, @b = p1, p2
  end
end
fred = Fred.new('cat', 99)
fred.instance_variable_get(:@a)    # =>   "cat"
fred.instance_variable_get("@b")   # =>   99
```

---

instance_variable_set   *obj*.instance_variable_set(*symbol, other_obj*) → *other_obj*

Sets the instance variable names by *symbol* to *other_obj*, thereby frustrating the efforts of the class's author to attempt to provide proper encapsulation.

```
class Fred
  def initialize(p1, p2)
    @a, @b = p1, p2
  end
end
fred = Fred.new('cat', 99)
fred.instance_variable_set(:@a, 'dog')   # =>   "dog"
fred.inspect                             # =>   "#<Fred:0x0a3c64
                                                @a=\"dog\", @b=99>"
```

---

instance_variables   *obj*.instance_variables → *array*

Returns an array of instance variable names for the receiver. Note that simply defining an accessor does not create the corresponding instance variable.

```
class Fred
  attr_accessor :a1
  def initialize
    @iv = 3
  end
end
Fred.new.instance_variables   # =>   [:@iv]
```

---

is_a?   *obj*.is_a?(*klass*) → true or false

Synonym for Object#kind_of?.

---

kind_of?   *obj*.kind_of?(*klass*) → true or false

Returns true if *klass* is the class of *obj* or if *klass* is one of the superclasses of *obj* or modules included in *obj*.

```
module M;    end
class A
  include M
end
class B < A; end
class C < B; end
```

Object

```
b = B.new
b.instance_of? A   # =>   false
b.instance_of? B   # =>   true
b.instance_of? C   # =>   false
b.instance_of? M   # =>   false
b.kind_of? A       # =>   true
b.kind_of? B       # =>   true
b.kind_of? C       # =>   false
b.kind_of? M       # =>   true
```

---

method   *obj*.method(*symbol*) → *meth*

Looks up the named method in *obj*, returning a Method object (or raising NameError). The
Method object acts as a closure in *obj*'s object instance, so instance variables and the value
of self remain available.

```
class Demo
  def initialize(n)
    @iv = n
  end
  def hello()
    "Hello, @iv = #{@iv}"
  end
end

k = Demo.new(99)
m = k.method(:hello)
m.call   # =>   "Hello, @iv = 99"

l = Demo.new('Fred')
m = l.method("hello")
m.call   # =>   "Hello, @iv = Fred"
```

---

methods   *obj*.methods(*regular*=true) → *array*

If *regular* is true, returns a list of the names of methods publicly accessible in *obj* and *obj*'s
ancestors. Otherwise, returns a list of *obj*'s singleton methods.

```
class Klass
  def my_method()
  end
end
k = Klass.new
def k.single
end
k.methods[0..9]    # =>   [:single, :my_method, :nil?, :===, :=~, :!~,
                   #      :eql?, :class, :clone, :dup]
k.methods.length   # =>   54
k.methods(false)   # =>   [:single]
```

---

nil?   *obj*.nil? → true or false

All objects except nil return false.

Object

object_id   *obj*.object_id → *fixnum*

Returns an integer identifier for *obj*. The same number will be returned on all calls to object_id for a given object, and no two active objects will share an ID. Object#object_id is a different concept from the :name notation, which returns the symbol ID of name. Replaces the deprecated Object#id.

private_methods   *obj*.private_methods → *array*

Returns a list of private methods accessible within *obj*. This will include the private methods in *obj*'s ancestors, along with any mixed-in module functions.

protected_methods   *obj*.protected_methods → *array*

Returns the list of protected methods accessible to *obj*.

public_method   *obj*.public_method(*symbol*) → *meth*

1.9 Looks up the named public method in *obj*, returning a Method object (or raising NameError if the method if not found or if it is found but not public).

```
class Demo
  def initialize(n)
    @iv = n
  end
  def hello()
    puts "Hello, @iv = #{@iv}"
  end
end
k = Demo.new(99)
m = k.public_method(:hello)
m.call
l = Demo.new('Fred')
m = l.public_method(:initialize)
m.call
```

produces:

```
Hello, @iv = 99
prog.rb:15:in `public_method': undefined private method `initialize' for class
`Demo' (NameError)
from /tmp/prog.rb:15:in `<main>'
```

public_methods   *obj*.public_methods → *array*

Synonym for Object#methods.

public_send   *obj*.public_send(*name*, ⟨ args ⟩⁺) → *obj*

1.9 Invokes *obj*'s public method *name*, passing in any arguments. Returns the value returned by the method. See also send, which will also call private and protected methods.

---

respond_to?   *obj*.respond_to?(*symbol, include_priv*=false) → true or false

Returns true if *obj* responds to the given method. Private methods are included in the search only if the optional second parameter evaluates to true.

---

send   *obj*.send(*symbol* ⟨ , *args* ⟩* ⟨ , *&block* ⟩) → *other_obj*

Invokes the method identified by *symbol*, passing it any arguments and block. You can use BasicObject#__send__ if the name send clashes with an existing method in *obj*.

```ruby
class Klass
  def hello(*args)
    "Hello " + args.join(' ')
  end
end
k = Klass.new
k.send :hello, "gentle", "readers"   # =>   "Hello gentle readers"
```

---

singleton_methods   *obj*.singleton_methods(*all*=true) → *array*

Returns an array of the names of singleton methods for *obj*. If the optional *all* parameter is true, the list will include methods in modules included in *obj*. (The parameter defaults to false in versions of Ruby prior to January 2004.)

```ruby
module Other
  def three() end
end

class Single
  def Single.four() end
end

a = Single.new

def a.one() end

class << a
  include Other
  def two() end
end

Single.singleton_methods      # =>   [:four]
a.singleton_methods(false)    # =>   [:one, :two]
a.singleton_methods(true)     # =>   [:one, :two, :three]
a.singleton_methods           # =>   [:one, :two, :three]
```

---

taint   *obj*.taint → *obj*

Marks *obj* as tainted. If the $SAFE level is greater than zero, some objects will be tainted on creation. See Chapter 26, which begins on page 425.

---

tainted?   *obj*.tainted? → true or false

Returns true if the object is tainted.

```
a = "cat"
a.tainted?  # =>   false
a.taint     # =>   "cat"
a.tainted?  # =>   true
a.untaint   # =>   "cat"
a.tainted?  # =>   false
```

---

tap   *obj*.tap {| *val* | *block* } → *obj*

1.9 Invokes the block, passing *obj* as a parameter. Returns *obj*. Allows you to write code that
takes part in a method chain but that does not affect the overall value of the chain.

```
puts "dog"
    .reverse
        .tap {|o| puts "Reversed: #{o}"}
    .capitalize
```

produces:

```
Reversed: god
God
```

---

to_enum   *obj*.to_enum(*using*=:each, ⟨ args ⟩⁺ → *enumerator*

1.9 Returns an Enumerator object that will traverse the content of *obj*. By default, this enumerator will invoke the each method of self, but this can be overridden by passing a different
method name as the first parameter. Any additional arguments passed to to_enum will be
passed to the enumerator method.

```
by_bytes = "cat".to_enum(:each_byte)
by_bytes.next   # =>   99
by_bytes.next   # =>   97
by_chars = "cat".to_enum(:each_char)
by_chars.next   # =>    "c"
by_chars.next   # =>    "a"
```

---

to_s   *obj*.to_s → *string*

Returns a string representing *obj*. The default to_s prints the object's class and an encoding
of the object ID. As a special case, the top-level object that is the initial execution context
of Ruby programs returns "main."

---

trust   *obj*.trust → *obj*

1.9 Marks *obj* as trusted. (See the section on trust starting on page 427.)

---

untaint   *obj*.untaint → *obj*

Removes the taint from *obj*.

---

untrust   *obj*.untrust → *obj*

1.9 Marks *obj* as untrusted. (See the section on trust starting on page 427.)

---

untrusted?   *obj*.untrusted → true or false

1.9 Returns true is *obj* is untrusted, false otherwise.

Private instance methods

initialize   initialize(⟨ *arg* ⟩⁺)

Called as the third and final step in object construction, initialize is responsible for setting up the initial state of the new object. You use the initialize method the same way you'd use constructors in other languages. If you subclass classes other than Object, you will probably want to call super to invoke the parent's initializer.

```ruby
class A
  def initialize(p1)
    puts "Initializing A: p1 = #{p1}"
    @var1 = p1
  end
end
class B < A
  attr_reader :var1, :var2
  def initialize(p1, p2)
    super(p1)
    puts "Initializing B: p2 = #{p2}"
    @var2 = p2
  end
end

b = B.new("cat", "dog")
puts b.inspect
```

produces:

```
Initializing A: p1 = cat
Initializing B: p2 = dog
#<B:0x0a2ea4 @var1="cat", @var2="dog">
```

---

remove_instance_variable   remove_instance_variable(*symbol*) → *other_obj*

Removes the named instance variable from *obj*, returning that variable's value.

```
class Dummy
  def initialize
    @var = 99
  end
  def remove
    remove_instance_variable(:@var)
  end
  def var_defined?
    defined? @var
  end
end
d = Dummy.new
d.var_defined?  # =>   "instance-variable"
d.remove        # =>   99
d.var_defined?  # =>   nil
```

singleton_method_added   singleton_method_added(*symbol*)

Invoked as a callback whenever a singleton method is added to the receiver.

```
module Chatty
  def Chatty.singleton_method_added(id)
    puts "Adding #{id.id2name} to #{self.name}"
  end
  def self.one()    end
  def two()         end
end
def Chatty.three() end
obj = "cat"
def obj.singleton_method_added(id)
  puts "Adding #{id.id2name} to #{self}"
end
def obj.speak
  puts "meow"
end
```

produces:

```
Adding singleton_method_added to Chatty
Adding one to Chatty
Adding three to Chatty
Adding singleton_method_added to cat
Adding speak to cat
```

singleton_method_removed   singleton_method_removed(*symbol*)

Invoked as a callback whenever a singleton method is removed from the receiver.

```
module Chatty
  def Chatty.singleton_method_removed(id)
    puts "Removing #{id.id2name}"
  end
  def self.one()    end
  def two()         end
```

```
    def Chatty.three() end
    class <<self
      remove_method :three
      remove_method :one
    end
  end
```

produces:

```
Removing three
Removing one
```

---

singleton_method_undefined   singleton_method_undefined(*symbol*)

Invoked as a callback whenever a singleton method is undefined in the receiver.

```
module Chatty
  def Chatty.singleton_method_undefined(id)
    puts "Undefining #{id.id2name}"
  end
  def Chatty.one()    end
  class << self
      undef_method(:one)
  end
end
```

produces:

```
Undefining one
```

Module
ObjectSpace

The ObjectSpace module contains a number of routines that interact with the garbage collection facility and allow you to traverse all living objects with an iterator.

ObjectSpace also provides support for object finalizers. These are procs that will be called when a specific object is about to be destroyed by garbage collection.

```
include ObjectSpace
a, b, c = "A", "B", "C"
puts "a's id is #{a.object_id}"
puts "b's id is #{b.object_id}"
puts "c's id is #{c.object_id}"
define_finalizer(a, lambda {|id| puts "Finalizer one on #{id}" })
define_finalizer(b, lambda {|id| puts "Finalizer two on #{id}" })
define_finalizer(c, lambda {|id| puts "Finalizer three on #{id}" })
```

produces:

```
a's id is 333080
b's id is 332950
c's id is 332880
Finalizer three on 332880
Finalizer two on 332950
Finalizer one on 333080
```

Module methods

_id2ref

ObjectSpace._id2ref(*object_id*) → *obj*

Converts an object ID to a reference to the object. May not be called on an object ID passed as a parameter to a finalizer.

```
s = "I am a string"          # =>  "I am a string"
oid = s.object_id            # =>  335730
r = ObjectSpace._id2ref(oid) # =>  "I am a string"
r                            # =>  "I am a string"
r.equal?(s)                  # =>  true
```

count_objects

ObjectSpace.count_objects → *histogram_hash*

1.9

Returns a hash where the keys are the interpreter-specific internal object types and the values are the number of objects of each type.

```
ObjectSpace.count_objects   # =>  {:TOTAL=>10639, :FREE=>412,
                                   :T_OBJECT=>7, :T_CLASS=>406,
                                   :T_MODULE=>18, :T_FLOAT=>5,
                                   :T_STRING=>2357, :T_REGEXP=>11,
                                   :T_ARRAY=>304, :T_HASH=>9,
                                   :T_STRUCT=>32, :T_BIGNUM=>2,
                                   :T_FILE=>4, :T_DATA=>153, :T_MATCH=>1,
                                   :T_COMPLEX=>1, :T_NODE=>6898,
                                   :T_ICLASS=>19}
```

define_finalizer   ObjectSpace.define_finalizer(*obj*, *a_proc*=proc())

Adds *a_proc* as a finalizer, called when *obj* is about to be destroyed. Note that if you use lambda to create the proc object, you must remember to include a parameter wih the block. If you don't, the invocation of the lambda will silently fail when the finalizer is called because of a mismatch in the expected and actual parameter count.

each_object   ObjectSpace.each_object(⟨ *class_or_mod* ⟩) {| *obj* | *block* } → *fixnum*

Calls the block once for each living, nonimmediate object in this Ruby process. If *class_or_mod* is specified, calls the block for only those classes or modules that match (or are a subclass of) *class_or_mod*. Returns the number of objects found. Immediate objects (Fixnums, Symbols true, false, and nil) are never returned. In the following example, each_object returns both the numbers we defined and several constants defined in the Math module:

```
a = 102.7
b = 95        # Fixnum: won't be returned
c = 12345678987654321
count = ObjectSpace.each_object(Numeric) {|x| p x }
puts "Total count: #{count}"
```

produces:

```
12345678987654321
102.7
(0+1i)
2.71828182845905
3.14159265358979
9223372036854775807
54184490433925379262241098507698327656
2.22044604925031e-16
1.79769313486232e+308
2.2250738585072e-308
Total count: 10
```

garbage_collect   ObjectSpace.garbage_collect → nil

Initiates garbage collection (see module GC on page 523).

undefine_finalizer   ObjectSpace.undefine_finalizer(*obj*)

Removes all finalizers for *obj*.

Class		
Proc	<	Object

Proc objects are blocks of code that have been bound to a set of local variables. Once bound, the code may be called in different contexts and still access those variables.

```
def gen_times(factor)
  return Proc.new {|n| n*factor }
end

times3 = gen_times(3)
times5 = gen_times(5)

times3.call(12)            # =>   36
times5.call(5)             # =>   25
times3.call(times5.call(4))  # =>   60
```

Class methods

new

$$Proc.new \{ block \} \rightarrow a\_proc$$
$$Proc.new \rightarrow a\_proc$$

Creates a new Proc object, bound to the current context. Proc.new may be called without a block only within a method with an attached block, in which case that block is converted to the Proc object.

```
def proc_from
  Proc.new
end
proc = proc_from { "hello" }
proc.call  # =>   "hello"
```

Instance methods

[ ]

$$prc[\langle params \rangle^*] \rightarrow obj$$

Synonym for Proc.call.

==

$$prc== other \rightarrow \text{true or false}$$

Returns true if *prc* is the same as *other*.

===

$$prc=== other \rightarrow obj$$

1.9

Equivalent to *prc*.call(other). Allows you to use procs in when clauses. Allows us to write stuff such as this:

```
even = lambda {|num| num.even? }
(0..3).each do |num|
  case num
  when even
    puts "#{num} is even"
  else
    puts "#{num} is not even"
  end
end
```

produces:

```
0 is even
1 is not even
2 is even
3 is not even
```

---

arity

prc.arity → *integer*

Returns the number of arguments required by the block. If the block is declared to take no arguments, returns 0. If the block is known to take exactly n arguments, returns n. If the block has optional arguments, return $-(n + 1)$, where n is the number of mandatory arguments. A proc with no argument declarations also returns -1, because it can accept (and ignore) an arbitrary number of parameters.

```
Proc.new {}.arity          # =>   0
Proc.new {||}.arity        # =>   0
Proc.new {|a|}.arity       # =>   1
Proc.new {|a,b|}.arity     # =>   2
Proc.new {|a,b,c|}.arity   # =>   3
Proc.new {|*a|}.arity      # =>   -1
Proc.new {|a,*b|}.arity    # =>   -2
```

1.9 In Ruby 1.9, arity is defined as the number of parameters that would not be ignored. In 1.8, Proc.new{}.arity returns -1, and in 1.9 it returns 0.

---

call

prc.call(⟨ *params* ⟩*) → *obj*

Invokes the block, setting the block's parameters to the values in *params* using something close to method-calling semantics. Returns the value of the last expression evaluated in the block.

```
a_proc = Proc.new {|a, *b| b.collect {|i| i*a }}
a_proc.call(9, 1, 2, 3)   # =>   [9, 18, 27]
a_proc[9, 1, 2, 3]        # =>   [9, 18, 27]
```

1.9 If the block being called accepts a single parameter and you give call more than one parameter, only the first will be passed to the block. This is a change from Ruby 1.8.

```
a_proc = Proc.new {|a| puts a}
a_proc.call(1,2,3)
```

produces:

```
1
```

If you want a block to receive an arbitrary number of arguments, define it to accept *args.

```
a_proc = Proc.new {|*a| p a}
a_proc.call(1,2,3)
```

produces:

```
[1, 2, 3]
```

Blocks created using Kernel.lambda check that they are called with exactly the right number of parameters.

```
p_proc = Proc.new {|a,b| puts "Sum is: #{a + b}" }
p_proc.call(1,2,3)
p_proc = lambda {|a,b| puts "Sum is: #{a + b}" }
p_proc.call(1,2,3)
```

produces:

```
Sum is: 3
prog.rb:4:in `call': wrong number of arguments (3 for 2) (ArgumentError)
from /tmp/prog.rb:5:in `<main>'
```

---

curry   *prc*.curry → *curried_proc*

1.9

If you have a proc that takes arguments, you normally have to supply all of those arguments if you want the proc to execute successfully. However, it is also possible to consider an n argument proc to be the same as a single argument proc that returns a new proc that has this first argument fixed and that takes $n - 1$ arguments. If you repeat this process recursively for each of these subprocs, you end up with a proc that will take from zero to n arguements. If you pass it all n, it simply executes the proc with those arguments. If you pass it m arguments (where $m < n$), it returns a new proc that has those arguments prebaked in and that takes $m - n$ arguements. In this way, it is possible to partially apply arguments to a proc.

```
add_three_numbers = lambda {|a,b,c| a + b + c}
add_10_to_two_numbers = add_three_numbers.curry[10]
add_33_to_one_number  = add_10_to_two_numbers[23]

add_three_numbers[1,2,3]     # =>   6
add_10_to_two_numbers[1,2]   # =>   13
add_33_to_one_number[1]      # =>   34
```

---

lambda?   *prc*.lambda? → true or false

1.9

Returns true if *prc* has lambda semantics (that is, if argument passing acts as it does with method calls). See the discussion starting on page 351.

---

source_location   *prc*.source_location → [*filename, lineno*] or nil

1.9

Returns the source filename and line number where *prc* was defined or nil if self was not defined in Ruby source.

```
variable = 123
prc = lambda { "some proc" }
prc.source_location   # =>   ["/tmp/prog.rb", 2]
```

---

to_proc   *prc*.to_proc → *prc*

Part of the protocol for converting objects to Proc objects. Instances of class Proc simply return themselves.

to_s
prc.to_s → *string*

Returns a description of *prc*, including information on where it was defined.

```
def create_proc
  Proc.new
end

my_proc = create_proc { "hello" }
my_proc.to_s   # =>   "#<Proc:0x001c7abc@prog.rb:5>"
```

yield
prc.yield(⟨ *params* ⟩*) → *obj*

1.9 Synonym for Proc#call.

Module

Process

The Process module is a collection of methods used to manipulate processes. Programs that want to manipulate real and effective user and group IDs should also look at the Process::GID, and Process::UID modules. Much of the functionality here is duplicated in the Process::Sys module.

Module constants

PRIO_PGRP	Process group priority.
PRIO_PROCESS	Process priority.
PRIO_USER	User priority.
WNOHANG	Does not block if no child has exited. Not available on all platforms.
WUNTRACED	Returns stopped children as well. Not available on all platforms.
RLIM[IT]_*xxx*	Used by getrlimit and setrlimit

.

Module methods

abort
abort
abort(msg)

Synonym for Kernel.abort.

---

daemon
Process.daemon(stay_in_dir = false, keep_stdio_open = false) → 0 or -1

Puts the current process into the background (either by forking and calling Process.setssid or by using the daemon(2) call if available). Sets the current working directory to / unless *stay_in_dir* is true. Redirects standard input, output, and error to /dev/null unless keep_stdio_open is true. Not available on all platforms.

---

detach
Process.detach(pid) → thread

Some operating systems retain the status of terminated child processes until the parent collects that status (normally using some variant of wait()). If the parent never collects this status, the child stays around as a *zombie* process. Process.detach prevents this by setting up a separate Ruby thread whose sole job is to reap the status of the process *pid* when it terminates. Use detach only when you do not intend to explicitly wait for the child to terminate. detach checks the status only periodically (currently once each second).

In this first example, we don't reap the first child process, so it appears as a zombie in the process status display.

```
pid = fork { sleep 0.1 }
sleep 1
system("ps -o pid,state -p #{pid}")
```

produces:

```
  PID STAT
48004 ZN+
```

In the next example, Process.detach is used to reap the child automatically—no child processes are left running.

```
pid = fork { sleep 0.1 }
Process.detach(pid)
sleep 1
system("ps -o pid,state -p #{pid}")
```

produces:

```
PID STAT
```

---

egid
Process.egid → *int*

Returns the effective group ID for this process.

```
Process.egid   # =>   501
```

---

egid=
Process.egid= *int* → *int*

Sets the effective group ID for this process.

---

euid
Process.euid → *int*

Returns the effective user ID for this process.

```
Process.euid   # =>   501
```

---

euid=
Process.euid= *int*

Sets the effective user ID for this process. Not available on all platforms.

---

exec
Process.exec(*command* ⟨ , *args* ⟩)

1.9 Synonym for Kernel.exec.

---

exit
Process.exit(*int*=0)

Synonym for Kernel.exit.

---

exit!
Process.exit!(true | false | *status*=1)

Synonym for Kernel.exit!. No exit handlers are run. 0, 1, or *status* is returned to the underlying system as the exit status.

```
Process.exit!(0)
```

---

fork
Process.fork ⟨ { *block* } ⟩ → *int* or nil

See Kernel.fork on page 561.

---

getpgid
Process.getpgid(*int*) → *int*

Returns the process group ID for the given process ID. Not available on all platforms.

```
Process.getpgid(Process.ppid())   # =>   44514
```

---

getpgrp   *Process.getpgrp → int*

Returns the process group ID for this process. Not available on all platforms.

```
Process.getpgid(0)   # =>   44514
Process.getpgrp      # =>   44514
```

---

getpriority   *Process.getpriority(kind, int) → int*

Gets the scheduling priority for specified process, process group, or user. *kind* indicates the kind of entity to find: one of Process::PRIO_PGRP, Process::PRIO_USER, or Process::PRIO_PROCESS. *int* is an ID indicating the particular process, process group, or user (an ID of 0 means *current*). Lower priorities are more favorable for scheduling. Not available on all platforms.

```
Process.getpriority(Process::PRIO_USER, 0)      # =>   19
Process.getpriority(Process::PRIO_PROCESS, 0)   # =>   19
```

---

getrlimit   *Process.getrlimit(name) → [current, max]*

1.9   Returns the current and maximum resource limit for the named resource. The name may be a symbol or a string from the following list. It may also be an operating-specific integer constant. The Process module defines constants corresponding to these integers: the constants are named RLIMIT_ followed by one of the following: AS, CORE, CPU, DATA, FSIZE, MEMLOCK, NOFILE, NPROC, RSS or STACK. Consult your operating systems *getrlimit(2)* man page for details. The return array may contain actual values, or one of the constants RLIM_INFINITY, RLIM_SAVED_CUR, or RLIM_SAVED_MAX. Not available on all platforms. See also Process.setrlimit.

```
Process.getrlimit(:STACK)                # =>   [67104768, 67104768]
Process.getrlimit("STACK")               # =>   [67104768, 67104768]
Process.getrlimit(Process::RLIMIT_STACK) # =>   [67104768, 67104768]
```

---

gid   *Process.gid → int*

Returns the group ID for this process.

```
Process.gid   # =>   501
```

---

gid=   *Process.gid= int → int*

Sets the group ID for this process.

---

groups   *Process.groups → groups*

Returns an array of integer supplementary group IDs. Not available on all platforms. See also Process.maxgroups.

```
Process.groups   # =>   [501, 98, 101, 102, 80]
```

groups=   Process.groups = *array* → *groups*

Sets the supplementary group IDs from the given array, which may contain either numbers or group names (as strings). Not available on all platforms. Available only to superusers. See also Process.maxgroups.

initgroups   Process.initgroups(*user, base_group*) → *groups*

Initializes the group access list using the operating system's initgroups call. Not available on all platforms. May require superuser privilege.

```
Process.initgroups("dave", 500)
```

kill   Process.kill(*signal,* ⟨ *pid* ⟩⁺) → *int*

1.9

Sends the given signal to the specified process ID(s) or to the current process if *pid* is zero. *signal* may be an integer signal number or a string or symbol representing a POSIX signal name (either with or without a SIG prefix). If *signal* is negative (or starts with a – sign), kills process groups instead of processes. Not all signals are available on all platforms.

```
pid = fork do
   Signal.trap(:USR1) { puts "Ouch!"; exit }
   # ... do some work ...
end
# ...
Process.kill(:USR1, pid)
Process.wait
```

produces:

```
Ouch!
```

maxgroups   Process.maxgroups → *count*

The Process module has a limit on the number of supplementary groups it supports in the calls Process.groups and Process.groups=. The maxgroups call returns that limit (by default 32), and the maxgroups= call sets it.

```
Process.maxgroups   # =>   32
Process.maxgroups = 64
Process.maxgroups   # =>   64
```

maxgroups=   Process.maxgroups= *limit* → *count*

Sets the maximum number of supplementary group IDs that can be processed by the groups and groups= methods. If a number larger that 4096 is given, 4096 will be used.

pid   Process.pid → *int*

Returns the process ID of this process. Not available on all platforms.

```
Process.pid   # =>   48034
```

Process

---

ppid   Process.ppid → *int*

Returns the process ID of the parent of this process. Always returns 0 on Windows. Not available on all platforms.

```
puts "I am #{Process.pid}"
Process.fork { puts "Dad is #{Process.ppid}" }
```

produces:

```
I am 48036
Dad is 48036
```

---

setpgid   Process.setpgid(*pid, int*) → 0

Sets the process group ID of *pid* (0 indicates this process) to *int*. Not available on all platforms.

---

setpgrp   Process.setpgrp → 0

Equivalent to setpgid(0,0). Not available on all platforms.

---

setpriority   Process.setpriority(*kind, int, int_priority*) → 0

See Process#getpriority.

```
Process.setpriority(Process::PRIO_USER, 0, 19)      # =>   0
Process.setpriority(Process::PRIO_PROCESS, 0, 19)   # =>   0
Process.getpriority(Process::PRIO_USER, 0)          # =>   19
Process.getpriority(Process::PRIO_PROCESS, 0)       # =>   19
```

---

setrlimit   Process.setrlimit(*name, soft_limit, hard_limit=soft_limit*) → nil

1.9 Sets the limit for the named resource. See Process.getrlimit for a description of resource naming. See your system's man page for setrlimit(2) for a description of the limits. Not available on all platforms.

---

setsid   Process.setsid → *int*

Establishes this process as a new session and process group leader, with no controlling tty. Returns the session ID. Not available on all platforms.

```
Process.setsid  # =>   48041
```

---

spawn   Process.spawn(*command* ⟨ *, args* ⟩*) → *pid*

1.9 Synonym for Kernel.spawn.

---

times   Process.times → *struct_tms*

Returns a Tms structure (see Struct::Tms on page 691) that contains user and system CPU times for this process.

```
t = Process.times
[ t.utime, t.stime ]  # =>   [0.0, 0.0]
```

uid _____ Process.uid → *int*

Returns the user ID of this process.

```
Process.uid  # =>   501
```

uid= _____ Process.uid= *int* → *numeric*

Sets the (integer) user ID for this process. Not available on all platforms.

wait _____ Process.wait → *int*

Waits for any child process to exit and returns the process ID of that child. Also sets $? to the Process::Status object containing information on that process. Raises a SystemError if there are no child processes. Not available on all platforms.

```
Process.fork { exit 99 }   # =>   48048
Process.wait               # =>   48048
$?.exitstatus              # =>   99
```

waitall _____ Process.waitall → [[*pid1*,*status*], ...]

Waits for all children, returning an array of *pid/status* pairs (where *status* is an object of class Process::Status).

```
fork { sleep 0.2; exit 2 }   # =>   48051
fork { sleep 0.1; exit 1 }   # =>   48052
fork {            exit 0 }   # =>   48053
Process.waitall              # =>   [[48053, #<Process::Status: pid 48053
                                      exit 0>], [48052, #<Process::Status:
                                      pid 48052 exit 1>], [48051,
                                      #<Process::Status: pid 48051 exit 2>]]
```

wait2 _____ Process.wait2 → [*pid*, *status*]

Waits for any child process to exit and returns an array containing the process ID and the exit status (a Process::Status object) of that child. Raises a SystemError if no child processes exist.

```
Process.fork { exit 99 }   # =>   48056
pid, status = Process.wait2
pid                        # =>   48056
status.exitstatus          # =>   99
```

waitpid _____ Process.waitpid(*pid*, *int*=0) → *pid*

Waits for a child process to exit depending on the value of *pid*:

< −1   Any child whose progress group ID equals the absolute value of *pid*.
 −1   Any child (equivalent to wait).
  0   Any child whose process group ID equals that of the current process.
 > 0   The child with the given PID.

int may be a logical or of the flag values Process::WNOHANG (do not block if no child available) or Process::WUNTRACED (return stopped children that haven't been reported). Not all flags are available on all platforms, but a flag value of zero will work on all platforms.

```
include Process
pid = fork { sleep 3 }          # =>   48059
Time.now                         # =>   2009-03-31 09:58:37 -0500
waitpid(pid, Process::WNOHANG)   # =>   nil
Time.now                         # =>   2009-03-31 09:58:37 -0500
waitpid(pid, 0)                  # =>   48059
Time.now                         # =>   2009-03-31 09:58:40 -0500
```

---

waitpid2   Process.waitpid2(*pid*, *int*=0) → [*pid*, *status*]

Waits for the given child process to exit, returning that child's process ID and exit status (a Process::Status object). *int* may be a logical or of the values Process::WNOHANG (do not block if no child available) or Process::WUNTRACED (return stopped children that haven't been reported). Not all flags are available on all platforms, but a flag value of zero will work on all platforms.

<table>
<tr><td>Module</td></tr>
</table>

Process::GID

Provides a higher-level (and more portable) interface to the underlying operating system's concepts of real, effective, and saved group IDs. Discussing of the semantics of these IDs is well beyond the scope of this book: readers who want to know more should consult POSIX documentation or read the intro(2) man pages on a recent Unix platform. All these methods throw NotImplementedError if the host operating does not support a sufficient set of calls. The descriptions that follow are based on notes in ruby-talk:76218 by Hidetoshi Nagai.

Module methods

change_privilege   Process::GID.change_privilege(*gid*) → *gid*

Sets the real, effective, and saved group IDs to *gid*, raising an exception on failure (in which case the state of the IDs is not known).

This method is not compatible with Process.gid=.

eid   Process::GID.eid → *egid*

Returns the effective group ID for this process. Synonym for Process.egid.

eid=   Process::GID.eid = *egid*

Synonym for Process::GID.grant_privilege.

grant_privilege   Process::GID.grant_privilege(*egid*) → *egid*

Sets the effective group ID to *egid*, raising an exception on failure. One some environments this may also change the saved group ID (see re_exchangeable?).

re_exchange   Process::GID.re_exchange → *egid*

Exchanges the real and effective group IDs, setting the saved group ID to the new effective group ID. Returns the new effective group ID.

re_exchangeable?   Process::GID.re_exchangeable → true or false

Returns true if real and effective group IDs can be exchanged on the host operating system and returns false otherwise.

rid   Process::GID.rid → *gid*

Returns the real group ID for this process. Synonym for Process.gid.

sid_available?   Process::GID.sid_available? → true or false

Returns true if the underlying platform supports saved group IDs and returns false otherwise. Currently, Ruby assumes support if the operating system has setresgid(2) or setegid(2) calls or if the configuration includes the POSIX_SAVED_IDS flag.

switch   Process::GID.switch → *egid*
                              Process::GID.switch { *block* } → *obj*

Handles the toggling of group privilege. In the block form, automatically toggles the IDs back when the block terminates (but only if the block doesn't use other calls into Process::GID calls, which would interfere). Without a block, returns the original effective group ID.

Class

Process::Status < Object

Process::Status encapsulates the information on the status of a running or terminated system process. The built-in variable $? is either nil or a Process::Status object.

```
fork { exit 99 }    # =>    47188
Process.wait        # =>    47188
$?.class            # =>    Process::Status
$?.to_i             # =>    25344
$? >> 8             # =>    99
$?.stopped?         # =>    false
$?.exited?          # =>    true
$?.exitstatus       # =>    99
```

POSIX systems record information on processes using a 16-bit integer. The lower bits record the process status (stopped, exited, signaled), and the upper bits possibly contain additional information (for example, the program's return code in the case of exited processes). Before Ruby 1.8, these bits were exposed directly to the Ruby program. Ruby now encapsulates these in a Process::Status object. To maximize compatibility, however, these objects retain a bit-oriented interface. In the descriptions that follow, when we talk about the integer value of *stat*, we're referring to this 16-bit value.

Instance methods

==   *stat* == *other* → true or false

Returns true if the integer value of *stat* equals *other*.

&   *stat* & *num* → *fixnum*

Logical AND of the bits in *stat* with *num*.

```
fork { exit 0x37 }
Process.wait
sprintf('%04x', $?.to_i)        # =>    "3700"
sprintf('%04x', $? & 0x1e00)    # =>    "1600"
```

>>   *stat* >> *num* → *fixnum*

Shifts the bits in *stat* right *num* places.

```
fork { exit 99 }    # =>    47194
Process.wait        # =>    47194
$?.to_i             # =>    25344
$? >> 8             # =>    99
```

coredump?   *stat*.coredump → true or false

Returns true if *stat* generated a coredump when it terminated. Not available on all platforms.

exited?   *stat*.exited? → true or false

Returns true if *stat* exited normally (for example using an exit call or finishing the program).

exitstatus

stat.exitstatus → *fixnum* or nil

Returns the least significant 8 bits of the return code of *stat*. Available only if exited? is true.

```
fork { }            # =>   47197
Process.wait        # =>   47197
$?.exited?          # =>   true
$?.exitstatus       # =>   0

fork { exit 99 }    # =>   47198
Process.wait        # =>   47198
$?.exited?          # =>   true
$?.exitstatus       # =>   99
```

pid

stat.pid → *fixnum*

Returns the ID of the process associated with this status object.

```
fork { exit }   # =>   47201
Process.wait    # =>   47201
$?.pid          # =>   47201
```

signaled?

stat.signaled? → true or false

Returns true if *stat* terminated because of an uncaught signal.

```
pid = fork { sleep 100 }
Process.kill(9, pid)    # =>   1
Process.wait            # =>   47204
$?.signaled?            # =>   true
```

stopped?

stat.stopped? → true or false

Returns true if this process is stopped. This is returned only if the corresponding wait call had the WUNTRACED flag set.

success?

stat.success? → nil, or true or false

Returns true if *stat* refers to a process that exited successfully, returns false if it exited with a failure, and returns nil if *stat* does not refer to a process that has exited.

stopsig

stat.stopsig → *fixnum* or nil

Returns the number of the signal that caused *stat* to stop (or nil if self is not stopped).

termsig

stat.termsig → *fixnum* or nil

Returns the number of the signal that caused *stat* to terminate (or nil if self was not terminated by an uncaught signal).

---

to_i *stat*.to_i → *fixnum*

Returns the bits in *stat* as a Fixnum. Poking around in these bits is platform dependent.

```
fork { exit 0xab }          # =>   47207
Process.wait                # =>   47207
sprintf('%04x', $?.to_i)    # =>   "ab00"
```

---

to_s *stat*.to_s → *string*

Equivalent to *stat*.to_i.to_s.

Module	
	Process::Sys

Process::Sys provides system call–level access to the process user and group environment. Many of the calls are aliases of those in the Process module and are packaged here for completeness. See also Process::GID and Process::UID for a higher-level (and more portable) interface.

Module methods

getegid   Process::Sys.getegid → *gid*

Returns the effective group ID for this process. Synonym for Process.egid.

geteuid   Process::Sys.getugid → *uid*

Returns the effective user ID for this process. Synonym for Process.euid.

getgid   Process::Sys.getgid → *gid*

Returns the group ID for this process. Synonym for Process.gid.

getuid   Process::Sys.getuid → *uid*

Returns the user ID for this process. Synonym for Process.uid.

issetugid   Process::Sys.issetugid → true or false

Returns true if this process was made setuid or setgid as a result of the last execve() system call and returns false if not. On systems that don't support issetugid(2), throws NotImplementedError.

setegid   Process::Sys.setegid(*gid*)

Sets the effective group ID to *gid*, failing if the underlying system call fails. On systems that don't support setegid(2), throws NotImplementedError.

seteuid   Process::Sys.seteuid(*uid*)

Sets the effective user ID to *uid*, failing if the underlying system call fails. On systems that don't support seteuid(2), throws NotImplementedError.

setgid   Process::Sys.setgid(*gid*)

Sets the group ID to *gid*, failing if the underlying system call fails. On systems that don't support setgid(2), throws NotImplementedError.

setregid   Process::Sys.setregid(*rgid, egid*)

Sets the real and effective group IDs to *rgid* and *egid*, failing if the underlying system call fails. On systems that don't support setregid(2), throws NotImplementedError.

setresgid   Process::Sys.setresgid(*rgid, egid, sgid*)

Sets the real, effective, and saved group IDs to *rgid, egid,* and *sgid*, failing if the underlying system call fails. On systems that don't support setresgid(2), throws NotImplementedError.

setresuid   Process::Sys.setresuid(*ruid*, *euid*, *suid*)

Sets the real, effective, and saved user IDs to *ruid*, *euid*, and *suid*, failing if the underlying system call fails. On systems that don't support setresuid(2), throws NotImplementedError.

setreuid   Process::Sys.setreuid(*ruid*, *euid*)

Sets the real and effective user IDs to *ruid* and *euid*, failing if the underlying system call fails. On systems that don't support setreuid(2), throws NotImplementedError.

setrgid   Process::Sys.setrgid(*rgid*)

Sets the real group ID to *rgid*, failing if the underlying system call fails. On systems that don't support setrgid(2), throws NotImplementedError.

setruid   Process::Sys.setruid(*ruid*)

Set the real user ID to *ruid*, failing if the underlying system call fails. On systems that don't support setruid(2), throws NotImplementedError.

setuid   Process::Sys.setuid(*uid*)

Sets the user ID to *uid*, failing if the underlying system call fails. On systems that don't support setuid(2), throws NotImplementedError.

Module	
Process::UID	

Provides a higher-level (and more portable) interface to the underlying operating system's concepts of real, effective, and saved user IDs. For more information, see the introduction to Process::GID on page 639.

Module methods

change_privilege   Process::UID.change_privilege(*uid*) → *uid*

Sets the real, effective, and saved user IDs to *uid*, raising an exception on failure (in which case the state of the IDs is not known). Not compatible with Process.uid=.

eid   Process::UID.eid → *euid*

Returns the effective user ID for this process. Synonym for Process.euid.

eid=   Process::UID.eid = *euid*

Synonym for Process::UID.grant_privilege.

grant_privilege   Process::UID.grant_privilege(*euid*) → *euid*

Sets the effective user ID to *euid*, raising an exception on failure. One some environments this may also change the saved user ID.

re_exchange   Process::UID.re_exchange → *euid*

Exchanges the real and effective user IDs, setting the saved user ID to the new effective user ID. Returns the new effective user ID.

re_exchangeable?   Process::UID.re_exchangeable → true or false

Returns true if real and effective user IDs can be exchanged on the host operating system and returns false otherwise.

rid   Process::UID.rid → *uid*

Returns the real user ID for this process. Synonym for Process.uid.

sid_available?   Process::UID.sid_available? → true or false

Returns true if the underlying platform supports saved user IDs and returns false otherwise. Currently, Ruby assumes support if the operating system has setresuid(2) or seteuid(2) calls or if the configuration includes the POSIX_SAVED_IDS flag.

switch   Process::UID.switch → *euid*
                                                             Process::UID.switch { *block* } → *obj*

Handles the toggling of user privilege. In the block form, automatically toggles the IDs back when the block terminates (as long as the block doesn't use other Process::UID calls to interfere). Without a block, returns the original effective user ID.

Range < Object

A Range represents an interval—a set of values with a start and an end. Ranges may be constructed using the *s..e* and *s...e* literals or using Range.new. Ranges constructed using .. run from the start to the end inclusively. Those created using ... exclude the end value. When used as an iterator, ranges return each value in the sequence.

```
(-1..-5).to_a      # =>   []
(-5..-1).to_a      # =>   [-5, -4, -3, -2, -1]
('a'..'e').to_a    # =>   ["a", "b", "c", "d", "e"]
('a'...'e').to_a   # =>   ["a", "b", "c", "d"]
```

Ranges can be constructed using objects of any type, as long as the objects can be compared using their <=> operator and they support the succ method to return the next object in sequence.

```
class Xs                   # represent a string of 'x's
  include Comparable
  attr :length
  def initialize(n)
    @length = n
  end
  def succ
    Xs.new(@length + 1)
  end
  def <=>(other)
    @length <=> other.length
  end
  def inspect
    'x' * @length
  end
end

r = Xs.new(3)..Xs.new(6)   # =>   xxx..xxxxxx
r.to_a                     # =>   [xxx, xxxx, xxxxx, xxxxxx]
r.member?(Xs.new(5))       # =>   true
```

In the previous code example, class Xs includes the Comparable module. This is because Enumerable#member? checks for equality using ==. Including Comparable ensures that the == method is defined in terms of the <=> method implemented in Xs.

Mixes in

Enumerable:

all?, any?, collect, count, cycle, detect, drop, drop_while, each_cons, each_slice, each_with_index, entries, find, find_all, find_index, first, grep, group_by, include?, inject, map, max, max_by, member?, min, min_by, minmax, minmax_by, none?, one?, partition, reduce, reject, select, sort, sort_by, take, take_while, to_a, zip

Class methods

new   Range.new(*start*, *end*, *exclusive*=false) → *rng*

Constructs a range using the given *start* and *end*. If the third parameter is omitted or is false, the range will include the end object; otherwise, it will be excluded.

Instance methods

==   *rng* == *obj* → true or false

Returns true if *obj* is a range whose beginning and end are the same as those in *rng* (compared using ==) and whose *exclusive* flag is the same as *rng*.

===   *rng* === *val* → true or false

If *rng* excludes its end, returns $rng.start \leq val < rng.end$. If *rng* is inclusive, returns $rng.start \leq val \leq rng.end$. Note that this implies that *val* need not be a member of the range itself (for example, a float could fall between the start and end values of a range of integers). Conveniently, the === operator is used by case statements.

```
case 74.95
when   1...50   then   puts "low"
when  50...75   then   puts "medium"
when  75...100  then   puts "high"
end
```

produces:

```
medium
```

Implemented internally by calling include?.

begin   *rng*.begin → *obj*

Returns the first object of *rng*.

cover?   *rng*.cover?(*obj*) → true or false

1.9   Returns true if *obj* lies between the start and end of the range. For ranges defined with *min..max*, this means $min \leq obj \leq max$. For ranges defined with *min...max*, it means $min \leq obj < max$.

```
(1..10).cover?(0)     # =>   false
(1..10).cover?(1)     # =>   true
(1..10).cover?(5)     # =>   true
(1..10).cover?(9.5)   # =>   true
(1..10).cover?(10)    # =>   true
(1...10).cover?(10)   # =>   false
```

each   *rng*.each {| i | *block* } → *rng*

Iterates over the elements *rng*, passing each in turn to the block. Successive elements are generated using the succ method.

```
(10..15).each do |n|
   print n, ' '
end
```

produces:

```
10 11 12 13 14 15
```

---

end   *rng*.end → *obj*

Returns the object that defines the end of *rng*.

```
(1..10).end    # =>   10
(1...10).end   # =>   10
```

---

eql?   *rng*.eql?(*obj*) → true or false

Returns true if *obj* is a range whose beginning and end are the same as those in *rng* (compared using eql?) and whose *exclusive* flag is the same as *rng*.

---

exclude_end?   *rng*.exclude_end? → true or false

Returns true if *rng* excludes its end value.

---

first   *rng*.first(*n* = 1) → *obj* or *array*

1.9   Returns the first (or first *n*) elements of *rng*.

```
('aa'..'bb').first      # =>   "aa"
('aa'..'bb').first(5)   # =>   ["aa", "ab", "ac", "ad", "ae"]
```

---

include?   *rng*.include?(*val*) → true or false

1.9   Returns true if *val* is one of the values in *rng* (that is if Range#each would return *val* at some point). If the range is defined to span numbers, this method returns true if the value lies between the start and end of the range, even if it is not actually a member (that is, it has the same behavior as Range#cover?). Otherwise, the parameter must be a member of the range.

```
r = 1..10
r.include?(5)        # =>   true
r.include?(5.5)      # =>   true
r.include?(10)       # =>   true
r = 1...10
r.include?(10)       # =>   false
r = 'a'..'z'
r.include?('b')      # =>   true
r.include?('ruby')   # =>   false
```

---

last   *rng*.last(*n* = 1) → *obj* or *array*

1.9   Returns the last (or last *n*) elements of *rng*.

```
('aa'..'bb').last       # =>   "bb"
('aa'..'bb').last(5)    # =>   ["ax", "ay", "az", "ba", "bb"]
```

max

$$rng.\text{max} \rightarrow obj$$
$$rng.\text{max} \{\,|\,a,b\,|\ block\ \} \rightarrow obj$$

Returns the maximum value in the range. The block is used to compare values if present.

```
(-3..2).max                    # =>   2
(-3..2).max {|a,b| a*a <=> b*b }  # =>   -3
```

member?

$$rng.\text{member?}(\ val\ ) \rightarrow \text{true or false}$$

Synonym for Range#include?.

min

$$rng.\text{min} \rightarrow obj$$
$$rng.\text{min} \{\,|\,a,b\,|\ block\ \} \rightarrow obj$$

1.9

Returns the minimum value in the range. The block is used to compare values if present.

```
(-3..2).min                    # =>   -3
(-3..2).min {|a,b| a*a <=> b*b }  # =>   0
```

step

$$rng.\text{step}(\ n=1\ ) \ \langle\ \{\,|\,obj\,|\ block\ \}\ \rangle \rightarrow rng \text{ or } enum$$

1.9

Iterates over *rng*, passing each nth element to the block. If the range contains numbers, addition by one is used to generate successive elements. Otherwise, step invokes succ to iterate through range elements. If no block is given, an enumerator is returned. The following code uses class Xs defined at the start of this section:

```
range = Xs.new(1)..Xs.new(10)
range.step(2) {|x| p x}
enum = range.step(3)
p enum.to_a
```

produces:

```
x
xxx
xxxxx
xxxxxxx
xxxxxxxxx
[x, xxxx, xxxxxxx, xxxxxxxxxx]
```

Here's step with numbers:

```
(1..5).step(1).to_a        # =>   [1, 2, 3, 4, 5]
(1..5).step(2).to_a        # =>   [1, 3, 5]
(1..5).step(1.5).to_a      # =>   [1.0, 2.5, 4.0]
(1.0..5.0).step(1).to_a    # =>   [1.0, 2.0, 3.0, 4.0, 5.0]
(1.0..5.0).step(2).to_a    # =>   [1.0, 3.0, 5.0]
(1.0..5.0).step(1.5).to_a  # =>   [1.0, 2.5, 4.0]
```

Range

Rational   <   Numeric

Rational numbers are expressed as the ratio of two integers. When the denominator exactly divides the numerator, a rational number is effectively an integer. Rationals allow exact representation of fractional numbers, but some real values cannot be expressed exactly and so cannot be represented as rationals.

Class Rational is normally relatively independent of the other numeric classes, in that the result of dividing two integers with the / operator will normally be a (truncated) integer (the quo method will always return a rational result). However, if the mathn library is loaded into a program, integer division may generate a Rational result. Also see the rational library on page 787 for additional methods on rational numbers.

```
r1 = Rational("1/2")   # =>   1/2
r2 = 4.quo(5)          # =>   4/5
r1 * r2                # =>   2/5
```

Instance methods

Arithmetic operations

Performs various arithmetic operations on self.

self	+	*numeric*	Addition
self	−	*numeric*	Subtraction
self	*	*numeric*	Multiplication
self	/	*numeric*	Division
self	%	*numeric*	Modulo
self	**	*numeric*	Exponentiation
self	-@		Unary minus

Comparisons

Compares self to other numbers.

<, <=, ==, >=, and >.

<=>   self <=> *numeric* $\rightarrow$ $-1, 0, +1$

Comparison—Returns -1, 0, or $+1$ depending on whether self is less than, equal to, or greater than *numeric*. Although Rational's grandparent, mixes in Comparable, Rational does not use that module for performing comparisons, instead implementing the comparison operators explicitly.

```
Rational("4/2") <=> Rational("98/49")   # =>   0
Rational("3/4") <=> 41                  # =>   -1
Rational("0") <=> 0.0                   # =>   0
```

==   self == *numeric*

Returns true is self has the same value as *numeric*. Comparisons against integers and rational numbers are exact; comparisons against floats first convert self to a float.

ceil   self.ceil → *numeric*

Returns the smallest integer greater than or equal to self.

```
Rational("22/7").ceil    # =>    4
Rational("-22/7").ceil   # =>    -3
```

denominator   self.denominator → *a_number*

Returns the denominator of self.

```
Rational("2/3").denominator   # =>    3
```

div   self.div(*numeric*) → *integer*

Returns the integral result of dividing self by *numeric*.

```
Rational("11/2") / 2     # =>    11/4
Rational("11/2").div 2   # =>    2
```

fdiv   self.fdiv(*numeric*) → *float*

Returns the floating-point result of dividing self by *numeric*.

```
Rational("11/2") / 2      # =>    11/4
Rational("11/2").fdiv 2   # =>    2.75
```

floor   self.floor → *numeric*

Returns the largest integer less than or equal to self.

```
Rational("22/7").floor    # =>    3
Rational("-22/7").floor   # =>    -4
```

numerator   self.numerator → *a_number*

Returns the numerator of self.

```
Rational("2/3").numerator   # =>    2
```

quo   self.quo(*numeric*) → *numeric*

1.9   Synonym for Rational#/.

round   self.round → *numeric*

Rounds self to the nearest integer.

```
Rational("22/7").round    # =>    3
Rational("-22/7").round   # =>    -3
```

to_f   self.to_f → *float*

Returns the floating-point representation of self.

```
Rational("37/4").to_f   # =>    9.25
```

to_i
self.to_i → *integer*

Returns the truncated integer value of self.

```
Rational("19/10").to_i    # =>    1
Rational("-19/10").to_i   # =>   -1
```

to_r
self.to_r → self

Returns self.

truncate
self.truncate → *numeric*

Returns self truncated to an integer.

```
Rational("22/7").truncate    # =>    3
Rational("-22/7").truncate   # =>   -3
```

Rational

Class
Regexp < Object

A Regexp holds a regular expression, used to match a pattern against strings. Regexps are created using the /.../ and %r... literals and using the Regexp.new constructor. Ruby 1.9 uses a different regular expression engine than previous versions.[4] See the reference on regular expressions starting 22 on page 320 for details.

1.9

Class constants

EXTENDED	Ignores spaces and newlines in regexp.
IGNORECASE	Matches are case insensitive.
MULTILINE	Newlines treated as any other character.

Class methods

compile   Regexp.compile(*pattern* ⟨ , *options* ⟨ , *lang* ⟩ ⟩) → *rxp*

Synonym for Regexp.new.

escape   Regexp.escape(*string*) → *escaped_string*

Escapes any characters that would have special meaning in a regular expression. For any string, Regexp.new(Regexp.escape(*str*))=~*str* will be true.

```
Regexp.escape('\\[]*?{}.')   # =>   \\\[\]\*\?\{\}\.
```

last_match   Regexp.last_match → *match*
                                               Regexp.last_match(*int*) → *string*

The first form returns the MatchData object generated by the last successful pattern match. This is equivalent to reading the global variable $~. MatchData is described on page 576. The second form returns the nth field in this MatchData object.

```
/c(.)t/ =~ 'cat'          # =>   0
Regexp.last_match         # =>   #<MatchData "cat" 1:"a">
Regexp.last_match(0)      # =>   "cat"
Regexp.last_match(1)      # =>   "a"
Regexp.last_match(2)      # =>   nil
```

new   Regexp.new(*string* ⟨ , *options* ⟨ , *lang* ⟩ ⟩) → *rxp*
                                               Regexp.new(*regexp*) → *new_regexp*

Constructs a new regular expression from the *string* or the *regexp*. In the latter case, that regexp's options are propagated, and new options may not be specified. If *options* is a Fixnum, it should be one or more of Regexp::EXTENDED, Regexp::IGNORECASE, and Regexp::MULTILINE, *or*-ed together. Otherwise, if the *options* parameter is not nil, the regexp will be case insensitive. The *lang* can be set to "N" or "n" to force the regular expression

---

4.   It is called *Oniguruma*.

to have ASCII-8BIT encoding;[5] otherwise, the encoding of the string determines the encoding of the regular expression.

```
# encoding: utf-8
r1 = Regexp.new('^[a-z]+:\\s+\w+')        # =>   /^[a-z]+:\s+\w+/
r2 = Regexp.new('cat', true)              # =>   /cat/i
r3 = Regexp.new('dog', Regexp::EXTENDED)  # =>   /dog/x
r4 = Regexp.new(r2)                       # =>   /cat/i
r5 = Regexp.new("δelta")                  # =>   /δelta/
r1.encoding                               # =>   #<Encoding:US-ASCII>
r5.encoding                               # =>   #<Encoding:UTF-8>
```

---

quote   Regexp.quote(*string*) → *escaped_string*

Synonym for Regexp.escape.

---

try_convert   Regexp.try_convert(*obj*) → *a_regexp* or nil

1.9   If *obj* is not already a regular expression, attempts to convert it to one by calling its to_regexp method. Returns nil if no conversion could be made.

```
Regexp.try_convert("cat")   # =>   nil
class String
  def to_regexp
    Regexp.new(self)
  end
end
Regexp.try_convert("cat")   # =>   /cat/
```

---

union   Regexp.union(⟨ pattern ⟩*) → *a_regexp*

1.9   Returns a regular expression that will match any of the given patterns. With no patterns, produces a regular expression that will never match. If a pattern is a string, it will be given the default regular expression options. If a pattern is a regular expression, its options will be honored in the final pattern. The patterns may also be passed in a single array.

```
Regexp.union("cat")           # =>   /cat/
Regexp.union("cat", "dog")    # =>   /cat|dog/
Regexp.union(%w{ cat dog })   # =>   /cat|dog/
Regexp.union("cat", /dog/i)   # =>   /cat|(?i-mx:dog)/
```

Instance methods

==   *rxp == other_regexp* → true or false

Equality—Two regexps are equal if their patterns are identical, they have the same character set code, and their casefold? values are the same.

```
/abc/  == /abc/x  # =>  false
/abc/  == /abc/i  # =>  false
/abc/u == /abc/n  # =>  false
```

===   *rxp === string* → true or false

Case Equality—Like Regexp#=~, but accepts nonstring arguments (returning false). Used in case statements.

```
a = "HELLO"
case a
when /^[a-z]*$/; print "Lower case\n"
when /^[A-Z]*$/; print "Upper case\n"
else             print "Mixed case\n"
end
```

produces:

```
Upper case
```

=~   *rxp =~ string* → int or nil

Match—Matches *rxp* against *string*, returning the offset of the start of the match or nil if the match failed. Sets $~ to the corresponding MatchData or nil.

```
/SIT/  =~ "insensitive"  # =>  nil
/SIT/i =~ "insensitive"  # =>  5
```

~   *~ rxp* → int or nil

Match—Matches *rxp* against the contents of $_. Equivalent to *rxp* =~ $_. You should be ashamed if you use this....

```
$_ = "input data"
~ /at/   # =>  7
```

---

casefold?   *rxp.casefold?* → true or false

Returns the value of the case-insensitive flag. Merely setting the i option inside *rxp* does not set this flag.

```
/cat/.casefold?       # =>  false
/cat/i.casefold?      # =>  true
/(?i:cat)/.casefold?  # =>  false
```

encoding

rxp.encoding → *an_encoding*

1.9 ⌐ Returns the character encoding for the regexp.

```
/cat/.encoding    # =>   #<Encoding:US-ASCII>
/cat/s.encoding   # =>   #<Encoding:Windows-31J>
/cat/u.encoding   # =>   #<Encoding:UTF-8>
```

fixed_encoding?

rxp.fixed_encoding? → true or false

1.9 ⌐ A regular expression containing only 7-bit characters can be matched against a string in any encoding. In this case, fixed_encoding? returns false. Otherwise, it returns true.

```
/cat/.fixed_encoding?    # =>   false
/cat/s.fixed_encoding?   # =>   true
/cat/u.fixed_encoding?   # =>   true
```

match

rxp.match(*string, offset=0*) → *match* or nil
rxp.match(*string, offset=0*) { | *match* | *block* } → *obj*

1.9 ⌐

1.9 ⌐ Returns a MatchData object (see page 576) describing the match or nil if there was no match. This is equivalent to retrieving the value of the special variable $~ following a normal match. The match process will start at *offset* into *string*. If a block is given and the match is successful, the block will be invoked with the MatchData object, and the value returned by the block will be the value returned by match.

```
md = /(.)(d)(.)/.match("abcdefabcdef")
md              # =>   #<MatchData "cde" 1:"c" 2:"d" 3:"e">
md[1]           # =>   "c"
md.begin(1)     # =>   2
md = /(.)(d)(.)/.match("abcdedcba", 4)
md              # =>   #<MatchData "edc" 1:"e" 2:"d" 3:"c">
md.begin(1)     # =>   4

result = /(...)...(...)/.match("catanddog") do |md|
  md[1] + "&" + md[2]
end
result          # =>   "cat&dog"
```

named_captures

rxp.named_captures → *hash*

1.9 ⌐ Returns a hash whose keys are the names of captures and whose values are each an array containing the number of the capture in *rxp*.

```
/(?<a>.).(?<b>.)/.named_captures          # =>   {"a"=>[1], "b"=>[2]}
/(?<a>.)(.)(?<b>.)/.named_captures        # =>   {"a"=>[1], "b"=>[2]}
/(?<a>.)(?<b>.)(?<a>.)/.named_captures    # =>   {"a"=>[1, 3], "b"=>[2]}
```

names

rxp.names → *array*

1.9 ⌐ Returns an array containing the names of captures in *rxp*.

```
/(.)(.)(.)/.names                      # =>   []
/(?<first>.).(?<last>.)/.names         # =>   ["first", "last"]
```

options   *rxp*.options → *int*

Returns the set of bits corresponding to the options used when creating this Regexp (see Regexp.new for details). Note that additional bits may be set in the returned options: these are used internally by the regular expression code. These extra bits are ignored if the options are passed to Regexp.new.

```
# Let's see what the values are...
Regexp::IGNORECASE            # =>   1
Regexp::EXTENDED              # =>   2
Regexp::MULTILINE             # =>   4

/cat/.options                 # =>   0
/cat/ix.options               # =>   3
Regexp.new('cat', true).options   # =>   1
Regexp.new('cat', 0, 'n').options # =>   32

r = /cat/ix
Regexp.new(r.source, r.options)   # =>   /cat/ix
```

source   *rxp*.source → *string*

Returns the original string of the pattern.

```
/ab+c/ix.source   # =>   "ab+c"
```

to_s   *rxp*.to_s → *string*

Returns a string containing the regular expression and its options (using the (?xx:yyy) notation). This string can be fed back in to Regexp.new to a regular expression with the same semantics as the original. (However, Regexp#== may not return true when comparing the two, because the source of the regular expression itself may differ, as the example shows.) Regexp#inspect produces a generally more readable version of *rxp*.

```
r1 = /ab+c/ix        # =>   /ab+c/ix
s1 = r1.to_s         # =>   "(?ix-m:ab+c)"
r2 = Regexp.new(s1)  # =>   /(?ix-m:ab+c)/
r1 == r2             # =>   false
r1.source            # =>   "ab+c"
r2.source            # =>   "(?ix-m:ab+c)"
```

Signal

Many operating systems allow signals to be sent to running processes. Some signals have a defined effect on the process, and others may be trapped at the code level and acted upon. For example, your process may trap the USR1 signal and use it to toggle debugging, and it may use TERM to initiate a controlled shutdown.

```
pid = fork do
  Signal.trap("USR1") do
    $debug = !$debug
    puts "Debug now: #$debug"
  end
  Signal.trap(:TERM) do   # symbols work too...
    puts "Terminating..."
    exit
  end
  # . . . do some work . . .
end

Process.detach(pid)

# Controlling program:
Process.kill("USR1", pid)
# ...
Process.kill(:USR1, pid)
# ...
Process.kill("TERM", pid)
```

produces:

```
Debug now: true
Debug now: false
Terminating...
```

The list of available signal names and their interpretation is system dependent. Signal delivery semantics may also vary between systems; in particular, signal delivery may not always be reliable.

Module methods

list

Signal.list → *hash*

Returns a list of signal names mapped to the corresponding underlying signal numbers.

```
Signal.list   # =>   {"ABRT"=>6, "ALRM"=>14, "BUS"=>10, "CHLD"=>20,
                      "CLD"=>20, "CONT"=>19, "EMT"=>7, "EXIT"=>0, "FPE"=>8,
                      "HUP"=>1, "ILL"=>4, "INFO"=>29, "INT"=>2, "IO"=>23,
                      "IOT"=>6, "KILL"=>9, "PIPE"=>13, "PROF"=>27,
                      "QUIT"=>3, "SEGV"=>11, "STOP"=>17, "SYS"=>12,
                      "TERM"=>15, "TRAP"=>5, "TSTP"=>18, "TTIN"=>21,
                      "TTOU"=>22, "URG"=>16, "USR1"=>30, "USR2"=>31,
                      "VTALRM"=>26, "WINCH"=>28, "XCPU"=>24, "XFSZ"=>25}
```

---

trap

Signal.trap(*signal, command*) → *obj*
Signal.trap(*signal*) { *block* } → *obj*

Specifies the handling of signals. The first parameter is a signal name (a string or symbol such as SIGALRM, SIGUSR1, and so on) or a signal number. The characters SIG may be omitted from the signal name. The command or block specifies code to be run when the signal is raised. If the command is nil, the string IGNORE or SIG_IGN, or the empty string, the signal will be ignored. If the command is DEFAULT or SIG_DFL, the operating system's default handler will be invoked. If the command is EXIT, the script will be terminated by the signal. Otherwise, the given command or block will be run.

The special signal name EXIT or signal number zero will be invoked just prior to program termination.

trap returns the previous handler for the given signal.

```
Signal.trap(0, lambda { |signo| puts "exit pid #{$$} with #{signo}" })
Signal.trap("CLD")  { |signo| puts "Child died (#{signo})" }
if fork   # parent
  do_something # ...
else
  puts "In child, PID=#{$$}"
end
```

produces:

```
In child, PID=48085
exit pid 48085 with 0
Child died (20)
exit pid 48084 with 0
```

Note that you must specify a block taking a parameter if you use lambda to create the proc object.

Class
String < Object

A String object holds and manipulates a sequence of bytes, typically representing characters. String objects may be created using String.new or as literals (see page 316).

Because of aliasing issues, users of strings should be aware of the methods that modify the contents of a String object. Typically, methods with names ending in ! modify their receiver, while those without a ! return a new String. However, exceptions exist, such as String#[]=.

In this description, I try to differentiate between the bytes in a string and the characters in a string. Internally, a string is a sequence of 8-bit bytes. These are represented externally as small Fixnums. At the same time, these byte sequences can be interpreted as a sequence of characters. This interpretation is controlled by the encoding of the string. In some encodings (such as US-ASCII and ISO-8859), each byte corresponds to a single character. In other encodings (such as UTF-8), a varying number of bytes comprise each character.

1.9 As of Ruby 1.9, String no longer mixes in Enumerable.

Mixes in

Comparable:

    <, <=, ==, >=, >, between?

Class methods

new String.new(*val*="") → *str*

Returns a new string object containing a copy of *val* (which should be a String or implement to_str). Note that the new string object is created only when one of the strings is modified.

```
str1 = "wibble"
str2 = String.new(str1)
str1.object_id   # =>   336070
str2.object_id   # =>   335970
str1[1] = "o"
str1             # =>   "wobble"
str2             # =>   "wibble"
```

try_convert String.try_convert(*obj*) → *a_string* or nil

1.9 If *obj* is not already a string, attempts to convert it to one by calling its to_str method. Returns nil if no conversion could be made.

```
String.try_convert("cat")   # =>   "cat"
String.try_convert(0xbee)   # =>   nil
```

Instance methods

%   *str % arg → string*

Format—Uses *str* as a format specification and returns the result of applying it to *arg*. If the format specification contains more than one substitution, then *arg* must be an Array containing the values to be substituted. See Kernel.sprintf on page 568 for details of the format string.

```
puts "%05d" % 123
puts "%-5s: %08x" % [ "ID", self.object_id ]
puts "%-5<name>s: %08<value>x" % { name: "ID", value: self.object_id }
```

produces:

```
00123
ID    : 000653ba
ID    : 000653ba
```

---

*   *str * int → string*

Copies—Returns a new String containing *int* copies of the receiver.

```
"Ho! " * 3    # =>    "Ho! Ho! Ho! "
```

+   *str + string → string*

Concatenation—Returns a new String containing *string* concatenated to *str*. If both strings contain non-7-bit characters, their encodings must be compatible.

```
"Hello from " + "RubyLand"   # =>    "Hello from RubyLand"
```

<<   *str << fixnum → str*
                                                               str << obj → str

Append—Concatenates the given object to *str*. If the object is a Fixnum, it is considered to be a codepoint in the encoding of *str* and converted to the appropriate character before being appended.

```
a = "hello world"
a.force_encoding("utf-8")
a << 33             # =>    "hello world!"
a << " Says the "   # =>    "hello world! Says the "
a << 8706           # =>    "hello world! Says the δ"
a << "og"           # =>    "hello world! Says the δog"
```

<=>   *str <=> other_string → −1, 0, +1*

Comparison—Returns −1 if *str* is less than, 0 if *str* is equal to, and +1 if *str* is greater than *other_string*. If the strings are of different lengths and the strings are equal when compared up to the shortest length, then the longer string is considered greater than the shorter one. In older versions of Ruby, setting $= allowed case-insensitive comparisons; you must now use String#casecmp.

<=> is the basis for the methods <, <=, >, >=, and between?, included from module Comparable. The method String#== does not use Comparable#==.

```
"abcdef" <=> "abcde"    # =>   1
"abcdef" <=> "abcdef"   # =>   0
"abcdef" <=> "abcdefg"  # =>   -1
"abcdef" <=> "ABCDEF"   # =>   1
```

==   *str* == *obj* → true or false

Equality—If *obj* is a String, returns true if *str* has the same encoding, length, and content as *obj*; returns false otherwise. If *obj* is not a String but responds to to_str, returns *obj* == *str*; otherwise, returns false.

```
"abcdef" == "abcde"    # =>   false
"abcdef" == "abcdef"   # =>   true
```

=~   *str* =~ *regexp* → *int* or nil

Match—Equivalent to *regexp* =~ *str*. Prior versions of Ruby permitted an arbitrary operand to =~; this is now deprecated. Returns the position the match starts or returns nil if there is no match or if *regexp* is not a regular expression.[6]

```
"cat o' 9 tails" =~ /\d/   # =>   7
"cat o' 9 tails" =~ 9      # =>   nil

"cat o' 9 tails" =~ "\d"
```

produces:

```
prog.rb:1:in `=~': type mismatch: String given (TypeError)
from /tmp/prog.rb:1:in `<main>'
```

[ ]   *str*[*int*] → *string* or nil
                                                        str[*int*, *int*] → *string* or nil
                                                        str[*range*] → *string* or nil
                                                        str[*regexp*] → *string* or nil
                                                    str[*regexp*, *int*] → *string* or nil
                                                        str[*string*] → *string* or nil

Element Reference—If passed a single *int*, returns the character at that position. (Prior to Ruby 1.9, an integer character code was returned.) If passed two *ints*, returns a substring starting at the offset given by the first, and a length given by the second. If given a range, a substring containing characters at offsets given by the range is returned. In all three cases, if an offset is negative, it is counted from the end of *str*. Returns nil if the initial offset falls outside the string and the length is not given, the length is negative, or the beginning of the range is greater than the end.

If *regexp* is supplied, the matching portion of *str* is returned. If a numeric parameter follows the regular expression, that component of the MatchData is returned instead. If a String is given, that string is returned if it occurs in *str*. In both cases, nil is returned if there is no match.

---

6.   Except for a strange corner case. If *regexp* is a string or can be coerced into a string, a TypeError exception is raised.

```
a = "hello there"
a[1]                      # =>   "e"
a[1,3]                    # =>   "ell"
a[1..3]                   # =>   "ell"
a[1...3]                  # =>   "el"
a[-3,2]                   # =>   "er"
a[-4..-2]                 # =>   "her"
a[-2..-4]                 # =>   ""
a[/[aeiou](.)\1/]         # =>   "ell"
a[/[aeiou](.)\1/, 0]      # =>   "ell"
a[/[aeiou](.)\1/, 1]      # =>   "l"
a[/[aeiou](.)\1/, 2]      # =>   nil
a[/(..)e/]                # =>   "the"
a[/(..)e/, 1]             # =>   "th"
a["lo"]                   # =>   "lo"
a["bye"]                  # =>   nil
```

[ ]=

                                    str[*int*] = *string*
                               str[*int, int*] = *string*
                                 str[*range*] = *string*
                                str[*regexp*] = *string*
                           str[*regexp, int*] = *string*
                                str[*string*] = *string*

Element Assignment—Replaces some or all of the content of *str*. The portion of the string affected is determined using the same criteria as String#[ ]. If the replacement string is not the same length as the text it is replacing, the string will be adjusted accordingly. If the regular expression or string is used as the index doesn't match a position in the string, IndexError is raised. If the regular expression form is used, the optional second *int* allows you to specify which portion of the match to replace (effectively using the MatchData indexing rules). The forms that take a Fixnum will raise an IndexError if the value is out of range; the Range form will raise a RangeError, and the Regexp and String forms will silently ignore the assignment.

```
a = "hello"
a[2] = "u"                       (a → "heulo")
a[2, 4] = "xyz"                  (a → "hexyz")
a[-4, 2] = "xyz"                 (a → "hxyzlo")
a[2..4] = "xyz"                  (a → "hexyz")
a[-4..-2] = "xyz"                (a → "hxyzo")
a[/[aeiou](.)\1(.)/] = "xyz"     (a → "hxyz")
a[/[aeiou](.)\1(.)/, 1] = "xyz"  (a → "hexyzlo")
a[/[aeiou](.)\1(.)/, 2] = "xyz"  (a → "hellxyz")
a["l"] = "xyz"                   (a → "hexyzlo")
a["ll"] = "xyz"                  (a → "hexyzo")
a[2, 0] = "xyz"                  (a → "hexyzllo")
```

ascii_only?

str.ascii_only? → true or false

_{1.9} Returns true if the string contains no characters with a character code greater than 127 (that is, it contains only 7-bit ASCII characters).

```
# encoding: utf-8
"dog".ascii_only?         # =>   true
"δog".ascii_only?         # =>   false
"\x00 to \x7f".ascii_only? # =>  true
```

bytes

str.bytes → *enum*
str.bytes {| *byte* | *block* } → *str*

_{1.9} Returns an enumerator for the bytes (integers in the range 0 to 255) in *str*. With a block, passes each byte to the block and returns the original string. See also String#chars and String#codepoints.

```
# encoding: utf-8
"dog".bytes.to_a                   # =>   [100, 111, 103]
"δog".bytes.to_a                   # =>   [226, 136, 130, 111, 103]
result = []
"δog".bytes.each {|b| result << b } # =>   "δog"
result                             # =>   [226, 136, 130, 111, 103]
```

bytesize

str.bytesize → *int*

_{1.9} Returns the number of bytes (not characters) in *str*. See also String#length.

```
# encoding: utf-8
"dog".length   # =>  3
"dog".bytesize # =>  3
"δog".length   # =>  3
"δog".bytesize # =>  5
```

capitalize

str.capitalize → *string*

Returns a copy of *str* with the first character converted to uppercase and the remainder to lowercase.

```
"hello world".capitalize  # =>   "Hello world"
"HELLO WORLD".capitalize  # =>   "Hello world"
"123ABC".capitalize       # =>   "123abc"
```

capitalize!

str.capitalize! → *str* or nil

Modifies *str* by converting the first character to uppercase and the remainder to lowercase. Returns nil if no changes are made.

```
a = "hello world"
a.capitalize!  # =>   "Hello world"
a              # =>   "Hello world"
a.capitalize!  # =>   nil
```

---

casecmp   *str*.casecmp(*string*) → −1, 0, +1

Case-insensitive version of String#<=>.

```
"abcdef".casecmp("abcde")     # =>   1
"abcdef".casecmp("abcdef")    # =>   0
"aBcDeF".casecmp("abcdef")    # =>   0
"abcdef".casecmp("abcdefg")   # =>   -1
"abcdef".casecmp("ABCDEF")    # =>   0
```

---

center   *str*.center(*int, pad=" "*) → *string*

If *int* is greater than the length of *str*, returns a new String of length *int* with *str* centered between the given padding (defaults to spaces); otherwise, returns *str*.

```
"hello".center(4)             # =>   "hello"
"hello".center(20)            # =>   "⌴⌴⌴⌴⌴⌴⌴hello⌴⌴⌴⌴⌴⌴⌴⌴"
"hello".center(4,  "_-^-")    # =>   "hello"
"hello".center(20, "_-^-")    # =>   "_-^-_-^hello_-^-_-^-"
"hello".center(20, "-")       # =>   "-------hello--------"
```

---

chars   *str*.chars → *enum*
                                                     str.chars {| *char* | *block* } → *str*

Returns an enumerator for the characters (single character strings) in *str*. With a block, passes each character to the block and returns the original string. See also String#bytes.

```
# encoding: utf-8
"dog".chars.to_a                        # =>   ["d", "o", "g"]
"δog".chars.to_a                        # =>   ["δ", "o", "g"]
result = []
"δog".chars.each {|b| result << b }     # =>   "δog"
result                                  # =>   ["δ", "o", "g"]
```

---

chr   *str*.chr → *string*

Returns the first character of *str*.

```
# encoding: utf-8
"dog".chr  # =>   "d"
"δog".chr  # =>   "δ"
```

---

clear   *str*.clear → *str*

Removes the content (but not the associated encoding) of *str*.

```
# encoding: utf-8
str = "δog"
str.clear       # =>   ""
str.length      # =>   0
str.encoding    # =>   #<Encoding:UTF-8>
```

---

chomp   *str*.chomp(*rs=$/*) → *string*

Returns a new String with the given record separator removed from the end of *str* (if

present). If $/ has not been changed from the default Ruby record separator, then chomp
also removes carriage return characters (that is it will remove \n, \r, and \r\n).

```
"hello".chomp              # =>    "hello"
"hello\n".chomp            # =>    "hello"
"hello\r\n".chomp          # =>    "hello"
"hello\n\r".chomp          # =>    "hello\n"
"hello\r".chomp            # =>    "hello"
"hello \n there".chomp     # =>    "hello \n there"
"hello".chomp("llo")       # =>    "he"
```

chomp!

str.chomp!($rs=\$/$) $\rightarrow$ str or nil

Modifies str in place as described for String#chomp, returning str or returning nil if no modifications were made.

chop

str.chop $\rightarrow$ $string$

Returns a new String with the last character removed. If the string ends with \r\n, both characters are removed. Applying chop to an empty string returns an empty string. String#chomp
is often a safer alternative, because it leaves the string unchanged if it doesn't end in a record
separator.

```
"string\r\n".chop    # =>    "string"
"string\n\r".chop    # =>    "string\n"
"string\n".chop      # =>    "string"
"string".chop        # =>    "strin"
"x".chop.chop        # =>    ""
```

chop!

str.chop! $\rightarrow$ str or nil

Processes str as for String#chop, returning str or returning nil if str is the empty string. See
also String#chomp!.

codepoints

str.codepoints $\rightarrow$ $enum$
str.codepoints { | $integer$ | $block$ } $\rightarrow$ str

1.9

Returns an enumerator for the codepoints (integers representation of the characters) in str.
With a block, passes each integer to the block and returns the original string. See also
String#bytes and String#chars.

```
# encoding: utf-8
"dog".codepoints.to_a                       # =>    [100, 111, 103]
"δog".codepoints.to_a                       # =>    [8706, 111, 103]
result = []
"δog".codepoints.each {|b| result << b }    # =>    "δog"
result                                      # =>    [8706, 111, 103]
```

concat

str.concat(int) $\rightarrow$ str
str.concat(obj) $\rightarrow$ str

Synonym for String#<<.

String

count str.count(⟨ $string$ ⟩$^{+}$) → int

Each *string* parameter defines a set of characters to count. The intersection of these sets defines the characters to count in *str*. Any parameter that starts with a caret (^) is negated. The sequence c_1–c_2 means all characters between c_1 and c_2.

```
a = "hello world"
a.count "lo"            # =>   5
a.count "lo", "o"       # =>   2
a.count "hello", "^l"   # =>   4
a.count "ej-m"          # =>   4
```

crypt str.crypt($settings$) → $string$

Applies a one-way cryptographic hash to *str* by invoking the standard library function crypt. The argument is to some extent system dependent. On traditional Unix boxes, it is often a two-character *salt* string. On more modern boxes, it may also control things such as DES encryption parameters. See the man page for crypt(3) for details.

```
# standard salt
"secret".crypt("sh")            # =>   "shRK3aVg8FsI2"
# On OSX: DES, 2 interactions, 24-bit salt
"secret".crypt("_...0abcd")     # =>   "_...0abcdROn65JNDj12"
```

delete str.delete(⟨ $string$ ⟩$^{+}$) → new_string

Returns a copy of *str* with all characters in the intersection of its arguments deleted. Uses the same rules for building the set of characters as String#count.

```
"hello".delete("l","lo")      # =>   "heo"
"hello".delete("lo")          # =>   "he"
"hello".delete("aeiou", "^e") # =>   "hell"
"hello".delete("ej-m")        # =>   "ho"
```

delete! str.delete!(⟨ $string$ ⟩$^{+}$) → str or nil

Performs a delete operation in place, returning *str* or returning nil if *str* was not modified.

```
a = "hello"
a.delete!("l","lo")   # =>   "heo"
a                     # =>   "heo"
a.delete!("l")        # =>   nil
```

downcase str.downcase → $string$

Returns a copy of *str* with all uppercase letters replaced with their lowercase counterparts. The operation is locale insensitive—only characters *A* to *Z* are affected. Multibyte characters are skipped.

```
"hEllO".downcase  # =>   "hello"
```

---

downcase!   *str*.downcase! → *str* or nil

Replaces uppercase letters in *str* with their lowercase counterparts. Returns nil if no changes
were made.

---

dump   *str*.dump → *string*

Produces a version of *str* with all nonprinting characters replaced by \nnn notation and all
special characters escaped.

---

each_byte   *str*.each_byte → *enum*
                                                  str.each_byte {| *byte* | *block* } → *str*

1.9   Synonym for String#bytes. The each_byte form is falling out of favor.

---

each_char   *str*.each_char → *enum*
                                                  str.each_char {| *char* | *block* } → *str*

1.9   Synonym for String#chars. The each_char form is falling out of favor.

---

each_codepoint   *str*.each_codepoint → *enum*
                                          str.each_codepoint {| *integer* | *block* } → *str*

1.9   Synonym for String#codepoints.

---

each_line   *str*.each_line(*sep=$/*) → *enum*
                                    str.each_line(*sep=$/*) {| *substr* | *block* } → *str*

1.9   Synonym for String#lines. The each_line form is falling out of favor.

---

empty?   *str*.empty? → true or false

Returns true if *str* has a length of zero.

```
"hello".empty?  # =>   false
"".empty?       # =>   true
```

---

encode   *str*.encode → *a_string*
                                          str.encode(*to_encoding* ⟨ , options ⟩) → *a_string*
                          str.encode(*to_encoding*, *from_encoding*, ⟨ , options ⟩) → *a_string*

1.9   Transcodes *str*, returning a new string encoded as *to_encoding*. If no encoding is given,
transcodes using default_internal encoding. The source encoding is either the current encoding of the string or *from_encoding*. May raise a RuntimeError if characters in the original
string cannot be represented in the target encoding. *options* defines the behavior for invalid
transcodings and other boundary conditions. It can be a hash or an or-ing of integer values.
I recommend the hash form—see Table 27.15 on page 671 for details. Encodings can be
passed as Encoding objects or as names.

```
# encoding: utf-8
ole_in_utf = "olé"
ole_in_utf.encoding    # =>    #<Encoding:UTF-8>
ole_in_utf.dump        # =>    "ol\u{e9}"

ole_in_8859 = ole_in_utf.encode("iso-8859-1")
ole_in_8859.encoding   # =>    #<Encoding:ISO-8859-1>
ole_in_8859.dump       # =>    "ol\xE9"
```

Using a default internal encoding of ISO-8859-1 and a source file encoding of UTF-8:

```
#!/usr/local/rubybook/bin/ruby -E:ISO-8859-1
# encoding: utf-8
utf_string = "olé"
utf_string.encoding    # =>    #<Encoding:UTF-8>
iso_string = utf_string.encode
iso_string.encoding    # =>    #<Encoding:ISO-8859-1>
```

Attempt to transcode a string with characters not available in the destination encoding:

```
# encoding: utf-8
utf = "δog"
utf.encode("iso-8859-1")
```

produces:

```
prog.rb:3:in `encode': "δ" from UTF-8 to ISO-8859-1
      (Encoding::UndefinedConversionError)
from /tmp/prog.rb:3:in `<main>'
```

You can replace the character in error with something else:

```
# encoding: utf-8
utf = "δog"
utf.encode("iso-8859-1", undef: :replace)                # =>    "?og"
utf.encode("iso-8859-1", undef: :replace, replace: "X" ) # =>    "Xog"
```

---

encode! str.encode! $\rightarrow$ str
str.encode!($to\_encoding$ $\langle$, options $\rangle$) $\rightarrow$ str
str.encode!($to\_encoding$, $from\_encoding$, $\langle$, options $\rangle$) $\rightarrow$ str

1.9   Transcodes str in place.

---

encoding str.encoding $\rightarrow$ $an\_encoding$

1.9   Returns the encoding of str.

```
# encoding: utf-8
"cat".encoding   # =>   #<Encoding:UTF-8>
"δog".encoding   # =>   #<Encoding:UTF-8>
```

---

end_with? str.end_with?($\langle$ suffix $\rangle^{+}$) $\rightarrow$ true or false

1.9   Returns true if str ends with any of the given suffices.

```
"Apache".end_with?("ache")                      # =>    true
"ruby code".end_with?("python", "perl", "code")  # =>    true
```

Table 27.15. Options to Encode and Encode!

Option	Meaning
:replace => *string*	Specifies the string to use if :invalid or :undef options are present. If not specified, uFFFD is used for Unicode encodings and ? for others.
:invalid => :replace	Replaces invalid characters in the source string with the replacement string. If :invalid is not specified or nil, raises an exception.
:undef => :replace	Replaces characters that are not available in the destination encoding with the replacement string. If :undef not specified or nil, raises an exception.
:universal_newline => true	Converts crlf and cr line endings to lf.
:crlf_newline => true	Converts lf to crlf.
:cr_newline => true	Converts lf to cr.
:xml => :text | :attr	After encoding, escape characters that would otherwise have special meaning in XML PCDATA or attributes. In all cases, converts & to &, < to <, > to >, and undefined characters to a hexadecimal entity (&#xhh;). For :attr, also converts " to ".

---

eql?   *str*.eql?(*obj*) → true or false

Returns true if *obj* is a String with identical contents to *str*.

```
"cat".eql?("cat")   # =>   true
```

---

force_encoding   *str*.force_encoding(*encoding*) → *str*

1.9

Sets the encoding associated with *str* to *encoding*. Note that this does not change the underlying bytes in *str*—it simply tells Ruby how to interpret those bytes as characters.

```
# encoding: utf-8
δog_in_bytes = [226, 136, 130, 111, 103]  # utf-8 byte sequence
str = δog_in_bytes.pack("C*")
str.encoding   # =>   #<Encoding:ASCII-8BIT>
str.length     # =>   5
str.force_encoding("utf-8")
str.encoding   # =>   #<Encoding:UTF-8>
str.length     # =>   3
str            # =>   "δog"
```

---

getbyte   *str*.getbyte(*offset*) → *int* or nil

1.9

Returns the byte at *offset* (starting from the end of the string if the offset is negative). Returns nil if the offset lies outside the string.

```
# encoding: utf-8
str = "δog"
str.bytes.to_a    # =>    [226, 136, 130, 111, 103]
str.getbyte(0)    # =>    226
str.getbyte(1)    # =>    136
str.getbyte(-1)   # =>    103
str.getbyte(99)   # =>    nil
```

---

gsub   *str*.gsub(*pattern, replacement*) → *string*
                          str.gsub(*pattern*) {| *match* | *block* } → *string str*.gsub(*pattern*) → *enum*

1.9   Returns a copy of *str* with *all* occurrences of *pattern* replaced with either *replacement* or the value of the block. The *pattern* will typically be a Regexp; if it is a String, then no regular expression metacharacters will be interpreted (that is /\d/ will match a digit, but '\d' will match a backslash followed by a *d*).

If a string is used as the replacement, special variables from the match (such as $& and $1) cannot be substituted into it, because substitution into the string occurs before the pattern match starts. However, the sequences \1, \2, and so on, may be used to interpolate successive numbered groups in the match, and \k<*name*> will substitute the corresponding named captures. These sequences are shown in Table 27.16 on the facing page.

In the block form, the current match is passed in as a parameter, and variables such as $1, $2, $`, $&, and $' will be set appropriately. The value returned by the block will be substituted for the match on each call.

The result inherits any tainting in the original string or any supplied replacement string.

```
"hello".gsub(/[aeiou]/, '*')                # =>    "h*ll*"
"hello".gsub(/([aeiou])/, '<\1>')           # =>    "h<e>ll<o>"
"hello".gsub(/./) {|s| s[0].to_s + ' '}     # =>    "h e l l o "
"hello".gsub(/(?<double>l)/, '-\k<double>-') # =>   "he-l--l-o"
```

1.9   If no block or replacement string is given, an enumerator is returned.

```
"hello".gsub(/../).to_a   # =>    ["he", "ll"]
```

1.9   If a hash is given as the replacement, successive matched groups are looked up as keys, and the corresponding values are substituted into the string.

```
repl = Hash.new("?")
repl["a"] = "*"
repl["t"] = "T"
"cat".gsub(/(.)/, repl)    # =>    "?*T"
```

---

gsub!   *str*.gsub!(*pattern, replacement*) → *str* or nil
                                      str.gsub!(*pattern*) {| *match* | *block* } → *str* or nil

---

Performs the substitutions of String#gsub in place, returning *str*, or returning nil if no substitutions were performed.

Table 27.16. Backslash Sequences in Substitution Strings

Sequence	Text That Is Substituted
\1, \2, ... \9	The value matched by the *n*th grouped subexpression
\&	The last match
\`	The part of the string before the match
\'	The part of the string after the match
\+	The highest-numbered group matched
\k<*name*>	The named capture

---

hex

$str.\text{hex} \rightarrow int$

Treats leading characters from *str* as a string of hexadecimal digits (with an optional sign and an optional 0x) and returns the corresponding number. Zero is returned on error.

```
"0x0a".hex     # =>    10
"-1234".hex    # =>    -4660
"0".hex        # =>    0
"wombat".hex   # =>    0
```

---

include?

$str.\text{include?}(\ string\ ) \rightarrow \text{true or false}$

1.9 Returns true if *str* contains the given string.

```
"hello".include? "lo"    # =>    true
"hello".include? "ol"    # =>    false
"hello".include? ?h      # =>    true
```

---

index

$str.\text{index}(\ string\ \langle\ , offset\ \rangle\ )$
$str.\text{index}(\ regexp\ \langle\ , offset\ \rangle\ ) \rightarrow int \text{ or nil}$

Returns the index of the first occurrence of the given substring or pattern in *str*. Returns nil if not found. If the second parameter is present, it specifies the position in the string to begin the search.

```
"hello".index('e')          # =>    1
"hello".index('lo')         # =>    3
"hello".index('a')          # =>    nil
"hello".index(/[aeiou]/, -3) # =>    4
```

---

insert

$str.\text{insert}(\ index, string\ ) \rightarrow str$

Inserts *string* before the character at the given *index*, modifying *str*. Negative indices count from the end of the string and insert *after* the given character. After the insertion, *str* will contain *string* starting at *index*.

```
"abcd".insert(0, 'X')    # =>    "Xabcd"
"abcd".insert(3, 'X')    # =>    "abcXd"
"abcd".insert(4, 'X')    # =>    "abcdX"
"abcd".insert(-3, 'X')   # =>    "abXcd"
"abcd".insert(-1, 'X')   # =>    "abcdX"
```

String

intern *str*.intern → *symbol*

Returns the Symbol corresponding to *str*, creating the symbol if it did not previously exist. Can intern any string, not just identifiers. See Symbol#id2name on page 694.

```
"Koala".intern   # =>   :Koala
sym = "$1.50 for a soda!?!?".intern
sym.to_s         # =>   "$1.50 for a soda!?!?"
```

length *str*.length → *int*

Returns the number of characters in *str*. See also String#bytesize.

lines *str*.lines(*sep=$/*) → *enum*
str.lines(*sep=$/*) { | *substr* | *block* } → *str*

1.9

Splits *str* using the supplied parameter as the record separator ($/ by default), passing each substring in turn to the supplied block. If a zero-length record separator is supplied, the string is split into paragraphs, each terminated by multiple \n characters. With no block, returns a enumerator.

```
print "Example one\n"
"hello\nworld".lines {|s| p s}
print "Example two\n"
"hello\nworld".lines('l') {|s| p s}
print "Example three\n"
"hello\n\n\nworld".lines('') {|s| p s}
```

produces:

```
Example one
"hello\n"
"world"
Example two
"hel"
"l"
"o\nworl"
"d"
Example three
"hello\n\n\n"
"world"
```

ljust *str*.ljust(*width, padding=" "*) → *string*

If *width* is greater than the length of *str*, returns a new String of length *width* with *str* left justified and padded with copies of *padding*; otherwise, returns a copy of *str*.

```
"hello".ljust(4)          # =>   "hello"
"hello".ljust(20)         # =>   "hello⎵⎵⎵⎵⎵⎵⎵⎵⎵⎵⎵⎵⎵⎵⎵"
"hello".ljust(20, "*")    # =>   "hello***************"
"hello".ljust(20, " dolly")  # =>   "hello⎵dolly⎵dolly⎵do"
```

lstrip

str.lstrip → *string*

Returns a copy of *str* with leading whitespace characters removed. Also see the methods String#rstrip and String#strip.

```
"  hello  ".lstrip       # =>   "hello␣␣"
"\000 hello  ".lstrip    # =>   "\x00␣hello␣␣"
"hello".lstrip           # =>   "hello"
```

lstrip!

str.lstrip! →
self or nil

Removes leading whitespace characters from *str*, returning nil if no change was made. See also String#rstrip! and String#strip!.

```
"  hello  ".lstrip!   # =>   "hello␣␣"
"hello".lstrip!       # =>   nil
```

match

str.match(*pattern*) → *match_data* or nil
str.match(*pattern*) { | *matchdata* | *block* } → *obj*

1.9

Converts *pattern* to a Regexp (if it isn't already one) and then invokes its match method on *str*. If a block is given, the block is passed the MatchData object, and the match method returns the value of the block.

```
'seed'.match('(.)\1')                      # => #<MatchData "ee" 1:"e">
'seed'.match('(.)\1')[0]                    # => "ee"
'seed'.match(/(.)\1/)[0]                     # => "ee"
'seed'.match('ll')                           # => nil
'seed'.match('ll') {|md| md[0].upcase }      # => nil
'seed'.match('xx')                           # => nil
```

next

str.next → *string*

Synonym for String#succ.

next!

str.next! → *str*

Synonym for String#succ!.

oct

str.oct → *int*

Treats leading characters of *str* as a string of octal digits (with an optional sign) and returns the corresponding number. Returns 0 if the conversion fails.

```
"123".oct       # =>   83
"-377".oct      # =>   -255
"bad".oct       # =>   0
"0377bad".oct   # =>   255
```

ord

str.ord → *int*

1.9

Returns the integer code point of the first character of *str*. Note that it isn't quite the inverse of Integer#chr, because the latter does not deal with encodings.

```
# encoding: utf-8
"d".ord     # =>   100
"dog".ord   # =>   100
"δ".ord     # =>   8706
```

partition

str.partition(*pattern*) → [*before, match after*]

1.9

Searches *str* for *pattern* (which may be a string or a regular expression). Returns a three-element array containing the part of the string before the pattern, the part that matched the pattern, and the part after the match. If the pattern does not match, the entire string will be returned as the first element of the array, and the other two entries will be empty strings.

```
"THX1138".partition("11")     # =>   ["THX", "11", "38"]
"THX1138".partition(/\d\d/)   # =>   ["THX", "11", "38"]
"THX1138".partition("99")     # =>   ["THX1138", "", ""]
```

replace

str.replace(*string*) → *str*

Replaces the contents, encoding, and taintedness of *str* with the corresponding values in *string*.

```
s = "hello"        # =>   "hello"
s.replace "world"  # =>   "world"
```

reverse

str.reverse → *string*

Returns a new string with the characters from *str* in reverse order.

```
# Every problem contains its own solution...
"stressed".reverse   # =>   "desserts"
```

reverse!

str.reverse! → *str*

Reverses *str* in place.

rindex

str.rindex(*string* ⟨ , *int* ⟩) → *int* or nil
str.rindex(*regexp* ⟨ , *int* ⟩) → *int* or nil

Returns the index of the last occurrence of the given substring, character, or pattern in *str*. Returns nil if not found. If the second parameter is present, it specifies the position in the string to end the search—characters beyond this point will not be considered.

```
"hello".rindex('e')         # =>   1
"hello".rindex('l')         # =>   3
"hello".rindex('a')         # =>   nil
"hello".rindex(/[aeiou]/, -2) # =>   1
```

rjust

str.rjust(*width, padding*=" ") → *string*

If *width* is greater than the length of *str*, returns a new String of length *width* with *str* right justified and padded with copies of *padding*; otherwise, returns a copy of *str*.

```
"hello".rjust(4)             # =>    "hello"
"hello".rjust(20)            # =>    "⌴⌴⌴⌴⌴⌴⌴⌴⌴⌴⌴⌴⌴⌴⌴hello"
"hello".rjust(20, "-")       # =>    "---------------hello"
"hello".rjust(20, "padding") # =>    "paddingpaddingphello"
```

---

rpartition
str.rpartition(*pattern*) → [*before, match after*]

Searches *str* for *pattern* (which may be a string or a regular expression), starting at the end of the string. Returns a three-element array containing the part of the string before the pattern, the part that matched the pattern, and the part after the match. If the pattern does not match, the entire string will be returned as the last element of the array, and the other two entries will be empty strings.

```
"THX1138".rpartition("1")    # =>    ["THX1", "1", "38"]
"THX1138".rpartition(/1\d/)  # =>    ["THX1", "13", "8"]
"THX1138".rpartition("99")   # =>    ["", "", "THX1138"]
```

---

rstrip
str.rstrip → *string*

Returns a copy of *str*, stripping first trailing NUL characters and then stripping trailing whitespace characters. See also String#lstrip and String#strip.

```
"  hello  ".rstrip     # =>    "⌴⌴hello"
"  hello \000 ".rstrip # =>    "⌴⌴hello"
"  hello  \000".rstrip # =>    "⌴⌴hello"
"hello".rstrip         # =>    "hello"
```

---

rstrip!
str.rstrip! → self or nil

Removes trailing NUL characters and then removes trailing whitespace characters from *str*. Returns nil if no change was made. See also String#lstrip! and #strip!.

```
"  hello  ".rstrip!  # =>    "⌴⌴hello"
"hello".rstrip!      # =>    nil
```

---

scan
str.scan(*pattern*) → *array*
str.scan(*pattern*) {| *match, ...* | *block* } → *str*

Both forms iterate through *str*, matching the pattern (which may be a Regexp or a String). For each match, a result is generated and either added to the result array or passed to the block. If the pattern contains no groups, each individual result consists of the matched string, $&. If the pattern contains groups, each individual result is itself an array containing one entry per group. If the pattern is a String, it is interpreted literally (in other words, it is not taken to be a regular expression pattern).

```
a = "cruel world"
a.scan(/\w+/)        # =>    ["cruel", "world"]
a.scan(/.../)        # =>    ["cru", "el ", "wor"]
a.scan(/(...)/)      # =>    [["cru"], ["el "], ["wor"]]
a.scan(/(..)(..)/)   # =>    [["cr", "ue"], ["l ", "wo"]]
```

And the block form:

```
a.scan(/\w+/) {|w| print "<<#{w}>> " }
puts
a.scan(/(.)(.)/) {|a,b| print b, a }
puts
```

produces:

```
<<cruel>> <<world>>
rceu lowlr
```

---

setbyte str.setbyte(*offset*, *byte*) → *byte*

1.9

Sets the byte at *offset* (starting from the end of the string if the offset is negative) to *byte*. Cannot be used to change the length of the string. Does not change the encoding of the string.

```
str = "defog"
# a utf-8 delta character
str.setbyte(0, 226)   # =>   226
str.setbyte(1, 136)   # =>   136
str.setbyte(2, 130)   # =>   130
str                   # =>   "\xE2\x88\x82og"
str.length            # =>   5
str.force_encoding("utf-8")
str.length            # =>   3
str                   # =>   "δog"
```

---

size str.size → *int*

Synonym for String#length.

---

slice str.slice(*int*) → *string* or nil
str.slice(*int*, *int*) → *string* or nil
str.slice(*range*) → *string* or nil
str.slice(*regexp*) → *string* or nil
str.slice(*match_string*) → *string* or nil

Synonym for String#[ ].

```
a = "hello there"
a.slice(1)        # =>   "e"
a.slice(1,3)      # =>   "ell"
a.slice(1..3)     # =>   "ell"
a.slice(-3,2)     # =>   "er"
a.slice(-4..-2)   # =>   "her"

a.slice(-2..-4)       # =>   ""
a.slice(/th[aeiou]/)  # =>   "the"
a.slice("lo")         # =>   "lo"
a.slice("bye")        # =>   nil
```

slice!

str.slice!(*int*) → *string* or nil
str.slice!(*int, int*) → *string* or nil
str.slice!(*range*) → *string* or nil
str.slice!(*regexp*) → *string* or nil
str.slice!(*match_string*) → *string* or nil

Deletes the specified portion from *str* and returns the portion deleted. The forms that take a Fixnum will raise an IndexError if the value is out of range; the Range form will raise a RangeError, and the Regexp and String forms will silently not change the string.

```
string = "this is a string"
string.slice!(2)        # =>   "i"
string.slice!(3..6)     # =>   " is "
string.slice!(/s.*t/)   # =>   "sa st"
string.slice!("r")      # =>   "r"
string                  # =>   "thing"
```

split

str.split(*pattern*=$;, ⟨ *limit* ⟩) → *array*

Divides *str* into substrings based on a delimiter, returning an array of these substrings.

If *pattern* is a String, then its contents are used as the delimiter when splitting *str*. If *pattern* is a single space, *str* is split on whitespace, with leading whitespace and runs of contiguous whitespace characters ignored.

If *pattern* is a Regexp, *str* is divided where the pattern matches. Whenever the pattern matches a zero-length string, *str* is split into individual characters. If pattern includes groups, these groups will be included in the returned values.

If *pattern* is omitted, the value of $; is used. If $; is nil (which is the default), *str* is split on whitespace as if "␣" were specified.

If the *limit* parameter is omitted, trailing empty fields are suppressed. If *limit* is a positive number, at most that number of fields will be returned (if *limit* is 1, the entire string is returned as the only entry in an array). If negative, there is no limit to the number of fields returned, and trailing null fields are not suppressed.

```
" now's   the time".split      # =>   ["now's", "the", "time"]
" now's   the time".split(' ')  # =>   ["now's", "the", "time"]
" now's   the time".split(/ /)  # =>   ["", "now's", "", "", "the",
                                #      "time"]
"a@1bb@2ccc".split(/@\d/)       # =>   ["a", "bb", "ccc"]
"a@1bb@2ccc".split(/@(\d)/)     # =>   ["a", "1", "bb", "2", "ccc"]
"1, 2.34,56, 7".split(/,\s*/)   # =>   ["1", "2.34", "56", "7"]
"hello".split(//)               # =>   ["h", "e", "l", "l", "o"]
"hello".split(//, 3)            # =>   ["h", "e", "llo"]
"hi mom".split(/\s*/)           # =>   ["h", "i", "m", "o", "m"]

"".split                        # =>   []
```

```
"mellow yellow".split("ello")    # =>   ["m", "w y", "w"]
"1,2,,3,4,,".split(',')          # =>   ["1", "2", "", "3", "4"]
"1,2,,3,4,,".split(',', 4)       # =>   ["1", "2", "", "3,4,,"]
"1,2,,3,4,,".split(',', -4)      # =>   ["1", "2", "", "3", "4", "", ""]
```

---

squeeze   *str*.squeeze(⟨ *string* ⟩*) → *squeezed_string*

Builds a set of characters from the *string* parameter(s) using the procedure described for
String#count on page 668. Returns a new string where runs of the same character that occur
in this set are replaced by a single character. If no arguments are given, all runs of identical
characters are replaced by a single character.

```
"yellow moon".squeeze              # =>   "yelow mon"
"  now   is  the".squeeze(" ")     # =>   " now is the"
"putters putt balls".squeeze("m-z") # =>  "puters put balls"
```

---

squeeze!   *str*.squeeze!(⟨ *string* ⟩*) → *str* or nil

Squeezes *str* in place, returning *str*. Returns nil if no changes were made.

---

start_with?   *str*.start_with?(⟨ *suffix* ⟩+) → true or false

1.9   Returns true if *str* starts with any of the given prefixes.

```
"Apache".start_with?("Apa")                        # =>   true
"ruby code".start_with?("python", "perl", "ruby")  # =>   true
```

---

strip   *str*.strip → *string*

Returns a copy of *str* with leading whitespace and trailing NUL and whitespace characters
removed.

```
"    hello    ".strip  # =>   "hello"
"\tgoodbye\r\n".strip  # =>   "goodbye"
"goodbye \000".strip   # =>   "goodbye"
"goodbye \000 ".strip  # =>   "goodbye"
```

---

strip!   *str*.strip! → *str* or nil

Removes leading whitespace and trailing NUL and whitespace characters from *str*. Returns
nil if *str* was not altered.

---

sub   *str*.sub(*pattern*, *replacement*) → *string*
                                               str.sub(*pattern*) {| *match* | *block* } → *string*

Returns a copy of *str* with the *first* occurrence of *pattern* replaced with either *replacement*
or the value of the block. See the description of String#gsub on page 672 for a description
of the parameters.

```
"hello".sub(/[aeiou]/, '*')                  # =>   "h*llo"
"hello".sub(/([aeiou])/, '<\1>')             # =>   "h<e>llo"
"hello".sub(/./) {|s| s[0].to_s + ' '}       # =>   "h ello"
"hello".sub(/(?<double>l)/, '-\k<double>-')  # =>   "he-l-lo"
```

sub!   *str*.sub!(*pattern*, *replacement*) → *str* or nil
                            str.sub!(*pattern*) {| *match* | *block* } → *str* or nil

Performs the substitutions of String#sub in place, returning *str*. Returns nil if no substitutions were performed.

succ   *str*.succ → *string*

Returns the successor to *str*. The successor is calculated by incrementing characters starting from the rightmost alphanumeric (or the rightmost character if there are no alphanumerics) in the string. Incrementing a digit always results in another digit, and incrementing a letter results in another letter of the same case. Incrementing nonalphanumerics uses the underlying character set's collating sequence.

If the increment generates a "carry," the character to the left of it is incremented. This process repeats until there is no carry, adding a character if necessary. An exception is when the carry is generated by a sequence of digits in a string containing digits, nonalpha characters, and more digits, in which case the carry applies to the digits. This allows for incrementing (for example) numbers with decimal places.

```
"abcd".succ        # =>   "abce"
"THX1138".succ     # =>   "THX1139"
"<<koala>>".succ   # =>   "<<koalb>>"
"1999zzz".succ     # =>   "2000aaa"
"ZZZ9999".succ     # =>   "AAAA0000"
"***".succ         # =>   "**+"
"1.9".succ         # =>   "2.0"
"1//9".succ        # =>   "2//0"
"1/9/9/9".succ     # =>   "2/0/0/0"
"1x9".succ         # =>   "1y0"
```

succ!   *str*.succ! → *str*

Equivalent to String#succ but modifies the receiver in place.

sum   *str*.sum(*n*=16) → *int*

Returns a basic *n*-bit checksum of the characters in *str*, where *n* is the optional parameter, defaulting to 16. The result is simply the sum of the binary value of each character in *str* modulo $2^n - 1$. This is not a particularly good checksum—see the digest libraries on page 736 for better alternatives.

```
"now is the time".sum      # =>   1408
"now is the time".sum(8)   # =>   128
```

swapcase   *str*.swapcase → *string*

Returns a copy of *str* with uppercase alphabetic characters converted to lowercase and lowercase characters converted to uppercase. The mapping depends on the string encoding, but not all encodings produce expected results.

```
# encoding: utf-8
"Hello".swapcase         # =>   "hELLO"
"cYbEr_PuNk11".swapcase  # =>   "CyBeR_pUnK11"
"δOg".swapcase           # =>   "δoG"
```

swapcase!   *str*.swapcase! → *str* or nil

Equivalent to String#swapcase but modifies *str* in place, returning *str*. Returns nil if no changes were made.

to_c   *str*.to_c → *float*

Returns the result of interpreting leading characters in *str* as a complex number. Extraneous characters past the end of a valid number are ignored. If there is not a valid number at the start of *str*, Complex(0,0) is returned. The method never raises an exception.

```
"123".to_c      # =>   123+0i
"4+5/6i".to_c   # =>   4+5/6i
"thx1138".to_c  # =>   0+0i
```

to_f   *str*.to_f → *complex*

Returns the result of interpreting leading characters in *str* as a floating-point number. Extraneous characters past the end of a valid number are ignored. If there is not a valid number at the start of *str*, 0.0 is returned. The method never raises an exception (use Kernel.Float to validate numbers).

```
"123.45e1".to_f       # =>   1234.5
"45.67 degrees".to_f  # =>   45.67
"thx1138".to_f        # =>   0.0
```

to_i   *str*.to_i(*base*=10) → *int*

Returns the result of interpreting leading characters in *str* as an integer base *base* (2 to 36). Given a base of zero, to_i looks for leading 0, 0b, 0o, 0d, or 0x and sets the base accordingly. Leading spaces are ignored, and leading plus or minus signs are honored. Extraneous characters past the end of a valid number are ignored. If there is not a valid number at the start of *str*, 0 is returned. The method never raises an exception.

```
"12345".to_i            # =>   12345
"99 red balloons".to_i  # =>   99
"0a".to_i               # =>   0
"0a".to_i(16)           # =>   10
"0x10".to_i             # =>   0
"0x10".to_i(0)          # =>   16
"-0x10".to_i(0)         # =>   -16
"hello".to_i            # =>   0
"hello".to_i(30)        # =>   14167554
"1100101".to_i(2)       # =>   101
"1100101".to_i(8)       # =>   294977
"1100101".to_i(10)      # =>   1100101
"1100101".to_i(16)      # =>   17826049
"1100101".to_i(24)      # =>   199066177
```

to_r

1.9
Returns the result of interpreting leading characters in *str* as a rational number. Extraneous characters past the end of a valid number are ignored. If there is not a valid number at the start of *str*, Rational(0,1) is returned. The method never raises an exception.

```
"123".to_r      # =>   123/1
"5/6".to_r      # =>   5/6
"25/100".to_r   # =>   1/4
"thx1138".to_r  # =>   (0/1)
```

to_s

Returns the receiver.

to_str

Synonym for String#to_s. to_str is used by methods such as String#concat to convert their arguments to a string. Unlike to_s, which is supported by almost all classes, to_str is normally implemented only by those classes that act like strings. Of the built-in classes, only Exception and String implement to_str.

to_sym

Returns the symbol for *str*. This can create symbols that cannot be represented using the :xxx notation. A synonym for String#intern.

```
s = 'cat'.to_sym        # =>   :cat
s == :cat               # =>   true
'cat and dog'.to_sym    # =>   :"cat and dog"
s == :'cat and dog'     # =>   false
```

tr

Returns a copy of *str* with the characters in *from_string* replaced by the corresponding characters in *to_string*. If *to_string* is shorter than *from_string*, it is padded with its last character. Both strings may use the c_1–c_2 notation to denote ranges of characters, and *from_string* may start with a ^, which denotes all characters except those listed.

```
"hello".tr('aeiou', '*')   # =>   "h*ll*"
"hello".tr('^aeiou', '*')  # =>   "*e**o"
"hello".tr('el', 'ip')     # =>   "hippo"
"hello".tr('a-y', 'b-z')   # =>   "ifmmp"
```

tr!

Translates *str* in place, using the same rules as String#tr. Returns *str* or returns nil if no changes were made.

---

tr_s   *str*.tr_s(*from_string*, *to_string*) → *string*

Processes a copy of *str* as described under String#tr and then removes duplicate characters in regions that were affected by the translation.

```
"hello".tr_s('l', 'r')    # =>    "hero"
"hello".tr_s('el', '*')   # =>    "h*o"
"hello".tr_s('el', 'hx')  # =>    "hhxo"
```

---

tr_s!   *str*.tr_s!(*from_string*, *to_string*) → *str* or nil

Performs String#tr_s processing on *str* in place, returning *str*. Returns nil if no changes were made.

---

unpack   *str*.unpack(*format*) → *array*

Decodes *str* (which may contain binary data) according to the format string, returning an array of the extracted values. The format string consists of a sequence of single-character directives, summarized in Table 27.17 on the next page. Each directive may be followed by a number, indicating the number of times to repeat this directive. An asterisk (*) will use up all remaining elements. The directives sSiIlL may each be followed by an underscore (_) or bang (!) to use the underlying platform's native size for the specified type; otherwise, it uses a platform-independent consistent size. Spaces are ignored in the format string. Comments starting with # to the next newline or end of string are also ignored. The encoding of the string is ignored; unpack treats the string as a sequence of bytes. See also Array#pack on page 448.

```
"abc \0\0abc \0\0".unpack('A6Z6')    # =>    ["abc", "abc "]
"abc \0\0".unpack('a3a3')            # =>    ["abc", " \x00\x00"]
"aa".unpack('b8B8')                  # =>    ["10000110", "01100001"]
"aaa".unpack('h2H2c')                # =>    ["16", "61", 97]
"\xfe\xff\xfe\xff".unpack('sS')      # =>    [-2, 65534]
"now=20is".unpack('M*')              # =>    ["now is"]
"whole".unpack('xax2aX2aX1aX2a')     # =>    ["h", "e", "l", "l", "o"]
```

---

upcase   *str*.upcase → *string*

Returns a copy of *str* with all lowercase letters replaced with their uppercase counterparts. The mapping depends on the string encoding, but not all encodings produce expected results.

```
# encoding: utf-8
"hEllO".upcase  # =>    "HELLO"
"δog".upcase    # =>    "δOG"
```

---

upcase!   *str*.upcase! → *str* or nil

Upcases the contents of *str*, returning nil if no changes were made.

Table 27.17. Directives for String#unpack

Format	Function	Returns
A	Sequence of bytes with trailing NULs and ASCII spaces removed.	String
a	Sequence of bytes.	String
B	Extracts bits from each byte (MSB first).	String
b	Extracts bits from each byte (LSB first).	String
C	Extracts a byte as an unsigned integer.	Fixnum
c	Extracts a byte as an integer.	Fixnum
d,D	Treat *sizeof(double)* bytes as a native double.	Float
E	Treats *sizeof(double)* bytes as a double in little-endian byte order.	Float
e	Treats *sizeof(float)* bytes as a float in little-endian byte order.	Float
f,F	Treats *sizeof(float)* bytes as a native float.	Float
G	Treats *sizeof(double)* bytes as a double in network byte order.	Float
g	Treats *sizeof(float)* bytes as a float in network byte order.	Float
H	Extracts hex nibbles from each byte (most significant first).	String
h	Extracts hex nibbles from each byte (least significant first).	String
I	Treats *sizeof(int)*[1] successive bytes as an unsigned native integer.	Integer
i	Treats *sizeof(int)*[1] successive bytes as a signed native integer.	Integer
L	Treats four[1] successive bytes as an unsigned native long integer.	Integer
l	Treats four[1] successive characters as a signed native long integer.	Integer
M	Extracts a quoted-printable string.	String
m	Extracts a Base64-encoded string. By default, accepts \n and \r. "m0" rejects these.	String
N	Treats four bytes as an unsigned long in network byte order.	Fixnum
n	Treats two bytes as an unsigned short in network byte order.	Fixnum
P	Treats *sizeof(char *)* bytes as a pointer and returns *len* bytes from the referenced location.	String
p	Treats *sizeof(char *)* bytes as a pointer to a null-terminated string.	String
Q	Treats eight bytes as an unsigned quad word (64 bits).	Integer
q	Treats eight bytes as a signed quad word (64 bits).	Integer
S	Treats two[1] bytes characters as an unsigned short in native byte order.	Fixnum
s	Treats two[1] successive bytes as a signed short in native byte order.	Fixnum
U	Extracts UTF-8 characters as unsigned integers.	Integer
u	Extracts a UU-encoded string.	String
V	Treats four bytes as an unsigned long in little-endian byte order.	Fixnum
v	Treats two bytes as an unsigned short in little-endian byte order.	Fixnum
w	BER-compressed integer (see Array#pack for more information).	Integer
X	Skips backward one byte.	—
x	Skips forward one byte.	—
Z	String with trailing NULs removed.	String
@	Skips to the byte offset given by the length argument.	—

[1] May be modified by appending _ or ! to the directive.

---

upto   *str*.upto(*string*) {| *s* | *block* } → *str* or *enumerator*

1.9   Iterates through successive values, starting at *str* and ending at *string* inclusive, passing each
value in turn to the block. The String#succ method is used to generate each value. Returns
an Enumerator object if no block is given.

```
"a8".upto("b6") {|s| print s, ' ' }
for s in "a8".."b6"
  print s, ' '
end
```

produces:

```
a8 a9 b0 b1 b2 b3 b4 b5 b6
a8 a9 b0 b1 b2 b3 b4 b5 b6
```

---

valid_encoding?   *str*.valid_encoding? → true or false

1.9   Returns true if *str* contains a valid byte sequence in its current encoding.

```
# encoding: binary
str = "\xE2"
str.force_encoding("utf-8")
str.valid_encoding?   # =>   false
str = "\xE2\x88\x82"
str.force_encoding("utf-8")
str.valid_encoding?   # =>   true
```

S tring

Class
Struct < Object

Subclasses: Struct::Tms

A Struct is a convenient way to bundle a number of attributes together, using accessor methods, without having to write an explicit class.

The Struct class is a generator of specific classes, each one of which is defined to hold a set of variables and their accessors. In these examples, we'll call the generated class *Customer*, and we'll show an example instance of that class as *joe*.

Also see OpenStruct on page 778.

In the descriptions that follow, the parameter *symbol* refers to a symbol, which is either a quoted string or a Symbol (such as :name).

Mixes in

Enumerable:

all?, any?, collect, count, cycle, detect, drop, drop_while, each_cons, each_slice, each_with_index, entries, find, find_all, find_index, first, grep, group_by, include?, inject, map, max, max_by, member?, min, min_by, minmax, minmax_by, none?, one?, partition, reduce, reject, select, sort, sort_by, take, take_while, to_a, zip

Class methods

new

$$\text{Struct.new(} \langle \textit{string} \rangle \langle \textit{, symbol} \rangle^+ \text{)} \rightarrow \textit{Customer}$$
$$\text{Struct.new(} \langle \textit{string} \rangle \langle \textit{, symbol} \rangle^+ \text{) \{ } \textit{block} \text{ \} } \rightarrow \textit{Customer}$$

Creates a new class, named by *string*, containing accessor methods for the given symbols. If the name *string* is omitted, an anonymous structure class will be created. Otherwise, the name of this struct will appear as a constant in class Struct, so it must be unique for all Structs in the system and should start with a capital letter. Assigning a structure class to a constant effectively gives the class the name of the constant.

Struct.new returns a new Class object, which can then be used to create specific instances of the new structure. The remaining methods listed next (class and instance) are defined for this generated class. See the description that follows for an example.

```
# Create a structure with a name in Struct
Struct.new("Customer", :name, :address)    # =>   Struct::Customer
Struct::Customer.new("Dave", "123 Main")   # =>   #<struct
                                                  Struct::Customer
                                                  name="Dave",
                                                  address="123 Main">

# Create a structure named by its constant
Customer = Struct.new(:name, :address)   # =>   Customer
Customer.new("Dave", "123 Main")         # =>   #<struct Customer
                                                name="Dave", address="123
                                                Main">
```

S
truct

A block passed to the constructor is evaluated in the context of the new struct's class and hence allows you conveniently to add instance methods to the new struct.

```
Customer = Struct.new(:name, :address) do
  def to_s
    "#{self.name} lives at #{self.address}"
  end
end
Customer.new("Dave", "123 Main").to_s   # =>    "Dave lives at 123 Main"
```

---

new   *Customer*.new(⟨ *obj* ⟩⁺) → *joe*

Creates a new instance of a structure (the class created by Struct.new). The number of actual parameters must be less than or equal to the number of attributes defined for this class; unset parameters default to nil. Passing too many parameters will raise an ArgumentError.

```
Customer = Struct.new(:name, :address, :zip)

joe = Customer.new("Joe Smith", "123 Maple, Anytown NC", 12345)
joe.name  # =>   "Joe Smith"
joe.zip   # =>   12345
```

[ ]   *Customer*[⟨ *obj* ⟩⁺] → *joe*

Synonym for new (for the generated structure).

```
Customer = Struct.new(:name, :address, :zip)

joe = Customer["Joe Smith", "123 Maple, Anytown NC", 12345]
joe.name  # =>   "Joe Smith"
joe.zip   # =>   12345
```

---

members   *Customer*.members → *array*

1.9   Returns an array of symbols representing the names of the instance variables.

```
Customer = Struct.new("Customer", :name, :address, :zip)
Customer.members   # =>   [:name, :address, :zip]
```

Instance methods

==   *joe* == *other_struct* → true or false

Equality—Returns true if *other_struct* is equal to this one: they must be of the same class as generated by Struct.new, and the values of all instance variables must be equal (according to Object#==).

```
Customer = Struct.new(:name, :address, :zip)

joe   = Customer.new("Joe Smith", "123 Maple, Anytown NC", 12345)
joejr = Customer.new("Joe Smith", "123 Maple, Anytown NC", 12345)
jane  = Customer.new("Jane Doe", "456 Elm, Anytown NC", 12345)

joe == joejr  # =>    true
joe == jane   # =>    false
```

[ ]

$$joe[\ symbol\ ] \rightarrow obj$$
$$joe[\ integer\ ] \rightarrow obj$$

Attribute Reference—Returns the value of the instance variable named by *symbol* or indexed (0..*length* − 1) by *int*. Raises NameError if the named variable does not exist or raises IndexError if the index is out of range.

```
Customer = Struct.new(:name, :address, :zip)
joe = Customer.new("Joe Smith", "123 Maple, Anytown NC", 12345)
joe["name"]   # =>   "Joe Smith"
joe[:name]    # =>   "Joe Smith"
joe[0]        # =>   "Joe Smith"
```

[ ]=

$$joe[\ symbol\ ] = obj \rightarrow obj$$
$$joe[\ int\ ] = obj \rightarrow obj$$

Attribute Assignment—Assigns to the instance variable named by *symbol* or *int* the value *obj* and returns it. Raises a NameError if the named variable does not exist or raises an IndexError if the index is out of range.

```
Customer = Struct.new(:name, :address, :zip)
joe = Customer.new("Joe Smith", "123 Maple, Anytown NC", 12345)
joe["name"] = "Luke"
joe[:zip]   = "90210"
joe.name   # =>   "Luke"
joe.zip    # =>   "90210"
```

each

$$joe.each\ \{\ |\ obj\ |\ block\ \}\ \rightarrow joe$$

Calls *block* once for each instance variable, passing the value as a parameter.

```
Customer = Struct.new(:name, :address, :zip)
joe = Customer.new("Joe Smith", "123 Maple, Anytown NC", 12345)
joe.each {|x| puts(x) }
```

produces:

```
Joe Smith
123 Maple, Anytown NC
12345
```

each_pair

$$joe.each\_pair\ \{\ |\ symbol,\ obj\ |\ block\ \}\ \rightarrow joe$$

Calls *block* once for each instance variable, passing the name (as a symbol) and the value as parameters.

```
Customer = Struct.new(:name, :address, :zip)
joe = Customer.new("Joe Smith", "123 Maple, Anytown NC", 12345)
joe.each_pair {|name, value| puts("#{name} => #{value}") }
```

produces:

```
name => Joe Smith
address => 123 Maple, Anytown NC
zip => 12345
```

Struct

---

length   *joe*.length → *int*

Returns the number of attributes.

```
Customer = Struct.new(:name, :address, :zip)
joe = Customer.new("Joe Smith", "123 Maple, Anytown NC", 12345)
joe.length  # =>  3
```

---

members   *joe*.members → *array*

Returns an array of strings representing the names of the instance variables.

```
Customer = Struct.new(:name, :address, :zip)
joe = Customer.new("Joe Smith", "123 Maple, Anytown NC", 12345)
joe.members  # =>  [:name, :address, :zip]
```

---

size   *joe*.size → *int*

Synonym for Struct#length.

---

to_a   *joe*.to_a → *array*

Returns the values for this instance as an array.

```
Customer = Struct.new(:name, :address, :zip)
joe = Customer.new("Joe Smith", "123 Maple, Anytown NC", 12345)
joe.to_a[1]  # =>  "123 Maple, Anytown NC"
```

---

values   *joe*.values → *array*

Synonym for to_a.

---

values_at   *joe*.values_at(⟨ *selector* ⟩*) → *array*

Returns an array containing the elements in *joe* corresponding to the given indices. The selectors may be integer indices or ranges.

```
Lots = Struct.new(:a, :b, :c, :d, :e, :f)
l = Lots.new(11, 22, 33, 44, 55, 66)
l.values_at(1, 3, 5)    # =>  [22, 44, 66]
l.values_at(0, 2, 4)    # =>  [11, 33, 55]
l.values_at(-1, -3, -5) # =>  [66, 44, 22]
```

Class
Struct::Tms < Struct

This structure is returned by Process.times. It holds information on process times on those platforms that support it. Not all values are valid on all platforms. This structure contains the following instance variables and the corresponding accessors:

utime	Amount of user CPU time, in seconds
stime	Amount of system CPU time, in seconds
cutime	Total of completed child processes' user CPU time, in seconds (always 0 on Windows)
cstime	Total of completed child processes' system CPU time, in seconds (always 0 on Windows)

See also Struct on page 687 and Process.times on page 636.

```
def eat_cpu
  100_000.times { Math.sin(0.321) }
end
3.times { fork { eat_cpu } }
eat_cpu
Process.waitall
t = Process::times
[ t.utime, t.stime]        # =>   [0.03, 0.0]
[ t.cutime, t.cstime ]     # =>   [0.07, 0.0]
```

Class **Symbol** < Object

Symbol objects represent names inside the Ruby interpreter. They are generated using the :name or :"arbitrary text" literal syntax and by using the various to_sym methods. The same Symbol object will be created for a given name string for the duration of a program's execution, regardless of the context or meaning of that name. Symbols can be arbitrary sequences of characters. Like strings, a symbol literal containing any characters with the top-bit set will have an encoding determined by the encoding of the source file containing the definition.

Ruby 1.9 adds a lot of new string-like functionality to symbols.

Mixes in

Comparable:

    <, <=, ==, >=, >, between?

Class methods

all_symbols   Symbol.all_symbols → *array*

Returns an array of all the symbols currently in Ruby's symbol table.

```
Symbol.all_symbols.size    # =>   1485
Symbol.all_symbols[1,20]   # =>   [:"<IFUNC>", :"<CFUNC>", :respond_to?,
                                   :"#__ThrowState__",
                                   :"core#set_method_alias",
                                   :"core#set_variable_alias",
                                   :"core#undef_method",
                                   :"core#define_method",
                                   :"core#define_singleton_method",
                                   :"core#set_postexe", :each, :length,
                                   :lambda, :intern, :gets, :succ,
                                   :method_missing, :send, :__send__,
                                   :initialize]
```

Instance methods

<=>   *sym* <=> *other_sym* → −1, 0, +1

Compares *sym* to *other_sym* after converting each to strings. <=> is the basis for the methods <, <=, >, >=, and between?, included from module Comparable. The method Symbol#== does not use Comparable#==.

```
:abcdef <=> :abcde    # =>   1
:abcdef <=> :abcdef   # =>   0
:abcdef <=> :abcdefg  # =>   -1
:abcdef <=> :ABCDEF   # =>   1
```

==   *sym* == *obj* → true or false

Returns true only if *sym* and *obj* are symbols with the same object_id.

```
:abcdef == :abcde    # =>   false
:abcdef == :abcdef   # =>   true
```

=~ sym =~ obj → int or nil

1.9 Converts *sym* to a string and matches it against *obj.* with the same object_id.

```
:abcdef =~ /.[aeiou]/   # =>   3
:abcdef =~ /xx/         # =>   nil
```

[ ] $sym[\ int\ ]$ → *string* or nil
$sym[\ int,\ int\ ]$ → *string* or nil
$sym[\ range\ ]$ → *string* or nil
$sym[\ regexp\ ]$ → *string* or nil
$sym[\ regexp,\ int\ ]$ → *string* or nil
$sym[\ string\ ]$ → *string* or nil

1.9 Converts *sym* to a string and then indexes it using the same parameters as String#[].

```
:"hello there"[1]                # =>   "e"
:"hello there"[1,3]              # =>   "ell"
:"hello there"[1..3]             # =>   "ell"
:"hello there"[1...3]            # =>   "el"
:"hello there"[-3,2]             # =>   "er"
:"hello there"[-4..-2]           # =>   "her"
:"hello there"[-2..-4]           # =>   ""
:"hello there"[/[aeiou](.)\1/]   # =>   "ell"
:"hello there"[/[aeiou](.)\1/, 0] # =>  "ell"
:"hello there"[/[aeiou](.)\1/, 1] # =>  "l"
:"hello there"[/[aeiou](.)\1/, 2] # =>  nil
:"hello there"[/(..)e/]          # =>   "the"
:"hello there"[/(..)e/, 1]       # =>   "th"
:"hello there"["lo"]             # =>   "lo"
:"hello there"["bye"]            # =>   nil
```

---

capitalize sym.capitalize → *symbol*

1.9 Returns a symbol with the first character of *sym* converted to uppercase and the remainder to lowercase.

```
:hello.capitalize          # =>   :Hello
:"HELLO WORLD".capitalize  # =>   :"Hello world"
:"123ABC".capitalize       # =>   :"123abc"
```

---

casecmp sym.casecmp(*other*) → $-1, 0, +1$, or nil

1.9 Case-insensitive version of Symbol#<=>. Returns nil if *other* is not a symbol.

```
:abcdef.casecmp(:abcde)   # =>   1
:abcdef.casecmp(:abcdef)  # =>   0
:abcdef.casecmp(:ABCDEF)  # =>   0
:aBcDeF.casecmp(:abcdef)  # =>   0
:abcdef.casecmp(:abcdefg) # =>   -1
:abcdef.casecmp("abcdef") # =>   nil
```

downcase
sym.downcase → *symbol*

1.9 Returns a symbol with all the characters of *sym* converted to lowercase.

```
:Hello.downcase          # =>   :hello
:"HELLO WORLD".downcase  # =>   :"hello world"
:"123ABC".downcase       # =>   :"123abc"
```

empty?
sym.empty → true or false

1.9 Returns true if the string representation of *sym* is empty.

```
:hello.empty?  # =>   false
:"".empty?     # =>   true
```

encoding
sym.encoding → *enc*

1.9 Returns the encoding of *sym*.

```
# encoding: utf-8
:hello.encoding  # =>   #<Encoding:US-ASCII>
:"δog".encoding  # =>   #<Encoding:UTF-8>
```

id2name
sym.id2name → *string*

Returns the string representation of *sym*.

```
:fred.id2name                # =>   "fred"
:"99 red balloons!".id2name  # =>   "99 red balloons!"
```

inspect
sym.inspect → *string*

Returns the representation of *sym* as a symbol literal.

```
:fred.inspect                # =>   :fred
:"99 red balloons!".inspect  # =>   :"99 red balloons!"
```

intern
sym.intern → *sym*

Synonym for Symbol#to_sym.

length
sym.length → *int*

1.9 Returns the number of characters in the string representation *sym*.

```
# encoding: utf-8
:dog.length   # =>   3
:δog.length   # =>   3
```

match
sym.match(*regexp*) → *int* or nil

1.9 Converts *self* to a string and then matches it against *regexp*. Unlike String#match, does not support blocks or non-regexp parameters.

```
:hello.match(/(.)\1/)  # =>   2
:hello.match(/ll/)     # =>   2
```

S ymbol

next   *sym*.next → *symbol*

1.9   Synonym for Symbol#succ.

---

size   *sym*.size → *int*

1.9   Synonym for Symbol#length.

---

slice   *sym*.slice(*int*) → *string* or nil
                                                              sym.slice(*int, int*) → *string* or nil
                                                              sym.slice(*range*) → *string* or nil
                                                              sym.slice(*regexp*) → *string* or nil
                                                        sym.slice(*match_string*) → *string* or nil

1.9   Synonym for Symbol#[ ].

---

succ   *sym*.succ → *symbol*

1.9   Returns the successor to *sym* using the same rules as String#succ.

```
:abcd.succ          # =>    :abce
:THX1138.succ       # =>    :THX1139
:"<<koala>>".succ   # =>    :"<<koalb>>"
:"1999zzz".succ     # =>    :"2000aaa"
:ZZZ9999.succ       # =>    :AAAA0000
:"***".succ         # =>    :"**+"
```

---

swapcase   *sym*.swapcase → *symbol*

1.9   Returns a symbol with the case of all the characters of *sym* swapped.

```
:Hello.swapcase       # =>    :hELLO
:"123ABC".swapcase    # =>    :"123abc"
```

---

to_proc   *sym*.to_proc → *proc*

1.9   Allows a symbol to be used when a block is expected. The symbol acts as a method invoked
on each parameter to the block. See page 368 for more information.

```
%w{ant bee cat}.map(&:reverse)   # =>    ["tna", "eeb", "tac"]
```

---

to_s   *sym*.to_s → *string*

Synonym for Symbol#id2name.

---

to_sym   *sym*.to_sym → *sym*

Symbols are symbol-like!

---

upcase   *sym*.upcase → *symbol*

1.9   Returns a symbol with of all the characters of *sym* in uppercase.

```
:Hello.upcase     # =>    :HELLO
:"123Abc".upcase  # =>    :"123ABC"
```

S ymbol

Class **Thread** < Object

Thread encapsulates the behavior of a thread of execution, including the main thread of the Ruby script. See the tutorial in Chapter 12, beginning on page 169.

In the descriptions that follow, the parameter *symbol* refers to a symbol, which is either a quoted string or a Symbol (such as :name).

Class methods

abort_on_exception
Thread.abort_on_exception → true or false

Returns the status of the global "abort on exception" condition. The default is false. When set to true or if the global $DEBUG flag is true (perhaps because the command-line option -d was specified), all threads will abort (the process will exit(0)) if an exception is raised in any thread. See also Thread.abort_on_exception=.

abort_on_exception=
Thread.abort_on_exception= *bool*→ true or false

When set to true, all threads will abort if an exception is raised. Returns the new state.

```
Thread.abort_on_exception = true
t1 = Thread.new do
  puts  "In new thread"
  raise "Exception from thread"
end
sleep(1)
puts "not reached"
```

produces:

```
In new thread
prog.rb:4:in `block in <main>': Exception from thread (RuntimeError)
```

current
Thread.current → *thread*

Returns the currently executing thread.

```
Thread.current  # =>   #<Thread:0x0ac684 run>
```

exclusive
Thread.exclusive { *block* } → *obj*

Executes the block and returns whatever the block returns. Internally uses a Mutex so that only one thread can be executing code under control of Thread.exclusive at a time.

exit
Thread.exit

Terminates the currently running thread and schedules another thread to be run. If this thread is already marked to be killed, exit returns the Thread. If this is the main thread, or the last thread, exits the process.

fork
Thread.fork { *block* } → *thread*

Synonym for Thread.start.

kill
Thread.kill(*thread*)

Causes the given thread to exit (see Thread.exit).

```
count = 0
a = Thread.new { loop { count += 1 } }
sleep(0.1)        # =>    0
Thread.kill(a)    # =>    #<Thread:0x0a3764 aborting>
count             # =>    964882
# give it time to die...
sleep 0.01
a.alive?          # =>    false
```

list
Thread.list → *array*

Returns an array of Thread objects for all threads that are either runnable or stopped.

```
Thread.new { sleep(200) }
Thread.new { 1000000.times {|i| i*i } }
Thread.new { Thread.stop }
Thread.list.each {|thr| p thr }
```

produces:

```
#<Thread:0x0ac684 run>
#<Thread:0x0a3b88 sleep>
#<Thread:0x0a3a70 run>
#<Thread:0x0a39a8 sleep>
```

main
Thread.main → *thread*

Returns the main thread for the process.

```
Thread.main   # =>    #<Thread:0x0ac684 run>
```

new
Thread.new(⟨ *arg* ⟩*) {| *args* | *block* } → *thread*

Creates and runs a new thread to execute the instructions given in *block*. Any arguments passed to Thread.new are passed into the block.

```
x = Thread.new { sleep 0.1; print "x"; print "y"; print "z" }
a = Thread.new { print "a"; print "b"; sleep 0.2; print "c" }
x.join; a.join # wait for threads to finish
```

produces:

```
abxyzc
```

pass
Thread.pass

Invokes the thread scheduler to pass execution to another thread.

```
a = Thread.new { print "a"; Thread.pass; print "b" }
b = Thread.new { print "x"; Thread.pass; print "y" }
a.join; b.join
```

produces:

```
axby
```

T hread

start   Thread.start(⟨ *args* ⟩*) {| *args* | *block* } → *thread*

Basically the same as Thread.new. However, if class Thread is subclassed, then calling start in that subclass will not invoke the subclass's initialize method.

stop   Thread.stop

Stops execution of the current thread, putting it into a "sleep" state, and schedules execution of another thread. Resets the "critical" condition to false.

```
a = Thread.new { print "a"; Thread.stop; print "c" }
Thread.pass
print "b"
a.run
a.join
```

produces:

```
a
b
c
```

Instance methods

[ ]   *thr*[*symbol*] → *obj* or nil

Attribute Reference—Returns the value of a thread-local variable, using either a symbol or a string name. If the specified variable does not exist, returns nil.

```
a = Thread.new { Thread.current["name"] = "A"; Thread.stop }
b = Thread.new { Thread.current[:name]  = "B"; Thread.stop }
c = Thread.new { Thread.current["name"] = "C"; Thread.stop }
Thread.list.each {|x| puts "#{x.inspect}: #{x[:name]}" }
```

produces:

```
#<Thread:0x0ac684 run>:
#<Thread:0x0a2ecc run>:
#<Thread:0x0a2e7c run>:
#<Thread:0x0a2cb0 run>:
```

[ ]=   *thr*[*symbol*] = *obj* → *obj*

Attribute Assignment—Sets or creates the value of a thread-local variable, using either a symbol or a string. See also Thread#[].

abort_on_exception   *thr*.abort_on_exception → true or false

Returns the status of the thread-local "abort on exception" condition for *thr*. The default is false. See also Thread.abort_on_exception=.

abort_on_exception=   *thr*.abort_on_exception= true or false→ true or false

When set to true, causes all threads (including the main program) to abort if an exception is raised in *thr*. The process will effectively exit(0).

alive?
thr.alive? → true or false

Returns true if *thr* is running or sleeping.

```
thr = Thread.new { }
thr.join                  # =>   #<Thread:0x0a49ac dead>
Thread.current.alive?     # =>   true
thr.alive?                # =>   false
```

exit
thr.exit → thr or nil

Terminates *thr* and schedules another thread to be run. If this thread is already marked to be killed, exit returns the Thread. If this is the main thread, or the last thread, exits the process.

group
thr.group → thread_group

1.9 Returns the ThreadGroup owning *thr*, or nil.

```
thread = Thread.new { sleep 99 }
Thread.current.group.list   # =>   [#<Thread:0x0ac684 run>,
                                    #<Thread:0x0a3764 run>]
new_group = ThreadGroup.new
thread.group.list           # =>   [#<Thread:0x0ac684 run>,
                                    #<Thread:0x0a3764 run>]
new_group.add(thread)
thread.group.list           # =>   [#<Thread:0x0a3764 run>]
Thread.current.group.list   # =>   [#<Thread:0x0ac684 run>]
```

join
thr.join → thr
thr.join(limit) → thr

1.9 The calling thread will suspend execution and run *thr*. Does not return until *thr* exits or until *limit* seconds have passed. If the time limit expires, nil will be returned; otherwise, *thr* is returned.

Any threads not joined will be killed when the main program exits. If *thr* had previously raised an exception and the abort_on_exception and $DEBUG flags are not set (so the exception has not yet been processed), it will be processed at this time.

```
a = Thread.new { print "a"; sleep(10); print "b"; print "c" }
x = Thread.new { print "x"; Thread.pass; print "y"; print "z" }
x.join # Let x thread finish, a will be killed on exit.
```

produces:

```
axyz
```

The following example illustrates the *limit* parameter.

```
y = Thread.new { loop { sleep 0.1; print "tick...\n" }}
y.join(0.25)
puts "Gave up waiting..."
```

produces:

```
tick...
tick...
Gave up waiting...
```

keys

thr.keys → array

Returns an array of the names of the thread-local variables (as symbols).

```
thr = Thread.new do
  Thread.current[:cat] = 'meow'
  Thread.current["dog"] = 'woof'
end
thr.join   # =>   #<Thread:0x0a44e8 dead>
thr.keys   # =>   [:cat, :dog]
```

key?

thr.key?(symbol) → true or false

Returns true if the given string (or symbol) exists as a thread-local variable.

```
me = Thread.current
me[:oliver] = "a"
me.key?(:oliver)   # =>   true
me.key?(:stanley)  # =>   false
```

kill

thr.kill

Synonym for Thread#exit.

priority

thr.priority → int

Returns the priority of *thr*. The default is zero; higher-priority threads will run before lower-priority threads.

```
Thread.current.priority   # =>   0
```

priority=

thr.priority= int → thr

Sets the priority of *thr* to *integer*. Higher-priority threads will run before lower-priority threads. If you find yourself messing with thread priorities to get things to work, you're doing something wrong.

```
count_high = count_low = 0
Thread.new do
  Thread.current.priority = 1
  loop { count_high += 1 }
end
Thread.new do
  Thread.current.priority = -1
  loop { count_low += 1 }
end

sleep 1
count_high   # =>   7509268
count_low    # =>   1886223
```

raise

thr.raise
thr.raise(*message*)
thr.raise(*exception* ⟨ , *message* ⟨ , *array* ⟩ ⟩)

1.9

Raises an exception (see Kernel.raise on page 566 for details) from *thr*. The caller does not
have to be *thr*.

```
Thread.abort_on_exception = true
a = Thread.new { sleep(200) }
a.raise("Gotcha")
a.join
```

produces:

```
prog.rb:2:in `sleep': Gotcha (RuntimeError)
from /tmp/prog.rb:2:in `block in <main>'
```

run

Wakes up *thr*, making it eligible for scheduling. If not in a critical section, then invokes the
scheduler.

```
a = Thread.new { puts "a"; Thread.stop; puts "c" }
Thread.pass
puts "Got here"
a.run
a.join
```

produces:

```
a
b
c
```

safe_level

Returns the safe level in effect for *thr*. Setting thread-local safe levels can help when implementing sandboxes that run insecure code.

```
thr = Thread.new { $SAFE = 3; sleep }
Thread.current.safe_level   # =>   0
thr.safe_level              # =>   0
```

status

Returns the status of *thr*: sleep if *thr* is sleeping or waiting on I/O, run if *thr* is executing,
aborting if *thr* is aborting, false if *thr* terminated normally, and nil if *thr* terminated with an
exception.

```
a = Thread.new { raise("die now") }
b = Thread.new { Thread.stop }
c = Thread.new { Thread.exit }
a.status                    # =>   nil
b.status                    # =>   "sleep"
c.status                    # =>   false
Thread.current.status       # =>   "run"
```

Thread

---

stop?   *thr*.stop? → true or false

Returns true if *thr* is dead or sleeping.

```
a = Thread.new { Thread.stop }
b = Thread.current
Thread.pass
a.stop?   # =>   false
b.stop?   # =>   false
```

---

terminate   *thr*.terminate

Synonym for Thread#exit.

---

value   *thr*.value → *obj*

Waits for *thr* to complete (via Thread#join) and returns its value.

```
a = Thread.new { 2 + 2 }
a.value   # =>   4
```

---

wakeup   *thr*.wakeup → *thr*

Marks *thr* as eligible for scheduling (it may still remain blocked on I/O, however). Does not invoke the scheduler (see Thread#run).

Thread

Class

ThreadGroup < Object

A ThreadGroup keeps track of a number of threads. A Thread can belong to only one ThreadGroup at a time; adding a thread to a group will remove it from its current group. Newly created threads belong to the group of the thread that created them.

ThreadGroup constants

Default   Default thread group.

Class methods

new   ThreadGroup.new → *thgrp*

Returns a newly created ThreadGroup. The group is initially empty.

Instance methods

add   *thgrp*.add(*thread*) → *thgrp*

Adds the given thread to this group, removing it from any other group to which it may have previously belonged.

```
puts "Default group is #{ThreadGroup::Default.list}"
tg = ThreadGroup.new
t1 = Thread.new { sleep }
t2 = Thread.new { sleep }
puts "t1 is #{t1}, t2 is #{t2}"
tg.add(t1)
puts "Default group now #{ThreadGroup::Default.list}"
puts "tg group now #{tg.list}"
```

produces:

```
Default group is [#<Thread:0x0ac684 run>]
t1 is #<Thread:0x0a35fc>, t2 is #<Thread:0x0a34f8>
Default group now [#<Thread:0x0ac684 run>, #<Thread:0x0a34f8 run>]
tg group now [#<Thread:0x0a35fc run>]
```

---

enclose   *thgrp*.enclose → *thgrp*

1.9   Prevents threads being added to and removed from *thgrp*. New threads may still be started.

```
thread = Thread.new { sleep 99 }
group = ThreadGroup.new
group.add(thread)
group.enclose
ThreadGroup::Default.add(thread)
```

produces:

```
prog.rb:5:in `add': can't move from the enclosed thread group (ThreadError)
	from /tmp/prog.rb:5:in `<main>'
```

---

enclosed?   *thgrp*.enclose → true or false

1.9   Returns true if this thread group has been enclosed.

---

list   *thgrp*.list → *array*

Returns an array of all existing Thread objects that belong to this group.

```
ThreadGroup::Default.list   # =>   [#<Thread:0x0ac684 run>]
```

Time   <   Object

Time is an abstraction of dates and times. Time is stored internally as the number of seconds and microseconds since the *epoch*, January 1, 1970 00:00 UTC. On some operating systems, this offset is allowed to be negative. Also see the Date library module on page 733.

The Time class treats GMT (Greenwich Mean Time) and UTC (Coordinated Universal Time)[7] as equivalent. GMT is the older way of referring to these baseline times but persists in the names of calls on POSIX systems.

All times are stored with some number of microseconds. Be aware of this fact when comparing times with each other—times that are apparently equal when displayed may be different when compared.

Mixes in

Comparable:

    <, <=, ==, >=, >, between?

Class methods

at
$$\text{Time.at(} time \text{)} \rightarrow time$$
$$\text{Time.at(} seconds \ \langle \text{ , } microseconds \ \rangle \text{)} \rightarrow time$$

Creates a new time object with the value given by *time* or the given number of *seconds* (and optional *microseconds*) from epoch. Microseconds may be a float—this allows setting times with nanosecond granularity on systems that support it. A nonportable feature allows the offset to be negative on some systems.

```
Time.at(0)           # =>   1969-12-31 18:00:00 -0600
Time.at(946702800)   # =>   1999-12-31 23:00:00 -0600
Time.at(-284061600)  # =>   1960-12-31 00:00:00 -0600
t = Time.at(946702800, 123.456)
t.usec               # =>   123
t.nsec               # =>   123456
```

gm
$$\text{Time.gm(} year \ \langle \text{, month } \langle \text{, day } \langle \text{, hour } \langle \text{, min } \langle \text{, sec } \langle \text{, usec } \rangle \rangle \rangle \rangle \rangle \rangle \text{)} \rightarrow time$$
$$\text{Time.gm(} sec, min, hour, day, month, year, wday, yday, isdst, tz \text{)} \rightarrow time$$

Creates a time based on given values, interpreted as UTC. The year must be specified. Other values default to the minimum value for that field (and may be nil or omitted). Months may be specified by numbers from 1 to 12 or by the three-letter English month names. Hours are specified on a 24-hour clock (0..23). Raises an ArgumentError if any values are out of range. Will also accept ten arguments in the order output by Time#to_a.

```
Time.gm(2000,"jan",1,20,15,1)   # =>   2000-01-01 20:15:01 UTC
```

---

7.   Yes, UTC really does stand for Coordinated Universal Time. There was a committee involved.

local   Time.local(*year* ⟨ , month ⟨ , day ⟨ , hour ⟨ , min ⟨ , sec ⟨ , usec ⟩ ⟩ ⟩ ⟩ ⟩ ⟩) → *time*
Time.local(*sec, min, hour, day, month, year, wday, yday, isdst, tz*) → *time*

Same as Time.gm but interprets the values in the local time zone. The second form accepts ten arguments in the order output by Time#to_a.

```
Time.local(2000,"jan",1,20,15,1)   # =>   2000-01-01 20:15:01 -0600
```

mktime Time.mktime(*year* ⟨ , month ⟨ , day ⟨ , hour ⟨ , min ⟨ , sec ⟨ , usec ⟩ ⟩ ⟩ ⟩ ⟩ ⟩) → *time*
Time.mktime(*sec, min, hour, day, month, year, wday, yday, isdst, tz*) → *time*

Synonym for Time.local.

new   Time.new → *time*

Returns a Time object initialized to the current system time. **Note:** The object created will be created using the resolution available on your system clock and so may include fractional seconds.

```
a = Time.new       # =>   2009-03-31 09:58:26 -0500
b = Time.new       # =>   2009-03-31 09:58:26 -0500
a == b             # =>   false
"%.6f" % a.to_f    # =>   "1238511506.962090"
"%.6f" % b.to_f    # =>   "1238511506.962514"
```

now   Time.now → *time*

Synonym for Time.new.

utc   Time.utc(*year* ⟨ , month ⟨ , day ⟨ , hour ⟨ , min ⟨ , sec ⟨ , usec ⟩ ⟩ ⟩ ⟩ ⟩ ⟩) → *time*
Time.utc(*sec, min, hour, day, month, year, wday, yday, isdst, tz*) → *time*

Synonym for Time.gm.

```
Time.utc(2000,"jan",1,20,15,1)   # =>   2000-01-01 20:15:01 UTC
```

Instance methods

+   *time + numeric* → *time*

Addition—Adds some number of seconds (possibly fractional) to *time* and returns that value as a new time.

```
t = Time.now         # =>   2009-03-31 09:58:27 -0500
t + (60 * 60 * 24)   # =>   2009-04-01 09:58:27 -0500
```

–   *time - time* → *float*
time - numeric → *time*

Difference—Returns a new time that represents the difference between two times or subtracts the given number of seconds in *numeric* from *time*.

```
t = Time.now       # =>   2009-03-31 09:58:27 -0500
t2 = t + 2592000   # =>   2009-04-30 09:58:27 -0500
t2 - t             # =>   2592000.0
t2 - 2592000       # =>   2009-03-31 09:58:27 -0500
```

<=>   *time* <=> *other_time* → −1, 0, +1
                                                              time <=> *other* → nil

1.9
1.9
Comparison—Compares *time* with *other_time* or with *numeric*, which is the number of
seconds (possibly fractional) since epoch. As of Ruby 1.9, nil is returned for comparison
against anything other that a Time object.

```
t = Time.now       # =>   2009-03-31 09:58:27 -0500
t2 = t + 2592000   # =>   2009-04-30 09:58:27 -0500
t <=> t2           # =>   -1
t2 <=> t           # =>   1
t <=> t            # =>   0
```

---

asctime   *time*.asctime → *string*

Returns a canonical string representation of *time*.

```
Time.now.asctime   # =>   "Tue Mar 31 09:58:27 2009"
```

---

ctime   *time*.ctime → *string*

Synonym for Time#asctime.

---

day   *time*.day → *int*

Returns the day of the month (1..*n*) for *time*.

```
t = Time.now   # =>   2009-03-31 09:58:27 -0500
t.day          # =>   31
```

---

dst?   *time*.dst? → true or false

Synonym for Time#isdst.

```
Time.local(2000, 7, 1).dst?   # =>   true
Time.local(2000, 1, 1).dst?   # =>   false
```

---

friday?   *time*.friday? → true or false

1.9
Returns true if *time*.wday is 5.

---

getgm   *time*.getgm → *time*

Returns a new Time object representing *time* in UTC.

```
t = Time.local(2000,1,1,20,15,1)   # =>   2000-01-01 20:15:01 -0600
t.gmt?                             # =>   false
y = t.getgm                       # =>   2000-01-02 02:15:01 UTC
y.gmt?                            # =>   true
t == y                           # =>   true
```

Time

---

getlocal   *time*.getlocal → *time*

Returns a new Time object representing *time* in local time (using the local time zone in effect for this process).

```
t = Time.gm(2000,1,1,20,15,1)   # =>   2000-01-01 20:15:01 UTC
t.gmt?                          # =>   true
l = t.getlocal                  # =>   2000-01-01 14:15:01 -0600
l.gmt?                          # =>   false
t == l                          # =>   true
```

---

getutc   *time*.getutc → *time*

Synonym for Time#getgm.

---

gmt?   *time*.gmt? → true or false

Returns true if *time* represents a time in UTC.

```
t = Time.now                    # =>   2009-03-31 09:58:27 -0500
t.gmt?                          # =>   false
t = Time.gm(2000,1,1,20,15,1)   # =>   2000-01-01 20:15:01 UTC
t.gmt?                          # =>   true
```

---

gmtime   *time*.gmtime → *time*

Converts *time* to UTC, modifying the receiver.

```
t = Time.now   # =>   2009-03-31 09:58:27 -0500
t.gmt?         # =>   false
t.gmtime       # =>   2009-03-31 14:58:27 UTC
t.gmt?         # =>   true
```

---

gmt_offset   *time*.gmt_offset → int

Returns the offset in seconds between the time zone of *time* and UTC.

```
t = Time.gm(2000,1,1,20,15,1)   # =>   2000-01-01 20:15:01 UTC
t.gmt_offset                    # =>   0
l = t.getlocal                  # =>   2000-01-01 14:15:01 -0600
l.gmt_offset                    # =>   -21600
```

---

gmtoff   *time*.gmtoff → *int*

Synonym for Time#gmt_offset.

---

hour   *time*.hour → *int*

Returns the hour of the day (0..23) for *time*.

```
t = Time.now   # =>   2009-03-31 09:58:27 -0500
t.hour         # =>   9
```

isdst

time.isdst → true or false

Returns true if *time* occurs during daylight saving time in its time zone.

```
Time.local(2000, 7, 1).isdst  # =>   true
Time.local(2000, 1, 1).isdst  # =>   false
```

localtime

time.localtime → *time*

Converts *time* to local time (using the local time zone in effect for this process) modifying the receiver.

```
t = Time.gm(2000, "jan", 1, 20, 15, 1)
t.gmt?         # =>   true
t.localtime    # =>   2000-01-01 14:15:01 -0600
t.gmt?         # =>   false
```

mday

time.mday → *int*

Synonym for Time#day.

monday?

time.monday? → true or false

1.9 Returns true if *time*.wday is 1.

min

time.min → *int*

Returns the minute of the hour (0..59) for *time*.

```
t = Time.now   # =>   2009-03-31 09:58:27 -0500
t.min          # =>   58
```

mon

time.mon → *int*

Returns the month of the year (1..12) for *time*.

```
t = Time.now   # =>   2009-03-31 09:58:27 -0500
t.mon          # =>   3
```

month

time.month → *int*

Synonym for Time#mon.

nsec

time.nsec → *int*

1.9 Returns just the number of nanoseconds for *time*.

```
t = Time.now       # =>   2009-03-31 09:58:27 -0500
"%10.6f" % t.to_f  # =>   "1238511507.341332"
t.nsec             # =>   341332000
t.usec             # =>   341332
```

saturday?

time.saturday? → true or false

1.9 Returns true if *time*.wday is 06.

---

sec *time*.sec → *int*

Returns the second of the minute (0..60)[8] for *time*.

```
t = Time.now    # =>   2009-03-31 09:58:27 -0500
t.sec           # =>   27
```

---

strftime *time*.strftime(*format*) → *string*

Formats *time* according to the directives in the given format string. See Table 27.18 on the next page for the available values. Any text not listed as a directive will be passed through to the output string. If an up arrow follows the % sign, any text returned for that directive will be mapped to uppercase.

```
t = Time.now
t.strftime("Printed on %m/%d/%Y")    # =>   "Printed on 03/31/2009"
t.strftime("at %I:%M%P")             # =>   "at 09:58am"
# force the am/pm flag to upper case
t.strftime("at %I:%M%^P")            # =>   "at 09:58AM"
```

---

succ *time*.succ → *later_time*

Returns a time object one second after *time*.

```
now = Time.now    # =>   2009-03-31 09:58:27 -0500
later = now.succ  # =>   2009-03-31 09:58:28 -0500
# preserves the fractional part
now.to_f          # =>   1238511507.40664
later.to_f        # =>   1238511508.40664
```

---

sunday? *time*.sunday? → true or false

Returns true if *time*.wday is 0.

---

thursday? *time*.thursday? → true or false

Returns true if *time*.wday is 4.

---

to_a *time*.to_a → *array*

Returns a ten-element *array* of values for *time*: [sec, min, hour, day, month, year, wday, yday, isdst, zone]. See the individual methods for an explanation of the valid ranges of each value. The ten elements can be passed directly to the methods Time.utc or Time.local to create a new Time.

```
now = Time.now    # =>   2009-03-31 09:58:27 -0500
t = now.to_a      # =>   [27, 58, 9, 31, 3, 2009, 2, 90, true, "CDT"]
```

---

8.   Yes, seconds really can range from zero to 60. This allows the system to inject leap seconds every now and then to correct for the fact time measured by atomic clocks differs from time measured by a spinning earth.

Table 27.18. Time#strftime Directives

Format	Meaning
%a	The abbreviated weekday name ("Sun")
%A	The full weekday name ("Sunday")
%b	The abbreviated month name ("Jan")
%B	The full month name ("January")
%c	The preferred local date and time representation
%d	Day of the month (01..31)
%H	Hour of the day, 24-hour clock (00..23)
%I	Hour of the day, 12-hour clock (01..12)
%j	Day of the year (001..366)
%m	Month of the year (01..12)
%M	Minute of the hour (00..59)
%p	Meridian indicator ("AM" or "PM")
%P	Meridian indicator ("am" or "pm")
%s	Number of seconds since 1970-01-01 00:00:00 UTC
%S	Second of the minute (00..60)
%U	Week number of the current year, starting with the first Sunday as the first day of the first week (00..53)
%W	Week number of the current year, starting with the first Monday as the first day of the first week (00..53)
%w	Day of the week (Sunday is 0, 0..6)
%x	Preferred representation for the date alone, no time
%X	Preferred representation for the time alone, no date
%y	Year without a century (00..99)
%Y	Year with century
%Z	Time zone name
%%	Literal % character

---

to_f _time_.to_f → _float_

Returns the value of _time_ as a floating-point number of seconds since epoch.

```
t = Time.now
"%10.5f" % t.to_f   # =>   "1238511507.44729"
t.to_i              # =>   1238511507
```

---

to_i _time_.to_i → _int_

Returns the value of _time_ as an integer number of seconds since epoch.

```
t = Time.now
"%10.5f" % t.to_f   # =>   "1238511507.46712"
t.to_i              # =>   1238511507
```

to_s   *time*.to_s → *string*

Returns a string representing *time*. Equivalent to calling Time#strftime with a format string of %a %b %d %H:%M:%S %Z %Y.

```
Time.now.to_s    # =>    "2009-03-31 09:58:27 -0500"
```

tuesday?   *time*.tuesday? → true or false

1.9 Returns true if *time*.wday is 2.

tv_nsec   *time*.tv_nsec → *int*

1.9 Synonym for Time#nsec.

tv_sec   *time*.tv_sec → *int*

Synonym for Time#to_i.

tv_usec   *time*.tv_usec → *int*

Synonym for Time#usec.

usec   *time*.usec → *int*

Returns just the number of microseconds for *time*.

```
t = Time.now        # =>    2009-03-31 09:58:27  -0500
"%10.6f" % t.to_f   # =>    "1238511507.508262"
t.nsec              # =>    508262000
t.usec              # =>    508262
```

utc   *time*.utc → *time*

Synonym for Time#gmtime.

```
t = Time.now    # =>    2009-03-31 09:58:27  -0500
t.utc?          # =>    false
t.utc           # =>    2009-03-31 14:58:27 UTC
t.utc?          # =>    true
```

utc?   *time*.utc? → true or false

Returns true if *time* represents a time in UTC.

```
t = Time.now                    # =>    2009-03-31 09:58:27  -0500
t.utc?                          # =>    false
t = Time.gm(2000,"jan",1,20,15,1)    # =>    2000-01-01 20:15:01 UTC
t.utc?                          # =>    true
```

utc_offset   *time*.utc_offset → *int*

Synonym for Time#gmt_offset.

wednesday?   *time*.wednesday? → true or false

1.9 Returns true if *time*.wday is 3.

Time

wday

Returns an integer representing the day of the week, 0..6, with Sunday == 0.

```
t = Time.now   # =>   2009-03-31 09:58:27 -0500
t.wday         # =>   2
```

yday

Returns an integer representing the day of the year, 1..366.

```
t = Time.now   # =>   2009-03-31 09:58:27 -0500
t.yday         # =>   90
```

year

Returns the year for *time* (including the century).

```
t = Time.now   # =>   2009-03-31 09:58:27 -0500
t.year         # =>   2009
```

zone

Returns the name of the time zone used for *time*.

```
t = Time.gm(2000, "jan", 1, 20, 15, 1)
t.zone   # =>   "UTC"
t = Time.local(2000, "jan", 1, 20, 15, 1)
t.zone   # =>   "CST"
```

Class
TrueClass < Object

The global value true is the only instance of class TrueClass and represents a logically true value in boolean expressions. The class provides operators allowing true to be used in logical expressions.

Instance methods

&

true & *obj* → true or false

And—Returns false if *obj* is nil or false and returns true otherwise.

^

true ^ *obj* → true or false

Exclusive Or—Returns true if *obj* is nil or false and returns false otherwise.

|

true | *obj* → true

Or—Returns true. Because *obj* is an argument to a method call, it is always evaluated; short-circuit evaluation is not performed in this case.

```
true |  puts("or")
true || puts("logical or")
```

produces:

```
or
```

UnboundMethod < Object

Ruby supports two forms of objectified methods. Class Method is used to represent methods that are associated with a particular object: these method objects are bound to that object. Bound method objects for an object can be created using Object#method.

Ruby also supports unbound methods, which are method objects that are not associated with a particular object. These can be created either by calling unbind on a bound method object or by calling Module#instance_method.

Unbound methods can be called only after they are bound to an object. That object must be a *kind_of?* the method's original class.

```ruby
class Square
  def area
    @side * @side
  end
  def initialize(side)
    @side = side
  end
end

area_unbound = Square.instance_method(:area)

s = Square.new(12)
area = area_unbound.bind(s)
area.call   # =>   144
```

Unbound methods are a reference to the method at the time it was objectified: subsequent changes to the underlying class will not affect the unbound method.

```ruby
class Test
  def test
    :original
  end
end
um = Test.instance_method(:test)
class Test
  def test
    :modified
  end
end
t = Test.new
t.test              # =>   :modified
um.bind(t).call     # =>   :original
```

Instance methods

arity

umeth.arity → *fixnum*

See Method#arity on page 582.

bind

umeth.bind(*obj*) → *method*

Bind *umeth* to *obj*. If Klass was the class from which *umeth* was originally obtained, obj.kind_of?(Klass) must be true.

```
class A
  def test
    puts "In test, class = #{self.class}"
  end
end
class B < A
end
class C < B
end
um = B.instance_method(:test)
bm = um.bind(C.new)
bm.call
bm = um.bind(B.new)
bm.call
bm = um.bind(A.new)
bm.call
```

produces:

```
In test, class = C
In test, class = B
prog.rb:16:in `bind': bind argument must be an instance of B (TypeError)
from /tmp/prog.rb:16:in `<main>'
```

name

umeth.name → *string*

1.9

Returns the name of the method *umeth*.

```
um = String.instance_method(:upcase)
um.name   # =>   :upcase
```

owner

umeth.owner → *module*

1.9

Returns the class or module in which *umeth* is defined.

```
um = String.instance_method(:upcase)
um.owner   # =>   String
```

source_location

umeth.source_location → [*filename*, *lineno*] or nil

1.9

Returns the source filename and line number where *umeth* was defined or nil if self was not defined in Ruby source. See Method#source_location for an example.

## Chapter 28

Standard Library

The Ruby interpreter comes with a large number of classes, modules, and methods built in—they are available as part of the running program. When you need a facility that isn't part of the built-in repertoire, you'll often find it in a library that you can require into your program. Sometimes you'll need to download one of these libraries (perhaps as a Ruby gem).

However, Ruby also ships as standard with a large number of libraries. Some of these are written in pure Ruby and will be available on all Ruby platforms. Others are Ruby extensions, and some of these will be present only if your system supports the resources that they need. All can be included into your Ruby program using require. And, unlike libraries you may find on the Internet, you can pretty much guarantee that all Ruby users will have these libraries already installed on their machines.

Ruby 1.9 has more than 100 standard libraries included in the distribution. For each of these libraries, this section shows a one- or a two-page summary. For each library, we give some introductory notes and typically give an example or two of use. You won't find detailed method descriptions here; for that, consult the library's own documentation.

It's all very well suggesting that you "consult the library's own documentation," but where can you find it? The answer is that it depends. Some libraries have already been documented using RDoc (see Chapter 19). That means you can use the ri command to get their documentation. For example, from a command line, you may be able to see the following documentation on the escapeHTML method in the CGI standard library member:

```
% ri CGI.escapeHTML
--------------------------------------------------- CGI::escapeHTML
     CGI::escapeHTML(string)
------------------------------------------------------------------
     Escape special characters in HTML, namely &"<>

       CGI::escapeHTML('Usage: foo "bar" <baz>')
           # => "Usage: foo &quot;bar&quot; &lt;baz&gt;"
```

If there's no RDoc documentation available, the next place to look is the library itself. If you have a source distribution of Ruby, these are in the ext/ and lib/ subdirectories. If instead you have a binary-only installation, you can still find the source of pure-Ruby library modules (normally in the lib/ruby/1.9/ directory under your Ruby installation). Often, library source directories contain documentation that the author has not yet converted to RDoc format.

If you still can't find documentation, turn to Google. Many of the Ruby standard libraries are also hosted as external projects. The authors develop them stand-alone and then periodically integrate the code into the standard Ruby distribution. For example, if you want detailed information on the API for the YAML library, googling *yaml ruby* may lead you to http://yaml4r.sourceforge.net. After admiring *why the lucky stiff's* artwork, a click will take you to his 40+ page reference manual.

The next port of call is the ruby-talk mailing list. Ask a (polite) question there, and chances are that you'll get a knowledgeable response within hours. See page 888 for pointers on how to subscribe.

And if you *still* can't find documentation, you can always follow Obi Wan's advice and do what we did when documenting Ruby—use the source. You'd be surprised at how easy it is to read the actual source of Ruby libraries and work out the details of usage.

Library Changes in Ruby 1.9

1.9

These are the library changes in Ruby 1.9:

- Much of the Complex and Rational libraries are now built in to the interpreter. However, requiring the external libraries adds some functionally. In the case of Rational, this functionality is minimal.

- The CMath library has been added.

- The Enumerator library is now built in.

- The Fiber library has been added (it adds coroutine support to fibers).

- ftools have been removed (and replaced by fileutils).

- The Generator library has been removed (use fibers).

- Notes on using irb from inside applications have been added.

- jcode has been removed in favor of built-in encoding support.

- The json library is added.

- The matrix library no longer requires that you include mathn.

- The mutex library is now built in.

- parsedate has been removed. The Date class handles most of its functionality.

- readbytes has been removed. IO now supports the method directly.

- A description of Ripper has been added.

- A description of SecureRandom has been added.

- I've omitted the shell library, because it seems more like a curiosity than something folks would use (and it's broken under 1.9).

- The soap library has been removed.

- I've omitted the sync library. It is broken under 1.9, and the monitor library seems to be cleaner.

- Win32API is now deprecated in favor of using the DL library.

Library
Abbrev
Generate Sets of Unique Abbreviations

Given a set of strings, calculates the set of unambiguous abbreviations for those strings and returns a hash where the keys are all the possible abbreviations and the values are the full strings. Thus, given input of "car" and "cone," the keys pointing to "car" would be "ca" and "car," and those pointing to "cone" would be "co," "con," and "cone."

An optional pattern or a string may be specified—only those input strings matching the pattern, or beginning with the string, are considered for inclusion in the output hash.

Including the Abbrev library also adds an abbrev method to class Array.

- Shows the abbreviation set of some words:

  `slabbrev_1.rb`

```
require 'abbrev'

Abbrev::abbrev(['ruby', 'rules'])    # =>    {"rub"=>"ruby",
                                             "rule"=>"rules",
                                             "rul"=>"rules",
                                             "ruby"=>"ruby",
                                             "rules"=>"rules"}

%w{ car cone }.abbrev              # =>    {"ca"=>"car",
                                             "con"=>"cone",
                                             "co"=>"cone", "car"=>"car",
                                             "cone"=>"cone"}

%w{ car cone }.abbrev("ca")        # =>    {"ca"=>"car", "car"=>"car"}
```

- A trivial command loop using abbreviations:

  `slabbrev_2.rb`

```
require 'abbrev'
COMMANDS = %w{ sample send start status stop }.abbrev
while line = gets
  line = line.chomp
  case COMMANDS[line]
  when "sample":  # ...
  when "send":    # ...
  # ...
  else
    STDERR.puts "Unknown command: #{line}"
  end
end
```

Library **Base64**   Base64 Conversion Functions

Performs encoding and decoding of binary data using a Base64 representation. This allows you to represent any binary data in purely printable characters. The encoding is specified in RFC 2045 (`http://www.faqs.org/rfcs/rfc2045.html`) and RFC 4648 (`http://www.faqs.org/rfcs/rfc4648.html`).

- Encodes and decodes strings. Note the newlines inserted into the Base64 string.

`slbase64_1.rb`

```
require 'base64'
str = "Now is the time for all good coders\nto learn Ruby"
converted = Base64.encode64(str)
puts converted
puts Base64.decode64(converted)
```

produces:

```
Tm93IGlzIHRoZSBOaW1lIGZvciBhbGwgZ29vZCBjb2RlcnMKdG8gbGVhcm4g
UnVieQ==
Now is the time for all good coders
to learn Ruby
```

- Now uses RFC 4648 variants:

`slbase64_2.rb`

```
require 'base64'
str = "Now is the time for all good coders\nto learn Ruby"
converted = Base64.strict_encode64(str)
puts converted
puts Base64.strict_decode64(converted)
```

produces:

```
Tm93IGlzIHRoZSBOaW1lIGZvciBhbGwgZ29vZCBjb2RlcnMKdG8gbGVhcm4gUnVieQ==
Now is the time for all good coders
to learn Ruby
```

Library
Benchmark   Time Code Execution

Allows code execution to be timed and the results tabulated. The Benchmark module is easier to use if you include it in your top-level environment.

See also: Profile (page 783)

- Compares the costs of four kinds of method dispatch:

slbenchmark_1.rb

```ruby
require 'benchmark'
include Benchmark
string = "Stormy Weather"
m = string.method(:length)
bm(6) do |x|
  x.report("direct") { 100_000.times { string.length } }
  x.report("call")   { 100_000.times { m.call } }
  x.report("send")   { 100_000.times { string.send(:length) } }
  x.report("eval")   { 100_000.times { eval "string.length" } }
end
```

produces:

```
             user      system      total          real
direct    0.010000   0.000000   0.010000 (   0.010877)
call      0.020000   0.000000   0.020000 (   0.022432)
send      0.020000   0.000000   0.020000 (   0.016415)
eval      0.770000   0.000000   0.770000 (   0.779643)
```

- Which is better: reading all of a dictionary and splitting it or splitting it line by line? Use bmbm to run a rehearsal before doing the timing:

slbenchmark_2.rb

```ruby
require 'benchmark'
include Benchmark
bmbm(6) do |x|
  x.report("all") do
    str = File.read("/usr/share/dict/words")
    words = str.scan(/[-\w']+/)
  end
  x.report("lines") do
    words = []
    File.foreach("/usr/share/dict/words") do |line|
      words << line.chomp
    end
  end
end
```

produces:

```
Rehearsal ----------------------------------------
all      0.200000   0.010000   0.210000 (   0.218893)
lines    0.250000   0.010000   0.260000 (   0.254882)
------------------------------- total: 0.470000sec

             user      system      total          real
all      0.220000   0.010000   0.230000 (   0.230821)
lines    0.230000   0.020000   0.250000 (   0.238031)
```

BigDecimal
Large-Precision Decimal Numbers

Ruby's standard Bignum class supports integers with large numbers of digits. The BigDecimal class supports decimal numbers with large numbers of decimal places. The standard library supports all the normal arithmetic operations. BigDecimal also comes with some extension libraries.

bigdecimal/ludcmp

Performs an LU decomposition of a matrix.

bigdecimal/math

Provides the transcendental functions *sqrt*, *sin*, *cos*, *atan*, *exp*, and *log*, along with functions for computing *PI* and *E*. All functions take an arbitrary precision argument.

bigdecimal/jacobian

Constructs the Jacobian (a matrix enumerating the partial derivatives) of a given function. Not dependent on BigDecimal.

bigdecimal/newton

Solves the roots of nonlinear function using Newton's method. Not dependent on BigDecimal.

bigdecimal/nlsolve

Wraps the bigdecimal/newton library for equations of BigDecimals.

You can find English-language documentation in the Ruby source distribution in the file ext/bigdecimal/bigdecimal_en.html.

slbigdecimal_1.rb

```ruby
require 'bigdecimal'
require 'bigdecimal/math'
include BigMath

pi = BigMath::PI(20)     # 20 is the number of decimal digits

radius = BigDecimal("2.14156987652974674392")

area = pi * radius**2

area.to_s                # =>  "0.1440835404468560441767200338066795616885
                                998464104450325832158247587804055458617
                                80909930190528E2"

# The same with regular floats

radius = 2.14156987652974674392

Math::PI * radius**2  # =>   14.4083540446856
```

C GI

The CGI class provides support for programs used as Common Gateway Interface (CGI) scripts in a web server. CGI objects are initialized with data from the environment and from the HTTP request, and they provide convenient accessors to form data and cookies. They can also manage sessions using a variety of storage mechanisms. Class CGI also provides basic facilities for HTML generation and class methods to escape and unescape requests and HTML.

See also: CGI::Session (page 726)

- Escapes and unescapes special characters in URLs and HTML. Numeric entities below 256 will be encoded based on the encoding of the input string. Other numeric entities will be left unchanged.

1.9

slcgi_1.rb

```ruby
require 'cgi'
CGI.escape('c:\My Files')              # =>   c%3A%5CMy+Files
CGI.unescape('c%3a%5cMy+Files')        # =>   c:\My Files
CGI::escapeHTML('"a"<b & c')           # =>   &quot;a&quot;&lt;b &amp; c

CGI.unescapeHTML('&quot;a&quot;&lt;=&gt;b')   # =>   "a"<=>b
CGI.unescapeHTML('&#65;&#x41;')               # =>   AA
str = '&#x3c0;r&#178;'
str.force_encoding("utf-8")
CGI.unescapeHTML(str)                         # =>   $\pi r^2$
```

- Accesses information from the incoming request:

slcgi_3.rb

```ruby
require 'cgi'
c = CGI.new
c.auth_type    # =>   "basic"
c.user_agent   # =>   "Mozscape Explorari V5.6"
```

- Accesses form fields from an incoming request. Assume that the following script is installed as test.cgi and the user linked to it using http://mydomain.com/test.cgi?fred=10&barney=cat:

slcgi_4.rb

```ruby
require 'cgi'
c = CGI.new
c['fred']    # =>   "10"
c.keys       # =>   ["fred", "barney"]
c.params     # =>   {"fred"=>["10"], "barney"=>["cat"]}
```

- If a form contains multiple fields with the same name, the corresponding values will be returned to the script as an array. The [] accessor returns just the first of these—index the result of the params method to get them all.

In this example, assume the form has three fields called "name":

slcgi_5.rb

```
require 'cgi'
c = CGI.new
c['name']           # =>   "fred"
c.params['name']    # =>   ["fred", "wilma", "barney"]
c.keys              # =>   ["name"]
c.params            # =>   {"name"=>["fred", "wilma", "barney"]}
```

• Sends a response to the browser. (Not many folks use this form of HTML generation. Consider one of the templating libraries—see page 295.)

slcgi_6.rb

```
require 'cgi'
cgi = CGI.new("html4Tr")
cgi.header("type" => "text/html", "expires" => Time.now + 30)
cgi.out do
  cgi.html do
    cgi.head{ cgi.title{"Hello World!"} } +
    cgi.body do
      cgi.pre do
        CGI::escapeHTML(
          "params: " + cgi.params.inspect + "\n" +
          "cookies: " + cgi.cookies.inspect + "\n")
      end
    end
  end
end
```

• Stores a cookie in the client browser:

slcgi_7.rb

```
require 'cgi'
cgi = CGI.new("html4")
cookie = CGI::Cookie.new('name' => 'mycookie',
                         'value' => 'chocolate chip',
                         'expires' => Time.now + 3600)
cgi.out('cookie' => cookie) do
  cgi.head + cgi.body { "Cookie stored" }
end
```

• Retrieves a previously stored cookie:

slcgi_8.rb

```
require 'cgi'
cgi = CGI.new("html4")
cookie = cgi.cookies['mycookie']
cgi.out('cookie' => cookie) do
  cgi.head + cgi.body { "Flavor: " + cookie[0] }
end
```

Library **CGI::Session** *CGI Sessions*

A CGI::Session maintains a persistent state for web users in a CGI environment. Sessions may be memory resident or may be stored on disk. See the discussion on page 300 for details.

See also: CGI (page 724)

`slcgisession_1.rb`

```ruby
require 'cgi'
require 'cgi/session'
cgi = CGI.new("html3")
sess = CGI::Session.new(cgi,
                        "session_key" => "rubyweb",
                        "prefix" => "web-session.")
if sess['lastaccess']
  msg = "<p>You were last here #{sess['lastaccess']}.</p>"
else
  msg = "<p>Looks like you haven't been here for a while</p>"
end
count = (sess["accesscount"] || 0).to_i
count += 1
msg << "<p>Number of visits: #{count}</p>"
sess["accesscount"] = count
sess["lastaccess"]  = Time.now.to_s
sess.close
cgi.out {
  cgi.html {
    cgi.body {
      msg
    }
  }
}
```

Library **CMath**   Complex Transcendental Functions

1.9   As of Ruby 1.9, Complex class is built in to the interpreter. There is no need to require
the complex library to create and manipulate complex numbers. However, if you want the
transcendental functions defined by the Math to work with complex numbers, you must also
require the cmath library. The functions affected are as follows: acosh, acos, asinh, asin,
atan2, atanh, atan, cosh, cos, exp, log10, log, sinh, sin, sqrt, tanh, and tan.

The Complex library makes these complex functions the default (so, if you require 'complex',
you can use Math::sin and not CMath::sin).

`slcmath_1.rb`

```ruby
require 'cmath'
point = Complex(2, 3)
CMath::sin(point)   # =>   (9.15449914691143-4.16890695996656i)
CMath::cos(point)   # =>   (-4.18962569096881-9.10922789375534i)
```

Complex   Complex Numbers

Loads the cmath library, which defines the transcendental functions for complex numbers. It then arranges things so that these complex-aware functions are the ones invoked when you use Math::. The net effect is that, after requiring complex, you can use functions such as Math::sin on any numeric value, including complex numbers.

Using transcendental numbers with complex arguments will, by default, cause an error:

slcomplex_1.rb

```
point = Complex(2, 3)
Math::sin(point)
```

produces:

```
prog.rb:2:in `to_f': can't convert 2+3i into Float (RangeError)
from /tmp/prog.rb:2:in `sin'
from /tmp/prog.rb:2:in `<main>'
```

However...

slcomplex_2.rb

```
require 'complex'
point = Complex(2, 3)
Math::sin(point)   # =>   (9.15449914691143-4.168906959966656i)
```

Library

Continuation

Continuations

Continuation objects are generated by the Kernel#callcc method, which becomes available only when the continuation library is loaded. They hold a return address and execution context, allowing a nonlocal return to the end of the callcc block from anywhere within a program. Continuations are somewhat analogous to a structured version of C's setjmp/longjmp (although they contain more state, so you may consider them closer to threads). This (somewhat contrived) example allows the inner loop to abandon processing early.

- Does a nonlocal exit when a condition is met:

slcontinuation_1.rb

```ruby
require 'continuation'
callcc do |cont|
  for i in 0..4
    print "\n#{i}: "
    for j in i*5...(i+1)*5
      cont.call() if j == 7
      printf "%3d", j
    end
  end
end
print "\n"
```

produces:

```
0:   0  1  2  3  4
1:   5  6
```

- The call stack for methods is preserved in continuations:

slcontinuation_2.rb

```ruby
require 'continuation'
def strange
  callcc {|continuation| return continuation}
  print "Back in method, "
end
print "Before method. "
continuation = strange()
print "After method. "
continuation.call if continuation
```

produces:

```
Before method. After method. Back in method, After method.
```

CSV

CSV   Comma-Separated Values

Comma-separated data files are often used to transfer tabular information (and are a *lingua franca* for importing and exporting spreadsheet and database information). As of Ruby 1.9, the old library has been replaced by James Edward Gray II's FasterCSV version. It has a few incompatibilities with the original. In particular, CSV.open now works like File.open, not File.foreach, and options are passed as a hash and not positional parameters.

Ruby's CSV library deals with arrays (corresponding to the rows in the CSV file) and strings (corresponding to the elements in a row). If an element in a row is missing, it will be represented as a nil in Ruby.

The files used in the following examples are as follows:

csvfile:
```
12,eggs,2.89,
2,"shirt, blue",21.45,special
1,"""Hello Kitty"" bag",13.99
```

csvfile_hdr:
```
Count,Description,Price
12,eggs,2.89,
2,"shirt, blue",21.45,special
1,"""Hello Kitty"" bag",13.99
```

- Reads a file containing CSV data and process line by line:

slcsv_1.rb
```
require 'csv'
CSV.foreach("csvfile") do |row|
  qty = row[0].to_i
  price = row[2].to_f
  printf "%20s: $%5.2f %s\n", row[1], qty*price, row[3] || "  ---"
end
```

produces:
```
             eggs: $34.68    ---
      shirt, blue: $42.90 special
"Hello Kitty" bag: $13.99    ---
```

- Processes a CSV file that contains a header line. Automatically converts fields that look like numbers.

slcsv_2.rb
```
require 'csv'
total_cost = 0
CSV.foreach("csvfile_hdr", headers: true, converters: :numeric) do |data|
  total_cost += data["Count"] * data["Price"]
end
puts "Total cost is #{total_cost}"
```

produces:
```
Total cost is 91.57
```

- Writes CSV data to an existing open stream (STDOUT in this case). Uses | as the column separator.

slcsv_3.rb

```ruby
require 'csv'
CSV(STDOUT, col_sep: "|") do |csv|
  csv << [ 1, "line 1", 27 ]
  csv << [ 2, nil, 123 ]
  csv << [ 3, "|bar|", 32.5]
end
```

produces:

```
1|line 1|27
2||123
3|"|bar|"|32.5
```

- You can access a CSV file as a two-dimensional table:

slcsv_4.rb

```ruby
require 'csv'
table = CSV.read("csvfile_hdr",
                  headers: true,
                  header_converters: :symbol)
puts "Row count = #{table.count}"
puts "First row = #{table[0].fields}"
puts "Count of eggs = #{table[0][:count]}"
table << [99, "red balloons", 1.23]
table[:in_stock] = [10, 5, 10, 10]
puts "\nAfter adding a row and a column, the new table is:"
puts table
```

produces:

```
Row count = 3
First row = ["12", "eggs", "2.89", nil]
Count of eggs = 12

After adding a row and a column, the new table is:
count,description,price,,in_stock
12,eggs,2.89,,10
2,"shirt, blue",21.45,special,5
1,"""Hello Kitty"" bag",13.99,10
99,red balloons,1.23,,10
```

Library

Curses

CRT Screen Handling

The Curses library is a fairly thin wrapper around the C curses or ncurses libraries, allowing applications a device-independent way of drawing on consoles and other terminal-like devices. As a nod toward object-orientation, curses windows and mouse events are represented as Ruby objects. Otherwise, the standard curses calls and constants are simply defined in the Curses module.

Only if: curses or ncurses installed in target environment

slcurses_1.rb

```ruby
# Draw the paddle of a simple game of 'pong'. It moves
# in response to the up and down keys
require 'curses'
include Curses
class Paddle
  HEIGHT = 4
  PADDLE = " \n" + "|\n"*HEIGHT + " "
  def initialize
    @top = (Curses::lines - HEIGHT)/2
    draw
  end
  def up
    @top -= 1 if @top > 1
  end
  def down
    @top += 1 if (@top + HEIGHT + 1) < lines
  end
  def draw
    setpos(@top-1, 0)
    addstr(PADDLE)
    refresh
  end
end
init_screen
begin
  crmode
  noecho
  stdscr.keypad(true)
  paddle = Paddle.new
  loop do
    case ch = getch
    when "Q".ord, "q".ord then    break
    when Key::UP           then    paddle.up
    when Key::DOWN         then    paddle.down
    else beep
    end
    paddle.draw
  end
ensure
  close_screen
end
```

Library ## Date/DateTime   Date and Time Manipulation

The date library implements classes Date and DateTime, which provide a comprehensive set of facilities for storing, manipulating, and converting dates with or without time components. The classes can represent and manipulate civil, ordinal, commercial, Julian, and standard dates, starting January 1, 4713 BCE. The DateTime class extends Date with hours, minutes, seconds, and fractional seconds, and it provides some support for time zones. The classes also provide support for parsing and formatting date and datetime strings. The classes have a rich interface—consult the ri documentation for details. The introductory notes in the file lib/date.rb are also well worth reading.

- Experiment with various representations:

sldate_1.rb

```ruby
require 'date'

d = Date.new(2000, 3, 31)
[d.year, d.yday, d.wday]        # =>   [2000, 91, 5]
[d.month, d.mday]              # =>   [3, 31]
[d.cwyear, d.cweek, d.cwday]   # =>   [2000, 13, 5]
[d.jd, d.mjd]                  # =>   [2451635, 51634]
d1 = Date.commercial(2000, 13, 7)
d1.to_s                        # =>   "2000-04-02"
[d1.cwday, d1.wday]            # =>   [7, 0]
```

- Essential information about Christmas:

sldate_2.rb

```ruby
require 'date'
now = DateTime.now
year = now.year
year += 1 if now.month == 12 && now.day > 25
xmas = DateTime.new(year, 12, 25)
diff = xmas - now
puts "It's #{diff.to_i} days to Christmas"
puts "Christmas #{year} falls on a #{xmas.strftime('%A')}"
```

produces:

```
It's 268 days to Christmas
Christmas 2009 falls on a Friday
```

Library
DBM   Interface to DBM Databases

DBM files implement simple, hashlike persistent stores. Many DBM implementations exist: the Ruby library can be configured to use one of the DBM libraries db, dbm (ndbm), gdbm, and qdbm. The interface to DBM files is similar to class Hash, except that DBM keys and values will be strings. This can cause confusion, because the conversion to a string is performed silently when the data is written. The DBM library is a wrapper around the lower-level access method. For true low-level access, see also the GDBM and SDBM libraries.

Only if: a DBM library is installed in target environment

See also: gdbm (page 749), sdbm (page 797)

- Creates a simple DBM file and then reopens it read-only and reads some data. Note the conversion of a date object to its string form.

sldbm_1.rb

```
require 'dbm'
require 'date'
DBM.open("data.dbm") do |dbm|
  dbm['name'] = "Walter Wombat"
  dbm['dob']  = Date.new(1997, 12,25)
end
DBM.open("data.dbm", nil, DBM::READER) do |dbm|
  p dbm.keys
  p dbm['dob']
  p dbm['dob'].class
end
```

produces:

```
["name", "dob"]
"1997-12-25"
String
```

- Reads from the system's *aliases* file. Note the trailing null bytes on all strings.

sldbm_2.rb

```
require 'dbm'
DBM.open("/etc/aliases", nil) do |dbm|
  p dbm.keys
  p dbm["postfix\000"]
end
```

produces:

```
["postmaster:\x00", "daemon:\x00", "ftp-bugs:\x00", "operator:\x00",
 "abuse:\x00", "decode:\x00", "mailer-daemon:\x00", "bin:\x00",
 "named:\x00", "nobody:\x00", "uucp:\x00", "www:\x00", "postfix:\x00",
 "manager:\x00", "dumper:\x00"]
nil
```

Library

Delegator   Delegate Calls to Other Object

Object delegation is a way of *composing* objects—extending an object with the capabilities of another—at runtime. The Ruby Delegator class implements a simple but powerful delegation scheme, where requests are automatically forwarded from a master class to delegates or their ancestors and where the delegate can be changed at runtime with a single method call.

See also: Forwardable (page 748)

- For simple cases where the class of the delegate is fixed, make the master class a subclass of DelegateClass, passing the name of the class to be delegated as a parameter. In the master class's initialize method, pass the object to be delegated to the superclass.

sldelegate_1.rb

```ruby
require 'delegate'

class Words < DelegateClass(Array)
  def initialize(list = "/usr/share/dict/words")
    words = File.read(list).split
    super(words)
  end
end

words = Words.new
words[9999]           # =>   "anticritique"
words.size            # =>   234936
words.grep(/matz/)    # =>   ["matzo", "matzoon", "matzos", "matzoth"]
```

- Use SimpleDelegator to delegate to a particular object (which can be changed):

sldelegate_2.rb

```ruby
require 'delegate'

words = File.read("/usr/share/dict/words").split
names = File.read("/usr/share/dict/propernames").split

stats = SimpleDelegator.new(words)
stats.size   # =>   234936
stats[226]   # =>   "abidingly"
stats.__setobj__(names)
stats.size   # =>   1323
stats[226]   # =>   "Dave"
```

Library

Digest
MD5, RIPEMD-160 SHA1, and SHA2 Digests

The Digest module is the home for a number of classes that implement message digest algorithms: MD5, RIPEMD-160, SHA1, and SHA2 (256, 384, and 512 bit). The interface to all these classes is identical.

- You can create a binary or hex digest for a given string by calling the class method digest or hexdigest.

- You can also create an object (optionally passing in an initial string) and determine the object's hash by calling the digest or hexdigest instance methods. In this case, you can then append to the string using the update method and then recover an updated hash value.

- Calculates some MD5 and SHA1 hashes:

sldigest_1.rb

```
require 'digest/md5'
require 'digest/sha1'
for hash_class in [ Digest::MD5, Digest::SHA1 ]
  puts "Using #{hash_class.name}"
  # Calculate directly
  puts hash_class.hexdigest("hello world")
  # Or by accumulating
  digest = hash_class.new
  digest << "hello"
  digest << " "
  digest << "world"
  puts digest.hexdigest
  puts
end
```

produces:

```
Using Digest::MD5
5eb63bbbe01eeed093cb22bb8f5acdc3
5eb63bbbe01eeed093cb22bb8f5acdc3

Using Digest::SHA1
2aae6c35c94fcfb415dbe95f408b9ce91ee846ed
2aae6c35c94fcfb415dbe95f408b9ce91ee846ed
```

Library
DL
Access Dynamically Loaded Libraries (.dll and .so)

Only if:
Windows, or
system
supports dl
library

The DL module interfaces to the underlying operating system's dynamic loading capabilities. On Windows boxes, it can be used to interface with functions in DLLs. Under Unix it can load shared libraries. Because Ruby does not have typed method parameters or return values, you must define the types expected by the methods you call by specifying their signatures. This can be done using a C-like syntax (if you use the high-level methods in dl/import) or using explicit type specifiers in the lower-level DL module. Good documentation is provided in the source tree's ext/dl/doc/ directory.

- Here's a trivial C program that we'll build as a shared library:

`sldl_1.rb`

```
#include <stdio.h>
int print_msg(text, number) {
  return printf("Text: %s (%d)\n", text, number);
}
```

- Generates a proxy to access the print_msg method in the shared library. The way this book is built, the shared library is in the subdirectory code/dl; this directory must be added to the directories searched when looking for dynamic objects.

`sldl_2.rb`

```
ENV['DYLD_LIBRARY_PATH'] = ":code/dl"  # Mac OS X
require 'dl/func'
lib = DL.dlopen("code/dl/lib.so")
cfunc = DL::CFunc.new(lib['print_msg'], DL::TYPE_INT, 'print_msg')
print_msg = DL::Function.new(cfunc, [DL::TYPE_VOIDP, DL::TYPE_INT])
msg_size = print_msg.call("Answer", 42)
puts "Just wrote #{msg_size} bytes"
```

produces:

```
Just wrote 18 bytes
Text: Answer (42)
```

- We can also wrap the method in a module:

`sldl_3.rb`

```
ENV['DYLD_LIBRARY_PATH'] = ":code/dl"  # Mac OS X
require 'dl/import'
module Message
  extend DL::Importer
  dlload "lib.so"
  extern "int print_msg(char *, int)"
end
msg_size = Message.print_msg("Answer", 42)
puts "Just wrote #{msg_size} bytes"
```

produces:

```
Just wrote 18 bytes
Text: Answer (42)
```

Library		
dRuby		Distributed Ruby Objects (drb)

dRuby allows Ruby objects to be distributed across a network connection. Although expressed in terms of clients and servers, once the initial connection is established, the protocol is effectively symmetrical: either side can invoke methods in objects on the other side. Normally, objects passed and returned by remote calls are passed by value; including the DRbUndumped module in an object forces it to be passed by reference (useful when implementing callbacks).

See also: Rinda (page 792), XMLRPC (page 821)

- This server program is *observable*—it notifies all registered listeners of changes to a count value:

sldrb_1.rb

```
require 'drb'
require 'drb/observer'
class Counter
  include DRb::DRbObservable
  def run
    5.times do |count|
      changed
      notify_observers(count)
    end
  end
end
counter = Counter.new
DRb.start_service('druby://localhost:9001', counter)
DRb.thread.join
```

- This client program interacts with the server, registering a listener object to receive callbacks before invoking the server's run method:

sldrb_2.rb

```
require 'drb'
class Listener
  include DRbUndumped
  def update(value)
    puts value
  end
end
DRb.start_service
counter = DRbObject.new(nil, "druby://localhost:9001")
listener = Listener.new
counter.add_observer(listener)
counter.run
```

Library

English

English Names for Global Symbols

Includes the English library file in a Ruby script, and you can reference the global variables such as $_ using less-cryptic names, listed in the following table.English. It is now predefined in the Ruby interpreter.

$*	$ARGV	$_	$LAST_READ_LINE
$?	$CHILD_STATUS	$"	$LOADED_FEATURES
$<	$DEFAULT_INPUT	$&	$MATCH
$>	$DEFAULT_OUTPUT	$.	$NR
$!	$ERROR_INFO	$,	$OFS
$@	$ERROR_POSITION	$\	$ORS
$;	$FIELD_SEPARATOR	$,	$OUTPUT_FIELD_SEPARATOR
$;	$FS	$\	$OUTPUT_RECORD_SEPARATOR
$=	$IGNORECASE	$$	$PID
$.	$INPUT_LINE_NUMBER	$'	$POSTMATCH
$/	$INPUT_RECORD_SEPARATOR	$`	$PREMATCH
$~	$LAST_MATCH_INFO	$$	$PROCESS_ID
$+	$LAST_PAREN_MATCH	$/	$RS

`slenglish_1.rb`

```ruby
require 'English'
$OUTPUT_FIELD_SEPARATOR = ' -- '
"waterbuffalo" =~ /buff/
print $., $INPUT_LINE_NUMBER, "\n"
print $', $POSTMATCH, "\n"
print $$, $PID
```

produces:

```
0 -- 0 --
 -- alo -- alo --
 -- 48223 -- 48223 --
```

Library
erb
Lightweight Templating for HTML

ERb is a lightweight templating system, allowing you to intermix Ruby code and plain text. This is sometimes a convenient way to create HTML documents but also is usable in other plain-text situations. For other templating solutions, see 295.

ERB breaks its input text into chunks of regular text and program fragments. It then builds a Ruby program that, when run, outputs the result text and executes the program fragments. Program fragments are enclosed between <% and %> markers. The exact interpretation of these fragments depends on the character following the opening <%, as shown in Table 28.1 on the facing page.

slerb_1.rb
```
require 'erb'
input = %{<% high.downto(low) do |n|    # set high, low externally %>
  <%= n %> green bottles, hanging on the wall
  <%= n %> green bottles, hanging on the wall
  And if one green bottle should accidentally fall
  There'd be <%= n-1 %> green bottles, hanging on the wall
<% end %>}
high,low = 10, 8
erb = ERB.new(input)
erb.run(binding)
```

produces:
```
  10 green bottles, hanging on the wall
  10 green bottles, hanging on the wall
  And if one green bottle should accidentally fall
  There'd be 9 green bottles, hanging on the wall
       . . .
```

An optional second parameter to ERB.new sets the safe level for evaluating expressions. If nil, expressions are evaluated in the current thread; otherwise, a new thread is created, and its $SAFE level is set to the parameter value.

The optional third parameter to ERB.new allows some control of the interpretation of the input and of the way whitespace is added to the output. If the third parameter is a string and that string contains a percent sign, then ERB treats lines starting with a percent sign specially. Lines starting with a single percent sign are treated as if they were enclosed in <%...%>. Lines starting with a double percent sign are copied to the output with a single leading percent sign.

```
str = %{\
% 2.times do |i|
  This is line <%= i %>
%end
%% done}
ERB.new(str, 0, '%').run
```
⇒
produces:
```
  This is line 0
  This is line 1
% done
```

If the third parameter contains the string < >, then a newline will not be written if an input line starts with an ERB directive and ends with %>. If the trim parameter contains >, then a newline will not be written if an input line ends %>.

Table 28.1. Directives for ERB

Sequence	Action
<% *ruby code* %>	Inserts the given Ruby code at this point in the generated program. If it outputs anything, include this output in the result.
<%= *ruby expression* %>	Evaluate expression and insert its value in the output of the generated program.
<%# ... %>	Comment (ignored).
<%% and %%>	Replaced in the output by <% and%> respectively.

slerb_4.rb

```
str1 = %{\
* <%= "cat" %>
<%= "dog" %>
}
ERB.new(str1, 0, ">").run
ERB.new(str1, 0, "<>").run
```

produces:

```
* catdog* cat
dog
```

The erb library also defines the helper module ERB::Util that contains two methods: html_escape (aliased as h) and url_encode (aliased as u). These are equivalent to the CGI methods escapeHTML and escape, respectively (except escape encodes spaces as plus signs, and url_encode uses %20).

slerb_5.rb

```
include ERB::Util
str1 = %{\
h(a) = <%= h(a) %>
u(a) = <%= u(a) %>
}
a = "< a & b >"
ERB.new(str1).run(binding)
```

produces:

```
h(a) = &lt; a &amp; b &gt;
u(a) = %3C%20a%20%26%20b%20%3E
```

You may find the command-line utility erb is supplied with your Ruby distribution. This allows you to run erb substitutions on an input file; see erb --help for details.

Library

Etc

Access User and Group Information in /etc/passwd

The Etc module provides a number of methods for querying the passwd and group facilities on Unix systems.

Only if: Unix or Cygwin

- Finds out information about the currently logged-in user:

```
sletc_1.rb
```

```ruby
require 'etc'

name = Etc.getlogin
info = Etc.getpwnam(name)
info.name    # =>   "dave"
info.uid     # =>   501
info.dir     # =>   "/Users/dave"
info.shell   # =>   "/bin/bash"

group = Etc.getgrgid(info.gid)
group.name   # =>   "dave"
```

- Returns the names of users on the system used to create this book:

```
sletc_2.rb
```

```ruby
require 'etc'

users = []
Etc.passwd {|passwd| users << passwd.name }
users[1,5].join(", ")   # =>   "_appowner, _appserver, _ard,
                                  _atsserver, _calendar"
```

- Returns the IDs of groups on the system used to create this book:

```
sletc_3.rb
```

```ruby
require 'etc'

ids = []
Etc.group {|entry| ids << entry.gid }
ids[1,5].join(", ")   # =>   "87, 81, 79, 67, 97"
```

Library		
expect		Expect Method for IO Objects

The expect library adds the method expect to all IO objects. This allows you to write code that waits for a particular string or pattern to be available from the I/O stream. The expect method is particularly useful with pty objects (see page 786) and with network connections to remote servers, where it can be used to coordinate the use of external interactive processes.

If the global variable $expect_verbose is true, the expect method writes all characters read from the I/O stream to STDOUT.

See also: pty (page 786)

- Connects to the local FTP server, logs in, and prints out the name of the user's directory. (Note that it would be a lot easier to do this using the net/ftp library.)

`slexpect_1.rb`

```ruby
# This code might be specific to the particular
# ftp daemon.
require 'expect'
require 'socket'
$expect_verbose = true
socket = TCPSocket.new('localhost', 'ftp')
socket.expect("ready")
socket.puts("user testuser")
socket.expect("Password required for testuser")
socket.puts("pass secret")
socket.expect("logged in.\r\n")
socket.puts("pwd")
puts(socket.gets)
socket.puts "quit"
```

produces:

```
220 localhost FTP server (tnftpd 20061217) ready.
331 Password required for testuser.
230 User testuser logged in.
257 "/Users/testuser" is the current directory.
```

Library   **Fcntl**   Symbolic Names for IO#fcntl Commands

The Fcntl module provides symbolic names for each of the host system's available fcntl constants (defined in fcntl.h). That is, if the host system has a constant named F_GETLK defined in fcntl.h, then the Fcntl module will have a corresponding constant Fcntl::F_GETLK with the same value as the header file's #define.

• Different operating system will have different Fcntl constants available. The value associated with a constant of a given name may also differ across platforms. Here are the values on my Mac OS X system:

`slfcntl_1.rb`

```
require 'fcntl'
Fcntl.constants.sort.each do |name|
  printf "%10s: 0x%06x\n", name, Fcntl.const_get(name)
end
```

produces:

```
FD_CLOEXEC: 0x000001
   F_DUPFD: 0x000000
   F_GETFD: 0x000001
   F_GETFL: 0x000003
   F_GETLK: 0x000007
   F_RDLCK: 0x000001
   F_SETFD: 0x000002
   F_SETFL: 0x000004
   F_SETLK: 0x000008
  F_SETLKW: 0x000009
   F_UNLCK: 0x000002
   F_WRLCK: 0x000003
 O_ACCMODE: 0x000003
  O_APPEND: 0x000008
   O_CREAT: 0x000200
    O_EXCL: 0x000800
  O_NDELAY: 0x000004
  O_NOCTTY: 0x020000
O_NONBLOCK: 0x000004
  O_RDONLY: 0x000000
    O_RDWR: 0x000002
   O_TRUNC: 0x000400
  O_WRONLY: 0x000001
```

Library **Fiber** Coroutines Using Fibers

The Fiber class that is built into Ruby provides a generator-lke capability—fibers may be created and resumed from some controlling program. If you want to extend the Fiber class to provide full, symmetrical coroutines, you need first to require the fiber library. This adds two instance methods, transfer and alive? to Fiber objects, and the singleton method current to the Fiber class.

- It is difficult to come up with a meaningful, concise example of symmetric coroutines that can't more easily be coded with asymetric (plain old) fibers. So, here's an artificial example....

slfiber_1.rb

```ruby
require 'fiber'
# take items two at a time off a queue, calling the producer
# if not enough are available
consumer = Fiber.new do |producer, queue|
  5.times do
    while queue.size < 2
      queue = producer.transfer(consumer, queue)
    end
    puts "Consume #{queue.shift} and #{queue.shift}"
  end
end

# add items three at a time to the queue
producer = Fiber.new do |consumer, queue|
  value = 1
  loop do
    puts "Producing more stuff"
    3.times { queue << value; value += 1}
    puts "Queue size is #{queue.size}"
    consumer.transfer queue
  end
end

consumer.transfer(producer, [])
```

produces:

```
Producing more stuff
Queue size is 3
Consume 1 and 2
Producing more stuff
Queue size is 4
Consume 3 and 4
Consume 5 and 6
Producing more stuff
Queue size is 3
Consume 7 and 8
Producing more stuff
Queue size is 4
Consume 9 and 10
```

FileUtils

Library		
FileUtils		File and Directory Manipulation

FileUtils is a collection of methods for manipulating files and directories. Although generally applicable, the model is particularly useful when writing installation scripts.

Many methods take a *src* and a *dest* parameter. If *dest* is a directory, *src* may be a single filename or an array of filenames. For example, the following copies the files a, b, and c to /tmp:

```
cp( %w{ a b c }, "/tmp")
```

Most functions take a set of options. These may be zero or more of the following:

Option	Meaning
:verbose	Traces execution of each function (by default to STDERR, although this can be overridden by setting the class variable @fileutils_output).
:noop	Does not perform the action of the function (useful for testing scripts).
:force	Overrides some default conservative behavior of the method (for example, over-writing an existing file).
:preserve	Attempts to preserve atime, mtime, and mode information from *src* in *dest*. (Setuid and setgid flags are always cleared.)

For maximum portability, use forward slashes to separate the directory components of file-names, even on Windows.

FileUtils contains three submodules that duplicate the top-level methods but with different default options: module FileUtils::Verbose sets the verbose option, module FileUtils::NoWrite sets noop, and FileUtils::DryRun sets verbose and noop.

See also: un (page 816)

`slfileutils_2.rb`

```
require 'fileutils'
include FileUtils::Verbose
cd("/tmp") do
  cp("/etc/passwd", "tmp_passwd")
  chmod(0666, "tmp_passwd")
  cp_r("/usr/include/net/", "headers")
  rm("tmp_passwd")       # Tidy up
  rm_rf("headers")
end
```

produces:

```
cd /tmp
cp /etc/passwd tmp_passwd
chmod 666 tmp_passwd
cp -r /usr/include/net/ headers
rm tmp_passwd
rm -rf headers
cd -
```

The Find module supports the top-down traversal of a set of file paths, given as arguments to the find method. If an argument is a file, its name is passed to the block associated with the call. If it's a directory, then its name and the name of all its files and subdirectories will be passed in. If no block is associated with the call, an Enumerator is returned.

Within the block, the method prune may be called, which skips the current file or directory, restarting the loop with the next directory. If the current file is a directory, that directory will not be recursively entered. In the following example, we don't list the contents of the local Subversion cache directories:

`slfind_1.rb`

```ruby
require 'find'
Find.find("/etc/passwd", "code/cdjukebox") do |f|
  type = case
         when File.file?(f)      then "File: "
         when File.directory?(f) then "Dir:  "
         else "?"
         end
  puts "#{type} #{f}"
  Find.prune if f =~ /.svn/
end
```

produces:

```
File:   /etc/passwd
Dir:    code/cdjukebox
File:   code/cdjukebox/Makefile
File:   code/cdjukebox/libcdjukebox.a
File:   code/cdjukebox/cdjukebox.o
File:   code/cdjukebox/cdjukebox.h
File:   code/cdjukebox/cdjukebox.c
Dir:    code/cdjukebox/.svn
```

Forwardable   Object Delegation

Forwardable provides a mechanism to allow classes to delegate named method calls to other objects.

See also: Delegator (page 735)

- This simple symbol table uses a hash, exposing a subset of the hash's methods:

  slforwardable_1.rb

  ```
  require 'forwardable'

  class SymbolTable
    extend Forwardable
    def_delegator(:@hash, :[],  :lookup)
    def_delegator(:@hash, :[]=, :add)
    def_delegators(:@hash, :size, :has_key?)
    def initialize
      @hash = Hash.new
    end
  end

  st = SymbolTable.new
  st.add('cat', 'feline animal')   # =>   "feline animal"
  st.add('dog', 'canine animal')   # =>   "canine animal"
  st.add('cow', 'bovine animal')   # =>   "bovine animal"

  st.has_key?('cow')               # =>   true
  st.lookup('dog')                 # =>   "canine animal"
  ```

- Forwards can also be defined for individual objects by extending them with the Single-Forwardable module. It's hard to think of a good reason to use this feature, so here's a silly one:

  slforwardable_2.rb

  ```
  require 'forwardable'
  TRICKS = [ "roll over", "play dead" ]
  dog = "rover"
  dog.extend SingleForwardable
  dog.def_delegator(:TRICKS, :each, :can)
  dog.can do |trick|
    puts trick
  end
  ```

  produces:

  ```
  roll over
  play dead
  ```

Library		
GDBM		Interface to GDBM Database

Only if: gdbm
library available

Interfaces to the gdbm database library.[1] Although the DBM library provides generic access to gdbm databases, it doesn't expose some features of the full gdbm interface. The GDBM library gives you access to underlying gdbm features such as the cache size, synchronization mode, reorganization, and locking. Only one process may have a GDBM database open for writing (unless locking is disabled).

See also: DBM (page 734), SDBM (page 797)

- Stores some values into a database and then reads them back. The second parameter to the open method specifies the file mode, and the next parameter uses two flags that (1) create the database if it doesn't exist, and (2) force all writes to be synced to disk. Create on open is the default Ruby gdbm behavior.

slgdbm_1.rb
```ruby
require 'gdbm'
GDBM.open("data.dbm", 0644, GDBM::WRCREAT | GDBM::SYNC) do |dbm|
  dbm['name'] = "Walter Wombat"
  dbm['dob']  = "1969-12-25"
  dbm['uses'] = "Ruby"
end
GDBM.open("data.dbm") do |dbm|
  p dbm.keys
  p dbm['dob']
  dbm.delete('dob')
  p dbm.keys
end
```

produces:
```
["uses", "dob", "name"]
"1969-12-25"
["uses", "name"]
```

- Opens a database read-only. Note that the attempt to delete a key fails.

slgdbm_2.rb
```ruby
require 'gdbm'
GDBM.open("data.dbm", 0, GDBM::READER) do |dbm|
  p dbm.keys
  dbm.delete('name')
end
```

produces:
```
["uses", "name"]
prog.rb:4:in `delete': Reader can't delete (GDBMError)
from /tmp/prog.rb:5:in `block in <main>'
from /tmp/prog.rb:3:in `open'
```

G DBM

---

1.   http://www.gnu.org/software/gdbm/gdbm.html

Library
GetoptLong   Parse Command-Line Options

Class GetoptLong supports GNU-style command-line option parsing. Options may be a minus sign (–) followed by a single character or may be two minus signs (- -) followed by a name (a long option). Long options may be abbreviated to their shortest unambiguous lengths.

A single internal option may have multiple external representations. For example, the option to control verbose output could be any of -v, --verbose, or --details. Some options may also take an associated value.

Each internal option is passed to GetoptLong as an array, containing strings representing the option's external forms and a flag. The flag specifies how GetoptLong is to associate an argument with the option (NO_ARGUMENT, REQUIRED_ARGUMENT, or OPTIONAL_ARGUMENT).

If the environment variable POSIXLY_CORRECT is set, all options must precede non-options on the command line. Otherwise, the default behavior of GetoptLong is to reorganize the command line to put the options at the front. This behavior may be changed by setting GetoptLong#ordering= to one of the constants PERMUTE, REQUIRE_ORDER, or RETURN_IN_ORDER. POSIXLY_CORRECT may not be overridden.

See also: OptionParser (page 776)

`sigetoptlong_1.rb`

```
# Call using "ruby example.rb --size 10k -v -q a.txt b.doc"
require 'getoptlong'
# specify the options we accept and initialize
# the option parser
opts = GetoptLong.new(
  [ "--size",    "-s",            GetoptLong::REQUIRED_ARGUMENT ],
  [ "--verbose", "-v",            GetoptLong::NO_ARGUMENT ],
  [ "--query",   "-q",            GetoptLong::NO_ARGUMENT ],
  [ "--check",   "--valid", "-c", GetoptLong::NO_ARGUMENT ]
)
# process the parsed options
opts.each do |opt, arg|
  puts "Option: #{opt}, arg #{arg.inspect}"
end
puts "Remaining args: #{ARGV.join(', ')}"
```

produces:

```
Option: --size, arg "10k"
Option: --verbose, arg ""
Option: --query, arg ""
Remaining args: a.txt, b.doc
```

Library **GServer**   Generic TCP Server

Simple framework for writing TCP servers. Subclasses the GServer class, sets the port (and potentially other parameters) in the constructor, and then implements a serve method to handle incoming requests.

GServer manages a thread pool for incoming connections, so your serve method may be running in multiple threads in parallel.

You can run multiple GServer copies on different ports in the same application.

- When a connection is made on port 2000, responds with the current time as a string. Terminates after handling three requests.

slgserver_1.rb

```ruby
require 'gserver'
class TimeServer < GServer
  def initialize
    super(2000)
    @count = 3
  end
  def serve(client)
    client.puts Time.now
    @count -= 1
    stop if @count.zero?
  end
end
server = TimeServer.new
server.audit = true    # enable logging
server.start
server.join
```

- You can test this server by reading from *localhost* on port 2000. We use curl to do this—you could also use telnet:

```
% curl -s localhost:2000
```

produces:

```
2009-03-31 09:58:47 -0500
```

conv

The Iconv class is an interface to the Open Group's iconv library, which supports the translation of strings between character encodings. For a list of the supported encodings on your platform, see the iconv_open man pages for your system.

Only if: libiconv installed

An Iconv object encapsulates a conversion descriptor, which in turn contains the information needed to convert from one encoding to another. The converter can be used multiple times, until closed.

The conversion method iconv can be called multiple times to convert input strings. At the end, it should be called with a nil argument to flush out any remaining output.

The new string transcoding functions in Ruby 1.9 make the basic Iconv functions redundant. However, Iconv has capabilities (such as transliteration) that are not part of the built-in Ruby functionality.

- Converts from ISO-8859-1 to UTF-16:

```
require 'iconv'
conv = Iconv.new("UTF-16", "ISO-8859-1")
result = conv.iconv("hello")
result << conv.iconv(nil)
result.dump   # =>   "\xFE\xFF\x00h\x00e\x00l\x00l\x00o"
```

- Does the same conversion using a class method. Note that we use Iconv.conv, which returns a single string, as opposed to Iconv.iconv, which returns an array of strings.

```
require 'iconv'
result = Iconv.conv("UTF-16", "ISO-8859-1", "hello")
result.dump   # =>   "\xFE\xFF\x00h\x00e\x00l\x00l\x00o"
```

- Converts *olé* from UTF-8 to ISO-8859-1:

```
require 'iconv'
result = Iconv.conv("ISO-8859-1", "UTF-8", "ol\303\251")
result.dump   # =>   "ol\xE9"
```

- Converts *olé* from UTF-8 to ASCII. This throws an exception, because ASCII doesn't have an *é* character.

```
require 'iconv'
result = Iconv.conv("ASCII", "UTF-8", "ol\303\251")
```

produces:

```
prog.rb:2:in `conv': "\xC3\xA9" (Iconv::IllegalSequence)
from /tmp/prog.rb:2:in `<main>'
```

- This time, converts to ASCII with transliteration, which shows approximations of missing characters:

```
require 'iconv'
result = Iconv.iconv("ASCII//TRANSLIT", "UTF-8", "ol\303\251")
result[0].dump   # =>   "ol'e"
```

Library

IO/Wait

Check for Pending Data to Be Read

Only if:
FIONREAD
feature in
ioctl(2)

Including the library io/wait adds the methods IO#nread, IO#ready?, and IO#wait to the standard IO class. These allow an IO object opened on a stream (not a file) to be queried to see whether data is available to be read without reading it and to wait for a given number of bytes to become available.

- Sets up a pipe between two processes and writes 10 bytes at a time into it. Periodically sees how much data is available.

`sliowait_1.rb`

```ruby
require 'io/wait'
reader, writer = IO.pipe
if (pid = fork)
  writer.close
  8.times do
    sleep 0.03
    len = reader.ready?
    if len
      puts "#{len} bytes available: #{reader.sysread(len)}"
    else
      puts "No data available"
    end
  end
  Process.waitpid(pid)
else
  reader.close
  5.times do |n|
    sleep 0.04
    writer.write n.to_s * 10
  end
  writer.close
end
```

produces:

```
No data available
10 bytes available: 0000000000
10 bytes available: 1111111111
No data available
10 bytes available: 2222222222
10 bytes available: 3333333333
10 bytes available: 4444444444
No data available
```

Library

IPAddr   Represent and Manipulate IP Addresses

Class IPAddr holds and manipulates Internet Protocol (IP) addresses. Each address contains three parts: an address, a mask, and an address family. The family will typically be AF_INET for IPv4 and IPv6 addresses. The class contains methods for extracting parts of an address, checking for IPv4 compatible addresses (and IPv4-mapped IPv6 addresses), testing whether an address falls within a subnet and many other functions. It is also interesting in that it contains as data its own unit tests.

```
require 'ipaddr'

v4 = IPAddr.new('192.168.23.0/24')
v4              # =>   #<IPAddr: IPv4:192.168.23.0/ 255.255.255.0>
v4.mask(16)     # =>   #<IPAddr: IPv4:192.168.0.0/ 255.255.0.0>
v4.reverse      # =>   "0.23.168.192.in-addr.arpa"
v6 = IPAddr.new('3ffe:505:2::1')
v6              # =>   #<IPAddr:
                       IPv6:3ffe:0505:0002:0000:0000:0000:0000:0001/
                       ffff:ffff:ffff:ffff:ffff:ffff:ffff:ffff>
v6.mask(48)     # =>   #<IPAddr:
                       IPv6:3ffe:0505:0002:0000:0000:0000:0000:0000/
                       ffff:ffff:ffff:0000:0000:0000:0000:0000>

# the value for 'family' is OS dependent. This
# value is for OS X
v6.family       # =>   30

other = IPAddr.new("192.168.23.56")
v4.include?(other)  # =>   true
```

Library
irb

The irb library is most commonly associated with the console command irb. However, you can also start an irb session from within your running application. A common technique is to trap a signal and start irb in the handler.

The following program sets up a signal handler that runs irb when the user hits ^C. The user can change the value of the instance variable @value. When they exit from irb, the original program continues to run with that new value.

slirb_1.rb

```ruby
require 'irb'
trap "INT" do
  IRB.start
end
count = 0
loop do
  count += 1
  puts count
  puts "Value = #{@value}" if defined? @value
  sleep 1
end
```

Here's a simple session using it:

```
$ ruby code/run_irb.rb
1
2
3
^C4
irb(main):001:0> @value = "wibble"
=> "wibble"
irb(main):002:0> exit
5
Value = wibble
6
Value = wibble
...
```

json

JSON is a language-independent data interchange format based on key/value pairs (hashes in Ruby) and sequences of values (arrays in Ruby).[2] JSON is frequently used to exchange data between JavaScript running in browsers and server-based applications. JSON is not a general-purpose object marshaling format. Although you can add to_json methods to your own classes, you will lose interoperability.   See also: yaml (page 822)

- Serializes a data structure into a string and write that to a file:

`sljson_1.rb`

```
require 'json'
data = { name: 'dave', address: [ 'tx', 'usa' ], age: 17 }
serialized = data.to_json
serialized  # =>   {"name":"dave","address":["tx","usa"],"age":17}
File.open("data", "w") {|f| f.puts serialized}
```

- Reads the serialized data from the file and reconstitute it:

`sljson_2.rb`

```
require 'json'
serialized = File.read("data")
data = JSON.parse(serialized)
data   # =>   {"name"=>"dave", "address"=>["tx", "usa"], "age"=>17}
```

- The methods j and jj convert their argument to JSON and write the result to STDOUT (jj prettyprints). This can be useful in irb.

`sljson_3.rb`

```
require 'json'
data = { name: 'dave', address: [ 'tx', 'usa' ], age: 17 }
puts "Regular"
j data
puts "Pretty"
jj data
```

produces:

```
Regular
{"name":"dave","address":["tx","usa"],"age":17}
Pretty
{
  "name": "dave",
  "address": [
    "tx",
    "usa"
  ],
  "age": 17
}
```

---

2.   http://www.ietf.org/rfc/rfc4627.txt

Logger

Writes log messages to a file or stream. Supports automatic time- or size-based rolling of log files. Messages can be assigned severities, and only those messages at or above the logger's current reporting level will be logged.

- During development, you may want to see all messages:

```
require 'logger'
log = Logger.new(STDOUT)
log.level = Logger::DEBUG
log.datetime_format = "%H:%M:%S"
log.info("Application starting")
3.times do |i|
  log.debug("Executing loop, i = #{i}")
  temperature = some_calculation(i)  # defined externally
  if temperature > 50
    log.warn("Possible overheat. i = #{i}")
  end
end
log.info("Application terminating")
```

produces:

```
I, [09:58:48#48356]  INFO -- : Application starting
D, [09:58:48#48356] DEBUG -- : Executing loop, i = 0
D, [09:58:48#48356] DEBUG -- : Executing loop, i = 1
D, [09:58:48#48356] DEBUG -- : Executing loop, i = 2
W, [09:58:48#48356]  WARN -- : Possible overheat. i = 2
I, [09:58:48#48356]  INFO -- : Application terminating
```

- In deployment, you can turn off anything below INFO:

```
require 'logger'
log = Logger.new(STDOUT)
log.level = Logger::INFO
log.datetime_format = "%H:%M:%S"
# as above...
```

produces:

```
I, [09:58:48#48358]  INFO -- : Application starting
W, [09:58:48#48358]  WARN -- : Possible overheat. i = 2
I, [09:58:48#48358]  INFO -- : Application terminating
```

- Logs to a file, which is rotated when it gets to about 10KB. Keeps up to five old files.

```
require 'logger'
log = Logger.new("application.log", 5, 10*1024)
log.info("Application starting")
# ...
```

The mathn library attempts to bring some unity to numbers under Ruby, making classes Bignum, Complex, Fixnum, Integer, and Rational work and play better together. It automatically includes the libraries complex, rational, matrix, and prime.

- Types will tend to convert between themselves in a more natural way (so, for example, Complex::I squared will evaluate to −1, rather than Complex[-1,0]).

- Division will tend to produce more accurate results. The conventional division operator (/) is redefined to use quo, which doesn't round (quo is documented on page 652).

- Related to the previous point, rational numbers will be used in preference to floats when possible. Dividing one by two results in the rational number $\frac{1}{2}$, rather than 0.5 (or 0, the result of normal integer division).

See also: Matrix (page 760), Rational (page 787), Complex (page 728), Prime (page 782)

- Without mathn:

`slmathn_1.rb`

```
require 'matrix'
36/16                    # =>   2
Math.sqrt(36/16)         # =>   1.4142135623731

Complex::I * Complex::I  # =>   (-1+0i)

(36/16)**-2              # =>   1/4
(36.0/16.0)**-2          # =>   0.197530864197531
(-36/16)**-2             # =>   1/9

(36/16)**(1/2)           # =>   1
(-36/16)**(1/2)          # =>   1

(36/16)**(-1/2)          # =>   1/2
(-36/16)**(-1/2)         # =>   -1/3
```

$$
\text{Matrix.diagonal(6,7,8)/3} \quad \# \Rightarrow \quad
\begin{pmatrix} 2 & 0 & 0 \\ 0 & 2 & 0 \\ 0 & 0 & 2 \end{pmatrix}
$$

- With mathn:

`slmathn_2.rb`

```
require 'mathn'
36/16                     # =>   9/4
Math.sqrt(36/16)          # =>   3/2

Complex::I * Complex::I   # =>   -1

(36/16)**-2               # =>   16/81
(36.0/16.0)**-2           # =>   0.197530864197531
(-36/16)**-2              # =>   16/81

(36/16)**(1/2)            # =>   3/2
(-36/16)**(1/2)           # =>   (9.18485099360515e-17+1.5i)

(36/16)**(-1/2)           # =>   2/3
(-36/16)**(-1/2)          # =>   (4.08215599715784e-17-0.666666666666667i)

Matrix.diagonal(6,7,8)/3  # =>
```

$$\begin{pmatrix} 2 & 0 & 0 \\ 0 & 7/3 & 0 \\ 0 & 0 & 8/3 \end{pmatrix}$$

Mathn

Library

Matrix

Matrix and Vector Manipulation

The matrix library defines classes Matrix and Vector, representing rectangular matrices and vectors. As well as the normal arithmetic operations, they provide methods for matrix-specific functions (such as rank, inverse, and determinants) and a number of constructor methods (for creating special-case matrices—zero, identity, diagonal, singular, and vector).

1.9 As of Ruby 1.9, matrices use quo internally for division, so rational numbers may be returned as a result of integer division. In prior versions of Ruby, you'd need to include the mathn library to achieve this.

slmatrix_1.rb

```
require 'matrix'

m1 = Matrix[ [2, 1], [-1, 1] ]          # =>   ( 2   1 )
                                        #      ( -1  1 )

m1[0,1]                                 # =>   1

m1.inv                                  # =>   ( 1/3   -1/3 )
                                        #      ( 1/3    2/3 )

m1 * m1.inv                             # =>   ( 1/1   0/1 )
                                        #      ( 0/1   1/1 )

m1.determinant                          # =>   3/1

m1.singular?                            # =>   false

v1 = Vector[3, 4]                       # =>   Vector[3, 4]

v1.covector                             # =>   ( 3   4 )

m1 * v1                                 # =>   Vector[10, 1]

m2 = Matrix[ [1,2,3], [4,5,6], [7,8,9] ]  # =>   ( 1  2  3 )
                                          #      ( 4  5  6 )
                                          #      ( 7  8  9 )

m2.minor(1, 2, 1, 2)                    # =>   ( 5  6 )
                                        #      ( 8  9 )
```

MiniTest

1.9   New in Ruby 1.9, MiniTest is now the standard unit testing framework supplied with Ruby. The MiniTest library contains classes for unit tests, mock objects, and a (trivial) subset of RSpec-style testing syntax.

The unit testing framework is similar to the original Test::Unit framework. However, if you want functionality that is the same as Test::Unit, use the Test::Unit wrappers for MiniTest—simply require "test/unit" as normal.

Chapter 13 on page 183 contains a tutorial on unit testing with Ruby.

Monitor   Monitor-Based Synchronization

Monitors are a mutual-exclusion mechanism. They allow separate threads to define shared resources that will be accessed exclusively, and they provide a mechanism for a thread to wait for resources to become available in a controlled way.

The monitor library actually defines three separate ways of using monitors: as a parent class, as a mixin, and as a extension to a particular object. In this section, we document the module form of Monitor. The class form is effectively identical. In both the class form and when including MonitorMixin in an existing class, it is essential to invoke super in the class's initialize method.

See also: Thread (page 696)

(The following example would be better written using fibers.)

slmonitor_1.rb

```ruby
require 'monitor'
require 'mathn'
numbers = []
numbers.extend(MonitorMixin)
number_added = numbers.new_cond
# Reporter thread
consumer = Thread.new do
  5.times do
    numbers.synchronize do
      number_added.wait_while { numbers.empty? }
      puts numbers.shift
    end
  end
end
# Prime number generator thread
generator = Thread.new do
  p = Prime.new
  5.times do
    numbers.synchronize do
      numbers << p.succ
      number_added.signal
    end
  end
end
generator.join
consumer.join
```

produces:

```
Prime::new is obsolete. use Prime::instance or class methods of Prime.
2
3
5
7
11
```

Mutex_m

Mutex Mix-In

mutex_m is a variant of class Mutex (documented on page 603) that allows mutex facilities to be mixed into any object.

The Mutex_m module defines methods that correspond to those in Mutex but with the prefix mu_ (so that lock is defined as mu_lock and so on). These are then aliased to the original Mutex names.

See also: Mutex (page 603), Thread (page 696)

`slmutexm_1.rb`

```
require 'mutex_m'

class Counter
  include Mutex_m
  attr_reader :count
  def initialize
    @count = 0
    super
  end
  def tick
    lock
    @count += 1
    unlock
  end
end

c = Counter.new

t1 = Thread.new { 100_000.times {  c.tick } }
t2 = Thread.new { 100_000.times {  c.tick } }

t1.join
t2.join

c.count   # =>   200000
```

Library **Net::FTP**   FTP Client

The net/ftp library implements a File Transfer Protocol (FTP) client. As well as data transfer commands (getbinaryfile, gettextfile, list, putbinaryfile, and puttextfile), the library supports the full complement of server commands (acct, chdir, delete, mdtm, mkdir, nlst, rename, rmdir, pwd, size, status, and system). Anonymous and password-authenticated sessions are supported. Connections may be active or passive.

See also: open-uri (page 773)

`slnetftp_1.rb`

```
require 'net/ftp'
ftp = Net::FTP.new('ftp.ruby-lang.org')
ftp.login
ftp.chdir('pub/ruby/doc')
puts ftp.list('*txt')
ftp.getbinaryfile('MD5SUM.txt', 'md5sum.txt', 1024)
ftp.close
puts File.read('md5sum.txt')
```

produces:

```
-rw-r--r-- 1 1027 100 3060 Jan 21 11:21 MD5SUM.txt
-rw-r--r-- 1 1027 100 3436 Jan 21 11:22 SHA1SUM.txt
d529768c828c930c49b3766d13dc1f2c ruby-man-1.4.6-jp.tar.gz
8eed63fec14a719df26247fb8384db5e ruby-man-1.4.6.tar.gz
623b5d889c1f15b8a50fe0b3b8ba4b0f ruby-man-ja-1.6.6-20011225-rd.tar.gz
5f37ef2d67ab1932881cd713989af6bf ruby-man-ja-html-20050214.tar.bz2
. . .
```

Net::HTTP HTTP Client

The net/http library provides a simple client to fetch headers and web page contents using the HTTP protocol.

The get post, and head methods return a response object, with the content of the response accessible through the response's body method.

See also: OpenSSL (page 775), open-uri (page 773), URI (page 817)

- Opens a connection and fetch a page, displaying the response code and message, header information, and some of the body:

```
require 'net/http'
Net::HTTP.start('www.pragprog.com') do |http|
  response = http.get('/categories/new')
  puts "Code = #{response.code}"
  puts "Message = #{response.message}"
  response.each {|key, val| printf "%-14s = %-40.40s\n", key, val }
  p response.body[0, 55]
end
```

produces:

```
Code = 200
Message = OK
server         = nginx/0.6.34
date           = Tue, 31 Mar 2009 14:58:49 GMT
content-type   = text/html; charset=UTF-8
transfer-encoding = chunked
connection     = keep-alive
set-cookie     = _pragmatic_session_id=5791920183398036f6
status         = 200 OK
x-runtime      = 89ms
etag           = "2b47fa92d9d8ea8cdbbe984ea70c96c7"
x-app-info     = master@854ad4d62c78ed239dd21d23eb27c8295
cache-control  = private, max-age=0, must-revalidate
"<!DOCTYPE html PUBLIC \"-//W3C//DTD XHTML 1.1//EN\"\n  \"ht"
```

- Fetches a single page, displaying the response code and message, header information, and some of the body:

```
require 'net/http'
response = Net::HTTP.get_response('www.pragprog.com',
                                  '/categories/new')
puts "Code = #{response.code}"
puts "Message = #{response.message}"
response.each {|key, val| printf "%-14s = %-40.40s\n", key, val }
p response.body[0, 55]
```

produces:

```
Code = 200
Message = OK
server         = nginx/0.6.34
```

```
date           = Tue, 31 Mar 2009 14:58:49 GMT
content-type   = text/html; charset=UTF-8
connection     = keep-alive
set-cookie     = _pragmatic_session_id=69cd2fbb961630200d
status         = 200 OK
x-runtime      = 78ms
etag           = "2b47fa92d9d8ea8cdbbe984ea70c96c7"
x-app-info     = master@854ad4d62c78ed239dd21d23eb27c8295
cache-control  = private, max-age=0, must-revalidate
content-length = 23283
"<!DOCTYPE html PUBLIC \"-//W3C//DTD XHTML 1.1//EN\"\n  \"ht"
```

- Follows redirections (the open-uri library does this automatically). This code comes from the RDoc documentation.

```
require 'net/http'
require 'uri'
def fetch(uri_str, limit=10)
  fail 'http redirect too deep' if limit.zero?
  puts "Trying: #{uri_str}"
  response = Net::HTTP.get_response(URI.parse(uri_str))
  case response
  when Net::HTTPSuccess     then response
  when Net::HTTPRedirection then fetch(response['location'], limit-1)
  else response.error!
  end
end
response = fetch('http://www.ruby-lang.org')
p response.body[0, 50]
```

produces:

```
Trying: http://www.ruby-lang.org
Trying: http://www.ruby-lang.org/en/
"<!DOCTYPE html PUBLIC \"-//W3C//DTD XHTML 1.1//EN\"\n"
```

- Searches our site for things about Ruby and lists the authors. (This would be tidier using Hpricot,[3] but this doesn't run on Ruby 1.9 as I write this.)

```
require 'net/http'
response = Net::HTTP.post_form(URI.parse('http://pragprog.com/search'),
                              "q" => "ruby")
puts response.body.scan(%r{<p class="by-line">by (.*?)</p>})[0,3]
```

produces:

```
Dave Thomas, with Chad Fowler and Andy Hunt
Bruce Tate
Lyle Johnson
```

3.   http://code.whytheluckystiff.net/hpricot/

Library

Net::IMAP

Access an IMAP Mail Server

The Internet Mail Access Protocol (IMAP) is used to allow mail clients to access mail servers. It supports plain-text login and the IMAP login and CRAM-MD5 authentication mechanisms. Once connected, the library supports threading, so multiple interactions with the server may take place at the same time.

The examples that follow are taken with minor modifications from the RDoc documentation in the library source file.

The TMail gem provides an interface for creating and parsing e-mail messages.

See also: Net::POP (page 768)

- Lists senders and subjects of messages to "dave" in the inbox:

`slnetimap_1.rb`

```
require 'net/imap'
imap = Net::IMAP.new('my.mailserver.com')
imap.authenticate('LOGIN', 'dave', 'secret')
imap.examine('INBOX')
puts "Message count: #{ imap.responses["EXISTS"]}"
imap.search(["TO", "dave"]).each do |message_id|
  envelope = imap.fetch(message_id, "ENVELOPE")[0].attr["ENVELOPE"]
     puts "#{envelope.from[0].name}: \t#{envelope.subject}"
end
```

- Moves all messages with a date in April 2008 from the folder Mail/sent-mail to Mail/sent-apr08:

`slnetimap_2.rb`

```
require 'net/imap'
imap = Net::IMAP.new('my.mailserver.com')
imap.authenticate('LOGIN', 'dave', 'secret')
imap.select('Mail/sent-mail')
if not imap.list('Mail/', 'sent-apr08')
  imap.create('Mail/sent-apr08')
end
imap.search(["BEFORE", "01-May-2008",
             "SINCE",  "1-Apr-2008"]).each do |message_id|
  imap.copy(message_id, "Mail/sent-apr08")
  imap.store(message_id, "+FLAGS", [:Deleted])
end
imap.expunge
```

Library
Net::POP
Access a POP Mail Server

The net/pop library provides a simple client to fetch and delete mail on a Post Office Protocol (POP) server.

The class Net::POP3 is used to access a POP server, returning a list of Net::POPMail objects, one per message stored on the server. These POPMail objects are then used to fetch and/or delete individual messages. The TMail gem provides an interface for creating and parsing e-mail messages.

The library also provides class APOP, an alternative to the POP3 class that performs authentication.

`slnetpop_1.rb`

```ruby
require 'net/pop'
pop = Net::POP3.new('server.ruby-stuff.com')
pop.start('joe', 'secret') do |server|
  msg = server.mails[0]
  # Print the 'From:' header line
  from = msg.header.split("\r\n").grep(/^From: /)[0]
  puts from
  puts
  puts "Full message:"
  text = msg.pop
  puts text
end
```

`slnetpop_2.rb`

produces:

```
From: dave@facet.ruby-stuff.com (Dave Thomas)

Full message:
Return-Path: <dave@facet.ruby-stuff.com>
Received: from facet.ruby-stuff.com (facet.ruby-stuff.com [10.96.0.122])
        by pragprog.com (8.11.6/8.11.6) with ESMTP id i2PJMW701809
        for <joe@carat.ruby-stuff.com>; Thu, 25 Mar 2008 13:22:32 -0600
Received: by facet.ruby-stuff.com (Postfix, from userid 502)
        id 4AF228B1BD; Thu, 25 Mar 2008 13:22:36 -0600 (CST)
To: joe@carat.ruby-stuff.com
Subject: Try out the new features!
Message-Id: <20080325192236.4AF228B1BD@facet.ruby-stuff.com>
Date: Thu, 25 Mar 2008 13:22:36 -0600 (CST)
From: dave@facet.ruby-stuff.com (Dave Thomas)
Status: RO

Ruby 1.9 has even more new features, both in
the core language and in the supplied libraries.

Try it out!
```

Net::SMTP Simple SMTP Client

The net/smtp library provides a simple client to send electronic mail using the Simple Mail Transfer Protocol (SMTP). It does not assist in the creation of the message payload—it simply delivers messages once an RFC822 message has been constructed. The TMail gem provides an interface for creating and parsing e-mail messages.

- Sends an e-mail from a string:

slnetsmtp_1.rb

```
require 'net/smtp'
msg = "Subject: Test\n\nNow is the time\n"
Net::SMTP.start('pragprog.com') do |smtp|
  smtp.send_message(msg, 'dave@pragprog.com', ['dave'])
end
```

- Sends an e-mail using an SMTP object and an adapter:

slnetsmtp_2.rb

```
require 'net/smtp'
Net::SMTP::start('pragprog.com', 25, "pragprog.com") do |smtp|
  smtp.open_message_stream('dave@pragprog.com', # from
                          [ 'dave' ]            # to
                          ) do |stream|
    stream.puts "Subject: Test1"
    stream.puts
    stream.puts "And so is this"
  end
end
```

- Sends an e-mail to a server requiring CRAM-MD5 authentication:

slnetsmtp_3.rb

```
require 'net/smtp'
msg = "Subject: Test\n\nNow is the time\n"
Net::SMTP.start('pragprog.com', 25, 'pragprog.com',
                'user', 'password', :cram_md5) do |smtp|
  smtp.send_message(msg, 'dave@pragprog.com', ['dave'])
end
```

Net::Telnet   Telnet Client

The net/telnet library provides a complete implementation of a telnet client and includes features that make it a convenient mechanism for interacting with nontelnet services.

Class Net::Telnet delegates to class Socket. As a result, the methods of Socket and its parent, class IO, are available through Net::Telnet objects.

- Connects to a localhost, runs the date command, and disconnects:

sinettelnet_1.rb

```
require 'net/telnet'
tn = Net::Telnet.new({})
tn.login "guest", "secret"
tn.cmd "date"   # =>    "Tue Mar 31 09:58:51 CDT 2009\n"
tn.close
```

- The methods new, cmd, login, and waitfor take an optional block. If present, the block is passed output from the server as it is received by the routine. This can be used to provide real-time output, rather than waiting (for example) for a login to complete before displaying the server's response.

sinettelnet_2.rb

```
require 'net/telnet'
tn = Net::Telnet.new({})        {|str| print str }
tn.login("guest", "secret")     {|str| print str }
tn.cmd("date")                  {|str| print str }
tn.close
```

produces:

```
Connected to localhost.
Darwin/BSD (dave-2.home) (ttys012)
login: guest
Password:Last login: Thu Mar  5 13:23:25 from 0.0.0.0
$ date
Tue Mar 31 09:58:51 CDT 2009
$
```

- Gets the time from an NTP server:

sinettelnet_3.rb

```
require 'net/telnet'
tn = Net::Telnet.new('Host'       => 'time.nonexistent.org',
                     'Port'       => 'time',
                     'Timeout'    => 60,
                     'Telnetmode' => false)
atomic_time = tn.recv(4).unpack('N')[0]
puts "Atomic time: " + Time.at(atomic_time - 2208988800).to_s
puts "Local time:  " + Time.now.to_s
```

produces:

```
Atomic time: 2009-03-31 09:58:51 -0500
Local time:  2009-03-31 09:58:54 -0500
```

Library

NKF

Interface to Network Kanji Filter

The NKF module is a wrapper around Itaru Ichikawa's Network Kanji Filter (NKF) library (version 1.7). It provides functions to guess at the encoding of JIS, EUC, and SJIS streams and to convert from one encoding to another. Even though Ruby 1.9 now supports these encodings natively, this library is still useful for guessing encodings.

1.9

1.9

- As of Ruby 1.9, NFK uses the built-in encoding objects:

  slnkf_1.rb

  ```
  require 'nkf'
  NKF::AUTO   # =>   nil
  NKF::JIS    # =>   #<Encoding:ISO-2022-JP (dummy)>
  NKF::EUC    # =>   #<Encoding:EUC-JP>
  NKF::SJIS   # =>   #<Encoding:Shift_JIS>
  ```

- Guesses at the encoding of a string. (Thanks to Nobu Nakada for the examples on this page.)

  slnkf_2.rb

  ```
  require 'nkf'
  p NKF.guess("Yukihiro Matsumoto")
  p NKF.guess("\e$B$^$D$b$H$f$-$R$m\e(B")
  p NKF.guess("\244\336\244\304\244\342\244\310\244\346\244\255\244\322\244\355")
  p NKF.guess("\202\334\202\302\202\340\202\306\202\344\202\253\202\320\202\353")
  ```

  produces:

  ```
  #<Encoding:US-ASCII>
  #<Encoding:ISO-2022-JP (dummy)>
  #<Encoding:EUC-JP>
  #<Encoding:Shift_JIS>
  ```

- The NKF.nfk method takes two parameters. The first is a set of options, passed on to the NKF library. The second is the string to translate. The following examples assume that your console is set up to accommodate Japanese characters. The text at the end of the three ruby commands is Yukihiro Matsumoto.

  ```
  $ ruby -e 'p *ARGV'  まつもと ゆきひろ

  "\244\336\244\304\244\342\244\310\244\346\244\255\244\322\244\355"

  $ ruby -rnkf -e 'p NKF.nfk(*ARGV)' - -Es  まつもと ゆきひろ

  "\202\334\202\302\202\340\202\306\202\344\202\253\202\320\202\353"

  $ ruby -rnkf -e 'p NKF.nfk(*ARGV)' - -Ej  まつもと ゆきひろ

  "\e$B$^$D$b$H$f$-$R$m\e(B"
  ```

Observable

The Observer pattern, also known as Publish/Subscribe, provides a simple mechanism for one object (the source) to inform a set of interested third-party objects when its state changes (see *Design Patterns* [GHJV95]). In the Ruby implementation, the notifying class mixes in the module Observable, which provides the methods for managing the associated observer objects. The observers must implement the update method to receive notifications.

`slobserver_1.rb`

```ruby
require 'observer'
class CheckWaterTemperature # Periodically check the water
  include Observable
  def run
    last_temp = nil
    loop do
      temp = Temperature.fetch   # external class...
      puts "Current temperature: #{temp}"
      if temp != last_temp
        changed                  # notify observers
        notify_observers(Time.now, temp)
        last_temp = temp
      end
    end
  end
end
class Warner
  def initialize(&limit)
    @limit = limit
  end
  def update(time, temp)         # callback for observer
    if @limit.call(temp)
      puts "--- #{time.to_s}: Temperature outside range: #{temp}"
    end
  end
end
checker = CheckWaterTemperature.new
checker.add_observer(Warner.new {|t| t < 80})
checker.add_observer(Warner.new {|t| t > 120})
checker.run
```

produces:

```
Current temperature: 83
Current temperature: 75
--- 2009-03-31 09:58:51 -0500: Temperature outside range: 75
Current temperature: 90
Current temperature: 134
--- 2009-03-31 09:58:51 -0500: Temperature outside range: 134
Current temperature: 134
Current temperature: 112
Current temperature: 79
--- 2009-03-31 09:58:51 -0500: Temperature outside range: 79
```

The open-uri library extends Kernel#open, allowing it to accept URIs for FTP and HTTP as well as local filenames. Once opened, these resources can be treated as if they were local files, accessed using conventional IO methods. The URI passed to open is either a string containing an HTTP or FTP URL or a URI object (described on page 817). When opening an HTTP resource, the method automatically handles redirection and proxies. When using an FTP resource, the method logs in as an anonymous user.

The IO object returned by open in these cases is extended to support methods that return metainformation from the request: content_type, charset, content_encoding, last_modified, status, base_uri, meta.

See also: URI (page 817)

`slopen-uri_1.rb`

```ruby
require 'open-uri'
require 'pp'
open('http://ruby-lang.org') do |f|
  puts "URI: #{f.base_uri}"
  puts "Content-type: #{f.content_type}, charset: #{f.charset}"
  puts "Encoding: #{f.content_encoding}"
  puts "Last modified: #{f.last_modified}"
  puts "Status: #{f.status.inspect}"
  pp f.meta
  puts "----"
  3.times {|i| puts "#{i}: #{f.gets}" }
end
```

produces:

```
URI: http://www.ruby-lang.org/en/
Content-type: text/html, charset: utf-8
Encoding: []
Last modified:
Status: ["200", "OK"]
{"date"=>"Tue, 31 Mar 2009 14:58:35 GMT",
 "server"=>
  "Apache/2.2.3 (Debian) DAV/2 SVN/1.4.2 mod_ruby/1.2.6 Ruby/1.8.5(2006-08-25)
mod_ssl/2.2.3 OpenSSL/0.9.8c",
 "transfer-encoding"=>"chunked",
 "content-type"=>"text/html;charset=utf-8"}
----
0: <!DOCTYPE html PUBLIC "-//W3C//DTD XHTML 1.1//EN"
1:    "http://www.w3.org/TR/xhtml11/DTD/xhtml11.dtd">
2: <html xmlns="http://www.w3.org/1999/xhtml">
```

open-uri

Open3
Run Subprocess and Connect to All Streams

Runs a command in a subprocess. Data written to *stdin* can be read by the subprocess, and data written to standard output and standard error in the subprocess will be available on the *stdout* and *stderr* streams. The subprocess is actually run as a grandchild, and as a result, Process#waitall cannot be used to wait for its termination (hence the sleep in the following example). Note also that you probably cannot assume that the application's output and error streams will not be buffered, so output may not arrive when you expect it to.

`slopen3_1.rb`

```ruby
require 'open3'
Open3.popen3('bc') do | stdin, stdout, stderr |
  Thread.new { loop { puts "STDOUT stream: #{stdout.gets}" } }
  Thread.new { loop { puts "STDERR stream: #{stderr.gets}" } }
  stdin.puts "3 * 4"
  stdin.puts "1 / 0"
  stdin.puts "2 ^ 5"
  sleep 0.1
end
```

produces:

```
STDOUT stream: 12
STDOUT stream: 32
STDERR stream: Runtime error (func=(main), adr=3): Divide by zero
```

OpenSSL

SSL Library

Only if:
OpenSSL
library available
(http://www.
openssl.org)

The Ruby OpenSSL extension wraps the freely available OpenSSL library. It provides the Secure Sockets Layer and Transport Layer Security (SSL and TLS) protocols, allowing for secure communications over networks. The library provides functions for certificate creation and management, message signing, and encryption/decryption. It also provides wrappers to simplify access to https servers, along with secure FTP. The interface to the library is large (roughly 330 methods), but the average Ruby user will probably use only a small subset of the library's capabilities.

See also: Net::FTP (page 764), Net::HTTP (page 765), Socket (page 802)

- Accesses a secure website using HTTPS. Note that SSL is used to tunnel to the site, but the requested page also requires standard HTTP basic authorization.

slopenssl_1.rb

```ruby
require 'net/https'
USER = "xxx"
PW   = "yyy"
site = Net::HTTP.new("www.securestuff.com", 443)
site.use_ssl = true
response = site.get2("/cgi-bin/cokerecipe.cgi",
                     'Authorization' => 'Basic ' +
                     ["#{USER}:#{PW}"].pack('m').strip)
```

- Creates a socket that uses SSL. This isn't a good example of accessing a website. However, it illustrates how a socket can be encrypted.

slopenssl_2.rb

```ruby
require 'socket'
require 'openssl'
socket = TCPSocket.new("www.secure-stuff.com", 443)
ssl_context = OpenSSL::SSL::SSLContext.new()
unless ssl_context.verify_mode
  warn "warning: peer certificate won't be verified this session."
  ssl_context.verify_mode = OpenSSL::SSL::VERIFY_NONE
end
sslsocket = OpenSSL::SSL::SSLSocket.new(socket, ssl_context)
sslsocket.sync_close = true
sslsocket.connect
sslsocket.puts("GET /secret-info.shtml")
while line =  sslsocket.gets
  p line
end
```

OpenSSL

Library

OptionParser

Option Parsing

OptionParser is a flexible and extensible way to parse command-line arguments. It has a particularly rich abstraction of the concept of an option.

- An option can have multiple short names (options preceded by a single hyphen) and multiple long names (options preceded by two hyphens). Thus, an option that displays help may be available as -h, -?, --help, and --about. Users may abbreviate long option names to the shortest nonambiguous prefix.

- An option may be specified as having no argument, an optional argument, or a required argument. Arguments can be validated against patterns or lists of valid values.

- Arguments may be returned as objects of any type (not just strings). The argument type system is extensible (we add Date handling in the example).

- Arguments can have one or more lines of descriptive text, used when generating usage information.

Options are specified using the on and def methods. These methods take a variable number of arguments that cumulatively build a definition of each option. The arguments accepted by these methods are listed in Table 28.2 on the next page.

See also: GetoptLong (page 750)

`sloptparse_2.rb`

```ruby
require 'optparse'
require 'date'
# Add Dates as a new option type
OptionParser.accept(Date, /(\d+)-(\d+)-(\d+)/) do |d, mon, day, year|
  Date.new(year.to_i, mon.to_i, day.to_i)
end
opts = OptionParser.new
opts.on("-x")                          {|val| puts "-x seen" }
opts.on("-s", "--size VAL", Integer) {|val| puts "-s #{val}" }
opts.on("-a", "--at DATE",  Date)    {|val| puts "-a #{val}" }
my_argv = [ "--size", "1234", "-x", "-a", "12-25-2008", "fred", "wilma" ]
rest = opts.parse(*my_argv)
puts "Remainder = #{rest.join(', ')}"
puts opts.to_s
```

produces:

```
-s 1234
-x seen
-a 2008-12-25
Remainder = fred, wilma
Usage: myprog [options]
    -x
    -s, --size VAL
    -a, --at DATE
```

Table 28.2. Option Definition Arguments

"-x" "-xARG" "-x=ARG" "-x[OPT]" "-x[=OPT]" "-x PLACE"
> Option has short name x. First form has no argument, next two have mandatory argument, next two have optional argument, last specifies argument follows option. The short names may also be specified as a range (such as "-[a-c]").

"--*switch*" "--*switch*=ARG" "--*switch*=[OPT]" "--*switch* PLACE"
> Option has long name switch. First form has no argument, next has a mandatory argument, the next has an optional argument, and the last specifies the argument follows the switch.

"--no-*switch*"
> Defines a option whose default value is false.

"=ARG" "=[OPT]"
> Argument for this option is mandatory or optional. For example, the following code says there's an option known by the aliases -x, -y, and -z that takes a mandatory argument, shown in the usage as N:
> ```
> opt.on("-x", "-y", "-z", "=N")
> ```

"description"
> Any string that doesn't start − or = is used as a description for this option in the summary. Multiple descriptions may be given; they'll be shown on additional lines.

/pattern/
> Any argument must match the given pattern.

array
> Argument must be one of the values from array.

proc or method
> Argument type conversion is performed by the given proc or method (rather than using the block associated with the on or def method call).

ClassName
> Argument must match that defined for ClassName, which may be predefined or added using OptionParser.accept. Built-in argument classes are
> **Object:** Any string. No conversion. This is the default.
> **String:** Any nonempty string. No conversion.
> **Integer:** Ruby/C-like integer with optional sign (0ddd is octal, 0bddd binary, 0xddd hexadecimal). Converts to Integer.
> **Float:** Float number format. Converts to Float.
> **Numeric:** Generic numeric format. Converts to Integer for integers, Float for floats.
> **Array:** Argument must be of list of strings separated by a comma.
> **OptionParser::DecimalInteger:** Decimal integer. Converted to Integer.
> **OptionParser::OctalInteger:** Ruby/C-like octal/hexadecimal/binary integer.
> **OptionParser::DecimalNumeric:** Decimal integer/float number. Integers converted to Integer, floats to Float.
> **TrueClass, FalseClass:** Boolean switch.

OptionParser

OpenStruct   Open (dynamic) Structure

An open structure is an object whose attributes are created dynamically when first assigned. In other words, if *obj* is an instance of an OpenStruct, then the statement obj.abc=1 will create the attribute *abc* in *obj* and then assign the value 1 to it.

slostruct_1.rb

```
require 'ostruct'

os = OpenStruct.new( "f1" => "one", :f2 => "two" )
os.f3 = "cat"
os.f4 = 99
os.f1   # =>   "one"
os.f2   # =>   "two"
os.f3   # =>   "cat"
os.f4   # =>   99
```

Because OpenStruct uses method_missing and because it is a subclass of Object, you can't name field with the same names as Object's instance methods. In the following example, the access to ice.freeze is a call to Object#freeze:

slostruct_2.rb

```
require 'ostruct'

ice = OpenStruct.new
ice.freeze = "yes"
ice.freeze   # =>   #<OpenStruct freeze="yes">
```

Pathname   Representation of File Paths

A Pathname represents the absolute or relative name of a file. It has two distinct uses. First, it allows manipulation of the parts of a file path (extracting components, building new paths, and so on). Second (and somewhat confusingly), it acts as a façade for some methods in classes Dir, File, and module FileTest, forwarding on calls for the file named by the Pathname object.

See also: File (page 497)

- Path name manipulation:

slpathname_1.rb

```
require 'pathname'

p1 = Pathname.new("/usr/bin")
p2 = Pathname.new("ruby")
p3 = p1 + p2
p4 = p2 + p1
p3.parent           # =>   #<Pathname:/usr/bin>
p3.parent.parent    # =>   #<Pathname:/usr>
p1.absolute?        # =>   true
p2.absolute?        # =>   false
p3.split            # =>   [#<Pathname:/usr/bin>, #<Pathname:ruby>]

p5 = Pathname.new("testdir")
puts p5.realpath
puts p5.children
```

produces:

```
/Users/dave/BS2/titles/RUBY3/Book/testdir
testdir/config.h
testdir/main.rb
```

- Path name as proxy for file and directory status requests:

slpathname_3.rb

```
require 'pathname'

p1 = Pathname.new("/usr/bin/ruby")
p1.file?                    # =>   true
p1.directory?               # =>   false
p1.executable?              # =>   true
p1.size                     # =>   38304

p2 = Pathname.new("testfile")    # =>   #<Pathname:testfile>

p2.read                     # =>   "This is line one\nThis is line
                            #       two\nThis is line three\nAnd so
                            #       on...\n"
p2.readlines                # =>   ["This is line one\n", "This is
                            #       line two\n", "This is line
                            #       three\n", "And so on...\n"]
```

PP

PP uses the PrettyPrint library to format the results of inspecting Ruby objects. As well as the methods in the class, it defines a global function, pp, which works like the existing p method but formats its output.

PP has a default layout for all Ruby objects. However, you can override the way it handles a class by defining the method pretty_print, which takes a PP object as a parameter. It should use that PP object's methods text, breakable, nest, group, and pp to format its output (see PrettyPrint for details).

See also: JSON (page 756), PrettyPrint (page 781), YAML (page 822)

- Compares "p" and "pp":

  `slpp_1.rb`
  ```
  require 'pp'
  Customer = Struct.new(:name, :sex, :dob, :country)
  cust = Customer.new("Walter Wall", "Male", "12/25/1960", "Niue")
  puts "Regular print"
  p cust
  puts "\nPretty print"
  pp cust
  ```
  produces:
  ```
  Regular print
  #<struct Customer name="Walter Wall", sex="Male", dob="12/25/1960",
   country="Niue">

  Pretty print
  #<struct Customer
   name="Walter Wall",
   sex="Male",
   dob="12/25/1960",
   country="Niue">
  ```

- You can tell PP not to display an object if it has already displayed it:

  `slpp_2.rb`
  ```
  require 'pp'
  a = "string"
  b = [ a ]
  c = [ b, b ]
  PP.sharing_detection = false
  pp c
  PP.sharing_detection = true
  pp c
  ```
  produces:
  ```
  [["string"], ["string"]]
  [["string"], [...]]
  ```

PrettyPrint   General Pretty Printer

PrettyPrint implements a pretty printer for structured text. It handles details of wrapping, grouping, and indentation. The PP library uses PrettyPrint to generate more legible dumps of Ruby objects.

See also: PP (page 780)

- The following program prints a chart of Ruby's classes, showing subclasses as a bracketed list following the parent. To save some space, we show just the classes in the Numeric branch of the tree.

`slprettyprint_1.rb`

```ruby
require 'prettyprint'
@children = Hash.new { |h,k| h[k] = Array.new }
ObjectSpace.each_object(Class) do |cls|
  @children[cls.superclass] << cls if cls <= Numeric
end
def print_children_of(printer, cls)
  printer.text(cls.name)
  kids = @children[cls].sort_by(&:name)
  unless kids.empty?
    printer.group(0, " [", "]") do
      printer.nest(3) do
        printer.breakable
        kids.each_with_index do |k, i|
          printer.breakable unless i.zero?
          print_children_of(printer, k)
        end
      end
      printer.breakable
    end
  end
end
printer = PrettyPrint.new($stdout, 30)
print_children_of(printer, Object)
printer.flush
```

produces:

```
Object [
   Numeric [
      Complex
      Float
      Integer [
         Bignum
         Fixnum
      ]
      Rational
   ]
]
```

prime   Prime Numbers

Provides facilities for generating prime numbers, as well as factoring numbers. Note that the Prime class is a singleton.

See also: mathn (page 758)

- The prime library extends the number classes to include new functionality and adds a new class Prime:

```
require 'prime'

# 60 = 2**2 * 3 * 5
60.prime?           # =>   false
60.prime_division   # =>   [[2, 2], [3, 1], [5, 1]]
```

- You can also use it to generate sequences of primes:

```
require 'prime'
Prime.each {|p| puts p; break if p > 20 }
```

produces:

```
2
3
5
7
11
13
17
19
23
```

Profile   Profile Execution of a Ruby Program

The profile library is a trivial wrapper around the Profiler module, making it easy to profile the execution of an entire program. Profiling can be enabled from the command line using the -rprofile option or from within a source program by requiring the profile module.

1.9 Unlike Ruby 1.8, Ruby 1.9 does not profile primitive methods such as Fixnum#== and iFixnum#+. This helps boost Ruby's performance.

See also: Benchmark (page 722), Profiler__ (page 784)

slprofile_1.rb

```
require 'profile'
def ackerman(m, n)
  if m == 0 then  n+1
  elsif n == 0 and m > 0 then ackerman(m-1, 1)
  else ackerman(m-1, ackerman(m, n-1))
  end
end
ackerman(3, 3)
```

produces:

%	cumulative	self		self	total	
time	seconds	seconds	calls	ms/call	ms/call	name
100.00	0.05	0.05	2432	0.02	0.55	Object#ackerman
0.00	0.05	0.00	1	0.00	0.00	Kernel.puts
0.00	0.05	0.00	1	0.00	0.00	IO#puts
0.00	0.05	0.00	1	0.00	0.00	Module#method_added
0.00	0.05	0.00	2	0.00	0.00	IO#write
0.00	0.05	0.00	1	0.00	50.00	#toplevel

Profiler__   Control Execution Profiling

The Profiler__ module can be used to collect a summary of the number of calls to, and the time spent in, methods in a Ruby program. The output is sorted by the total time spent in each method. The profile library is a convenience wrapper that profiles an entire program.

See also: Benchmark (page 722), profile (page 783)

slprofiler_1.rb

```
require 'profiler'
# Omit definition of connection and fetching methods
def calc_discount(qty, price)
  case qty
  when 0..10 then 0.0
  when 11..99 then price * 0.05
  else price * 0.1
  end
end
def calc_sales_totals(rows)
  total_qty =  total_price = total_disc = 0
  rows.each do |row|
    total_qty   += row.qty
    total_price += row.price
    total_disc  += calc_discount(row.qty, row.price)
  end
end
connect_to_database

rows = read_sales_data

Profiler__::start_profile
calc_sales_totals(rows)
Profiler__::stop_profile
Profiler__::print_profile(STDOUT)
```

produces:

```
  %   cumulative   self              self     total
 time   seconds   seconds    calls  ms/call  ms/call  name
37.50     0.03      0.03       648     0.05     0.08   Range#===
25.00     0.05      0.02       648     0.03     0.03   Range#include?
12.50     0.06      0.01       648     0.02     0.02   S#qty
12.50     0.07      0.01       648     0.02     0.02   S#price
12.50     0.08      0.01         1    10.00    80.00   Array#each
 0.00     0.08      0.00         3     0.00     0.00   Fixnum#+
 0.00     0.08      0.00       648     0.00     0.00   Fixnum#<=>
 0.00     0.08      0.00       324     0.00     0.15   Object#calc_discount
 0.00     0.08      0.00       648     0.00     0.00   Float#<=>
 0.00     0.08      0.00         1     0.00    80.00   Object#calc_sales_totals
 0.00     0.08      0.00         1     0.00    80.00   #toplevel
```

Library **PStore**   Persistent Object Storage

The PStore class provides transactional, file-based, persistent storage of Ruby objects. Each
PStore can store several object hierarchies. Each hierarchy has a root, identified by a key
(often a string). At the start of a PStore transaction, these hierarchies are read from a disk
file and made available to the Ruby program. At the end of the transaction, the hierarchies
are written back to the file. Any changes made to objects in these hierarchies are therefore
saved on disk, to be read at the start of the next transaction that uses that file.

In normal use, a PStore object is created and then is used one or more times to control a
transaction. Within the body of the transaction, any object hierarchies that had previously
been saved are made available, and any changes to object hierarchies, and any new hierarchies, are written back to the file at the end.

- The following example stores two hierarchies in a PStore. The first, identified by the
  key "names", is an array of strings. The second, identified by "tree", is a simple binary
  tree.

slpstore_1.rb
```ruby
require 'pstore'
require 'pp'
class T
  def initialize(val, left=nil, right=nil)
    @val, @left, @right = val, left, right
  end
  def to_a
    [ @val, @left.to_a, @right.to_a ]
  end
end
store = PStore.new("/tmp/store")
store.transaction do
  store['names'] = [ 'Douglas', 'Barenberg', 'Meyer' ]
  store['tree']  = T.new('top',
                    T.new('A', T.new('B')),
                    T.new('C', T.new('D', nil, T.new('E'))))
end
# now read it back in
store.transaction do
  puts "Roots: #{store.roots.join(', ')}"
  puts store['names'].join(', ')
  pp store['tree'].to_a
end
```
produces:
```
Roots: names, tree
Douglas, Barenberg, Meyer
["top",
 ["A", ["B", [], []], []],
 ["C", ["D", [], ["E", [], []]], []]]
```

PTY

Pseudo-Terminal Interface: Interact with External Processes

Only if: Unix
with pty support

Many Unix platforms support a *pseudo-terminal*—a device pair where one end emulates a process running on a conventional terminal, and the other end can read and write that terminal as if it were a user looking at a screen and typing on a keyboard.

The PTY library provides the method spawn, which starts the given command (by default a shell), connecting it to one end of a pseudo-terminal. It then returns the reader and writer streams connected to that terminal, allowing your process to interact with the running process.

Working with pseudo-terminals can be tricky. See IO#expect on page 743 for a convenience method that makes life easier. You might also want to track down Ara T. Howard's Session module for an even simpler approach to driving subprocesses.[4]

See also: expect (page 743)

- Runs irb in a subshell and asks it to convert the string "cat" to uppercase:

slpty_1.rb

```ruby
require 'pty'
require 'expect'
$expect_verbose = true
PTY.spawn("/usr/local/rubybook/bin/ruby /usr/local/rubybook/bin/irb") do |reader,
writer, pid|
  reader.expect(/irb.*:0> /)
  writer.puts "'cat'.upcase"
  reader.expect("=> ")
  answer = reader.gets
  puts "Answer = #{answer}"
end
```

produces:

```
irb(main):001:0> 'cat'.upcase
=> Answer = "CAT"
```

---

4. Currently found at http://www.codeforpeople.com/lib/ruby/session/.

1.9

The Rational class is now built in to Ruby. The vestigial Rational library simply defines a few aliases for backward compatibility. For the classes Fixnum and Bignum, the following aliases are defined:

Floating-point division

quof is an alias for fdiv.

Rational division

rdiv is an alias for quo.

Exponentiation

power! and rpower are aliases for **.

Library
Readline
Interface to GNU Readline Library

The Readline module allows programs to prompt for and receive lines of user input. The module allows lines to be edited during entry, and command history allows previous commands to be recalled and edited. The history can be searched, allowing the user to (for example) recall a previous command containing the text *ruby*. Command completion allows context-sensitive shortcuts: tokens can be expanded in the command line under control of the invoking application. In typical GNU fashion, the underlying readline library supports more options than any user could need and emulates both vi and emacs key bindings.

Only if: GNU readline present

• This meaningless program implements a trivial interpreter that can increment and decrement a value. It uses the Abbrev module (described on page 720) to expand abbreviated commands when the Tab key is pressed.

slreadline_1.rb

```
require 'readline'
include Readline
require 'abbrev'
COMMANDS = %w{ exit inc dec }
ABBREV = COMMANDS.abbrev
Readline.completion_proc = proc do |string|
  ABBREV[string]
end
value = 0
loop do
  cmd = readline("wibble [#{value}]: ", true)
  break if cmd.nil?
  case cmd.strip
  when "exit"
    break
  when "inc"
    value += 1
  when "dec"
    value -= 1
  else
    puts "Invalid command #{cmd}"
  end
end
```

```
% ruby code/readline.rb
wibble [0]: inc
wibble [1]: <up-arrow>    => inc
wibble [2]: d<tab>        => dec
wibble [1]: ^r i          => inc
wibble [2]: exit
%
```

The resolv library is a pure-Ruby implementation of a DNS client—it can be used to convert domain names into corresponding IP addresses. It also supports reverse lookups and the resolution of names in the local hosts file.

The resolv library exists to overcome a problem with the interaction of the standard operating system DNS lookup and the Ruby threading mechanism. On most operating systems, name resolution is synchronous: you issue the call to look up a name, and the call returns when an address has been fetched. Because this lookup often involves network traffic and because DNS servers can be slow, this call may take a (relatively) long time. During this time, the thread that issued the call is effectively suspended. Because Ruby does not use operating system threads, this means that the interpreter is effectively suspended while a DNS request is being executed from any running Ruby thread. This is sometimes unacceptable. Enter the resolv library. Because it is written in Ruby, it automatically participates in Ruby threading, and hence other Ruby threads can run while a DNS lookup is in progress in one thread.

Loading the additional library resolv-replace insinuates the resolv library into Ruby's socket library (see page 802).

- Uses the standard socket library to look up a name. A counter running in a separate thread is suspended while this takes place.

slresolve_1.rb

```
require 'socket'

count = 0
thread = Thread.new { Thread.pass; loop {  count += 1;  } }
IPSocket.getaddress("www.ruby-lang.org")   # =>   "221.186.184.68"
count                                      # =>   0
```

- Repeats the experiment but uses the resolv library to allow Ruby's threading to work in parallel:

slresolve_2.rb

```
require 'socket'
require 'resolv-replace'

count = 0
thread = Thread.new { Thread.pass; loop {  count += 1;  } }
IPSocket.getaddress("www.ruby-lang.org")   # =>   "221.186.184.68"
count                                      # =>   5055763
```

REXML

REXML is a pure-Ruby XML processing library, including DTD-compliant document parsing, XPath querying, and document generation. It supports both tree-based and stream-based document processing. Because it is written in Ruby, it is available on all platforms supporting Ruby. REXML has a full and complex interface—this section contains a few small examples.

- Assume the file demo.xml contains this:

```
<classes language="ruby">
  <class name="Numeric">
    Numeric represents all numbers.
    <class name="Float">
      Floating point numbers have a fraction and a mantissa.
    </class>
    <class name="Integer">
      Integers contain exact integral values.
      <class name="Fixnum">
        Fixnums are stored as machine ints.
      </class>
      <class name="Bignum">
        Bignums store arbitraty-sized integers.
      </class>
    </class>
  </class>
</classes>
```

- Reads and processes the XML:

slrexml_2.rb
```
require 'rexml/document'
xml = REXML::Document.new(File.open("demo.xml"))

puts "Root element: #{xml.root.name}"
puts "\nThe names of all classes"
xml.elements.each("//class") {|c| puts c.attributes["name"] }
puts "\nThe description of Fixnum"
p xml.elements["//class[@name='Fixnum']"].text
```

produces:

```
Root element: classes

The names of all classes
Numeric
Float
Integer
Fixnum
Bignum

The description of Fixnum
"\n        Fixnums are stored as machine ints.\n      "
```

- Reads in a document, adds and deletes elements, and manipulates attributes before writing it back out:

`slrexml_3.rb`

```ruby
require 'rexml/document'
include REXML
xml = Document.new(File.open("demo.xml"))
cls = Element.new("class")
cls.attributes["name"] = "Rational"
cls.text = "Represents complex numbers"
# Remove Integer's children, and add our new node as
# the one after Integer
int = xml.elements["//class[@name='Integer']"]
int.delete_at(1)
int.delete_at(2)
int.next_sibling = cls
# Change all the 'name' attributes to class_name
xml.elements.each("//class") do |c|
  c.attributes['class_name'] = c.attributes['name']
  c.attributes.delete('name')
end
# and write it out with a XML declaration at the front
xml << XMLDecl.new
xml.write(STDOUT, 0)
```

produces:

```
<?xml version='1.0'?>
<classes language='ruby'>
<class class_name='Numeric'>
 Numeric represents all numbers.
<class class_name='Float'>
 Floating point numbers have a fraction and a mantissa.
</class>
<class class_name='Integer'>
 Integers contain exact integral values.
</class>
<class class_name='Rational'>
Represents complex numbers
</class>
</class>
</classes>
```

Rinda   Tuplespace Implementation

Tuplespaces are a distributed blackboard system. Processes may add tuples to the blackboard, and other processes may remove tuples from the blackboard that match a certain pattern. Originally presented by David Gelernter, tuplespaces offer an interesting scheme for distributed cooperation among heterogeneous processes.

Rinda, the Ruby implementation of tuplespaces, offers some interesting additions to the concept. In particular, the Rinda implementation uses the === operator to match tuples. This means that tuples may be matched using regular expressions, the classes of their elements, and the element values.

See also: DRb (page 738)

- The blackboard is a DRb server that offers a shared tuplespace:

slrinda_1.rb

```
require 'rinda/tuplespace'
MY_URI = "druby://127.0.0.1:12131"
DRb.start_service(MY_URI, Rinda::TupleSpace.new)
DRb.thread.join
```

- The arithmetic agent accepts messages containing an arithmetic operator and two numbers. It stores the result back on the blackboard.

slrinda_2.rb

```
require 'rinda/rinda'
MY_URI = "druby://127.0.0.1:12131"
DRb.start_service
ts = Rinda::TupleSpaceProxy.new(DRbObject.new(nil, MY_URI))
loop do
  op, v1, v2 = ts.take([ %r{^[-+/*]$}, Numeric, Numeric])
  ts.write(["result", v1.send(op, v2)])
end
```

- The client places tuples on the blackboard and reads back the result of each:

slrinda_3.rb

```
require 'rinda/rinda'
MY_URI = "druby://127.0.0.1:12131"
DRb.start_service
ts = Rinda::TupleSpaceProxy.new(DRbObject.new(nil, MY_URI))
queries = [[ "+", 1, 2 ], [ "*", 3, 4 ], [ "/", 8, 2 ]]
queries.each do |q|
  ts.write(q)
  ans = ts.take(["result", nil])
  puts "#{q[1]} #{q[0]} #{q[2]} = #{ans[1]}"
end
```

produces:

```
1 + 2 = 3
3 * 4 = 12
8 / 2 = 4
```

Ripper

The ripper library gives you access to Ruby's parser. It can tokenize input, return lexical tokens, and return a nested S-expression. It also supports event-based parsing.

- Tokenize a line of Ruby code:

slripper_1.rb

```
require "ripper"
content = "a=1;b=2;puts a+b"
Ripper.tokenize(content)   # =>   ["a", "=", "1", ";", "b", "=", "2",
                                  ";", "puts", " ", "a", "+", "b"]
```

- Does a lexical analysis, returning token types, values, line and column numbers:

slripper_2.rb

```
require "ripper"
require "pp"
content = "a=1;b=2;puts a+b"
pp Ripper.lex(content)[0,5]
```

produces:

```
[[[1, 0], :on_ident, "a"],
 [[1, 1], :on_op, "="],
 [[1, 2], :on_int, "1"],
 [[1, 3], :on_semicolon, ";"],
 [[1, 4], :on_ident, "b"]]
```

- Returns the sexp representing a chunk of code:

slripper_3.rb

```
require "ripper"
require "pp"
content = "a=1;b=2;puts a+b"
pp Ripper.sexp(content)
```

produces:

```
[:program,
 [[:assign, [:var_field, [:@ident, "a", [1, 0]]], [:@int, "1", [1, 2]]],
  [:assign, [:var_field, [:@ident, "b", [1, 4]]], [:@int, "2", [1, 6]]],
  [:command,
   [:@ident, "puts", [1, 8]],
   [:args_add_block,
    [[:binary,
      [:var_ref, [:@ident, "a", [1, 13]]],
      :+,
      [:var_ref, [:@ident, "b", [1, 15]]]]],
    false]]]]
```

- As a (silly) example of event-based lexical analysis, here's a program that finds class definitions and their associated comment blocks. For each, it outputs the class name and the comment. It might be considered the zeroth iteration of an RDoc-like program.

The parameter to parse is an accumulator—it is passed between event handlers and can be used to construct the result.

`slripper_4.rb`

```ruby
require 'ripper'
# This class handles parser events, extracting
# comments and attaching them to class definitions
class BabyRDoc < Ripper::Filter
  def initialize(*)
    super
    reset_state
  end
  def on_default(event, token, output)
    reset_state
    output
  end
  def on_sp(token, output) output end
  alias on_nil on_sp
  def on_comment(comment, output)
    @comment << comment.sub(/^\s*#\s*/, "    ")
    output
  end
  def on_kw(name, output)
    @expecting_class_name = (name == 'class')
    output
  end
  def on_const(name, output)
    if @expecting_class_name
      output << "#{name}:\n"
      output <<  @comment
    end
    reset_state
    output
  end
  private
  def reset_state
    @comment = ""
    @expecting_class_name = false
  end
end
BabyRDoc.new(File.read(__FILE__)).parse(STDOUT)
```

produces:

```
BabyRDoc:
    This class handles parser events, extracting
    comments and attaching them to class definitions
```

Rich (or RDF) Site Summary, Really Simple Syndication—take your pick. RSS is the protocol of choice for disseminating news on the Internet. The Ruby RSS library supports creating and parsing streams compliant with RSS 0.9, RSS 1.0, and RSS 2.0.

- Reads and summarizes the latest stories from `http://ruby-lang.org`:

`slrss_1.rb`

```ruby
require 'rss/2.0'
require 'open-uri'
open('http://ruby-lang.org/en/feeds/news.rss') do |http|
  response = http.read
  result = RSS::Parser.parse(response, false)
  puts "Channel: " + result.channel.title
  result.items.each_with_index do |item, i|
    puts "#{i+1}. #{item.title}" if i < 3
  end
end
```

produces:

```
Channel: Ruby News
1. MountainWest RubyConf Schedule
2. Ruby 1.9.1 released
3. Server maintenance
```

- Generates some RSS information:

`slrss_2.rb`

```ruby
require 'rss/0.9'
rss  = RSS::Rss.new("0.9")
chan = RSS::Rss::Channel.new
chan.title       = "The Daily Dave"
chan.description = "Dave's Feed"
chan.language    = "en-US"
chan.link        = "http://pragdave.pragprog.com"
rss.channel      = chan
image = RSS::Rss::Channel::Image.new
image.url   = "http://pragprog.com/pragdave.gif"
image.title = "PragDave"
image.link  = chan.link
chan.image  = image
3.times do |i|
  item = RSS::Rss::Channel::Item.new
  item.title       = "My News Number #{i}"
  item.link        = "http://pragprog.com/pragdave/story_#{i}"
  item.description = "This is a story about number #{i}"
  chan.items << item
end
puts rss.to_s
```

Scanf Input Format Conversion

Implements a version of the C library scanf function, which extracts values from a string under the control of a format specifier.

The Ruby version of the library adds a scanf method to both class IO and class String. The version in IO applies the format string to the next line read from the receiver. The version in String applies the format string to the receiver. The library also adds the global method Kernel.scanf, which uses as its source the next line of standard input.

Scanf has one main advantage over using regular expressions to break apart a string: a regular expression extracts strings whereas scanf will return objects converted to the correct type.

- Splits a date string into its constituents:

slscanf_1.rb

```
require 'scanf'

date = "2004-12-15"
year, month, day = date.scanf("%4d-%2d-%2d")
year        # =>   2004
month       # =>   12
day         # =>   15
year.class  # =>   Fixnum
```

- The block form of scanf applies the format multiple times to the input string, returning each set of results to the block:

slscanf_2.rb

```
require 'scanf'
data = "cat:7 dog:9 cow:17 walrus:31"
data.scanf("%[^:]:%d ") do |animal, value|
  puts "A #{animal.strip} has #{value*1.4}"
end
```

produces:

```
A cat has 9.8
A dog has 12.6
A cow has 23.8
A walrus has 43.4
```

- Extracts hex numbers:

slscanf_3.rb

```
require 'scanf'

data = "decaf bad"
data.scanf("%3x%2x%x")   # =>   [3564, 175, 2989]
```

SDBM
Interface to SDBM Database

The SDBM database implements a simple key/value persistence mechanism. Because the underlying SDBM library itself is provided with Ruby, there are no external dependencies, and SDBM should be available on all platforms supported by Ruby. SDBM database keys and values must be strings. SDBM databases are effectively hashlike.

See also: DBM (page 734), GDBM (page 749)

- Stores a record in a new database and then fetches it back. Unlike the DBM library, all values to SDBM must be strings (or implement to_str).

`slsdbm_1.rb`

```ruby
require 'sdbm'
require 'date'
SDBM.open("data.dbm") do |dbm|
  dbm['name'] = "Walter Wombat"
  dbm['dob']  = Date.new(1997, 12,25).to_s
  dbm['uses'] = "Ruby"
end
SDBM.open("data.dbm", nil) do |dbm|
  p dbm.keys
  p dbm['dob']
  p dbm['dob'].class
end
```

produces:

```
["name", "dob", "uses"]
"1997-12-25"
String
```

SecureRandom   Access to Secure Random Number Generators

Provides access to one of your operating system's secure random number generators. If the OpenSSL library is installed, the module uses it's random_bytes method. Otherwise, the module looks for and uses /dev/urandom or the CryptGenRandom method in the Windows API.

- Generates some random numbers:

slsecurerandom_1.rb

```
require 'securerandom'
# Random floats such that 0.0 <= rand < 1.0
SecureRandom.random_number(0)      # =>   0.895090909365585
SecureRandom.random_number(0)      # =>   0.755652798349986

# Random integers such that 0 <= rand < 1000
SecureRandom.random_number(1000)   # =>   185
SecureRandom.random_number(1000)   # =>   718
```

- Generates 10 random bytes, returning the result as a hex string, a Base64 string, and a string of binary data. A different random string is returned for each call.

slsecurerandom_2.rb

```
require 'securerandom'
SecureRandom.hex(10)            # =>   "bcf15fbb8b2a83604555"
SecureRandom.base64(10)         # =>   "5/DqS9PYwqLouA=="
SecureRandom.random_bytes(10)   # =>   "\x91U\xC9\xBE\x86f\x8C8\xC0\xD3"
```

A Set is a collection of unique values (where uniqueness is determined using eql? and hash). Convenience methods let you build sets from enumerable objects.

- Basic set operations:

```
require 'set'

set1 = Set.new([:bear, :cat, :deer])

set1.include?(:bat)    # =>   false
set1.add(:fox)         # =>   #<Set: {:bear, :cat, :deer, :fox}>

partition = set1.classify {|element| element.to_s.length }

partition      # =>   {4=>#<Set: {:bear, :deer}>, 3=>#<Set: {:cat,
                      :fox}>}

set2 = [ :cat, :dog, :cow ].to_set
set1 | set2    # =>   #<Set: {:bear, :cat, :deer, :fox, :dog, :cow}>
set1 & set2    # =>   #<Set: {:cat}>
set1 - set2    # =>   #<Set: {:bear, :deer, :fox}>
set1 ^ set2    # =>   #<Set: {:dog, :cow, :bear, :deer, :fox}>
```

- Partitions the users in our /etc/passwd file into subsets where members of each subset have adjacent user IDs:

```
require 'etc'
require 'set'
users = []
Etc.passwd {|u| users << u }
related_users = users.to_set.divide do |u1, u2|
  (u1.uid - u2.uid).abs <= 1
end
related_users.each do |relatives|
  relatives.each {|u| print "#{u.uid}/#{u.name} " }
  puts
end
```

produces:

```
67/_ard
93/_calendar 92/_securityagent 91/_tokend
59/_devdocs 60/_sandbox 58/_serialnumberd
26/_lp 27/_postfix
54/_mcxalr 55/_pcastagent 56/_pcastserver
65/_mdnsresponder
4/_uucp
1/daemon 0/root
501/dave 502/juliet 503/testuser
```

Shellwords　　　　　　　　Manipulate Shell Lines Using POSIX Semantics

Given a string representative of a shell command line, splits it into word tokens according to POSIX semantics. Also allows you to create properly escaped shell lines from individual words.

- Spaces between double or single quotes are treated as part of a word.

- Double quotes may be escaped using a backslash.

- Spaces escaped by a backslash are not used to separate words.

- Otherwise, tokens separated by whitespace are treated as words.

slshellwords_1.rb

```
require 'shellwords'
include Shellwords

line = %{Code Ruby Be Happy!}
shellwords(line)                        # =>   ["Code", "Ruby", "Be",
                                        #       "Happy!"]

line = %{"Code Ruby" 'Be Happy'!}
shellwords(line)                        # =>   ["Code Ruby", "Be Happy!"]

line = %q{Code\ Ruby "Be Happy"!}
shellwords(line)                        # =>   ["Code Ruby", "Be Happy!"]

shelljoin(["Code Ruby", "Be Happy"])    # =>   Code\ Ruby Be\ Happy
```

In addition, the library adds shellsplit and shelljoin methods to classes String and CArray, respectively:

slshellwords_2.rb

```
require 'shellwords'
include Shellwords

%{Code\\ Ruby Be Happy!}.shellsplit     # =>   ["Code Ruby", "Be", "Happy!"]
["Code Ruby", "Be Happy"].shelljoin     # =>   "Code\\ Ruby Be\\ Happy"
```

Singleton

The Singleton Pattern

The Singleton design pattern ensures that only one instance of a particular class may be created for the lifetime of a program (see *Design Patterns* [GHJV95]).

The singleton library makes this simple to implement. Mix the Singleton module into each class that is to be a singleton, and that class's new method will be made private. In its place, users of the class call the method instance, which returns a singleton instance of that class.

In this example, the two instances of MyClass are the same object:

slsingleton_1.rb

```
require 'singleton'

class MyClass

  attr_accessor :data
  include Singleton
end

a = MyClass.instance     # =>   #<MyClass:0x128d4c>
b = MyClass.instance     # =>   #<MyClass:0x128d4c>

a.data = 123             # =>   123
b.data                   # =>   123
```

Socket   IP, TCP, Unix, and SOCKS Socket Access

The socket extension defines nine classes for accessing the socket-level communications of the underlying system. All of these classes are (indirect) subclasses of class IO, meaning that IO's methods can be used with socket connections.

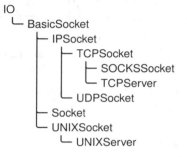

```
IO
  └─ BasicSocket
       ├─ IPSocket
       │    ├─ TCPSocket
       │    │    ├─ SOCKSSocket
       │    │    └─ TCPServer
       │    └─ UDPSocket
       ├─ Socket
       └─ UNIXSocket
            └─ UNIXServer
```

The hierarchy of socket classes reflects the reality of network programming and hence is somewhat confusing. The BasicSocket class largely contains methods common to data transfer for all socket-based connections. It is subclassed to provide protocol-specific implementations: IPSocket, UNIXSocket (for domain sockets), and (indirectly) TCPSocket, UDP-Socket, and SOCKSSocket.

BasicSocket is also subclassed by class Socket, which is a more generic interface to socket-oriented networking. Although classes such as TCPSocket are specific to a protocol, Socket objects can, with some work, be used regardless of protocol.

TCPSocket, SOCKSSocket, and UNIXSocket are each connection oriented. Each has a corresponding *xxxx*Server class, which implements the server end of a connection.

The socket libraries are something that you may never use directly. However, if you do use them, you'll need to know the details. For that reason, we've included a reference section covering the socket library methods in Appendix A on page 871.

The following code shows a trivial UDP server and client. For more examples see Appendix A:

slsocket_1.rb

```ruby
# Simple logger prints messages
# received on UDP port 12121
require 'socket'
socket = UDPSocket.new
socket.bind("127.0.0.1", 12121)
loop do
  msg, sender  = socket.recvfrom(100)
  host = sender[3]
  puts "#{Time.now}: #{host} '#{msg}'"
  STDOUT.flush
end
```

slsocket_2.rb

```ruby
# Exercise the logger
require 'socket'
log = UDPSocket.new
log.connect("127.0.0.1", 12121)
log.print "Up and Running!"
# process ... process ..
log.print "Done!"
```

produces:

```
2009-03-31 09:58:58 -0500: 127.0.0.1 'Up and Running!'
2009-03-31 09:58:58 -0500: 127.0.0.1 'Done!'
```

StringIO

In some ways the distinction between strings and file contents is artificial: the contents of a file is basically a string that happens to live on disk, not in memory. The StringIO library aims to unify the two concepts, making strings act as if they were opened IO objects. Once a string is wrapped in a StringIO object, it can be read from and written to as if it were an open file. This can make unit testing a lot easier. It also lets you pass strings into classes and methods that were originally written to work with files. StringIO objects take their encoding from the string you pass in or the default external encoding is no string is passed.

1.9

- Reads and writes from a string:

slstringio_1.rb

```ruby
require 'stringio'

sio = StringIO.new("time flies like an arrow")
sio.read(5)              # =>   "time "
sio.read(5)              # =>   "flies"
sio.pos = 19
sio.read(5)              # =>   "arrow"
sio.rewind               # =>   0
sio.write("fruit")       # =>   5
sio.pos = 16
sio.write("a banana")    # =>   8
sio.rewind               # =>   0
sio.read                 # =>   "fruitflies like a banana"
```

- Uses StringIO as a testing aid:

slstringio_2.rb

```ruby
require 'stringio'
require 'csv'
require 'test/unit'
class TestCSV < Test::Unit::TestCase
  def test_simple
    StringIO.open do |op|
      CSV(op) do |csv|
        csv << [ 1, "line 1", 27 ]
        csv << [ 2, nil, 123 ]
      end
      assert_equal("1,line 1,27\n2,,123\n", op.string)
    end
  end
end
```

produces:

```
Loaded suite /tmp/prog
Started
.
Finished in 0.001700 seconds.

1 tests, 1 assertions, 0 failures, 0 errors, 0 skips
```

S tringIO

StringScanner   Basic String Tokenizer

StringScanner objects progress through a string, matching (and optionally returning) tokens that match a given pattern. Unlike the built-in scan methods, StringScanner objects maintain a current position pointer in the string being examined, so each call resumes from the position in the string where the previous call left off. Pattern matches are anchored to this previous point.

- Implements a simple language:

`slstrscan_1.rb`

```
require 'strscan'
# Handle the language:
#   set <var> = <value>
#   get <var>
values = {}
while line = gets
  scanner = StringScanner.new(line.chomp)
  scanner.scan(/(get|set)\s+/) or fail "Missing command"
  cmd = scanner[1]
  var_name = scanner.scan(/\w+/) or fail "Missing variable"
  case cmd
  when "get"
    puts "#{var_name} => #{values[var_name].inspect}"
  when "set"
    scanner.skip(/\s+=\s+/) or fail "Missing '='"
    value = scanner.rest
    values[var_name] = value
  else
    fail cmd
  end
end
```

produces:

```
% ruby code/strscan.rb
set a = dave
set b = hello
get b
b => "hello"
get a
a => "dave"
```

Syslog

Only if: Unix system with syslog

The Syslog class is a simple wrapper around the Unix syslog(3) library. It allows messages to be written at various severity levels to the logging daemon, where they are disseminated according to the configuration in syslog.conf. The following examples assume the log file is /var/log/system.log.

- Adds to our local system log. We'll log all the levels configured for the user facility for our system (which is every level except debug and info messages).

slsyslog_1.rb

```ruby
require 'syslog'
log = Syslog.open("test")   # "test" is the app name
log.debug("Warm and fuzzy greetings from your program")
log.info("Program starting")
log.notice("I said 'Hello!'")
log.warning("If you don't respond soon, I'm quitting")
log.err("You haven't responded after %d milliseconds", 7)
log.alert("I'm telling your mother...")
log.emerg("I'm feeling totally crushed")
log.crit("Aarrgh....")
system("tail -6 /var/log/system.log")
```

produces:

```
Mar 31 09:58:46 dave-2 com.apple.ftpd[48252]: launchproxy[48252]: /usr/libexec/ftpd: Connection
from: ::1 on port: 56170
Mar 31 09:58:58 dave-2 test[48661]: I said 'Hello!'
Mar 31 09:58:58 dave-2 test[48661]: If you don't respond soon, I'm quitting
Mar 31 09:58:58 dave-2 test[48661]: You haven't responded after 7 milliseconds
Mar 31 09:58:58 dave-2 test[48661]: I'm telling your mother...
Mar 31 09:58:58 dave-2 test[48661]: I'm feeling totally crushed
```

- Logs only errors and above:

slsyslog_3.rb

```ruby
require 'syslog'
log = Syslog.open("test")
log.mask = Syslog::LOG_UPTO(Syslog::LOG_ERR)
log.debug("Warm and fuzzy greetings from your program")
log.info("Program starting")
log.notice("I said 'Hello!'")
log.warning("If you don't respond soon, I'm quitting")
log.err("You haven't responded after %d milliseconds", 7)
log.alert("I'm telling your mother...")
log.emerg("I'm feeling totally crushed")
log.crit("Aarrgh....")
system("tail -4 /var/log/system.log")
```

produces:

```
Mar 31 09:58:58 dave-2 test[48667]: You haven't responded after 7 milliseconds
Mar 31 09:58:58 dave-2 test[48667]: I'm telling your mother...
Mar 31 09:58:58 dave-2 test[48667]: I'm feeling totally crushed
Mar 31 09:58:58 dave-2 test[48667]: Aarrgh....
```

Syslog

Tempfile

Temporary File Support

Class Tempfile creates managed temporary files. Although they behave the same as any other IO objects, temporary files are automatically deleted when the Ruby program terminates. Once a Tempfile object has been created, the underlying file may be opened and closed a number of times in succession.

Tempfile does not directly inherit from IO. Instead, it delegates calls to a File object. From the programmer's perspective, apart from the unusual new, open, and close semantics, a Tempfile object behaves as if it were an IO object.

If you don't specify a directory to hold temporary files when you create them, the tmpdir library will be used to find a system-dependent location.

See also: tmpdir (page 813)

`sltempfile_1.rb`

```ruby
require 'tempfile'
tf = Tempfile.new("afile")
tf.path    # =>   "/var/folders/.../-Tmp-/afile20090331-48677-t3mrjh-0"
tf.puts("Cosi Fan Tutte")
tf.close
tf.open
tf.gets    # =>   "Cosi Fan Tutte\n"
tf.close(true)
```

Test::Unit is a unit testing framework based on the original SUnit Smalltalk framework. It provides a structure in which unit tests may be organized, selected, and run. Tests can be run from the command line or using one of several GUI-based interfaces.

Chapter 13 on page 183 contains a tutorial on Test::Unit.

We could have a simple playlist class, designed to store and retrieve songs:

sltestunit_1.rb

```ruby
require 'code/testunit/song.rb'
require 'forwardable'
class Playlist
  extend Forwardable
  def_delegator(:@list, :<<, :add_song)
  def_delegators(:@list, :size, :empty?)
  def initialize
    @list = []
  end
  def find(title)
    @list.find {|song| song.title == title}
  end
end
```

We can write unit tests to exercise this class. The Test::Unit framework is smart enough to run the tests in a test class if no main program is supplied.

sltestunit_2.rb

```ruby
require 'test/unit'
require 'code/testunit/playlist.rb'
class TestPlaylist < Test::Unit::TestCase
  def test_adding
    pl = Playlist.new
    assert_empty(pl)
    assert_nil(pl.find("My Way"))
    pl.add_song(Song.new("My Way", "Sinatra"))
    assert_equal(1, pl.size)
    s = pl.find("My Way")
    refute_nil(s)
    assert_equal("Sinatra", s.artist)
    assert_nil(pl.find("Chicago"))
    # .. and so on
  end
end
```

produces:

```
Loaded suite /tmp/prog
Started
.
Finished in 0.000413 seconds.

1 tests, 7 assertions, 0 failures, 0 errors, 0 skips
```

Test::Unit

thread
Utility Functionality for Threading

The thread library adds some utility functions and classes for supporting threads. Much of this has been superseded by the Monitor class, but the thread library contains two classes, Queue and SizedQueue, that are still useful. Both classes implement a thread-safe queue that can be used to pass objects between producers and consumers in multiple threads. The Queue object implements a unbounded queue. A SizedQueue is told its capacity; any producer that tries to add an object when the queue is at that capacity will block until a consumer has removed an object.

- The following example was provided by Robert Kellner. It has three consumers taking objects from an unsized queue. Those objects are provided by two producers, which each add three items.

sithread_1.rb

```
require 'thread'
queue = Queue.new
consumers = (1..3).map do |i|
  Thread.new("consumer #{i}") do |name|
    begin
      obj = queue.deq
      print "#{name}: consumed #{obj.inspect}\n"
    end until obj == :END_OF_WORK
  end
end
producers = (1..2).map do |i|
  Thread.new("producer #{i}") do |name|
    3.times do |j|
      queue.enq("Item #{j} from #{name}")
    end
  end
end
producers.each(&:join)
consumers.size.times { queue.enq(:END_OF_WORK) }
consumers.each(&:join)
```

produces:

```
consumer 1: consumed "Item 0 from producer 1"
consumer 1: consumed "Item 0 from producer 2"
consumer 2: consumed "Item 1 from producer 1"
consumer 3: consumed "Item 1 from producer 2"
consumer 1: consumed "Item 2 from producer 1"
consumer 2: consumed "Item 2 from producer 2"
consumer 1: consumed :END_OF_WORK
consumer 2: consumed :END_OF_WORK
consumer 3: consumed :END_OF_WORK
```

ThreadsWait

Wait for Multiple Threads to Terminate

Class ThreadsWait handles the termination of a group of thread objects. It provides methods to allow you to check for termination of any managed thread and to wait for all managed threads to terminate.

The following example kicks off a number of threads that each wait for a slightly shorter length of time before terminating and returning their thread number. Using ThreadsWait, we can capture these threads as they terminate, either individually or as a group.

`slthwait_1.rb`

```ruby
require 'thwait'

group = ThreadsWait.new

# construct threads that wait for 1 second, .9 second, etc.
# add each to the group

9.times do |i|
  thread = Thread.new(i) {|index| sleep 1.0 - index/10.0; index }
  group.join_nowait(thread)
end

# any threads finished?
group.finished?              # =>    false

# wait for one to finish
group.next_wait.value        # =>    8

# wait for 5 more to finish
5.times { group.next_wait }  # =>    5

# wait for next one to finish
group.next_wait.value        # =>    2

# and then wait for all the rest
group.all_waits              # =>    nil
```

Library	
Time	Extended Functionality for Class Time

The time library adds functionality to the built-in class Time, supporting date and/or time formats used by RFC 2822 (e-mail), RFC 2616 (HTTP), and ISO 8601 (the subset used by XML schema).

```
require 'time'
Time.rfc2822("Thu, 1 Apr 2008 16:32:45 CST")
                                → 2008-04-01 17:32:45 -0500


Time.rfc2822("Thu, 1 Apr 2008 16:32:45 -0600")
                                → 2008-04-01 17:32:45 -0500


Time.now.rfc2822                 → Tue, 31 Mar 2009 09:58:59 -0500

Time.httpdate("Thu, 01 Apr 2008 16:32:45 GMT")
                                → 2008-04-01 11:32:45 -0500


Time.httpdate("Thursday, 01-Apr-04 16:32:45 GMT")
                                → 2004-04-01 16:32:45 UTC


Time.httpdate("Thu Apr 1 16:32:45 2008")
                                → 2008-04-01 16:32:45 UTC


Time.now.httpdate               → Tue, 31 Mar 2009 14:58:59 GMT

Time.xmlschema("2008-04-01T16:32:45")
                                → 2008-04-01 16:32:45 -0500


Time.xmlschema("2008-04-01T16:32:45.12-06:00")
                                → 2008-04-01 22:32:45 UTC


Time.now.xmlschema              → 2009-03-31T09:58:59-05:00
```

Time

The Timeout.timeout method takes a parameter representing a timeout period in seconds, an optional exception parameter, and a block. The block is executed, and a timer is run concurrently. If the block terminates before the timeout, timeout returns the value of the block. Otherwise, the exception (default Timeout::Error) is raised.

`sltimeout_1.rb`

```ruby
require 'timeout'
for snooze in 1..2
  puts "About to sleep for #{snooze}"
  begin
    Timeout::timeout(1.5) do |timeout_length|
      puts "Timeout period is #{timeout_length}"
      sleep(snooze)
      puts "That was refreshing"
    end
  rescue Timeout::Error
    puts "Woken up early!!"
  end
end
```

produces:

```
About to sleep for 1
Timeout period is 1.5
That was refreshing
About to sleep for 2
Timeout period is 1.5
Woken up early!!
```

Be careful when using timeouts—you may find them interrupting system calls that you cannot reliably restart, resulting in possible data loss.

Library

Tk

Wrapper for Tcl/Tk

Of all the Ruby options for creating GUIs, the Tk library is probably the most widely supported, running on Windows, Linux, Mac OS X, and other Unix-like platforms.[5] Although it doesn't produce the prettiest interfaces, Tk is functional and relatively simple to program.

Only if: Tk library installed

`sltk_1.rb`

```ruby
require 'tk'
include Math
TkRoot.new do |root|
  title "Curves"
  geometry "400x400"
  TkCanvas.new(root) do |canvas|
    width 400
    height 400
    pack('side'=>'top', 'fill'=>'both', 'expand'=>'yes')
      points = [ ]
      10.upto(30) do |scale|
        (0.0).step(2*PI,0.1) do |i|
          new_x = 5*scale*sin(i) + 200  +  scale*sin(i*2)
          new_y = 5*scale*cos(i) + 200  + scale*cos(i*6)
          points << [ new_x, new_y ]
          f = scale/5.0
          r = (Math.sin(f)+1)*127.0
          g = (Math.cos(2*f)+1)*127.0
          b = (Math.sin(3*f)+1)*127.0
          col = sprintf("#%02x%02x%02x", r.to_i, g.to_i, b.to_i)
          if points.size == 3
            TkcLine.new(canvas,
                        points[0][0], points[0][1],
                        points[1][0], points[1][1],
                        points[2][0], points[2][1],
                        'smooth'=>'on',
                        'width'=> 7,
                        'fill'       => col,
                        'capstyle' => 'round')
            points.shift
          end
        end
      end
    end
  end
end
Tk.mainloop
```

---

5. All these environments require that the Tcl/Tk libraries are installed before the Ruby Tk extension can be used.

tmpdir   System-Independent Temporary Directory Location

The tmpdir library adds the tmpdir method to class Dir. This method returns the path to a temporary directory that *should* be writable by the current process. (This will not be true if none of the well-known temporary directories is writable and if the current working directory is also not writable.) Candidate directories include those referenced by the environment variables TMPDIR, TMP, TEMP, and USERPROFILE, the directory /tmp, and (on Windows boxes) the temp subdirectory of the Windows or System directory.

`sltmpdir_1.rb`

```
require 'tmpdir'

Dir.tmpdir   # =>   "/var/folders/a4/a4-daQQOG4anplm9DAY+TE+++TI/-Tmp-"

ENV['TMPDIR'] = "/wibble"    # doesn't exist
ENV['TMP']    = "/sbin"      # not writable
ENV['TEMP']   = "/Users/dave/tmp" # just right

Dir.tmpdir   # =>   "/Users/dave/tmp"
```

The mktmpdir method can be used to create a new temporary directory:

`sltmpdir_2.rb`

```
require 'tmpdir'
name = Dir.mktmpdir
# .. process, process, process ..
Dir.rmdir(name)
```

Tracer   Trace Program Execution

The tracer library uses Kernel.set_trace_func to trace all or part of a Ruby program's execution. The traced lines show the thread number, file, line number, class, event, and source line. The events shown are - for a change of line, > for a call, < for a return, C for a class definition, and E for the end of a definition.

- You can trace an entire program by including the tracer library from the command line:

```
class Account
  def initialize(balance)
    @balance = balance
  end
  def debit(amt)
    if @balance < amt
      fail "Insufficient funds"
    else
      @balance -= amt
    end
  end
end
acct = Account.new(100)
acct.debit(40)
```

```
% ruby -r tracer account.rb
#0:account.rb:1::-: class Account
#0:account.rb:1:Class:>: class Account
#0:account.rb:1:Class:<: class Account
#0:account.rb:1::C: class Account
#0:account.rb:2::-:   def initialize(balance)
#0:account.rb:2:Module:>:   def initialize(balance)
#0:account.rb:2:Module:<:   def initialize(balance)
#0:account.rb:5::-:   def debit(amt)
#0:account.rb:5:Module:>:   def debit(amt)
#0:account.rb:5:Module:<:   def debit(amt)
#0:account.rb:1::E: class Account
#0:account.rb:13::-: acct = Account.new(100)
#0:account.rb:13:Class:>: acct = Account.new(100)
#0:account.rb:2:Account:>:   def initialize(balance)
#0:account.rb:3:Account:-:     @balance = balance
#0:account.rb:13:Account:<: acct = Account.new(100)
#0:account.rb:13:Class:<: acct = Account.new(100)
#0:account.rb:14::-: acct.debit(40)
#0:account.rb:5:Account:>:   def debit(amt)
#0:account.rb:6:Account:-:     if @balance < amt
#0:account.rb:6:Account:-:     if @balance < amt
#0:account.rb:6:Fixnum:>:     if @balance < amt
#0:account.rb:6:Fixnum:<:     if @balance < amt
#0:account.rb:9:Account:-:       @balance -= amt
#0:account.rb:9:Fixnum:>:       @balance -= amt
#0:account.rb:9:Fixnum:<:       @balance -= amt
#0:account.rb:9:Account:<:       @balance -= amt
```

- You can also use tracer objects to trace just a portion of your code and use filters to select what to trace:

```
require 'tracer'

class Account
  def initialize(balance)
    @balance = balance
  end
  def debit(amt)
    if @balance < amt
      fail "Insufficient funds"
    else
      @balance -= amt
    end
  end
end

tracer = Tracer.new
tracer.add_filter lambda {|event, *rest| event == "line" }
acct = Account.new(100)
tracer.on do
  acct.debit(40)
end
```

```
#0:account.rb:20::-:   acct.debit(40)
#0:account.rb:8:Account:-:     if @balance < amt
#0:account.rb:8:Account:-:     if @balance < amt
#0:account.rb:11:Account:-:       @balance -= amt
```

Given a set of dependencies between nodes (where each node depends on zero or more other nodes and there are no cycles in the graph of dependencies), a topological sort will return a list of the nodes ordered such that no node follows a node that depends on it. One use for this is scheduling tasks, where the order means that you will complete the dependencies before you start any task that depends on them. The make program uses a topological sort to order its execution.

In this library's implementation, you mix in the TSort module and define two methods: tsort_each_node, which yields each node in turn, and tsort_each_child, which, given a node, yields each of that nodes dependencies.

- Given the set of dependencies among the steps for making a piña colada, what is the optimum order for undertaking the steps?

sltsort_1.rb

```ruby
require 'tsort'
class Tasks
  include TSort
  def initialize
    @dependencies = {}
  end
  def add_dependency(task, *relies_on)
    @dependencies[task] = relies_on
  end
  def tsort_each_node(&block)
    @dependencies.each_key(&block)
  end
  def tsort_each_child(node, &block)
    deps = @dependencies[node]
    deps.each(&block) if deps
  end
end
tasks = Tasks.new
tasks.add_dependency(:add_rum,       :open_blender)
tasks.add_dependency(:add_pc_mix,    :open_blender)
tasks.add_dependency(:add_ice,       :open_blender)
tasks.add_dependency(:close_blender, :add_rum, :add_pc_mix, :add_ice)
tasks.add_dependency(:blend_mix,     :close_blender)
tasks.add_dependency(:pour_drink,    :blend_mix)
tasks.add_dependency(:pour_drink,    :open_blender)
puts tasks.tsort
```

produces:

```
open_blender
add_rum
add_pc_mix
add_ice
close_blender
blend_mix
pour_drink
```

T Sort

un

Why un? When you invoke it from the command line with the -r option to Ruby, it spells -run. This pun gives a hint as to the intent of the library: it lets you run commands (in this case, a subset of the methods in FileUtils) from the command line. In theory this gives you an operating system–independent set of file manipulation commands, possibly useful when writing portable Makefiles.

See also: FileUtils (page 746)

- The available commands are as follows:

```
% ruby -run -e cp -- <options> source dest
% ruby -run -e ln -- <options> target linkname
% ruby -run -e mv -- <options> source dest
% ruby -run -e rm -- <options> file
% ruby -run -e mkdir -- <options> dirs
% ruby -run -e rmdir -- <options> dirs
% ruby -run -e install -- <options> source dest
% ruby -run -e chmod -- <options> octal_mode file
% ruby -run -e touch -- <options> file
```

Note the use of -- to tell the Ruby interpreter that options to the program follow.

You can get a list of all available commands with this:

slun_1.rb

```
% ruby -run -e help
```

For help on a particular command, append the command's name:

slun_2.rb

```
% ruby -run -e help mkdir
```

URI   RFC 2396 Uniform Resource Identifier (URI) Support

URI encapsulates the concept of a Uniform Resource Identifier (URI), a way of specifying some kind of (potentially networked) resource. URIs are a superset of URLs: URLs (such as the addresses of web pages) allow specification of addresses by location, and URIs also allow specification by name.

URIs consist of a scheme (such as http, mailto, ftp, and so on), followed by structured data identifying the resource within the scheme.

URI has factory methods that take a URI string and return a subclass of URI specific to the scheme. The library explicitly supports the ftp, http, https, ldap, and mailto schemes; others will be treated as generic URIs. The module also has convenience methods to escape and unescape URIs. The class Net::HTTP accepts URI objects where a URL parameter is expected.

See also: open-uri (page 773), Net::HTTP (page 765)

sluri_1.rb

```
require 'uri'

uri = URI.parse("http://pragprog.com:1234/mypage.cgi?q=ruby")
uri.class      # =>   URI::HTTP
uri.scheme     # =>   "http"
uri.host       # =>   "pragprog.com"
uri.port       # =>   1234
uri.path       # =>   "/mypage.cgi"
uri.query      # =>   "q=ruby"

uri = URI.parse("mailto:ruby@pragprog.com?Subject=help&body=info")
uri.class      # =>   URI::MailTo
uri.scheme     # =>   "mailto"
uri.to         # =>   "ruby@pragprog.com"
uri.headers    # =>   [["Subject", "help"], ["body", "info"]]

uri = URI.parse("ftp://dave@anon.com:/pub/ruby;type=i")
uri.class      # =>   URI::FTP
uri.scheme     # =>   "ftp"
uri.host       # =>   "anon.com"
uri.port       # =>   21
uri.path       # =>   "pub/ruby"
uri.typecode   # =>   "i"
```

URI

WeakRef   Support for Weak References

In Ruby, objects are not eligible for garbage collection if references still exist to them. Normally, this is a Good Thing—it would be disconcerting to have an object simply evaporate while you were using it. However, sometimes you may need more flexibility. For example, you might want to implement an in-memory cache of commonly used file contents. As you read more files, the cache grows. At some point, you may run low on memory. The garbage collector will be invoked, but the objects in the cache are all referenced by the cache data structures and so will not be deleted.

A weak reference behaves like any normal object reference with one important exception— the referenced object may be garbage collected, even while references to it exist. In the cache example, if the cached files were accessed using weak references, once memory runs low, they will be garbage collected, freeing memory for the rest of the application.

- Weak references introduce a slight complexity. Because the object referenced can be deleted by garbage collection at any time, code that accesses these objects must take care to ensure that the references are valid. Two techniques can be used. First, the code can reference the objects normally. Any attempt to reference an object that has been garbage collected will raise a WeakRef::RefError exception.

`slweakref_1.rb`

```
require 'weakref'
# Generate lots of small strings. Hopefully the early ones will have
# been garbage collected...
refs = (1..10000).map {|i| WeakRef.new("#{i}") }
puts "Last element is #{refs.last}"
puts "First element is #{refs.first}"
```

produces:

```
Last element is 10000
prog.rb:6:in `<main>': Invalid Reference - probably recycled
  (WeakRef::RefError)
```

- Alternatively, use the WeakRef#weakref_alive? method to check that a reference is valid before using it. Garbage collection must be disabled during the test and subsequent reference to the object. In a single-threaded program, you could use something like this:

`slweakref_2.rb`

```
ref = WeakRef.new(some_object)
# .. some time later
gc_was_disabled = GC.disable
if ref.weakref_alive?
  # do stuff with 'ref'
end
GC.enable unless gc_was_disabled
```

WEBrick

Web Server Toolkit

WEBrick is a pure-Ruby framework for implementing HTTP-based servers. The standard library includes WEBrick services that implement a standard web server (serving files and directory listings) and servlets supporting CGI, erb, file download, and the mounting of Ruby lambdas.

More examples of WEBrick start on page 301.

- The following code mounts two Ruby procs on a web server. Requests to the URI `http://localhost:2000/hello` run one proc, and requests to `http://localhost:2000/bye` run the other.

slwebrick_1.rb

```ruby
#!/usr/bin/ruby
require 'webrick'
include WEBrick
hello_proc = lambda do |req, resp|
  resp['Content-Type'] = "text/html"
  resp.body = %{
      <html><body>
        Hello. You're calling from a #{req['User-Agent']}
       <p>
        I see parameters: #{req.query.keys.join(', ')}
      </body></html>
  }
end
bye_proc = lambda do |req, resp|
  resp['Content-Type'] = "text/html"
  resp.body = %{
      <html><body>
        <h3>Goodbye!</h3>
      </body></html>
  }
end

hello =  HTTPServlet::ProcHandler.new(hello_proc)
bye   =  HTTPServlet::ProcHandler.new(bye_proc)
s = HTTPServer.new(:Port => 2000)
s.mount("/hello", hello)
s.mount("/bye",   bye)
trap("INT"){ s.shutdown }
s.start
```

WIN32OLE   Windows Automation

Interface to Windows automation, allowing Ruby code to interact with Windows applications. The Ruby interface to Windows is discussed in more detail in Chapter 21 on page 303.

Only if:
Windows

- Opens Internet Explorer and asks it to display our home page:

slwin32ole_1.rb

```
ie = WIN32OLE.new('InternetExplorer.Application')
ie.visible = true
ie.navigate("http://www.pragprog.com")
```

- Creates a new chart in Microsoft Excel and then rotates it:

slwin32ole_2.rb

```
require 'win32ole'
#    -4100 is the value for the Excel constant xl3DColumn.
ChartTypeVal = -4100;
excel = WIN32OLE.new("excel.application")
# Create and rotate the chart
excel['Visible'] = TRUE
excel.Workbooks.Add()
excel.Range("a1")['Value'] = 3
excel.Range("a2")['Value'] = 2
excel.Range("a3")['Value'] = 1
excel.Range("a1:a3").Select()
excelchart = excel.Charts.Add()
excelchart['Type'] = ChartTypeVal
30.step(180, 5) do |rot|
  excelchart.rotation = rot
  sleep(0.1)
end
excel.ActiveWorkbook.Close(0)
excel.Quit()
```

XMLRPC

Remote Procedure Calls using XML-RPC

XMLRPC allows clients to invoke methods on networked servers using the XML-RPC protocol. Communications take place over HTTP. The server may run in the context of a web server, in which case ports 80 or 443 (for SSL) will typically be used. The server may also be run stand-alone. The Ruby XML-RPC server implementation supports operation as a CGI script, as a mod_ruby script, as a WEBrick handler, and as a stand-alone server. Basic authentication is supported, and clients can communicate with servers via proxies. Servers may throw FaultException errors—these generate the corresponding exception on the client (or optionally may be flagged as a status return to the call).

See also: dRuby (page 738), WEBrick (page 819)

- The following simple server accepts a temperature in Celsius and converts it to Fahrenheit. It runs within the context of the WEBrick web server.

slxmlrpc_1.rb

```ruby
require 'webrick'
require 'xmlrpc/server'
xml_servlet = XMLRPC::WEBrickServlet.new
xml_servlet.add_handler("convert_celcius") do |celcius|
  celcius*1.8 + 32
end
xml_servlet.add_multicall # Add support for multicall
server = WEBrick::HTTPServer.new(:Port => 2000)
server.mount("/RPC2", xml_servlet)
trap("INT"){ server.shutdown }
server.start
```

- This client makes calls to the temperature conversion server. Note that in the output we show both the server's logging and the client program's output.

slxmlrpc_2.rb

```ruby
require 'xmlrpc/client'
server = XMLRPC::Client.new("localhost", "/RPC2", 2000)
puts server.call("convert_celcius", 0)
puts server.call("convert_celcius", 100)
puts server.multicall(['convert_celcius', -10],
                      ['convert_celcius', 200])
```

Produces:

```
localhost - - [10/Apr/2008:17:17:23 CDT] "POST /RPC2 HTTP/1.1" 200 124 - -> /RPC2
32.0
localhost - - [10/Apr/2008:17:17:23 CDT] "POST /RPC2 HTTP/1.1" 200 125 - -> /RPC2
212.0
localhost - - [10/Apr/2008:17:17:23 CDT] "POST /RPC2 HTTP/1.1" 200 290 - -> /RPC2
14.0
392.0
```

X MLRPC

YAML
Object Serialization/Deserialization

The YAML library (also described in the tutorial starting on page 422) serializes and deserializes Ruby object trees to and from an external, readable, plain-text format. YAML can be used as a portable object marshaling scheme, allowing objects to be passed in plain text between separate Ruby processes. In some cases, objects may also be exchanged between Ruby programs and programs in other languages that also have YAML support.

See also: json (page 756)

- YAML can be used to store an object tree in a flat file:

slyaml_1.rb
```ruby
require 'yaml'
tree = { :name => 'ruby',
         :uses => [ 'scripting', 'web', 'testing', 'etc' ]
       }
File.open("tree.yaml", "w") {|f| YAML.dump(tree, f)}
```

- Once stored, it can be read by another program:

slyaml_2.rb
```ruby
require 'yaml'
tree = YAML.load_file("tree.yaml")
tree[:uses][1]   # =>   "web"
```

- The YAML format is also a convenient way to store configuration information for programs. Because it is readable, it can be maintained by hand using a normal editor and then read as objects by programs. For example, a configuration file may contain the following:

slyaml_3.rb
```yaml
---
username: dave
prefs:
  background: dark
  foreground: cyan
  timeout: 30
```

We can use this in a program:

slyaml_4.rb
```ruby
require 'yaml'

config = YAML.load_file("code/config.yaml")
config["username"]                # =>   "dave"
config["prefs"]["timeout"] * 10   # =>   300
```

Zlib

Only if: zlib
library available

The Zlib module is home to a number of classes for compressing and decompressing streams and for working with gzip-format compressed files. They also calculate zip checksums.

- Compresses /etc/passwd as a gzip file and then reads the result back:

slzlib_1.rb

```
require 'zlib'
# These methods can take a filename
Zlib::GzipWriter.open("passwd.gz") do |gz|
  gz.write(File.read("/etc/passwd"))
end
system("ls -l /etc/passwd passwd.gz")
# or a stream
File.open("passwd.gz") do |f|
  gzip = Zlib::GzipReader.new(f)
  data = gzip.read.split(/\n/)
  puts data[15,3]
end
```

produces:

```
-rw-r--r--  1 root  wheel  2888 Sep 23  2007 /etc/passwd
-rw-rw-r--  1 dave  dave   1057 Mar 31 09:59 passwd.gz

daemon:*:1:1:System Services:/var/root:/usr/bin/false
_uucp:*:4:4:Unix to Unix Copy Protocol:/var/spool/uucp:/usr/sbin/uucico
_lp:*:26:26:Printing Services:/var/spool/cups:/usr/bin/false
```

- Compresses data sent between two processes:

slzlib_2.rb

```
require 'zlib'
rd, wr = IO.pipe
if fork
  rd.close
  zipper = Zlib::Deflate.new
  zipper << "This is a string "
  data = zipper.deflate("to compress", Zlib::FINISH)
  wr.write(data)
  wr.close
  Process.wait
else
  wr.close
  unzipper = Zlib::Inflate.new
  unzipper << rd.read
  puts "We got: #{unzipper.inflate(nil)}"
end
```

produces:

```
We got: This is a string to compress
```

## Chapter 29

Extending Ruby

It is easy to extend Ruby with new features by writing code in Ruby. But every now and then you need to interface to things at a lower level. Once you start adding in low-level code written in C, the possibilities are endless. Having said this, the stuff in this chapter is pretty advanced and should probably be skipped the first time through the book.

Extending Ruby with C is pretty easy. For instance, suppose we are building a custom Internet-ready jukebox for the Sunset Diner and Grill. It will play MP3 audio files from a hard disk or audio CDs from a CD jukebox. We want to be able to control the jukebox hardware from a Ruby program. The hardware vendor gave us a C header file and a binary library to use; our job is to construct a Ruby object that makes the appropriate C function calls.

Much of the information in this chapter is taken from the README.EXT file that is included in the distribution. If you are planning on writing a Ruby extension, you may want to refer to that file for more details as well as the latest changes.

Your First Extension

Just to introduce extension writing, let's write one. This extension is purely a test of the process—it does nothing that you couldn't do in pure Ruby. We'll also present some stuff without too much explanation; all the messy details will be given later.

The extension we write will have the same functionality as the following Ruby class:

```
extruby_1.rb
class MyTest
  def initialize
    @arr = Array.new
  end
  def add(obj)
    @arr.push(obj)
  end
end
```

That is, we'll be writing an extension in C that is plug-compatible with that Ruby class. The equivalent code in C should look somewhat familiar:

```
extruby_2.rb
#include "ruby.h"

static int id_push;

static VALUE t_init(VALUE self)
{
  VALUE arr;

  arr = rb_ary_new();
  rb_iv_set(self, "@arr", arr);
  return self;
}

static VALUE t_add(VALUE self, VALUE obj)
{
  VALUE arr;

  arr = rb_iv_get(self, "@arr");
  rb_funcall(arr, id_push, 1, obj);
  return arr;
}

VALUE cTest;

void Init_my_test() {
  cTest = rb_define_class("MyTest", rb_cObject);
  rb_define_method(cTest, "initialize", t_init, 0);
  rb_define_method(cTest, "add", t_add, 1);
  id_push = rb_intern("push");
}
```

Let's go through this example in detail, because it illustrates many of the important concepts in this chapter. First, we need to include the header file ruby.h to obtain the necessary Ruby definitions.

Now look at the last function, Init_my_test. Every extension defines a C global function named Init_*name*. This function will be called when the interpreter first loads the extension *name* (or on startup for statically linked extensions). It is used to initialize the extension and to insinuate it into the Ruby environment. (Exactly how Ruby knows that an extension is called *name* we'll cover later.) In this case, we define a new class named MyTest, which is a subclass of Object (represented by the external symbol rb_cObject; see ruby.h for others).

Next we set up add and initialize as two instance methods for class MyTest. The calls to rb_define_method establish a binding between the Ruby method name and the C function that will implement it. If Ruby code calls the add method on one of our objects, the interpreter will in turn call the C function t_add with one argument.

Similarly, when new is called for this class, Ruby will construct a basic object and then call initialize, which we have defined here to call the C function t_init with no (Ruby) arguments.

Now go back and look at the definition of t_init. Even though we said it took no arguments, it has a parameter here! In addition to any Ruby arguments, every method is passed an initial VALUE argument that contains the receiver for this method (the equivalent of self in Ruby code).

The first thing we'll do in t_init is create a Ruby array and set the instance variable @arr to point to it. Just as you would expect if you were writing Ruby source, referencing an instance variable that doesn't exist creates it. We then return a pointer to ourselves.

WARNING: Every C function that is callable from Ruby *must* return a VALUE, even if it's just Qnil. Otherwise, a core dump (or GPF) will be the likely result.

Finally, the function t_add gets the instance variable @arr from the current object and calls Array#push to push the passed value onto that array. When accessing instance variables in this way, the @ prefix is mandatory—otherwise, the variable is created but cannot be referenced from Ruby.

Despite the extra, clunky syntax that C imposes, you're still writing in Ruby—you can manipulate objects using all the method calls you've come to know and love, with the added advantage of being able to craft tight, fast code when needed.

Building Our Extension

We'll have a lot more to say about building extensions later. For now, though, all we have to do is follow these steps:

1. Create a file called extconf.rb in the same directory as our my_test.c C source file. The file extconf.rb should contain the following two lines:

   ```
   extruby_3.rb
   require 'mkmf'
   create_makefile("my_test")
   ```

2. Run extconf.rb. This will generate a Makefile:

   ```
   % ruby extconf.rb
   creating Makefile
   ```

3. Use make to build the extension. On an OS X system, you'd see:

   ```
   % make
   gcc -fno-common -g -02 -pipe -fno-common  -I.
       -I/usr/lib/ruby/1.9/powerpc-darwin7.4.0
       -I/usr/lib/ruby/1.9/powerpc-darwin7.4.0 -I.   -c my_test.c
   cc -dynamic -bundle -undefined suppress -flat_namespace
       -L'/usr/lib' -o my_test.bundle my_test.o  -ldl -lobjc
   ```

The result of all this is the extension, all nicely bundled up in a shared object (a .so, a .dll, or [on OS X] a .bundle).

Running Our Extension

We can use our extension from Ruby simply by require-ing it dynamically at runtime (on most platforms). We can wrap this up in a test to verify that things are working as we expect:

extruby_4.rb

```ruby
require 'my_test'
require 'test/unit'
class TestTest < Test::Unit::TestCase
  def test_test
    t = MyTest.new
    assert_equal(Object, MyTest.superclass)
    assert_equal(MyTest, t.class)
    t.add(1)
    t.add(2)
    assert_equal([1,2], t.instance_eval("@arr"))
  end
end
```

produces:

```
Finished in 0.000385 seconds.
1 tests, 3 assertions, 0 failures, 0 errors, 0 skips
```

Once we're happy that our extension works, we can then install it globally by running make install.

Ruby Objects in C

When we wrote our first extension, we cheated, because it didn't really do anything with the Ruby objects. For example, it didn't do calculations based on Ruby numbers. Before we can do this, we need to find out how to represent and access Ruby data types from within C.

Everything in Ruby is an object, and all variables are references to objects. When we're looking at Ruby objects from within C code, the situation is pretty much the same. Most Ruby objects are represented as C pointers to an area in memory that contains the object's data and other implementation details. In C code, all these references are via variables of type VALUE, so when you pass Ruby objects around, you'll do it by passing VALUEs.

This has one exception. For performance reasons, Ruby implements Fixnums, Symbols, true, false, and nil as so-called immediate values. These are still stored in variables of type VALUE, but they aren't pointers. Instead, their value is stored directly in the variable.

So, sometimes VALUEs are pointers, and sometimes they're immediate values. How does the interpreter pull off this magic? It relies on the fact that all pointers point to areas of memory aligned on 4- or 8-byte boundaries. This means that it can guarantee that the low 2 bits in a pointer will always be zero. When it wants to store an immediate value, it arranges to have at least one of these bits set, allowing the rest of the interpreter code to distinguish immediate values from pointers. Although this sounds tricky, it's actually easy to use in practice, largely because the interpreter comes with a number of macros and methods that simplify working with the type system.

This is how Ruby implements object-oriented code in C: a Ruby object is an allocated structure in memory that contains a table of instance variables and information about the class. The class itself is another object (an allocated structure in memory) that contains a table of the methods defined for that class. Ruby is built upon this foundation.

Working with Immediate Objects

As we said earlier, immediate values are not pointers: Fixnum, Symbol, true, false, and nil are stored directly in VALUE.

Fixnum values are stored as 31-bit numbers[1] that are formed by shifting the original number left 1 bit and then setting the LSB, or least significant bit (bit 0), to 1. When VALUE is used as a pointer to a specific Ruby structure, it is guaranteed always to have an LSB of zero; the other immediate values also have LSBs of zero. Thus, a simple bit test can tell you whether you have a Fixnum. This test is wrapped in a macro, FIXNUM_P. Similar tests let you check for other immediate values.

```
FIXNUM_P(value)  → nonzero if value is a Fixnum
SYMBOL_P(value)  → nonzero if value is a Symbol
NIL_P(value)     → nonzero if value is nil
RTEST(value)     → nonzero if value is neither nil nor false
```

Several useful conversion macros for numbers as well as other standard data types are shown in Table 29.1 on the next page.

The other immediate values (true, false, and nil) are represented in C as the constants Qtrue, Qfalse, and Qnil, respectively. You can test VALUE variables against these constants directly or use the conversion macros (which perform the proper casting).

Working with Strings

In C, we're used to working with null-terminated strings. Ruby strings, however, are more general and may well include embedded nulls. The safest way to work with Ruby strings, therefore, is to do what the interpreter does and use both a pointer and a length. In fact, Ruby String objects are actually references to an RString structure, and the RString structure contains both a length and a pointer field. You can access the structure via the RSTRING macros. This is a change in Ruby 1.9—prior to this you manipulated the C structure directly.

1.9

```
VALUE str;
RSTRING_LEN(str)  → length of the Ruby string
RSTRING_PTR(str)  → pointer to string storage
RSTRING_END(str)  → pointer to end of string
```

---

1.   Or 63-bit on wider CPU architectures

Table 29.1. C/Ruby Data Type Conversion Functions and Macros

C Data Types to Ruby Objects:

INT2NUM(*int*)	→ *Fixnum* or *Bignum*
INT2FIX(*int*)	→ *Fixnum* (faster)
LONG2NUM(*long*)	→ *Fixnum* or *Bignum*
LONG2FIX(*int*)	→ *Fixnum* (faster)
LL2NUM(*long long*)	→ *Fixnum* or *Bignum* (if native system supports *long long* type)
ULL2NUM(*long long*)	→ *Fixnum* or *Bignum* (if native system supports *long long* type)
CHR2FIX(*char*)	→ *Fixnum*
rb_str_new2(*char **)	→ *String*
rb_float_new(*double*)	→ *Float*

Ruby Objects to C Data Types:

int	NUM2INT(*Numeric*)	(Includes type check)
int	FIX2INT(*Fixnum*)	(Faster)
unsigned int	NUM2UINT(*Numeric*)	(Includes type check)
unsigned int	FIX2UINT(*Fixnum*)	(Includes type check)
long	NUM2LONG(*Numeric*)	(Includes type check)
long	FIX2LONG(*Fixnum*)	(Faster)
unsigned long	NUM2ULONG(*Numeric*)	(Includes type check)
char	NUM2CHR(*Numeric* or *String*)	(Includes type check)
double	NUM2DBL(*Numeric*)	
	see text for strings...	

However, life is slightly more complicated than that. Rather than using the VALUE object directly when you need a string value, you probably want to call the method StringValue, passing it the original value. It'll return an object that you can use the RSTRING_ macros on or throw an exception if it can't derive a string from the original. This is all part of Ruby duck typing conventions, described in more detail on pages 845 and 359. The StringValue method checks to see whether its operand is a String. If not, it tries to invoke to_str on the object, throwing a TypeError exception if it can't.

So, if you want to write some code that iterates over all the characters in a String object, you may write the following:

```
extruby_5.rb
static VALUE iterate_over(VALUE original_str) {
  int i;
  char *p;
  VALUE str = StringValue(original_str);
  p = RSTRING_PTR(str);    // may be null
  for (i = 0; i < RSTRING_LEN(str); i++, p++) {
    // process *p
  }
  return str;
}
```

If you want to bypass the length and just access the underlying string pointer, you can use the convenience method StringValuePtr, which both resolves the string reference and then returns the C pointer to the contents.

If you plan to use a string to access or control some external resource, you probably want to hook into Ruby's tainting mechanism. In this case, you'll use the method SafeStringValue, which works like StringValue but throws an exception if its argument is tainted and the safe level is greater than zero.

Working with Other Objects

When VALUEs are not immediate; they are pointers to one of the defined Ruby object structures—you can't have a VALUE that points to an arbitrary area of memory. The structures for the basic built-in classes are defined in ruby.h and are named R*Classname*: RArray, RBignum, RClass, RData, RFile, RFloat, RHash, RObject, RRegexp, RString, and RStruct.

You can check to see what type of structure is used for a particular VALUE in a number of ways. The macro TYPE(*obj*) will return a constant representing the C type of the given object: T_OBJECT, T_STRING, and so on. Constants for the built-in classes are defined in ruby.h. Note that the *type* we are referring to here is an implementation detail—it is not the same as the class of an object.

If you want to ensure that a VALUE pointer points to a particular structure, you can use the macro Check_Type, which will raise a TypeError exception if *value* is not of the expected *type* (which is one of the constants T_STRING, T_FLOAT, and so on):

```
Check_Type(VALUE value, int type)
```

Having said all this, you need to be careful about building too much dependence on checking types into your extension code. We have more to say about extensions and the Ruby type system on page 845.

Again, note that we are talking about "type" as the C structure that represents a particular built-in type. The class of an object is a different beast entirely. The class objects for the built-in classes are stored in C global variables named rb_c*Classname* (for instance, rb_cObject); modules are named rb_m*Modulename*.

It isn't advisable to alter the data in these C structures directly, however—you may look, but don't touch. Instead, you'll normally use the supplied C functions to manipulate Ruby data (we'll talk more about this in just a moment).

However, in the interests of efficiency, you may need to dig into these structures to obtain data. To dereference members of these C structures, you have to cast the generic VALUE to the proper structure type. ruby.h contains a number of macros that perform the proper casting for you, allowing you to dereference structure members easily. These macros are named R*CLASSNAME* (which returns the whole structure) and R*CLASSNAME_xxx*, which let you access the specific fields in the structure. For example, RSTRING(obj) will return a reference to the RString structure pointed to by obj; RSTRING_PTR(obj) and RSTRING_LEN(obj) return the contents and length. There are similar accessors for hashes (RHASH), files (RFILE), and so on. The full list is shown in 29.2 on page 833.

1.9

Pre-1.9 String Access

Prior to Ruby 1.8.6, you'd access RSTRING fields directly to get the length and string data pointer. So, how do you write an extension that works with either technique? Perhaps like this:

extruby_6.rb

```
#if !defined(RSTRING_LEN)
#  define RSTRING_LEN(x) (RSTRING(x)->len)
#  define RSTRING_PTR(x) (RSTRING(x)->ptr)
#endif
```

Global Variables

Most of the time, your extensions will implement classes, and the Ruby code uses those classes. The data you share between the Ruby code and the C code will be wrapped tidily inside objects of the class. This is how it should be.

Sometimes, though, you may need to implement a global variable, accessible by both your C extension and by Ruby code.

The easiest way to do this is to have the variable be a VALUE (that is, a Ruby object). You then bind the address of this C variable to the name of a Ruby variable. In this case, the $ prefix is optional, but it helps clarify that this is a global variable. Make sure you don't make a stack-based variable a Ruby global: it won't exist once the stack frame is gone.

```
static  VALUE hardware_list;

static VALUE Init_SysInfo() {
  rb_define_class(....);

  hardware_list = rb_ary_new();
  rb_define_variable("$hardware", &hardware_list);
  ...
  rb_ary_push(hardware_list, rb_str_new2("DVD"));
  rb_ary_push(hardware_list, rb_str_new2("CDPlayer1"));
  rb_ary_push(hardware_list, rb_str_new2("CDPlayer2"));
}
```

The Ruby side can then access the C variable hardware_list as $hardware:

```
$hardware   # =>  ["DVD", "CDPlayer1", "CDPlayer2"]
```

Sometimes, though, life is more complicated. Perhaps you want to define a global variable whose value must be calculated when it is accessed. You do this by defining *hooked* and *virtual* variables. A hooked variable is a real variable that is initialized by a named function when the corresponding Ruby variable is accessed. Virtual variables are similar but are never stored; their value purely comes from evaluating the hook function. See the API section that begins on page 860 for details.

Table 29.2. Object Accessor Macros

RClass c;	
RCLASS_M_TBL(c)	Pointer to table of methods
RCLASS_SUPER(c)	Pointer to superclass
RModule m;	
RMODULE_IV_TBL(m)	
RMODULE_M_TBL(m)	Same as classes
RMODULE_SUPER(m)	
RFloat v;	
RFLOAT_VALUE(v)	The value as a native float
RString str;	
RSTRING_LEN(str)	Length of the string
RSTRING_PTR(str)	Pointer to start of string data
RSTRING_END(str)	Pointer to end of string data
RArray a;	
RARRAY_LEN(a)	Number of elements in the array
RARRAY_PTR(a)	Pointer to start of array data (treat as being read-only)
RHash h;	
RHASH_TBL(h)	Pointer to the hash data (see st.c
RHASH_ITER_LEV(h)	If nonzero, hash is being traversed by an iterator
RHASH_IFNONE(h)	Default value for hash (may be a proc object)
RHASH_SIZE(h)	Number of entries in hash
RHASH_EMPTY_P(h)	True if RHASH_SIZE(h) is zero

If you create a Ruby object from C and store it in a C global variable *without* exporting it to Ruby, you must at least tell the garbage collector about it, lest ye be reaped inadvertently:

```
static VALUE obj;
// ...
obj = rb_ary_new();
rb_global_variable(obj);
```

The Threading Model

Previous Ruby interpreters implemented threading internally. These *green threads* relied on the interpreter periodically switching between Ruby-level threads. Even if your computer had eight cores, your Ruby program would run on only one of them at a time. And, if you called a long-running external function, your whole program would hang. DNS name resolution was a notorious culprit.

1.9 Ruby 1.9 now uses operating system threads. This allows your multithreaded Ruby programs to do more in parallel than was possible earlier. However, before you run cheering into the streets, I have to tell you a catch. Although the core interpreter is thread-safe, extension libraries probably aren't. And problems that arise when you run non-thread-safe code multithreaded are incredibly hard to diagnose, and they have a habit of being extremely damaging to data. So, Matz made a decision: the Ruby VM can run in multiple threads, but it will execute Ruby code in only one of those threads at a time.

This means that you probably won't be writing your next high-volume telephone exchange microcode in Ruby. But it still brings benefits. Whereas previously the DNS lookup would stall all your code, in Ruby 1.9 it will run in an operating system thread. If your program has other Ruby-level threads waiting to execute, they can run while the looking is executing. Another example is the multiplication of very large Bignum values. Whereas in the old interpreter the multiplication would hog the CPU and no other threads would run, Ruby 1.9 schedules such multiplications in one operating system thread and allows other Ruby-level threads to operate in true parallel.

When you write your own Ruby extensions, you need to make sure they play well in this new world. In particular, if they are about to undertake some long-running external operation, you need to make sure that other Ruby threads are allowed to run in parallel.

Ruby controls which threads can run using the GVL, or *Giant VM Lock*. The thread that's currently executing Ruby-level code will have claimed the GVL, and no other thread will be able to claim it (and hence execute Ruby code) until the lock is relinquished. Your extension code normally doesn't worry about this—Ruby handles it for you. But if your extension is about to make (say) a long-running I/O request, it will need to temporarily relinquish the GVL until that request completes. To do this, call the method rb_thread_blocking_region (which we'll abbreviate to rb_tbr in the description that follows—in your code you have to spell out the full name). This method takes the address of a C function and a pointer to a parameter to pass to that function. It also takes a second function/parameter pair, which we'll describe shortly.

Internally, rb_tbr releases the GVL and then calls the function you specify, passing it the parameter you gave in the call. When the function terminates, rb_tbr then reacquires the GVL before returning back to you. If it were written in Ruby, an incomplete implementation might look like this:

```
def rb_thread_blocking_region(param, unblock_function, unblock_flag)
  release_lock(GVL)
  begin
    yield(param)
  ensure
    acquire_lock(GVL)
  end
end
rb_thread_blocking_region(task_data, ...) do |data|
  # some long-running external call
end
```

Before we look at the C-level implementation, we need to discuss the second function/parameter pair that you pass to rb_thread_blocking_region. These represent an *unblocking function*, or *ubf*. There are times that Ruby needs to terminate the execution of code that's being run in a separate thread. For example, a thread may call your extension library to start some long-running operation, such as a file copy. Your code uses rb_tbr to allow the rest of the interpreter to run during this process. But maybe one of those other threads calls exit to shut down the interpreter. Ruby needs to coordinate this shutdown with the work that's taking place in your thread. It does this by calling the unblocking function that you pass to rb_tbr. This function is responsible for terminating whatever activity was initiated by rb_tbr.

Let's look at some C code that uses this feature. This example is taken from bignum.c in the main interpreter, but it applies to code that is in an extension, too.

First, the code defines a structure that is used to pass parameters to the function that executes in parallel. In this example, the same structure is also passed to the unblocking function:

```
struct big_mul_struct {
    VALUE x, y, z, stop;
};
```

Here's the body of the method that is called to multiply two bignums. I've cut out some of the boring stuff in the middle.

```
static VALUE
rb_big_mul0(VALUE x, VALUE y)
{
  struct big_mul_struct bms;
  volatile VALUE z;

  /* ... */
  bms.x = x;
  bms.y = y;
  bms.stop = Qfalse;
  if (RBIGNUM_LEN(x) + RBIGNUM_LEN(y) > 10000) {
    z = rb_thread_blocking_region(bigmul1, &bms, rb_big_stop, &bms.stop);
  }
  else {
    z = bigmul1(&bms);
  }
  return z;
}
```

The important code for us is at the end of the method. If the numbers being multiplied are big, it calls rb_thread_blocking_region, passing in the function to run (bigmul1), the parameter to pass to it (bms), and the unblocking function and parameter (rb_big_stop and bms). If instead the numbers are below the threshold, it calls bigmul1 directly.

Now let's look at the unblocking function, rb_big_stop:

```
static void
rb_big_stop(void *ptr)
{
    VALUE *stop = (VALUE*)ptr;
    *stop = Qtrue;
}
```

If called, it simply sets the location referenced by its parameter to Qtrue.

And how does this stop the calculation prematurely? Let's look at bigmul1 (again, omitting some gory details):

```
static VALUE
bigmul1(void *ptr)
{
    struct big_mul_struct *bms = (struct big_mul_struct*)ptr;
    long i, j;
    VALUE x = bms->x, y = bms->y, z = bms->z;

    /* ... */
    for (i = 0; i < RBIGNUM_LEN(x); i++) {
        if (bms->stop) return Qnil;
        /*
         * do the next digit...
         */
    }
    return z;
}
```

So, if the unblocking function is called, it sets the stop member of the structure to Qtrue. Then in the loop that's doing the multiplication and that is running in a separate thread, it notices that the flag has been set and exits early, returning nil.

Threads, Processes, and I/O

If the function you pass to rb_tbr executes I/O or synchronizes with an external process, you're left with a difficult decision when it comes time to write the unblocking function. Interrupting I/O is tricky and is most likely system-dependent. Luckily for you, Ruby provides a sledgehammer to crack that particular nut. If you pass RUBY_UBF_IO or RUBY_UBF_PROCESS as the third parameter (and NULL as the fourth), Ruby will use a default ubf function that simply kills the thread performing the processing. Here's the code from the interpreter method that reads from a file descriptor:

```
static int
rb_read_internal(int fd, void *buf, size_t count)
{
  struct io_internal_struct iis;
  iis.fd = fd;
  iis.buf = buf;
  iis.capa = count;

    return rb_thread_blocking_region(internal_read_func, &iis,
                                     RUBY_UBF_IO, 0);
}
```

You'll need to decide whether you should use these built-in ubfs in your own extension. For example, if updating a database table, you'll probably want to perform a more controlled shutdown than simply terminating the controlling thread.

The Jukebox Extension

We've covered enough of the basics now to return to our jukebox example—interfacing C code with Ruby and sharing data and behavior between the two worlds.

Wrapping C Structures

We have the vendor's library that controls the audio CD jukebox units, and we're ready to wire it into Ruby. The vendor's header file looks like this:

```
typedef struct _cdjb {
  int    statusf;
  int    request;
  void *data;
  char  pending;
  int    unit_id;
  void *stats;
} CDJukebox;
// Allocate a new CDJukebox structure
CDJukebox *new_jukebox(void);
// Assign the Jukebox to a player
void assign_jukebox(CDJukebox *jb, int unit_id);
// Deallocate when done (and take offline)
void free_jukebox(CDJukebox *jb);
// Seek to a disc, track and notify progress
void jukebox_seek(CDJukebox *jb,
                  int disc,
                  int track,
                  void (*done)(CDJukebox *jb, int percent));
// ... others...
// Report a statistic
double get_avg_seek_time(CDJukebox *jb);
```

This vendor has its act together; although they might not admit it, the code is written with an object-oriented flavor. We don't know what all those fields mean within the CDJukeBox structure, but that's OK—we can treat it as an opaque pile of bits. The vendor's code knows what to do with it; we just have to carry it around.

Any time you have a C-only structure that you would like to handle as a Ruby object, you should wrap it in a special, internal Ruby class called DATA (type T_DATA). Two macros do this wrapping, and one macro retrieves your structure back out again.

API: C Data Type Wrapping

VALUE **Data_Wrap_Struct**(VALUE class, void (*mark)(), void (*free)(), void *ptr)

> Wraps the given C data type *ptr*, registers the two garbage collection routines (explained in a moment), and returns a VALUE pointer to a genuine Ruby object. The C type of the resulting object is T_DATA, and its Ruby class is *class*.

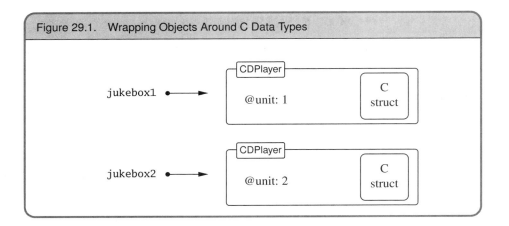

Figure 29.1. Wrapping Objects Around C Data Types

VALUE **Data_Make_Struct**(VALUE class, *c-type*, void (*mark)(), void (*free)(), *c-type* *)
> Allocates and sets to zero a structure of the indicated type first and then proceeds as Data_Wrap_Struct. *c-type* is the name of the C data type that you're wrapping, not a variable of that type.

Data_Get_Struct(VALUE obj,*c-type*,*c-type* *)
> Returns the original pointer. This macro is a type-safe wrapper around the macro DATA_PTR(obj), which evaluates the pointer.

The object created by Data_Wrap_Struct is a normal Ruby object, except that it has an additional C data type that can't be accessed from Ruby. As you can see in Figure 29.1, this C data type is separate from any instance variables that the object contains. But since it's a separate thing, how do you get rid of it when the garbage collector claims this object? What if you have to release some resource (close some file, clean up some lock or IPC mechanism, and so on)?

Ruby uses a "mark-and-sweep" garbage collection scheme. During the mark phase, Ruby looks for pointers to areas of memory. It marks these areas as "in use" (because something is pointing to them). If those areas themselves contain more pointers, the memory these pointers reference is also marked, and so on. At the end of the mark phase, all memory that is referenced will have been marked, and any orphaned areas will not have a mark. At this point, the sweep phase starts, freeing memory that isn't marked.

To participate in Ruby's mark-and-sweep garbage collection process, you must define a routine to free your structure and possibly a routine to mark any references from your structure to other structures. Both routines take a void pointer, a reference to your structure. The *mark* routine will be called by the garbage collector during its mark phase. If your structure references other Ruby objects, then your mark function needs to identify these objects using rb_gc_mark(*value*). If the structure doesn't reference other Ruby objects, you can simply pass 0 as a function pointer.

When the object needs to be disposed of, the garbage collector will call the *free* routine to free it. If you've allocated any memory yourself (for instance, by using Data_Make_Struct), you'll need to pass a free function—even if it's just the standard C library's free routine. For complex structures that you have allocated, your free function may need to traverse the structure to free all the allocated memory.

Let's look at our CD player interface. The vendor library passes the information around between its various functions in a CDJukebox structure. This structure represents the state of the jukebox and therefore is a good candidate for wrapping within our Ruby class. You create new instances of this structure by calling the library's CDPlayerNew method. You'd then want to wrap that created structure inside a new CDPlayer Ruby object. A fragment of code to do this may look like the following. (We'll talk about that magic *klass* parameter in a minute.)

```
CDJukebox *jukebox;
VALUE obj;
// Vendor library creates the Jukebox
jukebox = new_jukebox();
// then we wrap it inside a Ruby CDPlayer object
obj = Data_Wrap_Struct(klass, 0, cd_free, jukebox);
```

Once this code executed, *obj* would hold a reference to a newly allocated CDPlayer Ruby object, wrapping a new CDJukebox C structure. Of course, to get this code to compile, we'd need to do some more work. We'd have to define the CDPlayer class and store a reference to it in the variable cCDPlayer. We'd also have to define the function to free off our object, cdplayer_free. That's easy, because it just calls the vendor library dispose method:

```
static void cd_free(void *p) {
   free_jukebox(p);
}
```

However, code fragments do not a program make. We need to package all this stuff in a way that integrates it into the interpreter. And to do that, we need to look at some of the conventions the interpreter uses.

Object Creation

Let's start by looking at how you allocate the memory for a new object. The basic idea is simple. Let's say you're creating an object of class CDPlayer in your Ruby program:

```
cd = CDPlayer.new
```

Underneath the covers, the interpreter calls the class method new for CDPlayer. Because CDPlayer hasn't defined a method new, Ruby looks into its parent, class Class.

The implementation of new in class Class is fairly simple; it allocates memory for the new object and then calls the object's initialize method to initialize that memory.

So, if our CDPlayer extension is to be a good Ruby citizen, it should work within this framework. This means that we'll need to implement an allocation function and an initialize method.

Allocation Functions

The allocation function is responsible for creating the memory used by your object. If the object you're implementing doesn't use any data other than Ruby instance variables, then you don't need to write an allocation function—Ruby's default allocator will work just fine. But if your class wraps a C structure, you'll need to allocate space for that structure in the allocation function. The allocation function gets passed the class of the object being allocated. In our case, it will in all likelihood be a cCDPlayer, but we'll use the parameter as given, because this means that we'll work correctly if subclassed:

```
static VALUE cd_alloc(VALUE klass) {
  CDJukebox *jukebox;
  VALUE obj;
  // Vendor library creates the Jukebox
  jukebox = new_jukebox();
  // then we wrap it inside a Ruby CDPlayer object
  obj = Data_Wrap_Struct(klass, 0, cd_free, jukebox);
  return obj;
}
```

You then need to register your allocation function in your class's initialization code:

```
void Init_CDPlayer() {
  cCDPlayer = rb_define_class("CDPlayer", rb_cObject);
  rb_define_alloc_func(cCDPlayer, cd_alloc);
  // ...
}
```

Most objects probably need to define an initializer too. The allocation function creates an empty, uninitialized object, and we'll need to fill in specific values. In the case of the CD player, the constructor is called with the unit number of the player to be associated with this object:

```
static VALUE cd_initialize(VALUE self, VALUE unit) {
  int unit_id;
  CDJukebox *jb;
  Data_Get_Struct(self, CDJukebox, jb);
  unit_id = NUM2INT(unit);
  assign_jukebox(jb, unit_id);
  return self;
}
```

One of the reasons for this multistep object creation protocol is that it lets the interpreter handle situations where objects have to be created by "back-door means." One example is when objects are being deserialized from their marshaled form. Here, the interpreter needs to create an empty object (by calling the allocator), but it cannot call the initializer (because it has no knowledge of the parameters to use). Another common situation is when objects are duplicated or cloned.

One further issue lurks here. Because users can choose to bypass the constructor, you need to ensure that your allocation code leaves the returned object in a valid state. It may not contain all the information it would have had, had it been set up by #initialize, but it at least needs to be usable.

Cloning Objects

All Ruby objects can be copied using one of two methods, dup and clone. The two methods are similar. Both produce a new instance of their receiver's class by calling the allocation function. Then they copy across any instance variables from the original. clone then goes a bit further and copies the original's singleton class (if it has one) and flags (such as the flag that indicates that an object is frozen). You can think of dup as being a copy of the contents and clone as being a copy of the full object.

However, the Ruby interpreter doesn't know how to handle copying the internal state of objects that you write as C extensions. For example, if your object wraps a C structure that contains an open file descriptor, it's up to the semantics of your implementation whether that descriptor should simply be copied to the new object or whether a new file descriptor should be opened.

To handle this, the interpreter delegates to your code the responsibility of copying the internal state of objects that you implement. After copying the object's instance variables, the interpreter invokes the new object's initialize_copy method, passing in a reference to the original object. It's up to you to implement meaningful semantics in this method.

For our CDPlayer class, we'll take a fairly simple approach to the cloning issue. We'll simply copy across the CDJukebox structure from the original object.

There's a wee chunk of strange code in this example. To test that the original object is indeed something we can clone the new one from, the code checks to see that the original

- has a TYPE of T_DATA (which means that it's a noncore object), and

- has a free function with the same address as our free function.

This is a relatively high-performance way of verifying that the original object is compatible with our own (as long as you don't share free functions between classes). An alternative, which is slower, would be to use rb_obj_is_kind_of and do a direct test on the class:

```
static VALUE cd_init_copy(VALUE copy, VALUE orig) {
  CDJukebox *orig_jb;
  CDJukebox *copy_jb;
  if (copy == orig)
    return copy;
  // we can initialize the copy from other CDPlayers
  // or their subclasses only
  if (TYPE(orig) != T_DATA ||
      RDATA(orig)->dfree != (RUBY_DATA_FUNC)cd_free) {
    rb_raise(rb_eTypeError, "wrong argument type");
  }
  // copy all the fields from the original
  // object's CDJukebox structure to the
  // new object
  Data_Get_Struct(orig, CDJukebox, orig_jb);
  Data_Get_Struct(copy, CDJukebox, copy_jb);
  MEMCPY(copy_jb, orig_jb, CDJukebox, 1);
  return copy;
}
```

Our copy method does not have to allocate a wrapped structure to receive the original objects CDJukebox structure; the cd_alloc method has already taken care of that.

Note that in this case it's correct to do type checking based on classes. We need the original object to have a wrapped CDJukebox structure, and the only objects that have one of these are derived from class CDPlayer.

Putting It All Together

OK, finally we're ready to write all the code for our CDPlayer class:

```
extruby_24.rb
#include "ruby.h"
#include "cdjukebox.h"

static VALUE cCDPlayer;

// Helper function to free a vendor CDJukebox
static void cd_free(void *p) {
  free_jukebox(p);
}

// Allocate a new CDPlayer object, wrapping
// the vendor's CDJukebox structure
static VALUE cd_alloc(VALUE klass) {
  CDJukebox *jukebox;
  VALUE obj;
  // Vendor library creates the Jukebox
  jukebox = new_jukebox();
  // then we wrap it inside a Ruby CDPlayer object
  obj = Data_Wrap_Struct(klass, 0, cd_free, jukebox);
  return obj;
}

// Assign the newly created CDPLayer to a
// particular unit
static VALUE cd_initialize(VALUE self, VALUE unit) {
  int unit_id;
  CDJukebox *jb;
  Data_Get_Struct(self, CDJukebox, jb);
  unit_id = NUM2INT(unit);
  assign_jukebox(jb, unit_id);
  return self;
}

// Copy across state (used by clone and dup).  For jukeboxes, we
// actually create a new vendor object and set its unit number from
// the old
static VALUE cd_init_copy(VALUE copy, VALUE orig) {
  CDJukebox *orig_jb;
  CDJukebox *copy_jb;
  if (copy == orig)
    return copy;
```

```
    // we can initialize the copy from other CDPlayers or their
    // subclasses only
    if (TYPE(orig) != T_DATA ||
        RDATA(orig)->dfree != (RUBY_DATA_FUNC)cd_free) {
      rb_raise(rb_eTypeError, "wrong argument type");
    }
    // copy all the fields from the original object's CDJukebox
    // structure to the new object
    Data_Get_Struct(orig, CDJukebox, orig_jb);
    Data_Get_Struct(copy, CDJukebox, copy_jb);
    MEMCPY(copy_jb, orig_jb, CDJukebox, 1);

    return copy;
}
// The progress callback yields to the caller the percent complete
static void progress(CDJukebox *rec, int percent) {
  if (rb_block_given_p()) {
    if (percent > 100) percent = 100;
    if (percent < 0) percent = 0;
    rb_yield(INT2FIX(percent));
  }
}
// Seek to a given part of the track, invoking the progress callback
// as we go
static VALUE
cd_seek(VALUE self, VALUE disc, VALUE track) {
  CDJukebox *jb;
  Data_Get_Struct(self, CDJukebox, jb);

  jukebox_seek(jb,
               NUM2INT(disc),
               NUM2INT(track),
               progress);
  return Qnil;
}
// Return the average seek time for this unit
static VALUE
cd_seek_time(VALUE self)
{
  double tm;
  CDJukebox *jb;
  Data_Get_Struct(self, CDJukebox, jb);
  tm = get_avg_seek_time(jb);
  return rb_float_new(tm);
}
// Return this player's unit number
static VALUE
cd_unit(VALUE self) {
  CDJukebox *jb;
  Data_Get_Struct(self, CDJukebox, jb);
```

```
    return INT2NUM(jb->unit_id);
}


void Init_CDPlayer() {
    cCDPlayer = rb_define_class("CDPlayer", rb_cObject);
    rb_define_alloc_func(cCDPlayer, cd_alloc);

    rb_define_method(cCDPlayer, "initialize", cd_initialize, 1);
    rb_define_method(cCDPlayer, "initialize_copy", cd_init_copy, 1);

    rb_define_method(cCDPlayer, "seek", cd_seek, 2);
    rb_define_method(cCDPlayer, "seek_time", cd_seek_time, 0);
    rb_define_method(cCDPlayer, "unit", cd_unit, 0);
}
```

Now we can control our jukebox from Ruby in a nice, object-oriented way:

> extruby_25.rb

```ruby
require 'CDPlayer'
p = CDPlayer.new(13)
puts "Unit is #{p.unit}"
p.seek(3, 16) {|x| puts "#{x}% done" }
puts "Avg. time was #{p.seek_time} seconds"
p1 = p.dup
puts "Cloned unit = #{p1.unit}"
```

produces:

```
Unit is 13
26% done
79% done
100% done
Avg. time was 1.2 seconds
Cloned unit = 13
```

This example demonstrates most of what we've talked about so far, with one additional neat feature. The vendor's library provided a callback routine—a function pointer that is called every so often while the hardware is grinding its way to the next disc. We've set that up here to run a code block passed as an argument to seek. In the progress function, we check to see whether there is an iterator in the current context and, if there is, run it with the current percent done as an argument.

Memory Allocation

You may sometimes need to allocate memory in an extension that won't be used for object storage—perhaps you have a giant bitmap for a Bloom filter, an image, or a whole bunch of little structures that Ruby doesn't use directly.

To work correctly with the garbage collector, you should use the following memory allocation routines. These routines do a little bit more work than the standard malloc. For instance, if ALLOC_N determines that it cannot allocate the desired amount of memory, it will invoke the garbage collector to try to reclaim some space. It will raise a NoMemError if it can't or if the requested amount of memory is invalid.

API: Memory Allocation

type * **ALLOC_N**(*c-type*, n)

> Allocates *n c-type* objects, where *c-type* is the literal name of the C type, not a variable of that type.

type * **ALLOC**(*c-type*)

> Allocates a *c-type* and casts the result to a pointer of that type.

REALLOC_N(*var*, *c-type*, n)

> Reallocates *n c-type*s and assigns the result to *var*, a pointer to a variable of type *c-type*.

type * **ALLOCA_N**(*c-type*, n)

> Allocates memory for *n* objects of *c-type* on the stack—this memory will be automatically freed when the function that invokes ALLOCA_N returns.

Ruby Type System

In Ruby, we rely less on the type (or class) of an object and more on its capabilities. This is called *duck typing*. We describe it in more detail in Chapter 23 on page 359. You'll find many examples of this if you examine the source code for the interpreter itself. For example, the String class implements the method %. This treats the string object as a format specifier (just like the C sprintf function). The % method can take a single argument (if the string contains just one substitution) or an array of values (if the format string contains multiple substitutions).

```
irb(main):001:0> "You bought %d x %s" % [ 3, "widgets"]
=> "You bought 3 x widgets"
irb(main):002:0> "The total is %0.2f" % 5.678
=> "The total is 5.68"
```

Here's the code in string.c that implements the String.% method:

```
static VALUE
rb_str_format_m(VALUE str, VALUE arg)
{
    VALUE tmp = rb_check_array_type(arg);
    if (!NIL_P(tmp)) {
        return rb_str_format(RARRAY_LEN(tmp), RARRAY_PTR(tmp), str);
    }
    return rb_str_format(1, &arg, str);
}
```

The first parameter to this method is the *self* object—the format string. The arg argument is either an array or a single object. However, the code doesn't explicitly check the type of the argument. Instead, it first calls rb_check_array_type, passing in the argument. What does this method do? Let's see (the code is in array.c):

```
extruby_28.rb
VALUE
rb_check_array_type(ary)
    VALUE ary;
{
    return rb_check_convert_type(ary, T_ARRAY, "Array", "to_ary");
}
```

The plot thickens. Let's track down rb_check_convert_type in object.c:

```
extruby_29.rb
VALUE
rb_check_convert_type(VALUE val, int type, const char *tname,
                    const char *method)
{
    VALUE v;
    /* always convert T_DATA */
    if (TYPE(val) == type && type != T_DATA) return val;
    v = convert_type(val, tname, method, Qfalse);
    if (NIL_P(v)) return Qnil;
    if (TYPE(v) != type) {
        char *cname = rb_obj_classname(val);
        rb_raise(rb_eTypeError, "can't convert %s to %s (%s#%s gives %s)",
                cname, tname, cname, method, rb_obj_classname(v));
    }
    return v;
}
```

Now we're getting somewhere. If the object is the correct type (T_ARRAY in our example), then the original object is returned. Otherwise, we don't give up quite yet. Instead, we use the convert_type method to call our original object and ask whether it can represent itself as an array (we call its to_ary method). If it can, we're happy and continue. The code is saying "I don't need an Array; I just need something that can be represented as an array." This means that String.% will accept as an array any parameter that implements a to_ary method. We discuss these conversion protocols in more detail (but from the Ruby perspective) starting on page 365.

What does all this mean to you as an extension writer? There are two messages. First, try to avoid checking the types of parameters passed to you. Instead, see whether there's a rb_check_xxx_type method that will convert the parameter into the type that you need. If not, look for an existing conversion function (such as rb_Array, rb_Float, or rb_Integer) that'll do the trick for you. Second, if you're writing an extension that implements something that may be meaningfully used as a Ruby string or array, consider implementing to_str or to_ary methods, allowing objects implemented by your extension to be used in string or array contexts.

Creating an Extension

Having written the source code for an extension, we now need to compile it so Ruby can use it. We can either do this as a shared object, which is dynamically loaded at runtime, or statically link the extension into the main Ruby interpreter itself. The basic procedure is the same:

1. Create the C source code file(s) in a given directory.
2. Optionally create any supporting Ruby files in a lib subdirectory.
3. Create extconf.rb.
4. Run extconf.rb to create a Makefile for the C files in this directory.
5. Run make.
6. Run make install.

Creating a Makefile with extconf.rb

The overall workflow when building an extension is shown in Figure 29.2 on the following page. The key to the whole process is the extconf.rb program that you, as a developer, create. extconf.rb is simple program that determines what features are available on the user's system and where those features may be located. Executing extconf.rb builds a customized Makefile, tailored for both your application and the system on which it's being compiled. When you run the make command against this Makefile, your extension is built and (optionally) installed. If you have multiple versions of Ruby installed on your system, the one used when you run extconf.rb is the one your extension is built and installed against.

The simplest extconf.rb may be just two lines long, and for many extensions this is sufficient:

```
extruby_30.rb
require 'mkmf'
create_makefile("Test")
```

The first line brings in the mkmf library module (described starting on page 866). This contains all the commands we'll be using. The second line creates a Makefile for an extension called "Test." (Note that "Test" is the name of the extension; the file will always be called Makefile.) Test will be built from all the C source files in the current directory. When your code is loaded, Ruby will call its Init_Test method.

Let's say that we run this extconf.rb program in a directory containing a single source file, main.c. The result is a Makefile that will build our extension. On a Linux box, this executes the following commands (your commands will likely be different):

```
gcc -fPIC -I/usr/local/lib/ruby/1.9/i686-linux -g -O2 \
  -c main.c -o main.o
gcc -shared -o Test.so main.o -lc
```

The result of this compilation is Test.so, which may be dynamically linked into Ruby at runtime with require.

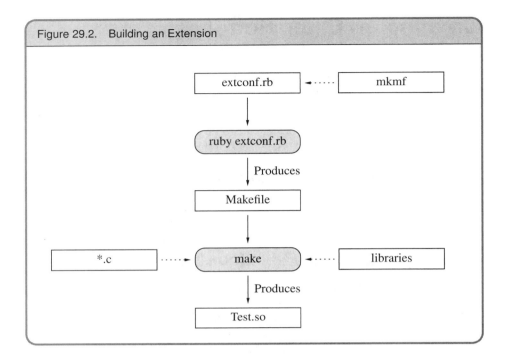

Figure 29.2.   Building an Extension

Under Mac OS X, the commands are different, but the result is the same; a shared object (a *bundle* on the Mac) is created:

```
gcc -fno-common -g -O2 -pipe -fno-common \
    -I/usr/lib/ruby/1.9.0/powerpc-darwin   \
    -I/usr/lib/ruby/1.9.0/powerpc-darwin -c main.c

cc -dynamic -bundle -undefined suppress -flat_namespace \
    -L'/usr/lib'  -o Test.bundle main.o -lruby -lpthread -ldl -lobjc
```

See how the mkmf commands have automatically located platform-specific libraries and used options specific to the local compiler. Pretty neat, eh?

Although this basic extconf.rb program works for many simple extensions, you may have to do some more work if your extension needs header files or libraries that aren't included in the default compilation environment or if you conditionally compile code based on the presence of libraries or functions.

A common requirement is to specify nonstandard directories where include files and libraries may be found. This is a two-step process. First, your extconf.rb should contain one or more dir_config commands. This specifies a tag for a set of directories. Then, when you run the extconf.rb program, you tell mkmf where the corresponding physical directories are on the current system.

> ### Dividing Up the Namespace
>
> Increasingly, extension writers are being good citizens. Rather than install their work directory into one of Ruby's library directories, they're using subdirectories to group their files together. This is easy with extconf.rb. If the parameter to the create_makefile call contains forward slashes, mkmf assumes that everything before the last slash is a directory name and that the remainder is the extension name. The extension will be installed into the given directory (relative to the Ruby directory tree). In the following example, the extension will still be named Test:
>
> ```
> require 'mkmf'
> create_makefile("wibble/Test")
> ```
>
> However, when you require this class in a Ruby program, you'd write this:
>
> ```
> require 'wibble/Test'
> ```

If extconf.rb contains the line dir_config(*name*), then you give the location of the corresponding directories with the command-line options:

--with-*name*-include=*directory*

> Adds *directory*/include to the compile command.

--with-*name*-lib=*directory*

> Adds *directory*/lib to the link command.

If (as is common) your include and library directories are subdirectories called include and lib of some other directory, you can take a shortcut:

--with-*name*-dir=*directory*

> Adds *directory*/lib and *directory*/include to the link command and compile command, respectively.

As well as specifying all these --with options when you run extconf.rb, you can also use the --with options that were specified when Ruby was built for your machine. This means you can discover and use the locations of libraries that are used by Ruby itself. It also means that you can specify the locations of all libraries just once and then rebuild extensions as many times as you like.

To make all this concrete, let's say you need to use the vendor's CDJukebox libraries and include files for the CD player we're developing. Your extconf.rb may contain this:

```
require 'mkmf'
dir_config('cdjukebox')
# .. more stuff
create_makefile("CDPlayer")
```

You'd then run extconf.rb with something like this:

```
% ruby extconf.rb --with-cdjukebox-dir=/usr/local/cdjb
```

The generated Makefile would assume that /usr/local/cdjb/lib contained the libraries and /usr/local/cdjb/include the include files.

The dir_config command adds to the list of places to search for libraries and include files. It does not, however, link the libraries into your application. To do that, you'll need to use one or more have_library or find_library commands.

have_library looks for a given entry point in a named library. If it finds the entry point, it adds the library to the list of libraries to be used when linking your extension. find_library is similar but allows you to specify a list of directories to search for the library. Here are the contents of the extconf.rb that we use to link our CD player:

```
require 'mkmf'
dir_config("cdjukebox")
have_library("cdjukebox", "new_jukebox")
create_makefile("CDPlayer")
```

A particular library may be in different places depending on the host system. The X Window system, for example, is notorious for living in different directories on different systems. The find_library command will search a list of supplied directories to find the right one (this is different from have_library, which uses only configuration information for the search). For example, to create a Makefile that uses X Windows and a JPEG library, extconf.rb may contain this:

```
require 'mkmf'

if have_library("jpeg","jpeg_mem_init") and
   find_library("X11", "XOpenDisplay",
                "/usr/X11/lib",       # list of directories
                "/usr/X11R6/lib",     # to check
                "/usr/openwin/lib")   # for library
then
    create_makefile("XThing")
else
    puts "No X/JPEG support available"
end
```

We've added some functionality to this program. All the mkmf commands return false if they fail. This means we can write an extconf.rb that generates a Makefile only if everything it needs is present. The Ruby distribution does this so that it will try to compile only those extensions that are supported on your system.

You also may want your extension code to be able to configure the features it uses depending on the target environment. For example, our CD jukebox may be able to use a high-performance MP3 decoder if the end user has one installed.

We can check by looking for its header file:

```
extruby_39.rb
require 'mkmf'
dir_config('cdjukebox')
have_library('cdjb', 'CDPlayerNew')
have_header('hp_mp3.h')
create_makefile("CDJukeBox")
```

We can also check to see whether the target environment has a particular function in any of the libraries we'll be using. For example, the setpriority call would be useful but isn't always available. We can check for it with this:

```
require 'mkmf'
dir_config('cdjukebox')
have_func('setpriority')
create_makefile("CDJukeBox")
```

Both have_header and have_func define preprocessor constants if they find their targets. The names are formed by converting the target name to uppercase and prepending HAVE_. Your C code can take advantage of this using constructs such as the following:

```
#if defined(HAVE_HP_MP3_H)
#  include <hp_mp3.h>
#endif

#if defined(HAVE_SETPRIORITY)
   err = setpriority(PRIOR_PROCESS, 0, -10)
#endif
```

If you have special requirements that can't be met with all these mkmf commands, your program can directly add to the global variables $CFLAGS and $LFLAGS, which are passed to the compiler and linker, respectively.

Sometimes you'll create an extconf.rb and it just doesn't seem to work. You give it the name of a library, and it swears that no such library has ever existed on the entire planet. You tweak and tweak, but mkmf still can't find the library you need. It would be nice if you could find out exactly what it's doing behind the scenes. Well, you can. Each time you run your extconf.rb script, mkmf generates a log file containing details of what it did. If you look in mkmf.log, you'll be able to see what steps the program used to try to find the libraries you requested. Sometimes trying these steps manually will help you track down the problem.

Installation Target

The Makefile produced by your extconf.rb will include an "install" target. This will copy your shared library object into the correct place on your (or your users') local file system. The destination is tied to the installation location of the Ruby interpreter you used to run extconf.rb in the first place. If you have multiple Ruby interpreters installed on your box, your extension will be installed into the directory tree of the one that ran extconf.rb.

In addition to installing the shared library, extconf.rb will check for the presence of a lib/ subdirectory. If it finds one, it will arrange for any Ruby files there to be installed along with your shared object. This is useful if you want to split the work of writing your extension between low-level C code and higher-level Ruby code.

Static Linking

Finally, if your system doesn't support dynamic linking or if you have an extension module that you want to have statically linked into Ruby itself, edit the file ext/Setup in the distribution and add your directory to the list of extensions in the file. In your extension's directory, create a file named MANIFEST containing a list of all the files in your extension (source, extconf.rb, lib/, and so on). Then rebuild Ruby. The extensions listed in Setup will be statically linked into the Ruby executable. If you want to disable any dynamic linking and link all extensions statically, edit ext/Setup to contain the following option.

```
extruby_42.rb
option nodynamic
```

A Shortcut

If you are extending an existing library written in C or C++, you may want to investigate SWIG (http://www.swig.org). SWIG is an interface generator: it takes a library definition (typically from a header file) and automatically generates the glue code needed to access that library from another language. SWIG supports Ruby, meaning that it can generate the C source files that wrap external libraries in Ruby classes.

Embedding a Ruby Interpreter

In addition to extending Ruby by adding C code, you can also turn the problem around and embed Ruby itself within your application. As of Ruby 1.9, you can no longer call ruby_run to invoke loaded code. Instead, you can call it either via the C API or by evaluating strings.

Let's start with the Ruby program we want to embed. Here's a simple Ruby class that implements a method to return the sum of the numbers from 1 to *max*:

```
extruby_43.rb
class Summer
  def sum(max)
    raise "Invalid maximum #{max}" if max < 0
    (max*max + max)/2
  end
end
```

Let's see how to invoke this from a C program.

First we'll interact by evaluating strings of Ruby code:

```
extruby_44.rb
#include "ruby.h"

int main(int argc, char **argv) {
  VALUE result;

  ruby_sysinit(&argc, &argv);
  RUBY_INIT_STACK;
  ruby_init();
  ruby_init_loadpath();

  rb_require("sum");   // or sum.rb
  rb_eval_string("$summer = Summer.new");
  rb_eval_string("$result = $summer.sum(10)");
  result = rb_gv_get("result");
  printf("Result = %d\n", NUM2INT(result));
  return ruby_cleanup(0);
}
```

To initialize the Ruby interpreter, you need to call ruby_sysinit() to pick up command-line arguments used by Ruby, RUBY_INIT_STACK to set up the Ruby stack, and ruby_init to initialize the interpreter itself. The call to ruy_init_loadpath adds any directories to be searched for libraries (for example if your RUBYLIB environment variable is set).

Once this prelude is out of the way, we can start using our external Ruby file. We load it into the interpreter using rb_require and then evaluate two lines of code using rb_eval_string. Notice that we assign the results of these two lines to global variables. We could also have used instance variables, but globals are easier to manipulate at the top level. We could not have used local variables: they don't persist across calls to eval.

Once our sum has been calculated, we need to get it back into our C code. The call to rb_gv_get gets the value of a global variable but returns it as a Ruby object. We convert it to a native integer via NUM2INT before printing the result (which is 55).

In order to compile this code, you need the Ruby include and library files accessible. When writing this book on my box (Mac OS X), I have the Ruby 1.9 interpreter installed in a private directory, so my Makefile looks like the following. (Note that Ruby 1.9 changes the location of the ruby.h file.)

1.9

```
extruby_45.rb
LIB=/usr/local/rubybook/lib
INC=/usr/local/rubybook/include/ruby-1.9.0/ruby
CFLAGS=-I$(INC) -g
LDFLAGS=-L$(LIB) -lruby -ldl -lobjc

embed:  embed.o
        $(CC) -o embed embed.o $(LDFLAGS)
```

This kind of hands-off manipulation of Ruby programs from within C code is easy, but it has two major drawbacks. First, it's indirect—we have to keep storing things in globals and extracting the values from these globals out to use them. Second, we're not doing any real error checking, which will definitely bite us later.

So, the second way to interact with Ruby code is to use the C API. This gives us much finer-grained control and also lets us handle errors. You do this by initializing the interpreter as normal. Then, rather than evaluating strings, you instead invoke specific methods in your Ruby code. When these methods return, your C code gets control back.

There's a wrinkle, though. If the Ruby code raises an exception and it isn't caught, your C program will terminate. To overcome this, you need to do what the interpreter does and protect all calls that could raise an exception. This can get messy. The rb_protect method call wraps the call to another C function. That second function should invoke our Ruby method. However, the method wrapped by rb_protect is defined to take just a single parameter. Passing more involves some ugly C casting.

Let's look at an example. Let's write a C program that calls an instance of this class multiple times.

To create the instance, we'll get the class object (by looking for a top-level constant whose name is the name of our class). We'll then ask Ruby to create an instance of that class— rb_class_new_instance is actually a call to Class.new. (The two initial 0 parameters are the argument count and a dummy pointer to the arguments themselves.) Once we have that object, we can invoke its sum method using rb_funcall.

extruby_46.rb

```
#include "ruby.h"
static int id_sum;
int Values[] = { 5, 10, 15, -1, 20, 0 };
static VALUE wrap_sum(VALUE args) {
  VALUE *values = (VALUE *)args;
  VALUE  summer = values[0];
  VALUE  max    = values[1];
  return rb_funcall(summer, id_sum, 1, max);
}
static VALUE protected_sum(VALUE summer, VALUE max) {
  int error;
  VALUE args[2];
  VALUE result;
  args[0] = summer;
  args[1] = max;
  result = rb_protect(wrap_sum, (VALUE)args, &error);
  return error ? Qnil : result;
}
int main(int argc, char **argv) {
  int value;
  int *next = Values;
  int error;
  ruby_sysinit(&argc, &argv);
  RUBY_INIT_STACK;
  ruby_init();
```

```
ruby_init_loadpath();
ruby_script("demo_embedder");   /* sets name in error messages */
rb_protect((VALUE (*)(VALUE))rb_require, (VALUE)"sum", &error);
// get an instance of Summer
VALUE summer = rb_class_new_instance(0, 0,
                    rb_const_get(rb_cObject, rb_intern("Summer")));
id_sum = rb_intern("sum");
while (value = *next++) {
  VALUE  result = protected_sum(summer, INT2NUM(value));
  if (NIL_P(result))
    printf("Sum to %d doesn't compute!\n", value);
  else
    printf("Sum to %d is %d\n", value, NUM2INT(result));
}
return ruby_cleanup(0);
}
```

The ugly part of this code is the protected_sum method. We want to use rb_funcall to call the sum method in our Summar object, but rb_funcall takes four parameters. The only way to handle exceptions raised in Ruby code from the C API is to wrap the call to Ruby code using the rb_protect method. But rb_protect wraps only those methods that have the following signature:

```
VALUE *method(VALUE arg)
```

To work around this, protected_sum creates a two-element array containing the parameters it wants to pass to rb_funcall and then uses a C cast to fake out that this array is a single VALUE argument. The first parameter to rb_protect is the name of a proxy method, wrap_sum, that unbundles these arguments and the calls rb_funcall. If you do a lot of this kind of work, it would be worthwhile writing a simple wrapper library to simplify this kind of coding.

One last thing: the Ruby interpreter was not originally written with embedding in mind. Probably the biggest problem is that it maintains state in global variables, so it isn't thread-safe. You can embed Ruby—just one interpreter per process.

API: Embedded Ruby API

void **ruby_init**( )

> Sets up and initializes the interpreter. This function should be called before any other Ruby-related functions.

void **ruby_init_loadpath**( )

> Initializes the $: (load path) variable; necessary if your code loads any library modules.

void **ruby_options**(int argc, char **argv)

> Gives the Ruby interpreter the command-line options.

void **ruby_script**(char *name)
        Sets the name of the Ruby script (and $0) to *name*.

void **rb_load_file**(char *file)
        Loads the given file into the interpreter.

void **ruby_run**( )
        Runs the interpreter.

void **ruby_finalize**( )
        Shuts down the interpreter.

For another example of embedding a Ruby interpreter within another program, see also eruby, which is described beginning on page 297.

Bridging Ruby to Other Environments

So far, we've discussed extending Ruby by adding routines written in C. However, you can write extensions in just about any language, as long as you can bridge the two languages with C. Almost anything is possible, including awkward marriages such as Ruby and C++.

There's a bigger story here, though. In the past, there was effectively only one Ruby implementation. But at the time of writing, we now have a number of alternative implementations. As well as Matz's original Ruby interpreter (commonly called MRI), there's JRuby,[2] Iron-Ruby,[3] Ruby.NET,[4] and Rubinius[5] (with other implementations waiting in the wings and not yet released).

So, if you're looking to integrate Ruby code and Java code, then you should probably consider JRuby. It allows you to bridge pretty much seamlessly between the two languages. It runs Ruby on Rails and provides adapters so that you can (for example) use existing entity beans as Rails model objects.

If you want to integrate Ruby into a Microsoft environment, IronRuby gives you an implementation targeted at the DLR, while Ruby.NET targets the CLR.

Rubinius is interesting—it uses the original Matz Ruby parser but contains a totally different VM implementation. Its goal it to have code run so fast that it is possible to write the majority of Ruby's libraries in Ruby itself (rather than having, for example, the String class written in C, as it is in MRI). Right now, it looks like they might be able to achieve this, which will be a major win for portability and extensibility.

---

2.   `http://jruby.codehaus.org/`

3.   `http://www.ironruby.net/`

4.   `http://rubydotnet.googlegroups.com/web/Home.htm`

5.   `http://rubini.us/`

However, be careful. Ruby does not really have an official specification, so these implementations may exhibit differing behaviors when dealing with edge conditions. Also, currently MRI implements only Ruby 1.9.

Ruby C Language API

Last, but by no means least, here are some C-level functions that you may find useful when writing an extension.

Some functions require an ID. You can obtain an ID for a string by using rb_intern and reconstruct the name from an ID by using rb_id2name.

Because most of these C functions have Ruby equivalents that are already described in detail elsewhere in this book, the descriptions here will be brief.

The following listing is not complete. Many more functions are available—too many to document them all, as it turns out. If you need a method that you can't find here, check ruby.h or intern.h for likely candidates. Also, at or near the bottom of each source file is a set of method definitions that describes the binding from Ruby methods to C functions. You may be able to call the C function directly or search for a wrapper function that calls the function you need. The following list, based on the list in README.EXT, shows the main source files in the interpreter.

Ruby Language Core
   class.c, error.c, eval*.c, gc.c, id.c, object.c, parse.y, variable.c

Utility Functions
   dln.c, reg*.c, st.c, util.c

Ruby Interpreter
   blockinlining.c, compile.c, debug.c, dmy*.c, inits.c, iseq.c, keywords, main.c, ruby.c, version.c, vm*.c

Encoding and Character Sets
   enc/*, encoding.c, transcode.c

Base Library
   array.c, bignum.c, compar.c, cont.c, dir.c, enum.c, enumerator.c, file.c, hash.c, io.c, marshal.c, math.c, numeric.c, pack.c, prec.c, process.c, random.c, range.c, re.c, signal.c, sprintf.c, string.c, struct.c, thread*.c, time.c

API: Defining Classes

VALUE **rb_define_class**(char *name, VALUE superclass)
>Defines a new class at the top level with the given *name* and *superclass* (for class Object, use rb_cObject).

VALUE **rb_define_module**(char *name)
>Defines a new module at the top level with the given *name*.

VALUE   **rb_define_class_under**(VALUE under, char *name, VALUE superclass)
> Defines a nested class under the class or module *under*.

VALUE   **rb_define_module_under**(VALUE under, char *name)
> Defines a nested module under the class or module *under*.

void   **rb_include_module**(VALUE parent, VALUE module)
> Includes the given *module* into the class or module *parent*.

void   **rb_extend_object**(VALUE obj, VALUE module)
> Extends *obj* with *module*.

VALUE   **rb_require**(const char *name)
> Equivalent to require *name*. Returns Qtrue or Qfalse.

API: Defining Structures

VALUE   **rb_struct_define**(char *name, char *attribute..., NULL)
> Defines a new structure with the given attributes.

VALUE   **rb_struct_new**(VALUE sClass, VALUE args..., NULL)
> Creates an instance of *sClass* with the given attribute values.

VALUE   **rb_struct_aref**(VALUE struct, VALUE idx)
> Returns the element named or indexed by *idx*.

VALUE   **rb_struct_aset**(VALUE struct, VALUE idx, VALUE val)
> Sets the attribute named or indexed by *idx* to *val*.

API: Defining Methods

In some of the function definitions that follow, the parameter *argc* specifies how many arguments a Ruby method takes. It may have the following values. If the value is not negative, it specifies the number of arguments the method takes. If negative, it indicates that the method takes optional arguments. In this case, the absolute value of *argc* minus one is the number of required arguments (so −1 means all arguments are optional, −2 means one mandatory argument followed by optional arguments, and so on).

In a function that has been given a variable number of arguments, you can use the C function rb_scan_args to sort things out (see below).

void   **rb_define_method**(VALUE classmod, char *name, VALUE(*func)(), int argc)
> Defines an instance method in the class or module *classmod* with the given *name*, implemented by the C function *func* and taking *argc* arguments.

void   **rb_define_alloc_func**(VALUE classmod, VALUE(*func)())
> Identifies the allocator for *classmod*.

void **rb_define_module_function**(VALUE module, char *name, VALUE(*func)(),
int argc))

    Defines a method in *module* with the given *name*, implemented by the C function *func* and taking *argc* arguments.

void **rb_define_global_function**(char *name, VALUE(*func)(), int argc)

    Defines a global function (a private method of Kernel) with the given *name*, implemented by the C function *func* and taking *argc* arguments.

void **rb_define_singleton_method**(VALUE classmod, char *name,
VALUE(*func)(), int argc)

    Defines a singleton (class) method in class *classmod* with the given *name*, implemented by the C function *func* and taking *argc* arguments.

int **rb_scan_args**(int argcount, VALUE *argv, char *fmt, ...)

    Scans the argument list and assigns to variables similar to scanf: *fmt* is a string containing zero, one, or two digits followed by some flag characters. The first digit indicates the count of mandatory arguments; the second is the count of optional arguments. A * means to pack the rest of the arguments into a Ruby array. A & means that an attached code block will be taken and assigned to the given variable (if no code block was given, Qnil will be assigned). After the *fmt* string, pointers to VALUE are given (as with scanf) to which the arguments are assigned.

    extruby_47.rb

```
VALUE name, one, two, rest;
rb_scan_args(argc, argv, "12", &name, &one, &two);
rb_scan_args(argc, argv, "1*", &name, &rest);
```

void **rb_undef_method**(VALUE classmod, const char *name)

    Undefines the given method *name* in the given *classmod* class or module.

void **rb_define_alias**(VALUE classmod, const char *newname,
const char *oldname)

    Defines an alias for *oldname* in class or module *classmod*.

API: Defining Variables and Constants

void **rb_define_const**(VALUE classmod, char *name, VALUE value)

    Defines a constant in the class or module *classmod*, with the given *name* and *value*.

void **rb_define_global_const**(char *name, VALUE value)

    Defines a global constant with the given *name* and *value*.

void **rb_define_variable**(const char *name, VALUE *object)

> Exports the address of the given *object* that was created in C to the Ruby namespace as *name*. From Ruby, this will be a global variable, so *name* should start with a leading dollar sign. Be sure to honor Ruby's rules for allowed variable names; illegally named variables will not be accessible from Ruby.

void **rb_define_class_variable**(VALUE class, const char *name, VALUE val)

> Defines a class variable *name* (which must be specified with a @@ prefix) in the given *class*, initialized to *value*.

void **rb_define_virtual_variable**(const char *name, VALUE(*getter)(), void(*setter)())

> Exports a virtual variable to a Ruby namespace as the global $*name*. No actual storage exists for the variable; attempts to get and set the value will call the given functions with the prototypes.

> `extruby_48.rb`

```
VALUE getter(ID id, VALUE *data,
             struct global_entry *entry);
void setter(VALUE value, ID id, VALUE *data,
            struct global_entry *entry);
```

> You will likely not need to use the *entry* parameter and can safely omit it from your function declarations.

void **rb_define_hooked_variable**(const char *name, VALUE *variable, VALUE(*getter)(), void(*setter)())

> Defines functions to be called when reading or writing to *variable*. See also rb_define_virtual_variable.

void **rb_define_readonly_variable**(const char *name, VALUE *value)

> Same as rb_define_variable but read-only from Ruby.

void **rb_define_attr**(VALUE variable, const char *name, int read, int write)

> Creates accessor methods for the given *variable*, with the given *name*. If *read* is nonzero, creates a read method; if *write* is nonzero, creates a write method.

void **rb_global_variable**(VALUE *obj)

> Registers the given address with the garbage collector.

API: Calling Methods

VALUE **rb_class_new_instance**((int argc, VALUE *argv, VALUE klass))

> Return a new instance of class *klass*. *argv* is a pointer to an array of *argc* parameters.

VALUE **rb_funcall**(VALUE recv, ID id, int argc, ...)

> Invokes the method given by *id* in the object *recv* with the given number of arguments *argc* and the arguments themselves (possibly none).

VALUE **rb_funcall2**(VALUE recv, ID id, int argc, VALUE *args)

> Invokes the method given by *id* in the object *recv* with the given number of arguments *argc* and the arguments themselves given in the C array *args*.

VALUE **rb_funcall3**(VALUE recv, ID id, int argc, VALUE *args)

> Same as rb_funcall2 but will not call private methods.

VALUE **rb_apply**(VALUE recv, ID name, VALUE args)

> Invokes the method given by *id* in the object *recv* with the arguments given in the Ruby Array *args*.

ID **rb_intern**(char *name)

> Returns an ID for a given *name*. If the name does not exist, a symbol table entry will be created for it.

char * **rb_id2name**(ID id)

> Returns a name for the given *id*.

VALUE **rb_call_super**(int argc, VALUE *args)

> Calls the current method in the superclass of the current object.

API: Exceptions

void **rb_raise**(VALUE exception, const char *fmt, ...)

> Raises an *exception*. The given string *fmt* and remaining arguments are interpreted as with printf.

void **rb_fatal**(const char *fmt, ...)

> Raises a Fatal exception, terminating the process. No rescue blocks are called, but ensure blocks will be called. The given string *fmt* and remaining arguments are interpreted as with printf.

void **rb_bug**(const char *fmt, ...)

> Terminates the process immediately—no handlers of any sort will be called. The given string *fmt* and remaining arguments are interpreted as with printf. You should call this function only if a fatal bug has been exposed. You don't write fatal bugs, do you?

void **rb_sys_fail**(const char *msg)

> Raises a platform-specific exception corresponding to the last known system error, with the given *msg*.

VALUE **rb_rescue**(VALUE (*body)(), VALUE args, VALUE(*rescue)(), VALUE rargs)
> Executes *body* with the given *args*. If a StandardError exception is raised, then execute *rescue* with the given *rargs*.

VALUE **rb_ensure**(VALUE(*body)(), VALUE args, VALUE(*ensure)(), VALUE eargs)
> Executes *body* with the given *args*. Whether or not an exception is raised, execute *ensure* with the given *eargs* after *body* has completed.

VALUE **rb_protect**(VALUE (*body)(), VALUE args, int *state)
> Executes *body* with the given *args* and returns nonzero in *result* if any exception was raised. The value in state corresponds to the various TAG_xxx macros. In Ruby 1.9, these are defined in eval_intern.h (although there's a strong argument for moving them to ruby.h, as eval_intern.h is not accessible to extension writers).

void **rb_notimplement**( )
> Raises a NotImpError exception to indicate that the enclosed function is not implemented yet or not available on this platform.

void **rb_exit**(int status)
> Exits Ruby with the given *status*. Raises a SystemExit exception and calls registered exit functions and finalizers.

void **rb_warn**(const char *fmt, ...)
> Unconditionally issues a warning message to standard error. The given string *fmt* and remaining arguments are interpreted as with printf.

void **rb_warning**(const char *fmt, ...)
> Conditionally issues a warning message to standard error if Ruby was invoked with the -w flag. The given string *fmt* and remaining arguments are interpreted as with printf.

API: Iterators

void **rb_iter_break**( )
> Breaks out of the enclosing iterator block.

VALUE **rb_each**(VALUE obj)
> Invokes the each method of the given *obj*.

VALUE **rb_yield**(VALUE arg)
> Transfers execution to the iterator block in the current context, passing *arg* as an argument. Multiple values may be passed in an array.

int **rb_block_given_p**( )
> Returns true if yield would execute a block in the current context—that is, if a code block was passed to the current method and is available to be called.

VALUE **rb_iterate**(VALUE (*method)(), VALUE args, VALUE (*block)(), VALUE arg2)
> Invokes *method* with argument *args* and block *block*. A yield from that method will invoke *block* with the argument given to yield and a second argument *arg2*.

VALUE **rb_catch**(const char *tag, VALUE (*proc)(), VALUE value)
> Equivalent to Ruby catch.

void **rb_throw**(const char *tag , VALUE value)
> Equivalent to Ruby throw.

API: Accessing Variables

VALUE **rb_iv_get**(VALUE obj, char *name)
> Returns the instance variable *name* (which must be specified with a @ prefix) from the given *obj*.

VALUE **rb_ivar_get**(VALUE obj, ID id)
> Returns the instance variable with ID *id* from the given *obj*.

VALUE **rb_iv_set**(VALUE obj, char *name, VALUE value)
> Sets the value of the instance variable *name* (which must be specified with an @ prefix) in the given *obj* to *value*. Returns *value*.

VALUE **rb_ivar_set**(VALUE obj, ID id, VALUE value)
> Sets the value of the instance variable with ID *id* in the given *obj* to *value*. Returns *value*.

VALUE **rb_gv_set**(const char *name, VALUE value)
> Sets the global variable *name* (the $ prefix is optional) to *value*. Returns *value*.

VALUE **rb_gv_get**(const char *name)
> Returns the global variable *name* (the $ prefix is optional).

void **rb_cvar_set**(VALUE class, ID id, VALUE val, int unused)
> Sets the class variable with ID *id* in the given *class* to *value*.

VALUE **rb_cvar_get**(VALUE class, ID id)
> Returns the class variable with ID *id* from the given *class*.

int **rb_cvar_defined**(VALUE class, ID id)
> Returns Qtrue if the class variable with ID *id* has been defined for *class*; otherwise, returns Qfalse.

void **rb_cv_set**(VALUE class, const char *name, VALUE val)
> Sets the class variable *name* (which must be specified with a @@ prefix) in the given *class* to *value*.

VALUE **rb_cv_get**(VALUE class, const char *name)
> Returns the class variable *name* (which must be specified with a @@ prefix) from the given *class*.

API: Object Status

OBJ_TAINT(VALUE obj)
> Marks the given *obj* as tainted.

int **OBJ_TAINTED**(VALUE obj)
> Returns nonzero if the given *obj* is tainted.

OBJ_FREEZE(VALUE obj)
> Marks the given *obj* as frozen.

int **OBJ_FROZEN**(VALUE obj)
> Returns nonzero if the given *obj* is frozen.

SafeStringValue(VALUE str)
> Raises SecurityError if current safe level > 0 and *str* is tainted or raises a TypeError if *str* is not a T_STRING or if $SAFE >= 4.

int **rb_safe_level**( )
> Returns the current safe level.

void **rb_secure**(int level)
> Raises SecurityError if *level* <= current safe level.

void **rb_set_safe_level**(int newlevel)
> Sets the current safe level to *newlevel*.

API: Commonly Used Methods

VALUE **rb_ary_new**( )
> Returns a new Array with default size.

VALUE **rb_ary_new2**(long length)
> Returns a new Array of the given *length*.

VALUE **rb_ary_new3**(long length, ...)
> Returns a new Array of the given *length* and populated with the remaining arguments.

VALUE **rb_ary_new4**(long length, VALUE *values)
> Returns a new Array of the given *length* and populated with the C array *values*.

void **rb_ary_store**(VALUE self, long index, VALUE value)
Stores *value* at *index* in array *self*.

VALUE **rb_ary_push**(VALUE self, VALUE value)
Pushes *value* onto the end of array *self*. Returns *value*.

VALUE **rb_ary_pop**(VALUE self)
Removes and returns the last element from the array *self*.

VALUE **rb_ary_shift**(VALUE self)
Removes and returns the first element from the array *self*.

VALUE **rb_ary_unshift**(VALUE self, VALUE value)
Pushes *value* onto the front of array *self*. Returns *value*.

VALUE **rb_ary_entry**(VALUE self, long index)
Returns array *self*'s element at *index*.

int **rb_respond_to**(VALUE self, ID method)
Returns nonzero if *self* responds to *method*.

VALUE **rb_thread_create**(VALUE (*func)(), void *data)
Runs *func* in a new thread, passing *data* as an argument.

VALUE **rb_hash_new**( )
Returns a new, empty Hash.

VALUE **rb_hash_aref**(VALUE self, VALUE key)
Returns the element corresponding to *key* in *self*.

VALUE **rb_hash_aset**(VALUE self, VALUE key, VALUE value)
Sets the value for *key* to *value* in *self*. Returns *value*.

VALUE **rb_obj_is_instance_of**(VALUE obj, VALUE klass)
Returns Qtrue if *obj* is an instance of *klass*.

VALUE **rb_obj_is_kind_of**(VALUE obj, VALUE klass)
Returns Qtrue if *klass* is the class of *obj* or *class* is one of the superclasses of the class of *obj*.

VALUE **rb_str_new**(const char *src, long length)
Returns a new String initialized with *length* characters from *src*.

VALUE **rb_str_new2**(const char *src)
Returns a new String initialized with the null-terminated C string *src*.

VALUE **rb_str_dup**(VALUE str)
Returns a new String object duplicated from *str*.

VALUE **rb_str_cat**(VALUE self, const char *src, long length)
> Concatenates *length* characters from the string *src* onto the String *self*.
> Returns *self*.

VALUE **rb_str_concat**(VALUE self, VALUE other)
> Concatenates *other* onto the String *self*. Returns *self*.

VALUE **rb_str_split**(VALUE self, const char *delim)
> Returns an array of String objects created by splitting *self* on *delim*.

MKMF Reference

Module		require
mkmf		"mkmf"

To build an extension, you create a program named extconf.rb, which may be as simple as this:

```
require 'mkmf'
create_makefile("Test")
```

When run, this script will produce a Makefile suited to the target platform. It also produces a log file, mkmf.log, which may help in diagnosing build problems.

mkmf contains several methods you can use to find libraries and include files and to set compiler flags.

mkmf takes configuration information from a variety of sources:

- The configuration used when Ruby was built

- The environment variable CONFIGURE_ARGS, a list of *key=value* pairs

- Command-line arguments of the form key=value or --key=value

You can examine the configuration by dumping the variable $configure_args:

```
% export CONFIGURE_ARGS="ruby=ruby18 --enable-extras"
% ruby -rmkmf -rpp -e 'pp $configure_args'  -- --with-cflags=-O3
{"--topsrcdir"=>".",
 "--topdir"=>"/Users/dave/Work/rubybook/tmp",
 "--enable-extras"=>true,
 "--with-cflags"=>"-O3",
 "--ruby"=>"ruby18"}
```

The following configuration options are recognized:

CFLAGS
> Flags passed to the C compiler (overridden by --with-cflags).

CPPFLAGS
> Flags passed to the C++ compiler (overridden by --with-cppflags).

curdir

Sets the global $curdir, which may be used inside the extconf.rb script. Otherwise, has no effect.

disable-xxx

Disables extension-specific option *xxx*.

enable-xxx

Enables extension-specific option *xxx*.

LDFLAGS

Flags passed to the linker (overridden by --with-ldlags).

ruby

Sets the name and/or path of the Ruby interpreter used in the Makefile.

srcdir

Sets the path to the source directory in the Makefile.

with-cflags

Flags passed to the C compiler. Overrides the CFLAGS environment variable.

with-cppflags

Flags passed to the C++ compiler. Overrides the CPPFLAGS environment variable.

with-ldflags

Flags passed to the linker compiler. Overrides the LDFLAGS environment variable.

with-make-prog

Sets the name of the make program. If running on Windows, the choice of make program affects the syntax of the generated Makefile (nmake vs. Borland make).

with-xxx-{dir|include|lib}

Controls where the dir_config method looks.

Instance methods

create_makefile
create_makefile(*target*, *srcprefix*=nil)

Creates a Makefile for an extension named *target*. The *srcprefix* can override the default source directory. If this method is not called, no Makefile is created.

dir_config
dir_config(*name*)

Looks for directory configuration options for *name* given as arguments to this program or to the original build of Ruby. These arguments may be one of the following:

--with-*name*-dir=*directory*
--with-*name*-include=*directory*
--with-*name*-lib=*directory*

The given directories will be added to the appropriate search paths (include or link) in the Makefile.

---

enable_config   enable_config(*name*, *default*=nil) → true or false or *default*

Tests for the presence of an --enable-*name* or --disable-*name* option. Returns true if the enable option is given, false if the disable option is given, and the default value otherwise.

---

find_library   find_library(*name*, *function*, ⟨ *path* ⟩⁺) → true or false

---

Same as have_library but will also search in the given directory paths.

---

have_func   have_func(*function*) → true or false

If the named function exists in the standard compile environment, adds the directive -D HAVE_*FUNCTION* to the compile command in the Makefile and returns true.

---

have_header   have_header(*header*) → true or false

If the given header file can be found in the standard search path, adds the directive -D HAVE_*HEADER* to the compile command in the Makefile and returns true.

---

have_library   have_library(*library*, *function*) → true or false

---

If the given function exists in the named library, which must exist in the standard search path or in a directory added with dir_config, adds the library to the link command in the Makefile and returns true.

Part V

Appendixes

Socket Library

Because the socket and network libraries are such important parts of integrating Ruby applications with the 'net, we've decided to document them in more detail than the other standard libraries.

The hierarchy of socket classes is shown in the following diagram:

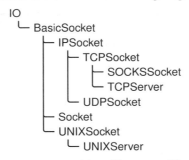

Because the socket calls are implemented in a library, you'll need to remember to add the following line to your code:

```
require 'socket'
```

Class	require
BasicSocket < IO	"mkmf"

BasicSocket is an abstract base class for all other socket classes.

This class and its subclasses often manipulate addresses using something called a struct sockaddr, which is effectively an opaque binary string.[1]

Class methods

do_not_reverse_lookup   BasicSocket.do_not_reverse_lookup → true or false

Returns the value of the global reverse lookup flag.

do_not_reverse_lookup=   BasicSocket.do_not_reverse_lookup = true or false

Sets the global reverse lookup flag. If set to true, queries on remote addresses will return the numeric address but not the host name.

By default the socket library performs this reverse lookup on connections. If for some reason this lookup is slow or times out, connecting to a host can take a long time. Set this option to false to fix this.

for_fd   BasicSocket.for_fd(*fd*) → *sock*

Wraps an already open file descriptor into a socket object.

Instance methods

close_read   *sock*.close_read → nil

Closes the readable connection on this socket.

close_write   *sock*.close_write → nil

Closes the writable connection on this socket.

getpeername   *sock*.getpeername → *string*

Returns the struct sockaddr structure associated with the other end of this socket connection.

getsockname   *sock*.getsockname → *string*

Returns the struct sockaddr structure associated with *sock*.

getsockopt   *sock*.getsockopt(*level, optname*) → *string*

Returns the value of the specified option.

recv   *sock*.recv(*len,* ⟨ *, flags* ⟩) → *string*

Receives up to *len* bytes from *sock*.

---

1.   In reality, it maps onto the underlying C-language struct sockaddr set of structures, documented in the man pages and in the books by Stevens.

recv_nonblock *sock*.recv_nonblock(*len*, ⟨ , *flags* ⟩) → *string*

1.9　Receives up to *len* bytes from *sock* after first setting the socket into nonblocking mode. If the underlying recvfrom call returns 0, an empty string is returned.

send *sock*.send(*string*, *flags*, ⟨ , *to* ⟩) → *int*

Sends *string* over *sock*. If specified, *to* is a struct sockaddr specifying the recipient address. *flags* are the sum of one or more of the MSG_ options (listed on the next page). Returns the number of characters sent.

setsockopt *sock*.setsockopt(*level*, *optname*, *optval*) → 0

Sets a socket option. *level* is one of the socket-level options (listed on the following page). *optname* and *optval* are protocol specific—see your system documentation for details.

shutdown *sock*.shutdown(*how*=2) → 0

Shuts down the receive (*how* == 0), sender (*how* == 1), or both (*how* == 2), parts of this socket.

Class		require
Socket < BasicSocket		"mkmf"

Class Socket provides access to the operating system socket implementation. It can be used to provide more system–specific functionality than the protocol-specific socket classes but at the expense of greater complexity. In particular, the class handles addresses using struct sockaddr structures packed into Ruby strings, which can be a joy to manipulate.

Class constants

Constants are available only on architectures that support the related facility.

Types:
SOCK_DGRAM, SOCK_PACKET, SOCK_RAW, SOCK_RDM, SOCK_SEQPACKET, SOCK_STREAM

Protocol families:
PF_APPLETALK, PF_AX25, PF_INET6, PF_INET, PF_IPX, PF_UNIX, PF_UNSPEC

Address families:
AF_APPLETALK, AF_AX25, AF_INET6, AF_INET, AF_IPX, AF_UNIX, AF_UNSPEC

Lookup-order options:
LOOKUP_INET6, LOOKUP_INET, LOOKUP_UNSPEC

Send/receive options:
MSG_DONTROUTE, MSG_OOB, MSG_PEEK

Socket-level options:
SOL_ATALK, SOL_AX25, SOL_IPX, SOL_IP, SOL_SOCKET, SOL_TCP, SOL_UDP

Socket options:
SO_BROADCAST, SO_DEBUG, SO_DONTROUTE, SO_ERROR, SO_KEEPALIVE, SO_LINGER, SO_NO_CHECK, SO_OOBINLINE, SO_PRIORITY, SO_RCVBUF, SO_REUSEADDR, SO_SNDBUF, SO_TYPE

QOS options:
SOPRI_BACKGROUND, SOPRI_INTERACTIVE, SOPRI_NORMAL

Multicast options:
IP_ADD_MEMBERSHIP, IP_DEFAULT_MULTICAST_LOOP, IP_DEFAULT_MULTICAST_TTL, IP_MAX_MEMBERSHIPS, IP_MULTICAST_IF, IP_MULTICAST_LOOP, IP_MULTICAST_TTL

TCP options:
TCP_MAXSEG, TCP_NODELAY

getaddrinfo error codes:
EAI_ADDRFAMILY, EAI_AGAIN, EAI_BADFLAGS, EAI_BADHINTS, EAI_FAIL, EAI_FAMILY, EAI_MAX, EAI_MEMORY, EAI_NODATA, EAI_NONAME, EAI_PROTOCOL, EAI_SERVICE, EAI_SOCKTYPE, EAI_SYSTEM

ai_flags values:
AI_ALL, AI_CANONNAME, AI_MASK, AI_NUMERICHOST, AI_PASSIVE, AI_V4MAPPED_CFG

Class methods

---

getaddrinfo　　　　　　　　　　　　　　　Socket.getaddrinfo(*hostname*, *port*,
⟨ *family* ⟨ , *socktype* ⟨ , *protocol* ⟨ , *flags* ⟩ ⟩ ⟩ ⟩) → *array*

Returns an array of arrays describing the given host and port (optionally qualified as shown). Each subarray contains the address family, port number, host name, host IP address, protocol family, socket type, and protocol.

```
require 'socket'
  for line in Socket.getaddrinfo('www.microsoft.com', 'http')
    puts line.join(", ")
  end
```

produces:

```
AF_INET, 80, wwwbaytest1.microsoft.com, 207.46.19.190, 2, 2, 17
AF_INET, 80, wwwbaytest1.microsoft.com, 207.46.19.190, 2, 1, 6
AF_INET, 80, wwwbaytest2.microsoft.com, 207.46.19.254, 2, 2, 17
AF_INET, 80, wwwbaytest2.microsoft.com, 207.46.19.254, 2, 1, 6
```

---

gethostbyaddr　　　　　　　　Socket.gethostbyaddr(*addr*, *type*=AF_INET) → *array*

Returns the host name, address family, and sockaddr component for the given address.

```
a = Socket.gethostbyname("198.145.243.54")
res = Socket.gethostbyaddr(a[3], a[2])
res.join(', ')   # =>   "mike.pragprog.com, , 2, \xC6\x91\xF36"
```

---

gethostbyname　　　　　　　　　　　Socket.gethostbyname(*hostname*) → *array*

Returns a four-element array containing the canonical host name, a subarray of host aliases, the address family, and the address portion of the sockaddr structure.

```
a = Socket.gethostbyname("63.68.129.130")
a.join(', ')   # =>   "63.68.129.130, , 2, ?D\x81\x82"
```

---

gethostname　　　　　　　　　　　　　　　Socket.gethostname → *string*

Returns the name of the current host.

```
Socket.gethostname   # =>   "dave-2.home"
```

---

getnameinfo　　　　　　　　　　　Socket.getnameinfo(*addr* ⟨ , *flags* ⟩) → *array*

Looks up the given address, which may be either a string containing a sockaddr or a three- or four-element array. If *addr* is an array, it should contain the string address family, the port (or nil), and the host name or IP address. If a fourth element is present and not nil, it will be used as the host name. Returns a canonical host name (or address) and port number as an array.

```
Socket.getnameinfo(["AF_INET", '23', 'www.ruby-lang.org'])
```

---

getservbyname　　　　　　　　　　Socket.getservbyname(*service*, *proto*='tcp') → *int*

Returns the port corresponding to the given service and protocol.

```
Socket.getservbyname("telnet")   # =>   23
```

---

getservbyport   Socket.getservbyport(*port*, *proto*='tcp') → *string*

1.9   Returns the port corresponding to the given service and protocol.

```
Socket.getservbyport(23)  # =>  "telnet"
```

---

new   Socket.new(*domain*, *type*, *protocol*) → *sock*

Creates a socket using the given parameters.

---

open   Socket.open(*domain*, *type*, *protocol*) → *sock*

Synonym for Socket.new.

---

pack_sockaddr_in   Socket.pack_sockaddr_in(port, host) → *str_address*

Given a port and a host, returns the (system dependent) sockaddr structure as a string of bytes.

```
require 'socket'
addr = Socket.pack_sockaddr_in(80, "pragprog.com")
# Pragprog.com is 65.74.171.137
addr.unpack("CCnC4")  # =>  [16, 2, 80, 65, 74, 171, 137]
```

---

pack_sockaddr_un   Socket.pack_sockaddr_un(path) → *str_address*

Given a path to a Unix socket, returns the (system dependent) sock_addr_un structure as a string of bytes. Available only on boxes supporting the Unix address family.

```
require 'socket'
addr = Socket.pack_sockaddr_un("/tmp/sample")
addr[0,20]  # =>  "\x00\x01/tmp/sample\x00\x00\x00\x00\x00\x00\x00"
```

---

pair   Socket.pair(*domain*, *type*, *protocol*) → *array*

Returns an array containing a pair of connected, anonymous Socket objects with the given domain, type, and protocol.

---

socketpair   Socket.socketpair(*domain*, *type*, *protocol*) → *array*

Synonym for Socket.pair.

---

sockaddr_in   Socket.sockaddr_in(port, host) → *str_address*

1.9   Synonym for pack_sockaddr_in.

---

sockaddr_un   Socket.sockaddr_un(path) → *str_address*

1.9   Synonym for pack_sockaddr_un.

---

socket_pair   Socket.socket_pair(*domain*, *type*, *protocol*) → *array*

Synonym for pair.

---

unpack_sockaddr_in   Socket.pack_sockaddr_in(string_address) → [*port*, *host*]

Given a string containing a binary addrinfo structure, return the port and host.

```
require 'socket'
addr = Socket.pack_sockaddr_in(80, "pragprog.com")
Socket.unpack_sockaddr_in(addr)   # =>   [80, "65.74.171.137"]
```

unpack_sockaddr_un   Socket.pack_sockaddr_in(*string_address*) → [*port, host*]

Given a string containing a binary sock_addr_un structure, returns the path to the Unix socket. Available only on boxes supporting the Unix address family.

```
require 'socket'
addr = Socket.pack_sockaddr_in(80, "pragprog.com")
Socket.unpack_sockaddr_in(addr)   # =>   [80, "65.74.171.137"]
```

Instance methods

accept   *sock*.accept → [*socket, address*]

Accepts an incoming connection returning an array containing a new Socket object and a string holding the struct sockaddr information about the caller.

accept_nonblock   *sock*.accept_nonblock → [*socket, address*]

1.9   Puts the listening socket into nonblocking mode and then accepts an incoming connection. Throws an exception if no connection is pending. You'll probably use this in conjunction with select.

bind   *sock*.bind(*sockaddr*) → 0

Binds to the given struct sockaddr, contained in a string.

connect   *sock*.connect(*sockaddr*) → 0

Connects to the given struct sockaddr, contained in a string.

listen   *sock*.listen(*int*) → 0

Listens for connections, using the specified *int* as the backlog.

recvfrom   *sock*.recvfrom(*len* ⟨ , *flags* ⟩) → [*data, sender*]

Receives up to *len* bytes from *sock*. *flags* is zero or more of the MSG_ options. The first element of the result is the data received. The second element contains protocol-specific information on the sender.

recvfrom_nonblock   *sock*.recvfrom_nonblock(*len* ⟨ , *flags* ⟩) → [*data, sender*]

1.9   Receives up to *len* bytes from *sock* in nonblocking mode. *flags* is zero or more of the MSG_ options. The first element of the result is the data received. The second element contains protocol-specific information on the sender.

sysaccept   *sock*.sysaccept → [*socket_fd, address*]

Accepts an incoming connection. Returns an array containing the (integer) file descriptor of the incoming connection and a string holding the struct sockaddr information about the caller.

Class
IPSocket < BasicSocket
require "mkmf"

Class IPSocket is a base class for sockets using IP as their transport. TCPSocket and UDP-Socket are based on this class.

Class methods

getaddress   IPSocket.getaddress(*hostname*) → *string*

Returns the dotted-quad IP address of *hostname*.

```
a = IPSocket.getaddress('www.ruby-lang.org')
a  # =>  "221.186.184.68"
```

Instance methods

addr   *sock*.addr → *array*

Returns the domain, port, name, and IP address of *sock* as a four-element array. The name will be returned as an address if the do_not_reverse_lookup flag is true.

```
u = UDPSocket.new
u.bind('localhost', 8765)
u.addr   # =>   ["AF_INET", 8765, "localhost", "127.0.0.1"]
BasicSocket.do_not_reverse_lookup = true
u.addr   # =>   ["AF_INET", 8765, "localhost", "127.0.0.1"]
```

peeraddr   *sock*.peeraddr → *array*

Returns the domain, port, name, and IP address of the peer.

recvfrom   *sock*.recvfrom(*len* ⟨ , *flags* ⟩) → [*data, sender*]

Receives up to *len* bytes on the connection. *flags* is zero or more of the MSG_ options (listed on page 874). Returns a two-element array. The first element is the received data, and the second is an array containing information about the peer. On systems such as my Mac OS X box where the native recvfrom() method does not return peer information for TCP connections, the second element of the array is nil.

```
require 'socket'
t = TCPSocket.new('127.0.0.1', 'ftp')
data = t.recvfrom(40)
data     # =>   ["220 localhost FTP server (tnftpd 2006121", nil]
t.close  # =>   nil
```

Class   **TCPSocket**   <   IPSocket   require   "mkmf"

```
t = TCPSocket.new('localhost', 'ftp')
t.gets   # =>   "220 localhost FTP server (tnftpd 20061217) ready.\r\n"
t.close  # =>   nil
```

Class methods

gethostbyname   TCPSocket.gethostbyname(*hostname*) → *array*

Looks up *hostname* and returns its canonical name, an array containing any aliases, the address type (AF_INET), and the dotted-quad IP address.

```
a = TCPSocket.gethostbyname('ns.pragprog.com')
a   # =>   ["pragprog.com", ["ns.pragprog.com"], 2, "65.74.171.137"]
```

new   TCPSocket.new(*hostname, port*) → *sock*

Opens a TCP connection to *hostname* on the *port*.

open   TCPSocket.open(*hostname, port*) → *sock*

Synonym for TCPSocket.new.

SOCKSSocket < TCPSocket

Class SOCKSSocket supports connections based on the SOCKS protocol.

Class methods

new SOCKSSocket.new(*hostname, port*) → *sock*

Opens a SOCKS connection to *port* on *hostname*.

open SOCKSSocket.open(*hostname, port*) → *sock*

Synonym for SOCKSSocket.new.

Instance methods

close *sock*.close → nil

Closes this SOCKS connection.

Class		require
TCPServer < TCPSocket		"mkmf"

A TCPServer accepts incoming TCP connections. Here is a web server that listens on a given port and returns the time:

```
require 'socket'
port = (ARGV[0] || 80).to_i
server = TCPServer.new('localhost', port)
while (session = server.accept)
  puts "Request: #{session.gets}"
  session.print "HTTP/1.1 200/OK\r\nContent-type: text/html\r\n\r\n"
  session.print "<html><body><h1>#{Time.now}</h1></body></html>\r\n"
  session.close
end
```

Class methods

new   TCPServer.new(⟨ *hostname,* ⟩ *port*) → *sock*

Creates a new socket on the given interface (identified by *hostname* and port). If *hostname* is omitted, the server will listen on all interfaces on the current host (equivalent to an address of 0.0.0.0).

open   TCPServer.open(⟨ *hostname,* ⟩ *port*) → *sock*

Synonym for TCPServer.new.

Instance methods

accept   *sock*.accept → *tcp_socket*

Waits for a connection on *sock* and returns a new tcp_socket connected to the caller. See the example on this page.

Class		require
UDPSocket < IPSocket		"mkmf"

UDP sockets send and receive datagrams. To receive data, a socket must be bound to a particular port. You have two choices when sending data: you can connect to a remote UDP socket and thereafter send datagrams to that port, or you can specify a host and port every time you send a packet. The following example is a UDP server that prints the message it receives. It is called by both connectionless and connection-based clients.

```
require 'socket'
PORT = 4321

server = UDPSocket.open
server.bind(nil, PORT)
server_thread = Thread.start(server) do |server|  # run server in a thread
  3.times { p server.recvfrom(64) }
end


# Ad-hoc client
UDPSocket.open.send("ad hoc", 0, 'localhost', PORT)

# Connection based client
sock = UDPSocket.open
sock.connect('localhost', PORT)
sock.send("connection-based", 0)
sock.send("second message", 0)
server_thread.join
```

produces:

```
["ad hoc", ["AF_INET", 49861, "localhost", "127.0.0.1"]]
["connection-based", ["AF_INET", 49862, "localhost", "127.0.0.1"]]
["second message", ["AF_INET", 49862, "localhost", "127.0.0.1"]]
```

Class methods

new   UDPSocket.new(*family* = AF_INET) → *sock*

Creates a UDP endpoint, optionally specifying an address family.

open   UDPSocket.open(*family* = AF_INET) → *sock*

Synonym for UDPSocket.new.

Instance methods

bind   *sock*.bind(*hostname, port*) → 0

Associates the local end of the UDP connection with a given *hostname* and *port*. As well as a host name, the first parameter may be "<broadcast>" or "" (the empty string) to bind to INADDR_BROADCAST and INADDR_ANY, respectively. Must be used by servers to establish an accessible endpoint.

---

connect   *sock*.connect(*hostname*, *port*) → 0

Creates a connection to the given *hostname* and *port*. Subsequent UDPSocket#send requests that don't override the recipient will use this connection. Multiple connect requests may be issued on *sock*: the most recent will be used by send. As well as a host name, the first parameter may be "<broadcast>" or "" (the empty string) to bind to INADDR_BROADCAST and INADDR_ANY, respectively.

---

recvfrom   *sock*.recvfrom(*len* 〈 , *flags* 〉) → [*data*, *sender*]

Receives up to *len* bytes from *sock*. *flags* is zero or more of the MSG_ options (listed on page 874). The result is a two-element array containing the received data and information on the sender. See the example on the facing page.

---

recvfrom_nonblock   *sock*.recvfrom_nonblock(*len* 〈 , *flags* 〉) → [*data*, *sender*]

<u>1.9</u>   Receives up to *len* bytes from *sock* in nonblocking mode.

---

send   *sock*.send(*string*, *flags*) → *int*
                                          sock.send(*string*, *flags*, *hostname*, *port*) → *int*

The two-parameter form sends *string* on an existing connection. The four-parameter form sends *string* to *port* on *hostname*.

Class		require
UNIXSocket < BasicSocket		**"mkmf"**

Class UNIXSocket supports interprocess communications using the Unix domain protocol. Although the underlying protocol supports both datagram and stream connections, the Ruby library provides only a stream-based connection.

```
require 'socket'
SOCKET = "/tmp/sample"
sock = UNIXServer.open(SOCKET)
server_thread = Thread.start(sock) do |sock|        # run server in a thread
  s1 = sock.accept
  p s1.recvfrom(124)
end
client = UNIXSocket.open(SOCKET)
client.send("hello", 0)
client.close
server_thread.join
```

produces:

```
["hello", ["AF_UNIX", ""]]
```

Class methods

new UNIXSocket.new(*path*) → *sock*

Opens a new domain socket on *path*, which must be a path name.

open UNIXSocket.open(*path*) → *sock*

Synonym for UNIXSocket.new.

Instance methods

addr *sock*.addr → *array*

Returns the address family and path of this socket.

path *sock*.path → *string*

Returns the path of this domain socket.

peeraddr *sock*.peeraddr → *array*

Returns the address family and path of the server end of the connection.

recvfrom *sock*.recvfrom(*len* ⟨ , *flags* ⟩) → *array*

Receives up to *len* bytes from *sock*. *flags* is zero or more of the MSG_ options (listed on page 874). The first element of the returned array is the received data, and the second contains (minimal) information on the sender.

Class		require
UNIXServer < UNIXSocket		"mkmf"

Class UNIXServer provides a simple Unix domain socket server. See UNIXSocket for example code.

Class methods

new   UNIXServer.new(*path*) → *sock*

Creates a server on the given *path*. The corresponding file must not exist at the time of the call.

open   UNIXServer.open(*path*) → *sock*

Synonym for UNIXServer.new.

Instance methods

accept   *sock*.accept → *unix_socket*

Waits for a connection on the server socket and returns a new socket object for that connection. See the example for UNIXSocket on the facing page.

Support

One of the major features of open source projects is the technical support. Articles in the mass media often criticize open source efforts for not having the same tech support that a commercial product has. And boy is that a good thing! Instead of dialing up some over-worked and understaffed help desk and being treated to music for an hour or so *without* ever getting the answer you need, we have a better solution: the Ruby community. The author of Ruby, the authors of this book, and many other Ruby users are willing and able to lend you a hand, should you need it.

The syntax of Ruby remains fairly stable, but as with all evolving software, new features are added every now and again. As a result, both printed books and the online documentation can fall behind. All software has bugs, and Ruby is no exception. There aren't many, but they do crop up.

If you experience a problem with Ruby, feel free to ask in the mailing lists. Generally you'll get timely answers from knowledgeable folks. However, as with all large communities, you may also find people with a less-than-perfect understanding of Ruby responding. As with all things on the 'net, use your judgment.

Before posting, do the right thing and search the Web for similar questions—by now most common questions have already been answered in the mailing lists or on someone's blog. But if you can't find the answer you need, ask, and a correct answer will usually show up with remarkable speed and precision.

Websites

Because the Web changes too fast, we've kept this list short. Visit one of the sites here, and you'll find a wealth of links to other online Ruby resources.

The official Ruby home page is `http://www.ruby-lang.org`.

RubyForge (`http://www.rubyforge.org`) hosts open source projects for Ruby developers. Each project has a Subversion repository, space to store releases, bug and feature request tracking, a WikiWiki web, and mailing lists. Anyone can apply to have a project hosted on this site. RubyForge is also the repository for downloadable RubyGems.

You'll also find a growing number of gems (and other goodies) at http://github.com. The gems on GitHub aren't automatically searched by the gem command, so you'll need to run this:

```
$  gem sources -a http://gems.github.com
```

to add GitHub to the list of places that RubyGems searches when running the gem command.

http://www.ruby-doc.org is a portal to various sources of Ruby documentation. Much of it comes from previous editions of this book.

While you're surfing, drop in on http://www.pragprog.com and see what we're up to.

Usenet Newsgroup

Ruby has its own newsgroup, comp.lang.ruby. Traffic on this group is archived and mirrored to the ruby-talk mailing list. It can be read via Google Groups.

Mailing Lists

You'll find many mailing lists talking about Ruby. The first three here are in English, and the remainder are mostly Japanese, but with some English language posts.

ruby-talk@ruby-lang.org	English language discussion of Ruby (mirrored to comp.lang.ruby)
ruby-doc@ruby-lang.org	Documentation standards and tools
ruby-cvs@ruby-lang.org	Notifications of CVS commits to Ruby source
ruby-core@ruby-lang.org	English discussion of core implementation topics
ruby-list@ruby-lang.org	Japanese language discussion of Ruby
ruby-dev@ruby-lang.org	List for Ruby developers
ruby-ext@ruby-lang.org	List for people writing extensions for or with Ruby
ruby-math@ruby-lang.org	Ruby in mathematics

See the "Mailing Lists" topic under http://www.ruby-lang.org/ for details on joining a mailing list.

The mailing lists are archived and can be searched here:

http://blade.nagaokaut.ac.jp/ruby/ruby-talk/index.shtml,

or here:

http://www.ruby-talk.org.

Bug Reporting

If you think you've spotted a bug in Ruby, you may want to browse the Ruby Issue Tracking System at `http://redmine.ruby-lang.org/`. You may also want to check to see whether a new version of Ruby is available—perhaps the bug you've found has already been fixed.

Before submitting a bug, it might be a good idea to post a question about it to the ruby-talk mailing list. Often, one person's bug is another person's language feature. Also, Ruby can be complicated, and sometimes its behavior can be subtle.

Once you've decided you have a genune bug, submit a bug report via the Ruby Issue Tracking site mentioned previosuly. When reporting a suspected bug, it's a good idea to include the output of running ruby -v along with any problematic source code. People will also need to know the operating system you're running. If you compiled your own version of Ruby, it may be a good idea to attach your rbconfig.rb file as well.

If you have a problem using irb, be aware of its limitations (see the reference section beginning on page 265). See what happens using just Ruby itself.

Appendix C

Bibliography

[Fri02]   Jeffrey E. F. Friedl. *Mastering Regular Expressions: Powerful Techniques for Perl and Other Tools*. O'Reilly & Associates, Inc., Sebastopol, CA, second edition, 2002.

[GHJV95]   Erich Gamma, Richard Helm, Ralph Johnson, and John Vlissides. *Design Patterns: Elements of Reusable Object-Oriented Software*. Addison-Wesley, Reading, MA, 1995.

[Mey97]   Bertrand Meyer. *Object-Oriented Software Construction*. Prentice Hall, Englewood Cliffs, NJ, second edition, 1997.

Index

Every built-in and library method described in this book is indexed at least twice, once under the method's name and again under the name of the class or module that contains it. These entries have the method and class/module names in typewriter font and have the word method, class, or module appended. If you want to know what methods class String contains, you can look up "String class" in the index. If instead you want to know which classes and modules support a method called index, look under "index method." A bold page number for these method listings shows the reference section entry.

When a class or method name corresponds with a broader concept (such as String), we've indexed the class separately from the concept.

Symbols are sorted using ASCII collation. The table on the right may help those who haven't yet memorized the positions of the punctuation characters (shame on you all).